PUBLIC RELATIONS THEORY II

LEA'S COMMUNICATION SERIES
Jennings Bryant/Dolf Zillmann, General Editors

Selected titles in Public Relations (James Grunig, Advisory Editor) include:

Austin/Pinkleton • Strategic Public Relations Management: Planning and Managing Effective Communication Programs

Berger/Reber • Gaining Influence in Public Relations: The Role of Resistance in Practice

Fearn-Banks • Crisis Communications: A Casebook Approach, Second Edition

Grunig/Grunig/Dozier • Excellent Public Relations and Effective Organizations: A Study of Communication Management in Three Countries

Ledingham/Brunig • Public Relations as Relationship Management: A Relational Approach to the Study and Practice of Public Relations

Lerbinger • The Crisis Manager: Facing Risk and Responsibility

Millar/Heath • Responding to Crisis: A Rhetorical Approach to Crisis Communication

Parkinson/Parkinson • Law for Advertising, Broadcasting, Journalism, and Public Relations: A Comprehensive Text for Students and Practitioners

Spicer • Organizational Public Relations: A Political Perspective

Sriramesh/Verčič • The Global Public Relations Handbook

PUBLIC RELATIONS THEORY II

EDITED BY

CARL BOTAN
GEORGE MASON UNIVERSITY

AND

VINCENT HAZLETON
RADFORD UNIVERSITY

LEA
LAWRENCE ERLBAUM ASSOCIATES, PUBLISHERS
2006 Mahwah, New Jersey   London

Senior Acquisitions Editor: Linda Bathgate
Assistant Editor: Karin Wittig Bates
Cover Design: Kathryn Houghtaling Lacey
Full-Service Compositor: TechBooks
Text and Cover Printer: Hamilton Printing Company

This book was typeset in 10.5/12 pt. Times, Italic, Bold, and Bold Italic.
The heads were typeset in Engravers Gothic, Zapf Humanist and Revival.

Lawrence Erlbaum Associates, Inc., Publishers
10 Industrial Avenue
Mahwah, New Jersey 07430
www.erlbaum.com

Library of Congress Cataloging-in-Publication Data

Public relations theory II / edited by Carl Botan and Vincent Hazleton.
   p. cm.—(LEA's communication series)
      Includes bibliographical references and indexes.
      ISBN 0-8058-3384-6 (casebound : alk. paper) – ISBN 0-8058-3385-4 (pbk. : alk. paper)
      1. Public relations.   I. Botan, Carl H.   II. Hazleton, Vincent.
   III Title: Public relations theory two.   IV. Series.
   HM1221.P825   2006
   659.201–dc22   2005029417

Books published by Lawrence Erlbaum Associates are printed on
acid-free paper, and their bindings are chosen for strength and durability.

Printed in the United States of America
10 9 8 7 6 5 4 3 2 1

Contents

Preface

In the preface to *Public Relations Theory* (1989), we said that "it should be possible to study public relations as an instance of applied communication [and that] we should be able to apply communication theory to explain and predict public relations practices, and use public relations practice as a site for the development of communication theory." We still believe this to be true; however, this book is a very different undertaking because of the changes (discussed in Chapter 1) in public relations since 1989.

Because the need for and role of theory in public relations is no longer disputed, *PRT II* dispenses with the introductory theory discussions that took up nearly a third of *PRT* (e.g., Chaps. 1, 4, 6, 9, 11, 16). For a current review of how theory has developed in public relations over the last quarter-century, see "Public relations: State of the field" (Botan & Taylor, 2004). This book moves directly to confront major theoretical issues that now characterize the field, including actual theories of public relations. It includes discussions of two important new areas: international/intercultural public relations and the role of new information technology in public relations.

Botan, C. H., & Taylor, M. (2004). Public relations: State of the field. *Journal of Communication*, *54*, 1–17.

Acknowledgments

Carl Botan wishes to thank several colleagues and students, particularly Maureen Taylor of Western Michigan University, for their support and ideas during the development of this book. He dedicates this book to Jennifer McCreadie, his wife, and to his current students at George Mason University.

Vince Hazleton wishes to thank his students and colleagues for their support and inspiration. Carl Botan, Bill Cupach, Bill Kennan, Juan Carlos Molleda, and Kelly Page Werder have all made significant contributions to both my view of the world of public relations and my work in this area. I have also benefited from the opportunities to interact and observe many helpful professionals in public relations over the last 27 years. I dedicate this work to the professionals who will benefit from the development of a useful body of knowledge.

Both of us also want to take this opportunity to note the passing of two of the chapter authors in *PRT* (1989), Gerald Miller and Ron Pearson. Both were outstanding scholars as well as outstanding people. The communications field, in general, and public relations, in particular, will not see their like soon.

Contributors

Carl Botan
George Mason University

Glen M. Broom
School of Communication
San Diego State University

W. Timothy Coombs
Eastern Illinois University

David M. Dozier
School of Communication
San Diego State University

Dawn Gilpin
Temple University

James E. Grunig
Department of Communication
University of Maryland

Larissa A. Grunig
Department of Communication
University of Maryland

Vincent Hazleton
Department of Communication
Radford University

Robert L. Heath
School of Communication
University of Houston

Dean Kazoleas
Department of Communication
Illinois State University

Michael L. Kent
Western Michigan University

William R. Kennan
Radford University

Dean Kruckeberg
Department of Communication
Studies
University of Northern Iowa

John A. Ledingham
Capital University

Juan-Carlos Molleda
University of Florida

Priscilla Murphy
Temple University

Michael Pfau
Department of Communication
University of Oklahoma

Cornelius B. Pratt
U.S. Department of Agriculture
Washington, DC

Benno Signitzer
Department of Communication
University of Salzburg, Austria

Kenneth Starck
College of Communication
and Media Science
Zayed University

Maureen Taylor
Western Michigan University

Lars Georg Teigen
Department of Communication
Illinois State University

Elizabeth L. Toth
University of Maryland

Marina Vujnovic
School of Journalism and Mass
Communication
University of Iowa

Gael Walker
University of Technology, Sydney

Carola Wamser
Department of Communication
University of Salzburg, Austria

Hua-Hsin Wan
Department of Communication
University of Texas, El Paso

Diane F. Witmer
Department of Communications
California State University,
Fullerton

Lynn M. Zoch
University of Miami

PUBLIC RELATIONS THEORY II

CHAPTER

1

Public Relations in a New Age

Carl Botan

George Mason University

Vincent Hazleton

Radford University

INTRODUCTION

When we sat down to write and edit *Public Relations Theory* more than a decade and a half ago, the public relations landscape was very much different than it is today. There are a few important similarities with the earlier book, but rather our current task is different enough that we do not consider this book a second edition of *Public Relations Theory* (1989, hereafter PRT) but rather a completely new project (hereafter, *PRT II*).

This book has an entirely different mission than *PRT* and it is about a field that has experienced huge changes since the late 1980s. For example, who would have thought back then that in 2003 the mean annual wage for public relations *managers* would be $74,750 while the mean for purchasing managers would be $73,479 and for food service managers $41,980 (U.S. Dept. of Labor, 2005)? On an hourly basis, the Bureau of Labor Statistics reported that in May of 2003 public relations managers' mean pay was $35.94 while that of judges was $37.94, physicists and astronomers $36.66, aerospace engineers $33.24, and psychologists $27.03 (U.S. Dept. of Labor, 2005). Even among nonmanagement jobs, Buckley (2002) reported that in 2000, of the 427 occupations listed by the U.S. Bureau of Labor Statistics, public relations specialists ranked 98th in income. We are ahead of architects, ranked 103, and computer programmers, ranked 104, and well ahead of social scientists, ranked 127, and construction supervisors, ranked 143. In 1989, the authors advocated a social scientific approach to public relations. Today, applying that recommendation too literally might result in a large pay cut for many public relations specialists.

In 1989, we all knew that public relations was practiced in other countries. But, who would have guessed then that several large firms would each have client lists with a dozen or more national governments on them? We simply had no idea that our field would move into a leadership role in as many ways as it has.

In the academic arena, public relations enrollments have continued to grow. In *PRT*, Neff (1989) reported graduate public relations programs in 48 departments. By 1999, the Commission on Public Relations Education reported 70 schools offering master's programs in the field. In 2005, GradSchools.com lists 64 graduate programs in public relations in the United States and 31 more internationally, although known programs in Germany, Brazil, and elsewhere had been left off that list.

Of the 64 U.S. graduate programs, 11 offer information on PhD programs. We have not seen consistent PhD graduations from the bulk of these, however, as discussed later. Public relations instructors almost unanimously agree that undergraduate enrollments have skyrocketed in the same period but reliable data on enrollments are not available.

GROWTH AND CHALLENGES

The demand for qualified faculty to teach in all these public relations programs continues to grow. Indeed, PR-education.org (2005) lists on its Web site alone 112 teaching jobs in public relations for the 2005–2006 school year, 72 for the 2004–2005 school year, and 113 for the 2003–2004 school year. Many of these go unfilled, and many of those that are filled are the result of recruiting existing faculty from other schools.

There is also a growing sense that public relations is an enrollment cash cow in more speech communication, mass communication, and journalism departments/schools than ever before. The field recognizes that this is a problem because when public relations generated tuition is used to support other areas, public relations students do not get as good a return on their tuition dollar as students in those other areas. This problem has gotten bad enough in some places that an ad hoc national committee of public relation educators is currently studying the feasibility and desirability of creating independent departments of public relations. Such an effort would, of course, have to find a way to address the shortage of qualified PhDs.

Although growth is generally a good thing, problems often accompany it. One such problem emerges from the fact that research universities that offer doctoral degrees have not been as quick to embrace public relations as for example, health communication, intercultural communication, international communication, or new information technology. This partially explains the discrepancy between the number of advertised faculty positions and the number of new public relations faculty that graduate annually with PhDs. In the late 1980s, we could identify two or three doctoral universities that regularly produced a small number of public relations graduates. Today, we can identify possibly two more universities that have developed public relations doctoral programs that regularly graduate new PhDs.

As a result of this shortage of PhD programs, many—perhaps most—new public relations faculty have never had a dedicated doctoral-level public relations theory course. Almost all have had one or more theory courses in mass communication, interpersonal communication, or freedom of the press, however. One consequence has been spotty development in public relations teaching, theory, and research. For example, public relations faculty that lack a PhD-level public relations theory course cannot be expected to explain or defend their area as well as faculty in subject areas where theories have been addressed directly as part of a graduate program. Of course, public relation faculty that lack theoretic training in public relations may read the published literature or attend conferences to partally compensate for this lack of education. This approach has an inherent bias built into it, however, and many do not avail themselves of such opportunities, resulting in some "professors" of public relations with zero academic training in the subject area. In addition, bias results from the tendency for theory learned later to be interpreted through the theoretic lens of one's first-learned theories. As a result, some public relation faculty understand and, therefore, teach their subject only from a mass communication, journalism, or organizational communication perspective rather than as a field with its own increasingly rich body of theory.

This book is not about economic status, enrollment, and teacher shortages, however. It is about a part of the field that may have changed even more than economics or enrollment; it is about public relations theory.

Different Times—Different Task

As we explain in more detail later, in the late 1980s we sought merely to give voice to the already widely recognized need for theory in public relations and to provide some conceptual tools for making that possible. *Public Relations Theory* (1989) was, to the best of our knowledge, the first theory book in the field. We did not set out to argue for or against any one theory. Rather, we set out to argue the need for more theory in PR. We explained why we thought that was true and how we thought such theory might be developed. We used the work of several outstanding colleagues to illustrate what we thought were significant contributions toward developing theory in public relations.

We divided that book into three sections and called them meta-theory, theory, and application. In the meta-theory section were chapters by us, J. Grunig, Miller (now deceased), Prior-Miller, Smilowitz, and Pearson (now deceased). In the theory section were chapters by Cheney and Dionisopoulos, Neff, Murphy, VanLeuven, Scott and O'Hair, and Cline, McBride, and Miller. In the application section were chapters by Johnson, Kreps, Terry, Anderson, Hamilton, and Gaudino, Fritch, and Haynes. Many of these chapter authors joined us in arguing that public relations is best understood as an applied social science.

A decade and a half later, that fight has largely been won. Now, we are engaged in the new task of giving voice to the need for diversity and competition between theories in public relations. We believe this task to be as critical in its time as the call for theory was in the late 1980s. In fact, we believe that our field cannot develop further without such a contest of ideas—without a real paradigm struggle.

Although we both still feel that it is useful to understand public relations as a social science, neither of us would argue today that a social, scientific perspective is necessarily the best way to understand public relations. In fact, we argue instead that what are needed today are actual theories of public relations, rather than just a social science approach. Hazleton's chapter in this book is an example of that. Although the chapter makes use of a social scientific theory for mapping and uses social science methodologies to test some of its contentions, it does not call for a social science approach but for a theory of public relations per se.

TRENDS 1988–2005

A number of changes and trends in public relations have set new tasks before us. These trends have not only helped emphasized the importance of theory in public relations but have helped to guide public relations education in directions that increasingly are integrating theory. Three such scholarly/academic trends are: (1) growth in scholarship and publishing, (2) development of scholarly organizations and conferences, and (3) development of a theoretic foundation, particularly through Symmetrical/Excellence theory.

Scholarship and Publishing

In the area of research, Botan and Taylor (2004) reported:

> With about 250 [research and theory] papers submitted to the public relations
> divisions in the Association for Education in Journalism and Mass Commu-
> nication (AEJMC), the International Communication Association (ICA), the
> National Communication Association (NCA), and the International Public Re-
> lations Research Conference (IPRRC) in 2003, public relations may be poised
> to become one of the most researched areas of communication. (p. 1)

Also, three academic journals in the United States are now solely or primarily dedicated to public relations: *Public Relations Review*, *Public Relations
Research*, and *International Journal of Strategic Communication* (starting in
2006), as well as two journals in England, *Corporate Communication: An International Journal* and *The Journal of Communication Management*. In 1989,
there was only one such journal, *Public Relations Review*, and two academic
divisions (*AEJMC* and *ICA*).

The growth in public relations journals and in the number of leading communication and mass communication journals that happily accept public relations scholarship have dramatically changed both the opportunities public
relations scholars have to publish their work and the probability that it will
be indexed by major sources like CommIndex and CommAbstracts. Indeed,
in 1989, we thought that there was a shortage of acceptable outlets for public
relations research and theorizing. Today, we are concerned that there may not
be enough good research to fill all the available outlets on a regular basis.
For example, although its founding editors and associate editors are all public
relations scholars, the *International Journal of Strategic Communication* still
casts a wide net in soliciting submissions, saying: "Submissions can address
problems grounded in any organizational or communication discipline, but
should have clear theoretical implications for how the organization functions
or responds to the environment in which it operates" (Hallahan, Holtzhauzen,
& van Ruler, 2005).

It is particularly gratifying is that several of the major national journals
in communication and mass communication, in addition to *Journalism and
Mass Communication Quarterly,* have begun to accept and even solicit public
relations articles. *Journal of Applied Communication Research* and *Journal
of Communication*, in particular, come to mind. This trend is by no means
universal, however, and public relations scholars are wise to check the policy
of individual editors and the composition of editorial boards before submitting
to non-PR journals. It is now realistic to expect that top-flight public relations
research may appear in any of up to about a dozen journals—a far cry from
1989, when most public relations research had to find its way into *Public
Relations Review* or, very occasionally, into what was then called *Journalism
Quarterly*.

Scholarly Organizations and Conferences

The growth in demand for public relations education has led to a concomitant growth in organizations where scholars can meet and present public relations research. Increases in membership and programming in both the International Communication Association and the National Communication Association has transferred what were public relations interest groups into public relations divisions. With these added to the existing divisions in the Association for Education in Journalism and Mass Communication and in the Public Relations Society of America, total divisional membership in public relations now exceeds 1,000 (although a few individuals hold dual, or even multiple, memberships). Public relations interest groups are also growing in regional communication associations in the United States.

Conferences in England, Slovenia, Australia, and Brazil, among others, have provided scholarly opportunities outside of the United States. The International Interdisciplinary Public Relations Research Conference, held in recent years in Miami, is in its eighth year and has emerged as the most important dedicated public relations research conference.

Such scholarly opportunities are important to the development of theory and research because a disciplinary community can develop around such venues. They are also important because most journal publications originate as conference papers. So, the number of conference papers is a good measure of the potential for future publications. Ideas and arguments are tested and refined through the give-and-take of scholarly discussion in formal programs as well as informally. Our own experiences at these conferences convince us that there are a generation of new scholars, with new ideas and interests, that assure the future development of public relations theory.

Theoretic Foundation

Botan and Taylor (2004) recently provided a summary of the state of public relations theory, so we will not repeat it here. They concluded the following:

> Over the last 20 years public relations has evolved into a major area of applied communication based in research of significant quantity and quality. Public relations has become much more than just a corporate communication practice. Rather, it is a theoretically grounded and research based area that has the potential to unify a variety of applied communication areas. (p. 659)

Over those 20 years, a leading body of work has developed around Symmetry/Excellence Theory, which has probably done more to develop public relations theory and scholarship than any other single school of thought. Its founder, James Grunig, is the most widely recognized public relations scholar.

Practitioners have, in our experience, become more appreciative and interested in scholarly research in recent years, probably in part because of research efforts based on the Symmetrical/Excellence approach.

Other foci have developed for public relations research, however, and have made substantial contributions. Botan and Taylor (2004) thought that over the past 20 years, the most striking trend in public relations has been the movement from a functionalist perspective to a co-creational one. Focusing on communication techniques, a functionalist perspective sees publics and communication as mere tools to achieve some corporate interest. Journalistic techniques are particularly valued because the relationship between practitioners and the media is seen as most important. A co-creational approach, on the other hand, focuses on publics as co-creators of meaning and emphasizes the building of relationships with all publics. Botan and Taylor cited several contributions to the emerging co-creational perspective, including Ferguson (1984), Crable and Vibbert (1985), Heath and Nelson (1986), Pearson (1989), J. Grunig (1992), Broom, Casey and Ritchey (1997), Botan (1997), Kent and Taylor (1998), Ledingham and Bruning (1998), and Grunig and Huang (2000), among others. They also predicted that the co-creational perspective would continue to grow and become the foundation for further developments in public relations theory.

THE CHALLENGE IN 2006

Many scholars and colleagues across the academy remain skeptical of the possibility of public relations developing as a self-standing theoretic discipline. To understand their arguments well enough to accept or reject them, we need to consider Kuhn's conceptualization of scientific paradigms.

Kuhn (1970) was a historian who was interested in how science advances. Rather than characterizing science as an orderly, logical progression of ideas, Kuhn characterized it as periods of what he calls normal science punctuated by revolutions. Quiet periods of normal science are directed and guided by paradigms, while revolutions are the period of conflict between old and new paradigms. Central to Kuhn's idea of revolutions is the concept of anomaly. An *anomaly* is an unexpected fact or a research finding that a paradigm in its original form did not anticipate. If the paradigm can be adjusted to incorporate the anomaly, normal science may continue. Failure to adequately incorporate anomalies can result in a crisis.

A *crisis* is best described as a widely spread recognition of the failures of a paradigm. According to Kuhn (1970), "crisis simultaneously loosens the stereotypes and provides the incremental data necessary for a paradigm change" (p. 89). So, one way to understand the difficulty that public relations has had in developing more than one major approach in the past two decades is to realize that our scholars have not identified major anomalies that existing models fail to address. Whether this is because public relations does not have any major unanswered questions—and so, can advance no further—or because we have just not identified them yet, only time will tell.

If a new paradigm provides a better account for both existing knowledge and the anomaly than does the existing approach, a scientific revolution may occur. The new paradigm replaces the old.

Unfortunately, *paradigm* is not a synonym for theory. It is a complex idea that refers not only to theory but also to the community of scholars that advocate and articulate particular theories, and to the body of research practices that theories generate. Masterman (1970) identifies three primary usages of the term *paradigm* by Kuhn. Each reflects a different level of abstraction.

Three Levels of Paradigm

Kuhn's (1970) interest was in the natural sciences and he was not certain that the social sciences or humanities follow similar paths. It is our belief that communication, like other social sciences, is naturally polyparadigmatic. That is, we think communication is best characterized by numerous competing paradigms, particularly at the construct and matrix levels, and not by the kinds of laws the natural sciences seek. Nevertheless, Kuhn's work informs our understanding of public relating theory. At the highest level, according to Masterman (1970), Kuhn uses paradigm to refer to a set of unquestioned presuppositions that provide an intellectual framework. Such presuppositions are fundamental but seldom articulated and discussed. Masterman refers to these fundamental beliefs as "metaphysical" paradigms. In the discipline of communication, for example, scholars may differ with respect to the extent to which intentionality is a defining characteristic of communication, or persuasion a defining characteristic of public relations. A position on such an issue limits and defines what groups or individuals take to be appropriate and inappropriate in the study of communication or public relations. Symmetrical/excellence theory, for example, reflects a metaphysical paradigm in its unquestioned presuppositions about persuasion.

At a secondary level, Kuhn describes paradigms as a disciplinary matrix. A disciplinary matrix is defined by the practices and beliefs of groups of scholars who cooperate in the work of normal science within a paradigm. Masterman (1970) refers to this as a sociological paradigm. At its third, and least abstract level, Kuhn describes a paradigm as an exemplar. *Exemplars* are reflected in the details of the research of a paradigm. Exemplar includes the questions in a survey, the manipulations in an experiment, measurement tools, and procedures. Masterman refers to this level as a construct paradigm and explains that this is the most important and fundamental use of the term paradigm.

Symmetrical/Excellence Theory, and the group of scholars working with it, is an example of a disciplinary matrix, in fact probably the only one in public relations. Disciplinary matrixes also often reflect construct paradigms, and Symmetrical/Excellence Theory may also be a construct paradigm that is defined partially by the questions and procedures of the Excellence project. Most scholars would agree that Symmetrical/Excellence Theory is, at least potentially, a paradigmatic theory. Most would also agree that it is the only such paradigmatic theory yet developed in public relations. This speaks well for the Symmetrical/Excellence folks, and ill for the rest of the field.

Critics of the Symmetrical/Excellence approach have spoken up, but either the field has failed to see enough merit in what they have said to develop their work into alternative paradigms, or they have limited their remarks to critiques and failed to conduct affirmative research, share their data, and sufficiently open their own theories to critical discourse. For example, Heath (Toth & Heath, 1992) joined Crable and Vibbert (1985), Pearson (1989), and Vasquez (1996) in arguing for what is essentially a rhetorically based approach to public relations. However, they did not provide the kind of systematic research results based on their theoretic perspective that the field could embrace. Others have also offered critically based analyses of Symmetric/Excellence Theory but, again, did not provide what the field needed in order to adopt their approach as a viable alternative to Symmetric/Excellence. Miller (1989) and Murphy (1989) also offered alternatives in *PRT* but, again, fell short of what the field needed to grant them a theoretic leadership role.

According to Kuhn (1970), theoretic paradigms frame and guide research in a field. However, they may also stifle and prevent the consideration of innovative ideas and theories. Regular and frequent public examinations of theories by scholars not directly tied to those theories may help a naturally polyparadigmatic field like public relations avoid the unhealthy condition of a lack of paradigmatic struggle.

Today's Challenge

The thrust of our argument is that in order to be more like our colleagues in the social sciences, humanities, and the rest of communication, we need to do at least two things. First, we need to encourage the development of additional and different theories of public relations, a primary goal toward which we hope this book makes a contribution. Second, we need to engage in frequent and public debates over the merits and weakness of all theories of public relations.

The value of our second goal is easily demonstrated by considering how Grunig and Hunt's original four models of public relations (Grunig & Hunt, 1984) became the Theory of Public Relations Excellence. Based on the distinctions between asymmetrical and symmetrical communication and one-way and two-way communication, Symmetrical Theory's first manifestation was as an explanation of the historical evolution of four models of public relations practice (Grunig & Hunt, 1984). Another important aspect of the theory was its grounding in concern for ethics. Rather than focusing on the technical issue of how to produce better communication, it attempted to explain how ethical communication was better—a strategic view of public relations.

The Theory of Public Relations Excellence presented in this book is substantively different from the theory articulated in 1984. Two different sources of influence account for the changes in the theory. First is an extensive and systematic program of empirical research. The theory was modified to account for discrepancies between the theory and actual data obtained in research. Most noticeable among these is acknowledgment that excellent public relations organizations use all four models of public relations practice. This is the kind of anomaly that can lead to the demise of a paradigm if not satisfactorily resolved.

The second source of influence was debate and dialogue with other theorists who disagreed with elements of the original theory. We know of at least one example of this working in the case of Symmetrical/Excellence Theory. In *PRT*, and in interpersonal communications at the conference at Illinois State University where the papers that evolved into the chapters of *PRT* were first presented, both Miller (1989) and Pearson (1989) fundamentally disagreed with Grunig's claim that persuasion was inherently unethical. At the time, the most influential of these was Pearson. In addition to acknowledging that persuasion is not always unethical, Excellence Theory has now incorporated persuasion into itself along with elements of the concept of dialogue, which Pearson articulated. Also in *PRT* Murphy (1989) indirectly challenged the idea that organizations were either symmetrical or asymmetrical and introduced the idea of mixed motives from game theory, a view we also think has influenced Excellence Theory.

In summary, reflecting on the past decade and a half, we feel that our earlier book made some small contributions to advancing both theoretic development and theory-based research in public relations. The challenge faced today is not just to contribute to theory development, however, but to contribute to the development of competing paradigms. The Pfau and Wan chapter in this book, among others, may be a step in that direction.

Use of Paradigm in Public Relations

When Botan (1993) first called for a paradigm struggle in the field in a special issue of *Public Relations Review,* he was careful to acknowledge that public relations was not yet at a developmental stage in which an actual paradigm struggle could occur. In fact, he referred to public relations as in a preparadigmatic state. Some may think it is still too early in our history to use the term *paradigm struggle.*

There have, no doubt, been times in human history when development was so slow that it literally took centuries for paradigm struggles to develop. In fact, one way we could describe the "Dark" or Middle Ages is as a historic period characterized by stagnation brought on by the lack of paradigm struggles in many fields.

Other historic epochs have been characterized by such rapid development that even identifying and explaining their paradigm struggles requires a retrospective analysis. The post–World War II period has certainly been one of the latter, and public relations theory is a child of that era. So, we are not surprised by how quickly our field has been moving through its developmental stages. We may be a fast mover in comparison to some fields, but we are veritable tortoises in comparison, for example, to information science.

Today, we are very heartened to say that the field has evolved a dominant paradigm. With the emergence of what serves as a dominant paradigm, a field has laid the necessary foundation for its next evolutionary stage—a struggle between paradigms—and public relations is no exception. This struggle between approaches to public relations will mark the coming decade or two, and it is this struggle that will be, quite literally, the engine that moves the field forward. We would expect any field that fails to develop a paradigm struggle to stagnate and even to slip backwards. Public relations will be no exception to this rule either, so just as we should celebrate the emergence of a dominant paradigm in the field, we should also celebrate the emergence of challenges to that paradigm and the eventual overthrow of that paradigm by new approaches.

In this book, you will find chapters by a substantial percentage of the leading scholars in the field. We make no predictions as to whether any, or which, of the works presented here may someday emerge as leading challenges to the then-dominant paradigm. What we do predict is that the next stage of development of the field will be a paradigm struggle, and we hope this book helps that process along.

PRT II

Given our goal of opening up the field to a variety of different theories of public relations, readers will find four different types of chapters in this book, which is divided into two major sections: "Foundations" and "Tools for Tomorrow." First are chapters addressing how public relations should be understood and practiced. Grunig, Grunig, and Dozier provide a summary description of their Excellence Theory of public relations. Although the theory is still grounded in the concepts of symmetrical and asymmetrical communication, it has changed substantially since it was first articulated and, later, discussed in *PRT*. This chapter plays a role somewhat parallel to Grunig's chapter in *PRT*. Pfau and Wan articulate a view of the role of persuasion in public relations that in *PRT II* plays a role that is somewhat parallel to the role which Miller's chapter played in *PRT*. Botan's chapter introduces the concept of grand strategy and seeks to provide some conceptual anchor points for strategic, tactical, and ethical decisions.

Second are in several chapters in which authors take theories that have been fruitful in other areas of communication, the social sciences, or business and consider their application to public relations. Hazleton takes research and theory on interpersonal competence and uses it as a framework to begin to develop a new theory of public relations competence. Walker explores the application of organizational communication's sense-making literature to public relations research. Witmer considers the potential of Structuration Theory from sociology for public relations. Kennan and Hazleton draw from sociology, political science, and economics for their Social Capital Theory of public relations. Gilpin and Murphy reframe crisis management through the lens of Complexity Theory. Finally, Pratt takes an international perspective on corporate social responsibility.

Third, some authors focus on theorizing about a specific area of public relations practice. Coombs' chapter on "Crisis Communication," Toth's chapter on "Building Public Affairs Theory," and Heath's chapter on "Issues Management," as well as Taylor and Kent's chapter on nation building, Kazoleas and Teigen's chapter on "Technology–Image Expectancy Gap," and Zoch and Molleda's chapter on "Media Relations" all represent such efforts. We feel that efforts to focus on specific areas of practice, or questions confronting the field, are necessary and are likely to be the starting point for generating midrange theories in public relations. The development of midrange theories is another part of the maturation process for public relations that we think the field should embrace. We think that these chapters may make insightful contributions toward that end.

Fourth are chapters in which authors reconsider public relations theories and research that we think may not have been given sufficient attention in the past or that we think hold particular promise for the future of public relations. In addition to some chapters in the third group that fall partially into this category, Dozier and Broom reexamine the research on public relations roles and suggest a more robust theory that incorporates concepts from the Excellence project. Kruckeberg, Starke, and Vujnovic revisit the concept of community that the first two authors articulated early in the last decade and suggest that it may aid in understanding the creation of special publics in a new century. Also included in this group is the chapter by Ledingham, which builds on his seminal work with Bruning in the application of theory from interpersonal communication to public relations, and one by Signitzer and Wamser that builds on Signitzer's earlier work in public diplomacy.

FUTURE OF THEORY DEVELOPMENT IN PUBLIC RELATIONS

Finally, although it is not the focus of any one chapter, we see one of the responsibilities of this book as commenting on where theory development in public relations is going in the next decade or two. In their recent review of the state of theory in the field, Botan and Taylor (2004) concluded that what they call the co-creational perspective has emerged at the center of public relations scholarship: "The co-creational perspective sees publics as co-creators of meaning and communication as what makes it possible to agree to shared meanings, interpretations and goals. This perspective is long term in its orientation and focuses on relationships among publics and organizations" (p. 652). Botan and Taylor argued that "in some ways, the ideas of the co-creational approach are not new because its foundation harkens back to Ferguson's 1984 call for relationships to be at the center of public relations research" (p. 652). Examples of co-creational research include the shift to organizational–public relationships, community theory, co-orientation theory, accommodation theory, and dialogue theory. Although not focused on co-creation of meaning, Symmetrical/Excellence Theory remains the most researched of the co-creational approaches.

There is no way to predict what the next generation of public relations theories will look like when we get there. We are confident, however, that co-creation—the idea that publics are a self-standing and often self-directing force in public relations—will be at the core of theory development in the next decade or two. We hope that, taken together, the works in this book will help readers develop their own feel for where public relations theory is going.

We conclude this chapter with some of our own guesses—and that is what they are, just guesses—about what we think will influence public relations theory development in the next few years.

PR Theory Now an International Undertaking

It is probably fair to say that the United States is the birthplace of public relations theory and has been dominant in public relations research in recent years. One of the most important developments in the field of public relations— perhaps, the most important—is that this U.S. dominance is fading. The rapid internationalization of our theoretic work and practice is critical to the future of the field because it brings new cultural insights, political perspectives, and histories to bear. We feel quite strongly that whatever emerges as public relations theory in the next couple of decades is likely to be fundamentally different from what has gone before, in part because it will be more international and intercultural in its assumptions, audiences, and challenges.

There are more emerging international contributors to public relations theory than we could possibly catalog in this chapter or even in a whole book dedicated to that task. In this book, for example, the chapters by Signitzer and Wamser and by Walker are international contributions. At least two other centers for theory work are emerging in the world with, possibly, two more starting to develop.

Europe

For many years, Europe has been the other major site for public relations research, most notably the German-speaking countries of Germany and Austria and, more recently, the United Kingdom. Since the publication of *PRT*, for example, three graduate-level edited books have been published in Germany (Armbrecht & Arvenarius, 1993; Armbrecht & Zabel, 1994; Avenarius & Armbrecht, 1992). These books came out of a series of conferences sponsored by the Herbert Quandt Stiftung and were coordinated by Benno Signitzer of the University of Salzburg. Several German universities also have very large public relations programs at both the graduate and undergraduate levels, with graduate students joining in theory development work. The book *Images of Nations* (1996) by Michael Kunczik of Mainz University in Germany has been well received in the U.S. since Lawrence Erlbaum Associates, the leading U.S. publisher of public relations books, republished that originally foundation-sponsored book.

Work is also moving forward in the United Kingdom. For example, as we mentioned earlier, two British journals are now largely, but not solely, dedicated to public relations.

The Lake Bled Conferences in Slovenia have contributed substantially to European public relations scholarships. Their coordinator, Dejan Vercic, is both coauthor of *The Global Public Relations Handbook: Theory, Research, and Practice* and associate editor of *International Strategic Communication Review*, in both cases with K. Sriramesh and in the latter case with Betteke von Ruler of The Netherlands.

The creation of the European Union has also benefited public relations scholarship. The EC has a branch for public relations called *Confederatione Europeanee* (CERP), which in turn has an educational division known as CERP-Education. CERP-Education has a Europe-wide student division made up of chapters and is comparable to PRSSA in the United States. CERP-Education's student division sponsors, among others, an annual conference where European public relations students can get together and exchange ideas. One of the editors of *PRT II* has served as a speaker at that conference.

Australia and New Zealand

Another region with an identifiable tradition in public relations scholarship is Australia and New Zealand. Australia in particular benefits from an uncommonly high level of support from the practitioner community represented by the Public Relations Institute of Australia (PRIA). Although having a population of only a little over 20 million, Australia is highly developed and its educational system is required to meet an ever-expanding demand not only for undergraduate education in public relations but also for graduate education.

After the United States and Germany, Australia may have the next largest number of public relations graduate students and the next highest quantity of published public relations scholarship. For example, both the *Australian Journal of Communication* and the *Asian Journal of Communication* are viable outlets for public relations scholarship.

Emerging Areas

In addition to the three well-established areas of the United States, EC, and Australia/New Zealand, we think that at least two other emerging eras will move into the mainstream of public relations scholarship in the coming years.

Brazil. A relatively small but impressive area of public relations scholarship is beginning to emerge in Brazil, particularly around Roberto Simones and his colleagues at the Catholic Pontifical University (PUCRS) and surrounding schools in the Porto Allegre area of Rio Grande du Sol in southern Brazil. This group and its connected scholars at Feevale and universities in the capital of Brasilia have been leading participants in the International Interdisciplinary Public Relations Research Conferences mentioned earlier. The group of young faculty and graduate students that has coalesced there bodes well for the future of public relations research and theory development in Brazil. The practitioner community in Brazil is not as united at the national level as in the United States, Europe, and Australia, so these scholars will probably not soon receive the kind of the support from their practitioner community that others have been enjoying from their practitioner communities.

China and Southeast Asia. We do not have specifics to share about how public relations is developing in China, other than to say that it is clearly emerging at least as a practice. We have not yet heard enough reports or seen enough scholarly publications from China to suggest that theory development has emerged as a major area of interest there. In addition, graduate students we have known and taught have confirmed that public relations is generally seen as just part of the economic revolution going on in China and that the rapidly growing number of educational programs addressing public relations in China, and in Southeast Asia, seem to be pitched at the technical level to meet market demands. Nevertheless, we fully expect that in a decade or so, there will be much more to report about theory development work in China and Southeast Asia.

NEGLECTED AREAS

Finally, we would like to mention three areas of research that are neglected in this book because the colleagues we invited to write about them were unable to write chapters. All three need to receive more attention from scholars in this field. Homeland security may emerge as a fourth such area in the coming months and years.

The first of the three areas is what we will call feminist research. Although the public relations field comprises mostly female practitioners, and women are the great majority of students, only a relative handful of scholars have directly addressed either a feminist perspective on public relations or women's issues within the field. With the publication of *Women in Public Relations* (L. Grunig, Toth, & Hon, 2001) this glaring weakness has been partially addressed. Much more still needs to be done, however, and theories that directly address the role of gender in public relations need to be developed so that body of literature can move beyond description and prescription into theory testing and development.

The second area is fundraising and social responsibility. This is a historically and socially important area of professional practice in public relations. Despite its importance, this area has received far too little attention, with research and theory development remaining almost the exclusively the domain of Kelly (1991, 1998). Fundraising and social responsibility is an area rich with potential for public relations scholars, with Pratt's chapter in this book addressing the latter area.

The third area is financial and investor relations. This is another significant area of professional practice that has been virtually ignored by public relations scholars. If we continue to ignore this area it will become the exclusive domain of the academic fields that do pay attention to it. Scholars in economics, finance, and management have legitimate, but not exclusive, interest in this area. We cannot name a public relations scholar with a defining interest in this potentially lucrative and important area of research.

CONCLUSION

Today our task is a very different one from the one we faced in the late 1980s. When we look at the theoretic landscape in public relations, we no longer see the almost desert-like view we thought we did in 1989. Instead, there is a respectable green garden of small growing ideas, research findings, and the beginnings of theories—and one moderately large tree, the Symmetric/ Excellence approach. More people have done more research using this theory than any other, and it has proved adaptable, as detailed earlier.

Nevertheless, having one clearly dominant theory raises its own questions. First, what might we have missed by focusing so much attention on a single theory? Second, scholarly research moves forward by competition between differing perspectives, not by the dominance of any one perspective. In fact, a lack of a paradigm struggle is a characteristic, not of having found the "truth," but of having given up the search. Indeed, we warned about this possibility in *PRT*. The lack of a dynamic, changing, and challenging theoretic landscape in public relations is not a criticism of the dominant paradigm, or its adherents. Rather, it is a criticism of the rest of the field for failing to develop, test, and defend other strong ideas.

REFERENCES

Armbrecht, W., & Avenarius, H. (1993). *Image und PR: Kann Image gegenstand einer Public Relations–Wissenschaft sein?* Opladen, Germany: Westdeutsher Verlag.
Armbrecht, W., & Zabel, U. (1994). *Normative Aspekte der Public Relations.* Opladen, Germany: Westdeutsher Verlag.
Avenarius, H., & Armbrecht, W. (1992). *Ist Public Relations eine Wissenschaft?* Opladen, Germany: Westdeutscher Verlag.
Botan, C. (1993). Introduction to the paradigm struggle. *Public Relations Review, 19*, 107–110.
Botan, C. (1997). Ethics in strategic communication campaigns: The case for a new approach to public relations. *Journal of Business Communication, 34*, 187–201.
Botan, C., & Hazleton, V. (Eds.). (1989). *Public relations theory.* Hillsdale, NJ: Lawrence Erlbaum Associates.
Botan, C., & Taylor, M. (2004). Public relations state of the field. *Journal of Communication, 54*, 645–661.
Broom, G. M., Casey, S., & Ritchey, J. (1997). Toward a concept and theory of organization—public relationships. *Journal of Public Relations Research, 9,* 2, 83–98.
Buckley, J. (2002, March). Rankings of full time occupations by earnings, 2000. *Monthly Labor Review.* U.S. Department of Labor. Retrieved February, 20, 2005, from http://www.bls.gov/ncs/ocs/sp/ncar0002.pdf.
Commission on Public Relations Education (1999). *Port of entry.* Available through Public Relations Society of America.
Crable, R. E., & Vibbert, S. L. (1985). Managing issues and influencing public policy. *Public Relations Review, 11*, 3–16.
Ferguson, M. A. (1984, August). *Building theory in public relations: Interorganizational relationships as public relations paradigm.* Paper presented at the conference of the Association for Education in Journalism and Mass Communication. Gainesville, FL.
GradSchools.com (2005). Retrieved March 5, 2005, from http://programs.gradschools.com/west/advertising_publicrelation.html.
Grunig, J. E. (1992). *Excellence in public relations and communication management.* Hillsdale, NJ: Lawrence Erlbaum Associates.
Grunig J. E., & Huang, Y. H. (2000). From organizational effectiveness to relationship indicators: Antecedents of relationships, public relations strategies, and relationship outcomes. In J. A. Ledingham & S. D. Bruning (Eds.), *Public relations as relationship management: A relational approach to the study and practice of public relations* (pp. 23–53). Mahwah NJ: Lawrence Erlbaum Associates.
Grunig, J., & Hunt, T. (1984). *Managing public relations.* New York: Holt, Rinehart & Winston.
Grunig, L., Toth, E., & Hon. L. (2001). *Women in public relations.* London: Guildford Press.
Hallahan, K, Holtzhauzan, D., & van Ruler, B. (2005). Editorial policy. Retrieved March 6, 2005, from https://www.erlbaum.com/shop/tek9.asp?pg=products&specific=1553-118X.
Heath, R. L., & Nelson, R. A. (1986). *Issues management: Corporate public policy making in an information society.* Beverly Hills, CA: Sage.

Kelly, K. S. (1991). *Fundraising and public relations: A critical analysis.* Hillsdale, NJ: Lawrence Erlbaum Associates.

Kelly, K. S. (1998). *Effective fundraising management.* Erlbaum: Mahwah, NJ: Lawrence Erlbaum Associates.

Kent, M. L., & Taylor, M. (2002). Toward a dialogic theory of public relations. *Public Relations Review, 28,* 1, 21–37.

Kuhn, T. S. (1970). *The structure of scientific revolutions.* Chicago: University of Chicago Press.

Kunczik, M. (1996). *Images of nations and international public relations.* Mahwah, NJ: Lawrence Erlbaum Associates.

Ledingham, J. A., & Bruning, S. D. (1998). Relationship management in public relations: Dimensions of an organization–public relationship. *Public Relations Review, 24,* 55–65.

Masterman, M. (1970). The nature of paradigms. In I. Lakatos & A. Musgrave (Eds.), *Criticism and the growth of knowledge* (pp. 61–65). Cambridge, UK: Cambridge University Press.

Miller, G. (1989). Persuasion and public relations: Two "P's" in a pod. In C. Botan & V. Hazleton (Eds.), *Public relations theory* (pp. 45–66). Hillsdale, NJ: Lawrence Erlbaum Associates.

Murphy, P. (1989). Game theory as a paradigm for the public relations process. In C. Botan & V. Hazleton (Eds.), *Public relations theory* (pp. 173–192). Hillsdale, NJ: Lawrence Erlbaum Associates.

Neff, B. (1989). The emerging theoretical perspective in PR: An opportunity for communication departments. In C. Botan & V. Hazleton (Eds.), *Public Relations Theory* (pp. 159–172). Hillsdale, NJ: Lawrence Erlbaum Associates.

Pearson, R. (1989). *A theory of public relations ethics.* Unpublished doctoral dissertation, Ohio University.

PR-Eduction.org (2005). Faculty vacancies. Retrieved March 7, 2005, from http://lamar.colostate.edu/~pr/vacancies05.htm.

Sriramesh, K., & Vercic, D. (2003). *The global public relations handbook: Theory, research, and practice.* Mahwah, NJ: Lawrence Erlbaum Associates.

Toth, E., & Heath, R. (1992) (Eds). *Rhetorical and critical approaches to public relations.* Hillsdale, NJ: Lawrence Erlbaum Associates.

U.S. Department of Labor, Bureau of Labor Statistics (2005). Occupational employment and wages, May 2003. Retrieved February 19, 2005, from http://www.bls.gov.oes/2003/may/oes112031.htm.

Vasquez, G. (1996). Public relations as negotiation: An issue development perspective. *Journal of Public Relations Research, 8,* 57–77.

The Foundations

2

The Excellence Theory[1]

James E. Grunig and Larissa A. Grunig
University of Maryland

David M. Dozier
San Diego State University

INTRODUCTION

In his highly influential book *The Structure of Scientific Revolutions,* Kuhn (1970) said that mature sciences differ from immature sciences because they are dominated by a single paradigm rather than being a battleground of multiple, conflicting theories. A *paradigm*, according to Kuhn, is a set of presuppositions, theories, methods, and exemplars of solutions to research problems that produce a unified worldview for the scientists associated with the paradigm. In mature sciences, scholars generally agree on common theories. In immature sciences, however, everyone seems to have his or her own theory, and debate rages among competing camps about which theories are preferable.

---

[1] This chapter has been developed from L. Grunig, J. Grunig, and D. M. Dozier (2002). The material herein is used with permission of Lawrence Erlbaum Associates, Publishers.

Some scholars in immature sciences mistakenly have interpreted Kuhn (1970) as suggesting that the discipline can be made more mature by imposing a single paradigm on the entire discipline. If others would adopt my theory, the reasoning goes, this discipline would mature. Scholars with competing theories understandably resist such attempts at theoretical imperialism. Instead, a dominant paradigm must emerge through research, conceptualization, and broadening and integrating of many theories rather than through imposing a single, narrow theory on the discipline.

In the Excellence study, we attempted to develop a broad, general theory of public relations by integrating most of the prominent middle-level theories that were available in the discipline at the time the study began in 1985. Our goal was not to impose a single theory on public relations but to try to bring both complementary and competing theories together in a way that would answer questions and solve problems of concern to most public relations practitioners and scholars.

Public relations research began in the 1950s and 1960s as an offshoot of mass communication research. Mass communication scholars then, as now, devoted most of their energy to explaining the effects of mass communication. At the time, most people, including scholars, believed the media had a major effect on elections, strongly influenced children, might be major contributors to crime and violence, created popular culture, influenced consumer choices, and affected decisions about war and peace. Most public relations practitioners in the 1950s and 1960s saw public relations primarily as an activity to influence the all-powerful media—through both day-to-day media relations activities and planned public information campaigns. Public relations researchers, therefore, joined with mass communication scholars to document the effectiveness of public relations (media relations/public information campaigns).

Research brought an end to the view that media have strong effects on attitudes and behaviors (often known as the *hypodermic needle theory*) and replaced it with the view that the media have limited effects (see, e.g., McQuail, 2000, for a history of mass communication research). Research then discredited the limited-effects view and replaced it with a different kind of powerful effects theory—a set of theories showing that the effects of the media are cognitive more than they are attitudinal and behavioral (they affect what people think about more than what they do) and that the media both influence and are influenced by culture.[2] From the vantage point of public relations, these new theories of media effects suggested that some people do

---

[2] The best-known of these theories of cognitive effects are the agenda-setting and framing theories. For an overview of agenda setting, see McCombs and Bell (1996) and Dearing and Rogers (1996). For an overview of framing, see Wallack, Dorfman, Jernigan, and Themba (1993), pp. 67–73.

indeed learn from the media in some situations, but that the media are not the solution to every public relations problem. Rather, public relations is a process in which organizations must communicate with publics in different ways in different situations. The public relations process, that is, must be managed—practitioners have to think about and plan what they do—in order to be effective.

Beginning in the 1950s, public relations textbooks such as Cutlip and Center's (1952) first edition began to claim that public relations is both a two-way communication process and a management function. However, ideas about the management of two-way communication processes remained vague until J. Grunig (1976) introduced organizational theory to public relations and developed the concept of symmetrical communication and Broom and Smith (1978, 1979) developed the concept of the public relations manager role. From that point on, public relations scholars began to think of public relations as both a management and a communication discipline—"the management of communication between an organization and its publics" (J. Grunig & Hunt, 1984, p. 6).

J. Grunig (1997) elaborated on this definition of public relations as communication management by emphasizing the management of an organization's communicative processes and the role of communication in management itself:

> I define communication as a behavior—of people, groups, or organizations—that consists of moving symbols to and from other people, groups, or organizations. Thus, we can say that public relations is an organization's managed communication behavior. Public relations professionals plan and execute communication for the entire organization or help parts of the organization to communicate. They manage the movement of messages *into* the organization, for example, when conducting research on the knowledge, attitudes, and behaviors of publics and then using the information to counsel managers on how to make the organization's policies or actions acceptable to publics. They may manage the movement of messages *out of* the organization when they help management decide how to explain a policy or action to a public and then write a news story or fact sheet to explain it. (pp. 242–243)

To this day, however, many public relations practitioners continue to think of public relations as mostly publicity and media relations. Many others have broadened their vision and see public relations as the part of the strategic management function through which organizations interact with their publics both before and after management decisions are made. In the early 1980s, the management approach was only beginning to enter public relations thinking. It was a preparadigm period of public relations in which scholars and practitioners, in particular, had widely differing views of the nature and purpose of public relations. This was the setting when the Foundation of the International

Association of Business Communicators issued a request for research proposals (RFP) in 1984 that gave birth to the Excellence study. The IABC's RFP
called for a study that would explain "how, why, and to what extent does
communication affect the achievement of organizational objectives."

For many years, public relations professionals have expressed great interest
in the third part of this research question: To what extent does communication
affect the achievement of organizational objectives? Public relations professionals generally feel underappreciated by other managers when they work
inside an organization or by clients when they work in a public relations firm.
Often they believe they are disadvantaged in competing for organizational resources because they cannot explain the value of their work. As a result, public
relations professionals long have searched for a statistical model or other evidence that would prove that public relations has value to an organization.

The IABC Foundation included two additional questions in the critical
sentence in its RFP that made it possible for us go beyond the widespread
interest in proving that public relations has value to an organization. The other
questions allowed us to build from the explanation of the extent to which
public relations has value, to develop a general theory that also explains why
it has value and how the communication function should be organized to best
provide this value. We collapsed these three questions into two major research
questions that guided the Excellence study:

- First, the Effectiveness Question asked why and to what extent public relations increases organizational effectiveness: How does public
  relations make an organization more effective, and how much is that
  contribution worth economically?

- Second, the Excellence Question asked how public relations should
  be organized and managed to be able to make the contribution to organizational effectiveness identified in the answer to the Effectiveness
  Question: What are the characteristics of a public relations function
  that are most likely to make an organization effective?

To answer these two research questions, we tried to use most existing public
relations theories as well as theories from related management and communication disciplines to build a general theory of public relations. This chapter
explains this general theory and summarizes the research conducted for the
Excellence study to apply and extend the theory. Although the Excellence theory by itself has not made public relations a mature science, it has provided
a comprehensive paradigm that has integrated and expanded public relations
research. At the same time, the Excellence theory has served as a focal point
for debate and criticism—a focus that Kuhn (1970) believed is a necessary
condition for a science to be mature.

AN OVERVIEW OF THE EXCELLENCE STUDY

When the IABC Foundation (now the IABC Research Foundation) issued its RFP in 1984, project director James Grunig assembled a research team of five scholars and practitioners from the United Kingdom and the United States. The team consisted of James Grunig and Larissa Grunig of the University of Maryland and David Dozier of San Diego State University; William Ehling, then of Syracuse University and now retired; Jon White, then of the Cranfield School of Management in the United Kingdom and now an independent consultant and teacher in London; and the now-deceased Fred Repper, who had recently retired as vice president of public relations for Gulf States Utilities in Beaumont, Texas.

The six members of the team wrote a proposal that promised to review the literature on organizational effectiveness to answer the question of how and why public relations has value to an organization. Because we believed that not all public relations units have value to their organizations, however, we also promised to do an extensive review of the literature on public relations and related disciplines to isolate the characteristics that make it more likely that a communication unit will add value to an organization. We could do such a review because each member of the team had been heavily involved in research on different, but complementary, aspects of communication management—such as strategic management, practitioner roles, gender and diversity, models of public relations, operations research, employee communication, organizational culture, and activism.

Conceptualization

In 1985, the IABC Foundation awarded us a grant for $400,000 to conduct the project we had outlined. The literature review started out as a paper but expanded into a book, *Excellence in Public Relations and Communication Management* (J. Grunig, 1992a). That first book presented the results of the extensive literature review that led to the conceptual framework for the study.

A number of excellence studies had been conducted for management practices in general, the most famous of which was Peters and Waterman's (1982) study, *In Search of Excellence.* We reviewed this study and similar ones and integrated the results in the chapter "What Is Excellence in Management?" in *Excellence in Public Relations and Communication Management* (J. Grunig, 1992c). Most previous studies of excellence, however, addressed only the *how* question of the three questions posed in the IABC Foundation's research question. Previous excellence researchers typically chose what they thought were excellent organizations using arbitrary criteria, such as six financial measures used by Peters and Waterman, and then searched for management practices that these excellent organizations shared. Generally, though, these researchers could not explain why the shared practices produced the observed financial results. That problem became especially acute when many of the excellent companies suffered financial declines or went out of business even though their management practices had not changed ("Who's Excellent Now," 1984).

In developing our study of excellence in public relations and communication management, by contrast, we began by reviewing the literature on the nature of organizational effectiveness, the nature of public relations, and the relationship between the two (L. Grunig, J. Grunig, & Ehling, 1992). That literature allowed us to answer the why question: For what reason does public relations contribute to organizational effectiveness?

With the answer to that question in mind, we then searched literature in public relations, communication, management, organizational sociology and psychology, social and cognitive psychology, feminist studies, political science, operations research, and culture to identify characteristics of public relations programs and departments and of the organizations in which they are found that answer the *how* question: By what means do excellent public relations departments make organizations more effective? Finally, we searched the literature for concepts that would explain the value of individual public relations programs and the value of the overall public relations function to an organization—the *to what extent* question (Ehling, 1992; L. Grunig, J. Grunig, & Ehling, 1992).

The result was a comprehensive, general theory of public relations. That general theory began with a premise of why public relations has value to an organization. We could use that premise to identify and connect attributes of the public relations function and of the organization that logically would be most likely to make the organization effective. Then we could link the outcomes of communication programs that make organizations effective to the characteristics of a public relations function that theoretically would contribute the most to organizational effectiveness.

Data Collection and Analysis

After completing the conceptualization, we submitted the general theory and the several middle-range theories and variables incorporated into it to empirical test—quantitative and qualitative research to look for evidence that excellent public relations programs were more valuable than less excellent functions.

The first phase of the Excellence study consisted of quantitative, survey research on 327 organizations in the United States, Canada, and the United Kingdom. Questionnaires were completed by 407 senior communication officers (some organizations had more than one public relations department), 292 CEOs or other executive managers, and 4,631 employees (an average of 14 per organization). The organizations included corporations, government agencies, nonprofit organizations, and trade and professional associations.

We analyzed the quantitative data by attempting first to reduce as much of the data as possible into a single index of excellence in communication management. We tried to reduce these variables to one index after first combining a number of indicators of variables into indices, or by using the statistical technique of factor analysis to combine related variables into broader variables. We then factor analyzed these indices and factors to isolate a single factor of excellence. Factor analysis looks for clusters of variables to which people respond with similar answers when they complete a questionnaire. In the case of communication Excellence, our theory suggested that most of the characteristics of excellence would cluster together, as would the characteristics of less excellent programs.

The factors produced by factor analysis represent underlying variables that are broader than the original variables analyzed. We expected that a factor would define an underlying variable of excellence in communication management, which would subsume the variables of the subtheories integrated into our general theory. Factor analysis allowed us to determine whether all of the characteristics of excellence clustered as we predicted so that we could use the underlying factor to identify the most and least excellent communication departments as well as average ones.

We then used this index to choose organizations for qualitative research, and the qualitative information provided insights on how excellent public relations came about in different organizations as well as detail on the outcomes produced by excellence. We also used the Excellence factor to determine whether other characteristics we measured correlated with the index—thus providing additional detail on conditions related to excellent public relations. For example, we had no theoretical reason to include the use of outside consulting firms for different purposes as a part of the theory of excellence but we could correlate the index of excellence with uses of consulting firms—thus determining whether excellent departments use outside firms differently than do less excellent departments.

We began the search for a single Excellence factor with the goal of including as much of the information from the three survey questionnaires as possible in the index. We could not include variables for which we did not have information for every organization, however. Therefore, we could not include the variables from the first part of the questionnaire completed by the senior communicator, which asked 8 1/2 pages of questions about how the organization identified publics and how it planned, executed, and evaluated communication programs for those publics. Top communicators answered this set of questions for the three publics they chose as receiving the most time and resources for public relations programs. Top communicators chose from a list of 17 stakeholder groups, but they chose only eight groups often enough to provide sufficient data for analysis.

Because top communicators chose different publics, the same data were not available for all organizations. Therefore, we could not include the data on programs for different publics in the Excellence factor without eliminating many organizations from the analysis. As a result, we built the Excellence factor from the rest of the three questionnaires. Later, we correlated the data from Part I of the public relations questionnaires with the Excellence factor public by public for organizations that had programs for each of the eight publics.

There also were several questions on the top communicator's and CEO's questionnaires that produced categorical data that could not be correlated with other variables. These questions asked about power of the public relations department; membership in the dominant coalition; organizational responses to activism; relationship to marketing and other managerial functions; gender of the top communicator; and country, type, and size of organization. We analyzed these variables later by comparing mean scores on the Excellence factor and its component variables for the categories of the categorical variables.

The Excellence factor we isolated strongly confirmed the theory developed in *Excellence in Public Relations and Communication Management* (J. Grunig, 1992). We found that CEOs with excellent public relations departments valued the communication function almost twice as much as did those with less excellent departments. CEOs who valued public relations most believed it should be practiced essentially as spelled out by our theory of excellence. Heads of excellent public relations departments also reported that their units practiced public relations according to these same principles of excellence. The first analysis also showed that the organizational and environmental context nurtured, but did not guarantee, excellent public relations. Finally, comparison of the Excellence index for different descriptive characteristics of organizations and communicators showed that excellence in public relations seemed to be generic to the three countries and the four types of organizations we studied. Size of the organization also made no difference. And, heads of excellent departments came from all age groups and were equally likely to be women or men.

When the survey was completed and the data analyzed, we provided a report to each of the organizations participating in the study. The report explained the theory behind the study and provided percentile scores showing each organization where it stood relative to the other organizations on overall Excellence and each of the component variables of an Excellence scale we constructed. The last phase of the study consisted of qualitative interviews of up to three people (the CEO, the head of communication, and a lower-level public relations professional) in 25 of the organizations that had the highest and lowest scores on the scale of excellence produced by the quantitative research.

After completing the research, we wrote two additional books reporting the results. The second book, *Manager's Guide to Excellence in Public Relations and Communication Management* (Dozier with L. Grunig & J. Grunig, 1995), included a user-friendly review and explanation of the theory and simplified results of both parts of the study, written mostly for public relations practitioners. A third and final book, *Excellent Public Relations and Effective Organizations: A Study of Communication Management in Three Countries* (L. Grunig, J. Grunig, & Dozier, 2002) presented the complete results of both the quantitative and qualitative segments of the study.

A Theoretical Benchmark of Best Practices

The result of 10 years of literature review, theory construction, and empirical research is a benchmarking study that identifies and describes critical success factors and best practices in public relations. We go beyond typical benchmarking studies, however, which usually are empirical but not explanatory. Typical studies identify organizations that are believed to be leaders in an area of practice and then describe how they practice public relations or some other management function. They answer the *how* question (how do the benchmarked companies practice public relations?), but not the *why* or *to what extent* questions. In his book on public affairs benchmarking, Fleisher (1995) said that it is important to measure what public relations units do, but that, "it is just as important to discover the qualitative factors—the how's and why's behind the numbers—associated with the attainment of the numbers" (p. 15).

The Excellence study provides a theoretical profile, a theoretical benchmark that we initially constructed from past research and by theoretical logic. In addition, we gathered empirical evidence from organizations to confirm that this theoretical profile explains best actual practice as well as best practice in theory. The theoretical and empirical benchmark provided by the Excellence study makes it possible for public relations units to compare themselves with what Fleisher (1995) called "higher performing and world-class units in order to generate knowledge and action about public affairs roles, processes, practice, products/services, or strategic issues which will lead to performance improvement" (p. 4).

In most benchmarking studies, communication units compare themselves with similar units in their industry or with similar functional units inside the organization. The Excellence study, by contrast, is an example of what Fleisher (1995) called "generic benchmarking"—identifying critical success factors across different types of organizations. Generic benchmarking is most valuable theoretically, because it is unlikely that one organization will be "a world-class performer across the board" (p. 29). In the Excellence study, a few organizations exemplified all of the best practices, many organizations exemplified some of them, and others exemplified few of the practices—i.e., the theoretical benchmark was normally distributed in the population of organizations.

A theoretical benchmark does not provide an exact formula or detailed description of practices that a public relations unit can copy in order to be excellent. Rather, it provides a set of principles that such units can use to generate ideas for specific practices in their own organizations. As a comprehensive model of excellence in public relations, therefore, this theoretical and empirical benchmark provides a model:

- For auditing and evaluating public relations departments;
- For explaining to the managers who make important decisions (dominant coalitions) why their organizations depend on public relations, how much value communication has to their organization, and how to organize and manage the function to achieve the greatest value from it; and
- For the teaching of public relations to both beginners and experienced practitioners.

The empirical results of the Excellence study provide strong and consistent support for the general theory that guided the study. As occurs in most research, however, the results also suggest how to improve and revise many of the middle-level theories that were incorporated into the general theory. The rest of this chapter summarizes the components of our general theory of public relations and discusses the insights provided by research for revising and improving that theory.

THE VALUE OF PUBLIC RELATIONS: THE BASIC PREMISE OF THE GENERAL THEORY

The question of the value of public relations has been of great concern to professional communicators for many years because of the belief among both communicators and other kinds of management professionals that public relations is an intangible management function in comparison with other functions whose value can be described, measured, and evaluated through systematic research. In fact, the elusive goal of determining the value of public relations was the major reason why the IABC Research Foundation requested proposals for the Excellence study. Because there has been no way to demonstrate its worth, public relations often has seemed to suffer at budget time and particularly during financial crises.

For at least 25 years, therefore, public relations professionals and researchers have struggled to develop measures that would establish that public relations is effective or adds value. Among other measures, they have attempted to determine the advertising value of press clippings; to establish the readership of publications; or to do surveys or experiments to determine whether communication campaigns or programs have had measurable effects on cognitions, attitudes, or behaviors. Many professional communicators have successfully demonstrated the effects of individual communication programs in one or more of these ways. Nevertheless, evaluation of communication programs falls short of demonstrating that the overall management function of public relations has value to an organization or to society.

Recently, public relations practitioners and firms have been on a quest to develop a single indicator of the value of organizational reputation. They believe that this indicator will establish that communication has a measurable monetary return that can be attributed to the public relations function (e.g., Jeffries-Fox Associates, 2000a; Fombrun, 1996). Many commercial research firms have developed a series of evaluative, attitudinal questions to measure reputation (Jeffries-Fox Associates, 2000b).

Levels of Analysis

These many forays into estimating the value of public relations have not been successful at least in part because of confusion over the organizational level at which public relations has value. We must recognize, to begin, that the value of communication can be determined at least at four levels[3]:

> *Program level.* Individual communication programs such as media relations, community relations, or customer relations are successful when they affect the cognitions, attitudes, and behaviors of both publics and members of the organization. The program level has been the traditional focus of evaluative research in public relations. However, effective communication programs may or may not contribute to organizational effectiveness; many operate independently of the organization's mission and goals.
>
> *Functional level.* The public relations or communication function as a whole can be audited by comparing the structure and processes of the department or departments that implement the function with the best practices of the public relations function in other organizations or with theoretical principles derived from scholarly research. Evaluation at this level can be called *theoretical* or *practical benchmarking.* Although the value of public relations at the program and functional level is different, public relations departments that meet evaluative criteria at the functional

---

[3] It is also possible to evaluate public relations at a lower level than the four described later—the level of the individual message or publication such as an annual report or a brochure. We have not addressed the individual level of evaluation in the Excellence study because the purpose of the study was to determine how the public relations function and its component programs contribute to organizational effectiveness. In general, though, evaluation can be done at the individual level using concepts similar to those used at the program level.

level should be likely to develop communication programs that meet their objectives more often than functions that do not meet these criteria.

Organizational level. For many years, organizational scholars have debated the question of what makes an organization effective. To show that, public relations has value to the organization, we must be able to show that effective communication programs and functions contribute to organizational effectiveness.

Societal level. Organizations have an impact beyond their own bottom line. They also affect other organizations, individuals, and publics in society. As a result, organizations cannot be said to be effective unless they also are socially responsible; and public relations can be said to have value when it contributes to the social responsibility of organizations.

The initial request for proposals from the IABC Research Foundation focused on the organizational level of value. The research team added the second question, the Excellence question, because we believed that public relations functions must be organized according to certain theoretical criteria before they could contribute value at the organizational level. We must address the societal level as well if we are to determine the value of public relations.

Organizational Effectiveness

In our review of relevant literature, conducted at the outset of this decade-long research, we began with the organizational level to develop a definition of organizational effectiveness. We reasoned that only by defining what we mean by an "effective" organization could we then determine the contribution that communication makes, or could make under conditions of excellent practice. The literature on organizational effectiveness is large and contradictory (overviews can be found in Goodman & Pennings, 1977; Hall, 1991, Price 1968; and Robbins, 1990). Robbins (1990) and Hall (1991), however, identified four main schools of thought on effectiveness, emanating primarily from organizational sociology and business management, which guided our initial conceptualization of the Excellence theory. These perspectives were systems, competing values, strategic constituencies, and goal attainment. We synthesized these approaches, culling the concepts within each one that offered the most promise in explaining the relationship between effectiveness and communication (see J. Grunig, 1997, pp. 257–258).

The *goal-attainment* approach states that organizations are effective when they meet their goals. However, the approach alone cannot explain effectiveness. Different individuals within an organization as well as different external stakeholders have different goals for the organization. Therefore, the organization might be effective with respect to some constituents but not with respect to others.

The *systems* approach recognizes the importance of the environment for an organization to be effective—the interdependence of organizations with their environments. Interdependence comes from mutual need. Presumably, organizations need resources from their environment—raw materials, a source of employees, clients or customers for the services or products they produce, and so forth. The environment, too, needs the organization for its products or services. The systems approach, however, defines the environment in vague terms and does not explain which elements of the environment are important for success.

The *strategic constituencies* approach puts meaning into the term *environment* by identifying the elements of the environment whose opposition or support can threaten the organization's goals or help to attain them. The fourth approach, *competing values,* provides a bridge between strategic constituencies and goals. It states that an organization must incorporate strategic constituencies' values into its goals so that the organization attains the goals of most value to its strategic constituencies. Thus different organizations with different strategic constituencies in their environments will have different goals, and their effectiveness will be defined in different ways.

This notion of specificity within the organization's environmental niche points to the value of public relations. As boundary spanners, managers of communication help the dominant coalition determine which elements of their domain are most important to reach. Organizational effectiveness is determined in part, then, by identifying those key publics. We also know that public relations departments can develop programs that build high-quality relationships with these strategic constituencies.

Relationships help the organization manage its interdependence with the environment. Of course, communication alone does not create and maintain these relationships; but it does play a vital role. Then, too, relationships may not be entirely beneficial to the organization. They have the capacity to both limit and enhance the organization's autonomy within its environment. Nevertheless, the notion of relationships is so central to the literature of organizational sociology, business management, and—of course—public relations that at least two scholars defined *business* as "a connected set of relationships among stakeholders where the emphasis is on the connectedness" (Freeman & Gilbert, 1992, p. 12).

Since the completion of the Excellence study, Post, Preston, and Sachs (2002) developed essentially the same theory of organizational effectiveness as we did, defining it as the *stakeholder* approach to organizational wealth:

> Our central proposition is that *organizational wealth* can be created (or destroyed) through relationships with stakeholders of all kind—resource providers, customers and suppliers, social and political actors. Therefore effective *stakeholder management*—that is managing relationships with stakeholders for mutual benefit—is a critical requirement for corporate success. (p. 1)

Post, Preston, and Sachs (2002), like many contemporary management theorists they cited, pointed out that corporations have *intangible assets* as well as physical and financial assets. The most original current approach to estimating the value of these intangible assets, they added, is that of *relational wealth*—"relationships, both among individuals and units within an organization and between any focal entity, or organization, on one hand, and other entities, groups, and organizations, on the other" (p. 40). "Organizational wealth," they concluded, "is the summary measure of the capacity of an organization to create benefits for any and all of its stakeholders over the long term" (p. 45).

The stakeholder approach to organizational effectiveness also makes it possible to integrate economic performance and the achievement of social goals into a definition of effectiveness. Freeman and Gilbert (1992) saw business "as a connected set of relationships among stakeholders where the emphasis is on the connectedness" (p. 12). They explained:

> We need to understand that stakeholders are in it together, rather than competing for limited and scarce resources, and that the fundamental reason that organizations as connected networks are effective is that they are built on the principles of cooperation and caring. Each stakeholder is "adding to the value" of others, creating a good deal for all. (p. 12)

The Contribution of Public Relations

Our review of the literature on organizational effectiveness led to the following premise, which we used to integrate a number of middle-range theories of public relations into a general theory:

> Public relations contributes to organizational effectiveness when it helps reconcile the organization's goals with the expectations of its strategic constituencies. This contribution has monetary value to the organization. Public relations contributes to effectiveness by building quality, long-term relationships with strategic constituencies. Public relations is most likely to contribute to effectiveness when the senior public relations manager is a member of the dominant coalition where he or she is able to shape the organization's goals and to help determine which external publics are most strategic. (L. Grunig, J. Grunig, & Dozier, 2002, p. 97)

Each of the key middle-range theories of public relations, which we integrated into a general theory, can be seen as a way of identifying publics with which an organization needs relationships to be effective and as a way of effectively cultivating relationships with these publics.

A key phrase in the foregoing proposition is that the contribution of public relations has monetary value. Although our search of the literature suggested that this monetary value comes mostly through intangible assets, many public relations professionals still would like researchers to determine an exact monetary value for the relationships created through the work of the public relations function. We explored this possibility when we conceptualized the Excellence study and rejected it as impossible for the following reasons flowing from the literature we reviewed in the first and last *Excellence* books:

•   Relationships provide a context for behavior by consumers, investors, employees, government, the community, the media, and other strategic constituencies. However, they do not determine this behavior alone. The behavior of these constituencies affects financial performance; but many other factors, such as competition and the economic environment, also affect that performance.

•   Relationships save money by preventing costly issues, crises, regulation, litigation, and bad publicity. It is not possible, however, to determine the cost of something that did not happen, or even to know that the negative event or behavior would have happened in the absence of excellent public relations.

•   The return on relationships is delayed. Organizations spend money on relationships for years to prevent events or behaviors such as crises, boycotts, or litigation that might happen many years down the road.

•   The return on relationships usually is lumpy. Good relationships with some constituencies such as consumers may produce a continuing stream of revenue, but for the most part the return comes all at once—e.g., when crises, strikes, boycotts, regulation, litigation, or bad publicity are avoided or mitigated. Similarly, relationships with potential donors must be cultivated for years before a donor makes a major gift. As a result, it is difficult to prorate the delayed returns on public relations to the monies invested in the function each year.

As a result, we concluded that the technique of compensating variation provided the best method known to date to estimate the value of relationships cultivated by public relations to the organization. Ehling (1992) developed that rationale for using this technique in the first *Excellence* book. We entered the data-gathering phase of the Excellence project with the understanding that public relations contributes both to the organization and to society. We also understand that the value of public relations lies in the value of relationships between the organization and publics in the internal and external environment of the organization. Public relations departments contribute this value at the organizational and societal levels through excellent practice at the functional and program levels. Public relations programs, for example, are effective when they accomplish objectives that help to build successful relationships with publics that have strategic value to the organization.

In our research, then, we attempted to measure the value of relationships as a means of estimating the value of public relations. After reviewing the literature on cost-benefit analysis, we identified a method for estimating the value of public relations and comparing it with the costs. Cost-benefit analysis of public relations is difficult, however, because of the intangibility of the benefit—the value of relationships. One method we identified in the literature, "compensating variation," offered promise.

Compensating variation, as economists term this process, provides a way of transforming nonmonetary values, such as the benefit of good relationships to the organization and to society, into monetary values. The idea behind the method is simple. You ask people how much they would be willing to pay to have something. For public relations, you ask members of the dominant coalition or public relations managers how much public relations is worth to them on either a monetary or nonmonetary scale.

A compensating variation is:

- The amount of money a beneficiary of a program (such as the dominant coalition) would be willing to pay for a program (such as public relations) so that he or she would be equally well off with the program or the payment he or she is willing to make for it, or

- The amount an entity (such as the dominant coalition) that is worse off because of the effects of a program (such as opposition from activists) would be willing to pay to eliminate the effects, so that the entity is equally well off without the program or the payment.

Our method was limited by the fact that we asked only one party to the relationships between organizations and publics to estimate the value of the relationship—the organization's side. Ideally, we also would have asked representatives of publics, such as leaders of activist groups, to estimate the value of each relationship. With a survey sample of more than 300 organizations and a set of 25 qualitative cases, the cost in time and money of interviewing representatives of publics was prohibitive. Researchers in the future should extend our analysis by choosing a smaller number of participating organizations and interviewing both sides of relationships.

Results Related to Value

In the survey research, we asked both the senior public relations executives and the CEOs who completed questionnaires to answer two questions based on the method of compensating variation. One of these questions asked both the CEO and the top communicator to provide a nonmonetary value for public relations in comparison with a typical department in the same organization.

They assigned a value on a scale called a *fractionation scale*, in which they were told that 100 would be the value of a typical department. In addition, the top communicator and the CEO were asked to assign a cost-benefit ratio to public relations—essentially a monetary value. The top communicators also were asked to predict how they thought members of the dominant coalition would respond to these same two questions.

Based on this method, our survey research showed that CEOs and communicators alike agree that public relations returns significantly more than it costs—and more than the typical department in their organization. CEOs estimated the average return-on-investment for public relations to be 186%. This ROI increased to 225% under conditions of excellence. It was 140% for the least excellent public relations departments. CEOs estimated values for public relations in comparison with other management functions to be 160 (where 100 was average) for all departments, 232 for excellent departments, and 109 for less excellent departments.

These estimates, of course, cannot be considered to be hard measures of the value of public relations. They are soft, comparative measures. However, the measures provided strong statistical evidence of the value of public relations. These measures of value had strong statistical correlations with the characteristics of excellent public relations—thus showing that excellent public relations contributes more value than less excellent public relations.

Our qualitative interviews with CEOs and public relations heads also confirmed our conceptualization of the value of public relations. Most were unwilling or unable to assign an exact value to public relations. However, those with excellent public relations departments were sure of the value of public relations; and they explained that value in essentially the same way we had theorized. In addition, we found no evidence that the financial success attributed to public relations had come at the cost of social responsibility. The most effective organizations we studied relied on public relations to help determine which stakeholder groups were strategic for it and then to help develop credible, long-term relationships with those constituencies. Such high-quality relationships only exist when the organization acknowledges the legitimacy of the public, listens to its concerns, and deals with any negative consequences it may be having on that public.

Undeniable evidence came from the chemical association. There, the head of public relations developed a program of citizen advisory panels that has changed his entire industry's way of operating and, concomitantly, its reputation. This program of social responsibility reflects the vice-president's belief in the legitimacy of the public interest. His accompanying public relations efforts have been characterized in the trade press as "sophisticated," "very aggressive," "skilled," "more open," "responsive," and "more effective." He himself believes the program is helping his industry change in ways that respond to citizens' concerns about health, safety, and the environment. As he was quoted as saying in a weekly trade publication, "Changing one's own performance, not 'educating' the public, is the only successful strategy" (as quoted in Begley, 1993, p. 23).

THE FUNCTIONAL LEVEL: CHARACTERISTICS OF EXCELLENT PUBLIC RELATIONS DEPARTMENTS

After answering the effectiveness question, both our theory building and research turned to the Excellence question: What are the characteristics of public relations departments and programs, and of the internal and environmental context of the organization, that increase the likelihood that the public relations function will have value for both the organization and for society? Answering this question required a number of critical middle-range theories that we integrated within the general theory of excellence in our first *Excellence* book. This section reviews the characteristics of the overall public relations department. In subsequent sections, we do the same for specific communication programs and for the environmental and organizational context of excellent public relations functions. The characteristics can be placed into four categories that represent major areas of study in public relations.

Empowerment of the Public Relations Function

The overarching theory integrating this category of concepts was the idea that the public relations function must be empowered as a distinctive and strategic managerial function if it is to play a role in making organizations effective. The senior public relations officer must play a role in making strategic organizational decisions, must be a member of the dominant coalition or have access to this powerful group of organizational leaders, and must have relative autonomy from excessive clearance rules to play this strategic role. In addition, the growth in the number of female practitioners should not hinder this empowerment of the public relations function; indeed, the growth should be valued for the diversity it brings to public relations. In addition, excellent departments should seek more of the scarce supply of minority practitioners to add to their ability to understand the environments faced by their organizations.

Specifically, we developed and tested three theoretical propositions:

1. *The senior public relations executive is involved with the strategic management processes of the organization, and communication programs are developed for strategic publics identified as a part of this strategic management process.* Public relations contributes to strategic management by scanning the environment to identify publics affected by the consequences of decisions or who might affect the outcome of decisions. An excellent public relations

department communicates with these publics to bring their voices into strategic management, thus making it possible for stakeholder publics to participate in organizational decisions that affect them.

2. *The senior public relations executive is a member of the dominant coalition of the organization, or the senior public relations executive has a direct reporting relationship to senior managers who are part of the dominant coalition.* The public relations function seldom will be involved in strategic management, nor will public relations have the power to affect key organizational decisions, unless the senior public relations executive is part of or has access to the group of senior managers with the greatest power in the organization. Public relations executives also must have a good deal of freedom to make decisions about public relations problems without excessive clearance by other managers.

The third characteristic of empowerment relates to the extent to which practitioners who are not white males are empowered in the public relations function:

3. *Diversity is embodied in all public relations roles.* The principle of requisite variety (Weick, 1979) suggests that organizations need as much diversity inside as in their environment. Excellent public departments empower both men and women in all roles as well as practitioners of diverse racial, ethnic, and cultural backgrounds.

To a great extent, the Excellence data provide sound empirical support for our overarching theory of empowerment. We found that many organizations, including some of the excellent ones, had not fully empowered their public relations professionals. But in excellent public relations departments, by and large, public relations professionals were involved in strategic management. In particular, their role is as environmental scanners, providing information needed about strategic publics affected by managerial decisions. They get this information through formal research and various informal methods of gaining information about organizational constituencies.

Although not all of the managers of excellent communication functions were in the dominant coalition, nearly two-thirds of top communicators in the top 10% of our organizations were in that powerful group, compared to about 45% in the overall sample. When public relations was in the dominant coalition, that elite group also tended to include more representatives of outside constituencies. The larger the dominant coalition, the more likely it was that the top communicator was a member. That result suggests that the more an organization empowers most of its employees and outside constituents, the more likely it is also to empower public relations.

We found that the knowledge base of public relations practitioners increased their chance of being involved in strategic management and being accepted by the dominant coalition. Public relations practitioners in excellent organizations had more expertise in public relations. They did not all have college degrees in the field, although several did. Instead, they seemed to be self-educated; at least one participant in the qualitative research alluded to enhancing his practice after reading and studying the *Excellence* theory book. Others emphasized what they had learned from mentors.

The research also showed that excellent communicators are more likely to be team players than independent operators. They cultivate relationships not only with members of their external publics but also with their counterparts inside the organization. They promote teamwork within their own departments as well, empowering middle managers there to develop and work toward achieving a vision. In particular, these effective communicators have earned a close working relationship with their CEO. This relationship is characterized by credibility. It tends to result from extensive knowledge of the business or industry; longevity plus a track record of successful performance in the organization; expertise in strategic planning and managerial decision-making that is not limited to communication; and a shared worldview of the value of two-way symmetrical public relations, in particular.

Having such an expert communicator in place tended to lead to high value for public relations, rather than having a CEO who valued public relations in the first place seeking and hiring someone with that expertise. However, there were many significant exceptions to this pattern. Several senior executives in our study seemed determined to hire and support the best communicator they could find. To them, that meant a person capable of going beyond functions typically associated with public relations. It also meant a person whose expertise in public relations extended well beyond publicity, promotion, or media relations to encompass conflict resolution, environmental scanning, and dialogue with key publics.

Most of the top communicators in our survey reported directly to the CEO or indirectly through another senior manager. Such a reporting relationship does not ensure excellence, but we found that without such a clear path to the CEO public relations cannot contribute much to organizational effectiveness. A direct relationship with the CEO provides the top communicator access to strategic management processes of the organization. A direct reporting relationship, therefore, appears to be a necessary, if not a sufficient, condition for participation in strategic management, which is one of the most critical components of excellent public relations.

The need to be team players also showed up in our data on clearance procedures. Most public relations heads in our survey cannot act unilaterally. They are required to clear their activities at times where the input of top management is needed to ensure the accuracy or involvement of management. They are not required to clear more routine activities. At the same time, we found that excellent departments are more empowered than less excellent departments, as evidenced by having somewhat more autonomy to make major decisions without interference from top management.

Finally, we found that departments are excellent as often when women are the senior communicator as when men are in that role. Likewise, increasing the number of women in the public relations department and in managerial roles had no effect on excellence. At the same time, however, we found that excellent public relations departments take active steps to include women in managerial roles and to promote them from inside rather than to bring in men from other managerial functions. Likewise, we found that excellent departments actively strive to increase racio-ethnic diversity in the public relations function—pushing for more requisite variety in public relations.

In short, excellent public relations departments are interesting and challenging places for capable and knowledgeable professionals to work. In these departments, public relations people are empowered, they play an active strategic role, their expertise in communication and environmental scanning is valued, and they are valued when they bring gender and racio-ethnic diversity into the function.

Public Relations Roles

Roles are abstractions about the patterned behaviors of individuals in organizations, a way of classifying and summarizing the myriad activities that an individual might perform as a member of an organization. By playing roles, individuals mesh activities, yielding predictable outcomes. Arguably, organizations are defined as systems of roles. In public relations, the concept of practitioner role has been systematically studied for about 25 years; such research places practitioner roles at the nexus of a network of important antecedent concepts and professional consequences. In the Excellence study, new role measures were developed and used to expand this important theoretical area.

Public relations researchers have conducted extensive research on four major roles that communicators play in organizations—the manager, senior adviser (also known as a communication liaison), technician, and media relations roles (for a review, see Dozier, 1992; L. Grunig, J. Grunig, & Dozier, 2002, Chapter 6). The manager and technician roles are the most common of the four. Communication technicians are essential to carry out most of the day-to-day communication activities of public relations departments, and many practitioners play both manager and technician roles. In less excellent departments, however, all of the communication practitioners—including the senior practitioner—are technicians. If the senior communicator is not a manager, it is not possible for public relations to be empowered as a management function because there are no managers in the department.

The Excellence study examined three theoretical propositions related to roles:

1. *The public relations unit is headed by a manager rather than a technician.* Excellent public relations units must have at least one senior communication manager who conceptualizes and directs public relations programs, or this direction will be supplied by other members of the dominant coalition who have little or no knowledge of communication management or of relationship building.

2. *The senior public relations executive or others in the public relations unit must have the knowledge needed for the manager role, or the communication function will not have the potential to become a managerial function.* Excellent public relations programs are staffed by people who have gained the knowledge needed to carry out the manager role through university education, continuing education, or self-study.

3. *Both men and women must have equal opportunity to occupy the managerial role in an excellent department.* The majority of public relations professionals in the three countries studied are women. If women are excluded from the managerial role, the communication function may be diminished because the majority of the most knowledgeable practitioners will be excluded from that role. When that is the case, the senior position in the public relations department typically is filled by a technician or by a practitioner from another managerial function who has little knowledge of public relations.

The results of the Excellence study solidly supported our proposition that the distinction between the manager and technician roles for the senior communicator in a public relations department is a core factor distinguishing excellent from less excellent departments. However, the results also showed the vital supporting role of technical expertise to the management role. More than any other variable, the availability of knowledge to perform a managerial role distinguishes excellent departments from less excellent ones. Excellent departments also have higher levels of technical expertise than less excellent departments. Nevertheless, technical expertise has value only when it is accompanied by managerial expertise. Public relations managers are most effective when they also possess technical expertise or have it available to them—especially technical knowledge in media relations. Expert technicians who have little managerial expertise or who are not supervised by expert managers have little value to the organization.

Our data also revealed more than one kind of managerial expertise. Public relations departments can possess strategic managerial expertise, administrative managerial expertise, or both. We found that excellent departments possess both kinds of expertise. We showed that strategic managers are most essential to the functioning of an excellent public relations department. In addition, our data showed that public relations departments need administrative expertise. Like technical expertise, however, administrative expertise has little value without accompanying knowledge of how to practice strategic public relations. At the same time, our data showed that communication departments possess less strategic knowledge than knowledge needed to practice any of the other roles.

The managerial role is equally important for public relations when the perspective of the dominant coalition is taken into account. Although CEOs view public relations roles in a more splintered and confusing way than do top communicators, the CEOs of organizations with excellent public relations departments expect their top communicators to be managers. Also, the greater the importance assigned to communication with outside groups by the dominant coalition, the stronger the coalition's expectation will be that the top communicator should be a manager rather than a technician.

CEOs also expect top communicators to be expert in media relations—more strongly than do top communicators. In addition, our results suggested that CEOs often hire top communicators because of their technical expertise but then learn that technical expertise is insufficient when a crisis or major internal upheaval requires more strategic communication skills. When top communicators have managerial as well as technical knowledge, as our qualitative results showed, they can meet such a challenge. When they have only technical expertise, they cannot.

We also found that gender makes little difference in the role enacted by top communicators, in the role expectations of CEOs, and in the expertise of the public relations department. However, we found that female public relations heads are more likely to play dual manager-technician roles than are men—even in organizations with excellent public relations departments. We also found that women may have less opportunity than men to gain strategic expertise because of the time they must spend doing technical tasks. The gender of the top communicator, therefore, does not help or hinder communication Excellence, but female top communicators may have to work harder to develop strategic expertise while they must engage in technical activities that are not expected of men.

Organization of the Communication Function, Relationship to Other Functions, and Use of Consulting Firms

Many organizations have a single department devoted to all communication functions. Others have separate departments for programs aimed at different publics such as employees, consumers, investors, or donors. Still others place communication under another managerial function such as marketing, human resources, legal, or finance. Many organizations also contract with or consult with outside firms for all or some of their communication programs or for such communication techniques as annual reports or newsletters.

Starting at about the time we began work on the Excellence project in 1985, there has been extensive debate about how the communication function should be organized in organizations and what its relationship should be to other management functions, especially marketing (see, e.g., Schultz, Tannenbaum & Lauterborn, 1993; Thorson & Moore, 1996). Numerous scholars and professionals have called for the integration of all communication activities in an organization into a single department or for communication to be coordinated in some way by a "communication czar" (Schultz et al., 1993, p. 168), "pope" (Gronstedt, 2000, p. 189), or "chief reputation officer" (Fombrun, 1996, p. 197).

Advertising scholars and practitioners originally advocated the integration of these communication activities though the marketing function or, on a smaller scale, through a marketing communication department or executive. Public relations scholars and practitioners largely resisted this integration, although some endorsed it as a way of empowering public relations through alignment with the more powerful marketing function. Public relations people pointed out that most communication activities other than marketing communication have long been integrated through the public relations function or through a chief public relations or communication officer. They feared that marketing encroachment or dominance of the public relations function would diminish the role of public relations in organizations.

By today, integrated marketing communication (IMC) scholars and practitioners (e.g., Duncan & Moriarty, 1997; Gronstedt, 2000) have moved away from integrated *marketing* communication to what they now call "integrated communication"—although most still concentrate their attention on consumers and marketing communication programs. This integrated communication differs little from the principle of integration of all communication activities under the public relations function that we proposed in the first Excellence book and tested in the Excellence study. Public relations scholars and practitioners, likewise, now seem to have embraced the idea of pulling marketing communication activities under the public relations umbrella—although data reported by Hunter (1999a) show that a large proportion of marketing communication programs still report to marketing rather than public relations.

For public relations to be managed strategically and to serve a role in the overall strategic management of the organization, therefore, the Excellence theory first states the theoretical principle that organizations must have an integrated communication function. An excellent public relations function integrates all public relations programs into a single department or provides a mechanism for coordinating programs managed by different departments. Only in an integrated system is it possible for public relations to develop new communication programs for changing strategic publics and to move resources from outdated programs designed for formerly strategic publics to the new programs.

Even though the public relations function is integrated in an excellent organization, the function should not be integrated into another department whose primary responsibility is a management function other than communication. Therefore, the Excellence theory also states that public relations should be a management function separate from other functions. Many organizations splinter the public relations function by making communication a supporting tool for other departments. When the public relations function is sublimated to other functions, it cannot be managed strategically because it cannot move communication resources from one strategic public to another—as an integrated public relations function can.

When we wrote Excellence in Public Relations and Communication Management (J. Grunig, 1992a), little research was available on the role of public relations consulting firms in excellent organizations. Therefore, the Excellence theory made no predictions about the role of outside firms, but in the quantitative study we asked questions on how organizations use these firms in the communication function.

The Excellence data and those reported by Hunter (1997, 1999a) from surveys of Fortune 500 companies showed that communication functions rapidly are being organized under the rubric of public relations or corporate communication. Organizations seem to be integrating communication activities through a central public relations department. Alternatively, they have several specialized communication departments that are coordinated both formally and informally by a chief communication officer, who usually holds the title of senior vice president or vice president of corporate communication. In addition to the coordinating role of this senior communication officer, organizations use a number of ways to coordinate their activities, such as organization-wide meetings, communication policies, and unstructured interaction of communication professionals in different departments or business units. Our data showed that this integration has occurred most often in organizations that have excellent public relations functions, as we have defined excellence.

These combinations of centralized or integrated, specialized departments also tend to have a matrix arrangement with other management functions—such as marketing, human resources, or finance. They work under an integrated philosophy of communication—a philosophy that is largely strategic and symmetrical. But the communication managers in these centralized and specialized departments work as peer professionals with their counterparts in other management functions. They collaborate with their peers. In excellent departments there is little conflict and competition with other management functions—including marketing. Inside excellent communication departments, professionals work as colleagues who are equally empowered. As the field becomes female-intensive, the implications are clear: Women must be included in the organization's power and information networks.

Excellent communication departments also seek support from outside firms. All public relations departments in our sample purchased a substantial proportion of their technical publicity activities from outside firms, as well as a large proportion of their research support. Excellent public relations departments also sought strategic counseling from outside firms when they had difficulties with their publics, although most seem to possess the knowledge themselves to deal with these problems.

Whereas the marketing function in excellent organizations seldom dominates public relations, communication departments in less excellent organizations have a strong tendency to provide little more than technical support to the marketing function—technical support that most communication departments purchase from outside firms. A few of the excellent departments do seem to have adopted marketing theory as the foundation for their communication programs—with its emphasis on customers, messages, and symbols. On the positive side, however, they also have adopted the strategic, two-way approach of modern marketing—although marketing theory has steered them toward an asymmetrical rather than a symmetrical approach to communication.

The challenge for public relations theorists and practitioners, therefore, seems to be to persuade their counterparts in marketing to adopt a more symmetrical approach to communication. Recent books by Gronstedt (2000) and Duncan and Moriarty (1997) suggest that this conversion already may be occurring.

Models of Public Relations

J. Grunig (1976) first introduced the concept of models of public relations as a way of understanding and explaining the behavior of public relations practitioners. At that time, public relations educators routinely advocated two-way communication; but few made a distinction in the purpose of public relations in an organization. J. Grunig (1984) conceptualized the press agentry and public information models to improve on the simple concept of one-way communication. He also did not believe that all two-way communication was the same. Some was asymmetrical: Public relations people did research and listened to publics in an effort to determine how best to change their behavior to benefit the organization. But, he believed that public relations professionals had a calling beyond this asymmetrical approach: serving as the organizational function that attempts to balance the interests of organizations with those of their publics, an approach he called "symmetrical" communication.

Over the years, these public relations models have been researched and debated (for reviews, see J. Grunig, 2001; J. Grunig & L. Grunig, 1989, 1992; L. Grunig, J. Grunig, & Dozier, 2002, Chapter 8). Do they really describe actual public relations practice? Is the symmetrical model only an idealized, normative model? Are critical scholars correct: Is it unlikely that a large organization with more power than its publics would ever deliberately choose to practice symmetrical public relations? Is symmetrical public relations simply a deceptive term used by educators and practitioners to cover up the damage that public relations does to the interests of publics?

In *Excellent Public Relations and Effective Organizations* (L. Grunig, J. Grunig, & Dozier, 2002), we summarized and responded to these questions. We concluded that the four models are both positive and normative and that the two-way symmetrical model still appears to be a normative ideal for public relations practice. We maintained that public relations professionals can use the power of their knowledge—if they have it, and if society recognizes the value of public relations—to advocate a symmetrical approach to public relations. They should be able to advocate symmetry in public relations for the same reason that a physician tells an overweight person to exercise—because it is good for the organization, just as exercise is good for one's health.

The Excellence theory, therefore, stated that excellent departments will design their communication programs on the two-way symmetrical model rather than the press agentry, public information, or two-way asymmetrical models. Two-way symmetrical public relations attempts to balance the interests of the organization and its publics, is based on research, and uses communication to manage conflict with strategic publics. As a result, two-way symmetrical communication produces better long-term relationships with publics than do the other models of public relations. Symmetrical programs generally are conducted more ethically than are other models and produce effects that balance the interests of organizations and the publics in society. Symmetrical practitioners, therefore, have mixed motives (they are loyal to both their employers and to the publics of their organizations).

Three specific propositions were based on the symmetrical model:

1. The public relations department and the dominant coalition share the worldview that the communication department should reflect the two-way symmetrical, or mixed-motive, model of public relations.

2. Communication programs developed for specific publics are based on the two-way symmetrical, mixed-motive model.

3. The senior public relations executive or others in the public relations unit must have the knowledge needed for the two-way symmetrical model, or the communication function will not have the potential to practice that excellent model.

The quantitative and qualitative data collected in the Excellence study provided the most comprehensive information ever collected on the models of public relations. As a result, the data suggested a significant reconceptualization of the models. We did find that the four models still provide an accurate and useful tool to describe public relations practice and worldview. Practitioners and CEOs do think about public relations in these ways, and the four models do describe the way communication programs are conducted for different types of publics. However, the differences among the two one-way and the two two-way models typically blur in the minds of CEOs and in the practice of some, but not all, programs. CEOs, in particular, view an excellent public relations function as including the two-way asymmetrical model as often as it does the two-way symmetrical model.

We found the answer to that dilemma in the two-way component of the two-way asymmetrical model. CEOs like the two-way asymmetrical model because they appreciate the systematic use of research in that model. Most do not distinguish research conducted for symmetrical purposes from research conducted for asymmetrical purposes. Most CEOs do not want asymmetrical communication programs, although we did find exceptions in our survey of cases. Organizations that define public relations as a marketing function, in particular, tend to see public relations only in asymmetrical terms—or in one-way terms.

We successfully isolated three dimensions underlying the four models—one-way versus two-way, symmetry versus asymmetry, and mediated and interpersonal techniques. We also suggested further research on a fourth dimension, the ethics of communication. The overlapping concepts and practices of the models that we had found before—such as practicing the two-way symmetrical, two-way asymmetrical, and public information models concurrently—seem to have occurred because an organization had a symmetrical public relations worldview, favored extensive research, and practiced mediated as well as interpersonal communication.

Excellent public relations, therefore, can be described better in terms of these underlying dimensions than in terms of the four discrete models themselves. Excellent public relations is research based (two-way), symmetrical (although organizations constantly struggle between symmetry and asymmetry when they make decisions), and based on either mediated or interpersonal communication (depending on the situation and public). We also believe it is more ethical, although we did not measure ethics as a component of the models in the Excellence study. Future research, we predict, will establish ethics as a crucial component of excellent public relations.

We also learned from both our quantitative and qualitative data that organizations typically turn to a symmetrical approach when activist pressure or a crisis makes an asymmetrical approach too costly. Then, the CEO tends to upgrade the communication function and hire a knowledgeable top communicator—although sometimes the top communicator comes first and convinces the CEO of the need to enhance the communication function. By and large, organizations practice symmetrical public relations when the CEO understands its value and demands it; and the senior communicator and his or her communication staff have the knowledge to supply it. Much of that knowledge comes from the ability to do research, to understand publics, and to collaborate and negotiate— skills that excellent communicators must have.

THE PROGRAM LEVEL: CHARACTERISTICS OF PROGRAMS TO COMMUNICATE WITH SPECIFIC PUBLICS

In addition to theorizing about and researching the characteristics of excellent public relations at the functional level, the Excellence study also examined the level of ongoing programs that excellent communication departments devise to develop and maintain relationships with their key publics. In particular, we addressed two concerns that pervade current discussions of public relations— strategic origination of programs and evaluation of their outcomes.

The questionnaire for the top communicator provided a list of 17 publics that serve as the focus of public relations programs in many organizations. Top communicators were asked to provide a detailed breakdown of the origins, management, and outcomes of communication programs for their top three publics, as defined by budget allocations. We analyzed communication programs for seven specific publics that were most often mentioned by top communicators: the media,[4] employees, investors, the community, customers, government, and members.

Our theory stated simply that communication programs organized by excellent departments should be managed strategically. To be *managed strategically* means that these programs are based on research and environmental scanning, that varying rather than routine techniques are used when they are implemented, and that they are evaluated either formally or informally. In addition, we predicted that the communication professionals who participated in our research would have evidence to show that these programs had improved the relationships between the organization and its publics.

We looked for support for our theoretical prediction that organizations and public relations departments that are excellent overall also will have specific communication programs that are excellent. We believed that communication programs in excellent departments would be more likely to have strategic origins and less likely to have historicist origins than those in less excellent departments. We also believed that excellent programs will be based on environmental scanning research and more likely to use evaluation research to gather evidence that shows positive outcomes from the programs. Less excellent

---

[4] The media cannot truly be said to be a public, because they are important only as a means of communicating with publics that interact with an organization. If a key public does not use the media for information about an organization or its decisions, the media have little importance in a communication program. However, journalists behave like members of other publics (J. Grunig, 1983) when they seek information, so we refer to them loosely in this chapter as a public.

programs, in contrast, continue year after year with little or no research to identify new or changing publics, without setting measurable objectives, and without conducting evaluation research to determine whether these objectives have
been met.

The results provide remarkably robust support for the proposition that excellent public relations programs are managed strategically. When the organization and the communication department are excellent overall, communication
programs for specific publics are more likely to have strategic origins and less
likely to have historicist origins. Excellent departments are more than the routine publicity mills of traditional departments. Excellent programs arise from
environmental scanning research, and they are evaluated through all forms
of evaluation (scientific, clip-file, and informal). Managers of excellent departments also reported the availability of evidence that their programs have
positive outcomes, such as meeting their objectives, changing relationships,
and avoiding conflict.

We also found that communication programs have strategic origins most often in organizations experiencing pressure from activist groups. When program
origins are strategic, top communicators also report greater success in dealing with activist pressure on the organization. Programs are more likely to
have strategic origins if the communication department has the expertise to
enact the manager role and the top communicator enacts that role frequently.
When organizations experience activist pressure, they are more likely to use
both formal and informal environmental scanning research. Communication
programs are more likely to be evaluated through scientific, clip file, and informal evaluation when activist pressure is high. Generally, organizations are
more successful in dealing with activists when the organizations evaluate their
communication programs. Formal and informal scanning and the three forms
of program evaluation all increase when the communication department has
higher levels of managerial expertise and the head of public relations enacts that
role frequently. Positive program outcomes increase as a function of overall
Excellence, manager role expertise, and manager role enactment.

Government relations programs, however, did not fit this pattern when they
were compared to programs for the six other publics. The explanation, we
believe, is that in many organizations, government relations programs and
especially lobbying functions are directly dominated by lawyers and CEOs.
Communication departments typically exert little control over these programs,
even if government relations is situated in the communication department on
the organizational chart. For this reason, government relations programs often
operate somewhat orthogonally to communication departments, independent
of both strengths and weaknesses in those departments, as indicated by various
measures of communication Excellence.

Lobbyists also seem to lean heavily on personal experience and interpersonal relations with legislators or regulators as the basis for their actions.

Compared to others under the public relations umbrella in organizations, these practitioners are less likely to have formal training in communication management. Since expertise (e.g., manager role and two-way symmetrical communication) in the communication function is at the core of overall Excellence, quasi-autonomous government relations programs appear to operate less directly as a function of communication Excellence.

ACTIVISM AND THE ENVIRONMENTAL CONTEXT FOR EXCELLENCE

A central part of most research on public relations as a management function before the Excellence study looked for reasons inside and outside the organization to explain when some public relations functions are more strategic, managerial, and symmetrical than others are. In the Excellence study, we also examined the organizational context to determine whether communication Excellence can survive more or less on its own, or whether it requires a nourishing external and internal context to flourish. In this section, we look at the external context. The Excellence theory predicted that a turbulent, complex environment with pressure from activist groups stimulates organizations to develop an excellent public relations function.

Previous research on activist groups showed that most organizations, at least in the United States, have experienced pressure from activism (L. Grunig, 1992a). In addition, research on power in organizations suggests that organizations are most likely to empower the public relations function when pressure from activists, or crises produced by that pressure, makes public relations expertise valuable (L. Grunig, 1992b). We hypothesized, therefore, that activism would push organizations toward excellence. Organizations that face activist pressure would be more likely to assign public relations a managerial role, include public relations in strategic management, communicate more symmetrically with a powerful adversary or partner, and develop more participative cultures and organic structures that would open the organization to its environment—the key variables in our index of excellence.

Our results showed that an effective organization exists in an environment characterized more by dynamism and even hostility than by stability. We confirmed that activism pushes organizations toward excellence as they try to cope with the expectations of their strategic constituencies—although activism did not guarantee excellence. The perceived incidence of activism correlated moderately and significantly with excellence in public relations, especially when estimated by the head of public relations. According to the estimates of both CEOs and senior communicators, organizations with excellent public relations were more likely to report success in dealing with activists than organizations with less excellent departments. The success of activists, however, did not correlate significantly with excellence. Importantly, these correlations were not negative: Communication Excellence seems to mean that activists do not fail to achieve their goals when organizations achieve their goals.

The quantitative data, therefore, suggested that activism stimulates excellence. The correlations probably were moderate, however, because most of the organizations studied reported facing activism. Many, but not all, seem to have responded by developing excellent public relations departments, which make them more successful in dealing with activists. Activists probably achieve some level of success regardless of how the organization responds; the difference provided by excellence is that the organization as well as the activists can achieve success—a symmetrical outcome.

Both our quantitative and qualitative data also showed that excellent public relations departments respond to activists with two-way communication, symmetrical communication, involvement of activists in organizational decisions, and both formative and evaluative research on the activists. That pattern of results fits the Excellence theory: Excellent public relations departments scan the environment and continuously bring the voices of publics, especially activist publics, into decision making. Then, they develop programs to communicate symmetrically with activists and involve them with managers throughout the organization. Finally, they use both formative and evaluative research to manage their communication programs strategically.

In our qualitative research, we heard a great deal about symmetry in response to our questions about activism in the environment. For example, the head of public relations of an industry association scoring at the top of the Excellence scale described a community program he had developed that has won national prominence and acclaim. The program's first principle is listening and responding to the community's concerns. He emphasized that responsiveness may include change on the organization's part when pressure groups do not agree with it. Perhaps in no case was this more obvious than in the chemical corporation we studied. Crises and improving company performance both helped the corporation overcome what might have been crippling pressure from outside groups. As its vice president explained, since the catastrophe in Bhopal, his entire industry has become more willing to be open to the public.

The qualitative data also showed that crises have the potential to enhance the career opportunities of public relations practitioners. Most participants in our 25 qualitative cases discussed at least one crisis situation that had resulted in a real shift both in their organization's culture and in its practice of public relations. Often, they spoke of increased appreciation for their function on the part of others in the organization; greater access to the dominant coalition as a result; more openness in communication; a new willingness to cooperate with pressure groups and the community at large; the concomitant likelihood of learning from these strategic constituencies; and greater support for or at least understanding of the organization from the community, the clients or customers, the media, and even government regulators.

THE ORGANIZATIONAL CONTEXT OF EXCELLENT PUBLIC RELATIONS

Inside the organization, previous research both by organizational and public relations scholars has examined the extent to which the organizational characteristics of structure, culture, communication system, treatment of men and women, and power of the dominant coalition predict organizational behavior, in general, and public relations practice, in particular.

After reviewing this research in *Excellence in Public Relations and Communication Management* (J. Grunig, 1992a), we concluded that a power-control theory explains organizational and public relations behavior best. That is, organizations behave in general, and practice public relations in particular, as they do because the dominant coalition chooses to organize and manage in that way. Nevertheless, previous research also suggested that the organizational context of a public relations function could nurture or impede excellent communication management, although to a lesser extent than could the dominant coalition.

Therefore, the Excellence theory included five theoretical propositions stating that organizations with excellent public relations have the following attributes:

1. Participative rather than authoritarian organizational cultures.
2. A symmetrical system of internal communication.
3. Organic rather than mechanical structures.
4. Programs to equalize opportunities for men and women and minorities.
5. High job satisfaction among employees.

The results of our research demonstrate conclusively that excellent public relations will thrive most in an organization with an organic structure, participative culture, and a symmetrical system of communication and in which opportunities exist for women and racio-ethnic minorities. Although we found that these conditions alone cannot produce excellent public relations, they do provide a hospitable environment for excellent public relations.

Most important, these conditions provide a favorable context in which all employees work most effectively—but especially women and minorities. Within such an organization employees are empowered to participate in decision-making. As a result, they are more satisfied with the organization and are more likely to support than to oppose the goals of the organization. In addition, employees who are empowered to participate in decision-making and to engage in symmetrical internal communication are likely also to be effective symmetrical communicators with members of external publics.

We also found that the effective organization provides a hospitable environment for its increasingly diverse workforce. The CEOs and employees we surveyed seemed to agree on all 22 measured aspects of how women, in particular, are treated in their organizations. Although top management's perceptions were more optimistic, we were encouraged by the general correspondence among the responses from the CEOs, top communicators, and employees. All three groups of respondents clearly differentiated areas in which women are most and least supported. The survey data suggested that equitable treatment of women, as evidenced primarily by economic equity, and programs to foster their careers (such as policies against sexual harassment and efforts to encourage women's leadership abilities) are an integral component of excellent organizations. Programs that provide a supportive work environment correlate especially highly with the other conditions found in excellent organizations. Likewise, excellent organizations are beginning to branch out and offer some proactive mentoring and advancement programs for women.

Our data showed that when the public relations function was given the power to implement symmetrical programs of communication, the result was a more participative culture and greater employee satisfaction with the organization. However, we also found that symmetrical communication is not likely in an organization with a mechanical structure and authoritarian culture. Organic structure and symmetrical communication interact to produce a participative culture, and participative culture contributes strongly to employee satisfaction with the organization.

An organic structure seems to be the key to an effective organization—triggering changes in culture, communication, and satisfaction. Symmetrical communication has a strong role in creating and implementing organic structure, but a communicator cannot step alone into any organization and implement an organic structure or symmetrical system of communication. The top communicator must work with the dominant coalition to develop an organic structure for the organization while he or she is developing a system of symmetrical communication. Our data on the internal context of an organization, therefore, did not just support the need for symmetrical communication. They also supported the need for the public relations function to be represented in the dominant coalition, in order to create the organic structural context for participative culture and subsequent employee satisfaction.

SUMMARIZING THE EXCELLENCE THEORY

The Excellence theory is a broad, general theory that begins with a general premise about the value of public relations to organizations and to society and uses that premise to integrate a number of middle-range theories about the orgaization of the public relations function, the conduct of public relations programs, and the environmental and organizational context of excellent public relations. Since completion of the study, we and other researchers have begun research to extend the theory beyond the three English-speaking countries in which it was conducted. Before introducing that research, however, it is useful to summarize this complex theory.

The Excellence study has shown that public relations is a unique management function that helps an organization interact with the social and political components of its environment. This institutional environment consists of publics that affect the ability of the organization to accomplish its goals and that expect organizations to help them accomplish their own goals. Organizations solve problems for society, but they also create problems for society. As a result, organizations are not autonomous units free to make money or to accomplish other goals they set for themselves. They have relationships with individuals and groups that help set the organization's goals, define what the organization is and does, and affect the success of its strategic decisions and behaviors.

The study showed that the value of public relations comes from the relationships that organizations develop and maintain with publics. It also showed that the quality of relationships results more from the behavior of the organization than from the messages that communicators disseminate. Public relations can affect management decisions and behavior if it is headed by a manager who is empowered to play an essential role in the strategic management of the organization. In that role, communicators have greater value when they bring information into the organization than when they disseminate information out of the organization. The study also showed how communication programs for publics such as employees, consumers, or investors can be planned and managed strategically and evaluated to demonstrate their effectiveness.

Our research showed that communicators can develop relationships more effectively when they communicate with publics symmetrically rather than asymmetrically. Symmetrical communication is especially important inside the organization, where it helps to build a participative culture that, in turn, increases employee satisfaction with the organization. Symmetrical communication inside the organization and participative culture largely result from the structure that top management chooses for the organization. Communicators cannot be successful, therefore, unless they have access to the top-management team that develops an organizational structure. Our research also demonstrated the importance of diversity in a public relations department and throughout the organization. Women and men are equally effective in top communication roles, but we also learned that women have a more difficult time than men developing the experiences needed for a top communication role.

The study showed that excellent communication functions are integrated. However, they are not integrated through another management function, such as marketing or human resources. They are integrated through a senior communication executive—who usually has a background in public relations— or through a single public relations department. We found that integrated marketing communication (IMC) programs, which combine marketing public relations and advertising, are part of an integrated public relations function. IMC should not be the concept that integrates communication.

Finally, the Excellence study showed that activism is good, rather than bads for an organization. Activism provides the impetus for excellent public relations. Excellent public relations departments develop programs to communicate actively, and symmetrically, with activists. Organizations that collaborate with activists develop a competitive advantage over organizations that do not because they behave in a way that is acceptable to publics and, therefore, make fewer decisions that result in negative publicity and regulation, litigation, and opposition.

GLOBALIZATION OF THE EXCELLENCE THEORY

Most organizations are affected by publics throughout the world or by competition or collaboration with organizations in other countries. As a result, all public relations is global or international. Thus, it becomes imperative for public relations professionals to have a broad perspective that will allow them to work in many countries—or to work collaboratively with public relations professionals, employees, or customers from many countries.

In public relations as well as in related fields such as management and marketing, scholars and practitioners have asked whether the principles and practices of their profession are the same regardless of the country in which they are practiced or whether the profession must be enacted differently in each country. Although the Excellence study was conducted in only three English-speaking countries, it has generated a great deal of interest among public relations scholars and practitioners worldwide. This interest suggests that the theoretical principles we have identified are not limited to the United States and that they are applicable to public relations practice outside the three Anglo countries where the study was conducted. Although the United States, Canada, and the United Kingdom are similar in many ways, they also exhibit cultural, political, and social differences. Thus, the fact that we found no difference in excellent public relations among the three countries provides some evidence that the principles are not limited strictly to the United States.

As a result, we have begun research to determine if the Excellence theory can fulfill the need for a global theory of public relations. There is a substantial literature already on international public relations, but it consists mostly of descriptive research on and case studies of public relations practice in many countries of the world (as found, e.g., in Culbertson & Chen, 1996). Many of these studies suggest that public relations is practiced in substantially different ways in different countries—often reflecting cultural differences. At the same time, research has shown that the same four models of public relations we have used to describe U.S. practice (press agentry, public information, two-way asymmetrical, and two-way symmetrical) also describe practice in other countries (J. Grunig, L. Grunig, Sriramesh, Huang, & Lyra, 1995).

We have proposed that, rather than continuing to conduct purely positive research on how public relations is practiced in different countries, scholars should construct a normative theory of excellent global public relations. A normative theory would specify how public relations should be practiced. A good normative theory is based on sound theory; but it also is built from research to identify the most effective existing, or positive, practices of public relations. This is exactly what we have done in the Excellence study.

Before we can adopt the Excellence principles as a normative theory for global practice, we must do research to ensure that they are not an ethnocentric theory. At the same time, we do not believe that different polycentric theories are necessary for each country, region, or culture of the world. Vercic, L. Grunig, and J. Grunig (1996), L. Grunig, J. Grunig, and Vercic (1998), and Wakefield (1996) have collaborated to propose a global public relations theory of generic principles and specific applications—a middle-ground theory between an ethnocentric theory and polycentric theories.

Generic principles means that in an abstract sense, the principles of public relations are the same worldwide. *Specific applications* means that these abstract principles must be applied differently in different settings. For example, the concept of employee participation in decision-making is the same concept throughout the world. However, when Stohl (1993) asked managers in Denmark, Germany, France, England, and The Netherlands how they implemented that principle, she found that they did so differently in each country—in ways that reflected the culture of that country.

As a starting point for research, we have proposed that our principles of excellence are generic principles. We also have proposed that public relations professionals must take six contextual conditions into account when they apply the principles:

- Culture, including language
- The political system
- The economic system
- The media system
- The level of economic development
- The extent and nature of activism

Our research to date has provided evidence supporting this theory of generic principles and specific applications. The most extensive test of the theory came in Slovenia. L. Grunig, J. Grunig, and Vercic (1998) replicated the quantitative portion of the Excellence study with 30 Slovenian firms with public relations departments. They found that the principles of excellence clustered into the same Excellence factor in Slovenia as they did in the United States, Canada, and the United Kingdom, in spite of a different cultural, political, and economic context.

At the same time, the research showed that Slovenian practitioners were less involved in strategic management and were less valued by senior management than practitioners in the English-speaking countries. We also found that privatization and political change in Slovenia had encouraged activism to the extent that activism in Slovenia is now similar to that of the other countries. However, the old Yugoslavian cultural, political, and economic context in Slovenia had left its remnants inside Slovenian organizations, which still had more authoritarian cultures, more asymmetrical communication systems, and lower levels of job satisfaction than did organizations in the Anglo countries.

To deal with these differences, public relations practitioners in Slovenia found it necessary to apply the generic principles differently than in the Anglo countries. For example, they learned that they needed to counsel CEOs to support and empower public relations managers. They also developed continuing education in public relations to deal with the lack of public relations knowledge, and they had to emphasize employee relations because of the negative context inside Slovenian organizations.

Wakefield (1997) asked a Delphi panel of 23 public relations experts in 18 countries to evaluate the extent to which they believed that the Excellence principles were generic principles that applied to their countries and whether additional principles were needed. He also asked them whether all of the six specific conditions were important for applying the generic principles. With the exception of the need for diversity in public relations departments, he found consensus that the principles are generic and that the list of specific conditions is complete. Wakefield (2000) conducted a second Delphi study, which extended the database to 54 experts in 29 countries, and again found support for the principles of excellence and the contextual variables.

Wakefield (2000, 2001) has conducted research on the implications of this theory of generic principles and specific applications for the organization of a public relations function in a multinational organization and of the implications for using public relations firms in different countries. He found that in organizations with what he called a "world class" public relations function the generic principles provided a framework for public relations practice in all countries. However, he found that these world-class companies did not centralize the function or control it through the headquarters office. Rather, they did the following:

- International public relations officers functioned as a global team with frequent interaction among headquarters and local officers and among local officers.

- The senior public relations officer at headquarters served as a team leader for achieving mutual goals, and not as the only decision-maker in a hierarchical structure.
- Ideas and solutions came from any source in the global team.
- The global team cooperatively set public relations values and guidelines, but every unit created and carried out local strategies based on these guidelines. (p. 69)

Another test of the theory came in Korea. Rhee (1999) replicated major portions of the Excellence study and also produced an index of excellence almost identical to the Excellence factor. As was true in Slovenia, however, she found that fewer Korean professionals were involved in strategic management than in the Anglo countries, and she learned that they had less knowledge of the two-way models and managerial role. She also found that symmetrical public relations in Korea had been adapted to fit Confucian culture, with its emphasis on hierarchical relationships combined with collective responsibility.

As we search for and test generic principles of public relations, we have found it beneficial to begin with the Excellence principles. However, it is important to remain open to revision of these principles and to the addition of new ones so that the generic principles are truly global and not ethnocentric. In that regard, Vercic, L. Grunig, and J. Grunig (1996) interviewed three principals of the public relations firm Pristop in Slovenia to determine if they agreed that the Excellence principles are generic, to ask them how they adapted the principles in their country, and to suggest additional principles.

The interviews confirmed the importance of the existing principles and provided examples of context-specific applications of the principles. In addition, the Slovenian professionals suggested a new generic principle: Ethics is a necessary component of excellent public relations. They pointed out that in the postsocialist context of Slovenia, corruption was common and the suspicion of corruption even more common. Therefore, they suggested that ethical practice was a crucial element of excellent public relations in order to avoid damage to their individual reputations as well as to the reputation of the public relations profession.

Although we referred to integrity tangentially throughout the three books on the Excellence project, we did not include it as a principle of excellence or ask questions about it directly in our research. At this point, however, we have added ethical practice to our list of generic principles and consider ethics an important area that needs additional study.

Research, therefore, is well underway on a normative theory of global public relations. However, much more research is needed in many countries of the world to confirm the importance of the generic principles, to refine existing principles, to identify new principles, and to provide positive examples of how to apply the principles in the different local contexts in which global public relations professionals work.

REFERENCES

Begley, R. (1993, Dec. 8). Selling Responsible Care to a critical public: CMA takes its message to the airwaves. *Chemical Week*, p. 23.

Broom, G. M., & Smith, G. D. (1978, August). *Toward an understanding of public relations roles: An empirical test of five role models' impact on clients*. Paper presented at the meeting of the Public Relations Division, Association for Education in Journalism, Seattle.

Broom, G. M., & Smith, G. D. (1979). Testing the practitioner's impact on clients. *Public Relations Review, 5*(3), 47–59.

Culbertson, H. M., & Chen, N. (Eds.). (1996). *International public relations: A comparative analysis*. Mahwah NJ: Lawrence Erlbaum Associates.

Cutlip, S. M., & Center, A. H. (1952). *Effective public relations*. Englewood Cliffs, NJ: Prentice Hall.

Dearing, J. W., & Rogers, E. M. (1996). *Agenda-setting*. Thousand Oaks, CA: Sage.

Dozier, D. M. (1992). The organizational roles of communications and public relations practitioners. In J. E. Grunig (Ed.), *Excellence in public relations and communication management* (pp. 327–356). Hillsdale, NJ: Lawrence Erlbaum Associates.

Dozier, D. M., with Grunig, L. A., & Grunig, J. E. (1995). *Manager's guide to excellence in public relations and communication management. Hillsdale*, NJ: Lawrence Erlbaum Associates.

Duncan, T., & Moriarty, S. (1997). *Driving brand value: Using integrated marketing to manage profitable stakeholder relationships*. New York: McGraw-Hill.

Ehling, W. P. (1992). Estimating the value of public relations and communication to an organization. In J. E. Grunig (Ed.), *Excellence in public relations and communication management* (pp. 617–638). Hillsdale, NJ: Lawrence Erlbaum Associates.

Fleisher, C. S. (1995). *Public affairs benchmarking*. Washington: Public Affairs Council.

Fombrun, C. J. (1996). *Reputation: Realizing value from the corporate image*. Boston: Harvard Business School Press.

Freeman, R. E., & Gilbert, D. R. Jr. (1992, Spring). Business, ethics and society: A critical agenda. *Business and Society*, pp. 9–17.

Goodman, P. S., & Pennings, J. M. (Eds.). (1977). *New perspectives on organizational effectiveness*. San Francisco: Jossey-Bass.

Gronstedt, A. (2000). *The customer century: Lessons from world-class companies in integrated marketing and communication*. New York: Routledge.

Grunig, J. E. (1976). Organizations and publics relations: Testing a communication theory. *Journalism Monographs, 46*.

Grunig, J. E. (1983). Washington reporter publics of corporate public affairs programs. *Journalism Quarterly, 60*, 603–615.

Grunig, J. E. (1984). Organizations, environments, and models of public relations. *Public Relations Research & Education, 1*(1), 6–29.

Grunig, J. E. (Ed.). (1992a). *Excellence in public relations and communication management*. Hillsdale, NJ: Lawrence Erlbaum Associates.

Grunig, J. E. (1992b). Symmetrical systems of internal communication. In J. E. Grunig (Ed.), *Excellence in public relations and communication management* (pp. 531–576). Hillsdale, NJ: Lawrence Erlbaum Associates.

Grunig, J. E. (1992c). What is excellence in management? In J. E. Grunig (Ed.), *Excellence in public relations and communication management* (pp. 219–250). Hillsdale, NJ: Lawrence Erlbaum Associates.

Grunig, J. E. (1997). Public relations management in government and business. In J. L. Garnett & A. Kouzmin (Eds.), *Handbook of administrative communication* (pp. 241–283). New York: Marcel Dekker.

Grunig, J. E. (2001). Two-way symmetrical public relations: Past, present, and future. In R. L. Heath (Ed.), *Handbook of public relations* (pp. 11–30). Thousand Oaks, CA: Sage.

Grunig, J. E., & Grunig, L. A. (1989). Toward a theory of the public relations behavior of organizations: Review of a program of research. In J. E. Grunig & L. A. Grunig (Eds.), *Public relations research annual* (Vol. 1, pp. 27–66.). Hillsdale, NJ: Lawrence Erlbaum Associates.

Grunig, J. E., & Grunig, L. A. (1992). Models of public relations and communication. In J. E. Grunig (Ed.), *Excellence in public relations and communication management* (pp. 285–326). Hillsdale, NJ: Lawrence Erlbaum Associates.

Grunig, J. E., Grunig, L. A., Sriramesh, K., Huang, Y. H., & Lyra, A. (1995). Models of public relations in an international setting. *Journal of Public Relations Research, 7*, 163–186.

Grunig, J. E., & Hunt, T. (1984). *Managing public relations.* New York: Holt, Rinehart & Winston.

Grunig, L. A. (1992a). Activism: How it limits the effectiveness of organizations and how excellent public relations departments respond. In J. E. Grunig (Ed.), *Excellence in public relations and communication management* (pp. 503–530). Hillsdale, NJ: Lawrence Erlbaum Associates.

Grunig, L. A. (1992b). Power in the public relations department. In J. E. Grunig (Ed.), *Excellence in public relations and communication management* (pp. 483–502). Hillsdale, NJ: Lawrence Erlbaum Associates.

Grunig, L. A., Grunig, J. E., & Dozier, D. M. (2002). *Excellent public relations and effective organizations: A study of communication management in three countries.* Mahwah, NJ: Lawrence Erlbaum Associates.

Grunig, L. A., Grunig, J. E., & Ehling, W. P. (1992). What is an effective organization? In J. E. Grunig (Ed.), *Excellence in public relations and communication management* (pp. 65–90). Hillsdale, NJ: Lawrence Erlbaum Associates.

Grunig, L. A., Grunig, J. E., & Vercic, D. (1998). Are the IABC's excellence principles generic? Comparing Slovenia and the United States, the United Kingdom and Canada. *Journal of Communication Management, 2*, 335–356.

Hall, R. H. (1991). *Organizations: Structures, processes, and outcomes* (5th ed.). Englewood Cliffs, NJ: Prentice-Hall.

Hunter, T. (1997). *The relationship of public relations and marketing against the background of integrated communications: A theoretical analysis and empirical study at US-American corporations.* Unpublished master's thesis, University of Salzburg, Salzburg, Austria.

Hunter, T. (1999a). *Integrated communications: Current and future developments in integrated communications and brand management, with a focus on direct communication and new information and communication technologies, such as the Internet and stakeholder databases.* Unpublished doctoral dissertation, University of Salzburg, Salzburg, Austria.

Hunter, T. (1999b). The relationship of public relations and marketing. *Integrated Marketing Communications Research Journal, 5*(1), 41–44.

Jeffries-Fox Associates (2000a, March 3). *Toward a shared understanding of corporate reputation and related concepts: Phase I: Content analysis.* Basking Ridge, NJ: Report Prepared for the Council of Public Relations Firms.

Jeffries-Fox Associates (2000b, June 16). *Toward a shared understanding of corporate reputation and related concepts: Phase III: Interviews with client advisory committee members.* Basking Ridge, NJ: Report Prepared for the Council of Public Relations Firms.

Kuhn, T. S. (1970). *The structure of scientific revolutions* (2nd ed.). Chicago: University of Chicago Press. (A third edition of Kuhn's classic book also was published in 1996.)

McCombs, M., & Bell, T. (1996). The agenda-setting role of mass communication. In M. B. Salwen & D. Stacks (Eds.), *An integrated approach to communication theory and research* (pp. 93–110). Mahwah, NJ: Lawrence Erlbaum Associates.

McQuail, D. (2000). *McQuail's mass communication theory* (4th ed.). Newbury Park, CA: Sage.

Peters, T. J., & Waterman, R. H., Jr. (1982). *In search of excellence.* New York: Warner.

Post, J. E., Preston, L. E., & Sachs, S. (2002). *Redefining the corporation: Stakeholder management and organizational wealth.* Stanford, CA: Stanford Business Books.

Price, J. L. (1968). *Organizational effectiveness: An inventory of propositions.* Homewood, IL: Richard D. Irwin.

Rhee, Y. (1999). *Confucian culture and excellent public relations: A study of generic principles and specific applications in South Korean public relations practice.* Unpublished master's thesis, University of Maryland, College Park.

Robbins, S. P. (1990). *Organization theory: Structure, design, and application* (3rd ed.). Englewood Cliffs, NJ: Prentice-Hall.

Schultz, D. E., Tannenbaum, S. I., & Lauterborn, R. E. (1993). *Integrated marketing communications.* Chicago: NTC Business Books.

Stohl, C. (1993). European managers' interpretations of participation: A semantic network analysis. *Human Communication Research, 20,* 97–117.

Thorson, E., & Moore, J. (Eds.). (1996). *Integrated communication: Synergy of persuasive voices.* Mahwah, NJ: Lawrence Erlbaum Associates.

Vercic, D., Grunig, L. A., & Grunig, J. E. (1996). Global and specific principles of public relations: Evidence from Slovenia. In H. M. Culbertson & N. Chen (Eds.), *International public relations: A comparative analysis* (pp. 31–65). Mahwah NJ: Lawrence Erlbaum Associates.

Wakefield, R. I. (1996). Interdisciplinary theoretical foundations for international public relations. In H. M. Culbertson & N. Chen (Eds.), *International public relations: A comparative analysis* (pp. 17–30). Mahwah NJ: Lawrence Erlbaum Associates.

Wakefield, R. I. (1997). *International public relations: A theoretical approach to excellence based on a worldwide Delphi study.* Unpublished doctoral dissertation, University of Maryland, College Park.

Wakefield, R. I. (2000). World-class public relations: A model for effective public relations in the multinational. *Journal of Communication Management, 5*(1), 59–71.

Wakefield, R. I. (2001). Effective public relations in the multinational organization. In R. E. Heath (Ed.), *Handbook of public relations* (pp. 639–647). Thousand Oaks, CA: Sage.

Wallack, L., Dorfman, L., Jernigan, D., & Themba, M. (1993). *Media advocacy and public health: Power for prevention.* Newbury Park, CA: Sage.

Weick, K. E. (1979). *The social psychology of organizing* (2nd ed.). Reading, MA: Addison-Wesley.

Who's excellent now? (1984, November 5). *BusinessWeek*, pp. 76–87.

3

A Rhetorical Theory Approach to Issues Management

Robert L. Heath
University of Houston

A RHETORICAL THEORY APPROACH TO ISSUES MANAGEMENT

Issues management has grown as an applied and research discipline to compensate for what some believed was an insufficient approach to the practice of public relations in the mid-1970s. The inadequacy of the then state-of-the art approach to activist criticism was repeatedly demonstrated by strategic responses to corporate critics through counter publicity efforts, rather than solid issues engagement and corporate strategic planning adjustments. Instead of taking more sound responses to such criticism, many organizations engaged in stonewalling, expressed outrage at what were alleged to be presumptuous outbursts by critics of big business, and blamed the problems of society on the persons who were trying to call attention to and offer ways to solve those problems. This reactionary response, which often tried to blame the messenger, seemed to imply that no civil-rights, consumer-rights, or environmental-rights problems would exist if the critics would cease their clamor.

To formulate new ways to meet this challenge to the prerogatives of corporate governance, leading practitioners, academics, and business leaders developed issues management through many heated discussions at the senior executive level. Tradition has it that W. Howard Chase (1977) drew on his experience at American Can Company to develop the concept: a means of strengthening large organizations' ability to monitor, analyze, and respond to challenges voiced by myriad critics of private sector practices and policies. His efforts were supported by others, such as John E. O'Toole (1975a, 1975b), O'Toole may have coined the term *advocacy advertising* which was offered to strengthen the corporate voice in response to strident challenges by critics.

The turbulent 1960s and 1970s had caught America's private sector leadership off guard. At the start of that era, public relations was a feel-good discipline devoted to media relations, publicity, promotion, and integrated marketing communication. In partial response to this narrowness of response options, public affairs had grown as a substitute for public relations. Public affairs quickly achieved substantial popularity with the managements of larger corporations. Today the Public Affairs Council and the Public Relations Society of America see proactive strategic response to marketplace and public policy issues as a vital and central challenge to corporate leadership.

Issues management was not the brainchild of any one person. Several academics, corporate leaders, public affairs/public relations practitioners, and even some advertising persons decided that a new or renewed array of strategic options was needed to respond to and even combat the broad and resilient challenges to corporate America and the U.S. government that were voiced during the activist era of the 1970s. To review the leadership of this movement, Heath and Cousino (1990) examined several hundred articles and other publications to better understand leaders' analysis and responses to deficiencies in organizations' preparedness to respond to their critics.

Critics of government and business eventually reshaped the culture and ideology of society on civil rights, environmental rights, consumer rights, worker rights—and the list continues. New sociopolitical dynamics began in the 1960s to guide government policies and private sector practices. Businesses lost much of their public policy clout as the result of four dramatic changes: (a) Activists claimed that natural resources, found to be limited and rhetorically defined as the property of the citizens of the nation, and even the world, were to be managed in the collective interest. (b) Society became sensitive to the increasing heterogeneity of values, attitudes, beliefs, interests, and cultures, which destroyed the business-first policy consensus that prevailed at the start of the 1960s. (c) Citizens became less willing to act with deference toward business and government; they lost confidence in the ability of large institutions, such as government, media, and business, to recognize and solve problems. Citizens placed their confidence in activist groups and called on them to exert their collective power. (d) Standards of corporate responsibility changed (Pfeffer, 1981). This fertile ground fed the growth of business criticism and issues management.

Building out of this perspective, the purpose of this chapter is to provide a comprehensive survey of the leading commentary on issues management and to investigate its theoretical underpinnings. In broad measures, this chapter features three topic areas: the definition and theoretical underpinnings of issues and issues management; the implications of these underpinnings for future research and theory development; and a discussion of the implications of the theory and research for the practice of issues management in conjunction with public relations and public affairs.

This review is designed to explore in specific the rhetorical implications for issues management. Given that latitude, this author elects to draw on Western Civilization's rhetorical heritage, in particular the works of teachers in the golden age of Greece and Rome, the writings of Kenneth Burke, and the implications of the narrative view of rhetoric. Also, a couple of social scientific underpinnings are valuable to this discussion as well—social exchange theory and information integration theory. The central theme extracted from this literature can lead one to conclude that the rhetoric of issues management examines the rationale, motives, processes, and outcomes of advocacy discourse on public policy matters that influence the relationships between corporate entities and their stakeholders/stakeseekers. The ultimate effort of this rhetoric is to create enough concurrence that interested members of the general public, business, government, media, and nonprofit sectors can forge mutually beneficial policies. The upshot of this dialogue is a constant revision of citizens' expectations as to how business, government, media, and nonprofit organizations should conduct their business.

LITERATURE REVIEW

Defining Issues Management and Issues: The Legitimacy Gap

How we study issues management, and especially the rhetoric of issues management, depends on how we define the practice. How one defines issues management also reflects one's definition of public relations. Some see public relations as the umbrella concept under which issues management is one of many specialty functions. This view of the discipline would assume that public relations was always interested in public policy issues and routinely engaged in identifying, monitoring, analyzing, and strategically responding to them. To date, no definition of issues management has achieved consensus, nor has the discipline achieved its potential (Gaunt & Ollenburger, 1995).

Persons who see issues management as embracing but going beyond public relations and even public affairs are likely to conclude that especially during the activism of the 1960s, public relations practitioners were primarily interested in marketing publicity and promotion and simply dropped the ball when asked for advice on how to deal with activist critics. Advocates of a broader view of issues management are likely to ask whether public relations is seriously engaged in top-level organizational planning, development and implementation of standards of corporate responsibility, and advocacy—dialogue and collaborative decision making—that defends the interests of each organization by building effective relationships with its critical publics.

Any reasonable definition must acknowledge the challenge put down by Sethi (1977), one of the contributors to the research legacy of issues management. He believed that issues arise when large organizations suffer a legitimacy gap between what they do and what their markets and publics expect (prefer) them to do. The gap can result from differences of fact, value, and policy (Heath, 1997). It can foster division instead of merger. It can result in the enactment of competing narratives. It can strain the resource balances between organizations and the persons they affect. It can result in conflicting attitudes and behaviors between organizations and those of the persons whose goodwill they need. These strains can be managed rhetorically, but are more than differences of opinion. They often entail battles for power resource management. Activists learned to use power resources to force change that businesses would not make voluntarily.

Some who discuss this topic may argue that issues management entails only spirited defense and symbolic protection of the actions, rights, policies, and prerogatives of an organization—a stonewall approach to issues management, which presumes that the organization is always correct and critics are inherently wrong. This view of issues management urges that the symbolic boundaries of the organization should be defended by convincing critics that their challenges are unwarranted, unsubstantiated, and unmerited. A "purely rhetorical approach" to issues management can presume that the organization is correct and does not need to change itself to abate the challenges of its critics. Such views of issues managements can lead to tactical victories, but are likely to lose the strategic battles and eventually the war of public policy. They simply do not address the root causes of the friction between organizations and their critics.

Strategic Options: Denying the Legitimacy Gap or Stewarding Change

On the one end of a spectrum we have the symbolic view of issues management. On the other end rests the operational approach, which suggests that executive managements of organizations need to constantly adjust their policies to please and appease their external critics. Between these two polar extremes, one can find variations and a blend of the positions: a stewardship commitment to communication, to the extent that rhetorical stances can solve the legitimacy gap, with the proviso that the organization may also need to make small or even dramatic policy and management changes to reduce that gap.

The rhetorical principles of issues management can and probably do have a strong persuasive element. Critics advocate change. The organization can defend current actions and the new policy positions it proposes that may be adopted to end the criticism. This dialogue can be strident. It can be cordial, an honest effort to engage in collaborative decision making. The process entails multiple stakeholder (and stakeseeker) publics. Some of these publics may agree with the issue positions and management policy changes advocated by the organization; others may oppose them. The rhetorical enactment of issues management entails multiple and varied voices who advocate various issues and policy positions—who challenge the best efforts to achieve consensus. Some stakeholders are likely to praise corporate policy changes at the same time other stakeholders oppose and are even outraged by them.

Given these dynamics, the rhetoric of issues management is best conceived of as dialogue. Both—sides have views they express and preferences they advocate. This dialogue is the product of statement and counter statement, voiced expressions of what organizations do and what they should do, what they prefer as ideology and policy principles.

The optimal outcome of such advocacy is the resolution of some or all of the differences, which can foster social harmony. To do so requires, from an organization's point of view, that it reduce the legitimacy gap by moving closer to the expectations of its stakeholders, or that it must convince the stakeholders that their expectations are incorrect or unwise.

In a limited sense, a rhetorical view of issues management can assume that the organization is always correct and that a variety of rhetorical strategies can win the day. As Cheney and Dionisopoulos (1989) have observed, the ultimate struggle is for "control over the (value) premises that shape basic and applied policy decisions. In essence, corporate discourse seeks to establish public frames of reference for interpreting information concerning issues deemed important by Corporate America" (p. 144).

At one end of the rhetorical continuum, Sproule (1989) reasoned, "Organizations try to privatize public space by privatizing public opinions; that is, skillfully (one-sidedly) turning opinion in directions favorable to the corporation" (p. 264). At the other end, critics seek to impose public policy controls on the private decisions of corporate leaders. Both sides devote their efforts to deciding which actions and policies are best and to defining the value premises of society that privilege some actions and prohibit others. Stressing this view of issues management, Ewing (1987) concluded that it "developed within the business community as an educational task aimed at preserving the proper balance between the legitimate goals and rights of the free enterprise system and those of society" (p. 5). The battle over public policy and value principle hegemony is best when it seeks and achieves a mutually beneficial middle ground between interested parties.

Without doubt, the organization can be correct in the opinions it holds and the policies it implements. Thus, it can be expected to shoulder the stewardship responsibility of defending itself and the policy positions it prefers through strategic communication. Likewise, the organization can be incorrect and therefore need to change its policies, actions, and missions to adopt new and better standards of corporate responsibility or to be more effective in implementing the standards that its critics have become convinced are the most acceptable. The requirement is to reduce the legitimacy gap between the organization and its stakeholders and stakeseekers. Following this logic, issues-oriented communication is best when it aspires to be collaborative rather than combative.

This section has argued that the battle over the legitimacy gap is the heart and soul of the issues management process. People and organizations can be at peace or at war with one another. Such battles are the rationale for issues management rhetoric.

Defining Issues Management and Issues: Organizational Program or Public Relations Function

What we carve out as the theory of issues management rhetoric depends on how we define the discipline. Several corporate executives, academics, and communication professionals working in the 1970s observed that the standard practice of public relations left corporations without an adequate rationale and set of strategies to counter allegations that eventually eroded much of the privilege the private sector had enjoyed. New public policies grew from a culture that had come to reflect increased sensitivities about myriad issues: civil rights, environmental quality standards, working conditions, consumer rights, women's rights, and the "beat goes on."

In its efforts to respond to these tensions, issues management was recommended to be an early issues detection system, a means for creating less contentious corporate policy and planning, a device for better meeting key publics' standards of corporate responsibility, and a function assigned the responsibility to create rhetorical responses to the organization's critics. Proponents of the discipline tend to feature issues management as performing some or all of these functions. They tend either to view the discipline as larger than public relations—often a senior-level management or staff function—or a strategic option or function of public relations.

Topics of this kind became more widely discussed and relevant to corporate success in the 1970s. In that decade, companies were brought to task for their actions and policies. They suffered public condemnation for the same policies that many corporate and governmental leaders believed were effective in ending the Great Depression and winning the Second World War. The heady feeling of those successes had been increased by a new sense of postwar consumer prosperity. Corporations could do no wrong. Then, activist challenges came fast and furious. Every part of society was reevaluated. The undergirding of business was assaulted.

Although the term was new—a product of the 1970s—the concept and practice of issues management were not. As Heath (1997) has documented, the origins of contemporary issues management can be traced back to the battles by corporate leaders to forge favorable public policy even before the turn of the 20th century. The clearest instance of that tradition was the evolution of state and federal policy that tolerated and even supported ever larger industrial complexes. Issues management efforts were brought onto the public policy battlefield by industry leaders who a century later would be household names: Edison and Westinghouse. One of the great issues management efforts was the "battle of the currents," in which these titans of the electric generating industry fought over industry standards, pitting direct and alternating currents against one another.

Evidence such as this can support the conclusion that issues management has long been a tool of corporations, labor, government, and even activists. Labor— the great era of labor organization around the turn of the 20th century—adopted the device of organizational advocacy to champion better working conditions. The Populist Farmers and the Progressive young professionals fought serious battles to oppose the threats to health, safety, and the public welfare brought about by the economic tyranny of burgeoning industrial combines formed by executives who had come to bear the name Robber Barons. All of this turmoil and struggle to forge corporate and public policy has become part of the legacy of the rhetoric of issues management.

At the rhetorical level, public policy contests of this sort entail the public examination of facts, evaluations, and policies. Symbolic positioning results in the creation and dissolution of identifications. It results in the creation of one set of narratives that subsequently is challenged by a competing set of narratives. Burke (1969) called this clash of voices "the Scramble, the Wrangle of the Marketplace, the flurries and flare-ups of the Human Barnyard, Give and Take, the wavering line of pressure and counter pressure, the Logomachy, the onus of ownership, the War of Nerves, the War" (p. 23).

Competing voices produce new standards with which to define and evaluate "the good organization." Privileges seem to go to the "good organization that communicates effectively." Although the paradigm of the public spokesperson has been the corporate entity defining and protecting its symbolic boundaries (Cheney, 1992; Cheney & Dionisopoulos, 1989) for the better part of a century, the conception of the effective corporate citizen is as ancient as the prescriptive preferences of Quintilian (1951), who reasoned that the paradigm of the effective citizen was the good person who could speak well.

Thus, one element of the paradigm of the rhetoric of issues management is the organization that seeks and achieves concurrence as to the best standards of corporate social responsibility. Another factor in that paradigm is that the organization must be capable of the stewardship of promoting and defending the sound policies and principles that support corporate operations in the mutual best interest of society.

To be an effective advocate for such standards requires the effective speaker to be above moral reproach. The next requirement is to communicate effectively. Advocates for higher moral standards must be able to demonstrate that they have met the challenges that they advocate for others. To examine the relationship between issues management and public relations assumes that we start with Quintilian's challenge. Can a bad organization communicate effectively? If it can do so in the near term, can such an organization sustain its privilege in the dialogue over the long haul?

The Requirements of a Rhetorical Theory of Issues Management

To address that question drives us to the heart of what issues management is, and what its relationship to public relations is. Here we can explore the requirements for issues management rhetoric.

This analysis results in a clash of perspectives—a challenge of definitions that become institutionalized public and marketplace policies. Thus we can ask, is issues management a subfunction of public relations or an umbrella that encompasses it? How does issues management relate to strategic business planning? Is the function expected to reactively justify strategic planning, or is it vital to proactive strategic planning? In either case, the function cannot succeed without executive-level authority and budgetary support (Lukasik, 1981; Spitzer, 1979; Zraket, 1981).

Is issues management merely public relations revisited (Ehling & Hesse, 1983; Fox, 1983), and in that way more or less a subfunction of public relations (Cutlip, Center, & Broom, 2000; J. Grunig & Repper, 1992)? The Special Committee on Terminology of the Public Relations Society of America defined as "issues management systematic identification and action regarding public policy matters of concern to an organization" (Public Relations Society of America, 1987, p. 9).

Is it a program to help companies enjoy more effective involvement in the public policy process (Public Affairs Council, 1978)? Is it an executive-level staff function and community-oriented sense of organizational culture that empower public relations by giving it greater involvement in corporate strategic business planning and management (Heath, 1988, 1997; Lauzen, 1994; Lauzen & Dozier, 1994; Nelson & Heath, 1986)? Is it a new organizational discipline that features "public policy foresight and planning for an organization" (Ewing, 1987, p. 1)?

If public relations is limited to media relations and publicity and promotion—even integrated marketing communication, then it simply does not enjoy a corporate-level perspective and does not see and constructively deal with the big picture of the quality of fit between the organization and its stakeholders. In that case, public relations is not defined and implemented in a way that can even have issues management as a subfunction.

How issues management is defined depends not only on its organizational status but also on the functions that it performs. If issues management is only issues identification and response, it could be a public relations and public affairs function, if these disciplines engage in customer relations, community relations, government relations, and other efforts to adjust the relationship between the organization and its key publics and markets. If issues management is invested into the strategic planning and management of the organization—if the organization's executives want to position it so that it can affect as well as strategically adapt to its public policy arena and marketplace—then public relations simply may not be up to the challenge. However, as this discussion suggests, it's all in the definition.

In that regard, the turbulent 1970s demonstrated to many leaders—planning and operations executives as well as communication executives—that if public relations was not engaged in issues management—planning, monitoring, becoming a better organization, and responding to the voices of change—then the new discipline Chase, Ewing, and other corporate leaders had proposed could add value to the organization. Such challenges called on many if not most practitioners to increase the array of skills and strategic options that they needed to master. Under this challenge, many public relations and public affairs departments learned to take an issues management perspective.

Participants in this challenge engaged in "old hat" and "new stuff" debates. Some leading organizations created issues management teams and even departments that drew together personnel from the public relations department as well as from planning and operational departments. Those committees reported to executive management, not to the manager of public relations.

Putting a New Face on an Old Challenge

One way to examine the nature of issues management is to explore the incentives that led important thinkers in the 1970s to believe they needed new corporate strategies to deal with turbulence created by critics. This turmoil went beyond what these leaders had experienced and seemed to challenge the very foundations of the private sector.

Witnessing these trends, Bateman (1975) advised companies "to move from an information base to an advocacy position" in their responses to their critics and to build relationships with key publics (p. 5). This stance, he rationalized, was needed because "companies should not be the silent children of society"

(p. 3). Taking a cautious step to advise companies to make more bold responses to their critics, the International Association of Advertising (IAA), in its global study of issues communication, urged adoption of the less contentious term *controversy advertising* (Barnet, 1975). By 1976, terms such as *issue advertising* and *advocacy advertising* were being used in business publication discussions of the aggressive op-ed campaign made famous by Mobil Oil Corporation (Ross, 1976). Making the connection between advertising and issues, Dinsmore (1978) contended that "ideas could be sold like soap" (p. 16), but only if their presentation was complete and truthful. Advertising sought to provide the answer (Pincus, 1980).

Nevertheless, corporate leaders were convinced that they needed substantial revisions in the practice of advertising and public relations. Perhaps a new discipline was needed. Corporate executives and senior practitioners worked to define effective and ethical strategic responses their companies needed to take to counter their critics. In September 1978, Kalman B. Druck, Chairman, Harshe-Rotman & Druck, Inc. told the Houston Chapter of the Public Relations Society of America that "enormous opportunities await those who are willing to make the commitment, to apply professional management and public relations skills to the bitter confrontations industry is now facing" (p. 114).

Some proponents of issues management were communication specialists who worked for executives guided by the assumption that critics of business could be shouted down. This organizational function exhibited a business-is-sacred bias that featured issues advertising, a concept that produced a backlash (Ehrbar, 1978). Corporate leaders and their communication specialists had taken the status of their organizations for granted, heady with the accomplishments of victory over the Great Depression and the foes defeated by Allied forces in World War II. Without realizing the trend, they had slowly become politicized.

In 1979, *BusinessWeek* commented on this trend, featuring the political challenge facing the private sector with its governmental allies and speculating on the communication options that would solve this problem: "The corporation is being politicized and has assumed another dimension in our society that it did not have as recently as 10 years ago." What was needed, the publication asked? Featuring public relations, it concluded that a new breed of practitioners was required to defend business by "articulating its positions more clearly and urgently to government agencies, legislators, shareholders, employees, customers, financial institutions, and critical audiences" ("The Corporate Image," 1979, p. 47).

The Rhetorical Paradigm of the Good Organization Communicating Well

What was needed, some thought, was not more articulate advocates, but advocates who had achieved higher standards of corporate responsibility. Thus, in the spirit of Quintilian (1951), the ancient Roman teacher of speakers, critics called for the organization to be good as a first step to becoming more articulate. One such critic, management professor S. Prakesh Sethi (1976a, 1976b, 1977) strenuously argued that merely explaining the corporate point of view could never be efficacious. Companies that shout loudest often may deserve regulation most. Sensitive to the limitations of a communication bias, some companies, such as Prudential Insurance Company of America (MacNaughton, 1976), institutionalized standards of corporate responsibility, especially in their governmental relations programs (Bradt, 1972).

Although a communication perspective dominated discussions of how companies could handle their critics, some executives recognized that issues analysis must be incorporated into strategic business planning. William S. Sneath, President of Union Carbide Corporation, said in 1977 that his company was using "scenario evaluation" to project its business planning efforts 20 years into the future. Public policy issues, such as environmentalism, were a vital part of the planning effort at Union Carbide. Sneath said that only time could judge "our legacy not only in terms of the economic accuracy of our business planning but in the way we committed our best minds and our best intentions to meet the needs and aspirations of a free society in an increasingly interdependent world" (p. 199). Corporate leaders who supported the innovation of issues management recognized that slick issue advertising could not manipulate opinion and thereby "manage issues."

Giving substance to this sort of preference, Archie R. Boe (1979), CEO of Allstate Insurance Companies (1972–1982) and later President of Sears (1982–1984), created a Strategic Planning Committee in 1977 and an Issues Management Committee in 1978. The two groups had interlocking memberships. The vice president who chaired the Issues Management Committee was also a member of the Strategic Planning Committee. Supported by this level of corporate leadership, issues management's struggle for prominence did not rely exclusively on communication options. Leaders in the formation of this new discipline recognized the need for a well-integrated mix of strategic business planning, public policy analysis, and business ethics, along with advocacy communication.

Meeting Challenges Through Multilevel Responses

One of the strongest and most well-developed statements supporting issues management was published in 1978 by the Public Affairs Council. In a pamphlet titled *The Fundamentals of Issue Management*, the Council explained, "Issues management is a program which a company uses to increase its knowledge of the public policy process and enhance the sophistication and effectiveness of its involvement in that process" (p. 1). Rather than relying only on communication as the savior of corporate privilege, the Council featured the need for several interlocking functions: "Identifying issues and trends, evaluating their impact and setting priorities, establishing a company position, designing company action and response to help achieve the position (e.g., communication, lobbying, lawsuits, and advertising, etc.), and implementing the plans" (p. 2). Communication was the heart of issues management, the Council believed. It proclaimed, "Public affairs has increasingly come to mean not merely a response to change, but a positive role in the management of change itself—in the shaping of public policies and programs, and in the development of corporate activities to implement change constructively" (p. 2).

Sponsored by The Conference Board's Public Affairs Research Council, James K. Brown (1979) conducted a research project to determine how public affairs practitioners and corporate executives defined issues management. The study's findings could be used to help public affairs practitioners "and their colleagues in top management do a better job of planning" (p. ii). Rather than being limited to concerns regarding how issues mature into legislation or regulation, the study argued that issues management must be integrated into all management planning and be focused on the central task of helping the company—through its strategic management. What functions were needed for effective issues management? Brown advocated planning, monitoring, analyzing, and communicating.

What principle guides this activity? Strategic planning personnel need to spot, analyze, and know what can and cannot (should and should not) be done to communicate on public policy issues and how to adjust products and services to hostile environments as well as to take advantage of favorable ones. Brown (1979) reasoned that "if management should accustom itself routinely to ask the full range of questions that ought to be asked about vital corporate decisions, taking into account all the relevant external environments as well as the internal environment, this business of issues would become, properly, a non-issue" (p. 74). No single issues management function can accomplish that goal. Thus, any commitment to issues management rhetoric that lacks substantial management planning and issues analysis support could render corporate responses hollow outbursts of moral outrage.

Recognition of such limitations led issues management innovators to recognize the virtue of subtle but firm integration of strategic business planning and issues monitoring. Strategic business planning and environmental scanning become partners—at least in the literature, if not in practice. In 1979, *Business-Week* reported on the fledgling trend by some companies to use environmental scanning to improve strategic business plans and to alert line managers to changes in public sentiments regarding operating procedures ("Capitalizing on social change;" 1979).

Proponents of new approaches to corporate positioning often associated themselves with public affairs. In this way, one attempt to identify the key functions of issues management reasoned that it involved three activities: "issue identification, corporate proaction, and the inclusion of public affairs issues in established decision-making processes and managerial functions" (Fleming, 1980, p. 35). Business professors such as Fleming led this innovation by advising executives to realize that when corporate planning and public policy issues were on a collision trajectory, the company was likely to lose or waste valuable resources. Other business faculty, in particular Post (1978, 1979) and Buchholz (1982, 1985), produced seminal studies to expose the important role public policy plays in corporate planning and operation.

Reflecting on this trend, Renfro (1993), a pioneer in the theory and practice of issues management, stressed the need to identify and monitor issues as a preliminary to strategic planning. He made this case as he reflected on the history of the discipline: "The field of issues management emerged as public relations or public affairs officers included more and more forecasting and futures research in their planning and analysis of policy" (Renfro, 1993, p. 23). In this sense, "issues management is an intelligence function that does not get involved in the 'operations side' unless specifically directed to do so" (Renfro, 1993, p. 89).

The Rhetoric of Issues Management: Internal and External Dialogues

As it has emerged, issues management is a reaction to activism and the increasing intra- and interindustry pressures by corporations to define and implement higher standards of corporate responsibility—as well as debate in public what those standards should be. Issues management encompasses all efforts corporations must make to create harmony with key players in their public policy arena—by sensing changing standards of the norms of business practice preferred by key publics, especially those who have become activists. Corporate leaders and business college faculty led the discussion of corporate responsibility. Leaders in the discipline recognized the need to integrate strategic planning, public policy analysis, and communication (Marx, 1986). One of those leaders, Monsanto Corporation, has used issues management to determine which product lines are advisable in light of public policy trends (Fleming, 1980; Stroup, 1988). Describing Monsanto's contingency approach, Stroup (1988) observed: "Early knowledge of these trends would give the company more time to change negative attitudes toward business or to adapt business practices proactively if attitudes and expectations could not be swayed from the identified path" (p. 89).

This brief review of literature about the definition and functions of issues management demonstrates that even though no perspective prevails, several functions recur in the discussion. To some, issues management is "the organized activity of identifying emerging trends, concerns, or issues likely to affect an organization in the next few years and developing a wider and more positive range of organizational responses toward that future" (Coates, Coates, Jarratt, & Heinz, 1986, p. ix). Chase (1984) and Coates et al. (1986) were leaders in the efforts to increase management's awareness of issues while they were emerging. The assumption was that more leverage could be exerted on issues if responses could be made at the earliest stages of each issue's development. As Hainsworth and Meng (1988) contended, doing so gives "senior management the means to intelligently participate in the public policy process" (p. 28). Authors such as Crable and Vibbert (1985) developed models of the issues emergence process trying to demonstrate how early detection and response could be achieved.

Thus, corporate social responsibility and issues development awareness seem vital for effective strategic business planning and communication. But issues awareness, identification, and analysis alone do no good. At some point actions are needed, whether they are refinements of the organization's strategic business plan, its standards of corporate responsibility, its public policy plans, or its communication plan.

Issues management can link the public relations function and the management function to help the organization be outer directed and to have a participative organizational culture. Blending these functions is vital for organizations that seek harmonious relationships in an environment that is complex because of the number of publics and the variety of issues to be considered. Astute public relations practitioners used issues management to "expand the role of public relations beyond media relations and product publicity to a senior management problem-solving function critical to the survival of an organization" (Tucker, Broom, & Caywood, 1993, p. 38). The new discipline appealed to management as a "process whose goal is to help preserve markets, reduce risk, create opportunities and manage image as an organization asset for the benefit of both an organization and its primary shareholders" (Tucker et al., 1993, p. 38).

As long ago as the late 1970s, astute observers noted that issues management is an amalgamation of several disciplines and specialty functions. It includes identifying, monitoring, and analyzing trends in key publics' opinions that can mature into public policy and regulatory or legislative constraint of the private sector. It involves a staff function that, along with technical and managerial personnel support, can develop a corporate or industry stance to be executed through strategic business plans and communication campaigns. No other corporate function more completely stresses the inseparability of ethical corporate behavior, public judgment, responsible production and delivery of goods and services, and internal and external attempts to inform and persuade targeted constituencies to gain their support. Issues management goes beyond communication with various constituencies. It can penetrate all operations. The underpinning principle of issues management is not to shield an organization against emerging legislation or regulation, but to balance the interests of all segments of the community, so that each enjoys the proper amount of reward or benefit in proportion to the cost of allowing industry free rein to impose its own operating standards.

Issues Management as Four Functions

Taking one of the earliest and most comprehensive views of issues management, the Public Affairs Council (1978) described it as "a program which a company uses to increase its knowledge of the public policy process and enhance the sophistication and effectiveness of its involvement in that process" (p. 1). The Council endorsed an issues management model that consists of (a) monitoring the public policy arena to determine which trends will demand a reorientation of corporate policy and communication process, (b) identifying those issues of greatest potential importance to the organization, (c) evaluating their operational and financial impact through issues analysis, (d) prioritizing and establishing company policy positions by coordinating and assisting senior management decision making, (e) creating the company response from among a range of issue change strategy options, and (f) implementing the plans through issue action programming.

Through the years, four functions have come to define issues management (Heath, 1997; Heath & Cousino, 1990):

- Engage in strategic planning in ways that consider the threats and opportunities of public policy changes
- Embrace and implement the highest standards of corporate responsibility to achieve credibility, to be above reproach, and thereby to earn the right to be a public policy steward
- Identify, analyze, and monitor issues to constantly understand the public policy formation processes to be able to exert influence as well as avoid collisions
- Voice facts, opinions, and policy positions that support collaborative decision making and foster an ever more sound society, create and sustain identification, and ensure that the narratives enacted by the dominant forces of society correspond rather than compete in ways that lead to disharmony.

However various proponents view the discipline, they realize that the product of its efforts must be an executive-level staff effort that can create harmony between the sponsoring entity and its key stakeholder publics. That is the challenge, by whatever name. This view of issues management assumes that no entity can wisely or rightfully think that it can manage issues, but can engage in the collective efforts of society to manage issues. Also, this view of the discipline knows that the management of issues is not synonymous with the manipulation of issues. The term *issues management* assumes that savvy organizations take a management approach to issues to reduce friction and maximize harmony. They do so because conflict—unproductive conflict—is an unnecessary cost and therefore not a position that wise management would support.

Speaking as chairperson of the Issues Management Association, W. Howard Chase (1982) offered a widely quoted definition: "Issues management is the capacity to understand, mobilize, coordinate, and direct all strategic and policy planning functions, and all public affairs/public relations skills, toward achievement of one objective: meaningful participation in creation of public policy that affects personal and institutional destiny" (p. 1). Although wise supporters of the discipline realize that a bad organization cannot be defended by articulate communication, Chase stressed the proactive aspect of issues management, which "rejects the hypothesis that any institution must be the pawn of the public policy determined solely by others" (p. 2). To be a major player in the public policy arena, the organization must strive to meet or exceed the ethical standards expected by its constituents and critics. Once it has a strong moral center, it can be the good organization communicating well.

Stressing outcomes deliverable by issues management, former Allstate Insurance Company executive for public affairs Raymond Ewing (1987) defined it as "simply public policy research, foresight, and planning for an organization in the private sector impacted by decisions made by others in the public sector" (p. 18). Issues management can help fill "the policy hole in the center of corporate management, making it possible for the CEO and senior management to strategically manage their enterprise as a whole, as a complete entity capable of helping create the future and 'grow' their company into it" (p. 18). The greatest contribution of issues management is gained by early and proactive efforts "to intervene consciously and effectively and participate early in the process, instead of waiting passively until the organization finds itself a victim at the tail end of the process" (p. 19).

Issues management entails efforts to achieve understanding and increase satisfaction between parties and to negotiate their exchange of stakes. It engages interlocking cultures that are in various states of compatibility and similarity. It fosters the interests of the stakeholders by helping an organization achieve its goals in a community of complementary and competing interests.

To achieve its potential, issues management must add value by allocating, defining, and distributing resources: human, financial, and material. It serves its sponsoring organization by engaging in a field in which each player seeks its own advantage. Although these competing and conflicting interests are such that not all can be equally satisfied, issues management serves best when it assists in the planning, analysis, communication, and coalition-building efforts by which mutual interests are sought and appropriate resource allocation is achieved.

Learning From Three Decades of Thinking About Issues Management

Before this chapter can explore in detail the topic of the rhetorical theory of issues management, we must understand the literature that has struggled to define issues management. One reasonable version of the discipline is that it is *the management of organizational and community resources through the public policy process to advance organizational interests and rights by striking a mutual balance with those of stakeholders.* This view of issues management adopts the underpinning rationale that is provided by social exchange theory. Any person in a relationship—or an organization in a relationship—will suffer the consequences of constraints if that relationship is seen as causing greater social, health, safety, environmental quality, political, and economic costs than it delivers. Activist and other public policy initiatives seek to employ power resources—including the rhetorical redefinitions of the value premises of society—to challenge and constrain organizational prerogatives.

Any sound view of issues management rhetoric requires an understanding that the limits of one set of actions is a counter, opposing set. Likewise, the limits on the statement advocated by one entity is the counter advocacy of many other voices. Any rhetorical statement is only as strong as its ability to sustain itself in the public debate and achieve concurrence.

This line of analysis features a view that issues management supports strategic business planning and management by understanding public policy, meeting standards of corporate responsibility expected by key stakeholders, and using two-way communication to foster understanding and minimize conflict. It adapts products, services, or operations to policy or seeks to change policy to support products, services, or operations. It is not limited to media relations, customer relations, or government relations. It is engaged in strategic business planning options that may change operations, products, or services as well as communicate to establish mutual interests and achieve harmony with stakeholders. It is expected to keep the firm ethically attuned to its community and positioned to exploit, mitigate, and foster public policy changes as they relate to the corporate mission.

Defining Issues Management and Issues: Rhetorical Underpinnings

As Burke (1973b) said, democracy institutionalizes "the dialectic process, by setting up a political structure that gives full opportunity for the use of competition to a cooperative end" (p. 444). This view of the rhetorical process can suggest that some organizational relationship problems require issues management rhetoric. Thus, to adopt the proper perspective for understanding issues management rhetoric, we should examine key issues that are central to the heritage of rhetoric in order to grasp the relevant assumptions and theoretical underpinnings.

Many views of rhetoric can be found. They range from the conception of rhetoric as the dialogue of assertion and counter assertion, focused on careful analysis of fact and value, to a sharply contrasting view of discourse based on statements devoid of a basis in fact and value. This range of views on rhetoric is between one devoted to a search for the best available truth to one dedicated to the self-serving expedience of deception and manipulation that is associated with the popular conception of "spin."

Examining the rhetorical heritage, Campbell (1996) championed this form of discourse as "the study of what is persuasive. The issues it examines are social truths, addressed to others, justified by reasons that reflect cultural values. It is a humanistic study that examines all the symbolic means by which influence occurs" (p. 8). Although some critics of rhetoric might not agree, it is certainly acceptable to reason that ideas are likely to become better when subjected to public scrutiny through statement and counter statement. Defending that process, Lentz (1996) reasoned: "Truth should prevail in a market-like struggle where superior ideas vanquish their inferiors and achieve audience acceptance" (p. 1).

On the one hand, many rhetorical theorists have argued that one of the assumptions of rhetoric is that even though we cannot know reality absolutely(because of that reality), we must be willing to accept relative truth as a standard of rhetoric. Thus, people can concur and share beliefs on various issues until more agreeable and accurate views on those issues become available. At one end of the continuum, the purview of rhetoric is the search for truth through discourse that engages the best analytical efforts of interested parties. In the spectrum of rhetorical opinions, we have a symbolic view of rhetoric, which suggests that people create attachments and bridge natural estrangements through a variety of strategic identifications. People identify because they share symbolic substance that reflects their shared identity and mutual interest.

At the purely symbolic end of the continuum, rhetoric can be manipulative: Say what is acceptable to the audience and what needs to be said to win the issue without regard to the truth or some higher order of virtue or integrity. A company can take a stand that symbolically states its agreement with a public, even if that stance is not honest or genuine. Symbolic rhetoric can resort to plays on tricky definitions and attempts to shift the burden of responsibility or reframe the issue so that it becomes distorted. This manipulative approach to rhetoric can ascertain what people believe and then falsely position the organization as though it agreed with them.

The best form of rhetoric, in sharp contrast to those symbolic and manipulative ones, is devoted to using discourse to seek the best available truth and set of value priorities to help the community of interested parties to make sound and principled decisions. These decisions advance the interests of the entire community, rather than more narrowly privileging the advocate of the position.

The purely symbolic end of the continuum of rhetorical options is fraught with deceit and is committed to winning advantage for one side of a controversy by tricking the other side. It is often devoted to using any of a list of logical fallacies such as turning the tables, reframing the issue to the advantage of the advocate rather than in the mutual interest of the involved parties. This view advises the use of apology, even if it is not genuine, in order to make the offending organization appear to be the victim deserving of sympathy. It allows for stalling tactics that postpone a thoughtful and timely discussion of issues. Such strategies not only are morally repugnant, but are also likely to increase the legitimacy gap because they foster distrust over the long haul.

One central premise of the Western rhetorical heritage is that communicators design statements to address an important issue and thereby seek to solve a rhetorical problem shared by a community of interested persons. Rhetorical problems arise from needs or problems—exigencies—that can be solved by strategically developed and contextually meaningful actions and discourse (Bitzer, 1968). Customers' class action complaints may be a legal or public relations rhetorical problem. Activists' challenge to environmental emissions levels is a rhetorical problem. Consumers' complaints about foods being less nutritious than advertised is a rhetorical problem. Critics' appeal for companies to be forced to pay more taxes or create safer working conditions is a rhetorical problem. Whether these issues are of such magnitude that they require rhetorical response is part of issues management rhetoric.

Not all problems that an organization faces are rhetorical problems. A rhetorical problem is one that can be solved through discourse—essentially the dynamics of advocacy and counter advocacy. Some organizational problems require more savvy and sophisticated strategic planning and improved standards of corporate responsibility hence the need for issues management. If the leaderships of organizations encounter some isolated complaints and minor differences of opinions, they hardly need a sophisticated issues management program. As issues become more likely to damage the planning and operational preferences of the organization, its leadership needs to implement programs for identifying, analyzing, and tracking them (Dutton, 1993; Dutton & Ashford, 1993; Dutton & Duncan, 1987; Dutton & Jackson, 1987; Dutton & Ottensmeyer, 1987).

A Rhetorical Definition of Issues

An *issue*, a rhetorical problem, is a contestable matter of fact, evaluation, or policy. It is a difference of opinion that can result from or lead to a legitimacy gap. An emerging public policy issue attracts significant attention to the way an organization plans and operates. It can result from marketplace practices, such as the sale of hazardous materials (asbestos) or products (tobacco). It may arise as the value premises of various publics become more persuasive in the public policy arena. An issue can mature into substantial changes in the public policy or market arenas that have serious implications for the operating standards and practices of an organization.

Issues that are part of the purview of issues management rhetoric fall into the following categories:

- Issues of fact, value, and policy that can have implications for the development and implementation of regulation or legislation (perhaps even adjudication), as well as collaborative decision making. Thus, if genetic engineering results in actual health hazards, or even leads to substantial concerns, this documentation can be used by critics of genetic engineering to argue for specific legislative and regulatory guidelines. If genetic engineering is alleged to cause such problems, that claim is contestable as an issue of fact and may even be an issue of evaluation. Perhaps the gains achieved by genetic engineering offset the risks. But that balance is likely to be an issue that some voices in society contest as fact, evaluation, and policy.

- Issues of fact, value, and policy that can have implications for the development of the organization's reputation. For instance, an automobile company that has a corporate mission to be seen as the technological leader in its industry can legitimately be expected to challenge claims by critics that its technology is not as good as it claims. The issues arise from the claims of critics. The organization needs to defend its reputation by challenging those claims to demonstrate where they are inaccurate.

- Issues of identification that can lead to merger or division that has implications for the development and implementation of regulation or legislation (perhaps even adjudication), as well as collaborative decision making. A wise organization seeks to create identifications by fostering shared identity and social reality with its stakeholders and stakeseekers. The assumption, which will be expanded later, is that identification leads to *merger*—a sharing of interests. The opposite of identification is division. Environmentalists may divide themselves from organizations that they believe harm the environment. They identify or merge with organization that they believe improve the environment. Thus, issues management rhetoric can be a contest of identifications.

- Issues of identification that can lead to merger or division that has implications for the development and enactment of the organization's reputation. People are variously attracted to certain organizational personae. These personae can feature issues that have public policy or marketplace positioning implications. In both senses, issues managers should be interested in the differentiations that can be created because of issues stances their organizations take. They can strategically seek to foster association (and even dissociation) merger rather than division. The persona of the organization is vital to persons' coming to see it as a good organization, one they want to associate with, as differentiated from organizations they want to dissociate from. The persona can be enacted through its identity including its goodwill (Heath, 1997).

- Issues of narrative interpretations that can position the organization to be a moral leader, one of many that have adopted acceptable narratives to guide their corporate responsibility; a moral follower; or a violator of moral standards. One of the key narrative themes is the morality of the personae (the characters in a story). One of the standards narrative—stakeholder of the mind (Mitroff, 1983)—is constant improvement of the quality of goods and services as well as advocate of better public policies.
- Issues of narrative interpretations where claims of fact, value, policy, and identification are interpreted as exhibiting fidelity and probability.
- Issues of stakeholder relationships where the social exchange is balanced so that mutually beneficial relationships occur rather than legitimacy gaps in which organizations violate the expectations held by their key publics.

Themes that give rise to issues management typically have been those that are at play and become resolved in the public policy arena. However, some organizations are coupling an issues management perspective with their marketing and reputation management strategies. For instance, if an automobile company wants to be known as the technological leader of its industry, it may also use an issues management approach to manage its reputation. In that regard, if an automobile editorialist or even a technical reporter doubts this company's technological superiority, the corporation can engage in dialogue to present, bolster, and even win its case on the specific issues. These responses involve the presentation and examination of fact and the advocacy and counter advocacy of evaluative claims. This is the essence—form and substance—of issues management rhetoric.

Given this review, we can pause to examine the rhetoric of issues management. It needs to address facts, values, and policies. It creates and adapts to identifications. It fosters and applies narratives. The savvy issues manager becomes an advocate externally seeking to engage in the dialogues of these kinds that have an impact on the policies—public arena and marketplace—that shape the destiny of organizations and affect their relationships with markets, audiences, and publics. Issues managers do more than communicate to external audiences. They communicate through dialogic advocacy. They advocate changes to key internal stakeholder audiences as well as support specific interpretations of fact or policy for the consideration of external stakeholder audiences. This engagement is the essence of issues management rhetoric.

DIRECTIONS FOR RESEARCH AND THEORY DEVELOPMENT

Given this overview that has helped to define the rhetorical context of issues management, we shift attention to the rhetorical options that are essential to reducing the legitimacy gaps that plague the planning and operations of organizations. One option is to use rhetorical positioning to convince management to alter policies that result in abrasive relationships with their stakeholders.

Another option is to rhetorically manage differences by advocating that critics should take on more accurate perspectives.

The venues of this discussion can vary from public advocacy, through issues advertising, to collaborative decision-making sessions in which persons who have vested interests come together to work for the best solutions to shared problems. Several lines of rhetorical analysis help define the directions that research and theory development can take to improve the quality of issues management rhetoric. These themes are discussed in the following sections.

Issues Management Rhetoric: A Rational Process

With some literature on rhetoric shunning attempts to deal constructively with the difficulties of analyzing propositions of fact, value, and policy, we could adopt an extreme relativism and simply conclude that issues management rhetoric is purely symbolic. Extreme relativism suggests that rational efforts to generate and interpret facts and seek better evaluations and policies becomes meaningless. All truth and knowledge are relevant. Cynicism is the outcome of any rhetorical process that is not founded on good reasoning or good reasons (Wallace, 1963; Weaver, 1953, 1970). At its worst, symbolic rhetoric becomes nothing more than a form of facile impression management. For this reason, the research challenge is to improve the ability of issue management rhetors to link analytical and rhetorical processes to achieve better conclusions of fact, value, and policy.

If issues management cannot help people to obtain a better, more accurate, and more useful view of the problems they confront, then it is likely to lead them to be ever more cynical about the role that the search for truth plays in the rhetorical process. If public policy and marketplace policy are driven by image without efforts to get and refine substance, then cynicism can become the standard approach to problem solving.

A substantial body of literature in rhetoric and philosophy asks that we guard against a naive approach to the nature of fact and the role that interpretations of fact plays in the rhetorical process. Does issues management have a privileged means to discover and reveal the truth? The answer to this epistemic question is, probably not (Rorty, 1979; see also Bernstein, 1983; and Brummett, 1990; and Cherwitz & Hikins, 1986, who contended "all ways of knowing are inherently rhetorical" p. 92). But like the rhetorical tradition, issues management rhetoric is best when it engages in the refinement of knowledge, values, and truth to the mutual good of interested parties.

Relativism is a timeless issue. It cannot be solved here. But one cannot reasonably ignore the relevance of fact for policy or market decisions. It is the crux of the rhetorical process in the minds of many. Taking a perspective on this issue, Campbell (1996) compared scientists for whom "the most important concern is the discovery and testing of certain kinds of truths," to "rhetoricians (who study rhetoric and take a rhetorical perspective) [and who] would say, 'Truths cannot walk on their own legs. They must be carried by people to other people. They must be explained, defended, and spread through language, argument, and appeal'" (p. 3). From this foundation, Campbell reasoned, rhetoricians take the position "that unacknowledged and unaccepted truths are of no use at all" (p. 3).

The rhetoric of issues management, toward these ends, must begin with a consideration of the quality of facts, values/evaluations, and policy positions that are advocated and eventually enacted. As difficult as it is to achieve certain knowledge and truth, those outcomes need to be the constant goal of issues management rhetoric. Without a commitment to better facts, evaluations, and policies, the discipline devolves into the worst of "spin." The public will not tolerate a callous commitment to relativity. Relativity carried to its ultimate extreme suggests that because no truth or knowledge is superior, people are legitimately justified in taking a cynical commitment to abandon the pursuit of truth and knowledge. Nihilism or the power grab thus become alternative strategies. The preferred option is a good-faith effort to use the dialogue of rhetoric to produce and refine facts, evaluations, and policies in the public view through the processes of advocacy and counter advocacy. This is the essence of the rational approach to issues management rhetoric.

The substance of the rational approach to issues management rhetoric centers on the quality of information (fact), the sense that some principles are superior to others (evaluation), and the proposition that some policies bring better business, nonprofit, and governmental practices, products, and services. This search is in keeping with Kenneth Burke's (1966) observation that humans are rotten with perfection (p. 16). Burke noted the human propensity to seek the perfect identification, perfect values, perfect enemy, perfect identity, and so forth. As Burke continued:

> There is a kind of "terministic compulsion" to carry out the implications of one's terminology, quite as, if an astronomer discovered by his [or her] observations and computations that a certain wandering body was likely to hit the earth and destroy us, he [she] would nonetheless feel compelled to *argue for the correctness of his [her] computations*, despite the ominousness of the outcome (p. 19).

The incentive toward perfection assumes the perfect fact, perfect evaluation, and perfect policy. That rhetorical incentive translates into the perfect challenges launched by activists to motivate improved operating and planning principles on the part of businesses, nonprofits, and governmental organizations.

The process of issues management rhetoric assumes that better conclusions can be derived if issues of fact, evaluation, and policy are subject to public and private debate. The range of communication options and tools is substantial. It can include comments made to customers or activists as well as to reporters and legislators. Such communication can entail collaborative decision making, within the context of a conference room, a senate chamber, or public discussion in media or on the Internet. Venues change. Best practices suggest many options where ideas have the best opportunity for scrutiny.

Short of consensus, the process can at least achieve concurrence. From each step in the process additional steps are possible. This approach to decision making can result not only in better solutions and policy positions but also in ones that the participants are more committed to support because of their participation in the process. This process is likely to be unending as the dialogue continues and new problems, issues, facts, evaluations, and policy positions give motive to advocates to offer their views.

Viewed from the vantage point of issues management rhetoric, a strategic issue "is anything that may substantially impact your organization. Other ways to think of strategic issues are: all major questions needing answers; decisions needing to be made; things about the organization that need to be changed, corrected, or improved; or the primary challenges the organization faces" (Bandrowski, 1990, p. 18). In short, an issue is a contestable proposition of fact, evaluation, and policy that is of mutual concern to two or more parties.

The magnitude of issues can range from one reporter's statement about the quality of a company's product all the way to controversy about global warming. Matters of fact are judged within the analytical context of what observations of phenomena are more or less true. Evaluations are likely to be founded on fact, but extend to issues of preference. For instance, a timber company may clear-cut (fact) and science may show that clear-cutting has some detrimental effects on the environment. The real issue, however, may be the evaluations—perhaps pitting corporate financial interests against environmental aesthetics—of whether the damage is tolerable. Policy matters are stated as preferences, as *oughts* in debate and *shalls* and *shoulds* in operation. This operation can include matters of issue enacted by government or the private preferences of customers based on demonstrable claims about the quality of products, services, and organizational reputation.

In this case, issues count. For that reason, they need to be subjected to dialogue. They can affect the future of individuals, corporate entities, and society. The research and theory challenge is to improve the quality of analytical dialogue, which can sustain and foster the search for the value truths, knowledge, and policy positions in the interest of the community.

Issues Management Rhetoric: Courtship Battles for Identification

Organizations invite individuals as well as other organizations to identify with them. Members of an industry, such as agriculture, have reason to identify with one another. They share interests, needs, wants, values, policy preferences, goals, and opinions. Even then, differences of opinion can occur. Such differences, however, are likely to be greater when there is less apparent justification for individuals to identify with one another, where estrangement exists. Burke (1969) suggested that courtship is the essence of the rhetoric of identification. If we have estrangement, then we can have motives and appeals to come together. This coming together in an interpersonal sense is courtship. That premise can extend to the rhetorical appeals of issues management. The research challenge for the rhetoric of issues management is to improve the understanding of the substance and forms of appeal to end estrangement through courtship.

The rhetoric of issues management entails appeals to share substance and thereby to engage in the courtship of identification. Organizations position themselves as being different. People think of themselves as being different. In this sense, they are estranged.

Society cannot operate with total estrangement. Communication must bridge estrangement. But it cannot succeed for long in creating bridges that are asymmetrical. The essence of courtship is people's need to join, cooperate, with others. As much as it implies cooperation, it also entails competition. Recognizing this phenomenon, Burke (1969) built his rhetorical theory around the dialectic of merger and division, between cooperative competition. Herein lies a rationale for issues management rhetoric founded on the dialectics of identification.

Although many competing versions of reality (social reality) exist, groups share enough social knowledge and a common identity that they can coordinate their efforts toward mutually beneficial ends. These give them the ability to live and work in varying degrees of cooperation and competition. Identification through a shared social knowledge allows them to band together, even if that banding puts them at odds with other groups.

Rhetoric deals with "the ways in which the symbols of appeal are stolen back and forth by rival camps" (Burke, 1937, p. 365). Burke (1965) cautioned, "Let the system of cooperation become impaired, and the communicative equipment is correspondingly impaired, while this impairment of the communicative medium in turn threatens the structure of rationality itself" (p. 163). The dialectic goes like this. Environmentalists argue that green is good, including green products, to create that identification. Extending that logic, manufacturers of consumer products appeal for identification based on claims that their products are green and environmentally sound. Thus, we have competing calls for identification.

At the organizational level, people identify through a commitment to their modes of production. "Modes of cooperation," wrote Burke (1973a), "(production and distribution) give form to modes of communication. The modes of communication thus refer back to the modes of cooperation" (p. 312). In this sense, for Burke, *cooperation* is a means by which individuals form a group with its own identity. To sustain that group is some common mission of the members of the group. They collaborate. They conspire. They compete.

Through competitive competition, people engage in self-governance. Through the rhetoric of identification, they engage in the dialectic of merger and division. They unite with some people and polarize against others. What facilitates this movement? It results from the sharing of symbolic substance by which the identities of individuals can become the basis for their identifications.

Burke (1966) featured that logic in the development of his definition of *rhetoric* as "identification." Rhetoric, he reasoned, is "the use of language as a symbolic means of inducing cooperation in beings that by nature respond to symbols" (p. 43).

By this logic, the environmentalist challenges the business or industry to share the substance of environmental responsibility (identify with that substance) or to be at odds with that substance. In addition, the environmentalist seeks to define this substance. The company can respond to these definitions. It can contest these definitions. It can contest the extent to which its actions meet or exceed those definitions.

Such definitions and the enactment of those definitions can lead an organization to position itself in public policy or marketplace debates. Several personae can be the basis of the positioning an organization (corporate, nonprofit, and governmental) takes in its issues management. These strategic options include its differentiation—setting itself out as being unique because of its persona on issues; its association—coupling its symbolic substance to that preferred by those stakeholders it courts; and its identity—taking on one of several archetypal persona such as bold advocate or technically expert adviser (Heath, 1997).

All of those strategic options are part of issues management rhetoric derived from the rhetoric of identification. Two interesting and valuable contributions to the issues management literature help to demonstrate these principles. Mobil Oil Company is the focal point of the analysis of both discussions. Crable and Vibbert (1983) interpreted the 1970s issue positioning of Mobil as fitting the Prometheus icon. It sought to identify with persons who were convinced that a strong corporate voice—a bold advocate—was needed to counter the false claims by reporters who were eroding public confidence in business decision makers. Simons (1983) saw the Mobil issue advertising campaign from a different perspective. He claimed that Mobil, like the male bower bird (bold corporate advocate), was using its anti-media appeals to lure the unsuspecting female bower bird (passive follower who preferred pro-corporation to more democratic interpretations of corporate criticism) into his lair to take advantage of it.

These appeals elicit different courtship identifications. Schmertz (1986), one of the designers of the Mobil campaign, concluded that it had positive marketplace and public opinion impact. People like to identify with a company that takes aggressive stances on public policy issues that support its business practices. This aggressive stance—bold advocate—Schmertz concluded, even leads some consumers to prefer doing business with such companies.

Thus, issues management rhetoric can be understood as courtship appeals to build and bolster cooperation through shared symbolic substance and social knowledge. It can build on this foundation to call for additional perspectives and actions because of shared symbolic substance. As Kruckeberg and Starck (1988) have argued, the ultimate identification is the community—the shared interests of persons who have a common identification. Caution, however, is expressed by Brummett (1995), who suggests that one rhetorical stance used by the defenders of the status quo is to challenge counter advocates—typically critics of some prevailing point of view—as taking stances that threaten the sense of community. Can we better understand the dynamics of the rhetoric of courtship and identification? To do so is likely to entail better understanding of the ways in which critics can challenge the assumptions of the community in the name of improving the community. These are research challenges of the issues management rhetoric of identification.

Issues Management Rhetoric: Corporate Narrans

Another research challenge is to improve our understanding of the dynamics of rhetorical use of narratives. Establishing the intellectual rationale for this approach to rhetoric, Fisher (1985, 1987, 1989) characterized humans as storytellers—*Homo narrans*. By extension, we can frame issues management rhetoric as "corporate narrans"—the organization as storyteller (Heath, 1994). Stories are the eternal and compelling substance of human communication. They help people to achieve shared knowledge, identity, and practices that allow for a workable society. People not only tell stories, but also frame their actions, opinions, and lives in narrative form and substance. They frame one set of stories in terms of other stories. Those stories either agree with and complement or compete with and challenge one another.

Stories, Fisher (1987) concluded, become more compelling rhetorically if they exhibit *fidelity*—if they fit the facts that others know or believe to be true. If the story presents facts that differ from those others know or believe to be true, then the storyteller is handicapped rhetorically. If a corporate narrative lacks fidelity, it is less persuasive.

Stories also need to be *probable* (Fisher, 1987): They must present details that are internally and thematically consistent. Part of the interpretative frame of probability is the likelihood that the specific story is sustained by a specific account of details and actions.

We can suggest, as well, that stories are lived experience (Mangham & Overington, 1987) that take on different levels of generality or universality. Thus, there are societal-level narratives, such as those representing and justifying the free market system (Narrative1). Each company (nonprofit activist group or governmental agency) constitutes a narrative variation of that societal narrative (Narrative2). Units within organizations are a third level of narrative; persons in these units enact narratives that take their substance from the two more embracing narratives (Narrative3). Individual actions constitute the fourth level of narrative (Narrative4).

Such narratives can be contested rhetorically in terms of their fidelity and probability. They can be challenged by other narratives. Thus, the free market narrative that features corporate efficiency and productivity at the expense of environmental quality can be challenged by the environmental responsibility narrative that suggests that the outcome of the free market narrative is a world unfit for human existence.

Issues management rhetoric, in this way, can capture perspectives of fact, value, and policy and express them in narrative form and substance. Narratives have personae (enactors of the story), plots, themes, and scripts. People—individually and on behalf of organizations—communicate to define the scene. A scene defines which acts are appropriate and inappropriate given the nature of the scene. Issues management rhetoric can consist of contests of narrative fidelity and probability, as well as clashes of narratives.

Narrative analysis fits comfortably with news gathering and reporting protocols. News is narrative. Even more specific, this line of analysis supports the issues management rhetoric of crisis response. Each crisis is a story. Persons engaged in the crisis tell stories. Crisis response teams can rhetorically respond to and participate in the generation of stories. The public seeks the resolution of a story in "happily ever after" terms. The public does not like stories that fail to demonstrate fidelity and probability as well as to achieve resolution. Thus, one research challenge of issues management rhetoric is to continue to refine our understanding of the competing narratives that offer form and substance by which people contest mutually agreeable outcomes.

Issues Management Rhetoric: Social Exchange

Part of the challenge of issues management rhetoric is to strike a balance between competing and conflicting interests. This aspect of issues management rhetoric assumes that relationships that balance interests and tend toward mutual benefit are empowering and therefore more desirable. When the position advocated or the values enacted privilege the interest of one party at the expense of one or more others, then frictions are likely to occur and become the motives for issues management debates and collaborative decision making. The research challenge of this aspect of issues management rhetoric is to better understand how power resource management and mutual benefit can be achieved through collaborative decision making.

To explain these dynamics, we can briefly turn to social exchange theory. Prior-Miller (1989) has offered a compatible rationale for issues management issues, as has Heath (1997). This perspective suggests that as one party violates the obligations for a balanced and mutually beneficial relationship, a legitimacy gap can occur (Sethi, 1977). Imbalance exists in a relationship, leading competing interests to advocate issues positions, when the actions of one entity aggrieve the interests and standards of one or more other parties.

To balance this equation—to achieve or restore harmony—requires a change in the way the organization behaves or performs, a new standard or approach to corporate responsibility. It may entail a rhetorical stance that can persuade the critic that the standards preferred by the organization are best and do not constitute an imbalance in the relationship. It may require that the ostensibly offending party not do what is thought to be offensive.

In this way, we have a rationale for issues management rhetoric that centers on the issues of mutually beneficial interests and the balance of relational outcomes. Thus, we introduce the issues management rhetorical implications of power, control, cognitive involvement, problem recognition, trust, knowledge, and support/opposition. Participants can rhetorically contest the norms and social exchange ratios that lead to the achievement of mutually beneficial relationships and the resolution of conflict. This rationale can challenge us to better understand the efforts to use collaborative decision making to resolve differences and achieve win-win outcomes.

Issues Management Rhetoric: Information Integration/Expectancy Value

In addition to the more humanistic approaches, issues management rhetoric is enriched with the more social scientific theory and research of information integration/expectancy value. Ajzen and Fishbein (1980; Fishbein & Ajzen, 1975, 1981) are instrumental researchers and theorists in the effort to explain the connections between beliefs as subjective probabilities, evaluations, subjective norms, and behavioral intentions. The assumption, relevant to issues management rhetoric, is that people create attitudes (including yielding to persuasive messages they encounter) in an effort to achieve rewarding outcomes and avoid or prevent unrewarding ones.

This line of analysis fits nicely with the principles of the rational approach to rhetoric, the Greek and Roman rhetorical heritage. It supports the interest of public relations theorists in estimating the influence that people's opinions and preferences have on one another (subjective norms), and on decisions to take some actions in preference to others. This line of analysis has also been used to describe and evaluate the opinions of policy makers and publics (Thomas, Swaton, Fishbein, & Otway, 1980), a key theme in issues management rhetoric.

In essence, this line of analysis is comfortable with the reasoning that information affects beliefs—subjective probabilities. Evaluations result from many sources, including the influence of significant others. Based on attitudes (beliefs coupled to evaluations) and subjective norms, people create and even execute their behavioral attentions. In this way, we have empirical means of assessing some of the rhetorical principles implied in the humanistic approaches discussed earlier.

This line of analysis can also be used to measure and estimate the goodness of fit between the opinion positions of organizations, stakeholders, and stakeseekers. In this way, we can measure the legitimacy gap and imagine the shifts in opinion that increase or decrease the gap.

Conclusion

Issues management rhetoric can take its foundations from the lines of analysis outlined in this section, and even go beyond them. Key themes have been selected from the rhetorical heritage to offer underpinnings for issues management rhetoric.

Analysis has stressed the essential role that information, facts, and evaluations play in public-arena and marketplace policy discussions. Policy that is devoid of a sensitivity to fact and evaluation as preferences is likely not to last and may even result in cynicism. The search for order (Heath, 1997) constitutes a need for vigilant attention to the data that can bring about a sharper, clearer, and better view of reality. The policies, narratives, and identifications that surround, influence, and result from this policy are assumed to become better when subjected to the processes featured in the rhetorical tradition. This tradition, concluded Bryant (1953), consists of the processes and substance by which people are adjusted to ideas and ideas are adjusted to people. Issues management rhetoric is a process in which key participants voice their preferences, on behalf of organizations and as individuals—to create a social dialogue that can lead to a higher sense of value and a refined sense of social order.

THEORY AND RESEARCH IN PRACTICE

The practice of issues management entails coupling issues analysis, a continually refined sense of corporate responsibility, and communicative strategies—directed internally and externally—to achieve each organization's strategic business plan. The limits of this planning process are set by the abilities of corporate rhetors to define and delimit the standards of acceptance that reduce rather than enlarge the legitimacy gap. This line of analysis assumes that people cannot continue to operate organizations in ways that offend the limits set by the larger community.

In practice, therefore, we are likely to be interested in the rhetorical processes, message content, and delivery tools. These topics are developed in this section.

Rhetorical Processes

Rhetoric at heart is the process of advocacy and counter advocacy. It is the rationale for suasive discourse. Rhetoric assumes that ideas appropriately framed and presented can affect strategic and ethical changes. It assumes that the symmetry of relationships is best defined by the ability of ideas to sustain themselves under the scrutiny of public discourse.

Starting from this premise, we can explore some of the practices of issues management rhetoric. Some of these applications have been implied in previous sections. They are presented here in outline form rather than with full rationale, based on the assumption that they draw their rationale, from the analysis presented in earlier sections.

This line of analysis needs to be undertaken with sensitivity to the challenges of functionalism by scholars of the critical theory and cultural studies perspective. Crass functionalism trivializes the rhetorical process and can lead users to believe that it can be reduced to its functionalist extremes: Load a message, lock the strategy, fire, and hit the target. The process is more complex than this. A strongly functionalistic approach is paternalistic, assuming that a strong source of influence can, perhaps even should, dominate a passive persuadee. The practices that follow feature functions that should be taken in the most embracing manner.

To demonstrate: Since the age of Aristotle (1952), rhetoricians have recognized the ethical responsibility rhetors have to produce information in support of the conclusions they advocate. If ideas count, they do so because of their ability to achieve concurrence for a preferred, more accurate and detailed understanding of some issue.

To evaluate: Rhetoric is more than description. It is not limited to achieving understanding. It presumes the ability of humans to convince one another that something is better or worse than something else. It deals with evaluations and preferences.

To recommend: Policy statements traditionally are framed as *oughts*, *shoulds*, and *shalls*. They are the culmination of the evaluative examination of facts and values. They are designed and employed to discriminate between good outcomes and negative outcomes.

To identify through courtship: In one sense, any thing is no more than what people believe it to be. An organization, in this case, is what others perceive it to be. If in actuality it is inaccurately perceived, then communication must put this right. If the organization wants to achieve identification, it begins by understanding the essence of the substance available for it to share in identification with others. In this sense, it must demonstrate that others can and should identify with it—merge with it in interest and symbolic action. It can differentiate itself from some members of society as a means of demonstrating a higher commitment to the good of the community.

To narrate: Each narrative exists as part of the shared social reality of a people at a time and place. Issues management rhetoric can be used to convince management that it must adopt a story that is shared with those with whom it wants to achieve mutually beneficial relationships. This story needs to be enacted by the organization. The story can be shaped through statements as it evolves and changes through social discourse.

To foster community through social exchange: Interests can be narrow or those which embrace the good of the community. Such interests are definable rhetorically. They are subject to evaluation and the development of policy that guides choices—preferring positive to negative outcomes. The rhetorical effort consists of the constant search for the essence of community, which leads to mutual benefits for its members. In this social exchange ratio, an organization cannot legitimately expect to achieve rewards that are disproportionate to the costs it creates and the rewards it provides to the other interested parties in the community.

Message Content

Issues management rhetoric can be reduced to organizations saying what they think others will believe. Messages can be scientifically adjusted to appear to address issues and manipulate opinions without truly addressing the issues that are on the minds of the stakeholders of society.

The rhetorical tradition suggests that message content can be evaluated in terms of positions preferred by advocates. However, such messages are vetted for their informativeness and the evaluative preferences they contain in terms of the larger interests of the community. In this case we can ask whether the messages add value to discussions that frame, negotiate, and foster the interests of the community.

Message content can voice the interests of the dominant members of society. To the extent that it does this to the exclusion of other voices, the community is asymmetrical and resources are out of balance. Messages gain strength to the extent that they capture the interests of even the silent voices of society. As previously silent voices emerge, they may support and express reservations to the voice and dominant messages of society; they become part of the dialogue as others are willing to listen to them.

Message content consists of information, evaluation, preferences, courtship, and narrative. Through this content, not only do members of society learn and evaluate the ideas that are best, but they also have the opportunity to accommodate themselves and their interests to these ideas. People use rhetoric to adjust ideas to people and people to ideas.

Tools

The tools employed for issues management rhetoric cover the gamut. In the 1970s, issues management was often associated with issue advertising. This is a narrow, and likely dysfunctional, view of the range of options for the dialogue of issues management rhetoric.

Tools include the gamut of mediated communication options: books, articles, talk show appearances, videos, movies (for instance, *The Insider*, which criticized the tobacco industry, or *China Syndrome*, which challenged practices of nuclear power generation), and billboards. Advertising, news releases, congressional hearings, lawsuits, and Web site debates as town meetings (Coombs, 1998; Heath, 1998)—all of these and many more are the tools of issues management rhetoric.

Organizations have also discovered the value of other communication tools that are more specifically devoted to collaborative decision making. They can invite critics to engage in planning and positioning dialogues. They can create and sustain public decision-making sessions. They can listen. They can protest. They can demonstrate. They can boycott.

This list suggests the arsenal of tools available to the advocates who engage in public and private discourse as a means of reconciling differences, and achieving concurrence, as good people and organizations work to communicate effectively with one another.

CONCLUSION

Rhetoric may be thought of as manipulative, or invitational. Advocating an invitational view of rhetoric, Foss and Griffin (1995) argued against persuasive strategies that "constitute a kind of trespassing on the personal integrity of others when they convey the rhetor's belief that audience members have inadequacies that in some way can be corrected if they adhere to the viewpoint of the rhetor" (p. 3). The trespass view of persuasion is patriarchal; it enacts the values of source-centered change, competition, and domination. The invitational approach to rhetoric can temper the privileging of an advocate's point of view. Any arena where multiple advocates compete is healthier by definition and more likely to engage in invitation than patriarchy.

REFERENCES

Ajzen, I., & Fishbein, M. (1980). *Understanding attitudes and predicting social behavior.* Englewood Cliffs, NJ: Prentice Hall.

Aristotle. (1952). Rhetoric. (Trans. by W. R. Roberts). In R. M Hutchins, (Series Ed.), *Great books* (Vol. 2, pp. 593–675). Chicago: Encyclopaedia Briticannica.

Bandrowski, J. F. (1990). *Corporate imagination—plus.* New York: The Free Press.

Barnet, S. M., Jr. (1975). A global look at advocacy. *Public Relations Journal, 31*(11), 17–21.

Bateman, D. N. (1975). Corporate communications of advocacy: Practical perspectives and procedures. *Journal of Business Communication, 13*(1), 3–11.

Bitzer, L. (1968). The rhetorical situation. *Philosophy and Rhetoric, 1,* 1–15.

Bernstein, R. J. (1983). *Beyond objectivism and relativism: Science, hermeneutics and praxis.* Philadelphia: University of Pennsylvania Press.

Boe, A. R. (1972, October). The good hands of Allstate: A Spectator exclusive interview with Archie Boe, Allstate's Chairman of the Board. *Spectator,* pp. 1–3.

Bradt, W. R. (1972). *Current trends in public affairs.* New York: The Conference Board.

Brown, J. K. (1979). *The business of issues: Coping with the company's environments.* New York: Conference Board.

Brummett, B. (1990). Relativism and rhetoric. In R. A. Cherwitz (Ed.), *Rhetoric and philosophy* (pp. 79–103). Hillsdale, NJ: Lawrence Erlbaum Associates.

Brummett, B. (1995). Scandalous rhetorics. In W. N. Elwood (Ed.), *Public relations inquiry as rhetorical criticism: Case studies of corporate discourse and social influence* (pp. 13–23). Westport, CT: Praeger.

Bryant, D. C. (1953). Rhetoric: Its function and its scope. *Quarterly Journal of Speech, 39,* 401–424.

Buchholz, R. A. (1982). Education for public issues management: Key insights from a survey of top practitioners. *Public Affairs Review, 3,* 65–76.

Buchholz, R. A. (1985). *The essentials of public policy for management.* Englewood Cliffs, NJ: Prentice Hall.

Burke, K. (1937, January 20). Synthetic freedom. *New Republic, 89,* 365.

Burke, K. (1965). *Permanence and change* (2nd. revised ed.). Indianapolis: Bobbs-Merrill.

Burke, K. (1966). *Language as symbolic action.* Berkeley, CA: University of California Press.

Burke, K. (1969). *A rhetoric of motives.* Berkeley, CA: University of California Press.

Burke, K. (1973a). *The philosophy of literary form* (3rd. ed.) Berkeley, CA: University of California Press.

Burke, K. (1973b). The rhetorical situation. In L. Thayer (Ed.), *Communication: Ethical and moral issues* (pp. 263–275). New York: Gordon and Breach.

Campbell, K. K. (1996). *The rhetorical act* (2nd ed.). Belmont, CA: Wadsworth Publishing Company.

Capitalizing on social change. (1979, October 29). *BusinessWeek,* 105–106.

Chase, W. H. (1977). Public issue management: The new science. *Public Relations Journal, 32*(10), 25–26.

Chase, W. H. (1982, December 1). Issue management conference—a special report. *Corporate Public Issues and Their Management, 7,* pp. 1–2.

Chase, W. H. (1984). *Issue management: Origins of the future.* Stamford, CT: Issue Action Publications.

Cheney, G. (1992). The corporate person (re)presents itself. In E. L. Toth & R. L. Heath (Eds.), *Rhetorical and critical approaches to public relations* (pp. 165–183). Hillsdale, NJ: Lawrence Erlbaum Associates.

Cheney, G., & Dionisopoulos, G. N. (1989). Public relations? No, relations with publics: A rhetorical-organizational approach to contemporary corporate communications. In C. H. Botan & V. T. Hazleton, Jr. (Eds.), *Public relations theory* (pp. 135–157). Hillsdale, NJ: Lawrence Erlbaum Associates.

Cherwitz, R. A., & Hikins, J. W. (1986). *Communication and knowledge: An investigation in rhetorical epistemology.* Columbia, SC: University of South Carolina Press.

Coates, J. F., Coates, V. T., Jarratt, J., & Heinz, L. (1986). *Issues management: How you can plan, organize and manage for the future.* Mt. Airy, MD: Lomond.

Coombs, W. T. (1998). The Internet as potential equalizer: New leverage for confronting social irresponsibility. *Public Relations Review, 24,* 289–303.

Crable, R. E., & Vibbert, S. L. (1983). Mobil's epideictic advocacy: "Observations" of Prometheus-Bound. *Communication Monographs, 50,* 380–394.

Crable, R. E., & Vibbert, S. L. (1985). Managing issues and influencing public policy. *Public Relations Review, 11*(2), 3–16.

Cutlip, S. M., Center, A. H., & Broom, G. M. (2000). *Effective public relations* (8th ed.). Upper Saddle River, NJ: Prentice Hall.

Dinsmore, W. H. (1978). Can ideas be sold like soap? *Public Relations Quarterly, 23*(3), 16–18.

Druck, K. B. (1978). Dealing with exploding social and political forces. *Vital Speeches, 45*(4), 110–114.

Dutton, J. E. (1993). Interpretations on automatic: A different view of strategic issue diagnosis. *Journal of Management Studies, 30*, 339–357.

Dutton, J. E., & Ashford, S. J. (1993). Selling issues to top management. *Academy of Management Review, 18*, 397–428.

Dutton, J. E., & Duncan, R. B. (1987). The creation of momentum for change through the process of strategic issue diagnosis. *Strategic Management Journal, 8*, 279–295.

Dutton, J. E., & Jackson, S. E. (1987). Categorizing strategic issues: Links to organizational action. *Academy of Management Review, 12*(1), 76–90.

Dutton, J. E., & Ottensmeyer, E. (1987). Strategic issue management systems: Forms, functions, and contexts. *Academy of Management Review, 12*(2), 355–365.

Ehling, W. P., & Hesse, M. B. (1983). Use of "issue management" in public relations. *Public Relations Review, 9*(2), 18–35.

Ehrbar, A. F. (1978). The backlash against business advocacy. *Fortune, 98*(4), 62–64; 68.

Ewing, R. P. (1987). *Managing the new bottom line: Issues management for senior executives.* Homewood, IL: Dow Jones-Irwin.

Fishbein, M., & Ajzen, I. (1975). *Belief, attitude, intention, and behavior.* Reading, MA: Addison-Wesley.

Fishbein, M., & Ajzen, I. (1981). Acceptance, yielding and impact: Cognitive processes in persuasion. In R. E. Petty, T. M. Ostrom, & T. C. Brock (Eds.), *Cognitive responses in persuasion* (pp. 339–359). Hillsdale, NJ: Lawrence Erlbaum Associates.

Fisher, W. R. (1985). The narrative paradigm: An elaboration. *Communication Monographs, 52*, 347–367.

Fisher, W. R. (1987). *Human communication as narration: Toward a philosophy of reason, value, and action.* Columbia, SC: University of South Carolina Press.

Fisher, W. R. (1989). Clarifying the narrative paradigm. *Communication Monographs, 56*, 55–58.

Fleming, J. E. (1980). Linking public affairs with corporate planning. *California Management Review, 23*(2), 35–43.

Foss, S. J., & Griffin, C. L. (1995). Beyond persuasion: A proposal for an invitational rhetoric. *Communication Monographs, 62*, 1995.

Fox, J. F. (1983). Communicating on issues: The CEO's changing role. *Public Relations Review, 9*(11), 11–23.

Gaunt, P., & Ollenburger, J. (1995). Issues management revisited: A tool that deserves another look. *Public Relations Review, 21*, 199–210.

Grunig, J. E., & Repper, F. C. (1992). Strategic management, publics, and issues. In J. E. Grunig (Ed.) *Excellence in public relations and communication management* (pp. 117–157). Hillsdale, NJ: Lawrence Erlbaum Associates.

Hainsworth, B., & Meng, M. (1988). How corporations define issue management. *Public Relations Review, 14*(4), 18–30.

Heath, R. L. (Ed). (1988). *Strategic issues management: How organizations influence and respond to public interests and policies.* San Francisco: Jossey-Bass Publishers.

Heath, R. L. (1994). *Management of corporate communication: From interpersonal contacts to external affairs.* Hillsdale, NJ: Lawrence Erlbaum Publishers.

Heath, R. L. (1997). *Strategic issues management: organizations and public policy challenges.* Thousand Oaks, CA: Sage Publications.

Heath, R. L. (1998). New communication technologies: An issues management point of view. *Public Relations Review, 24,* 273–288.

Heath, R. L., & Cousino, K. R. (1990). Issues management: End of first decade progress report. *Public Relations Review, 17*(1), 6–18.

Kruckeberg, D., & Starck, K. (1988). *Public relations and community: A reconstructed theory.* New York: Praeger.

Lauzen, M. M. (1994). Public relations practitioner role enactment in issues management. *Journalism Quarterly, 71,* 356–369.

Lauzen, M. M., & Dozier, D. M. (1994). Issues management mediation of linkages between environmental complexity and management of public relations function. *Journal of Public Relations Research, 6,* 163–184.

Lentz, C. S. (1996). The fairness in broadcasting doctrine and the Constitution: Forced one-stop shopping in the "marketplace of ideas." *University of Illinois Law Review, 271,* 1–39.

Lukasik, S. J. (1981). Information for decision making. *Public Relations Quarterly, 26*(3), 19–22.

MacNaughton, D. S. (1976, December). Managing social responsiveness. *Business Horizons, 19,* 19–24.

Mangham, I. L., & Overington, M. A. (1987). *Organizations as theatre: A social psychology of dramatic appearances.* New York: Wiley.

Marx, T. G. (1986). Integrating public affairs and strategic planning. *California Management Review, 29*(1), 141–147.

Mitroff, I. I. (1983). *Stakeholders of the organizational mind: Toward a new view of organizational policy making.* San Francisco: Jossey-Bass.

Nelson, R. A., & Heath, R. L. (1986). A systems model for corporate issues management. *Public Relations Quarterly, 31*(3), 20–24.

O'Toole, J. E. (1975a). Advocacy advertising—act II. *Cross Currents in Corporate Communications,* No. 2, pp. 33–37.

O'Toole, J. E. (1975b). Advocacy advertising shows the flag. *Public Relations Journal, 31*(11), 14–16.

Pfeffer, J. (1981). *Power in organizations.* Boston: Pitman.

Pincus, J. D. (1980). Taking a stand on the issues through advertising. *Association Management, 32*(12), 58–63.

Post, J. E. (1978). *Corporate behavior and social change.* Reston, VA: Reston.

Post, J. E. (1979). Corporate response models and public affairs management. *Public Relations Quarterly, 24*(4), 27–32.

Prior-Miller, M. (1989). Four major social scientific theories and their value to the public relations researcher. In C.H. Botan & V. Hazleton, Jr. (Eds.), *Public relations theory* (pp. 67–81). Hillsdale, NJ: Lawrence Erlbaum Associates.

Public Affairs Council (1978). *The fundamentals of issue management.* Washington, DC: Public Affairs Council.

Public Relations Society of America. (1987). Report of Special Committee on Terminology. *International Public Relations Review, 11*(2), 6–11.

Quintilian, M. F. (1951). *The institutio oratoria of Marcus Fabius Quintilianus* (C. E. Little, Trans.). Nashville, TN: George Peabody College for Teachers.

Renfro, W. L. (1993). *Issues management in strategic planning.* Westport, CT: Quorum Books.

Rorty, R. (1979). *Philosophy and the mirror of nature.* Princeton, NJ: Princeton University Press.

Ross, I. (1976). Public relations isn't kid glove stuff at Mobil. *Fortune, 94*(9), 106–111; 196–202.

Schmertz, H. (1986). *Good-bye to the low profile: The art of creative confrontation.* Boston: Little, Brown.

Sethi, S. P. (1976a). Dangers of advocacy advertising. *Public Relations Journal, 32*(11), 42, 46–47.

Sethi, S. P. (1976b, Summer). Management fiddles while public affairs flops. *Business and Society Review*, No. 18, pp. 9–11.

Sethi, S. P. (1977). *Advocacy advertising and large corporations: Social conflict, big business image, the news media, and public policy.* Lexington, MA: D. C. Heath.

Simons, H. W. (1983). Mobil's system-oriented conflict rhetoric: A generic analysis. *Southern Speech Communication Journal, 48*, 243–254.

Sneath, W. S. (1977). Managing for an uncertain future. *Vital Speeches, 43*(7), 196–199.

Spitzer, C. E. (1979). Where are we getting all this information and what are we doing with it? *Public Relations Journal, 35*(2), 8–11.

Sproule, J. M. (1989). Organizational rhetoric and the public sphere. *Communication Studies, 40*, 258–265.

Stroup, M. A. (1988). Identifying critical issues for better corporate planning. In R. L. Heath (Ed.), *Strategic issues management: How organizations influence and respond to public interests and policies* (pp. 87–97). San Francisco: Jossey-Bass.

The corporate image: PR to the rescue. (1979, January 22). *BusinessWeek*, pp. 47–61.

Thomas, K., Swaton, E., Fishbein, M., & Otway, H. J. (1980). Nuclear energy: The accuracy of policy makers' perceptions of public beliefs. *Behavioral Science, 25*, 332–344.

Tucker, K., Broom, G., & Caywood, C. (1993). Managing issues acts as bridge to strategic planning. *Public Relations Journal, 49*(11), 38–40.

Wallace, K. R. (1963). The substance of rhetoric: Good reasons. *Quarterly Journal of Speech, 49*, 239–249.

Weaver, R. M. (1953). *The ethics of rhetoric.* Chicago: Henry Regnery Company.

Weaver, R. M. (1970). *Language is sermonic* (Ed. by R. L. Johannesen, R. Strickland, & R. T. Eubanks). Baton Rouge, LA: Louisiana State University Press.

Zraket, C. A. (1981). New challenges of the information society. *Public Relations Quarterly, 26*(3), 12–15.

4

Persuasion: An Intrinsic Function of Public Relations

Michael Pfau

University of Oklahoma

Hua-Hsin Wan

University of Texas, El Paso

The role of persuasion in public relations is the focus of considerable controversy. Edward Bernays (1955) initially posited that persuasion was integral to public relations. Bernays defined the function of public relations in terms of using "information, persuasion, and adjustment to engineer public support for an activity, cause, movement, or institution" (1955, pp. 3–4). He and Ivy Ledbetter Lee viewed the role of the public relations practitioner as an advocate in the arena of public opinion, much as a lawyer is an advocate in the courtroom: as "pleader to the public of a point of view" (Bernays, 1923, p. 57). Unlike Lee, however, Bernays was the first to view public relations as in the modern vernacular of strategic communication. He argued that the public relations practitioner "engineers consent" by "creating symbols which the public will respond to, analyzing the responses of the public, finding strategies that resonate with receivers, and adapting communication to receivers" (1923, p. 173). In Bernays' vision of public relations, persuasion is an integral function of public relations and, given the essential role that he envisioned public relations would play in democratic society, "persuasion ... is an inseparable part of a democratic way of life" (1955, p. 8).

More recently, James Grunig proposed an alternative vision of the nature of public relations. Grunig maintains that Bernays' perspective is based on "manipulating publics for the benefit of organizations" (1989b, p. 18), which results in ineffective and/or unethical practices. Grunig led the way for the many public relations scholars, and a more limited number of public relations practitioners, who sought to distance themselves from persuasion. He maintains that a two-way symmetrical approach to public relations, which is grounded more in shared interests and dialogue involving communicator and receiver, is superior to the Bernays persuasion-based model, which Grunig characterized as a "two-way asymmetrical approach."

This chapter argues that, although both "asymmetrical" and "symmetrical" approaches are needed, depending on the circumstances, persuasion continues to be an essential function of contemporary public relations, especially in campaigns designed to establish, change, and/or reinforce an organization's image and in the role that public relations plays in an organization's commercial or social marketing efforts. In addition, the chapter maintains that the controversy over whether public relations should operate from an asymmetrical or symmetrical model is misguided; that public relations is best viewed as a form of strategic communication, in which persuasion plays an integral role; and that the controversy over optimal approach has stunted public relations scholarship. Finally, the chapter explores potential applications of select theories of persuasion in public relations, as exemplars of how future scholarship might inform both persuasion theory and public relations practices.

NATURE AND ROLE OF PERSUASION IN PUBLIC RELATIONS

Persuasion, which we define as the use of communication in an attempt to shape, change, and/or reinforce perception, affect (feelings), cognition (thinking), and/or behavior, plays a pivotal role in many public relations activities, particularly in those dealing with external publics. Many of the core functions of public relations, such as community relations, media relations, crisis communication, and others, manifest an implicit, if not explicit, goal of cultivating or maintaining a positive organizational image. Persuasion is intrinsic to this process. Other functions of public relations, including fundraising, lobbying, commercial or social marketing, and others, embody explicit suasory goals.

As a result, public relations scholars and educators have long acknowledged the central role that persuasion plays in public relations. The late Gerald

Miller, in the first edition of *Public Relations Theory* (1989, p. 45) referred to persuasion and public relations as "two 'ps' in a pod." This is because "public relations [at least in its functions that involve external publics] is, in practice, advocacy" (Jones, 1955, p. 156). Barney and Black (1994) explain: "The public relations professional finds herself wearing the mantle of single-minded advocate in the arena of public opinion. This requires the tools of persuasion" (p. 240). Even the Grunigs, who champion an alternative model that downplays the role of persuasion, acknowledge, "Many, if not most, practitioners consider themselves to be advocates for or defenders of their organizations and cite the advocacy system in law as an analogy" (J. Grunig & L. Grunigs, 1990, p. 32). Thus, Pavlik (1987) acknowledges that "public relations has traditionally been viewed as a form of persuasive communication" (p. 26).

Public relations texts have traditionally recognized a key role for persuasion in public relations. Marston (1979) describes public relations as "the use of planned persuasive communication designed to influence significant publics" (p. 3). Moore and Canfield (1977) characterize the nature of public relations work as "the development of favorable public opinion" (p. 5), thereby placing attitude formation and maintenance at the forefront of public relations practice. Cutlip, Center, and Broom (1985) argue that the work of public relations involves "ethically and effectively plead[ing] the cause of a client or organization in the forum of public debate" (pp. 450–451). Center and Jackson (1995) describe the goal of "effective public relations" as eliciting "mutually favorable behavior from the organization and its publics": such behaviors as getting publics to act or not act, or winning their consent to let the organization act (p. 3). Robinson (1969) adds, "The goal of nearly all PR problem situations is to change attitudes and behaviors" (p. x).

CONTROVERSY OVER MODELS

Despite the obvious role that persuasion plays in public relations, Grunig led an effort to reconceptualize public relations in terms of his two-way symmetrical model. His model assumes a more level playing field involving organizations and publics and implies use of communication practices based on shared interests and dialogue involving communicators and receivers (Grunig & Grunig, 1992). Grunig posits that two-way symmetrical public relations constitutes the ideal approach: a minority, but an emerging view of public relations (Grunig, 1989b). Grunig claims that his model is superior to the traditional press agentry and public information approaches because it is scientific, it is grounded in research as to what publics think, and it is superior to a two-way asymmetrical paradigm because it is not manipulative and, therefore, is more ethical. Advocates of two-way symmetrical model believe "understanding . . . is the principal objective of public relations rather than persuasion" (Grunig & Grunig, 1992, p. 289).

Grunig's two-way symmetrical model has received a great deal of attention in public relations scholarship. The search for an alternative to a persuasion-based model of public relations has intrigued academics, in part because of the desire to carve out a distinctive niche for a fledgling discipline, and in part as a result of a queasiness over the ethical basis of public relations work. Grunig's alternative model has appeal to many academics because it is distinctly rooted in public relations domain—in contrast to persuasion, whose conceptual and empirical foundations are not even located in the broad terrain of journalism, which gave birth to public relations as an academic domain, but rather are firmly rooted in the disciplines of communication and social psychology. The ethical question has proven particularly troublesome to many academics and practitioners, prompting the recent retreat from use of the name of "public relations" in job titles, replaced by what Seitel (1998) terms "euphemisms," such as corporate communications, public affairs, and other titles (p. 3). Barney and Black (1994) observe that "public relations practitioners . . . often appear uneasy, and somewhat defensive, about the moral basis of their profession" (p. 236).

We take issue with Grunig's model on two grounds. First, the model presumes goal compatibility and a relatively even playing field between organizations and their external publics. Vasquez (1996) terms the assumption of goal compatibility as an "idealistic presupposition about the role of public relations in society" (p. 62). In fact, organizations and publics often manifest disparate goals. An oil company proposes offshore drilling that environmental groups oppose; a manufacturing firm wants to locate a plant on a site that community groups oppose; tobacco, alcohol, or gun manufacturers seek unfettered marketing of their products, which opponents deem harmful to the public health; a company disputes the news media's claims that question the safety or the performance of its products; and so on. Zealous advocates of the symmetrical model argue that, in those circumstances in which goals appear disparate, public relations can serve as the vehicle for a compromise solution that benefits the organization, all interested publics, and even society as a whole (Grunig & Grunig, 1992). Vasquez (1996) terms this line of reasoning as "tautological," since incompatible goals are, by their very nature, often intractable and defy magical transformation into compatible goals by virtue of the use of public relations processes. Not surprisingly, one study of the approach that 31 organizations used in dealing with activist groups espousing different goals than the organization reported that none of them employed two-way symmetrical methods (Grunig, 1986). The fact is that public relations frequently involves conflicting goals, in which the interests of an organization and interested publics inherently clash (Murphy, 1991; Tuleja, 1985; Vasquez, 1996). In those situations involving mixed motives, the process of negotiation may yield compromise through accommodation (Dozier, Grunig, & Grunig, 1995). [Ironically, persuasion plays a critical role in negotiation (Heath, 1993).] Often, however, such situations "are adversarial in their essence" and defy solution (Leichty, 1997; Murphy, 1991; Tuleja, 1985; Vasquez, 1996).

In addition, the communications playing field is more often than not uneven, especially in the corporate arena. A corporation, which possesses an enormous resource advantage over most publics with which it deals, is in a position to bring to bear tremendous power in achieving its goals. Yet, Pavlik's game theory results (1989) reveal that, because organizations can optimize their interests by practicing asymmetrical communication, two-way symmetrical communication simply won't happen until publics gain equal power. Given an uneven playing field, Barney and Black's (1994) admonition is right on target: "The unstructured public relations marketplace offers no guarantees of equity in public discussion" (p. 241).

The truth is that the continuing controversy over whether public relations should operate from a two-way symmetrical or asymmetrical model is a classic "straw man," which has stunted public relations scholarship. There is no single best approach, and attempts to suggest otherwise fly in the face of reality. Research indicates that most public relations practitioners use both approaches, depending on the circumstances (Katzman, 1993). Long (1987), Hellweg (1989), Murphy (1991), and Cancel, Cameron, Sallot, and Mitrook (1997) have argued that the public relations practitioner is first and foremost a problem solver, who "must typically choose, either consciously or by default, a stance somewhere between pure advocacy and pure accommodation" (Cancel et al., 1997, p. 37). They view most situations as involving considerable nuance, with strategic decisions made using either the perspective of a continuum that ranges at the poles from circumstances requiring either pure advocacy or pure cooperation (Dozier et al., 1995; Hellweg, 1989; Murphy, 1991), or the perspective that diagnoses situations in terms of "clusters of activities, techniques, and strategies." In either case, the professional operates from the maxim "What is going to be the most effective method at a given time" (Cancel et al., 1997, p. 35). Sometimes the best approach involves use of cooperation and dialogue between communicator and receiver, but at other times, especially in dealing with external publics, the optimal approach requires influence. Even the Excellence study, which equates excellence and symmetrical practices, acknowledges that "In the rough and tumble, everyday world ... communicators alternately negotiate and persuade, depending on the situation. The excellent communicator ... knows how to use both ... symmetrical and asymmetrical models of communication" (Dozier et al., 1995, pp. 13–14).

The second reason we take issue with Grunig's model is that it is based on erroneous assumptions about the nature of persuasion. Grunig (1989b) maintains that the "Bernay's paradigm," which emphasizes persuasion, has "steered research and theory in the field in a direction that I consider to be both ineffective and ethically questionable" (p. 18). This position is echoed by Grunig and White (1992), who maintain that the "asymmetrical worldview steers public relations practitioners toward actions that are unethical...and ineffective" (p. 40). Is the use of persuasion in public relations ineffective? The many successes organizations have achieved in promoting and maintaining positive image, fundraising, lobbying, or marketing products, services, and causes provide a resounding rebuttal to this claim.

We suspect that the charge of ineffectiveness is based on two erroneous assumptions. The first is that persuasion is, at times, an inappropriate response to a public relations problem. We concur. In those situations that require simple information or use of cooperation and dialogue, an asymmetrical approach would be inappropriate and, if utilized, would probably prove to be ineffective. It is not our position that persuasion is the sine qua non of public relations practices, but rather that persuasion plays an important role in many public relations activities. Clearly, the professional's choice of approaches requires an insightful diagnosis of the situation.

The second assumption is that persuasion seeks conversation or attitude change, and that this is problematic. Grunig (1992) asserts that an asymmetrical view "suggest[s] that organizations can achieve powerful effects with communication." However, "these effects seldom occur,...and thus asymmetrical public relations programs usually fail" (1992, p. 10). This view of persuasion is simply outdated. It was once in vogue. It was referred to as the "change" or "conversion" model, and it assumed that the process of influence is unidirectional, in which an active communicator works his/her magic on a passive receiver (Miller, 1989). Based on this view of persuasion, Grunig is correct that most attempts at influence are destined to fail. This was the prevailing view at the time classic studies were conducted that subsequently ushered in the limited effects view of the influence of the mass media (Berelson, Lazarsfeld, & McPhee, 1954; Katz & Lazarsfeld, 1955; Klapper, 1960; Lazarsfeld, Berelson, & Gaudet, 1948). However, persuasion scholars long ago abandoned this linear view and, along with it, the conversion model of influence.

Most contemporary persuasion scholars view persuasion from a transactional paradigm, involving the dynamic interplay of all elements in the communication's process (Pfau & Parrott, 1993) and view the process of persuasion as incremental, in which communicators seek specific objectives chosen from a broad spectrum of influence possibilities (Miller & Burgoon, 1973). Operating from this perspective, single persuasive messages seek small movements in receivers: initially forming or shaping thoughts, feelings, or behaviors where none existed before; reducing hostility levels in opponents; winning over apathetic, uninformed, or conflicted receivers; or intensifying thoughts, feelings, and/or behaviors among supporters. In the context of public relations, attaining these outcomes is only possible via persuasive campaigns, fully integrated and sustained communication efforts, which consist of multiple messages that seek clearly defined objectives (Pfau & Parrott, 1993).

The charge that persuasion is "ethically questionable" is grounded on the assumption that Bernays' perspective of public relations is based on "manipulating publics for the benefit of organizations" (in Grunigs 1989b, p. 18). This argument is somewhat more intricate.

Is persuasion inherently manipulative, as Grunig claims? Yes! Persuasive communication in all forms either explicitly or implicitly seeks to frame messages for optimal effectiveness and, thereby, affect receivers. Subsequently, all persuaders, whether operating in the realm of public relations, social marketing, commercial advertising, or politics, "rationalize their persuasive efforts in terms of the public interest" (Salmon, 1989, p. 47). As a result, effective persuasion is inherently manipulative. Is manipulation, de facto, unethical? No! It isn't manipulation, per se, that is ethically suspect. "The persuasive ethic is defensible and laudable, in a participatory democracy" (Barney & Black, 1994, p. 233).

As Gerald Miller (1989) reasons, persuasion is a means or vehicle that is designed to accomplish specific ends. There is nothing inherently unethical about means or ends. Rather, both means and ends require scrutiny for their ethical appropriateness. Miller (1989) explains, "Ethical issues ... are ... relevant to *particular* political, policy, or product ends and to the *specific* persuasive means used to pursue these ends" (p. 48). Concerning means, it is ethically proper to employ legitimate tools of persuasion in the pursuit of legitimate ends. However, it is ethically wrong to employ "deceptive or dishonest message strategies" (p. 48), no matter how laudable an end, such as making up information in order to make a claim appear even more compelling, a practice that has become all too common (Crossen, 1994). In terms of ends, it is ethically wrong to use persuasion to market products that harm workers, consumers, or the environment, or to use persuasion to deny or conceal these outcomes.

In assailing persuasion as "manipulation," Grunig is placing the ethical onus on means as opposed to ends. However, instead of examining means for ethical appropriateness, he offers a blanket indictment of all persuasion as ethically suspect because it involves manipulation. In doing so, he believes his symmetrical model resolves the ethical quagmire because "it defines ethics as a process of public relations rather than as an outcome" (Grunig & Grunig, 1992, p. 308). As we will argue shortly, symmetrical public relations does not resolve what critics term the "marked relativism [which] ... undergirds public relations work" (Jackall, 1995, p. 380). Indeed, in providing a blanket panacea for ethical nuances involved in process or means, Grunig oversimplifies what is an intricate problem area.

The public relations profession should ensure that practitioners employ appropriate means, but in doing so, it should concentrate its efforts on what most experts would agree are actual ethical violations. This is precisely what the profession is attempting to do.

Public relations professionals have acted to provide ethical standards for the profession. Their canons of appropriate conduct focus on means, attempting to regulate the way that public relations' practitioners conduct themselves. For example, the profession requires honesty in public relations communications. Both the Code of Professional Standards for the Practice of Public Relations, authored by the Public Relations Society of America (PRSA), and the Code of the International Association of Business Communicators (IABC) focus on honesty. The fifth article of the PRSA Code states: "A member shall not knowingly disseminate false or misleading information and shall act promptly to correct erroneous communication for which he or she is responsible." The second article of the IABC Code prescribes that "Professional communicators disseminate accurate information," and admonishes that they act "promptly" to "correct any erroneous communications for which they may be responsible."

Of course, efforts to regulate conduct, even obvious cases involving dishonesty, are difficult. Indeed, both the PRSA and IABC codes lack effective enforcement mechanisms, which renders them little more than prescriptive. However, even if such codes could be enforced, they would not quell ethical criticisms of the public relations profession because the real ethical battleground in contemporary public relations, one that can't be resolved via professional codes of conduct, is over ends.

The most serious ethical issues in public relations today concern ends, not means. When critics assail public relations as "flackery," "manipulation," "coverup," and "spin," they address what public relations does, more than how it does it. Some go so far as to argue that all public relations is ethically suspect (Ewen, 1996; Gandy, 1982; Herman & Chomsky, 1988; Jackall, 1995; Olasky, 1987; Stauber & Rampton, 1995). What public relations does is to tip the balance of power in favor of large corporate interests. Greider (1992) argues that large corporations employ public relations, coupled with ease of media access and use of campaign contributions and lobbying, to influence politicians at all levels, and that this unbridled use of power has undermined American democracy.

> At the highest levels of government, the power to decide things has ... gravitated from the many to the few ... Instead of popular will, the government now responds more often to narrow webs of power—the interests of major economic organizations and concentrated wealth and the influential elites surrounding them (p. 12).

Stauber and Rampton (1995), among the most unabashed critics of the profession, indict public relations for usurping democratic values: for harnessing the power of public relations "on behalf of wealthy special interests," thereby enabling corporate interests to dominate debate, discussion, and decision-making (p. 205). As a result, they charge that public relations often has been used for unsavory ends: to promote unhealthy and/or unsafe products, to damage the environment, and to silence individuals and groups who are critical of these practices.

The net result of this distortion of process is that public relations has contributed to the elevation of corporate values, as manifested in individual acquisitiveness, and the undermining of public values. Stauber and Rampton (1995) claim that "The values that dominate our lives today are corporate, not democratic values" (p. 203). Ewen (1996) argues that, public relations has "played a critical role" in demeaning public institutions (e.g., public housing, education, broadcasting, assistance, and health) (p. 407). Ewen charges that since the 1970s, corporate interests have taken the initiative in the effort to "dismantle" public policies: in essence, to transform people's perception of public services into something undesirable (p. 407).

These ethical issues concern what public relations does, not so much how it does it. They are about ends, as opposed to means. Those of us who are interested in the ethics of public relations must address these core issues, which have practically nothing to do with whether the profession employs a two-way asymmetrical or symmetrical approach.

PUBLIC RELATIONS AS STRATEGIC COMMUNICATION

As we indicated at the outset of this chapter, neither the asymmetrical nor the symmetrical model offers a single optimal approach to the practice of public relations, and the dispute over approaches is misguided. The public relations professional inevitably confronts unique circumstances: organizations vary in their size, function, and culture, which McElreath (1997) posits affects response options; furthermore, the nature of problems to be confronted are often unique.

We echo Bernays, who maintains that public relations should be viewed as a form of strategic communication, in which persuasion plays an integral role. Early in the century, Bernays advised that the public relations council affects public opinion "by creating symbols which the public will respond to, analyzing the responses of the public, finding strategies that resonate with receivers, and adapting communication to receivers" (1923, p. 173). Bernays viewed strategic communication as putting the receiver first and, through research, devising communication to achieve specific objectives with targeted receivers.

Strategic communication views the public relations person as problem solver who, when confronted with a situation, researches it, determines what needs to be done, and selects, implements, and monitors strategies that are designed to achieve predetermined objectives. If objectives are suasory, as will often be the case in dealing with external publics, communication approach can and should feature persuasion. Within ethical parameters, strategic communicators are principally concerned with "what is going to be the most effective method at a given time" (Cancel et al., 1997, p. 35).

Critical elements in strategic communication include use of environmental scanning to examine the organization's overarching goals, discern relevant publics, and identify potential problems or opportunities. In terms of a specific campaign, it uses formative research to set overall goals, segment audiences, set specific communication objectives for each audience, and devise optimal communication strategies for attaining these objectives; then, it implements the campaign and employs impact studies to monitor its progress and summative evaluation to assess effectiveness. Strategic communication, at its core, relies on quality research to determine both direction and strategy. Unfortunately, most public relations practitioners continue to view their work in technician terms, disdaining research and, with it, strategic communication (Dozier, 1990; Dozier & Repper, 1992; Gronstedt, 1997; Pavlik, 1987). We agree with the Excellence study (1995), which calls for a strategic approach to public relations (Grunig & Repper, 1992), but we disagree with the conclusion that excellence should be operationalized as symmetrical practices that, in essence, eschew the role of persuasion in public relations (Grunig, 1992).

THE ROLE OF THEORY IN PUBLIC RELATIONS

The unfortunate downside to the controversy concerning two-way symmetrical versus asymmetrical approaches is that it has stunted public relations scholarship. The search for an alternative to a persuasion-based model of public relations fascinates academics, in part, because of the desire to locate a theoretical base for the fledgling discipline within the confines of public relations, instead of relying on theory and research in the more established disciplines. Grunig (1989b) advanced precisely this argument as the rationale for his two-way symmetrical model in the first edition of *Public Relations Theory*. In his essay addressing "symmetrical presuppositions," he acknowledged that "public relations is an infant scholarly field" (p. 18). The abstract of the essay provides a blueprint for the field's maturation:

> Public relations theorists have borrowed theories from communication science and other social sciences, but few have developed unique theories of public relations. Scientific disciplines always have borrowed from one another, but they do not advance unless they build original theories from the borrowed concepts. (p. 17)

He is quite correct about the absence of theory in public relations scholarship. In the opening essay in the same edition, Hazleton and Botan (1989) lament that, "there has been little of public relations research that is theory driven" (p. 14). Botan (1989) adds that "public relations has not systematically addressed the development of theory or the relationship of practice to research and theory building" (p. 101). Instead, what has been the emphasis in public relations scholarship? Pavlik observed more than a decade ago that "almost all research on public relations is limited to description" (1987, p. 41).

We hasten to add that very little has changed since Pavlik's characterization. Many public relations scholars continue to add to the litany of case studies in public relations, settling for what amounts to anecdotal evidence. Others, preoccupied with the mission of carving out a distinct niche for the discipline, have focused their efforts on the two-way symmetrical model, ignoring relevant theories in other disciplines. The downside of both of these approaches is that they mire public relations scholarship in a narrow niche, in what amounts to a scholarly ghetto. Scholarly output appears in public relations books or journals, which are read by public relations academics and practitioners, but are of interest to no one else, particularly in the academy. The price public relations pays for this tunnel vision is steep: It is extracted in the form of diminished credibility of public relations scholars and the discipline, both in academic units where public relations is housed and across the university. This in evident in growing pedagogical debate in journalism programs, in particular, over "the fit" of public relations study (Habermann, Kupenhauer, & Martinson, 1988), and in the difficulty many scholars, who publish almost exclusively in public relations outlets, experience in tenure and promotion processes at Tier I research universities.

The contextual approach to public relations scholarship has accelerated in recent years, during the same period that public relations academics abandoned persuasion. Today, most academics define public relations as building and maintaining mutually beneficial relationships between an organization and its publics (e.g., Caywood, 1997; Crable & Vibert, 1986; Cutlip et al., 1985; Grunig & Hunt, 1984; McElreath, 1997; Seitel, 1992; Wilcox, Ault, & Agee, 1992). Although this definition provides a good start in describing what public relations is, it doesn't go far enough. The definition ignores the many functions of public relations, above and beyond building and maintaining relationships, which contribute to organizational effectiveness (e.g., fundraising, lobbying, promoting organizational image, marketing). These functions are largely suasory. Further, the definition says nothing about how public relations works. How does public relations build and maintain relationships or perform the other functions identified earlier? We maintain that communication, more often than not persuasive communication, is the essential means/vehicle in this process. Thus, we agree with Botan and Hazleton's (1989) position in the preface to the first edition of *Public Relations Theory* that the primary emphasis in public relations scholarship should focus on communication.

> Public relations can be best understood as a specialized kind of communica-
> tion . . . [and, therefore, that] it should be possible to study public relations as an

instance of applied communication. We should be able to apply communication theory to explain and predict public relations practice, and use public relations practice as a site for the development of communication theory. (p. xiii)

The choice for scholars interested in public relations or other applied communications domain (e.g., health communication, political communication) is simple: They can address core functional issues, usually dealing with communication processes, or they can focus narrowly on context. Functional questions deal with theoretical content about communication. Although research on functional questions is set in a specific context and its results inform communication practices in that context, the results of research on functional questions also carry important theoretical implications that cross contexts and, therefore, are of interest to a broad array of communication scholars. We urge scholars to make communication theory, and not context, the engine that propels their research.

THEORIES OF PERSUASION: SELECT EXEMPLARS

This chapter has argued that persuasion continues to be an integral function of public relations. As a result, theory and research in persuasion constitute fruitful ground in the search for functional questions, which are theoretically important in their own right and which may inform public relations practices. This section explores the potential applications of theories of persuasion in public relations, in the form of select exemplars, including involvement and information processing, affect, medium theory, functional theory, and inoculation. The exemplars chosen are intended to be illustrative, not exhaustive.

Involvement and Information Processing

Until the 1970s, scholars and practitioners operated on the assumption that receivers process messages actively. The active message processing model assumes that thinking *is* information processing (Lodge & Stroh, 1993, p. 231). In order to persuade, communicators are advised to employ good arguments and evidence, operating on the premise that well-crafted messages force attention, affect beliefs and, ultimately, exert influence. The active model elevates messages to center stage.

Today, the active approach guides many, perhaps most, public relations practitioners. They operate from an implicit premise that information is the key: that it triggers cognitive responses in people, thereby affecting attitudes and behaviors. Most social action messages, which seek to affect thinking and behavior about using child restraints, protecting against crime, or avoiding various deleterious behaviors (e.g., smoking, drug use, excessive drinking), rely heavily on specific content. Wallack (1989, p. 366) summarized the dominant message approach employed in the health area: "We tend to define fundamental health problems as a basic lack of information and then to rely on the mass media to provide the right information in the right way to the right people at the right time." Traditional public relations messages manifest a similar bias. A number of content analyses of organizations' communication in community relations, crisis communication, and other contexts reported heavy reliance on information appeals grounded in argument (see Heath, 1994).

During the 1960s and 1970s, theorists and practitioners began questioning the underlying assumptions of the active model. They were founders of what came to be known as the passive, heuristic, or low-elaborative message processing model. Krugman (1965, 1971) was one of the first to articulate a low-involvement perspective of message processing. Krugman reasoned that most contemporary influence attempts occur in low-involvement circumstances, where there is little, if any, active cognition. Krugman reasoned that this was true of most television content, whether it takes the form of news, advertising, or entertainment. Krugman argued that receiver involvement dictated how people process communication. Although Krugman's thesis was the first major step in formulating an alternative conceptualization of message processing, his view of involvement was subsequently challenged for generalizing about media while not taking into consideration differences in message content (Salmon, 1986).

Today, most scholars accept the thesis of Krugman's position that receiver involvement determines whether people will seek out and actively process public relations messages (see Grunig, 1980, 1989a; Heath, Seshadri, & Lee, 1998), and that there are distinct methods of message processing and, therefore, "two different 'routes' to attitude change" (Batra & Ray, 1985, p. 15). Passive or heuristic message processing bypasses active cognition. It assumes a more mindless processing. As Chaiken (1987) describes, "Opinion change in response to persuasive communications is often the outcome of only a minimal amount of information processing" (p. 3).

During the 1980s, the dual explanations for the process of influence were combined in two processing explanations that sought to predict circumstances when one or the other would prove predominant. The explanations, the Elaboration Likelihood Model (ELM) developed by Petty and Cacioppo (1986) and the Heuristic Systematic Model (HSM) articulated by Chaiken (1987), are similar, although there are subtle differences between them.

The ELM and HSM feature two distinct paths in influence: one that is active and thoughtful, termed *central* in the ELM and *systematic* in the HSM, and another that is more passive and less thoughtful. This route is called *peripheral* in the ELM and features such cues as source factors, the number of arguments contained in a message, or the feelings triggered by a message, any one of which may be responsible influence in low-elaboration conditions (Alba & Marmorstein, 1987; Axsom, Yates, & Chaiken, 1987; Maheswaran &

Chaiken, 1991; Petty & Cacioppo, 1979, 1984a, 1984b, 1986; Petty, Cacioppo, & Kasmer, 1988; Wood, Kellgren, & Preisler, 1985). The more passive and less thoughtful route in the HSM is termed *heuristic*. It is more narrowly conceptualized than peripheral processing in the ELM. Heuristic cues constitute decision rules that people employ, such as (Chaiken, 1987, p. 4) "experts are always right"; "people I like usually have correct opinions on issues"; "more arguments" are indicative of stronger positions; "arguments based on expert opinions are valid"; and so forth.

Heuristics are learned decision rules that people acquire over time. People employ heuristics because, in those situations when they are not motivated to attend communication, which is a frequent circumstance for public relations messages, they become "minimalist" information processors, expending only the minimum effort needed to get the job done (Chaiken, 1980, 1987; Chaiken, Liberman & Eagly, 1989). Research supports the basic logic of the HSM, particularly for the heuristic cues of consensus (Hazlewood & Chaiken, 1990) and communicator likability (Chaiken, 1980, 1987; Chaiken & Eagly, 1983; Roskos-Ewoldson & Fazio, 1992).

The main difference with the ELM, and one that makes the HSM an attractive alternative, is that it accommodates use of parallel or complementary processing (Stiff, 1994). To date, however, the HSM has not received the same level of scrutiny or extent of empirical support as the ELM.

Because of its theoretical promise, and because the HSM has not been researched as extensively as the ELM, it is a fruitful area for further research. What should render the HSM attractive for public relations scholars is the fact that heuristic message processing is, in all likelihood, the dominant processing mode for most public relations content. The information age probably has not produced more informed decisions, but it most certainly has caused information overload (Patterson, 1993). Furthermore, an organization's internal or external communication, regardless of its intended purpose, is not particularly involving, at least not for most people in most circumstances. So, are people likely to process an organization's communication actively or passively? We suspect that people typically employ information shortcuts to draw inferences. These shortcuts consist of decision rules, or heuristics.

Exploring circumstances in which an organization's messages result in systematic or heuristic processing carries important implications for public relations professionals. Where heuristic processing dominates, determining what shortcuts are more likely to be employed by specific receiver groups in what circumstances would inform public relations practices. Results of research that addresses these issues should be of interest to academics and practitioners: offering additional nuance about the HSM, and providing invaluable guidelines for strategic communicators, who strive to make informed decisions about message design, sources, communication outlets, and so on.

Affect

Affect is an umbrella term that encompasses a variety of states, including reflex, drive, feeling, emotion, mood, and personality trait (Izard, 1993). Affect is positive or negative valence of an emotional experience (Clore, Schwartz, & Conway, 1994). Batra (1986) refers to it as "feelings toward a stimulus that lead to relative preferences toward that stimulus out of a class of similar stimuli," and thus involve preferences as opposed to emotional states (p. 54). Affect tends to be subjective and consists of assertions that can be viewed as points on two independent continua, ranging from bad to good (Eagly & Chaiken, 1993) and negative to positive (Dillard, 1998). Affect can enter the communication process at one or more of three points: it may precede, perhaps induce, communication; communication, itself, can manifest emotion; and communication may elicit an emotional response (Dillard, 1998).

The role and influence of affect in persuasion, especially in applied social influence, has not received as much attention as is warranted (Ottati & Wyer, 1993). Jorgensen (1998) characterizes the overemphasis in persuasion research on message design and source considerations, and the resulting dearth of studies on affect, as "lamentable" (p. 404). Social psychologists led early research on affect, but there is growing appreciation of the integral role that emotion plays in influence (Arnold, 1985; Dillard & Wilson, 1993; Jorgensen, 1998).

Advertisers have long had "an intuitive understanding of the importance of affect" in consumer behavior (Peterson, Hoyer, & Wilson, 1986, p. 151). More recently, the results of preliminary advertising research suggest that affect can play a "major role" in consumer decisions (p. 143). Public relations scholars have yet to acknowledge the role and influence of affect in people's decision processes (Scott & O'Hair, 1989).

Early research indicates that affect, above and beyond mere cognition, exerts sizable impact on human perception. As Zajonc (1980) observes, "In nearly all cases ... feeling is not free of thought, not is thought free of feelings ... thoughts enter feelings at various stages of the affective sequence, and the converse is true for cognitions" (p. 154). Affect and cognition often have an impact on people's attitudes independently of one other (Edell & Burke, 1987; Zajonc, 1984). The fact that affect can function wholly independent of conscious thought (Wilson, 1979; Zajonc, 1984) makes it a useful tool in the arsenal of influence. Affect can even manifest itself absent *any* stimulus recognition (see Fink, Monahan & Kaplowitz, 1989; Moreland & Zajonc, 1977; Zajonc, 1980, 1984; Zajonc & Markus, 1982). Most of the time, however, feeling and thinking occur conjointly (Lazarus, 1982; Zajonc, 1980; Zuwerink & Devine, 1996) but, even then, extant research indicates that affect precedes cognition (Zajonc, 1980, 1981, 1984), suggesting that it may be the more instrumental of the two (Edell & Burke, 1987; Holbrook & Batra, 1987).

Affect is actively employed in commercial advertising and public relations campaigns. One strategy involves directly eliciting affect in receivers. Such messages stress "emotional quotient," seeking to trigger happiness, pleasure, warmth, or other feelings. In public relations, feel-good, image-oriented corporate campaigns are common. Spurred, in part, by the success of General Electric's "We bring good things to life" campaign, total spending on corporate advertising tripled between 1975 and 1984, exceeding $1 billion (Pavlik, 1987). Greider (1992) argues that corporations that are the most active in these image-based promotional campaigns are those with known substantive problems, including Chevron, Dow, General Electric, and Northrup. Research in commercial advertising indicates that messages that utilize affect are quite effective in eliciting emotional response, often during the first seconds of a message, which produces a positive impact on consumer behavior (Aaker, Stayman, & Hagarty, 1986; Holbrook & Batra, 1987). No comparable data are available for corporate image campaigns.

A second strategy involves association of a corporation or its products with stimuli that elicit positive emotions. This is the basis of the classical conditioning model, which posits that, following pairing over time of an unconditioned stimulus, capable on its own of eliciting a response, with a conditioned stimulus, normally not capable of eliciting the response, the conditioned stimulus alone becomes capable of eliciting the response (Watson, 1925). This strategy is prevalent in contemporary commercial television advertising, in which brands are paired with pleasant emotional stimuli, often elicited by "scenes of good times and beautiful surroundings" (Breckler, 1993; Pechman & Stewart, 1989; Peterson et al., 1986, p. 151; Pfau & Parrott, 1993). Research indicates that such advertising appeals are capable of eliciting the desired emotional response quickly (Stuart, Shimp, & Engle, 1987), and that they contribute to positive attitudes toward the advertised brand and to purchase intention (Edell & Burke, 1987; Hitchon & Thorson, 1995).

It is also a frequent strategy in public relations efforts. Organizations try to associate themselves with popular activities (e.g., extensive corporate sponsorship of the arts and sporting events), special events (e.g., the Olympics), and popular causes (e.g., missing children or the environment). These associations constitute more than an opportunity for corporations to be seen. They enable sponsors to establish linkages based on affect. These linkages function as image enhancers for sponsors, which boost public perceptions of a corporation or its products/services. One executive explained that, "You attach yourself to . . . events, piggybacking on them" (in Harris, 1991). Research suggests that an organization's image can be enhanced through association with positive events and causes (Denbow & Culbertson, 1985; Young, 1996; Zbar, 1993). Jackall (1995) claims that such "indirect methods" of promoting corporate image or persona "are thought to be particularly effective" (p. 368).

Despite extensive use of affect in corporate advertising campaigns that seek to enhance image and the use of corporate sponsorships to establish perceptual linkages based on affect, public relations scholars have largely ignored this domain. Scott and O'Hair (1989) call attention to "the paucity of emotional assessment in public relations" (p. 212), speculating that the seeming lack of interest may stem from the perception that "the concept of emotion is rather arbitrary and elusive" and defies clear conceptualization (p. 212). It is true that affect is "a messy construct to investigate either theoretically and empirically" (Lazarus, 1999; Peterson et al., 1986, p. 144). Nonetheless, it has generated a growing interest among social psychology and communication scholars during the past decade (Dalgleish & Power, 1999).

Although affect is an integral element in persuasion and, therefore, relevant to applied persuasion contexts such as public relations, there is much to be learned about its use and impact in persuasion (Jorgensen, 1998). Jorgensen argues that study of the types of messages that are most effective in eliciting specific emotional responses is "perhaps the single greatest contribution that communication scholars can make to the study of emotion" (p. 417). Other unresolved questions include the relationship involving affective appeal, communication form, and elicited emotional response; how specific affective appeals work, both alone and in conjunction with other emotional and cognitive appeals; and optimal sequencing of emotional appeals (Jorgensen, 1998).

Dillard (1998) recommends that emotion should be studied in the context of the process of persuasion, and Dalgleish and Power (1999) call for further research dealing with the role and impact of cognition and emotion, especially studies that apply findings in basic research to "real-life" contexts. Scholars interested in investigating influence in the context of public relations should heed their call.

Medium Theory

One implication of theories involving dual processing models and affect is that individual mass media vary in the way in which they exercise influence. Thus is the underlying premise of *medium theory*, which posits that, independent of the particular content communicated, media forms manifest unique symbol systems that shape both what is communicated and how it is received (Chesebro, 1984; McLuhan 1964; Meyrowitz, 1985; Salomon, 1987). Television, because it relies significantly on a "pictorial symbol system" (Salomon, 1981, p. 205), communicates a different message than other media; and, because its visually laden messages require less active processing (Chesebro, 1984; Graber, 1987; Krugman, 1971; Salomon, 1987, 1981; Wright, 1974), television exercises influence differently. Receiver involvement level dictates

the appropriate medium which, in turn, determines how receivers are likely
to respond to messages. Chaudhuri and Buck (1995) report that television is
the optimal medium for advertising appeals on behalf of low-involving products. Their research indicates that television, since it can transport emotions,
is uniquely able to "create an emotional bond with the brand" (p. 122). In all
likelihood, the same rationale applies to the communication of messages about
organizations, although the thesis hasn't been investigated in a public relations
context.

Meyrowitz (1985) contrasts television and print messages. Television, as
a result of the primacy of the visual channel, is expressive, stressing images
and impressions, whereas print is communicative, grounded in symbols and,
consequently, ideally suited to the presentation of arguments and facts. Television is presentational, emphasizing visual images, while print is more discursive, featuring more abstract messages. Finally, television is analogic, stressing more intimate relational messages, whereas print is digital, emphasizing
content.

Messages communicated via each communication form manifest unique
possibilities. The distinctions drawn by Meyrowitz between television and print
communication can by distilled to a single overarching difference: Television is
more about the source of messages and print is about the content of messages.
The primacy of source over content is further magnified by differences in
message processing. Because television is less involving, it is much more likely
to elicit peripheral (ELM) or heuristic (HSM) message processing, in which
influence can be accomplished "with only a minimal amount of information
processing" (Chaiken, 1987, p. 3; Chaiken & Eagly, 1976, 1983; Graber, 1987;
Markus & Zajonc, 1985; Salomon, 1981). In the dual processing models,
source cues function as peripheral or heuristic devices, thus suggesting an
elevated role in the process of influence.

This rationale is supported in research which points to an accented role
for source cues in television influence (Andreoli & Worchel, 1978; Chaiken,
1987; Chaiken & Eagly, 1983; Gold, 1988). Pfau (1990) compared the relative
influence of five communication modalities, including print, television, and
radio media, plus public address and interpersonal communication. Results
indicated that all communication forms were persuasive, as compared with a
control condition, but there were no differences in influence between modalities. However, results revealed that the factors responsible for influence varied
across modalities. The contribution of source overwhelmed content with television and interpersonal modalities, but content dominated source in print and
public address forms.

Television's emphasis on communicator expressiveness and more intimate
relational messages suggests greater emphasis on affect in influence. Relational
messages consist of how people perceive their relationship with a communicator (Burgoon & Hale, 1984) and derive from what Watzlawick, Beavin, and

Jackson (1967) termed the "command" dimension of messages. Relational messages have been reported to exert considerable impact in the process of persuasion in those instances where communication form facilitates real or perceived personal contact between a source and a receiver, as is obvious in the example of interpersonal communication (Burgoon, 1980; Burgoon & Hale, 1987), but just as real, although less apparent, in the case of television (Pfau, 1990). Television creates the perception of contact (Levy, 1979; Rubin & McHugh, 1987). It fosters the illusion of interpersonal contact, even a sense of intimacy (Beniger, 1987; Jamieson, 1988; Horton & Wohl, 1956; Keating & Latane, 1976; Perse & Rubin, 1989).

As a result of the primacy of source over content, coupled with a heightened sense of intimacy, the video modality rewards a warmer, much more casual communication style (Jamieson, 1988; Keating & Latane, 1976; Meyrowitz, 1985; Pfau, 1990), similar to what is required in effective interpersonal communication (Levy, 1979). This manifests itself in terms of more positive relational messages. Relational messages communicate the way people perceive their relationship with another (Burgoon & Hale, 1984, p. 193).

Pfau's (1990) study of factors that facilitate influence across communication modalities found that relational messages exerted much more influence than content in television, whereas the reverse was true for print communication. The dimensions of relational communication that have proven most influential in studies focusing specifically on television communication are those that manifest positive affect: receptivity/trust, which involves perception of source interest in the receiver, honesty, and sincerity; immediacy/affection, which includes perceptions of enthusiasm, warmth, and involvement; and similarity/depth, which features perceptions of friendliness, similarity, caring, and getting to know another better (Pfau, 1990; Pfau, Diedrich, Larson, & Van Winkle, 1993; Pfau & Kang, 1991).

As indicated previously, medium theory hasn't been studied in the context of public relations. Yet, the same logic applies, indicating that different media manifest unique message features, which contribute to influence. Because public relations expands the range of media options available to communicators, it would be an ideal domain to study medium theory.

Holbert (2002) calls for systematic empirical assessment of media form in persuasion. He advocates a shift in the focus of medium theory, from a macro emphases (e.g., Meyrowitz, 1994), as in the examples above, to more of a micro orientation, based on human sensorial involvement. The approach applies basic tenets of medium theory to recent work on cognitive function in the fields of communication and psychology. Holbert (in press) argues that the next generation of empirical studies of medium theory should stress the way particular media forms impact the construction and development of human schematic structures (e.g., Markus & Zajonc, 1985). Studies that address such theoretical content within the context of public relations provide an opportunity to contribute both to further understanding of persuasion and to public relations practices.

Functional Theory

In a general sense, functional theory constitutes a family of theories with their origins in sociology, which trace their philosophical roots to Emile Dirkheim. The functional approach is unique in that it focuses on why people hold attitudes, as opposed to how their attitudes are structured or whether they may change (Eagly & Chaiken, 1993, p. 479). People's behaviors are grounded in attitudes, which in turn serve functions, which are based on psychological motives. Functions are perceived as psychologically useful, which implies that attitudes are both active and mindful. Functional theory suggests that, in order to understand people's attitudes and the way that communication might affect them, communicators must understand the individual's motivation for holding an attitude (Kiesler, Collins, & Miller, 1969).

Although functional theory constitutes a family of theories, Katz's psychological need theory is particularly representative. Katz (1960) posits that attitudes may serve one or more functions for people.

First, attitudes serve a utilitarian function. Katz (1960) refers to this function as "instrumental" or "adjustment" function. The utilitarian function "recognizes the fact that 'people strive to maximize rewards in their external environment and to minimize the penalties'" (Katz, 1960, p. 171). For example, people develop and maintain favorable attitudes toward those organizations that facilitate their goals and negative attitudes toward those that impede their goals.

In order to create or to maintain attitudes, communicators attempt to link an attitude object with personal goal attainment. Many public relations campaigns are designed to help people to achieve personal goals. This is a common technique in community relations efforts. For example, hospitals offer information about diet, exercise, blood pressure, and other health concerns. Banks and insurance companies conduct seminars about personal finance, investing, and retirement. This approach also is characteristic of many internal public relations efforts. For instance, firms conduct sessions for employees to explain their health insurance options or 403B choices, or to preview retirement conditions.

To change utilitarian attitudes, communicators may create new needs, shift the balance of benefits and costs associated with needs, or provide superior vehicles for need satisfaction. Because needs are difficult to create or change, Katz (1960) advocates that communicators focus on the latter strategies. "The area of freedom for changing utilitarian attitudes is ... much greater in dealing with methods of satisfying needs than with the needs themselves" (p. 178).

A second function that attitudes serve is value expressive. Katz (1960) maintains that some attitudes serve the main purpose of expressing to other people the kind of person we think we are, or that we want to be. Such attitudes express people's sense of self, including their core values. They signal to others who we are: our moral values, religious beliefs, group attachments and affiliations, political philosophy, and tastes; and they allow us to verify and confirm our self-concept (Greenwald, 1989). This function stresses expression, which implies that those attitudes that serve this function will manifest a very strong behavioral component. The main approach used in attempting to modify value expressive attitudes is for a communicator to demonstrate "the inappropriateness of their present ways of expressing their values" (Katz, 1960, p. 189).

Communication based on value expressive attitudes is common in public relations. It manifests itself in a variety of ways. Stockholder relations stress the organization's contribution to the environment. Corporations sponsor those sporting or cultural events that reflect their public image. Companies in the United States during the early 1990s were spending about $1.5 billion per year sponsoring major sporting events plus $1 billion sponsoring the arts (Harris, 1993). Furthermore, total spending on sponsorships doubled between the late 1980s and the middle 1990s (Cornwell & Maignan, 1998). In addition to sponsorships, many companies also employ corporate advertising designed to promote a public image, or engage in advocacy advertising to speak out on controversial issues not directly relevant to the company's mission, thus fostering the perception of corporate citizenship.

A third function attitudes serve is knowledge. This doesn't imply a pure quest for knowledge per se, but rather a desire for order in the face of ambiguity. Katz (1960) notes, "People are not avid seekers after knowledge as judged by what the educator or social reformer would desire. But they do want to understand the events that impinge directly on their own life" (p. 176). What this means is that attitudes serve to clarify and simplify events for people. Attitudes serve as schemas, providing a useful "frame of reference" (Katz, 1960, p. 175) for the purpose of "organizing and simplifying ... perceptions of an often complex or ambiguous information environment" (Eagly & Chaiken, 1993, p. 480). Katz (1960) recommends that, in order to change knowledge-based attitudes, communicators should stress "inadequacies of existing attitudes to deal with new and changing situations. . . . People's intolerance for ambiguity exerts pressure to "either modify his beliefs to impose structure or accept some new formula presented by others" (pp. 190–191).

The knowledge function explains people's desire for simple answers for complicated issues. Communicators who can simplify complicated content for receivers can be very effective. However, it also explains people's vulnerability to negative political and issue advocacy advertising, such as when the nation's health care providers launched an extensive advertising campaign in 1993 in response to the proposed Clinton health care proposal. More than half of the spots, which attempted to boil the Clinton plan down to a few essentials that then could be the focus of attack, were judged by Jamieson and colleagues to be "unfair, misleading, or false" (Annenberg School, 1994).

The fourth function that attitudes serve is ego-defensive. Attitudes protect people's self-image or ego (Katz, 1960). This function is less relevant to public relations.

Functional theory is heuristically provocative. The theory provides a new way of thinking about attitudes, placing emphasis on underlying motivations for attitudes (Eagly & Himmelfarb, 1974). As a result, functional theory initially sparked a great deal of scholarly interest following its introduction. However, interest soon waned. The main reason was the dearth of empirical data in support of the theory (Kiesler et al., 1969). Functional theory poses special challenges for researchers. The problem is that it is difficult to operationalize in advance the functions served by attitudes, which makes it impossible to conduct a fair test the theory (Eagly & Chaiken, 1993). As Snyder and DeBono (1987) observe, "[R]esearchers need to know the functional underpinnings of people's attitudes before . . . persuasive messages are delivered, in order to choose the message appropriate to an attitude serving that function" (p. 110). Inability to identify functions in advance renders functional theory nonfalsifiable, which Synder and DeBono claim was the primary cause of reduced interest in the theory. This problem is compounded by subsequent research indicating that, not only do attitudes serve different functions for different people, but they often serve multiple functions for any one individual (Eagly & Chaiken, 1993). As a result, Kiesler and colleagues (1969) conclude, "Functional theories leave us powerless to predict" (p. 326).

To overcome this problem, Snyder and DeBono (1987) suggest a "global strategy," based on "identifying categories of people for whom attitudes may be serving different functions" (p. 110). The authors suggest that the attitudes of people who are "high self-monitors" may serve an adjustment or utilitarian function, whereas those of people who are "low self-monitors" may serve a value expressive function. Research by Herek (1987) has developed improved techniques for measuring attitude functions.

More recently scholars have shown renewed interest in the functions which underpin attitudes (Eagly & Chaiken, 1993; Shah, Domke, & Wackman, 1996). Contemporary perspectives continue to explore the original functions, but they accept that attitudes typically serve multiple functions for people (Eagly & Chaiken, 1993). One new wrinkle in recent work on functional theory is the assumption that, irrespective of the traditional functions that attitudes may serve, they provide a schematic function, offering a frame of reference for understanding and ordering attitude objects (Fazio, 1986, 1989; Shaw et al., 1996), although "the schematic function may be limited to strong, well established attitudes" (Eagly & Chaiken, 1993, p. 483).

Another recent development involves reconceptualization of attitude functions. Some researchers recommend recategorization of the basic functions into two. The first function focuses on the attitude object itself and is utilitarian or evaluative, stressing the benefits/rewards and costs/punishments associated with object (Herek, 1986). "In this scheme, the utilitarian function emerges as the *evaluative* function of attitudes" (Eagly & Chaiken, 1993, p. 483). The second function stresses attitude expression and is termed "value expressive" (Herek, 1986). This category would subsume the original social adjustment and ego-defensive functions (Eagly & Chaiken, 1993). Other researchers suggest the presence of three functions: social identity, which is a composite of adjustment and value expressive; self-esteem; and knowledge (Shavitt, 1989, 1990).

Functional theory is a viable potential domain for scholars in public relations. It has generated renewed interest, and yet manifests as-yet-unresolved theoretical and measurement issues (Abelson & Prentice, 1989; Shavitt, 1989). Further, utilitarian, value expressive, and knowledge functions, in particular, may undergird people's attitudes in a wide array of public relations contexts, as the examples just given demonstrate.

Inoculation Theory

In contemporary society, tremendous emphasis is placed on influencing others. The irony is that, given all the emphasis in contemporary society on influencing people, there has been little emphasis on conferring resistance to—defending people against—influence. However, this is changing. As Eagly and Chaiken (1993) observe: "Despite the obvious importance of studying mechanisms of resistance, few formal theories of attitudinal resistance have flourished." The exception, they argue, is inoculation theory, whose purpose is specifically intended "to explain resistance to influence" (p. 560).

Inoculation is a strategy designed to strengthen existing opinion against change. It is a resistance theory. The theory posits that refutational treatments, which introduce challenges to existing attitudes while simultaneously offering preemptive refutation of those challenges, threaten the individual, which triggers the person's motivation to bolster attitudes against change and, as a result, confers resistance to counterarguments which a person might be exposed to (Papageorgis & McGuire, 1961).

Inoculation stands as an alternative to a supportive, bolstering approach to strengthening attitudes. McGuire (1964) explains that the supportive defense is nonthreatening since it consists solely of bolstering content. Because it doesn't expose receivers to challenges against attitudes, it tends to make them overconfident and, therefore, vulnerable. The supportive defense leaves the individual unaware of potential weaknesses in his or her position and both unmotivated to, and unpracticed in, defending his or her attitudes (Wyer, 1974). Subsequent studies confirmed that refutational defenses are superior to supportive in protecting attitudes against subsequent influence (Anderson & McGuire, 1965; Crane, 1962; McGuire, 1962, 1964, 1966; McGuire & Papageorgis, 1961, 1962; Papageorgis & McGuire, 1961; Suedfeld & Borrie, 1978; Tannenbaum,

McCaulay, & Norris, 1966; Tannenbaum & Norris, 1965), although a combination of both is superior to either approach alone (McGuire, 1961, 1962; Tannenbaum & Norris, 1965).

Although early research on inoculation was limited to laboratory studies and conducted using noncontroversial topics, recent studies have returned to inoculation's core logic in an effort to further refine the workings of the theory. The results confirm McGuire's thesis that threat and refutational preemption function as critical ingredients in inoculation (Pfau et al., 1997, 1999). Threat involves the forewarning of impending challenges to attitudes. It is designed to get individuals to acknowledge the vulnerability of their attitudes to potential attack and, as a result, to trigger the internal process of cognitive reinforcement. Threat operates in tandem with refutational preemption. Refutational preemption consists of systematically raising, and then answering, one or more specific challenges to existing attitudes. Threat motivates motivates the individual to bolster attitudes, and refutational preemption provides both the specific cognitive content to use in answering potential challenges and rehearsal of the process used to strengthen attitudes. These studies indicate that inoculation elicits both threat and counterarguing, that threat functions to immediately strengthen initial attitudes and further contributes to counterarguing and elicited anger, and that counterarguing and anger promote resistance. In addition, refutational preemption directly fosters resistance (Pfau et al., 1997, 1999).

Inoculation has received considerable attention in applied influence settings. It has been found to confer resistance to the influence of comparative advertising appeals (Hunt, 1973; Pfau, 1992), social marketing messages (Bither, Dolich, & Nell, 1971; Szybillo & Heslin, 1973); political campaign attacks (Pfau & Burgoon, 1988; Pfau, Kenski, Nitz, & Sorenson, 1990), and to the counterattitudinal pressures on younger adolescents to initiate cigarette smoking (Pfau, Van Bockern, 1994; Pfau, Van Bockern, & Kang, 1992). In a public relations context, Burgoon, Pfau, and Birk (1995) reported that Mobil Oil Corporation's extensive issue advocacy advertising campaign functions to inoculate. When faced with counterattitudinal issue attacks, the company's advertorials inoculate readers against attitude slippage and protect Mobil's overall credibility rating.

One promising application of inoculation in public relations is as a preemptive, proactive approach in crisis communication. The crisis communication literature recommends use of preemptive, proactive strategies because of the inevitability of crises. As Coombs (1999) advises, "It is a mistake to believe that an organization can avoid or prevent all possible crises. Eventually, a crisis will befall an organization" (p. 126). Therefore, Coombs and others recommend strategies to prevent crises from occurring in the first place, which is obviously the ideal. However, acknowledging the inevitability of crises, many scholars and professionals advise the use of proactive strategies designed to soften their impact (Druckenmiller, 1993).

The latter strategies typically involve establishing a base of goodwill that might serve to partially deflect the damage to an organization's image that typically accompanies a crisis. This approach operates on the assumption that accumulation of "image credits," earned via positive performance, can serve to "offset the reputational damage generated by the crisis" (Coombs, 1998, p. 182). This approach makes intuitive sense, and there is some anecdotal evidence suggesting that it works. However, there are no hard data documenting efficacy; instead "untested assumptions" prevail in crisis communication, at both proactive and reactive levels (Coombs, 1999, p. 126). This proactive preemptive approach is conceptually similar to a supportive, or bolstering, message in inoculation theory and research. In inoculation, supportive treatments provide positive arguments designed to bolster original attitudes, thus protecting against attitude slippage in the face of subsequent challenges, much as good deeds enhance attitudes toward an organization, thereby protecting against the erosion of attitudes in the event of a crisis.

Inoculation provides an untested, but promising, alternative proactive approach in crisis communication. Inoculation, which would raise an organization's potential vulnerabilities and the specter of crisis, and then preemptively refute them, delineating what the organization is doing to address these vulnerabilities, may prove to provide greater protection once a crisis occurs than prior efforts to enhance positive image, much as refutational defenses confer greater resistance than supportive defenses (Anderson & McGuire, 1965; Crane, 1962; McGuire, 1962, 1964, 1966; McGuire & Papageorgis, 1961, 1962; Papageorgis & McGuire, 1961; Suedfeld & Borrie, 1978; Tannenbaum, McCaulay, & Norris, 1966; Tannenbaum & Norris, 1965). Or, use of inoculation in conjunction with an image-enhancing strategy may provide the optimal protection for an organization in a crisis, safeguarding its image better than either approach alone, much as extant research reveals that the use of a combined bolstering and inoculation strategy confers more resistance than either defense alone (McGuire, 1961, 1962; Tannenbaum & Norris, 1965).

Hua-Hsin Wan (2000) has launched an investigation that compares the efficacy of image-enhancing and inoculation proactive approaches in crisis communication. In addition, Wan's investigation probes whether use of inoculation, because organizations would expose their vulnerabilities, carries the intrinsic risk of undermining an organization's image absent a crisis.

Inoculation is a source of potential applications in public relations. It has demonstrated efficacy in advocacy advertising to strengthen public attitudes consonant with the organization's position on issues, and may offer a viable proactive strategy to protect an organization's image in event of a crisis. These and other applications warrant further investigation. In addition, there are unresolved theoretical questions in inoculation that additional research needs to address. For example, in addition to the mechanisms of threat and counterarguing, which have been proven to play an active role in conferring resistance

(Pfau et al., 1997, 2003), what process might explain the direct impact of refutational preemption in resistance? One possibility is that inoculation treatments make attitudes more accessible for the receiver, perhaps by priming them (Szabo & Pfau, 2002). Other questions also require resolution (Pfau, 1997; Szabo & Pfau, 2002). What is the most appropriate message approach: use of content-oriented or peripheral or systematic messages? What is the best community modality for delivering inoculation messages? What is the ideal timing of inoculation treatments and booster messages in relation to subsequent attacks?

CONCLUSION

We have argued in this chapter that persuasion continues to be an integral function of public relations. It is intrinsic to public relations activities aimed at external publics. Persuasion plays an implicit role in community relations, media relations, crisis communication, and other public relations tasks. Persuasion is more explicit in such endeavors as fundraising, lobbying, and commercial and social marketing. We also argued that the controversy over whether public relations should operate from an asymmetrical or symmetrical model is misguided; that public relations is a form of strategic communication in which persuasion plays an intrinsic role.

Finally, we explored potential applications of theories of persuasion in the context of public relations in the form of select exemplars. These exemplars, all drawn from the extant literature in persuasion, illustrate how persuasion theory and research offer fruitful ground for public relations scholars. If scholars make functional issues, many of which are grounded in persuasion, the focus of their research, the results of their efforts can simultaneously enhance understanding of persuasion and inform public relations practices. This approach would enable public relations scholars, and the discipline as a whole, to rise above the limitations inherent in the present preoccupation with context.

REFERENCES

Aaker, D. A., Stayman, D. M., & Hagarty, M. R. (1986). Warmth in advertising: Measurement, impact, and sequence effects. *Journal in Consumer Research, 12*, 365–381.

Abelson, R. P., & Prentice, D. A. (1989). In A. R. Pratkanis, S. J. Breckler, & A. G. Greenwald (Eds.), *Attitude structure and function* (pp. 361–381). Columbus: Ohio State University Press.

Alba, J. W., & Marmorstein, H. (1987). The effects of frequency knowledge on consumer decision making. *Journal of Consumer Research, 14*, 14–25.

Anderson, L. R., & McGuire, W, J. (1965). Prior reassurance of group consensus as a factor in producing resistance to persuasion. *Sociometry, 28*, 44–56.

Andreoli, V., & Worchel, S. (1978). Effects of media, communicator, and message position on attitude change. *Public Opinion Quarterly, 42*, 59–70.

Annenberg School for Communication, University of Pennsylvania (1994, Fall). Advertising and the health care debate. *News Link, 4*(3), p. 6.

Arnold, V. D. (1985). The importance of pathos in persuasive appeals. *The Bulletin*, 26–27.

Axsom, D., Yates, S. M., & Chaiken, S. (1987). Audience response as a heuristic cue in persuasion. *Journal of Personality and Social Psychology, 53*, 30–40.

Barney, R. D., & Black, J. (1994). Ethics and professional persuasive communications. *Public Relations Review, 20*, 233–248.

Batra, R. (1986). Affective advertising: Role, process, and measurement. In R. A. Peterson, W. D. Hoyer, & W. R. Wilson (Eds.), *The role of affect in consumer behavior: Emerging theories and applications* (pp. 53–85). Lexington, MA: Lexington Books.

Batra, R., & Ray, M. L. (1985). How advertising works at contact. In L. F. Alwitt & A. A. Mitchell (Eds.), *Psychological processes and advertising effects: Theory, research, and applications* (pp. 13–43). Hillsdale, NJ: Lawrence Erlbaum Associates.

Beniger, J. R. (1987). Personalization of mass media and the growth of pseudo-community. *Communication Research, 14*, 352–370.

Berelson, B., Lazarsfeld, P., & McPhee, W. (1954). *Voting: A study of opinion formation in a presidential campaign*. Chicago: University of Chicago Press.

Bernays, E. L. (1923). *Crystallizing public opinion*. New York: Boni and Liveright.

Bernays, E. L. (1955). The theory and practice of public relations: A resume. In E. L. Bernays (Ed.), *The engineering of consent* (pp. 3–25). Norman: University of Oklahoma Press.

Bither, S. W., Dolich, I. J., & Nell, E. B. (1971). The application of attitude immunization techniques in marketing. *Journal of Marketing Research, 18*, 56–61.

Botan, C. H. (1989). Theory development in public relations. In C. H. Botan and V. Hazleton, Jr. (Eds.), *Public relations theory* (pp. 99–110). Hillsdale, NJ: Lawrence Erlbaum Associates.

Breckler, S. J. (1993). Emotion and attitude change. In M. Lewis & J. Haviland (Eds.), *Handbook of emotions* (pp. 461–473). New York: Guilford.

Broom, G. M., & Dozier, D. M. (1990). *Using research in public relations: Applications to program management*. Englewood Cliffs, NJ: Prentice Hall.

Burgoon, J. K. (1980). Nonverbal communication research on the 1970s: An overview. In D. Nimmo (Ed.), *Communication yearbook 4* (pp. 179–197). New Brunswick, NJ: Transaction Books.

Burgoon, J. K., & Hale, J. L. (1984). The fundamental topoi of relational communication. *Communication Monographs, 51*, 193–214.

Burgoon, J. K., & Hale, J. L. (1987). Validation and measurement of the fundamental themes of relational communication. *Communication Monographs, 54*, 19–41.

Burgoon, M., Pfau, M., & Birk, T. (1995). An inoculation theory explanation for the effects of corporate issue/advocacy advertising campaigns. *Communication Research, 22*, 485–505.

Cancel, A. E., Cameron, G. T., Sallot, L. M., & Mitrook, M. A. (1997). It depends: A contingency theory of accommodation in public relations. *Journal of Public Relations Research, 9*, 31–63.

Caywood, C. L. (1997). Twenty-first century public relations: The strategic stages of integrated communications. In C. L. Caywood (Ed.), *The handbook of strategic public relations & integrated communications* (pp. xi–xxvi). New York: McGraw-Hill.

Center, A. H., & Jackson, P. (1995). *Public relations practices: Managerial case studies & problems* (5th ed.). Englewood Cliffs, NJ: Prentice Hall.

Chaiken, S. (1980). Heuristic versus systematic information processing and the use of source versus message cues in persuasion. *Journal of Personality and Social Psychology, 39*, 752–766.

Chaiken, S. (1987). The heuristic model of persuasion. In M. P. Zanna & C. P. Herman (Eds.), *Social influence: The Ontario symposium* (Vol. 5, pp. 3–39). Hillsdale, NJ: Lawrence Erlbaum Associates.

Chaiken, S., & Eagly, A. H. (1976). Communication modality as a determinant of message persuasiveness and message comprehensibility. *Journal of Personality and Social Psychology, 34,* 605–614.

Chaiken, S., & Eagly, A. H. (1983). Communication modality as a determinant of persuasion: The role of communicator silence. *Journal of Personality and Social Psychology, 45,* 241–256.

Chaiken, S., Liberman, A., & Eagly, A. H. (1989). Heuristic and systematic processing within and beyond the persuasion context. In J. S. Uleman & J. A. Bargh (Eds.), *Unintended thought* (pp. 212–252). New York: Guilford.

Chaudhuri, A., & Buck, R. (1995). Media differences in rational and emotional responses to advertising. *Journal of Broadcasting & Electronic Media, 39,* 109–125.

Chesebro, J. W. (1984). The media reality: Epistemological functions of media in cultural systems. *Critical Studies in Mass Communication, 1,* 111–130.

Clore, G. L., Schwartz, N., & Conway, M. (1994). Affective causes and consequences of social information processing. In R. S. Wyer & T. K. Srull (Eds.), *Handbook of social cognition* (Vol. 1, pp. 323–417). Hillsdale, NJ: Lawrence Erlbaum Associates.

Coombs, W. T. (1998). An analytic framework for crisis situations: Better responses from a better understanding of the situation. *Journal of Public Relations Research, 10,* 177–191.

Coombs, W. T. (1999). Information and compassion in crisis responses: A test of their effects. *Journal of Public Relations Research, 11,* 125–142.

Cornwell, T. B., & Maignan, I. (1998). An international review of sponsorship research. *Journal of Advertising, 27*(1), 15–21.

Crable, R. E., & Vibert, S. L. (1986). *Public relations as communication management.* Edina, MN: Bellwether Press.

Crane, E. (1962). Immunization—with and without use of counterarguments. *Journalism Quarterly, 39,* 445–450.

Crossen, C. (1994). *Tainted truth: The manipulation of fact in America.* New York: Simon & Schuster.

Cutlip, S. M., Center, A. H., & Broom, G. M. (1985). *Effective public relations* (6th ed.). Englewood Cliffs, NJ: Prentice Hall.

Dalgleish, T., & Power, M. J. (1999). Cognition and emotion: Future directions. In T. Dalgleish & M. J. Power (Eds.), *Handbook of cognition and emotion* (pp. 799–805). New York: Wiley.

Denbow, C. H., & Culbertson, H. M. (1985). Linking beliefs and diagnosing an image. *Public Relations Review, 11,* 29–37.

Dillard, J. P. (1998). Foreword: The role of affect in communication, biology, and social relationships. In P. A. Andersen & L. K. Guerrero (Eds.), *Handbook of communication and emotion: Research, theory, applications, and contexts* (pp. xvii–xxxii). San Diego, CA: Academic Press.

Dillard, J. P., & Wilson, B. J. (1993). Communication and affect: Thoughts, feelings, and issues for the future. *Communication Research, 20,* 637–646.

Dozier, D. M. (1990). The innovation of research in public relations practice: Review of a program of studies. In L. A. Grunig & J. E. Grunig (Eds.), *Public relations research annual* (vol. 2, pp. 3–28). Hillsdale, NJ: Lawrence Erlbaum Associates.

Dozier, D. M., Grunig, L., & Grunig, J. (1995). *Manager's guide to excellence in public relations and communication management.* Hillsdale, NJ: Lawrence Erlbaum Associates.

Dozier, D. M., & Repper, F. C. (1992). Research firms and public relations practices. In J. E. Grunig, D. M. Dozier, W. P. Ehling, L. A. Grunig, F. C. Repper, & J. White (Eds.), *Excellence in public relations and communication management* (pp. 185–215). Hillsdale, NJ: Lawrence Erlbaum Associates.

Druckenmiller, B. (1993). Crises provide insights on image. *Business Marketing, 78*, 40. Eagly, A. H., & Chaiken, S. (1993). *The psychology of attitudes.* Orlando, FL: Harcourt Brace Jovanovich.

Eagly, A. H., & Himmelfarb, S. (1974). Current trends in attitude theory and research. In S. Himmelfarb & A. H. Eagly (Eds.), *Readings in attitude change* (pp. 594–610). New York: Wiley.

Edell, J. A., & Burke, M. C. (1987). The power of feelings in understanding advertising effects. *Journal of Consumer Research, 14*, 421–433.

Ewen, S. (1996). *PR! A social history of spin.* New York: Basic Books.

Fazio, R. H. (1986). How do attitudes guide behavior? In R. M. Sorrentino & E. T. Higgins (Eds.), *Handbook of motivation and cognition: Foundations of social behavior* (pp. 204–243). New York: Guilford.

Fazio, R. H. (1989). On the power and functionality of attitudes: The role of attitude accessibility. In A. R. Pratkanis, S. J. Breckler, & A. G. Greenwald (Eds.), *Attitude structure and function* (pp. 153–179). Hillsdale, NJ: Lawrence Erlbaum Associates.

Fink, E. L., Monahan, J. L., & Kaplowitz, S. A. (1989). A spatial model of the mere exposure effect. *Communication Research, 16*, 746–769.

Gandy, O. H., Jr. (1982). *Beyond agenda setting: Information subsidies and public policy.* Norwood, NJ: Ablex.

Gold, E. R. (1988). Ronald Reagan and the oral tradition. *Central States Speech Journal, 39*, 159–176.

Graber, D. A. (1987). Television news without pictures? *Critical Studies in Mass Communication, 4*, 74–78.

Greenwald, A. G. (1989). Why attitudes are important: Defining attitudes and attitude theory 20 years later. In A. R. Pratkanis & S. J. Breckler (Eds.), *Attitude structure and function* (pp. 429–440). Hillsdale, NJ: Lawrence Erlbaum Associates.

Greider, W. M. (1992). *Who will tell the people: The betrayal of American democracy.* New York: Simon & Schuster.

Gronstedt, A. (1997). The role of research in public relations strategy and planning. In C. L. Caywood (Ed.), *The handbook of strategic public relations & integrated communications* (pp. 34–59). New York: McGraw-Hill.

Grunig, J. E. (1980). Communication of scientific information to nonscientists. In B. Dervin & M. J. Voight (Eds.), *Progress in communication sciences* (Vol. 2, pp. 167–214). Norwood, NJ: Ablex.

Grunig, J. E. (1989a). Sierra Club study shows who become activists. *Public Relations Review, 15*, 3–24.

Grunig, J. E. (1989b). Symmetrical presuppositions as a framework for public relations theory. In C. H. Botan and V. Hazleton, Jr. (Eds.), *Public relations theory* (pp. 17–44). Hillsdale, NJ: Lawrence Erlbaum Associates.

Grunig, J. E. (1992). Communication, public relations, and effective organizations: An overview. In J. E. Grunig, D. M. Dozier, W. P. Ehling, L. A. Grunig, F. C. Repper, & J. White (Eds.), *Excellence in public relations and communication management* (pp. 1–28). Hillsdale, NJ: Lawrence Erlbaum Associates.

Grunig, J. E., & Grunig, L. A. (1990, August). *Models of public relations: A review and reconceptualization.* Paper presented at the annual meeting of the Association for Education in Journalism and Mass Communication, Minneapolis, MN.

Grunig, J. E., & Grunig, L. A. (1992). Models of public relations and communication. In J. E. Grunig, D. M. Dozier, W. P. Ehling, L. A. Grunig, F. C. Repper, & J. White (Eds.), *Excellence in public relations and communication management* (pp. 285–326). Hillsdale, NJ: Lawrence Erlbaum Associates.

Grunig, J. E., & Hunt, T. (1984). *Managing public relations.* New York: Holt, Rinehart & Winston.

Grunig, J. E., & Repper, F. C. (1992). Strategic management, publics, and issues. In J. E. Grunig, D. M. Dozier, W. P. Ehling, L. A. Grunig, F. C. Repper, & J. White (Eds.), *Excellence in public relations and communication management* (pp. 117–157). Hillsdale, NJ: Lawrence Erlbaum Associates.

Grunig, J. E., & White, J. (1992). The effect of worldviews on public relations theory and practice. In J. E. Grunig, D. M. Dozier, W. P. Ehling, L. A. Grunig, F. C. Repper, & J. White (Eds.), *Excellence in public relations and communication management* (pp. 31–64). Hillsdale, NJ: Lawrence Erlbaum Associates.

Grunig, L. A. (1986, August). *Activism and organizational response: contemporary cases of collective behavior.* Paper presented at the annual meeting of the Association for Education in Journalism and Mass Communication, Norman, OK.

Habermann, P., Kupenhauer, L. L., & Martinson, D. L. (1988). Sequence faculty divided over PR value, status, and news orientation. *Journalism Quarterly, 65,* 490–496.

Harris, T. L. (1991). *The marketer's guide to public relations: How today's top companies are using the new PR to gain a competitive advantage.* New York: Wiley.

Hazleton, V., Jr., & Botan, C. G. (1989). The role of theory in public relations. In C. H. Botan and V. Hazleton, Jr. (Eds.), *Public relations theory* (pp. 3–15). Hillsdale, NJ: Lawrence Erlbaum Associates.

Hazlewood, J. D., & Chaiken, S. (1990, August). *Personal relevance, majority influence, and the law of large numbers.* Paper presented at the annual meeting of the American Psychological Association, Boston.

Heath, R. L. (1993). A rhetorical approach to zones of meaning and organizational prerogatives. *Public Relations Review, 19,* 141–155.

Heath, R. L. (1994). *Management of corporate communication: From interpersonal contacts to external affairs.* Hillsdale, NJ: Lawrence Erlbaum Associates.

Heath, R. L., Seshadri, S., & Lee, J. (1998). Risk communication: A two-community analysis of proximity, dread, trust/involvement, uncertainty, openness/accessibility, and knowledge on support/opposition toward chemical companies. *Journal of Public Relations Research, 10,* 35–56.

Hellweg, S. A. (1989, May). *The application of Grunig's symmetry-asymmetry public relations models to internal communications systems.* Paper presented at the annual meeting of the International Communication Association, San Francisco.

Herek, G. M. (1986). The instrumentality of attitudes: Towards a neo-functional theory. *Journal of Social Issues, 42,* 99–114.

Herek, G. N. (1987). Can functions be measured? A new perspective on the functional approach to attitudes. *Social Psychology Quarterly, 50,* 285–303.

Herman, E. S., & Chomsky, N. (1988). *Manufacturing consent: The political economy of the mass media.* New York: Pantheon Books.

Hitchon, J. C., & Thorson, E. (1995). Effects of emotion and product involvement on the experience of repeated commercial viewing. *Journal of Broadcasting & Electronic Media, 39,* 376–389.

Holbert, R. L. (in press). The embodied meaning of media form. In J. P. Dillard & M. Pfau (Eds.), *The persuasion handbook: Theory and practice.* (pp. 749–763). Newbury Park, CA: Sage.

Holbrook, M. B., & Batra, R. (1987). Assessing the role of emotions as mediators of consumer responses to advertising. *Journal of Consumer Research, 14,* 404–420.

Horton, D., & Wohl, R. R. (1956). Mass communication and parasocial interaction: Observations on intimacy at a distance. *Psychiatry, 19,* 215–229.

Hunt, H. K. (1973). Effects of corrective advertising. *Journal of Advertising Research, 13,* 15–22.

Izard, C. E. (1993). Four systems for emotion activation: Cognitive and noncognitive processes. *Psychological Review, 100,* 68–90.

Jackall, R. (1995). The magic lantern: The world of public relations. In R. Jackall, *Propaganda* (pp. 351–399). New York: New York University Press.

Jamieson, K. H. (1988). *Eloquence in an electronic age: The transformation of political speechmaking.* New York: Oxford University Press.

Jones, J. P. (1955). Organization for public relations. In E. L. Bernays (Ed.), *The engineering of consent* (pp. 156–184). Norman: University of Oklahoma Press.

Jorgensen P. F. (1988). Affect, persuasion, and communication processes. In P. A. Andersen & L. K. Guerrero (Eds.), *Handbook of communication and emotion: Research, theory, applications, and contexts* (pp. 403–422). San Diego, CA: Academic Press.

Katz, D. (1960). The functional approach to the study of attitudes. *Public Opinion Quarterly, 24,* 163–204.

Katz, E., & Lazarsfeld, P. F. (1955). *Personal influence: The part played by people in the flow of mass communications.* New York: The Free Press.

Katzman, J. B. (1993). What's the role of public relations? *Public Relations Journal, 49*(4), 11–16.

Keating, J. P., & Latane, B. (1976). Politicians on TV: The image is the message. *Journal of Social Issues, 32,* 116–132.

Kiesler, C. A., Collins, B. E., & Miller, N. (1969). *Attitude change: A critical analysis of theoretical approaches.* New York: Wiley.

Klapper, J. T. (1960). *The effects of mass communication.* New York: The Free Press.

Krugman, H. E. (1965). The impact of television advertising: Learning without involvement. *Public Opinion Quarterly, 29,* 349–356.

Krugman, H. E. (1971). Brain wave measures of media involvement. *Journal of Advertising Research, 11,* 3–9.

Lazarsfeld, P., Berelson, B., & Gaudet, H. (1948). *The people's choice.* New York: Columbia University Press.

Lazarus, R. S. (1982). Thoughts on the relations between emotion and cognition. *American Psychologist, 37,* 1019–1024.

Lazarus, R. S. (1999). The cognition-emotion debate: A bit of history. In T. Dalgleish & M. J. Power (Eds.), *Handbook of cognition and emotion* (pp. 3–19). New York: Wiley.

Leichty, G. (1997). The limits of collaboration. *Public Relations Review, 23,* 47–55.

Levy, M. R. (1979). Watching TV as parasocial interaction. *Journal of Broadcasting, 23,* 69–80.

Lodge, M., & Stroh, P. (1993). Inside the mental voting booth: An impression-driven process model of candidate evaluation. In S. Iyengar & W. J. McGuire (Eds.), *Explorations in political psychology* (pp. 225–263). Durham, NC: Duke University Press.

Long, R. K. (1987). Comments on "Professional advocacy in public relations." *Business and Professional Ethics Journal, 6*, 91–93.

Maheswaran, D., & Chaiken, S. (1991). Promoting systematic processing in low motivation settings: Effect of incongruent information on processing and judgment. *Journal of Personality and Social Psychology, 61*, 13–25.

Markus, H., & Zajonc, R. B. (1985). The cognitive perspective in social psychology. In G. Lindzey & E. Aronson (Eds.), *Handbook of social psychology* (Vol. 1, pp. 137–230). New York: Random House.

Marston, J. E. (1979). *Modern public relations.* New York: McGraw-Hill.

McLuhan, M. (1964). *Understanding media: The extensions of man.* New York: McGraw-Hill.

McElreath, M. P. (1997). *Managing systematic and ethical public relations campaigns* (2nd ed.). Dubuque, IA: Brown & Benchmark.

McGuire, W. J. (1961). The effectiveness of supportive and refutational defenses in immunizing and restoring beliefs against persuasion. *Sociometry, 24*, 184–197.

McGuire, W. J. (1962). Persistence of the resistance to persuasion induced by various types of prior belief defenses. *Journal of Abnormal and Social Psychology, 64*, 241–248.

McGuire, W. J. (1964). Inducing resistance to persuasion. Some contemporary approaches. In L. Berkowitz (Ed.), *Advances in experimental social psychology* (Vol. 1, pp. 191–229). New York: Academic Press.

McGuire, W. J. (1966). Persistence of the resistance to persuasion induced by various types of prior belief defenses. In C. W. Backman & P. F. Secord (Eds.), *Problems in social psychology* (pp. 128–135). New York: McGraw-Hill.

McGuire, W. J., & Papageorgis, D. (1961). The relative efficacy of various types of prior belief-defense in producing immunity against persuasion. *Journal of Abnormal and Social Psychology, 62*, 327–337.

McGuire, W. J., & Papageorgis, D. (1962). Effectiveness of forewarning in developing resistance to persuasion. *Public Opinion Quarterly, 26*, 24–34.

Meyrowitz, J. (1985). *No sense of place.* New York: Oxford University Press.

Meyrowitz, J. (1994). Medium theory. In D. Crowley & D. Mitchell (Eds.), *Communication theory today* (pp. 50–77). Stanford, CA: Stanford University Press.

Miller, G. R. (1989). Persuasion and public relations: Two "ps" in a pod. In C. H. Botan and V. Hazleton, Jr. (Eds.), *Public relations theory* (pp. 45–66). Hillsdale, NJ: Lawrence Erlbaum Associates.

Miller, G. R., & Burgoon, M. (1973). *New techniques of persuasion.* New York: Harper & Row.

Moore, H. F., & Canfield, B. R. (1977). *Public relations: Principles, cases, and problems* (7th ed.). Homewood, IL: Richard D. Irwin.

Moreland, R. L., & Zajonc, R. B. (1977). Is stimulus recognition a necessary condition for the occurrence of exposure effects? *Journal of Personality and Social Psychology, 35*, 191–199.

Murphy, P. (1991). The limits of symmetry: A game theory approach to symmetric and asymmetric public relations. In J. Grunig and L. Grunig (Eds.), *Public relations research annual* (Vol. 1, pp. 87–96). Hillsdale, NJ: Lawrence Erlbaum Associates.

Olasky, M. N. (1989). The aborted debate within public relations: An approach through Kuhn's paradigm. In J. E. Grunig & L. A. Grunig (Eds.), *Public relations research annual* (Vol. 1, pp. 87–96). Hillsdale, NJ: Lawrence Erlbaum Associates.

Ottati, V. C., & Wyer, Jr., R. S. (1993). Affect and political judgment. In S. Iyengar & W. J. McGuire (Eds.), *Explorations in political psychology* (pp. 296–315). Durham, NC: Duke University Press.

Papageorgis, D., & McGuire, W. J. (1961). The generality of immunity to persuasion produced by pre-exposure to weakened counterarguments. *Journal of Abnormal and Social Psychology, 62*, 475–481.

Patterson, T. E. (1993). *Out of order*. New York: Alfred A. Knopf.

Pavlik, J. V. (1987). *Public relations: What research tells us*. Newbury Park, CA: Sage.

Pavlik, J. V. (1989). Public relations: Public relations research annual, vol. 1. *Journalism and Mass Communication Quarterly, 66*, 759.

Pechmann, C., & Stewart, D. W. (1989). The multidimensionality of persuasive communications: Theoretical and empirical foundations. In P. Cafferata & A. M. Tybout (Eds.), *Cognitive and affective responses to advertising* (pp. 31–56). Lexington, MA: Lexington Books.

Perse, E. M., & Rubin, R. B. (1989). Attribution in social and parasocial relationships. *Communication Research, 16*, 59–77.

Peterson, R. A., Hoyer, W. D., & Wilson, W. R. (1986). Reflections on the role of affect in consumer behavior. In R. A. Peterson, W. D. Hoyer, & W. R. Wilson (Eds.), *The role of affect in consumer behavior: Emerging theories and applications* (pp. 141–159). Lexington, KY: Lexington Books.

Petty, R. E., & Cacioppo, J. T. (1979). Issue involvement can increase or decrease persuasion by enhancing message-relevant cognitive responses. *Journal of Personality and Social Psychology, 37*, 1915–1926.

Petty, R. E., & Cacioppo, J. T. (1984a). The effects of involvement on responses to argument quantity and quality: Central and peripheral routes to persuasion. *Journal of Personality and Social Psychology, 46*, 69–81.

Petty, R. E., & Cacioppo, J. T. (1984b). Source factors and the elaboration likelihood model of persuasion. *Advances in Consumer Research, 11*, 668–672.

Petty, R. E., & Cacioppo, J. T. (1986). *Communication and persuasion: Central and peripheral routes to attitude change*. New York: Springer-Verlag.

Petty, R. E., Cacioppo, J. T., & Kasmer, J. A. (1988). The role of affect in the elaboration likelihood model pf persuasion. In L. Donohew, H. E. Sypher, & E. T. Higgins (Eds.), *Communication, social cognition, and affect* (pp. 117–146). Hillsdale, NJ: Lawrence Erlbaum Associates.

Pfau, M. (1990). A channel approach to television influence. *Journal of Broadcasting & Electronic Media, 34*, 195–214.

Pfau, M. (1992). The potential of inoculation in promoting resistance to the effectiveness of comparative advertising messages. *Communication Quarterly, 40*, 26–44.

Pfau, M. (1997). The inoculation model of resistance to influence. In G. A. Barnett & F. J. Boster (Eds.), *Progress in communication sciences: Advances in persuasion* (Vol. 13, pp. 133–171). Greenwich, CT: Ablex.

Pfau, M., & Burgoon, M. (1988). Inoculation in political campaign communication. *Human Communication Research, 15*, 91–111.

Pfau, M., Diedrich, T., Larson, K. M., & Van Winkle, K. M. (1993). Relational and competence perceptions of presidential candidates during primary election campaigns. *Journal of Broadcasting & Electronic Media, 37*, 275–292.

Pfau, M., & Kang, J. G. (1991). The impact of relational messages on candidate influence in televised political debates. *Communication Studies, 42*, 114–128.

Pfau, M., Kenski, H. C., Nitz, M., & Sorenson, J. (1990). Efficacy of inoculation strategies in promoting resistance to political attack messages: Application to direct mail. *Communication Monographs, 57*, 1–12.

Pfau, M., & Parrott, R. (1993). *Persuasive communication campaigns*. Boston: Allyn & Bacon.

Pfau, M., Roskos-Ewoldsen, D., Wood, M., Yin, S., Cho, J., Lu, K.-S., & Shen, L. (2003). Attitude accessibility as an alternative explanation for how inoculation confers resistance. *Communication Monographs, 70*, 39–51.

Pfau, M., Szabo, E. A., Anderson, J., Morrill, J., Zubric, J., & Wan, H.-H. (2001). The role and impact of affect in the process of resistance to provision. *Human Communication Research, 27*, 216–252.

Pfau, M., Tusing, K. J., Koerner, A. F., Lee, W., Godbold, L. C., Penaloza, L. J., Yang, V. S., & Hong, Y. (1997). Enriching the inoculation construct: The role of critical components in the process of resistance. *Human Communication Research, 24*, 187–215.

Pfau, M., & Van Bockern, S. (1994). The persistence of inoculation in conferring resistance to smoking initiation among adolescents: The second year. *Human Communication Research, 20*, 413–430.

Pfau, M., Van Bockern, S., & Kang, J. G. (1992). Use of inoculation to promote resistance to smoking initiation among adolescents. *Communication Monographs, 59*, 213–230.

Robinson, E. J. (1969). *Public relations and survey research: Achieving organizational goals in a communication context*. New York: Appleton-Century Crofts.

Roskos-Ewoldson, D. R., & Fazio, R. H. (1992). The accessibility of source likability as a determinant of persuasion. *Personality and Social Psychology Bulletin, 18*, 19–25.

Rubin, R. B., & McHugh, M. P. (1987). Development of parasocial interaction relationships. *Journal of Broadcasting & Electronic Media, 31*, 279–292.

Salmon, C. T. (1986). Perspectives on involvement in consumer and communication research. In B. Dervin & M. J. Voight (Eds.), *Progress in communication sciences* (Vol. 7, pp. 243–268). Norwood, NJ: Ablex Publishing Corporation.

Salmon, C. T. (1989). Campaigns for social "improvement": An overview of values, rationales, and impacts. In C. T. Salmon (Ed.), *Information campaigns: Balancing social values and social change* (pp. 19–53). Newbury Park, CA: Sage.

Salomon, G. (1981). *Communication and education: Social and psychological interactions*. Beverly Hills, CA: Sage.

Salomon, G. (1987). *Interactions of media, cognition, and learning: An exploration of how symbolic forms cultivate mental skills and affect knowledge acquisition*. San Francisco: Jossey-Bass.

Scott, J. C., Jr., & O'Hair, D. (1989). Expanding psychographic concepts in public relations: The composite audience profile. In C. H. Botan and V. Hazleton, Jr. (Eds.), *Public relations theory* (pp. 203–219). Hillsdale, NJ: Lawrence Erlbaum Associates.

Seitel, F. P. (1992). *The practice of public relations*. New York: Macmillan.

Seitel, F. P. (1998). *The practice of public relations* (7th ed.). Upper Saddle River, NJ: Prentice Hall.

Shavitt, S. (1989). Operationalizing functional theories of attitude. In A. R. Pratkanis, S. J. Breckler, & A. G. Greenwald (Eds.), *Attitude structure and function* (pp. 311–337). Columbus: Ohio State University Press.

Shavitt, S. (1990). The role of attitude objects in attitude functions. *Journal of Experimental Social Psychology, 26*, 124–148.

Shah, D. V., Domke, D., & Wackmann, D. B. (1996). "To thine own self be true": Values, framing, and voter decision-making strategies. *Communication Research, 23*, 509–560.

Snyder, M., & DeBono, K. G. (1987). A functional approach to attitudes and persuasion. In M. P. Zanna, J. M. Olson, & C. P. Herman (Eds.), *Social influence: The Ontario symposium, Volume 5* (pp. 107–125). Hillsdale, NJ: Lawrence Erlbaum Associates.

Stauber, J., & Rampton, S. (1996). *Toxic sludge is good for you: Damn lies and the public relations industry.* Monroe, ME: Common Courage Press.

Stiff, J. B. (1994). *Persuasive communication.* New York: Guilford Press.

Stuart, E. W., Shimp, T. A., & Engle, R. W. (1987). Classical conditioning of consumer attitudes: Four experiments in an advertising context. *Journal of Consumer Research, 14*, 334–349.

Suedfeld, P., & Borrie, R. A. (1978). Sensory deprivation, attitude change, and defense against persuasion. *Canadian Journal of Behavioral Science, 10*, 16–27.

Szabo, E. A., & Pfau, M. (2002). Nuances in inoculation: Theory and applications. In J. P. Dillard & M. Pfau (Eds.), *The persuasion handbook: Theory and practice* (pp. 233–258). Newbury Park, CA: Sage.

Szybillo, G. J., & Heslin, R. (1973). Resistance to persuasion: Inoculation theory in a marketing context. *Journal of Marketing Research, 10*, 396–403.

Tannenbaum, P. H., Macaulay, J. R., & Norris, E. L. (1966). Principle of congruity and reduction in persuasion. *Journal of Personality and Social Psychology, 2*, 223–238.

Tannenbaum, P. H., & Norris, E. L. (1965). Effects of combining congruity principle strategies for the reduction of persuasion. *Sociometry, 28*, 145–157.

Tuleja, T. (1985). *Beyond the bottom line.* New York: Facts on File Publications.

Vasquez, G. M. (1996). Public relations as negotiation: An issue development perspective. *Journal of Public Relations Research, 8*, 57–77.

Wallack, L. (1989). Mass communication and health promotion: A critical perspective. In R. E. Rice & C. K. Atkin (Eds.), *Public communication campaigns* (2nd ed., pp. 353–367). Newbury Park, CA: Sage Publications.

Wan, H.-H. (2000). *Priming and inoculation in the context of crisis communication.* Unpublished doctoral dissertation, University of Wisconsin—Madison.

Watson, J. B. (1925). *Behaviorism.* New York: Norton.

Watzlawick, P., Beavin, J. H., & Jackson, D. D. (1967). *Pragmatics of human communication: A study of interactional patterns, pathologies, and paradoxes.* New York: W. W. Norton.

Wilcox, D. L., Ault, P. H., & Agee, W. K. (1992). *Public relations strategies and tactics.* New York: HarperCollins.

Wilson, W. R. (1979). Feeling more than we can know: Exposure effects without learning. *Journal of Personality and Social Psychology, 37*, 811–821.

Wood, W., Kallgren, C. A., & Priesler, R. M. (1985). Access to attitude-relevant information in memory as a determinant of persuasion: The role of message attributes. *Journal of Experimental Social Psychology, 21*, 73–85.

Wright, P. L. (1974). Analyzing media effects on advertising responses. *Public Opinion Quarterly, 38*, 192–205.

Wyer, R. S., Jr. (1974). *Cognitive organization and change: An information processing approach.* New York: Wiley.

Young, D. (1996). *Building your company's good name: How to create and protect the reputation your organization wants & deserves.* New York: American Management Association.

Zajonc, R. B. (1980). Feeling and thinking: Preferences need no inferences. *American Psychologist, 35*, 151–175.

Zajonc, R. B. (1981). A one-factor mind about mind and emotion. *American Psychologist, 36,* 102–103.

Zajonc, R. B. (1984). On the primacy of affect. *American Psychologist, 39,* 117–123.

Zajonc, R. B., & Markus, H. (1982). Affective and cognitive factors in preferences. *Journal of Consumer Research, 9,* 123–131.

Zbar, J. D. (1993, June 28). Environmental marketing. *Advertising Age,* pp. S1–S3.

Zuwerink, J. R., & Devine, P. G. (1996). Attitude importance and resistance to persuasion: It's not just the thought that counts. *Journal of Personality and Social Psychology, 70,* 931–944.

CHAPTER

5

The Centrality
of Practitioner Roles
to Public Relations
Theory

David M. Dozier
and Glen M. Broom
San Diego State University

Organizational *roles* are abstractions, conceptual maps that summarize the most salient features of day-to-day behaviors of organizational members. In public relations, the organizational role of practitioners has been one of the most studied areas in recent years (Pasadeos, Renfro, & Hanily, 1999). This attention to practitioner roles is due, in part, to the centrality of this concept to a wide range of professional and organizational antecedents and outcomes.

In this chapter, we explicate the concept of practitioner roles and typologies used to classify practitioner roles. We examine alternative approaches to measuring practitioner roles. We also review several feminist critiques of roles research, and then examine biases and presuppositions reflected in our own roles research. We then posit a theoretical model of practitioner roles and related professional issues at the individual level of analysis, highlighting important theoretical problems related to this level of analysis. To resolve those difficulties, we then posit a model that addresses the role of the public relations function at the organizational level of analysis, recommending this as a useful heuristic for further research. We clarify some of the normative implications that follow from this shift in level of analysis, arguing that such a shift eliminates the seeming normative denigration of the creative, artistic work done by communication technicians, an organizational role enacted predominantly by women. We conclude by suggesting a four-point agenda for future roles research, emphasizing ongoing refinement of role measures, new studies in the area of role expertise, further studies of role enactment and job satisfaction, and continuing research on gender-income disparities as a function of role enactment and role choice opportunities.

EXPLICATION OF KEY CONCEPTS

Katz and Kahn (1966, 1978) treated roles as central to understanding organizations. After Linton (1936), Newcomb (1950), Parsons (1951), and Merton (1957), Katz and Kahn argued that organizations are best understood as open systems, involving acts and events of people linked together through behaviors and ongoing relationships. Individuals in organizations occupy offices, such as vice president for corporate communications or audiovisual production specialist. An *office* is a point in organizational space located by virtue of its relationships to other offices and to the organization as a whole. A behavioral set is expected from the occupant of that office.

Office defines behavioral sets in a relatively static and formal manner. Organizational *role*, on the other hand, is defined as "recurring actions of an individual, appropriately interrelated with the repetitive activities of others so as to yield a predictable outcome" (Katz & Kahn, 1978, p. 189). Therefore, roles can be abstracted through induction from observed behaviors, as well as deductively from theoretical expectations.

Role behavior does not occur in a social/organizational vacuum; role expectations are transferred to organizational members through role sending and role receiving. *Role sending* is the social process whereby relevant officeholders in an organization prescribe and proscribe behaviors that define role expectations for an individual officeholder. With particular regard to practitioner roles, relevant officeholders include members of the *dominant coalition*—those members of organizations with the collective power to make strategic choices and change organizational structure (Robbins, 1990, p. 251). *Role expectations*, the aggregate of behaviors sought from the officeholder, are especially important when those of the practitioner do not mesh with those of the dominant coalition. Role expectations generally reflect cognitions regarding the role held by others, modified by "impressions of the abilities and personality of the officeholder" (Katz & Kahn, 1978, p. 190).

As traditionally conceptualized in practitioner roles research, role is treated and measured at the individual level of analysis, as an attribute of the practitioner. However, findings from the Excellence Study (Dozier, Grunig, & Grunig, 1995; J. Grunig, 1992; Grunig, Grunig & Dozier, 2002) suggest that the role of the public relations unit or department is of considerable importance in a comprehensive theory of practitioner roles. That is, dominant coalitions have role expectations of their public relations departments, which are communicated in various ways to the department. Public relations departments, in turn, enact roles as departments in organizations that do not necessarily have one-to-one correspondences to individual practitioner roles. For example, various members of the public relations department may be involved with the organization's interdepartmental strategic planning team from time to time, although strategic planning may not be reflected in their individual, day-to-day roles. Indeed, the whole of the departmental role may be greater than the sum of individual role enactments of practitioners that make up that department.

Organizational Roles in Public Relations

Launched by Glen Broom in the 1970s (Broom & Smith, 1978, 1979), roles research sought to develop a typology of practitioner roles that would adequately account for the myriad day-to-day activities of public relations professionals. Broom conceived of practitioners as consultants to dominant coalitions, with each role type providing a distinct form of assistance. Initially, Broom explicated five roles; however, a pretest led Broom to reduce the number to four.

Drawing from the literature, Broom defined the *expert prescriber* as the organization's acknowledged expert on all matters relating to public relations (Broom, 1982; Broom & Smith, 1978, 1979; Cutlip & Center, 1971; Newsom & Scott, 1976). Much like the traditional doctor-patient relationship, the expert prescriber makes recommendations and the dominant coalition complies. Broom drew from the consulting literature (Kurpius & Brubaker, 1976; Walton, 1969) to conceptualize the *communication facilitator* role. Serving as "go-betweens," communication facilitators are deeply involved in process, monitoring and improving the quality and quantity of information flowing between the dominant coalition and key publics. Broom conceptualized the *problem-solving process facilitator* as those assisting dominant coalitions to systematically analyze and solve public relations problems for the organization. The elements of this role were drawn from organization theory and development (Baker & Schaffer, 1969; Schein, 1969). The fourth role was the *communication technician*. In this role, the practitioner provides technical services, generating collateral materials needed to implement public relations programs developed by others. Broom described practitioners enacting this

TABLE 5.1

Factor Loadings for Manager Role Items in 1979 and 1991 PRSA Surveys

Ave	1979	1991	Item Description
.84	.83	.84	I plan and recommend courses of action for solving public relations problems [PF]
.83	.80	.85	I diagnose public relations problems and explain them to others in the organization [PF]
.81	.82	.80	Because of my experience and training, others consider me the organization's expert in solving public relations problems [EP]
.81	.79	.83	I operate as a catalyst in management's decision making [PF]
.79	.82	.76	In meetings with management, I point out the need to follow a systematic public relations planning process [PF]
.79	.77	.80	I take responsibility for the success or failure of my organization's public relations program [EP]
.75	.76	.74	I keep management informed of public reactions to organizational policies, procedures, and/or actions [CF]
.75	.75	.74	I observe that others in the organization hold me accountable for the success or failure of public relations programs [EP]
.73	.74	.71	I encourage management participation when making the important public relations decisions [PF]
.73	.73	.73	I work with managers to increase their skills in solving and/or avoiding public relations problems [PF]
.72	.73	.71	When working with managers on public relations, I outline alternative approaches for solving problems [PF]
.70	.70	.70	I make the communication policy decisions [EP]
.64	.61	.67	I report public opinion survey results to keep management informed of the opinions of various publics [CF]
.57	.61	.53	I create opportunities for management to hear the views of various internal and external publics [CF]
.57	.56	.57	I conduct communication audits to identify communication problems between the organization and various publics [CF]

Identification of conceptual role for each measure: EP, Expert Prescribe; PF, Process Facilitator; CF, Communication Facilitator.

role predominantly as journalists-in-residence, hired away from news organizations for their media relations and production skills.

The Manager-Technician Dichotomy

Following up on experiments in the classroom, Broom conducted a systematic sample survey of Public Relations Society of America (PRSA) members in 1979 (Broom, 1982). He discovered that three roles he had originally conceptualized as distinct were, at the operational level, highly correlated (p. 20). Although the expert prescriber, the communication facilitator, and the problem-solving process facilitator roles remain conceptually distinct roles,

TABLE 5.2

Factor Loadings for Technician Role Items in 1979 and 1991 PRSA Surveys

Ave	1979	1991	Item Description
.83	.82	.83	I handle the technical aspects of producing public relations materials [TECH]
.74	.77	.70	I produce brochures, pamphlets and other publications [TECH]
.64	.72	.55	I maintain media contacts and place press releases [TECH]
.63	.67	.58	I am the person who writes public relations materials presenting information on issues important to the organization [TECH]
.63	.61	.65	I do photography and graphics for public relations materials [TECH]
.55	.50	.59	I edit and/or rewrite for grammar and spelling the materials written by others in the organization [TECH]

Identification of Conceptual Role for Each Measure: TECH, Communication Technician.

practitioners tend to enact these three roles simultaneously in their actual, day-to-day work. The three conceptual roles are not correlated with the communication technician role, however.

Broom's finding prompted Dozier (1983, 1984c) to conduct exploratory factor analysis on data from three practitioner surveys, from which he inductively generated what he labeled the *communication manager* role. The factor structure has proved very stable over numerous studies of different practitioner populations (e.g., PRSA, International Association of Business Communicators, etc.) and over time. Table 5.1 provides a summary of the factor loadings for two surveys of PRSA members, conducted 12 years apart. The communication manager enacts aspects of the expert prescriber, problem-solving process facilitator, and communication facilitator roles. Those enacting the communication manager role make communication policy decisions and are held accountable—by themselves and by others—for the success or failure of public relations programs. The communication manager role involves the dominant coalition in a systematic planning process and serves as a catalyst for decision making. Such practitioners also facilitate communication between the dominant coalition and publics by informing management of public reactions to organizational policies, procedures, and/or actions. The *communication technician* role emerged from the factor analysis largely as Broom had originally operationalized it (see Table 5.2).

Predominant Role

For certain analytic purposes, scores on the manager and technician scales can be compared and practitioners classified as either predominantly managers or predominantly technicians, depending on the higher role score. *Predominant role* is an operational indicator that a communicator is either a manager or a technician predominantly, based on role activities most frequently enacted.

Predominant role can be determined by comparing the means of items that make up the manager and technician roles, assigning predominant role status to the higher of the two means. A second approach is to compare factor scores for the two roles, where role scores are first normalized. The predominant role is assigned to the higher of the two factor scores, yielding about a 50/50 split in the number of practitioners classified as predominantly managers or predominantly technicians.[1]

Regardless of the method used to operationalize predominant role, this dichotomy allows practitioner role status to be reduced to its most simple structure. Operationally, this variable permits certain statistical analyses (e.g., chi-square, F-test). However, use of predominant role is not without cost, since it loses the rich nuances captured by the original 24-item role set. Every practitioner enacts aspects of the manager and technician roles, as well as all four of the original conceptual roles. Further, the role set itself is a simplification of the fluid and complex organizational activities that practitioners enact each day.

Simplification of practitioner role behavior serves an important nomothetic purpose, however. The goal of using abstractions such as organizational roles is to provide a partial description and explanation of practitioner behavior across a wide range of organizational settings, as well as to test relationships between role indicators and the hypothesized antecedents and consequences of role enactment. The utility of such simplification is best judged by their contributions to the theory, education, and practice of public relations. In public relations research, both the four-way and two-way typologies of practitioner roles have proven both extremely efficacious and stimulating of intellectual debate (see Acharya, 1983; Ahlwardt, 1984; Anderson, Reagan, Sumner, & Hill, 1989; Anderson & Reagan, 1992; Broom, 1982, 1986; Broom & Dozier, 1985, 1986; Broom & Smith, 1978, 1979; Creedon, 1991; Culbertson, 1991; Dozier, 1981, 1983, 1984a, 1984b, 1984c, 1986, 1987, 1988a, 1988b, 1989, 1990, 1992, Dozier & Broom, 1995; Dozier, Chapo, & Sullivan, 1983; Dozier & Gottesman, 1982; Ferguson, 1979; Johnson & Acharya, 1982; Johnson, 1997; Lauzen, 1990, 1991, 1992, 1993, 1994, 1997; Lauzen & Dozier, 1992; Leichty & Springston, 1996; Morton, 1996; Pasadeos, Renfro, & Hanily, 1999; Piekos & Einsiedel, 1990; Serini, Toth, Wright, & Emig, 1997; Sullivan, Dozier, & Hellweg, 1984, 1985; Toth & Grunig, 1993; Toth, Serini, Wright, & Emig, 1998).

Role Ambiguity

Office holders are not passive recipients of roles sent messages (Katz & Kahn, 1978). Rather, members of organizations actively construct their roles from

---

[1] Normalization causes this 50/50 split. For each role score distribution, a practitioner may score below the mean, at the mean, or above the mean. When the higher of the two normalized scores is used to determine predominant role, the resulting dichotomy tends to be equally divided among those who are predominantly technicians and those who are predominantly managers.

the myriad of messages they receive about what's expected of their office, moderated by the consequences that flow from attending or not attending to particular role sent messages. *Role ambiguity* is the degree to which messages sent about roles and the consequences that follow are unclear or inconsistent. Ahlwardt (1984) provided evidence that public affairs officers in the U.S. Navy are subject to high levels of role ambiguity, because the role sent by the dominant coalition and immediate supervisor may be at odds with the officer's professional role expectations learned through formal education or professional associations.

Role ambiguity may create stress and uncertainty, but it also provides some wiggle room to selectively enact role behaviors in a strategic and proactive manner, a process called role taking. *Role taking* is a concept similar to role received, except that it places greater emphasis on the office holder as an active, reflexive agent, able to enact role behaviors outside those held by dominant coalitions. Culbertson (1991, p. 54), for example, argued that the technician role is "highly codified and repetitive," whereas process facilitation aspects of the manager role allow "subtle role taking." This, in turn, allows communicators to use role enactment as a means of defining or redefining the public relations function.

ALTERNATIVE APPROACHES TO MEASURING PRACTITIONER ROLES

Two streams of research have considered the concept of practitioner roles in organizations. In the first stream, the basic presuppositions of roles research are accepted; however, alternative strategies to Broom's 24-item role set have been employed to operationalize and measure practitioner roles. A second stream of research has challenged several of the underlying presuppositions of roles research. This second stream raises important criticisms of roles research. No discussion of practitioner roles theory would be complete without a review of these alternative theoretical frameworks, alternative operationalizations, and criticisms implicit in both.

Different Role Measurement Strategies

Broom's 24-item set of practitioner role measures (Dozier & Broom, 1995) has been used extensively to measure practitioner roles. This item set has been used to operationalize the four roles as originally conceptualized by Broom (Broom, 1982; Broom & Smith, 1979), the two-role dichotomy proposed by Dozier (1983), or both. However, some researchers have operationalized practitioner roles using alternative role conceptualizations and measurement strategies.

Ferguson (1979) constructed a universe of practitioner activities by reviewing the relevant literature, as well as examining surveys completed by public relations practitioners. After eliminating duplications, she reduced her set of measures to 45 items. Ferguson's measurement strategy (1979, p. 3) sought to operationalize role norms of public relations practitioners by asking "how appropriate or proper" each activity would be for a practitioner to perform. As framed by Katz and Kahn (1978), such role activities might be described as the role received, the expectations associated with the practitioner's office in the organization, as understood by the practitioner. As such, these measures are not direct indicators of role behaviors enacted, although they may be highly correlated with role enactments.

More recently, Berkowitz and Hristodoulakis (1999) developed a set of 13 items to operationalize the norms or ideals that apply to public relations work. These norms were derived from the discussion of activities and functions of public relations in Cutlip, Center, and Broom (1994). Members of a campus chapter of the Public Relations Student Society of America were asked to complete a self-administered questionnaire. In addition, the item set was mailed to a sample of PRSA members in a nearby city. Data were subjected to cluster analysis, specifying a two-cluster solution. The first cluster was interpreted as a management orientation, with high value placed on counseling management decision making. The second cluster was interpreted as a technician orientation, with high value placed on being a "people person" and regarding public relations primarily as a creative activity.

A set of 10 items was developed by Guth (1995) to measure the technician role. Some items were similar to Broom's technician items (e.g., write news releases, serve as photographer); others were quite different (e.g., take dictation, cannot be fired except for policy violation). A 20-item manager role index was also developed. The item set included measures similar to Broom's expert prescriber (e.g., develop organizational policy), problem solving process facilitator (e.g., counsel others on public relations concerns), and communication facilitator (e.g., serve as organizational spokesperson) role measures. Other items were strikingly different (e.g., serve at the pleasure of the CEO, have private office, have four-year college degree).

Wright (1995) used intensive observation of 148 senior-level communication executives; all were members of the Arthur Page Society, a professional organization of senior-level practitioners. Wright suggested the existence of a "third major role for public relations—communication executive, comprised mainly of corporate senior vice presidents who report directly to CEOs" (Wright, 1995, p. 181).

Leichty and Springston (1996) used Broom's (1982) 24-item set, which they supplemented with 14 additional items adapted from the literature on organizational boundary spanning. Members of the Public Relations Council of Alabama completed 137 questionnaires. When subjected to exploratory factor analysis, eight factors with eigenvalues greater than 1.0 emerged. Two factors, however, consisted only of two items, rendering them difficult to interpret. Factor 2 consisted of four items associated with the manager role factor (see

Dozier & Broom, 1995); none of 14 boundary spanning items loaded heavily on this factor. Factor 6 consisted of four technician role measures from the Broom set, with no heavy loadings for any of the 14 additional boundary-spanning activities. Factor scores were generated for each respondent for each of the eight factors. Next, factor scores were subjected to a series of cluster analyses. A five-cluster solution was deemed superior to other solutions and interpreted as internals, generalists, externals, traditional managers, and outliers.

Toth, Serini, Wright, and Emig (1998) conducted large sample surveys of PRSA members in 1990 ($N = 1,027$) and in 1995 ($N = 678$). A 17-item role set was used in each survey, using items similar or identical to Broom's four-role typology, including expert prescriber (e.g., making communication policy decisions), problem solving process facilitator (e.g., counseling management), and communication facilitator (e.g., meeting with clients/executives) roles, as well as measures of the communication technician (e.g., writing, editing, producing messages). Data for women and men were factor analyzed separately for both surveys. Exploratory factor analysis of the 1990 data yielded two factors for both men and women; the two factors closely parallel the manager and technician role factors.

The factors became less distinguishable when the same analysis was conducted on the 1995 data, with many items posting lower factor loadings than in 1990. Exploratory factor analysis revealed a third factor in 1995 data, a factor that Toth et al. interpreted as the *agency profile* factor. Items with high loadings on the agency profile factor included the following: meeting with peers, meeting with clients/executives, evaluating program results, handling correspondence, and making phone calls.

Some Reflections on Role Measures

Since roles are abstractions of the myriad activities of communicators in their day-to-day work, conceptualizing and measuring roles is inherently problematic. Roles research in public relations has used quantitative methods extensively, drawing items from a review of the literature (e.g., hypotheticodeductive approach) in order to construct nomothetic models of explanation. These presuppositions are built into much of the roles research in public relations. Within those broad assumptions, factor analysis or cluster analysis as data reduction tools add additional wrinkles. In exploratory factor analysis, the number of factors increase somewhat as a function of the number of items analyzed. In confirmatory factor analysis and cluster analysis, data reduction is forced. In any case, there is no one right number of roles, nor is there one right way to measure them.

Theoretically speaking, a purely inductive approach to constructing role measures leads to an infinite regress. As new items are added to or subtracted from the item set, new factor analytic or cluster analytic solutions emerge.

These new measures do not permit direct comparisons to findings from prior research, since differences among studies may be due to theoretically interesting issues or they may simply reflect differences in operationalization with little theoretical import. Further, the reliability of idiosyncratic role measures cannot be established across studies.

More important, however, is the theoretical utility of various role measures. How has a particular approach to role measurement contributed to our understanding of public relations? Clearly, Broom's 24-item role set and the manager-technician dichotomy has contributed the lion's share of new understanding about how roles relate to a myriad of interesting professional and social issues. At the same time, the evolution of communication as a profession suggests that the original 24-item role set may need constant reinvention through intensive observation of what communicators do in their day-to-day work. The dialogue over the operationalization of roles constitutes a narrow critique of role research in public relations. However, roles research also has been criticized more broadly in terms of its theoretical presuppositions.

CRITICISMS OF ROLES RESEARCH

Criticisms of roles research in public relations ranges from the methodological to the ideological. Starting with the narrowest methodological criticism, some argue (Leichty & Springston, 1996; Toth & Grunig, 1993, Toth et al., 1998) that the manager-technician role dichotomy oversimplifies the complexities of role enactment. Corrective strategies include using Broom's original four-way typology and expanding the number of items (Leichty & Springston, 1996), as well as attending to cross-loadings and factor analyzing women and men communicators separately (Toth & Grunig, 1993; Toth et al., 1998). Culbertson (1991) recommended further research into the process of role received and role taking, rather than focusing exclusively on role enactment.

A broader critique of roles research is embedded in liberal and radical feminist theory. Creedon first provided a comprehensive critique of roles research from this perspective in 1991. Other scholars such as Toth and Grunig (1993), Hon (1995), and Toth et al. (1998) have contributed to and provided further elaboration of this critique. This critique has five important elements relevant to theories of practitioner roles.

First, the gender of researchers (and worldviews embedded their socialization as either men or women) arguably affects what research questions investigators consider important and how those questions are investigated. This perspective is not uniquely feminist; rather, it reflects presuppositions that favor intensive observation, the value of subjectivity, the relationship between the scholar and those being studied, idiographic modeling, and reflexivity. These presuppositions parallel those found in ethnography (Fetterman, 1998; Rossman & Rallis, 1998).

Somewhat as a consequence of the first, a second element involves the way men and women studying roles look for different things, find different information in the data, and make sense of findings in different ways. Dozier's manager and technician role typology, for example, "homogenized and dichotomized the meaning of work in the field" (Creedon, 1991, p. 78). Creedon argued that women who study roles found liaison and decision-making activities among technicians, activities that male researchers had treated as part of the manager role.

Third, much roles research places greater normative value on the manager role than the technician role, devaluing the work that most women do in public relations. Such preference for the manager role emanates from male socialization to favor hierarchy and categorization. Further, open systems theory provides a larger paradigm in which roles theory is embedded. The structural/functional presuppositions of open systems theory, in turn, treat conflict as problematic, rather than potentially liberating. Feminist criticism has challenged these normative justifications for manager role preference.

Fourth, strategies for reducing gender discrimination against women practitioners (e.g., Dozier, 1988c) often treat organizational biases as a constant, suggesting that women change (e.g., do more research, enact the manager role) so that they may overcome institutionalized mechanisms of gender discrimination. This tendency reflects the status quo bias of structural/functionalism in organizational theory. A radical feminist critique of such liberal incrementalism is that the "victim is blamed" (Creedon, 1991, p. 73) for her condition. Further, women are urged to enact the manager role within the existing discriminatory structures by "aligning themselves with the masculine stereotype (power and control)" (Hon, 1995, p. 33).

Fifth, the liberal incrementalism that underlies much roles research (as it relates to gender discrimination) never challenges patterns of privilege and marginalization inherent in presuppositions of the open systems model of organizations or the liberal pluralistic model of society as a whole (Hon, Grunig, & Dozier, 1992). At core is the manifest unequal distribution of power in organizations and in society. Moreover, according to this critique, the solution to power inequities in organizations and in society is not simply to redistribute power. As L. Grunig (1992) argued, empowerment is a more useful concept. *Empowerment* means sharing power as in a positive-sum game, as opposed to aggregating or losing power in a zero-sum game. Hon (1995) provided a plan for empowering women in public relations by fusing liberal feminist tactics with a radical feminist strategy to change organizations and the social systems in which those organizations operate.

The feminist critique plays an important part in theorizing about practitioner roles. Public relations in the United States is a female-majority profession. According to the U.S. Department of Labor (2005), women constitute over 61% of the 133,000 practitioners (designated as *public relations specialists* by the

Department of Labor) employed in the U.S. labor force. As such, practitioner role theory cannot be separated from issues of gender and gender discrimination in the labor force. At the same time, considerable value is gleaned from construction of nomothetic models of explanation, based on abstract concepts of practitioner roles, as well as other key concepts. Although this approach to research may run counter to ethnographic presuppositions embedded in much of the feminist critique, this chapter seeks to build a nomothetic explanation, while being mindful of the legitimate concerns of our feminist critics and incorporating that critique into normative theory.

BIASES, REFLEXIVITY, AND PRESUPPOSITIONS

Our goal in theory construction here is to provide a positivist, nomothetic model of practitioner roles in organizations. As a positivist theory, it seeks to explain what is rather than what should be. As a nomothetic model, it seeks to identify a few useful concepts and how they are related, providing a partial explanation of practitioner roles in most or all organizations. As such, nuances of any one practitioner's role in any particular organization are never fully accounted for. Despite our goal, however, we are not without our own normative biases that undoubtedly influenced construction of these models. As in ethnography, permit us to clarify our own identified normative biases.

First, as former practitioners and current educators in the field, we regard public relations as an emerging profession. As widely defined (e.g., Cutlip, Center, & Broom, 1999; Grunig & Hunt, 1984), we regard public relations as a management function; therefore, the manager role is seen as an essential aspect of the public relations function. As noted earlier (Creedon, 1991), however, this hierarchical preference for the manager role may have the unintended effect of denigrating the technician role, perhaps reflecting a bias against the work that women practitioners perform disproportionately in public relations practice.

Second, we regard the internal operations and decision making of organizations as inherently political, an orientation to organizational theory best represented by the power-control perspective. In doing so, we do not reject the utility of the environmental imperative from organizational theory. Indeed, the boundary-spanning function performed by practitioners is an important value they add to strategic decision making. However, turbulent and threatening environments become important to decision makers only to the degree that those environmental conditions are deemed significant in the subjective worldviews of decision makers. That is, environmental pressures matter to strategic decision making only when the decision makers regard those pressures as important. The power-control perspective helps in the construction of theories regarding the effectiveness of public relations departments. With regard to scarce resource allocation, decision makers in organizations treat such allocations as zero-sum games. In this regard, empowerment is not as useful for nomothetic explanations as is the concept of power as traditionally defined. However, the concept of empowerment is critically important when we consider the normative aspects of roles theory in public relations.

Third, we regard gender discrimination in public relations work as an important, ongoing concern of practitioners, educators, and researchers in this female-majority profession. Much of our research on roles (Broom, 1982; Broom & Dozier, 1985, 1986; Dozier, 1987, 1988c, Dozier & Broom, 1995; Dozier, Chapo, & Sullivan, 1983) has documented patterns of gender discrimination. Ending gender discrimination specifically, and all other forms of discrimination in the workplace generally, are efforts we support and values we hold.

We find it useful, however, to build and test a positivist, nomothetic model first, then construct a normative model later. In that regard, we first treat gender as an important concept in describing and explaining role behaviors of practitioners, without regard to what should be. Obviously, as humans, we will not be wholly successful at bifurcating what is from what should be. However, we strive for the former in the section that follows. We return to normative theory later in this chapter.

A THEORETICAL MODEL OF INDIVIDUAL PRACTITIONER ROLES

The model displayed in Fig. 5.1 synthesizes findings of various practitioner role studies over the last 25 years into a single theoretical model at the individual level of analysis. This model elaborates findings of the Broom and Dozier survey of PRSA members in 1991 (Dozier & Broom, 1995). This model locates practitioner roles in a path model of antecedents and consequences.

Manager Role Expertise and Enactment

In Fig. 5.1, manager role expertise and manager role enactment are regarded as tightly linked but distinct concepts. Expertise is prerequisite to enactment—a necessary but not sufficient condition for role enactment. Whereas role enactment has been studied extensively (Anderson, Reagan, Sumner, & Hill, 1989; Anderson & Reagan, 1992; Broom, 1982; Broom & Dozier, 1985, 1986; Broom & Smith, 1978, 1979; Dozier, 1981, 1983, 1984a, 1984c, 1986, 1988c, 1990; Dozier & Broom, 1995; Ekachai, 1995; Johnson & Acharya, 1982; Lauzen, 1992, 1994; Lauzen & Dozier, 1992, 1994; Morton, 1996; Piekos & Einsiedel, 1990; Sullivan, Dozier, & Hellweg, 1984, 1985; Tam, Dozier, Lauzen, & Real, 1995; Toth, Serini, Wright, & Emig, 1998), role expertise has been studied less frequently as a separate concept (Dozier, Grunig, & Grunig, 1995; Grunig, Grunig, & Dozier, 2002). Whereas expertise is necessary to enact the manager

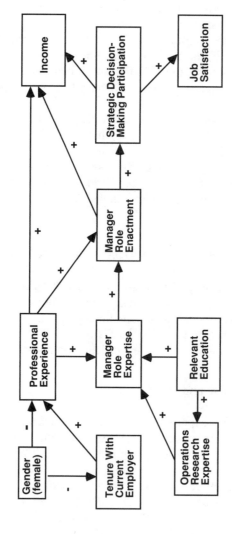

FIG. 5.1   Role enactment and professional advancement at the individual level of analysis.

role, the opportunity to employ that expertise can be constrained by a number of factors, including the worldview of the dominant coalition. If top managers in an organization equate public relations with publicity, as a technical support function of decisions made by others, then managerial expertise may not lead automatically to manager role enactment. As detailed later, dominant coalitions often need some catalyzing event as a "wake-up call" to utilize the managerial expertise that already exists in (or needs to be added to) the public relations department.

As indicated in the findings of the Excellence Study (Dozier, Grunig, & Grunig, 1995; Grunig, Grunig, & Dozier, 2002), manager role expertise consists of two empirically and conceptually distinct components. *Administrative management expertise* includes the requisite competencies to develop goals and objectives for programs, prepare departmental budgets, and manage organizational responses to issues. *Strategic management expertise* includes competencies to conduct evaluation research, use research to segment publics, and perform environmental scanning. Both types of expertise are critical to effective management of the public relations function.

Professional Experience and Manager Role Expertise

What factors help individual practitioner acquire the various competencies to enact the manager role? Previous research indicates that professional experience is a key determinant of manager role expertise and subsequent manager role enactment. Regarding enactment, years of professional experience accounted for 31% of variance in manager role enactment in Broom's 1979 study of PRSA members (Broom, 1982) and 18% of variance in manager role enactment in the 1991 survey of PRSA members (Dozier & Broom, 1995).

Professional experience is posited to contribute to both manager role expertise and manager role enactment, even though the relationship has not been directly tested in prior research. Through professional experience, practitioners learn the requisite skills to develop administrative manager expertise, perhaps supplemented by formal training and professional development workshops. Strategic management expertise may be acquired primarily through formal training, but professional experience provides the crucible where such strategic knowledge is tempered.

Further, professional experience is posited to contribute directly to manager role enactment, independent of role expertise. According to the power-control perspective, a seasoned and experienced practitioner may enact the manager role simply because environmental imperatives demand it. In the qualitative phase of the Excellence Study, practitioners with traditional (technical) training and professional experience sometimes were compelled to take on new managerial role responsibilities when an environmental crisis or catalyzing event required someone to take charge.

Formal Education and Manager Role Expertise

For those who teach public relations, the contribution of formal education to manager role expertise and enactment is somewhat disappointing. In 1979, formal education contributed little to manager role enactment (less than 1% explained variance, which was not statistically significant) in Broom's (1982) PRSA survey. In the 1991 survey of PRSA members, formal education contributed to manager role enactment, accounting for about 2% of variance (Dozier & Broom, 1995).

We speculate that measures of formal education in public relations are not sufficiently focused. We asked respondents in the 1979 and 1991 PRSA surveys how many years of formal education beyond high school the practitioner had completed. If the respondent had completed a college degree, we asked their major. The theoretical model in Fig. 5.1 emphasizes education that is specifically relevant to manager role enactment. Arguably, much formal education in public relations favors technical competencies that are key to entry-level work in public relations. Majoring in allied areas (e.g., journalism, speech communication) may provide even fewer opportunities to acquire strategic and administrative manager role expertise. Better measures would focus on specific coursework, workshops, and seminars that address specific manager role competencies.

Further, as posited in Fig. 5.1, the relationship between formal, relevant education and manager role enactment is not a direct one. A better theoretical model argues that relevant education contributes to manager role expertise (both administrative and strategic). Organizational exigencies, as articulated in the power-control perspective, mediate the degree to which manager role expertise is put to use.

Operations Research and Manager Role Expertise

In Fig. 5.1, operations research expertise is treated as a conceptually distinct area of specialized knowledge. This is because such expertise is relatively scarce among public relations practitioners (Grunig, Grunig, & Dozier, 2002), yet essential to the strategic management (as opposed to the operations management) role expertise. In the context of public relations, *operations research* is defined as environmental scanning and program evaluation expertise. Research indicates that operations research in public relations ranges in rigor from formal scanning activities (e.g., formal research, surveys, audits) to informal techniques (talking informally with field personnel, phone calls with publics to keep in touch, informal checking of reactions to special events, etc.). Likewise, program evaluation ranges from scientific evaluation (e.g., before-after measures of publics), to clip file evaluation (e.g., ongoing content analysis of media coverage), to informal, seat-of-the-pants evaluation (e.g., keeping eyes and ears open to reactions to PR programs). Prior studies indicate that practitioners enacting the manager role utilize a range of scanning and evaluation techniques, but are highly constrained by time, budget, and/or the sophistication of decision makers in the organization (Austin, Pinkleton, & Dixon, 2000; Broom & Dozier, 1990; Dozier, 1986, 1987, 1990; Dozier, Grunig, & Grunig, 1995; Grunig, Grunig, & Dozier, 2002; Hon, 1997, 1998). As Lindenmann (2001) argued, however, time and budget constraints can be overcome by prudent, creative use of low-cost research options.

As boundary spanners, a key scarce resource that practitioners bring to strategic planning tables is specialized knowledge about key publics and the possible impact of strategic choices on relationships with publics. As we have argued (Broom & Dozier, 1990; White & Dozier, 1992), such operations research is not useful to the dominant coalition unless the practitioner can translate scanning and evaluation data into information that makes sense to other managers and clarifies implications of vying decision options.

Operations Research and Two-Way Communication

In Grunig's models of public relations (1976; Grunig & Grunig, 1992), the concept of operations research is nested within the two-way symmetrical and two-way asymmetrical models. Whereas asymmetrical public relations practices seek to manipulate publics to go along with what the practitioner's organization wants in a zero-sum game, symmetrical public relations seeks mutually beneficial outcomes that sustain stable, long-term relationships in a positive-sum game. One of the interesting findings of the Excellence Study (also indicated in earlier research) is that both symmetrical and asymmetrical values are intertwined in a mixed-motive game, wherein organizations and publics seek "good enough" solutions to conflicts or disputes inside a range of choices that Dozier, Grunig, and Grunig (1995) termed the *win-win zone*. Thus, excellent public relations involves striving for tactical advantage (an asymmetrical orientation) that does not jeopardize the stability of long-term relationships that both parties can live with, inside a symmetrical worldview.

Since 1995, the Excellence research team has further analyzed the seeming paradox of high positive correlations of symmetrical and asymmetrical models with each other and with overall excellence. Based on its analysis of the Excellence data, the team concluded that two-way communication should be measured as a dimension separate from symmetry and asymmetry (Grunig, Grunig, & Dozier, 2002). One reason that symmetrical and asymmetrical values correlate positively—in addition to those provided earlier—is that these value measures also incorporate measurement of two-way communication (e.g., formal and informal operations research). The strong showing of the two-way asymmetrical model on the Excellence Factor may have more to do with the research activities measured by the index, rather than the asymmetrical purposes of that research.

Two-way communication means that the public relations function acts as the eyes and ears of the organization, as well as its official voice. As with the human body, different organs are involved and different competencies are relevant. When scanning and evaluation embrace the full range of formal and informal techniques delineated earlier, operations research closes the communication loop and makes the process two-way.

The Centrality of Manager Role Expertise

In the Excellence Study (J. Grunig, 1992; Dozier, Grunig, & Grunig, 1995; Grunig, Grunig, & Dozier, 2002), measures of manager role expertise were included in a battery of items administered to the public relations department. Department heads assessed the specialized expertise and knowledge available in their departments to enact a series of professional activities. When all the data from the Excellence Study were summarized in a single Excellence Factor (via factor analysis), manager role expertise and two-way communication skills ranked highest with regard to centrality to excellence. This knowledge core accounts for the lion's share of variance in the Excellence Factor. Manager role expertise posted the highest loading on the Excellence Factor (loading = .72), followed closely by two-way symmetrical communication expertise (loading = .67) and two-way asymmetrical communication expertise (loading = .64).

Gender, Tenure, and Professional Experience

Early roles research (Broom, 1982) indicated that enactment of the conceptual components of the manager role tended to be lower for women practitioners, when compared to their enactment of the technician role.[2] Subsequent research indicated that role segregation might serve as a mechanism whereby women in public relations work are paid less than men (Dozier, Chapo, & Sullivan, 1983; Dozier, 1988c).

A confounding factor is the role that professional experience, as well as length of service (tenure) with current employer, plays in mediating the relationship between gender and manager role enactment. Indeed, the transformation of public relations—from a male majority profession in the 1960s (Smith, 1968), when only a quarter of practitioners were women, to female majority in the mid-1980s, to more than 61% women in the 21st century—results in large disparities in the professional experience of men and women practitioners.

---

[2] The designation of gender as female in Fig. 5.1 was somewhat arbitrary, a designation used to clarify the meaning of path signs.

When comparing manager role enactment, relatively inexperienced women are compared to relatively experienced men.

However, persistent low enactment of the manager role (when compared to the technician role enactment) remained for women, even when professional experience was controlled statistically. As summarized (Dozier & Broom, 1995), this pattern has declined over time. In the 1979 PRSA survey, a significant negative relationship existed between being female and manager role enactment, after tenure and professional experience were controlled (Dozier & Broom, 1995, p. 14). By 1991, low predominant manager role enactment by women was insignificant, once tenure and professional experience were controlled (p. 16). Although significance was harder to achieve in the 1991 survey because of smaller sample size, the path coefficient for gender on predominant manager role enactment was only .08, less than 1% of explained variance in predominant manager role enactment. In 1991, the lower levels of predominant manager role enactment by women were largely accounted for by differences in professional experience and tenure. Inadequately studied to date, however, is the role that time out from professional work (for a short or extended periods of time) and part-time professional work play in gender differences in manager role enactment.

Further, no known research has been conducted on the relationship between gender and manager role expertise. The Excellence Study suggests that manager role expertise is a powerful concept, but data collected in the Excellence Study treated expertise of the public relations department, rather than individuals, as the unit of analysis. In the absence of empirical support, the model in Fig. 5.1 does not posit gender differences in manager role expertise. In 1998, women constituted a large majority (62%) of master's degree recipients and a slight majority (53%) of doctoral degree recipients in journalism and mass communication (Becker et al., 1999). Based on the historical distribution of women by major in mass communication, the percentages are much higher for public relations. What's not known from such aggregate data is whether advanced degrees in mass communication and public relations mean that such alumni are, in fact, more knowledgeable about the requisite expertise necessary for manager role enactment. Clearly, further research is needed.

Manager Role Enactment and Strategic Decision Making

Research findings indicate a strong relationship between manager role enactment and participation in the strategic processes in organizations. In the 1979 PRSA survey, the path coefficient between manager role enactment and strategic decision-making participation was .35, increasing to .40 in the 1991 survey of the same population.

This is the essential relationship in Fig. 5.1, because it links manager role enactment with a key professional outcome—participation in strategic decision making. Arguably, practitioners cannot effectively perform the function if they are not participants in *strategic decision making*, the choices made about long-term goals, required courses of action, and allocation of resources (Robbins, 1990). This is due to the following reasons:

1. Relationships with key constituencies are often defined by the strategic choices that organizations make. Grunig and Hunt (1984) argued that publics are usually created as a consequence of organizational behavior, including strategic choices.

2. Mutually beneficial, reciprocal relationships with publics often require organizations to initiate action strategies as a precursor to the media and message strategies that are often mistaken as the essence of public relations. An *action strategy* is defined as acts that change organizational policies, procedures, products, services, and behavior. To do so, the practitioner must have access to those in the organization with the power to make such strategic decisions, the dominant coalition.[3]

3. As boundary spanners, practitioners use formal and informal mechanisms of environmental scanning and public relations program evaluation to help inform strategic decision making. Such information gathering is of no value to organizations if practitioners cannot make such information available in a meaningful form to their dominant coalitions when strategic decisions are made.

Income

At the individual level of analysis, the theoretical model in Fig. 5.1 posits three direct relationships between income and antecedent constructs: professional experience, manager role enactment, and strategic decision-making participation. Professional experience is posited to exert a positive influence on salary, even after manager role enactment and decision making participation are controlled. Manager role enactment is posited to exert a positive influence on salary, even after decision-making participation is controlled.

Historically, salary tends to increase with professional experience in most occupational categories, even without a change in organizational office (e.g., promotion) or role. Manager role enactment reflects acknowledged expertise and responsibility for the success or failure of public relations programs. As

---

[3] From a normative perspective, action strategies are restricted to only those that are socially responsible. However, as a positivist model, action strategies must be defined as all steps taken within an organization to affect relationships with key publics, whether such actions are symmetrical or asymmetrical.

such, dominant coalitions are posited to increase the salaries of practitioners as a function of manager role enactment, rewarding employees who provide valuable services to their organizations. This reward is in addition to extra compensation received for participating in strategic decision making, since manager role enactment involves both administrative and strategic competencies.

Participation in strategic decision making implies that the practitioner is a member of the dominant coalition, on either a formal or informal basis. As such, practitioners who are de facto members of dominant coalitions are among the most valued employees in organizations. All the posited relationships with income are consistent with earlier research, including the 1979 and 1991 surveys of PRSA members (Dozier & Broom, 1995).

Figure 5.1 posits no simple, direct relationship between income and gender. The significant path coefficient between gender and income in the 1979 PRSA survey (beta = .25) dropped to near zero (beta = .03) in the 1991 survey of the same population (Dozier & Broom, 1995). This does not mean that all income disparities between men and women are explained away by professional experience, manager role enactment, and decision-making participation. In a secondary analysis of the 1991 PRSA survey data, we discovered that income disparities depend on women's stages in their careers. Specifically, we discovered a significant difference in income between men and women with 9 to 18 years of professional experience, the middle years of their careers. When this cohort was analyzed separately, men earned an average of $63,460 (in 1991 dollars). Women earned only $48,480, or about 76% of what men make, $F = 4.56$, d.f. $= 1, 51$, $p < .05$. These figures reflect salaries after the influences of professional experience, manager role enactment, and decision-making participation were controlled statistically. Significant income differences between men and women were not found in the 0–8 year and the 19+ cohorts of professional experience.

Job Satisfaction

If one assumes that public relations practitioners seek to move from the technical role at the time of entry to the manager role as their careers advance, then one would posit a significant positive path coefficient between manager role enactment and job satisfaction. Such is not the case in Fig. 5.1. Although previous research indicates that being included in management decision making is positively linked to job satisfaction, manager role playing is not, once decision-making participation is controlled. In fact, a panel study of PRSA members in 1979 and 1985 indicated that technicians who continued to play that role predominantly over the 6-year study period showed the largest increase in job satisfaction. Regarding job satisfaction, technicians who advanced to managers (predominantly) posted a much smaller gain (less than half) during that same period (Broom & Dozier, 1986).

A survey and a follow-up Q-study of practitioners by Dozier and Gottesman (1982) indicated a strong link between creative-artistic practitioners and technician role enactment. As defined by the Q-factor structure, the *creative-artistic practitioner* prefers the spontaneous, intuitive, and creative aspects of the practice. These practitioners want more say in organizational decision making, but would prefer to spend the bulk of their time immersed in creating messages. More recently, McGoon (1993) reported the results of an informal fax poll. Most practitioners responding indicated they preferred writing, editing, producing publications, and other activities of technical role enactment. Only 11% said they liked managing the public relations department. Only 2% picked working with top management as their preferred work activity. When asked what they would like to be doing in 10 years, responses included: "writer collecting royalties on a runaway best seller children's book," "living in Italy writing books," "on a beach," "owning my own greenhouse," and "in France working as an English professor." Zoch, Patterson, and Olson (1997) surveyed practitioners in South Carolina school districts; respondents rated creativity as one of five factors more important than salary in contributing to job satisfaction.

Dozier and Gottesman (1982) found no relationship between gender and creative-artistic practitioner beliefs. However, their sample size was too small to provide conclusive evidence. If gender is, indeed, related to the creative-artistic belief system, then Creedon's feminist critique of roles research takes on new meaning. Women may be segregated through their predominant technician role status into less powerful, lower-paying positions, as argued elsewhere (Dozier, 1998c; Dozier, Chapo, & Sullivan, 1983).

On the other hand, women may self-select technician role enactment in greater numbers because they seek the job satisfaction that comes from the creative and artistic aspect of their work. In a survey of college students preparing for careers in public relations using a national sample of Public Relations Student Society of America (PRSSA) members, Farmer and Waugh (1999) found that women majoring in public relations did not differ significantly from men in their desire to make communication policy decisions, take responsibility of the success or failure of public relations programs, be the organizations expert in public relations, plan and manage budgets, and counsel senior management. However, women were significantly higher than men in their desire to plan and implement special events, handle correspondence, make media contacts, and implement the technical/creative aspects of decisions made by others. Farmer and Waugh's findings are consistent with our own research. Women enact the manager role less frequently than men, but the gap is small and often not significant, once professional experience is controlled. However, women do enact the technician role with significantly higher frequency, after controlling for professional experience. Following our analytic strategy of using predominant role, Farmer and Waugh likely would have found that women majoring in public relations prefer the technician role predominantly, whereas men favor the manager role predominantly.

These role preferences among college students provide indirect support for a relationship between gender and preferences for creative-artistic aspects of public relations work. The absence of gender differences regarding the desire to play the manager role is consistent with previous research showing that job satisfaction (among working practitioners) is positively related to participating in strategic decision making, but not manager role enactment, after controlling for decision-making participation (see Fig. 5.1). This also squares with the finding of Dozier and Gottesman (1982) that creative-artistic practitioners want to be involved in decision making, but are distrustful of the cost in intrinsic satisfaction with climbing the corporate ladder.

In any case, the status of the technician role and the creative-artistic practitioner is a serious professional issue. The normative preference for manager role enactment implicitly denigrates the work of a large number of practitioners enacting the technician role predominantly, the majority of whom happen to be women. The problem, however, is resolved if the role of public relations is addressed at the organizational rather than individual level of analysis.

A MODEL OF ROLE ENACTMENT AT THE ORGANIZATIONAL LEVEL

Figure 5.2 takes the concept of practitioner role and re-conceptualizes it at the departmental and organizational level of analysis. This re-conceptualization of practitioner roles at the meso level reflects some of the work on practitioner roles conducted in the Excellence Study (Dozier, Grunig, & Grunig, 1995; Grunig, Grunig, & Dozier, 2002). The model in Fig. 5.2 is presented as a work in progress, with suggestions for its further development addressed at the end of this chapter. The model is circular in that key concepts are seen as interacting over time, with outcomes at Time 1 serving as inputs at Time 2. These mechanisms are reflected in the demand-delivery loop and the power-control loop in Fig. 5.2.

Three seemingly unrelated findings from the Excellence Study stimulated the creation of the theoretical model in Fig. 5.2. First, the qualitative portion of the study sought to determine how excellent public relations departments became excellent. In case after case, top communicators and members of dominant coalitions reported some kind of crisis as thrusting the public relations function to center stage. These included industry-wide crises such as the *Exxon Valdez* oil spill in Alaska and the Bhopal gas leak in India, as well as crises specific to individual organizations, such as opposition to construction of a nuclear power plant. In each instance, organizations seemed to need a catalyzing event to precipitate a rapid redefinition of public relations functions in

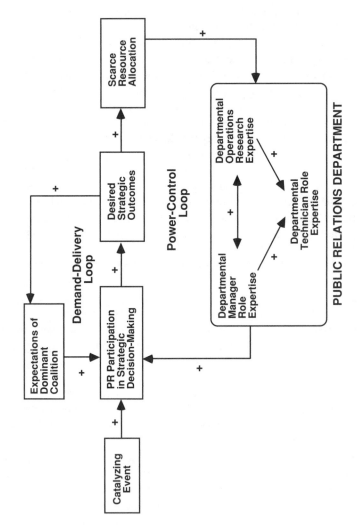

FIG. 5.2   A dynamic model of role enactment at the organizational level of analysis.

organizations. Such crises led dominant coalitions to take advantage of untapped talent in their existing public relations departments or to hire additional practitioners and consultants to enhance the public relations function.

Second, the case studies also revealed how public relations departments evolved, once a catalyzing event gave such departments a chance to do their stuff. This evolution is represented by the demand-delivery loop, which is more fully described elsewhere (Dozier, Grunig, & Grunig, 1995). In essence, representatives of the public relations department are brought to the strategic decision-making table in times of crisis. If the public relations function performs well (e.g., assists meaningfully with the strategic issues involved), desired outcomes are created for the organization. These desired outcomes are recognized by dominant coalitions, who then alter their perceptions of public relations and what the function can do. This leads to increased expectations from dominant coalitions that public relations contribute meaningfully to making strategic choices.

Third, the Excellence Study suggests that manager role expertise and operations research expertise (as reflected in Grunig's two-way models) are the most central attributes of excellent public relations departments (Grunig, Grunig, & Dozier, 2002). However, technical role expertise is also highly correlated with manager role expertise, operations research expertise, and overall excellence. To make sense of this theoretically, the power-control perspective provides a useful heuristic. When effective public relations departments produce desired strategic outcomes for organizations, the power-control perspective suggests some kind of quid pro quo with regard to the allocation of scarce resources. Public relations departments that produce desired strategic outcomes for dominant coalitions can maneuver to acquire scarce resources for the public relations department.

Whereas dominant coalitions may have little appreciation for technicians or creative-artistic practitioners, highly effective public relations departments clearly do. According to the Excellence Study, departments with the requisite expertise to enact the manager role and conduct operations research also acquire the best creative artistic talent. The power-control loop describes a reciprocal reward system for excellence in public relations. Although rewards are earned for the achievement of desired strategic outcomes, such outcomes arguably rest on excellence in program implementation as well as planning. Inside excellent public relations departments, people with different talents and competencies work together to plan, implement, and evaluate public relations programs. Not everyone in the public relations department needs to enact the manager role or conduct operations research. In fact, the best departments may well be those in which managers and technicians are clearly differentiated and career opportunities provide different ways for practitioners to gain satisfaction from their work. With this in mind, consider the implications for normative models of public relations practices.

TOWARD AN INCLUSIVE NORMATIVE MODEL
OF PUBLIC RELATIONS PRACTICES

The literature on public relations as an emerging profession has emphasized the practice as a management function in organizations. Major textbooks for introductory public relations courses (e.g., Cutlip, Center, & Broom, 1999; Grunig & Hunt, 1984) specifically define public relations as a management function.

Druck and Hiebert's (1979) guidebook laid out a professional advancement strategy that presumed the movement of practitioners from largely technical roles at the beginning of their careers into managerial roles as they gained more professional experience. The subtext, of course, is that individual practitioners who do not advance into management roles are stuck in essentially entry-level work of little value. As noted by various feminist critics, this denigrates the work that most women do most frequently as practitioners.

We are probably as guilty of this as were Druck and Hiebert. Our first joint publication for an academic journal, which reported findings of the panel study of PRSA members in 1979 and 1985, was titled *Role Advancement* on the cover of *Public Relations Review.* In retrospect, this seeming denigration of the technician role was never personal. Rather, it reflected a lack of precision about the appropriate level of analysis for consideration of key normative issues.

Indeed, public relations is a management function. To be excellent, the public relations department must have the expertise to enact the manager role and perform operations research (environmental scanning and program evaluation). To be excellent, the public relations function must be present, either formally or informally, when the dominant coalition makes strategic choices that affect relationships with publics. To earn a place at the strategic planning table, the public relations department must bring scarce and unique resources to the decision-making process. This often involves departmental expertise regarding what's going on in the organization's environment.

However, these imperatives for the function or department do not imply that every individual practitioner must be a manager. If the exploratory research in this area is correct (Dozier & Gottesman, 1982; McGoon, 1993), many public relations practitioners value the creative-artistic aspects of their work. Although they want to be included in decision making, these practitioners do not want to be managers. Nor should they. As the Excellence Study clearly indicates, the very best public relations departments support high levels of both manager and technical expertise.

The well-functioning public relations department might be understood best by invoking the metaphor of the human brain and its two distinctly different hemispheres (Springer & Deutsch, 1998). The left hemisphere favors the logical, analytic sequential tasking commonly associated with the management function; the right hemisphere favors the subjective, simultaneous, and synthetic activities associated with the creative production of message strategies.

Just as the human brain functions best when both hemispheres work in unison to solve problems, so too do effective public relations departments. Given that many working practitioners may be closet novelists, poets, and artists (McGoon, 1993) and given that the most excellent departments have high levels of such creative competencies (Grunig, Grunig, & Dozier, 2002), we must think constructively about parallel career tracks for those who derive satisfaction from the strategic management aspects of public relations work and those who derive satisfaction from the creative, artistic aspects of public relations work. We also need to think constructively about how these two orientations to public relations work can be integrated into an effective department. To be effective, the creative, artistic practitioner cannot function in a strategic vacuum, generating creative products as an end in themselves. Rather, through mutually beneficial relationships among members of the department, creative works must be seen as a means to an end, as relevant to the strategic goals of the program.

Just as effective public relations departments need to provide a hospitable work environment for creative, artistic practitioners, the needs of women employees must also be considered. In the Excellence Study, organizations with the best public relations departments also had clear policies banning sexual harassment and discrimination, provided a supportive work environment for women, and established mentoring programs for women (Dozier, Grunig, & Grunig, 1995). As a female-majority profession, the effectiveness of public relations departments clearly is intertwined with the treatment of women in organizations. Diversity within the public relations department, with regard to both gender and manager/technician roles, is more easily recognized as strengths when managerial definitions of the public relations *function* are not applied inappropriately to the *individual*. The creative, artistic work of practitioners, whether men or women, ought to be recognized and rewarded for its contribution to the excellent planning and execution of strategic public relations programs.

AN AGENDA FOR FUTURE ROLES RESEARCH

After a quarter century of research on the organizational roles of practitioners, further research is needed. We suggest the following.

1. *Continue the re-invention of role measures, but avoid the infinite regress of induction.* As public relations evolves as a profession and as studies of practitioner roles are conducted in nations other than the United States and Canada, measures of public relations roles must remain dynamic. At the same time, we ought not let our statistical tools bully us. Because "redefinition"

of practitioner roles is often based on exploratory factor analysis of altered item sets, the discovery of "new" roles becomes somewhat tautological. By its inductive nature, factor analysis typically generates "new" factors (roles) when different items are added to the initial correlation matrix. Newly discovered factors may be more artifacts of the analytic procedure used than important theoretical contributions. Such "new" roles are difficult to compare to studies that used Broom's original 24-item set. A more useful approach is to treat new role set measures as separate constructs for purpose of analysis, then correlate them with the original item set (see Tables 5.1 and 5.2). In this way, direct comparisons can be made between new role measures and the old.

2. *Measure manager role expertise as a separate concept and find out where that expertise comes from.* As the Excellence Study indicates, knowing how to enact the manager role is more central to excellence in public relations than is the actual execution of those role behaviors by the department head. Further, manager role expertise ought not be regarded as an individual attribute; rather, manager role expertise is an attribute of the public relations department. To move beyond the Excellence Study, however, data must be collected from all members of the public relations department, and then aggregated to represent a departmental attribute. Only in this way will we be able to determine empirically where specific role competencies reside within departments. This stream of research has important implications for the study of gender, roles, decision making, income, and job satisfaction. Aggregate data indicate that women practitioners are seeking advanced degrees in greater numbers than men. However, women also constitute the majority of practitioners. It therefore remains an empirical question whether women have greater manager role expertise than men. If women do have greater manager role expertise, then our theoretical models (see Figs. 5.1 and 5.2) need to be reconsidered.

3. *Study the creative, artistic practitioner and the strategic manager practitioner in terms of occupational role and job satisfaction.* Job satisfaction and organizational roles are concepts that have not received the attention they deserve. In all likelihood, extrinsic job satisfaction (e.g., job title, decision-making participation, income) may well be higher for those practitioners enacting the manager role. However, evidence suggests (Broom & Dozier, 1986; Dozier & Gottesman, 1982; McGoon, 1993) that many practitioners derive great intrinsic satisfaction for the creative and artistic aspects of technician role enactment. As a profession, public relations needs to provide viable career tracks in which both the creative, artistic practitioner and the strategic management practitioner receive both extrinsic and intrinsic rewards from their work. The large trend study of PRSA members in 1990 and 1995 (Serini et al., 1997; Toth et al., 1998) indicated that men and women derive satisfaction from public relations work in different ways; however, the specific relationship between role enactment and job satisfaction was not tested.

4. *Continue to study the relations among gender, income, and roles.* In our trend study of PRSA members in 1979 and 1991 (Dozier & Broom, 1995), we found that many of the overt patterns of gender-income discrimination in 1979 had declined substantially by 1991, with income and role differences largely accounted for by gender differences in professional experience. We cautioned then against making too much of this change. Strong patterns of income differences remained in 1991, with women making 76% of the income of men with equal professional experience. However, this effect was specified to the middle years of their professional lives (practitioners with 9–18 years of professional experience). Prior research on income, gender, and roles has not adequately measured the impact of career interruptions on salary and role enactment. We do know, based on substantial research, that manager role enactment is positively related to income, after controlling for professional experience. We also know that women enact the technician role predominantly, even after controlling for professional experience. However, researchers have not measured or analyzed the way in which role enactment choices affect income, and whether the opportunity to choose the role one enacts is affected by gender.

ACKNOWLEDGMENTS

The authors gratefully acknowledge the contributions of James Grunig (Principal Investigator), Larissa Grunig, William Ehling, Jon White, Fred Repper, and the IABC Research Foundation for the Excellence Study and its contribution to our understanding of practitioner roles.

REFERENCES

Acharya, L. (1983, August). *Practitioner representations of environmental uncertainty: An application of discriminant analysis.* Paper presented at the meeting of the Public Relations Division, Association for Education in Journalism and Mass Communication, Corvallis, OR.

Ahlwardt, E. (1984). *Coorientational states as predictors of organizational role ambiguity and conflict: An analysis of U.S. Navy commanding officer and public affairs officer dyads.* Unpublished master's thesis, San Diego State University, San Diego.

Anderson, R., & Reagan, J. (1992). Practitioner roles and uses of new technologies. *Journalism Quarterly, 69*(1), 156–165.

Anderson, R., Reagan, J., Sumner, J., & Hill, S. (1989). A factor analysis of Broom and Smith's public relations roles scale. *Public Relations Review, 15*(3), 54.

Austin, E. W., Pinkleton, B. E., & Dixon, A. (2000). Barriers to public relations program research. *Public Relations Review, 12*(3), 235–253.

Baker, J. K., & Schaffer, R. H. (1969). Making staff consulting more effective. *Harvard Business Review, 47*(1), 68.

Becker, L. B., Kosicki, G. R., Hammatt, H., Lowrey, W., Shin, S. C., & Wilson, J. M. (1999). Enrollment and degrees awarded continue 5-year growth trend. *Journalism & Mass Communication Educator, 54*(3), 5–22.

Berkowitz, D., & Hristodoulakis, I. (1999). Practitioner roles, public relations education, and professional socialization: An exploratory study. *Journal of Public Relations Research, 11*(1), 91–103.

Broom, G. M. (1982). A comparison of sex roles in public relations. *Public Relations Review, 8*(3), 17–22.

Broom, G. M. (1986, May). *Public relations roles and systems theory. Functional and historicist causal models.* Paper presented at the meeting of the Public Relations Interest Group, International Communication Association, Chicago.

Broom, G. M., & Dozier, D. M. (1985, August). *Determinants and consequences of public relations roles.* Paper presented at the meeting of the Public Relations Division, Association for Education in Journalism and Mass Communication, Memphis.

Broom, G. M., & Dozier, D. M. (1986). Advancement for public relations role models. *Public Relations Review, 7*(1), 37–56.

Broom, G. M., & Dozier, D. M. (1990). *Using research in public relations: Applications to program management.* Englewood Cliffs, NJ: Prentice Hall.

Broom, G. M., & Smith, G. D. (1978, August). *Toward an understanding of public relations roles: An empirical test of five role models' impact on clients.* Paper presented at the meeting of the Public Relations Division, Association for Education in Journalism, Seattle.

Broom, G. M., & Smith, G. D. (1979). Testing the practitioner's impact on clients. *Public Relations Review, 5*(3), 47–59.

Creedon, P. J. (1991). Public relations and "women's work": Toward a feminist analysis of public relations roles. In J. E. Grunig & L. A. Grunig (Eds.), *Public relations research annual* (Vol. 3, pp. 67–84). Hillsdale, NJ: Lawrence Erlbaum Associates.

Culbertson, H. M. (1991). Role taking and sensitivity: Keys to playing and making public relations roles. In J. E. Grunig & L. A. Grunig (Eds.), *Public relations research annual* (Vol. 3, pp. 37–65). Hillsdale, NJ: Lawrence Erlbaum Associates.

Cutlip, S. M., & Center, A. H. (1971). *Effective public relations* (4th ed.). Englewood Cliffs, NJ: Prentice Hall.

Cutlip, S. M., Center, A. H., & Broom, G. M. (1994). *Effective public relations* (7th ed.). Englewood Cliffs, NJ: Prentice Hall.

Cutlip, S. M., Center, A. H., & Broom, G. M. (1999). *Effective public relations* (8th ed.). Englewood Cliffs, NJ: Prentice Hall.

Dozier, D. M. (1981, August). *The diffusion of evaluation methods among public relations practitioners.* Paper presented at the meeting of the Public Relations Division, Association for Education in Journalism, East Lansing, MI.

Dozier, D. M. (1983, November). *Toward a reconciliation of 'role conflict' in public relations research.* Paper presented at the meeting of the Western Communication Educators Conference, Fullerton, CA.

Dozier, D. M. (1984a, June). *The evolution of evaluation methods among public relations practitioners.* Paper presented at the Educator Academy meeting of the International Association of Business Communicators, Montreal.

Dozier, D. M. (1984b, August). *Priority research issues in public relations.* Paper presented at the meeting of the Foundation for Public Relations Research and Education Meeting, Gainesville, FL.

Dozier, D. M. (1984c). Program evaluation and roles of practitioners. *Public Relations Review, 10*(2), 13–21.

Dozier, D. M. (1986, August). *The environmental scanning function of public relations practitioners and participation in management decision making.* Paper presented at the meeting of the Public Relations Division, Association for Education in Journalism and Mass Communication, Norman, OK.

Dozier, D. M. (1987, May). *Gender, environmental scanning, and participation in management decision making.* Paper presented at the meeting of the Public Relations Interest Group, International Communication Association, Montreal.

Dozier, D. M. (1988a, May). *The vertical location of the public relations function in organizations.* Paper presented at the meeting of the Public Relations Interest Group, International Communication Association, New Orleans, LA.

Dozier, D. M. (1988b, July). *Organic structure and managerial environmental sensitivity as predictors of practitioner membership in the dominant coalition.* Paper presented at the meeting of the Association for Education in Journalism and Mass Communication, Portland, OR.

Dozier, D. M. (1988c). Breaking public relations' glass ceiling. *Public Relations Review, 14*(3), 6–14.

Dozier, D. M. (1989, May). *Implementing public relations strategies and theories with high technology.* Paper presented at the meeting of the Public Relations Interest Group, International Communication Association, San Francisco.

Dozier, D. M. (1990). The innovation of research in public relations practice: Review of a program of studies. In J. E. Grunig & L. A. Grunig (Eds.), *Public relations research annual* (Vol. 2, pp. 3–28). Hillsdale, NJ: Lawrence Erlbaum Associates.

Dozier, D. M. (1992). The organizational roles of communications and public relations practitioners. In J. E. Grunig (Ed.), *Excellence in public relations and communication management.* (pp. 327-356). Hillsdale, NJ: Lawrence Erlbaum Associates.

Dozier, D. M., & Broom, G. M. (1995). Evolution of the manager role in public relations practice. *Journal of Public Relations Research, 7*(1), 3–26.

Dozier, D. M., Chapo, S., & Sullivan, B. (1983, August). *Sex and the bottom line: Income differences between women and men in public relations.* Paper presented at the meeting of the Public Relations Division, Association for Education in Journalism and Mass Communication, Corvallis, OR.

Dozier, D. M., & Gottesman, M. (1982, July). *Subjective dimensions of organizational roles among public relations practitioners.* Paper presented at the meeting of the Public Relations Division, Association for Education in Journalism, Athens, OH.

Dozier, D. M., Grunig, L. A., & Grunig, J. E. (1995). *Manager's guide to excellence in public relations and communication management.* Hillsdale, NJ: Lawrence Erlbaum Associates.

Druck, K. B., & Hiebert, R. E. (1979). *Your personal guidebook to help you chart a more successful career in public relations.* New York: Public Relations Society of America.

Ekachai, D. G. (1995). Applying Broom's role scales to Thai public relations practitioners. *Public Relations Review, 21*(4), 325–336.

Farmer, B., & Waugh, L. (1999). Gender differences in public relations students' career attitudes: A benchmark study. *Public Relations Review, 25,* 235–250.

Ferguson, M. A. (1979). *Role norms, implicit relationship attributions and organizational communication: A study of public relations practitioners.* Unpublished master's thesis, University of Wisconsin, Madison.

Fetterman, D. M. (1998). *Ethnography: Step by step* (2nd ed.). Thousand Oaks, CA: Sage.

Grunig, J. E. (1976). Organizations and public relations: Testing a communication theory. *Journalism Monographs, 46.*

Grunig, J. E. (Ed.). (1992). *Excellence in public relations and communication management.* Hillsdale, NJ: Lawrence Erlbaum Associates.

Grunig, J. E., & Grunig, L. A. (1992). Models of public relations and communication. In J. E. Grunig (Ed.), *Excellence in public relations and communication management* (pp. 285–325). Hillsdale, NJ: Lawrence Erlbaum Associates.

Grunig, J. E., & Hunt, T. (1984). *Managing public relations.* New York: Holt, Rinehart & Winston.

Grunig, L. A. (1992). Power in the public relations department. In J. E. Grunig (Ed.), *Excellence in public relations and communication management* (pp. 483–501). Hillsdale, NJ: Lawrence Erlbaum Associates.

Grunig, L. A., Grunig, J. E., & Dozier, D. M. (2002). *Excellent public relations and effective organizations: A study of communication management in three countries.* Mahwah, NJ: Lawrence Erlbaum Associates.

Guth, D. W. (1995). Organizational crisis experience and public relations roles. *Public Relations Review, 21*(2), 123–136.

Hon, L. C. (1997). What have done for me lately? Exploring effectiveness in public relations. *Journal of Public Relations Research, 9*(1), 1–30.

Hon, L. C. (1995). Toward a feminist theory of public relations. *Journal of Public Relations Research, 7*(1), 27–88.

Hon, L. C. (1998). Demonstrating effectiveness in public relations: Goals, objectives, and evaluation. *Journal of Public Relations Research, 10*(2), 103–136.

Hon, L. C., Grunig, L. A., & Dozier, D. M. (1992). Women in public relations: Problems and opportunities. In J. E. Grunig (Ed.), *Excellence in public relations and communication management* (pp. 419–438). Hillsdale, NJ: Lawrence Erlbaum Associates.

Johnson, D. J., & Acharya, L. (1982, July). *Organizational decision making and public relations roles.* Paper presented at the meeting of the Public Relations Division, Association for Education in Journalism, Athens, OH.

Johnson, M. A. (1997). Public relations and technology: Practitioner perspectives. *Journal of Public Relations Research, 9*(3), 213–236.

Katz, D., & Kahn, R. L. (1966). *The social psychology of organizations.* New York: Wiley.

Katz, D., & Kahn, R. L. (1978). *The social psychology of organizations* (rev. ed.). New York: Wiley.

Kurpius, D. J., & Brubaker, J. C. (1976). *Psychoeducational consultation: Definition, functions, and preparation.* Bloomington: Indiana University Press.

Lauzen, M. M. (1991). *When marketing imperialism matters: An examination of marketing imperialism at the managerial level.* Paper presented at the meeting of the Public Relations Division, Association for Education in Journalism and Mass Communication, Boston, MA.

Lauzen, M. M. (1992). Public relations roles, intraorganizational power, and encroachment. *Journal of Public Relations Research, 4*(2), 61–80.

Lauzen, M. M. (1993). When marketing involvement matters at the manager level. *Public Relations Review, 19*(3), 247–259.

Lauzen, M. M. (1994). Public relations practitioner role enactment in issues management. *Journalism Quarterly, 71*(2), 356–368.

Lauzen, M. M. (1997). Understanding the relation between public relations and issues management. *Journal of Public Relations Research, 9*(1), 65–82.

Lauzen, M. M., & Dozier, D. M. (1992). The missing link: The public relations manager role as mediator of organizational environments and power consequences for the function. *Journal of Public Relations Research, 4*(4), 205–220.

Lauzen, M. M., & Dozier, D. M. (1994). Issues management mediation of linkages between environmental complexity and management of the public relations function. *Journal of Public Relations Research, 6*(3), 163–184.

Leichty, G., & Springston, J. (1996). Elaborating public relations roles. *Journalism & Mass Communication Quarterly, 73*(2), 467–477.

Lindenmann, W. K. (2001). *Research doesn't have to put you in the poorhouse.* Retrieved April 7, 2001, from http://www.instituteforpr.com/printables/m&e_poorhouse.htm

Linton, R. (1936). *The study of man.* New York: Appleton-Century.

McGoon, C. (1993). Life's a beach, for communicators. *Communication World, 10*(1), 12–15.

Merton, R. K. (1957). *Social theory and social structure* (rev. ed.). New York: Free Press.

Morton, L. P. (1996). Do public relations managers and technicians value news releases differently? *Public Relations Review, 22*(4), 355–368.

Newcomb, T. M. (1950). *Social psychology.* New York: Dryden.

Newsom, D. A., & Scott, A. (1976). *This is PR: The realities of public relations.* Belmont, CA: Wadsworth.

Parsons, T. (1951). *The social system.* New York: Free Press.

Pasadeos, Y., Renfro, R. B., & Hanily, M. L. (1999). Influential authors and works of the public relations scholarly literature: A network of recent research. *Journal of Public Relations Research, 11*(1), 29–52.

Piekos, J. M., & Einsiedel, E. F. (1990). Roles and program evaluation techniques among Canadian public relations practitioners. In J. E. Grunig (Ed.), *Excellence in public relations and communication management.* (Vol. 2, pp. 95–113). Hillsdale, NJ: Lawrence Erlbaum Associates.

Robbins, S. P. (1990). *Organization theory: Structure, design and applications.* Englewood Cliffs, NJ: Prentice Hall.

Rossman, G. B., & Rallis, S. F. (1998). *Learning in the field: An introduction to qualitative research.* Thousand Oaks, CA: Sage.

Schein, E. H. (1969). *Process consultation: Its role in organizational development.* Reading, MA: Addison-Wesley.

Serini, S. A., Toth, E., Wright, D. K., & Emig, A. G. (1997). Watch for falling glass … women, men, and job satisfaction in public relations: A preliminary analysis. *Journal of Public Relations Research, 9*(2), 99–118.

Smith, R. (1968). Women in public relations. *Public Relations Journal, 24*(10), 26–29.

Springer, S. P., & Deutsch, G. (1998). *Left brain, right brain: Perspectives from cognitive neuroscience* (5th ed.). New York: Freeman.

Sullivan, B. S., Dozier, D. M., & Hellweg, S. A. (1984, August). *A test of organizational role hierarchy among public relations practitioners.* Paper presented at the meeting of the Public Relations Division, Association for Education in Journalism and Mass Communication, Gainesville, FL.

Sullivan, B. S., Dozier, D. M., & Hellweg, S. A. (1985). Practitioner pursuit of the ideal role. *IPRA Review, 9*(2), 14–18.

Tam, S. Y., Dozier, D. M., Lauzen, M. M., & Real, M. R. (1995). The impact of superior-subordinate gender on the career advancement of public relations practitioners. *Journal of Public Relations Research, 7*(4), 259–272.

Toth, E. L., & Grunig, L. A. (1993). The missing story of women in public relations. *Journal of Public Relations Research, 5*(3), 153–175.

Toth, E. L., Serini, S. S., Wright, D. K., & Emig, A. G. (1998). Trends in public relations roles: 1990–1995. *Public Relations Review, 24*(2), 145–163.

U.S. Department of Labor, Bureau of Labor Statistics. (2005, January). *Employment and earnings.* Washington, DC: U.S. Government Printing Office.

Walton, R. E. (1969). *Interpersonal peacemaking: Confrontations and third party consultation.* Reading, MA: Addison-Wesley.

White, J., & Dozier, D. M. (1992). Public relations and management decision making. In J. E. Grunig (Ed.), *Excellence in public relations and communication management* (pp. 91–108). Hillsdale, NJ: Lawrence Erlbaum Associates.

Wright, D. K. (1995). The role of corporate public relations executives in the future of employee communications. *Public Relations Review, 21*(3), 181–198.

Zoch, L. M., Patterson, B. S., & Olson, D. L. (1997). The status of the school public relations practitioner: A statewide exploration. *Public Relations Review, 23*(4), 361–375.

6

Crisis Management: A Communicative Approach

W. Timothy Coombs

Eastern Illinois University

Although the crisis response research is vibrant and growing, it remains in an early stage of theoretical development with the literature being largely descriptive. The extant prescriptive research is based almost exclusively on case studies or accepted wisdom. As crisis management increases in importance as an organizational function, the research should rise to a higher level of rigor to provide a sturdy foundation for that function. This chapter offers a review and synthesis of lessons learned from the crisis response research. The crisis response research can be can be divided into two categories that reflect different emphases: form and content. Form indicates what should be done. For instance, crisis managers are told to respond quickly. Content addresses what is actually said in the messages. For example, crisis managers are urged to express sympathy for crisis victims. The chapter begins with the distinction between the form and content lines of research. Situational Crisis Communication Theory (SCCT), a prescriptive system for matching crisis responses to the crisis situation, is used to organize the discussion of the content research and as a foundation for the explication of future research and theory development.

The chapter concludes with the implications of the form and content research for both researchers and practitioners.

CRISIS RESPONSE: THE VALUE OF FORM

The form of a crisis response represents the most basic and primitive line of research concerning crisis response. The research tends to be composed of lists of what to do and what not to do that are devoid of guiding theory. However, often the lists are developed from experience, so they do offer a grounded perspective on crisis responses. This section will review the lessons learned about crisis response form and map the state of research support for those lessons.

LESSONS FOR CRISIS RESPONSE FORM

When analyzing the crisis communication/management literature, three form lessons consistently appear: be quick, be consistent, and be open. "Being quick" is the most commonly recited lesson (e.g., Darling, 1994; Kempner, 1995). Crisis experts preach the need to get the word out within the first hour of the crisis (Lukaszweski, 1997). "Getting the word out" means letting stakeholders, primarily the media, know what information the organization-in-crisis has about the crisis event. The objective is to fill the information vacuum with accurate information. When a crisis hits, an information vacuum forms. Stakeholders, led by the mass media, do not know what happened but want to know what happened. The crisis creates a demand for information (Augustine, 1995; Darling, 1994; Fearn-Banks, 1996; Hearit, 1994; Heath, 1994; Maynard, 1993). A quick response is an active response because it tries to fill the vacuum with facts. A slow response allows others to fill the vacuum with speculation and/or misinformation. Those others could be ill informed or could use the opportunity to attack the organization (Coombs, 1999b). Consider this example. A rather harmless chemical leak is caused by a faulty valve. A neighborhood group that is angry with the organization could portray the crisis as a dangerous threat brought on by indifference to safety. The neighborhood group fills the vacuum with speculation designed to damage the organization's reputation.

A quick response may also help to create the perception that the organization is in control of the crisis situation (Lukaszewski, 1997). A crisis disrupts the organization's routine (Barton, 2001; Coombs, 1999b). Stakeholders will perceive that the organization has lost at least a modicum of control over its operations. A response indicates action—that the organization is regaining the control lost during the crisis. Perceptions of control may be helpful in restoring confidence in the organization and building/protecting its reputation (Coombs, 1999a; Egelhoff & Sen, 1992).

The second form lesson, "be consistent," requires that the various messages sent by an organization are free of contradictions (Carney & Jorden, 1993;

Seitel, 1983). Consistency is another name for speaking with one voice. It is not always possible nor desirable for one person to speak for an organization during a crisis. However, the crisis team must work to insure that different spokespersons, whom may be at different geographic locations, deliver a consistent message (Barton, 2001; Lukaszewski, 1997). Inconsistency erodes the believability of a message (Clampitt, 1991; Garvin, 1996).

Openness is the only "controversial" recommendation. The controversy arises from the two different interpretations of the terms. On one level, openness simply refers to organizational members being available to stakeholders for comment on the crisis. The crisis team is willing to talk to stakeholders, primarily the mass media. Being unavailable sends a number of negative messages. Those negative messages include that the organization is not in control, it is stonewalling, or it is trying to hide something (Barton, 2001; Kaufmann, Kesner & Hazen, 1994).

On another level, openness means full disclosure; the organization should tell stakeholders everything they know about the crisis as soon the organization receives the information. Legal interests often recommend limited disclosure (Fitzpatrick & Rubin, 1995; Kaufmann et al., 1994; Martinelli & Briggs, 1998) because full disclosure can increase an organization's legal exposure and financial loss. An organization must balance its concern for financial stakeholders (e.g., stockholders and creditors) against concerns for stakeholders injured by the crisis (e.g., community members, customers, or employees). Full disclosure is recommended because of the fear that partial disclosure could create negative, long-range problems for the organization-stakeholder relationship (Kaufman et al., 1994). Stakeholders may become angry if they learn months or years later than an organization withheld certain information about a crisis (Bradford, 1999).

If an organization chooses partial disclosure, how does it choose what information to release and what to withhold? As of now little attention has been paid to the concern over guidelines for partial disclosure. Only a guide based on financial practicality has been offered. Scant attention has been given to any of the ethical choices made in crisis communication, let alone the ethical implications of partial disclosure (Ulmer & Sellnow, 1997). Kaufmann et al. (1994) outline five conditions when full disclosure can be used:

1. There is a continuing danger. If stakeholders do not receive the information they will remain at risk from the crisis. People need to know to evacuate an area if there is a risk of contamination from radioactive gases released by a facility or to return a dangerous child's toy. Any risk to stakeholder safety should be disclosed.

2. When the organization is the victim of a crisis such as a product tampering or terrorist action. An organization is likely to gain sympathy when it is the victim of a crisis. Johnson & Johnson seemed to benefit from being seen

as a victim, a point they actively promoted, during the first Tylenol poisonings (Berg & Robb, 1992).

3.   When the rumors circulating about the crisis are more damaging than the truth. A crisis must be thoroughly explained if people misperceive the cause and/or damage to be worse than it really is. If reports of damage and injuries are exaggerated, an organization must provide the correct details for each. Furthermore, an erroneously named cause of a crisis can look worse for an organization than the real cause. Full disclosure is needed when the truth is preferable to the rumors about the crisis.

4.   The organization must be able to afford the corrective actions. If an organization discloses failures and does not correct them, the organization is increasing its legal liability. Stakeholders expect an organization to correct its mistakes. It follows that if an organization discloses its error but cannot afford to correct it, stakeholders will become even angrier.

5.   A failure to disclose and respond could financially cripple an organization. When a product that has problems is central to the financial success of an organization, full disclosure is needed to restore order and sales. Full disclosure reveals the cause of the problem and how the solution is working to correct and prevent a reoccurrence of the problem. If customers do not have faith that the product is safe, sales will remain depressed, and the organization remains at risk if that product is its key to profits (Kaufmann et al., 1994).

The foregoing guidelines are based on financial concerns. Full disclosure can also be used to preserve relationships with stakeholders and maintain the organization's social responsibilities—ethical concerns (Tyler, 1997). Obviously crisis managers and researchers have only begun the debate of the ethics of crisis responses. We will return to this topic in the discussion of future research and implications for practice.

Research Support for Form Lessons

There is a general lack of research to support the form lessons. The form lessons are born from direct experience with crises or case analyses. The lessons are a type of everyday knowledge (Barton, 2001; Druckenmiller, 1993; Kempner, 1995; Lukaszweski, 1997) and represent accepted wisdom in the field. Many crisis experts would view testing the form lessons as researching the obvious. However, closer examination of the form lessons can only serve to enhance our understanding and refine the utilization of crisis responses.

CRISIS RESPONSE: THE VALUE OF CONTENT

Content research is a recent development in crisis management and has proven to be more rigorous than the form research. Researchers from the fields of communication and management have developed detailed case analyses and some experimental studies of the message content of crisis responses. Still the research lacks a theoretical orientation that would permit the movement from description to prescription. The Situational Crisis Communication Theory (SCCT) has been offered as a theoretical framework to integrate the various ideas that have emerged from the crisis response content research (Coombs & Holladay, 2002). This section offers an explanation of SCCT, including the research lines that informed it and a review of two related lines of content research, financial/legal concerns and instructing responses.

SCCT is built around protecting the organization's reputation during a crisis. The crisis responses, what an organization says and does after a crisis, will affect its reputation. SCCT identifies a set of crisis response strategies and recommends which strategy(ies) would be most effective in particular crisis situations. The match between the situation and the response is based on attribution theory. Crises are events that will elicit a search for attributions—stakeholders will seek to assign responsibility for the crisis. Crisis responsibility, the perception that the organization is the reason for the crisis, is the linchpin. Different crisis situations will lead to different attributions of crisis responsibility. Similarly, the crisis response strategies imply different degrees of accepting crisis responsibility. To protect a reputation, the responsibility acceptance of the organization's crisis response must be consistent with the stakeholder attributions of crisis responsibility generated by the crisis situation. SCCT articulates a system for evaluating crisis situations and matching them to the most desirable crisis response. SCCT's workings will be discussed in more detail after a review of the literature that informed its creation.

Conceptual Influences

There is a long-held belief in communication that the situation influences our selection of communicative responses. The belief in the power of the situation influences both rhetorical studies (e.g., Ware & Linkugel, 1973) and interpersonal communication (e.g., Sharkey & Stafford, 1990). Benson (1988) acknowledged the power of communication and the situational influences in crisis communication. Benson posited that crisis communication could significantly diminish the harm wrought by a crisis or magnify the harm if mismanaged. The key to proper management resided in the crisis situation. As later crisis researchers have concurred, crisis situations can be grouped into families or categories (Lerbinger, 1997; Mitroff, 1988; Pauchant &Mitroff, 1992). Benson argued that certain crisis response strategies should work better in certain crisis situations. Benson (1988) believed a future goal of crisis research should be to identify the crisis situations, articulate the options for crisis response, and determine which crisis responses would be best suited to which crisis situation. Basically, the content of the crisis response should match the crisis situation. A list of crisis response strategies, a means for understanding crisis situations, and a system for matching the two are essential to fulfill Benson's (1988) vision.

Situational Crisis Communication Theory attempts to fulfill Benson's (1988) vision. The three central elements are (1) a list of crisis response strategies, (2) a framework for categorizing crisis situations, and (3) a method for matching the crisis response strategy(ies) to the crisis situation. These three points structure the literature review of research relevant to SCCT.

Crisis Response Strategies

Discussions of various options for responding to a crisis are scattered across the crisis communication literature. The most detailed discussions of crisis response strategies are found in the work on corporate apologia, corporate impression management, and image restoration theory.

Corporate Apologia

The corporate apologia research was the first to systematically identify crisis response strategies. Apologia is a well-established genre of self-defense. Individuals use certain patterns of self-defense when they respond to attacks on their character (Kruse, 1981; Ryan, 1982). Dionisopolous and Vibbert (1988) were the first to posit that the apologia genre could be applied to organizations. They argued that organizations have a public persona and are generally perceived as individuals by their various stakeholders. If organizations are considered to be individuals and have personas, it is possible to experience attacks on character and the need to engage in self-defense (apologia). The authors used case studies to show how the process of corporate apologia could work. Dionisopolous and Vibbert (1988) provided an early framework for the analysis of the content of crisis messages. Often overlooked, their efforts have been needlessly duplicated by some researchers. This "neglect" reinforces the notion that crisis communication researchers should consider a bigger piece of the research picture when engaging in their own work.

Although Dionisopolous and Vibbert (1988) did not specify apologia's application to crisis situations, they did open the potential for its application. Because a crisis situation can involve character attacks, corporate apologia might be appropriate. Three researchers have made specific applications of apologia to crisis communication. Of the three, only Hearit (1994, 1995a, 1996) developed a line of research in the area. Hearit's work will be examined last to demonstrate the evolution of crisis response strategy development in corporate apologia.

Ice (1991) was the first to publish research utilizing corporate apologia's crisis applications. Ice (1991) used apologia to understand the different responses Union Carbide offered to different stakeholder groups following the Bhopal tragedy. Apologia provided a tool for identifying, categorizing, and analyzing the different crisis responses. The list of potential crisis responses included (1) denial, claim no responsibility for the crisis; (2) bolstering, accept responsibility but link the organization to something positive; (3) differentiation, separate the crisis from some larger context; and (4) transcendence, place the crisis in a new, higher context (Ice, 1991).

Ice (1991) found that Union Carbide used the different responses in order to mend various stakeholder relationships. Stakeholders vary in terms of the information they need and the interest they have in the crisis. For instance, consumers experience a product recall much differently than do stockholders. It follows that the different stakeholders may require different types of responses—responses that fit their needs during the crisis. Meeting stakeholder needs is a central aspect of managing the organization-stakeholder relationship. Crisis managers do try to use communication strategies in order to manage/repair relationships with stakeholders. Ice (1991) recognized the value of communication strategies for repairing the relationship damage inflicted by a crisis and the need to tailor the response to the needs of the stakeholder. A situation with multiple stakeholders who had specific, unique communicative demands would require an organization to produce a number of different communicative responses designed to address each demand.

Hobbs (1995) extended corporate apologia with a focus on identification. A crisis serves to break the identification (relationship) between the organization and stakeholder. Crisis responses based in apologia can be used to rebuild identification (restore the relationship). The selection of the crisis response strategy was said to be dependent on the situation. The same four apologia factors identified by Ice (1991) were identified by Hobbs (1995): denial, bolstering, differentiation, and transcendence. Denial and bolstering are reformative factors because they try to revise how stakeholders feel. Differentiation and transcendence are transformative factors because they try to change the meaning of the crisis. The reformative and transformative strategies can be paired together to form four postures/crisis responses: (1) absolution, differentiation and denial; (2) vindication, denial and transcendence; (3) explanation, bolstering and differentiation, and (4) justification, bolstering and transcendence (Hobbs, 1995). Hobbs was among the first to look at combinations of strategies.

Hobbs (1995) applied corporate apologia to a case study involving Toshiba being caught selling submarine technology to the Soviets. Toshiba had limited options in the situation because they were clearly guilty and the United States would not accept any form of justification—the situation influenced the selection of the crisis response. Hobbs (1995) went on to echo Benson (1988) when he called for more research into discovering the types of response strategies available to crisis managers and a better understanding of the situational factors that shape the selection of response strategies. Both Ice (1991) and Hobbs (1995) recognized the content of the crisis response as a valuable relationship building resource for the crisis manager and offered a few crisis responses for crisis managers to consider.

The works of Ice and Hobbs were merely exploratory and showed that corporate apologia could be used to understand crisis management. Keith Hearit (1994) defined the corporate apologia line of research by establishing a program of research on the topic. Hearit moved beyond the early applications by articulating a coherent perspective from which to apply corporate apologia to crisis communication. His perspective integrated ideas from social legitimacy and rhetoric theory. Hearit developed a framework and vocabulary for integrating corporate apologia and crisis management.

Hearit keys corporate apologia to social legitimacy, the match between organizational values and stakeholder values. An organization achieves legitimacy by being competent at its task and meeting stakeholder expectations. A crisis can be a threat to social legitimacy. The crisis may make an organization appear incompetent (e.g., an industrial accident) and/or in violation of stakeholder expectations (e.g., violation of environmental or social policies). The social legitimacy violation is a form of character attack that triggers the need for apologia (Hearit, 1994, 1995b). Through a series of case studies, Hearit identified the various responses a crisis manager might employ and some situational factors that shape the communicative decisions. The research revealed two different patterns, one for when an organization takes some responsibility for the crisis and another for when the organization denies a crisis exists through the use of a counterattack.

When an organization takes some responsibility for the crisis, the response uses five elements: (1) The organization presents its account of the crisis by offering its frame for the crisis events. (2) A statement of regret is issued (express compassion). (3) The organization uses one of three dissociation strategies in order to distance itself from the crisis. The *opinion/knowledge dissociation* argues that the complaint against the organization is based on opinion and does not match the facts of the situation. The *individual/group dissociation* is a form of scapegoating whereby an employee or part of the organization, not the entire organization, is declared responsible for the crisis event. The *act/essence dissociation* argues that the crisis is not representative of the "real" organization: The crisis is a deviation from normal. (4) An organization takes action to identify and to resolve the problem which caused the crisis. (5) The organization explains how it has acted to restore the values violated by the crisis (Hearit, 1994, 1995b).

Hearit's work moved beyond the simple application of apologia to crisis management. He expanded upon the existing view of corporate apologia to reveal additional response options and to identify potential situational factors that would affect the selection of response strategies. Hearit revealed the limits of corporate apologia as a crisis management tool, and his case studies serve as a model for those who wish to go beyond apologia.

Corporate Impression Management

Allen and Caillouet (1994) take a similar tack to Hearit, as they see crises being tied to legitimacy. Legitimacy is taken to be the stakeholders' evaluation that an organization is good—it conforms to the social rules held by the stakeholders. (Their conceptualization of legitimacy is consistent with Hearit's.) A crisis occurs when stakeholders see a violation of the social rules and begin to question an organization's legitimacy. Hence, an important goal during a crisis is to reestablish legitimacy. The organization in crisis must demonstrate that it is still adhering to social rules. An organization will use communication (a crisis response) in an attempt to show that there is no crisis (no violation has occurred), to have stakeholders judge the crisis event less harshly (the violation is minor), or to have the stakeholders view the organization more positively (the organization still follows the social rules). Crisis responses are a strategic use of communication designed to restore perceptions of organizational legitimacy. Allen and Caillouet (1994) turned to impression management to develop a list of potential crisis responses since efforts to reestablish legitimacy were viewed as a form of impression management. Figure 6.1 provides a list and definition of what Allen and Caillouet call impression management strategies.

Allen and Caillouet focused on developing and testing their typology of crisis response strategies. Their work began a movement to integrate impression management into the crisis communication literature. Both of their empirical studies reaffirmed Ice's (1991) finding that an organization may use different response strategies for different stakeholder groups. The first study specifically searched for and found the response strategy differences by stakeholder group (Allen & Caillouet, 1994). The second study found different response strategies in different external media (Caillouet & Allen, 1996). External media are targeted to different stakeholders; hence, the media difference is more evidence for adapting response strategies to stakeholders. Their research offers little insight into how the situation influences the selection of crisis responses. Most of the insights are just general observations from the impression management literature, such as that justifications are commonly used in threatening situations (Caillouet & Allen, 1996). Impression management expanded the list of crisis response options and reinforced the notion that different crisis responses can be targeted to different stakeholders.

Image Restoration Theory

Image restoration theory has produced the most voluminous line of research using a variety of crisis case studies (e.g., Benoit, 1995b; Benoit & Brinson, 1999; Brinson & Benoit, 1996, 1999). William Benoit synthesized concepts from communication (including apologia) and sociology (including account analysis) to develop image restoration theory. Situations arise where an organization is accused of bad/objectionable behavior. The situations can damage

1. Excuse: tries to reduce the organization's responsibility for the crisis.

    E1: Denial of Intention

    E2: Denial of Volition—could not control the event

    E3: Denial of Agency—organization did not produce the trigger event

2. Justification: organization tries to deflect the negatives associated with the crisis while accepting some responsibility for the crisis.

    J1: Denial of Injury—no injuries or only minor problems

    J2: Denial of Victim—the victim deserved the injury

    J3: Condemnation of Condemner—others commit similar or worse crises, so this crisis is irrelevant

    J4: Negative Events Misrepresented—crisis is not as bad as people say it is

3. Ingratiation: try to gain stakeholder approval of the organization

    I1: Self-enhancing Communication: remind stakeholders of the organization's positive qualities.

        I1a: Role Model: the organization is an exemplar of behavior

        I1b: Social Responsibility: the organization claims it accepts social responsibility

    I2: Other-enhancing Communication: offer praise or flattery to stakeholders

    I3: Opinion Conformity: organization expresses beliefs or values similar to stakeholders

4. Intimidation: organization states it has power and will use it against stakeholders or condemners. Often it will include a threat.

5. Apology: the organization accepts responsibility for the crisis and aks to be punished

6. Denouncement: the organization blames some external person or group for the crisis.

7. Factual Distortion: organization claims statements or descriptions of the crisis are untrue in some way or simply taken out of context.

FIG. 6.1   Impression management strategies (Allen & Caillouet, 1994).

an organization's reputation. Communication strategies are used by the organization to explain its behavior and to restore its image (Benoit, 1995a). Benoit identifies five general image restoration strategies: denial, evasion of responsibility, reducing offensiveness of the event, corrective action, and mortification. The Figure 6.2 lists and defines the various strategies and subcategories, including the separation strategy that was added in 1999.

Coombs (1995, 1999b) combined the work of corporate apologia, corporate impression management, and image restoration theory to develop a list of crisis response strategies for SCCT. See Fig. 6.3 for a list and definition of those crisis response strategies. Benoit (1995a) had argued that there can be many different lists of crisis responses. The lists will vary in terms of abstractness of the category. He believed there is no one, perfect list, so we should apply ones that are useful. The synthesized list for SCCT tried to follow that advice. The list initially was based on the accommodative-defensive continuum developed by Marcus and Goodman (1991). Accommodative responses accept responsibility, admit a problem exists, and/or attempt to take corrective action.

1. Denial: organization claims there is no crisis
   Simple Denial: organization says it did not perform act in question
   Shift the Blame: organization blames another actor for the crisis
2. Evasion of Responsibility: organization attempts to reduce responsibility for the crisis
   Provocation: another actor forced the organization into the crisis situation
   Defeasibility: organization lacked the information or ability to prevent the crisis
   Accident: organization made a mistake
   Good Intentions: organization meant the action to be positive
3. Reducing Offensiveness of the Event: organization makes the crisis appear more positive
   Bolstering: organization reinforces its good traits
   Minimization: organization notes that the crisis is not serious
   Differentiation: organization explains that the crisis is not as bad as similar crises
   Transcendence: organization explains that the crisis event was related to achieving some larger goal
   Attack Accuser: organization attacks the credibility of its accuser
   Compensation: organization offers some form of aid to the victims
4. Corrective Action: organization takes steps to solve the problem and/or prevent a repetition of the crisis
5. Mortification: organization accepts responsibility and apologizes
6. Separation: organization explains that the act violated its policies, identifies a separate scapegoat within the organization, and initiates corrective action

FIG. 6.2 Image restoration strategies (Benoit, 1995; Brinson & Benoit, 1999).

Defensive responses insist there is no problem, reassure the stakeholders that the organization can generate future revenues, and/or take action to restore normal operations. Mitigating strategies demonstrate concern for the victims injured or threatened by the crisis. Aggravation strategies seek to protect the organization in crisis from further damage.

The accommodative-defensive continuum was found to be problematic because of the distinction between protecting the victim and protecting the organization. Respondents indicated that some strategies could do both. Moreover, the accommodative-defensive continuum is very similar to the mitigation-aggravation continuum found in interpersonal communication (McLauglin, Cody, & O'Hair, 1983). The mitigation-aggravation continuum has come under question with recent research (Dunn & Cody, 2000). The categorization of crisis response strategies was reframed to reflect the amount of responsibility each strategy is perceived to accept. The emphasis on responsibility is consistent with the attribution theory roots of SCCT and provides a useful linkage for matching crisis response strategies and crisis situations. The new responsibility acceptance categorization is included in Fig.6.3.

Crisis Situation

In SCCT, the crisis situation is evaluated using a two-step process. Step one is to identify the basic crisis type that is involved. A number of researchers have

1. Full Apology: the organization takes full responsibility for the   Very High Acceptance
   crisis and requests forgiveness from stakeholders. It can also
   include some form of compensation.

2. Corrective Action: the organization takes steps to repair the crisis   High Acceptance
   damage and/or prevent a recurrence of the crisis.

3. Ingratiation: the organization reminds stakeholders of past good   Mild Acceptance
   works by the organization or praises the stakeholders in
   some fashion.

4. Justification: the organization tries to minimize the perceived   Mild Acceptance
   damage related to the crisis. Includes claiming that the damage
   was minimal or that the victim deserved it.

5. Excuse: the organization tries to minimize its responsibility for   Mild Acceptance
   the crisis. Includes denying intent or control over the crisis event.

6. Denial: the organization maintains that no crisis occurred. The   No Acceptance
   response may include efforts to explain why there was no crisis.

7. Attack the Accuser: the organization confronts the people or group   No Acceptance
   who say that a crisis exists. The response may include a threat
   such as lawsuit.

FIG. 6.3   Crisis response strategies by level of responsibility acceptance (Coombs, 1999).

developed lists of crisis types (i.e., Lerbinger, 1997; Mitroff, 1988; Pauchant & Mitroff, 1992). SCCT distilled the list to the crisis types found in the Fig. 6.4. The distillation involved reviewing the major lists of crisis types and retaining only those crisis types that appeared on more than one list. Figure 6.4 provides a definition of each crisis type.

Attribution theory states that people will search for the causes of unusual events such as crises. SCCT argues that each crisis type will generate certain attributions of crisis responsibility—how much a stakeholder believes the organization is responsible for the crisis event. The foundation of crisis responsibility is personal control, perceptions that the organization could control the crisis event. Originally personal control and crisis responsibility were treated as separate constructs, but recent research has shown them to be the same construct (Coombs & Holladay, 2002). Coombs and Holladay (2002) have identified the general level of crisis responsibility that stakeholders will assign to the crisis types in Fig.6.4. Those levels of crisis responsibility are identified in Fig.6.4.

Step 2 in the crisis situation is the evaluation of the *modifiers*: variables that can alter attributions generated by the crisis type. There are two modifiers in SCCT, performance history and crisis severity. *Performance history* refers to the organization's past record of crises and good works. Past, similar crises have been found to intensify perceptions of organizational responsibility (Griffin, Babin, & Attaway, 1991). Good works were believed to reduce perceptions of responsibility by creating a halo effect (Coombs, 1999b). Thus far, research has only found the "Velcro effect": A negative performance history intensifies attributions of crisis responsibility, whereas a positive performance history has no significant effect on attributions of crisis responsibility (Coombs &

Stakeholders Hold Strong Attributions of Organizational Crisis Responsibility
Organizational Misdeeds: organization purposefully places stake holders at risk

  Management Misconduct: knowingly violate laws or regulations
  With No Injuries: External stakeholders deceived but not harmed
  With Injuries: External stakeholders deceived and harmed

Human Breakdown Product Recall: recall caused by human error
Human Breakdown Accident: industrial accident caused by human error

Stakeholders Hold Moderate Attributions of Organizational Crisis Responsibility
Technical Breakdown Product Recall: product recalled because of technology or equipment failure
Technical Breakdown Accident: industrial accident caused by technology or equipment failure
Megadamage: significant environmental damage from a technical error
Challenge: confronted by stakeholders who claim the organization is operating in an inappropriate manner

Stakeholders Hold Weak Attributions of Organizational Crisis Responsibility
Rumors: untrue information about the organization circulates among stakeholders
Natural Disasters: acts of nature such are hurricanes or tornadoes
Malevolence/Product Tampering: damage by an external agent against an organization
Workplace Violence: attack by an employee or former employee against co-workers and/or customers

FIG. 6.4   Crisis types by level of crisis responsibility.

Holladay, 2001). *Crisis severity* is the amount of damage inflicted by a crisis. Limited tests show that as the severity of personal injuries increases, so too do perceptions of organizational responsibility (Coombs & Holladay, in 2004). Thus far, the research shows the modifiers act to intensify attributions of crisis responsibility. As a result, either a negative performance history and/or severity will raise a crisis type with low crisis responsibility to the moderate level, or a crisis type at the moderate level, to the high level, thus affecting the type of crisis response strategy that is appropriate for the crisis situation. The crisis situation is a combination of assessments of the crisis type and modifiers (assessments of performance history and crisis severity).

Matching Process

The crisis response strategy and crisis type discussions are meant to guide crisis response selection. The basic idea is that as attributions of organization crisis responsibility intensify, crisis managers should use strategies that reflect greater acceptance of responsibility. The crisis managers need to meet the expectations of stakeholders, reflecting the legitimacy concerns found in corporate apologia and corporate impression management. Marcus and Goodman (1991) found some support for this contention when examining the financial impact of accommodative and defensive responses in accidents and scandals. Accommodative strategies were found to benefit victims of the crisis, whereas defensive strategies benefit shareholders by protecting stock values. The evidence suggested that investors react more positively when an accommodative strategy is used during a scandal and when a defensive strategy is used in an accident (Marcus & Goodman, 1991). Marcus and Goodman (1991) identified the financial costs associated with two types of crisis responses and provided some evidence to support matching crisis responses and crisis situations. SCCT focuses on reputation rather than financial costs, so the study is only indirect support for the theory.

In SCCT, a crisis manager begins by identifying the basic crisis type to determine the initial level of crisis responsibility stakeholders will attribute to the crisis situation. Next, performance history and the amount of damage are considered to determine if adjustment should be made to the original crisis responsibility assessment (Coombs, 1999b). After the final adjustment, the crisis managers select the crisis response strategy(ies) to fit the level of crisis responsibility. Empirical research has generated support for this system of evaluating organizational crisis responsibility and some of the claims made about matching crisis responses to the specific crisis situations on the continuum (Coombs, 1998, 1999a; Coombs & Holladay, 1996, 2001, 2002). SCCT does provide a mechanism for assessing the crisis situation and selecting crisis responses that fit the situation.

RELATED RESEARCH IN CRISIS RESPONSE CONTENT

Admittedly, reputation is a limited focus in crisis management. However, SCCT does take into account two other important foci, human and financial/legal concerns. Examining these two lines of research will provide a richer context for SCCT by placing it within the larger crisis communication literature.

Instructing Responses

The primary concern during a crisis is human lives and safety—people come first. After a crisis hits, stakeholders must learn how the crisis might/will affect them and what, if any, actions they must take to protect themselves (Bergman, 1994; Trahan, 1993). Sturges (1994) refers to this information as *instructing information*. Instructing responses address one or both of two stakeholder information needs: (1) an explanation of what happened—a description of the actual event (e.g., stakeholders want to know the general nature of the crisis); and (2) recommendations for what the stakeholders should do to protect themselves from the effects of the crisis (e.g., should neighbors near a chemical spill shelter in place or be evacuated?) (Ammerman, 1995; Bergman, 1994; Sturges, 1994).

Stakeholders will expect to receive instructing information after a crisis, so an organization should utilize the instructing responses. Although many crisis experts recommend the instructing responses (Birch, 1994; Darling, 1994; Egelhoff & Sen, 1992; Gonzalez-Herrero & Pratt, 1995; Maynard, 1993; Sturges, 1994), scant evidence exists to support or to explain its use. One study did examine the effects of vague and detailed instructing responses. The results found no effect on organizational reputation, accepting the organization's story, or being willing to engage in supportive behaviors for the organization (Coombs, 1999a). We must keep in mind that study had a rather simplistic view of instructing responses and may have found the existence of a very low threshold for what constitutes effective instructing information. The study is more of a call for additional research into instructing response than a definitive statement on the topic. SCCT maintains that instructing information should be taken as a given in any crisis situation. None of the crisis response strategies should be employed until the instructing information is delivered (Coombs & Holladay, 2002).

Financial/Legal Concerns

Crisis communication has financial/legal implications. Legal is considered part of financial because the legal ramifications will come with a price tag. SCCT holds that any crisis communication effort will have to consider the limitations imposed by the financial/legal concerns (Coombs & Holladay, 2002). A review of the financial/legal crisis literature will support this conclusion. Fitzpatrick and Rubin (1995) developed a set of crisis response strategies built on the legal-public relations conflict that can arise during crisis management. They identified four strategy types: traditional public relations strategies, traditional legal strategies, mixed strategies, and diversionary strategies. Traditional public relations strategies included stating the organizational policy, investigating allegations, being candid, admitting if the problem truly does exist, and announcing and implementing corrective actions as soon as possible. Traditional legal strategies include saying nothing, saying as little as possible, denying guilt and/or acting indignant, and shifting or sharing blame with the plaintiff if necessary. Mixed strategies involved denying fault while expressing remorse for the crisis. Diversionary strategies attempt to divert attention from the accusations by claiming organizational outrage over the situation but taking no corrective action, claiming the problem is solved, or reporting that the alleged offender is leaving the organization for other reasons.

Their examination of crisis cases found the legal response to be the most common. However, they did not consider whether the organization was found guilty as part of the analysis. If a company is innocent, that situational factor confounds a system which uses denial of guilt as a defining element of a legal strategy (Fitzpatrick & Rubin, 1995). Under their system, an organization that is innocent will choose a legal strategy because the organization will deny its guilt. It should be noted that some organizations are known to deny guilt but accept punishments (e.g., pay fines) simply to resolve a crisis. The organization may find that the punishment is less of a financial burden than fighting the charges. The organization may be pragmatic and use a mixed response. The research does not get into the relative advantages of each strategy.

Martinelli and Briggs (1998) used the Fitzpatrick and Rubin (1995) strategies to examine the Odwalla *E.coli* poisoning case. The strategies were useful in showing that both concerns were taken into account by Odwalla. The legal-public relations strategies have limited application beyond this point. The strategies are not as well defined or as distinct as other lists of crisis responses, nor does the research take into account situational influences on response selection. However, the system was developed at a rather high level of abstraction, trying merely to separate legal and public relations concerns. It is an accurate measure of the degree to which a legal perspective is influencing the response.

What these studies show is that organizations in crisis are often constrained by financial/legal concerns—use "legal" strategies. Tyler (1997) argued that legal strategies are used to protect financial assets. Organizations cannot always fully accept responsibility for a crisis because of the financial impact. Publicly accepting guilt means that an organization has no defense in litigation arising from the crisis (Tyler, 1997). At times, financial/legal constraints will prohibit an organization from using a crisis response strategy that openly accepts responsibility (Coombs & Holladay, 2002).

On a related note, an organization can express compassion without accepting responsibility. Compassion is when an organization expresses concern for the victims of a crisis—those injured in some way by the event. A number of experts recommended expressing compassion/concern for victims, people injured by the crisis (Augustine, 1995; Carney & Jorden, 1993; Mitchell, 1986; Sen & Egelhoff, 1991; Wilson & Patterson, 1987). Demonstrating compassion may be a way to enhance organizational credibility, a valuable aspect of the reputation. The organization demonstrates trustworthiness when it expresses concern for the victims. However, compassion is not the same as accepting responsibility (Fitzpatrick, 1995; Tyler, 1997). When demonstrating compassion, an organization shows concern without taking responsibility for the crisis.

Two studies have found empirical support for the compassion-reputation linkage. With product defect crises, Siomkos and Shrivastava (1993) tested the effect of four different responses: denial of a problem, a forced recall, voluntary recall, and a "super effort" that included compensation and a very easy return process. The four strategies marked a progression in social responsibility and compassion. Results found that the organizational reputation improved significantly as the responses became more compassionate (Siomkos & Shrivastava, 1993). Coombs (1998) compared the effect of compassion and no-compassion responses in an industrial accident crisis (a chlorine gas leak). The respondents in the compassion condition reported more positive perceptions of the organization's reputation, stronger honoring of the organization's account, and a greater intention to engage in supportive behavior for the organization (Coombs, 1998). Compassion is consistent with SCCT. Compassion is a very broad response including any statement or action designed to recognize or address victim needs; hence it is a part of many of the crisis response strategies identified in SCCT.

Summary

Situational Crisis Communication Theory integrates ideas from a variety of crisis communication research lines to produce a comprehensive and prescriptive perspective for selecting crisis response strategies. SCCT concentrates on crisis response strategies that will maximize protection of the organization's, reputation. However, efforts to protect the organizational reputation are undertaken only after human safety is secured through instructing information. SCCT holds that as attributions of crisis responsibility increase, the crisis managers should use crisis response strategies that progressively accept more responsibility for the crisis. There are financial/legal limits to the selection of crisis response strategies. SCCT recognizes that crisis managers may be forced to use suboptimal crisis response strategies because the organization cannot afford the financial and legal liabilities of strategies that accept full responsibility for the crisis. SCCT provides a framework for future research, as many of its assumptions and prescriptions remain untested.

FUTURE RESEARCH AND THEORY DEVELOPMENT

There is ample room for further research and theory development in both the areas of crisis response form and content. Researchers have just begun to move beyond the simple articulation of concepts and typologies to the identification of relationships and predictions.

Crisis Response Form

Although considered obvious, there is value to the further exploration of the form lessons. We can go beyond testing the obvious to gain a better understanding of how these form lessons work. The better we understand how they work, the more effectively crisis managers can apply the form lessons in their crisis communication efforts.

The quick response lessons can be rooted in media frames. The mass media select what to include and what to exclude from a story (Iyengar & Kinder, 1987; Pan & Kosicki, 1993). This selection process frames the story, tells people how to interpret it, as it "limits or defines the message's meaning by shaping the inference that individuals make about the message" (Hallahan, 1999, p. 207). The speed of the response may be an important step in establishing the frame for the crisis event. In the earlier crisis example of the chemical release, a delayed response allowed a disgruntled stakeholder group to develop a frame that would have very negative repercussions for the organization. Researchers could use a sample of media coverage from a variety of similar crises as a data base. The crises must be similar to reduce a potential confounding factor— different types of crises can be covered differently. The coverage could be examined to determine if the speed of the response affects the type of frame used for the crisis story.

In a very crude sense, discussions of "spin" are addressing issues of framing. Public relations practitioners are often in a contest with others to control the language used to describe an organization and its actions (Dionisopolous & Crable, 1988; Hearit, 1994; Heath, 1997). The crisis is another context in which practitioners try to control the interpretation of events by controlling the words used to describe the events. In a crisis, the crisis managers try to control the terms used to describe the crisis and the organization-in-crisis (Martinelli & Briggs, 1998). Given the ramifications of crisis framing, it would be instructive to know the impact that response speed has on the framing process.

The persuasion research in communication supports the belief that consistency increases credibility while inconsistency erodes it (McCroskey, 1997). Using real or created crisis responses, researchers could test the effect of inconsistencies on people's perceptions of the organization and its handling of the crisis. A starting point would be to identify different types of inconsistencies. Some inconsistencies may be minor, the wrong statistics or information, and easy to correct (Berg & Robb, 1992), whereas others are seen as reversing the organization's entire response to the crisis (Benoit, 1995b). For instance, in the first Tylenol poisoning, Johnson & Johnson wrongly stated there was no cyanide used at the manufacturing facility. They then had to correct themselves and admit there was some cyanide used in a testing laboratory on site, but none in the manufacturing area. Compare this to Mitsubishi, who, when charged with widespread sexual harassment, first attacked the Equal Employment Opportunity Commission, including sending workers to protest EEOC offices. They then decided to "play nice" and work with the same agency they had bashed (Coombs, 1999a). There should be a quantifiable difference between mistakes anyone can make and reversals of direction.

For openness, we still have much to learn about what facilitates perceptions of openness. Are there verbal cues; and even nonverbal ones for television, that help to create perceptions of openness as opposed to perceptions of stonewalling and deception? Testing sample messages for their effect on perceptions of organizational openness would provide valuable information about the form of responses. A crisis manager would benefit from knowing that the same information presented in different ways can create radically different perceptions of openness. Such research does not address the larger ethical concerns. There is a need to expose and examine the ethical issues of full and partial disclosure. However, we must keep in mind financial realities when we enter this debate. The concern over staying in business is not new for business ethics so we should consult that literature for some models. The deeper ethical and moral debate over full verses partial disclosure has just begun. We must begin to outline the positions and options in order to start constructing a code of conduct for the disclosure of crisis-related information. The debate highlights the financial-social tension which underlies the entire crisis communication process.

CRISIS RESPONSE CONTENT

The future research directions for crisis response content fall into six areas: (1) instructing information, (2) improved understanding of crisis response strategies, (3) limitations of case studies, (4) accepting responsibility, (5) testing elements of SCCT, and (6) testing SCCT prescriptions. Instructing information and crisis response strategies are at the core of SCCT but have received limited study. The bulk of previous crisis response research has been case studies. The limits of this method must be addressed along with the viability of its recommendations, especially the emphasis on accepting responsibility. As the legal research indicates, there are practical limits to accepting responsibility, a point that warrants further analysis. Finally, the elements and prescriptions of SCCT are only in the initial stages of analysis. Further research is needed to refine and to test the theory.

Instructing Information

Little is known about the most effective use of instructing information. In fact, the idea of instructing information is a vague concept. The first step in future research should be to unpack what is meant by *instructing information.* We need to know the different types of instructing information, how different stakeholders value the various types of instructing information, and how stakeholders use instructing information. Different crises might trigger the need for different types of instructing information. Crisis managers would benefit from knowing what instructing information will be in demand. Moreover, various stakeholders may want different types of instructing information. This concern is consistent with the apologia and impression management research showing different crisis responses being sent to different stakeholders. Crisis managers would benefit from knowing which stakeholders will want which type of instructing information.

Part of understanding instructing information is discovering how stakeholders use it. Uncertainty reduction theory (communication is triggered by a need to reduce uncertainty) could offer some guidance in understanding stakeholder use. Understanding how stakeholders use instructing information will bring a deeper appreciation of matching instructing information to stakeholders. The crisis managers not only know what type of instructing information a stakeholder might desire, but why it is desired. Efforts to understand the process should include the notion of threshold. Crisis managers have an easier task when they know how much instructing information is required as well as what type. By knowing how much, crisis managers will have a better understanding of when they can send messages to stakeholders—crisis managers can send messages once the minimum amount of instructing information is known.

Improved Understanding of Crisis Response Strategies

We need a better understanding of the list of crisis responses strategies assembled by SCCT. Coombs and Holladay (2002) suggest a continuum based on acceptance of responsibility. Published research has yet to evaluate how stakeholders perceived the crisis response strategies in terms of taking responsibility. We currently have projections based on parallel ideas in interpersonal communication. It would be useful to assess how receivers view the crisis response strategies and not just rely on a sender interpretation of the strategies. Another option would be to use multidimensional scaling (MDS) to examine the possible dimensionality of the crisis responses. Similar types of studies have been conduced using sets of communicative strategies (i.e., Geddes & Linnehan, 1996). MDS would give crisis managers and researchers a more complete understanding of the crisis response list. The hope is that understanding the list better will improve their ability to utilize the list.

Limitations of Case Studies

The case studies used in corporate apologia and image restoration theory have generated a number of prescriptive recommendations for the use of crisis strategies. Four stand out as noteworthy. The dominant recommendation is for an organization to admit fault/accept responsibility for the crisis immediately (Benoit, 1995a; Brinson & Benoit, 1996, 1999). Second, an organization should take corrective actions and publicize those actions (Benoit, 1995a; Sellnow, Ulmer & Snider, 1998). Third, bolstering is most effective when it is directly related to the charge. Fourth, denial is an effective strategy when the organization is innocent (Benoit, 1995a). Image restoration theory is the dominant line of research generating these recommendations. The most common recommendations suggest using the mortification and corrective action crisis response when an organization is guilty. However, the descriptive case studies are little better than hunches when untested. An example is the way image restoration theory promotes the use of mortification (accepting responsibility) and corrective action. Two recent SCCT-based, empirical tests of crisis response use found no support for always using mortification and corrective action. In a criminal violation crisis (racial discrimination), the mortification and corrective action strategies had no greater effect on organizational reputation or account honoring than a simple bolstering strategy (Coombs & Schmidt, 2000). In an industrial accident crisis (explosion), defeasibility (saying it was unintentional) had the same effect on reputation and account honoring as mortification or corrective action (Fediuk, 1999).

We must consider a closer examination of the case study claims. The case studies should be used to generate ideas for further research into strategy use. As Sellnow, Ulmer, and Snider (1998) noted, the case studies can offer glimpses into the use of combinations of crisis responses. I would add that we should subject those insights to closer scrutiny before offering them to crisis managers as facts. One option is to follow SCCT's lead and use empirical tests of the case study findings using quasi-experimental designs. Another option is to be more rigorous and move beyond single to multiple case studies. Following genre criticism, a number of similar crises should be examined for patterns of strategy use and effect or a large number of cases could be coded and subjected to loglinear analysis in order to identify patterns. Whichever option is used, researchers can gain additional insights into the use of crisis responses.

Accepting Responsibility

The import of these findings are linked to the legal debate over accepting responsibility. Fitzpatrick (1995) provides one of the first in-depth treatments of the need to balance legal liability with the demand to show concern for victims. Although it is laudable to accept responsibility for a crisis and show compassion for victims, there are serious legal ramifications of these actions. Crisis managers are counseled against accepting responsibility if an organization cannot afford to do so. However, organizations can still express regret and concern for victims without accepting responsibility. "Regret for the occurrence and consequences of a particular event can be expressed without accepting responsibility for causing it. The goal is to demonstrate the company's concerns for the affected parties and avoid public anger directed at the organization" (Fitzpatrick, 1995, p. 36). Although accepting responsibility is often recommended by crisis experts, it is not always wise. Compassion can be expressed in a less costly manner.

Tyler (1997) has expanded on Fitzpatrick's (1995) work, in part as a response to image restoration theory's promotion of accepting responsibility. Organizations may use *equivocal communication*, responses that appear to be ambiguous or contradictory. An organization may deny or not accept responsibility while simultaneously expressing remorse for the crisis and/or taking actions designed to eliminate a repeat of the crisis. Not taking responsibility runs the risk of intensifying stakeholder anger. An organization can appear to be arrogant or defensive. The alternative is to incur the legal liability of accepting responsibility. However, an organization may not be able to afford the legal liability. Although frequently recommended by image restoration theory, accepting responsibility (mortification) may be avoided for legitimate, legal reasons (Tyler, 1997). There is empirical evidence to support the value of simply addressing victims with a positive response that falls short of accepting responsibility. More research is required to establish the parameters of accepting responsibility as a crisis response.

Testing Elements of SCCT

SCCT has been using experimental and quasi-experimental designs to test some of the relationships, assumptions, and predictions for crisis response use. The core variables of crisis responsibility and organizational reputation are related as anticipated, and some evidence of the impact of performance history has been revealed (Coombs & Holladay, 2001, 2002). The examination of SCCT is still in the early stages of mapping out crisis situations and matching crisis responses to crisis situations. The nature of crisis situations has been refined (Coombs, 1998; Coombs & Holladay, 2002), but SCCT is still rough in how it accounts for financial and legal factors in the situation. Performance history and crisis severity also require further attention. More research should be conducted to see whether the Velcro effect is the only impact of performance history and that past good works (a general positive reputation) have no real effect on perceptions of the crisis situation. On a related note, what happens when the crisis strikes at the core of an organization's reputation? Consider a company that prides itself on fair treatment of workers. Suddenly it is revealed that the company is using sweatshops in Asia. How does the impact of a crisis involving a core reputational element differ from the impact of a crisis involving more peripheral elements of the reputation? The study of crisis severity as a modifier is very limited, with only one study focused on that variable. The results were mixed, so more research is needed to ascertain if and when crisis severity is a modifier of crisis responsibility attributions (Coombs & Holladay, 2004).

Testing SCCT Prescriptions

Only a few of the prescriptions recommended by SCCT for matching crisis responses have been tested. More research is needed to verify or disprove the other recommendations. Recent studies have also pointed to unintended effects of many crisis strategies. A variety of accommodative strategies have been found to create perceptions of corrective action being taken, even when it was not part of the response (Coombs, 1999a; Coombs & Schmidt, 2000). For instance, when just bolstering is used, respondents still assumed that the organization was taking corrective action (Coombs & Schmidt, 2000). Further research is needed to understand which strategies can create the desired perceptions—especially corrective action, because it is one of the strategies recommended by image restoration theory. It could be that image restoration theory has identified desired effects, and that strategies or combinations of strategies can create the desired effects even when the strategy(ies) do not seem to directly address that effect. Compassion and corrective action are two very important effects that require additional study.

IMPLICATIONS FOR THEORY AND PRACTICE

Crisis management transpires in an arena where small errors can be very costly. With reduced time to communicate and increased pressure to respond to stakeholders, crisis managers have precious little room for error. Bad advice can cost an organization financial and reputational resources (Barton, 2001; Coombs, 1999a). For public relations practitioners, the crisis team is a method of entry into the dominant coalition. As a member of the team, the public relations practitioner is part of the decision-making unit of the organization. In other words, the stakes are high for crisis communication. The public relations people must make their contributions about crisis communication meaningful in order to justify their inclusion within the dominant coalition. The advice that they offer should be guided by established research, not hunches or guesses. Like other social scientists, public relations people must be able to give reasons/evidence to support their chosen course of action. Basing actions on past research does not guarantee success, but it shows that there is logic and reason behind the choices. Respect is gained from others in management when the public relations recommendations are based upon reasoned action.

SCCT is an attempt to build crisis communication theory. Integrating more theory into crisis communication will help to demonstrate the danger of utilizing untested recommendations. Crisis managers will know that the recommendations are not simple wisdom or observations from a case study or two. SCCT can provide theoretically derived and tested recommendations—there will be evidence to support the selection or avoidance of particular response strategies in specific crisis situations. The evidence provided by SCCT is based on social science and created through developing and testing theory-based assumptions about crisis communication.

As noted throughout this chapter, the crisis communication literature is ripe with recommendations for crisis managers. However, we know little about how or why the recommendations are effective. The study of crisis responses, what organizations say and do after a crisis hits, is still in its infancy. As noted in the section on future research and theory development, there are a number of points that still need theoretical development and testing. Crisis communication is strengthened when we infuse theory into our analyses. We move away from everyday knowledge toward actions that are grounded in social science. Although research cannot guarantee success, it can improve decision making about the selection of crisis responses during a crisis. Research into crisis response can make its contribution to the crisis management body of knowledge by using and testing theory in its research. SCCT tries to move crisis communication further along its theoretical evolutionary line.

REFERENCES

Allen, M. W., & Caillouet, R. H. (1994). Legitimation endeavors: Impression management strategies used by an organization in crisis. *Communication Monographs, 61*, 44–62.

Ammerman, D. (1995). What's a nice company like yours doing in a story like this? In L. Barton (Ed.), *New Avenues in Risk and Crisis Management* (Vol. III, pp. 3–8). Las Vegas: UNLV Small Business Development Center.

Augustine, N. R. (1995, November/December). Managing the crisis you tried to prevent. *Harvard Business Review, 73*(6), 147–158.

Barton, L. (2001). *Crisis in organizations: II* (2nd ed.). Cincinnati, OH: College Divisions South-Western.

Benoit, W. L. (1995a). *Accounts, excuses, and apologies: A theory of image restoration.* Albany, NY: State University of New York Press.

Benoit, W. L. (1995b). Sears' repair of its auto service image: Image restoration discourse in the corporate sector. *Communication Studies, 46*, 89–105.

Benoit, W. L., & Brinson, S. L. (1999). Queen Elizabeth's image repair discourse: Insensitive royal or compassionate Queen? *Public Relations Review, 25*, 145–156.

Benson, J. A. (1988). Crisis revisited: An analysis of the strategies used by Tylenol in the second tampering episode. *Central States Speech Journal, 39*, 49–66.

Berg, D. M. & Robb, S. (1992). Crisis management and the "paradigm case." In E. L. Toth & R. L. Heath (Eds.), *Rhetorical and critical approaches to public relations* (pp. 93–110). Hillsdale, NJ: Lawrence Erlbaum Associates.

Bergman, E. (1994). Crisis? What crisis? *Communication World, 11*(4), 9–13.

Birch, J. (1994, Spring). New factors in crisis planning and response. *Public Relations Quarterly, 39*, 31–34.

Bradford, M. (1999, Aug. 9). Companies err on side of recalls. *Business Insurance*, 3–7.

Brinson, S. L., & Benoit, W. L. (1996). Dow Corning's image repair strategies in the breast implant crisis. *Communication Quarterly, 44*, 29–41.

Brinson, S. L., & Benoit, W. L. (1999). The tarnished star: Restoring Texaco's damaged public image. *Management Communication Quarterly, 12*, 483–510.

Caillouet, R. H., & Allen, M. W. (1996). Impression management strategies employees use when discussing their organization's public image. *Journal of Public Relations Research, 8*, 211–227.

Carney, A., & Jorden, A. (1993, August). Prepare for business-related crises. *Public Relations Journal, 49*, 34–35.

Clampitt, P. G. (1991). *Communicating for managerial effectiveness.* Newbury Park, CA: Sage.

Coombs, W. T. (1995). Choosing the right words: The development of guidelines for the selection of the "appropriate" crisis response strategies. *Management Communication Quarterly, 8*, 447–476.

Coombs, W. T. (1998). An analytic framework for crisis situations: Better responses from a better understanding of the situation. *Journal of Public Relations Research, 10*(3), 179–193.

Coombs, W. T. (1999a). Information and compassion in crisis responses: A test of their effects. *Journal of Public Relations Research, 11*, 125-142.

Coombs, W. T. (1999b). *Ongoing crisis communication: Planning, managing, and responding.* Thousand Oaks, CA: Sage.

Coombs, W. T., & Holladay, S. J. (1996). Communication and attributions in a crisis: An experimental study of crisis communication. *Journal of Public Relations Research, 8*(4), 279–295.

Coombs, W. T. & Holladay, S. J. (2001). An extended examination of the crisis situation: A fusion of the relational management and symbolic approaches. *Journal of Public Relations Research, 13,* 321–340.

Coombs, W. T. & Holladay, S. J. (2002). Helping managers protect reputational assets: Initial tests of the situational crisis communication theory. *Management Communication Quarterly, 16,* 165–186.

Coombs, W. T., & Holladay, S. J. (2004). Matching crisis response strategies to crisis situations: An attribution theory-based approach to crisis management. In D. P. Millar & R. L. Heath (Eds.), *Responding to Crisis: A Rhetorical Approach of Crisis Communication* (pp. 95–115). Mahwah, NJ: Lawrence Erlbaum Associates.

Coombs, W. T., & Schmidt, L. (2000). An empirical analysis of image restoration: Texaco's racism crisis. *Journal of Public Relations Research, 12*, 163–178.

Darling, J. R. (1994). Crisis management in international business: Keys to effective decision making. *Leadership & Organizational Development Journal Annual, 15*(8), 3–8.

Dionisopolous, G. N., & Crable, R. (1988). Definitional hegemony as a public relations strategy: The rhetoric of nuclear power after Three Mile Island. *Central States Speech Journal, 39*, 134–145.

Dionisopolous, G. N., & Vibbert, S. L. (1988). CBS vs Mobil Oil: Charges of creative bookkeeping. In H. R. Ryan (Ed.), *Oratorical encounters: Selected studies and sources of 20th century political accusation and apologies* (pp. 214–252). Westport, CT: Greenwood Press.

Druckenmiller, B. (1993, August). Crises provide insights on image. *Business Marketing, 78(8)*,40.

Dunn, D. & Cody, M.J. (2000). Account credibility and public image: Excuses, justifications, denials, and sexual harassment. *Communication Monographs, 67,* 4, 372–391.

Egelhoff, W. G., & Sen, F. (1992). An information-processing model of crisis management. *Management Communication Quarterly, 5*, 443–484.

Fearn-Banks, K. (1996). *Crisis communications: A casebook approach.* Mahwah, NJ: Lawrence Erlbaum Associates.

Fediuk, T. A. (1999). *Corrective action and concern during an accident: An analysis of responses communicated in a crisis situation.* Unpublished master's thesis, Illinois State University, Normal, IL.

Fitzpatrick, K. R. (1995, Summer). Ten guidelines for reducing legal risks in crisis management. *Public Relations Quarterly, 40* (2), 33–38.

Fitzpatrick, K. R., & Rubin, M. S. (1995). Public relations vs. legal strategies in organizational crisis decisions. *Public Relations Review, 21*(1), 21–33.

Garvin, A. P. (1996). *The art of being well informed.* Garden City Park, NY: Avery.

Geddes, D., & Linnehan, F. (1996). Exploring the dimensionality of positive and negative performance feedback. *Communication Quarterly, 44*, 326–344.

Gonzalez-Herrero, A., & Pratt, C. B. (1996). An integrated symmetrical model of crisis-communications management. *Journal of Public Relations Research, 8*(2), 79–106.

Griffin, M., Babin, B. J., & Attaway, J. S. (1991). An empirical investigation of the impact of negative public publicity on consumer attitudes and intentions. *Advances in Consumer Research, 19*, 870–877.

Hallahan, K. (1999). Seven models of framing: Implications for public relations. *Journal of Public Relations Research, 11(3)*, 205–242.

Hearit, K. M. (1994, Summer). Apologies and public relations crises at Chrysler, Toshiba, and Volvo. *Public Relations Review, 20(2)*, 113–125.

Hearit, K. M. (1995a). "Mistakes were made": Organizations, apologia, and crises of social legitimacy. *Communication Studies, 46*, 1–17.

Hearit, K. M. (1995b). From "we didn't do it" to "it's not our fault": The use of apologia in public relations crises. In W. N. Elwood (Ed.), *Public relations inquiry as rhetorical criticism: Case studies of corporate discourse and social influence.* Westport, CT: Praeger.

Hearit, K. M. (1996, Fall). The use of counter-attack in apologetic public relations crises: The case of General Motors vs. *Dateline NBC. Public Relations Review, 22(3)*, 233–248.

Heath, R. L. (1994). *Management of corporate communication: From interpersonal contacts to external affairs.* Hillsdale, NJ: Lawrence Erlbaum Associates.

Heath, R. L. (1997). *Strategic issues management: Organizations and public policy challenges.* Thousand Oaks, CA: Sage.

Hobbs, J. D. (1995). Treachery by any other name: A case study of the Toshiba public relations crisis. *Management Communication Quarterly, 8*, 323–346.

Ice, R. (1991). Corporate publics and rhetorical strategies: The case of Union Carbide's Bhopal crisis. *Management Communication Quarterly, 4*, 341–362.

Iyengar, S., & Kinder, D. R. (1987). *News that matters: Television and American opinion.* Chicago: University of Chicago Press.

Kaufmann, J. B., Kesner, I. F., & Hazen, T. L. (1994, July/August). The myth of full disclosure: A look at organizational communications during crises. *Business Horizons, 37*, 29–39.

Kempner, M. W. (March 1995). Reputation management: How to handle the media during a crisis. *Risk Management, 42(3)*, 43–47.

Kruse, N. W. (1981). Apologia in team sport. *Quarterly Journal of Speech, 67*, 273–283.

Lerbinger, O. (1997). *The crisis manager: Facing risk and responsibility.* Mahwah, NJ: Lawrence Erlbaum Associates.

Lukaszewski, J. E. (1997, Fall). Establishing individual and corporate crisis communication standards: The principles and protocols. *Public Relations Quarterly, 42*, 7–14.

Marcus, A. A., & Goodman, R. S. (1991). Victims and shareholders: The dilemmas of presenting corporate policy during a crisis. *Academy of Management Journal, 34*, 281–305.

Martinelli, K. A., & Briggs, W. (1998). Integrating public relations and legal responses during a crisis: The case of Odwalla. *Public Relations Review, 24*, 443–457.

Maynard, R. (1993, December). Handling a crisis effectively. *Nation's Business*, 54–55.

McCroskey, J. C. (1997). *An introduction to rhetorical communication* (7th ed.). Boston: Allyn and Bacon.

McLauglin, J. C., Cody, M. J., & O'Hair, H. D. (1983). The management of failure events: Some contextual determinants of accounting behavior. *Human Communication Research, 9*, 208–224.

Mitchell, T. H. (1986, Autumn). Coping with a corporate crisis. *Canadian Business Review, 13*, 17–20.

Mitroff, I. I. (1988, Winter). Crisis management: Cutting through the confusion. *Sloan Management Review, 29*, 15–20.

Pan, Z., & Kosicki, G. M. (1993). Framing analysis: An approach to discourse. *Political Communication, 10,* 55–75.

Pauchant, T. C., & Mitroff, I. I. (1992). *Transforming the crisis-prone organization: Preventing individual, organizational, and environmental tragedies.* San Francisco: Jossey-Bass.

Ryan, H. R. (1982). Kategoria and apologia: On their rhetorical criticism as a speech set. *Quarterly Journal of Speech, 68,* 254–261.

Seitel, F. P. (1983, May). 10 myths of handling bad news. *Bank Marketing, 15,* 12–14.

Sellnow, T. L., Ulmer, R. R., & Snider, M. (1998). The compatibility of corrective action in organizational crisis communication. *Communication Quarterly, 46,* 60–74.

Sen. F., & Egelhoff, W. G. (1991, Spring). Six years and counting: Leaning from crisis management at Bhopal. *Public Relations Review, 17*(1), 69–83.

Sharkey, W. F., & Stafford, L. (1990). Responses to embarrassment. *Human Communication Research, 17,* 315–342.

Siomkos, G. & Shrivastava, P. (1993). Responding to product liability crises. *Long Range Planning, 26*(5), 72–79.

Sturges, D. L. (1994). Communicating through crisis: A strategy for organizational survival. *Management Communication Quarterly, 7*(3), 297–316.

Trahan, J. V. III. (1993, Summer). Media relations in the eye of the storm. *Public Relations Quarterly, 38*(2), 31–33.

Tyler, L. (1997). Liability means never being able to say you're sorry: Corporate guilt, legal constraints, and defensiveness in corporate communication. *Management Communication Quarterly, 11*(1), 51–73.

Ulmer, R. R., & Sellnow, T. L. Strategic ambiguity and the ethic or significant choice in the tobacco industry's crisis communication. *Communication Studies, 48,* 215–233.

Ware, B. L., & Linkugel, W. A. (1973). They spoke in defense of themselves: On the generic criticism of apologia. *Quarterly Journal of Speech, 59,* 273–283.

Wilson, S., & Patterson, B. (1987, November). When the news hits the fan. *Business Marketing, 72,* 92–94.

Toward a Theory of Public Relations Competence

Vincent Hazleton
Radford University

No one would disagree with the observation that the quality of public relations varies widely. How and why such variances occur are fundamental theoretic questions for public relations. This essay proposes a theory of public relations competence to account for such variances. *Competence* is a synonym for *quality*. The theory is different from other theories of public relations in several significant and beneficial ways. First, the theory considers the potential for a variety of outcomes from public relations activities. Second, the theory recognizes publics as active participants in the public relations process. And finally, the theory recognizes context as a central feature of public relations.

It is somewhat ironic that a field like public relations—which is totally consumed by questions of competence in its daily practice—has not addressed the issue systematically. Many PR writers have, of course, discussed issues of competence, but they have not done so in any systematic fashion. They have discussed one aspect of competence or another, one effect of a lack of competence or another, one way to achieve competence or another. The Excellence

Theory, for example, is concerned with competence from a source perspective and deals with communication balance. However, it does not equally privilege publics as actors in the public relations process. Numerous authors have written about the characteristics of effective tactical practices such as news releases or events. However, in spite of some excellent work sponsored by the Institute for Public Relations Research in recent years, these writers have generally neglected issues of strategic appropriateness.

This chapter seeks to attain three goals. First, it develops and presents the essential elements of the theory through a mapping or modeling process useful in theory development. Second, it reports empirical data that partially test the viability of the proposed theory and lead to a clearer understanding of the uniqueness of the new theory. Finally, it presents a discussion of the implications of the theory for both practice and future research.

The theory of public relations competence is developed from and grounded in theories of interpersonal or communication competence (McCroskey, 1982, 1984; Ruben, Martin, Bruning, & Powers, 1993; Spitzberg and Cupach, 1983; Wieman, 1977). Public relations are substantively different from interpersonal relations. However, theories of interpersonal competence provide an analogic structure from which a theory of public relations competence may be developed. Hawes (1975) defines models as analogues, well-developed analogies.

> Given two objects or processes, which are dissimilar in many respects, one is an analogue of the other to the extent that the physical or logical structure of one re-presents the physical or logical structure of the other. It is the identification of the significant structural and/or functional similarities, ones which generate new insights and questions, that is the challenge in the art of model building. (p. 110)

The developing of theories through analogues involves a process that Hawes (1975) describes as *mapping*. The substance (conceptual material) of the analogue, the theory to be modeled, must be stripped away, leaving only its structure. The mapping process involves projecting the substance of the less developed theory onto the structure of the more developed theory. What is important is that the process is not one of simply using the old theory. The substance of the new theory is in fact different from the substance of the old theory. In the present case, the substance of public relations is projected onto the structure of a theory of interpersonal communication competence (Spitzberg & Cupach, 1984), producing a new theory of public relations.

The choice of this theory of interpersonal communication competence is neither random nor objective. Cupach was a colleague of mine at Illinois State University between 1980 and 1993, and we cooperated on several projects using this theory of interpersonal competence (Hazleton & Cupach, 1986; Hazleton, Cupach, & Canary, 1987). In fact, we discussed on numerous occasions the potential application of the theory to the study of public relations, and particularly the potential of this theory to expand our understanding of public relations roles. Rather than simply observing that there are managers and technicians, the theory of public relations competence may allow us to understand why some people are better at performing public relations roles than others, and to understand why and how individuals make the transition from technical to managerial roles. If the theory of public relations competence is viable and useful, much is owed to Bill Cupach. If it is not viable and useful, the fault is all mine.

INTERPERSONAL COMPETENCE ASSUMPTIONS

The model of interpersonal competence is grounded in seven assumptions identified by Spitzberg and Cupach. They are: (1) Competence is perceived appropriateness and effectiveness; (2) competence is contextual; (3) competence is a matter of degree; (4) competence is both molar and molecular; (5) competent communication is functional; (6) competence is an interdependent process; and (7) competence is an interpersonal impression. From these assumptions a model consisting of five components is generated. The components are: (1) communicator knowledge; (2) communicator skill; (3) communicator motivation; (4) outcomes; and (5) context. Each of these elements is explained in more detail next.

Competence is perceived appropriateness and effectiveness. This assumption is grounded in the common sense observation that it is possible to be appropriate without being effective and possible to be effective without being appropriate. In this sense appropriateness references the expectations of other interactants in a situation that constitute "norms" of behavior. Effectiveness refers to the explicit goals or needs of an interactant.

Competence is contextual. Research has shown that context or "situation" is a construct of central importance in the explanation of social behavior (Argyle, Furnham & Graham, 1981; Forgas, 1979; Hazleton, Cupach & Canary, 1987). Situational variables significantly influence the selection of communication strategies (see Lustig & King, 1980; McLaughlin, Cody & Robey, 1980; Miller, Boster, Roloff & Seibold, 1977; Roloff & Barnicott, 1978), as well as the standards for effectiveness of communication strategies (Spitzburg & Cupach, 1984). Communication strategies are enacted to accomplish specific objectives relevant to specific situations; therefore, strategies are best conceived as situational constructs.

Competence is a matter of degree. Judgments of appropriateness and effectiveness may be arrayed along a continuum. Competence does not represent a dichotomous judgment. Individuals and organizations may be more or less competent. In the same sense, observers *with* different criteria or expectations may judge or rate an identical performance differently.

Competence is both molar and molecular. Judgements of competence may be applied to single episodes or behaviors, and they may also reflect global judgments of multiple episodes or clusters of behavior. Conceptualizations of competence, as general phenomena tend to focus on adaptability as a central definitional component. Competence is an ability to adapt to a variety of different situations or changes in environmental conditions successfully. Underlying this conceptualization of competence as adaptability is the idea of a behavioral or strategic repertoire, which is situationally effective.

Competent communication is functional. People "do" things through communication. Functional analysis of communication can provide meaningful explanations of the relationships among source (goals), message (symbols), and receiver (effects).

Competence is an interdependent process. According to Harris (1993), identifying communication as a process is one of the most important additions to communication theory in the past 20 years. The widely recognized interactional model of communication defines *communication* as a process of reciprocal message exchange between a source and a receiver. Goals of the source, messages, and expectations of receivers are all relevant to judgements of competence. Competence exists only within the context of relationships. Wieman (1977) observed that individuals successful in accomplishing personal goals could be "incompetent in an interpersonal sense if such effectiveness precludes the possibility of others accomplishing their goals" (p. 196).

Competence is an interpersonal impression. Competence is dynamic and changes from moment to moment. It is a judgment made by both observers and participants in interaction. Behavior is not objectively appropriate or effective. Communication and consequently meanings are learned. As Spitzberg and Cupach (1984) note, "If it is possible for a given behavior to be perceived as competent in one context and incompetent in another, then the ability to perform the behavior does not seem to be the source of competence" (pp. 116–117).

THE MODEL OF INTERPERSONAL COMPETENCE

From the assumptions mentioned earlier, a model of interpersonal competence is generated. The first four components of the model are specific to the communicators. First, competent communicators must possess adequate *knowledge* about interactants and contexts to behave strategically. The information that people possess, its organization, and its accessibility are factors with the potential to directly influence behavior. Differences between specific and general forms of knowledge may account for some variation in competence across situations.

Second, competent communicators must possess *skill* at enacting selected interpersonal behaviors and managing interaction. Skill references a potential for performance: what a communicator can do. Experience and natural attributes both may enhance skilled performance. Physical attraction, for example, may distract receivers from aspects of performance that are less competent.

Third, competent communicators must possess *motivation* to use knowledge and skills effectively. At the interpersonal level, motivations may be expressed simply as approachavoidance behavior. Alternative conceptualizations grounded in physiology and psychology include anxiety and arousal.

The fourth component, *outcomes*, clearly references concepts of appropriateness and effectiveness. Although a wide array of outcomes are possible, those relevant to fundamental needs and relationships seem most appropriate. Each participant in interaction brings these four components to the process.

Context, the final element in the model, has been discussed in some detail earlier. Rather than as objective features of situations, contemporary approaches to context conceptualize it as "subjective perceptions of inhabitants." Cultural and social norms as well as specific experiences with communicators constrain and influence interpretations of behavior. Whereas Spitzberg and Cupach identify six questions that reference context, suggesting an extremely complex set of alternatives, there are likely to be practical limits on the complexity of conceptualizations used by communicators. This observations tends to be supported by extant research on perceptions of context (e.g. Argyle et al., 1981; Forgas, 1979; McLaughlin et al., 1980).

With a basic understanding of communication competence in place, it is now appropriate to begin mapping. In the following section, Spitzberg's & Cupach's model of interpersonal competence is used as a model for a theory of public relations competence. The structure of the old theory serves as the model for the structure of the new theory. The substance of the new theory, public relations, is different from the substance of the model theory, interpersonal relations. The assumptions and components of the model are considered.

Mapping the Assumptions

Competent public relations is conceptualized as both effective and appropriate. This understanding of competence is derived from a consideration of public relations as a goal directed activity. Public relations, like other forms of communication, may be viewed as a goal directed activity (Hazleton & Long, 1985; 1988; Long & Hazleton, 1986). There are two fundamental types of goals underlying purposeful communication and public relations: instrumental goals and relational goals.

Instrumental goals directly reference the communicator in terms of outcomes or actions. For organizations, instrumental goals include such traditional concepts as market share, return on investment, profit, cost of sales, and employee turnover. This is the bottom line, and these types of goals are primary to the existence of organizations and therefore public relations. If organizations do not achieve reasonable instrumental goals, they cease to exist. Effectiveness is the concept that references successful achievement of instrumental goals.

Relational goals reference both the communicator and the recipient of his/her message. Grunig and Hunt (1984) defined public relations in terms of relational goals, as the management of relationships between an organization and its publics. Successful achievement of instrumental goals in a democratic society requires the cooperation of others: sales require customers; charity requires philanthropists; and service requires clients. In a democratic society communication (public relations) is the legal and ethical means for securing social cooperation (Hazleton, 1993). We judge communication in relationships using a different criterion from effectiveness. Behavior that maintains or facilitates the achievement of relational goals is judged "appropriate."

Most interactions between organizations and their publics include both instrumental and relational goals. Competent public relations practitioners successfully balance concerns for instrumental and relational goal achievement. The communication of competent public relations practitioners therefore is both effective and appropriate.

Public relations competence is contextual. Context has largely been an ignored variable in public relations research (see, for example, Botan's chapter elsewhere in this book). Grunig's excellence theory (Grunig, 1992), for example, focuses primarily on the symmetrical and asymmetrical motivations of organizations and public relations strategies to explain effectiveness. In contrast, a more comprehensive model proposed by Hazleton and Long (Hazleton, 1992; Hazleton and long, 1985, 1988; Long and Hazleton, 1987) clearly privileges contextual features. Grounded in systems theory, the Hazleton and Long model proposes that environmental factors, as well as attributes of organizations, and attributes of publics influence public relations behavior. Specifically, Hazleton (1992) argues that characteristics of messages and attributes of publics are important factors in the use of communication strategies by organizations and the effectiveness of those strategies in achieving organizational goals.

A study by Page and Hazleton (1999) demonstrates an empirical relationship between contextual variables and frequency of public relations strategy use and public relations strategy effectiveness. Four variables from Hazleton and Long's Public Relations Process Model accounted for most of the significant relationships in their data: (1) The extent to which publics recognized the existence of a problem; (2) The extent to which publics saw the problem the same way as the respondents' organization; (3) The perceived level of information seeking activity by target publics; and (4) perceived goal compatibility between target publics and respondents organizations. More recently, Werder (2005) replicated these findings.

Goal compatibility is the extent to which the goals or objectives of an individual are similar to and coincide with the goals and objectives of another individual. The lack of similar goals, or goal incompatibility, has been identified as a primary characteristic of bargaining and negotiation strategies (Vasquez, 1996; Putnam & Roloff, 1992). According to Vasquez (1996), "parties in a negotiation are perceived to hold different interests or goals. Each party has the ability to constrain or prevent the other from attaining a goal. Within a framework of competition, negotiators must cooperate to reach individual goals in such a way that one party's gain is the other's loss" (p. 60).

The degree of compatibility of goals between organizations and publics has impact on determining the public relations strategy that will be most appropriate and effective in achieving organizational goals. If members of a public perceive that an organization's goals are similar to their own, they will likely be more receptive to messages from the organization. Similarly, a public may resist messages if its goals are not aligned with those of the organization. Furthermore, if a high degree of goal incompatibility exists, it may indicate the need for a bargaining strategy, which is defined by goal incompatibility.

It is clear that theories of public relations intended to predict and explain must clearly define and account for the influence of context in public relations. In public relations, context as reflected in knowledge of interactants may be both general and specific. The concepts identified by Paige and Hazleton represent general variables that may have considerable power across contexts. The concepts articulated by Coombs (1998), crisis responsibility and performance history, may in fact be specific to crisis contexts. Certainly both types of conceptualizations warrant further research.

Public relations competence is a matter of degree. As noted earlier, outcomes in relationships are seldom dichotomous. The same may be said to be true for both instrumental goals and relational goals that organizations seek to achieve. Profits and losses, market share, employee turnover, and other instrumental goals are clearly incremental. Relational goals are more difficult to measure and conceptualize, but common sense and experience suggest that we can express our evaluations of public relationships in at least ordinal terms. We can rank organizations in terms of both effectiveness and the quality of their relationships with key publics.

Public relations competence is both molar and molecular. Professionals are also capable of distinguishing between a competent instance of public relations, a molecular evaluation, and a competent public relations program, a molar evaluation. Organizations may be competent in a single instance but incompetent when programs are considered. The opposite is also true.

Understanding the relationship between molar and molecular evaluations is an important theoretical problem. How competent individual components must be and which components of performance influence molar perceptions are both significant research questions. Flexibility, or adaptability, is probably an important element in organizations' ability to be perceived as competent by multiple publics and across multiple contexts. Both general and specific knowledge components probably are important.

Competent public relations is functional. According to Hazleton (1993), public relations behavior in organizations is enacted through communication strategies designed to achieve organizational goals. Instrumental and relational goals can be influenced by public relations communications. Opportunities are exploited or missed and relationships can be enhanced or damaged through more or less competent public relations. Competent investor relations can enhance stock values and investor loyalty, such as decisions to buy or sell (Hazleton & Strough, 1997). Competent public affairs can result in a favorable policy environment and strategic alliances with government agencies.

Competent public relations is an interdependent process. Judgments of competence are based not only on the behavior of organizations being judged. Responses from targeted publics clearly influence judgements of competence. Theories of public relations must account for the relationships among source, message, and receiver and clearly acknowledge the fact that public relations, like other forms of communication, is "interactive." Comments from media or activist publics have the potential to frame or alter the meanings of carefully planned public relations activities.

Competent public relations is a social impression. Grunig (1992) neatly captured the problem of defining effectiveness in public relations by the question, "By whose criteria?" If, as we have suggested earlier, competence judgements are perceptions, then relationships and specific publics must be the meaningful unit of analysis. The same public relations activity may be judged competent by publics with compatible goals and incompetent by publics with incompatible goals. This does not imply that there are not standards or criteria that are meaningful and useful, and it is certainly not intended to imply that sender-centered models of public relations are, therefore, necessary. It merely means that we must understand how contextual aspects of relationships influence perceptions. Organizations that do not establish meaningful and positive relationships with key publics are not likely to be successful. But success is explained by the relationship, not by the behaviors that accomplish the relationship.

Mapping the Model

In the previous section, structural and content similarities between interpersonal competence and public relations competence are identified by applying seven basic assumptions to our understanding of public relations. However, there are fundamental and important differences between interpersonal communication and public relations. The unique characteristics that distinguish the new theory from the old theory are discovered in the mapping of the differences within the model. In the following sections, we recognize that public relations is frequently a collective activity characterized by the separation of strategic decision making and message production. In the interpersonal context, these activities are seldom discreet and frequently overlap, as they are the product of individuals. This leads to a linking of public relations competence to the study of public relations roles. We propose that the theory of public relations competence may invigorate the study of public relations roles by suggesting answers to unaddressed questions. We begin the process by considering the model elements.

Context for public relations has both general and specific components. Variables that reference publics and relationships between publics and communicators, such as those used by Paige and Hazleton (1999), are likely to be generalizable across a broad variety of contexts. Some aspects of context, such as "crisis responsibility" (Coombs, 1998), are context specific. Other contexts such as media relations, investor relations, public affairs, and employee relations are also likely to have specific contextual components. Contextual knowledge, general and specific, or skills essential to generate such knowledge, are necessary for competent public relations under most circumstances.

Outcomes of interest may be instrumental, relational, or both. Again, different areas of public relations may have preferences for different outcomes. Organizational image, reputation, and strategic alliances are outcomes that reference relational goals of public relations. Liability, profit, returns on investment, and productivity are outcomes that reference instrumental outcomes. Organizations that achieve their instrumental goals are effective. Appropriateness is considered a necessary condition for the achievement of relational goals.

Knowledge, skill, and motivation of interactants are primary factors influencing performance and competence judgments. However, the knowledge, skill, and motivation necessary for interpersonal competence is different from the knowledge, skill, and motivation required for public relations competence. Specifically, the message production function of public relations is different from the strategic analysis and planning function of communication. In fact, different people may perform these activities. Public relations is frequently a collective rather than an individual activity. These differences are embodied in the role approach to public relations. The message production function is the technical role, and the strategic analysis and planning function is the managerial role.

Managerial and technical public relations roles are both conceptually and empirically distinct. It seems reasonable therefore to assume that different knowledge bases, different skills, and different sources of motivation are related to competent role performance and role identification. These issues are discussed next.

Public Relations Technicians

Technicians are responsible for producing public relations messages. They write. They edit. They design graphics. They lay out and design messages consumed by publics as part of the public relations process. These tasks clearly define the skills necessary to being a competent public relations technician.

Knowledge represents an underlying conceptual framework for performance. Competent public relations technicians must possess knowledge of writing styles and forms, options and principles of layout, and design and editing styles, as well as other knowledge that facilitates message production. For example, in writing media releases and preparing media kits, public relations practitioners must know and understand the "five W's" of journalistic writing and the use of the inverted pyramid.

Motivation for technical roles is derived from the performance of the task and grounded in esthetic principle (Dozier, 1992; Dozier & Gottesman, 1982). Technicians enjoy the tasks associated with message production and judge messages as objects independent of their context.

Public Relations Managers

Public relations managers are responsible for a variety of tasks that are different from those performed by public relations technicians. Managers establish policies and are responsible for the outcomes of public relations programs. They do research and segment publics. They counsel other managers. They plan and budget public relations programs, and they sometimes supervise the work of public relations technicians.

Knowledge necessary to competently perform the managerial role is defined by role tasks. Knowledge of research methods is necessary to conduct and use research. Knowledge of management theories should be useful in performing tasks such as supervision, planning, and budgeting. Understanding of the organizational environment, what Katz and Kahn (1978) call *systemic perspective,* is necessary to successfully identifying problems and their solutions.

Skill at performing the regular tasks of public relations management is necessary to perform competently. Competent public relations managers are skilled at planning, budgeting, and motivating employees. They can estimate costs and effectively allocate resources.

Motivations for public relations managers are different from motivations for public relations technicians. Competent public relations managers enjoy managing public relations. They enjoy the intellectual challenges of planning public relations programs. They are also motivated by ethical concerns. Managers tend to view public relations as a profession based on social scientific principles, rather than as an art focused on creativity and judged by esthetic criteria. Managers believe that it is important to belong to professional organizations, and they are more likely to be loyal to their profession than to their employer.

The basic elements of a theory of public relations competence have been outlined. The theory defines competence in terms of balanced concerns for appropriateness and effectiveness. Competence is situational and tied to elements of context. Underlying both competent performance and perceptions of competence are the knowledge, skills, and motivations of practitioners. These concepts clearly have implications for increasing our understanding of public relations roles.

Hazleton and Botan (1989) identified four criteria for evaluating or comparing theories. Good theories are descriptive, promote understanding, allow for prediction and control of phenomena of interest, and are heuristic (they generate additional theory and research). The first two criteria reflect the goodness of fit between concepts and structure of the theory and the observer's experience of the phenomena of interest. Do the concepts adequately allow us to describe public relations in a satisfying way, and do the relationships between the concepts appear to reflect what we observe? The second two criteria are both tied to the ability of the initial theory to promote additional work. At this point a reader should only be able to speak to the first two criteria. The next section of this chapter reports two preliminary studies that will allow the reader to make a judgment about the theory's potential to meet the last two criteria.

STUDY 1

The first study focuses upon the development of reliable measures of public relations competence as reflected in knowledge, skill, and motivation. Second, the ability to predict public relations role identification, an outcome variable, is examined.

I am aware of no other theory that suggests why some people are managers and some people are technicians, or why some people spend more time in one role than the other. Role identification, the amount of effort or time people expend in a role, is the dependent variable in the present study. Public relations competence measured as knowledge, skill, and motivation should predict role identification. The reasoning that produces two hypotheses is presented in more detail next.

Successful performance is one aspect of behavior that facilitates role identification. People are more likely to be assigned to or to seek out roles in which they are more successful. Public relations practitioners who are more knowledgeable, more skilled, and more motivated are more likely to perform their roles more competently than public relations practitioners who are less knowledgeable, less skilled, and less motivated. Because the managerial and technical roles are different, we would expect that measures of knowledge, skill, and motivation that predict one role would not necessarily predict the other. Following this reasoning we sought to test the following two hypotheses.

H:1 *Technical skill, technical knowledge, and technical motivation will be significant predictors of technical role identification.*

H:2 *Managerial skill, managerial knowledge, and managerial motivation will be significant predictors of managerial role identification.*

Methods and Procedures

Participants in this research were a convenience sample of members of PRSA guests attending chapter meetings in Hampton Roads, VA; Roanoke, VA; Richmond, VA; Winston-Salem, NC; and Charlotte, NC; in February and March of 1996. Questionnaires with stamped and addressed return envelopes were distributed at the meetings. Respondents were asked to complete the questionnaire on site or at their convenience and return it to the authors.

Items used by Grunig and his colleagues (Grunig, 1992; Dozier, Grunig, & Grunig, 1995) in the IABC Excellence Project measured technical and managerial role identification.

The author and a graduate student developed a self-report instrument with items used to measure aspects of public relations competence (see Fig. 7.1). Competence in this study refers to measures of knowledge, skill, and motivation. Knowledge, skill and motivation measures for each role were constructed to reflect role differences observed in prior research and published discussions of technical and managerial roles. Five items each were used to measure technical knowledge, technical skill, technical motivation, managerial knowledge, and managerial skill. Eight items were used to measure managerial motivation. All items were presented in a five-point Likert format.

Results

A total of 252 questionnaires were distributed, and 122 were returned. One returned questionnaire was unusable, yielding an effective response rate of 48.01%. Response rates by site ranged from a low of 41.43% ($N = 29$) at Virginia Beach to a high of 61.54% ($N = 16$) at Winston-Salem.

Statistical tests were performed using SPSS-PC. Regression analysis was used to test hypotheses. The .05 level of significance was required to consider relationships for interpretation.

Reliability of independent and dependent variables was assessed using Cronbach's Alpha. Values obtained for independent measures were moderate to low. Measures of technical competence yielded the following alpha values: skill, .476; knowledge, .724; and motivation, .460. Measures of managerial competence yielded the following alpha values: skill, .715; knowledge, .756; and motivation, .528. The measure of technical role identification yielded an alpha value of .669. The measure of managerial role identification yielded an alpha value of .817.

Although some of the obtained reliabilities were low, a decision was made to use all the measures in subsequent analyses. Low reliability is more likely to cause Type II errors than Type I errors. Therefore, the measures were considered a conservative test of the research hypotheses.

Technical Knowledge

I understand the theory of photographic composition.
I have knowledge of the elements needed to compose an article, press release, and other materials.
I understand how to edit text.
I know graphic design and layout principles.
I understand the aesthetic composition of pieces.

Technical Skill

I am an excellent writer of articles, press releases, and other materials.
I am skilled at desktop publishing.
I follow business goals and objectives developed by management.
I am skilled at expressing my organization's responses to issues through message production.
I am excellent at adapting messages to different publics.

Technical Motivation

I enjoy working with the media.
I enjoy editing material.
There is nothing I enjoy more than crafting a public relations message.
I enjoy doing layout and design work.
I feel it is generally unethical to withhold information from media and publics.

Managerial Knowledge

I know how to evaluate survey research.
I understand concepts utilized for problem and solution identification.
I am familiar with management theories.
I understand how to scan the organizational environment.
I know how to estimate the cost and availability of resources.

Managerial Skill

I am good at identifying potential problems which my organization faces.
I am excellent at estimating resources and developing a budget for projects.
I am good at identifying solutions to problems my organizations face.
I am skilled at evaluating survey research.
I am good at segmenting publics.

Managerial Motivation

There is nothing more satisfying than planning a public relations program.
I am excited with the fulfillment of organizational goals.
I enjoy being involved in organizational politics and decision making.
It is important to belong to professional organizations such as PRSA.
I enjoy managing public relations.
It is more important to be ethical than to keep my job.
Loyalty to management is more important than protecting the "public interest."
It is more important to make management feel good than to tell them the truth.

FIG. 7.1   Items used to measure knowledge, skill, and motivation for public relations technicians and public relations managers in Study 1.

Regression analysis was used to test the hypothesis that technical skill, technical knowledge, and technical motivation are significant predictors of identification with the technical role of public relations. A regression model was developed that used all six independent variables as predictors of technical role identification. All predictors were entered into the equation simultaneously. Analysis of the data yielded an R-value of .581 ($F = 9.68$; $DF = 6$, 114; $p < .000$), indicating that the predictors accounted for 33.8% of the variance in technical role identification.

Consistent with the research hypothesis technical skill ($t = 2.48$, $p = 0.014$, $\beta = 0.371$), technical knowledge ($t = 2.40$, $p = 0.018$, $\beta = 0.2$, 40), and technical motivation ($t = 2.99$, $p = 0.003$, $\beta = 0.332$) were statistically significant predictors of technical role identification. Results indicated that managerial skill ($t = -0.15$, $p = .879$, $\beta = -0.023$), managerial knowledge ($t = -1.74$, $p = .085$, $\beta = -0.218$), and managerial motivation ($t = -0.019$, $p = .852$, $\beta = -0.019$) were not statistically significant predictors of technical role identification.

To test the hypothesis that managerial skill, managerial knowledge, and managerial motivation are significant predictors of identification with the managerial role of public relations, a regression model was developed that used all six independent variables as predictors of technical role identification. All predictors were entered into the equation simultaneously. Analysis of the data yielded an R value of 0.652 ($F = 14.03$; $DF = 6$, 114; $p < .000$), indicating that the predictors accounted for 42.5% of the variance in managerial role identification.

Results provided partial support for the research hypothesis. Managerial skill ($t = 5.12$, $p = .000$, $\beta = 0.131$) and managerial motivation ($t = 2.31$, $p = .023$, $\beta = 0.404$) were statistically significant predictors of managerial role identification. Managerial knowledge ($t = -1.03$, $p = 0.305$, $\beta = -0.224$) technical skill ($t = 0.190$, $p = .060$, $\beta = 0.4901$), technical knowledge ($t = 0.40$, $p = 0.690$, $\beta = 0.081$), and technical motivation ($t = -1.24$, $p = .216$, $\beta = -0.238$) were not statistically significant predictors of managerial role identification.

Discussion of Study 1

Two hypotheses were proposed and tested in this research project. Underlying both hypotheses is the assumption that the knowledge, skill, and motivations of public relations technicians and public relations managers are different. The first hypothesis stated that measures of technical knowledge, technical skills, and technical motivation would be statistically significant predictors of identification with the technical public relations role.

Results clearly supported the first hypothesis. Together the three variables accounted for 33.8% of the variance in respondents' identification with the technical role. As scores on the technical skills measure, the technical knowl-edge measure, and the technical motivation measure increased, scores in-creased on the technical role measure. Measures of managerial skill, man-agerial knowledge, and managerial motivation were not significant predictors of technical role identification.

Technicians are responsible for producing public relations messages. Ex-cellence and skill at desktop publishing, writing news releases, and writing brochures; knowledge of graphic design, editing, and aesthetics; and pleasure with the creative and aesthetic activities of technical tasks all were associated with increased identification with the technical role.

The second hypothesis stated that measures of managerial skill, managerial knowledge, and managerial motivation would be statistically significant pre-dictors of identification with the managerial role. Results partially supported the hypothesis. Measures of managerial skill and managerial motivation ac-counted for 42.5% of the variance in managerial role identification. Managerial knowledge was not a statistically significant predictor.

Failure of the managerial knowledge measure to predict managerial role identification is problematic. It could imply that the theory of public relations competence is not viable, but we do not feel that this is the case. Retrospec-tive examination of the items used to measure managerial knowledge led us to believe that more items directly reflecting the social scientific knowledge underlying public relations management might yield better results. This is a content validity issue, because our measure did not adequately capture the concept.

STUDY 2

The second study was designed to see if the measurement of public relations competence could be improved by adding items to the measurement instru-ment. Theoretic validity would be addressed by examining the structural rela-tionship among items in the measure to assess their goodness of fit with the theory as it was initially proposed.

Methods and Procedures

The 1999–2000 Public Relations Society of America's Register, known as *The Blue Book,* was used as the sampling frame for this study. The register lists the current members of PRSA at the time of publication. The respondents ($N = 242$) came from a sample of 710 chosen by a systematic sampling method with a random start.

Each respondent in the study was mailed a questionnaire booklet contain-ing, among other items, an expanded set of items designed to measure public relations, competence and a set of demographic questions. To test the validity

Item	Professional Skill & Knowledge	Graphic Skill & Knowledge	Semantic Skill & Knowledge	Organizational Skill & Knowledge	Technical Motivation	Professional Motivation
I understand the principles of planning and budgeting for public relations.	.724					
I know how to estimate the cost and availability of resources.	.710					
I know how to evaluate survey research.	.700					
I am excellent at estimating resources and developing a budget for projects.	.700		.351			
I am skilled at evaluating survey research.	.694					
I am good at segmenting publics.	.634					
I understand concepts utilized for identifying organizational problems and solutions to problems.	.633			.423		
I am good at identifying potential problems which my organization faces.	.620			.451		
I know how to counsel other managers concerning public relations issues.	.598		.336	.573		
I have a good understanding of communication theory.	.559					
I have a good understanding of management theory.	.553			.397		
I understand how to scan the organizational environment.	.541			.368		
I am good at running meetings.	.499			.431		
I am skilled at graphic design.		.826				
I enjoy doing layout and design work.		.777				
I know graphic design and layout principles.		.722				
I am skilled at Desktop publishing.		.685				
I am skilled at web design.		.674				
I know a lot about web page design and implementation.		.630				
I understand the aesthetic composition of graphics and text.		.617	.347			
I am an excellent photographer.		.458				.338
I understand the theory of photographic composition.		.455	.334			.362
I am an excellent writer of articles, press releases, and other materials.			.726			
I understand how to edit text.			.652			
I have knowledge of the elements needed to compose an article, press release, and other materials.			.626			

Item					
I possess a great deal of knowledge about producing public relations messages.	.570	.584	.390		
I am excellent at adapting messages to different publics.	.546	.561	.384	.351	
I enjoy editing material.		.509			
I am skilled at expressing my organization's responses to issues through message production.	.474	.504	.416		
I am excellent at performing the technical tasks of message production.		.495	.374		
I know the most important goals of my organization.		.421			
I am good at identifying solutions to problems my organization faces.	.625		.684		
I am successful at counseling other managers.	.578		.639		
I know who "the real decision makers" are in my organization.			.587		
I am good at negotiating compromises in difficult situations.	.504		.558		
I am good at getting others to see my point of view.			.539		
I know more about my organization than most other employees.			.523		
I enjoy being involved in organizational politics and decision making.			.462		
I enjoy managing public relations.	.349		.400		
There is nothing I enjoy more than crafting a public relations message.				.850	
There is nothing more satisfying than planning a public relations program.	.362			.778	
The most satisfying aspect of public relations work is producing messages.				.638	
I enjoy working with the media.				.421	
Loyalty to management is more important than protecting the "public interest."					.603
It is more important to be ethical than to keep my job.					.543
It is more important to make management feel good than to tell them the truth.					.468
I am excited with the fulfillment of organizational goals.			.381	.359	.428
I feel it is generally unethical to withhold information from media and publics.					.395
It is important to belong to professional organizations such as PRSA.					.395

FIG. 7.2 Nonorthogonal factor pattern for measures of public relations competence in Study 2. (Items with loadings of less than .33 [10% of item variance] were omitted to make the table easier to interpret. Items are interpreted in terms of their highest loadings.)

of the theory of public relations, competence data were factor analyzed to see if interpretable technical and managerial factors reflecting knowledge, skill, and motivation would emerge. Because components of knowledge and skill are likely to be moderately correlated, a nonorthogonal solution was deemed appropriate. Data were analyzed using SPSS-PC version 9. A principal components factor analysis with a promax rotation was used. Six factors were specified and examined. Items were interpreted in terms of their highest factor loading. Given this criterion, some items with lower factor loadings than others may be interpreted as loading on a factor simply because it is their highest loading, not the highest loading for the other item. This procedure places more importance on theoretic interpretability than on statistical independence. Multicollinearity is a risk in using such a procedure and correlations between factors were examined to determine whether a problem was created (see Fig. 7.3). Reliability estimates were calculated for obtained measures.

Results

Of the survey packets that were mailed to practitioners, eight were returned unopened because of errors in the address or because the organization returned the survey. After accounting for returned packets, the number of completed or partially completed questionnaires totaled 242. This resulted in an effective response rate of 35%, which was considered to be an adequate rate to proceed with the study. Because of the nature of the survey instrument, partially completed questionnaires were used in the data analysis, so the number of respondents varied for each statistical test used for data analysis.

Before beginning the analysis of the hypotheses, standard descriptive statistics were run on the data to determine the generalizability of the sample to the parent population. Of the individuals responding to the demographic portion of the questionnaire, 40.1% were male and 59.9% were female. Respondents worked for a variety of types of organizations: Trade and Professional Associations ($N = 10$, 4.1%), Not-for-profit ($N = 29$, 12%), Agencies and Firms ($N = 63, 26\%$), Corporations ($N = 52, 21.5\%$), Government ($N = 21, 8.7\%$), Education ($N = 12$, 5%), Health Care ($N = 19$, 7.9%), and Other ($N = 36$, 14.9%).

The respondents had significant experience as public relations practitioners. Years of professional experience reported by respondents ranged from 1 to 47. The average number of years of experience was 14.7 ($SD = 10.2$). The average time respondents had been with their present employer was 5.9 years ($SD = 6.75$). Almost 35% ($N = 83$) of the respondents were accredited in public relations.

Results of the factor analysis are reported in Fig. 7.2. The analysis did yield six interpretable factors; however, the factors were not as hypothesized. Cronbach's alpha was used to estimate the measurement reliability of the obtained factors. The six factors accounted for 44% of total item variance.

The first factor consisted of 13 items. Items in this factor appeared to reflect a broad range of professional skills and knowledge, ranging from research, and budgeting, to communication theory and management theory. The items appeared to reflect knowledge and skills that were general and would be useful in any organization. This factor was labeled Professional Skill & Knowledge. Cronbach's alpha for these items was .876.

The second factor consisted of nine items. The items in this factor were from the technical domain and appeared to be limited to production of graphics. It included skills such as photography, desktop publishing, and Web design. This factor was labeled Graphic Skill & Knowledge. Cronbach's alpha for these items was .842.

The third factor consisted of nine items. These items also came from the technical domain. However, the items in this factor reflected skills related to writing to produce messages. Because of the emphasis on symbolic ma-nipulation in writing, this factor was labeled Semantic Skill & Knowledge. Cronbach's alpha for these items was .719.

The fourth factor consisted of eight items. These items came from the man-agerial domain and tended to reflect knowledge and skill acquired through experience in the organization. Knowledge and skills of this type are not likely to be generalizable from organization to organization. This factor was labeled Organizational Skill and Knowledge. Cronbach's alpha for these items was .790.

The fifth factor consisted of four items. All of the items in this factor came from the technical motivation items. This factor was labeled Technical Moti-vation. The fourth item loaded weakly on the factor, and removing the item from the scale resulted in a significant improvement in the reliability estimate. Cronbach's alpha for the three items is .771.

The sixth factor consisted of six items. The items in this factor reflected ethical issues and professionalism. This factor was labeled Professional Mo-tivation. Most of the items in this factor had moderate or low loadings on the factor. Cronbach's Alpha for this factor was .427.

Correlations between the factors and reliability estimates are reported in Fig. 7.3. A nonorthogonal solution assumes the possibility of a relationship between factors. Correlations range between .002 and .60 in absolute values. The largest correlation of .60 between professional skill and knowledge and organizational skill and knowledge indicates 36% shared variance. All other correlations between factors are considerably smaller.

Discussion of Study 2

The theory of Public Relations Competence is modeled from a theory of in-terpersonal competence. At the beginning of this chapter it was claimed that

	Professional Skill & Knowledge	Organizational Skill & Knowledge	Professional Motivation	Graphic Skill & Knowledge	Semantic Skill & Knowledge	Technical Motivation
Organizational Skill & Knowledge	.60					
Professional Motivation	.232	.221				
Graphic Skill & Knowledge	.10	−.002	.049			
Semantic Skill & Knowledge	.447	.323	.140	.201		
Technical Motivation	.265	.188	.188	−.002	.295	
Reliability	.876	.790	.427	.842	.719	.77

FIG. 7.3 Pearson correlation matrix and alpha reliabilities for competence factors in Study 2.

public relationships are different from interpersonal relationships. The results of the second study demonstrate that public relations competence is different from interpersonal competence. This is in fact a good result. Our goal was to use the interpersonal theory as a map to begin an exploration of public relations. To learn that a different map is necessary helps to distinguish public relations as a unique area for communication research. We are not merely borrowing a theory. We are creating a unique theory of public relations competence.

Specifically, two differences stand out. First, it is apparent that practitioners responding to the survey items do not distinguish between knowledge and skill in the professional, graphic, semantic, or organizational context (Factors 1–4, Fig. 7.2).

Second, it is apparent that the Knowledge/Skill aspect of public relations competence is multidimensional for both the managerial role and the technical role of public relations. For the managerial role two different types of knowledge and skill emerge: professional and organizational. For the technical role two different types of knowledge and skill emerge: semantic and graphic.

That there are two technical skill/knowledge factors (graphic and semantic) is not surprising. Some technicians specialize in the design and production of graphics, whereas others write copy. A practitioner who can do both is more valuable and more competent.

One of the basic assumptions of the theory is that competence is contextual. The Organizational Skill/Knowledge factor supports and demonstrates this assumption. Competence in public relations practice is at least partly a result of organization-specific knowledge and skills. Knowing the key decision makers is probably a necessary characteristic for becoming a part of the dominant coalition in any organization. Second, specific knowledge of interpersonal style and preferences influences the potential for being appropriate and effective in interaction in all of the public relations tasks of management.

The Professional Skill/Knowledge factor reflects the general knowledge and skills that all competent practitioners must possess. Knowledge of communication and management theories, knowledge and skills related to research, and skills and knowledge related to the budgeting and allocation of resources are clearly valuable to managers. In the first study, items measuring managerial knowledge were not significant predictors of role identification. The results of the second study suggest a strong relationship between skills and knowledge. It may be that in the first study the managerial knowledge items did not contribute any unique explanatory knowledge because of shared variance with managerial skill, and therefore did not emerge as statistically significant. In the second, the number of items reflecting managerial knowledge, specifically social science of theory, was expanded. This difference may also influence results if the first study is replicated using the expanded theory.

The two motivational factors (technical and professional) conceptually appear to distinguish between technical aspects of public relations and managerial aspects of public relations. However, the failure to achieve adequate levels of measurement reliability for the Professional Motivation factor is problematic. The reason for this is not apparent at the moment, and the issue demands additional development of an appropriate measurement tool.

Although there is clearly a need to improve the measure of managerial motivation, all other factors yielded acceptable levels of reliability. Correlations between the obtained factors were also moderate to low. This suggests that most of the dimensions of competence may be theoretically as well as statistically important. Clearly, multicollinearity is not a problem.

These results are consistent with personal experience. We have all known good technicians who made poor managers. On the other hand, movement from the technical role to the managerial role may require a certain level of technical competence.

It is likely that these measures can provide researchers with useful tools to expand our understanding of public relations role performance. Specifically, the skill and knowledge factors potentially provide a framework for exploring both of the important theoretic issues identified at the beginning of this chapter. Although previous research has identified and distinguished between managerial and technical roles, little attention has been paid to variance in role performance and to the transition between roles. The theory of public relations competence provides a theoretically useful framework for addressing these issues.

CONCLUSION

In this chapter the assumptions and basic variables that define a theory of public relations competence have been articulated and modified, based on research results. In the first study, components of technical knowledge, technical skill, and technical motivation predicted identification with the technical public relations role by public relations practitioners. Components of managerial skill and motivation were significantly related to identification with the managerial role of public relations by public relations practitioners. In the second study a model emerged that combines elements of knowledge and skill, and that is itself multidimensional. Although the results do not fit the initial knowledge, skill, motivation dimensional structure based on the elements of the interpersonal theory, the results do make theoretic sense based on personal knowledge and experience in observing public relations practices.

The value and validity of any theory are rarely dependent on the results of a single research project. It is hoped that the heuristic and empirical potential of this theory is apparent, so that other researchers will explore the factors determining public relations competence and their relationships to other variables of theoretic interest.

REFERENCES

Anderson, R., & Reagan, J. (1992). Practitioner roles and uses of technology. *Journalism Quarterly, 69*(1), p. 156–165.

Argyle, M., Furnham, A. and Graham, J. A. (1981). *Social situations.* Cambridge: Cambridge University Press.

Botan, C., & Hazleton, V. (1989). The role of theory in public relations. In C. Botan & V. Hazleton (Eds.), *Public relations theory* (pp. 11–15). Hillsdales NJ: Lawrence Erlbaum Associates.

Broom, G. M., & Dozier, D. M. (1985, August). *Determinants and consequences of public relations roles.* Paper presented at the meeting of the Association for Education in Journalism and Mass Communication, Memphis.

Broom, G. M., & Dozier, D. M. (1986). Advancement for public relations role model. *Public Relations Review, 12,* 37–55.

Broom, G. M., & Smith, G. (1978, August). *Toward an understanding of public relations roles: An empirical test of five role models' impact on clients.* Paper presented at the meeting of the Association for Education in Journalism, Seattle.

Broom, G. M., & Smith, G. (1979). Testing the practitioner's impact on clients. *Public Relations Review, 5,* 47–59.

Coombs, W. T. (1998). An analytic framework for crisis situations: Better responses from a better understanding of the situation. *Journal of Public Relations Research, 10*(3), 179–193.

Culbertson, H. M. (1991). Role taking and sensitivity: Keys to playing and making public relations roles. In L. A. Grunig & J. E. Grunig (Eds.), *Public relations research annual* (vol. 3, pp. 37–65). Hillsdale, NJ: Lawrence Erlbaum Associates.

Dozier, D. M. (1983, November). *Toward a reconciliation of "role conflict" in public relations research.* Paper presented at the meeting of the Western Communication Educators Conference, Fullerton, CA.

Dozier, D. M. (1984). Program evaluation and roles of practitioners. *Public Relations Review, 10*(2), 13–21.

Dozier, D. M. (1992). The organizational roles of communications and public relations practitioners. In J. E. Grunig (Ed.), *Excellence in public relations and communication management* (pp. 327–356). Hillsdale, NJ: Lawrence Erlbaum Associates.

Dozier, D. M., & Gottesman, M. (1982, July). *Subjective dimensions of organizational roles among public relations practitioners.* Paper presented at the Association for Education in Journalism, Athens, OH.

Dozier, D. M., Grunig, L. A., & Grunig, J. E. (1995). *Manager's guide to excellence in public relations and communication management.* Hillsdale, NJ: Lawrence Erlbaum Associates.

Ferguson, M. A. (1979). *Role norms, implicit relationship attributions and organizational communication: A study of public relations practitioners.* Unpublished master's thesis, University of Wisconsin, Madison.

Forgas, J. P. (1979). *The study of interaction routines.* New York, Academic Press.

Grunig, J. E. (Ed.). (1992). *Excellence in public relations and communication management.* Hillsdale, NJ: Lawrence Erlbaum Associates.

Grunig, J. E., & Grunig, L. S. (1986, May). *Application of open systems theory to public relations: Review of program research.* Paper presented at the meeting of the International Communication Association, Chicago, IL.

Grunig, J. E., & Grunig, L. S. (1989). Toward a theory of public relations behavior in organizations: A review of program research. In J. E. Grunig and L. S. Grunig (Eds.), *Public relations research annual* (Vol. 1, pp. 27–63). Hillsdale, NJ: Lawrence Erlbaum Associates.

Grunig, J. E., & Hunt, T. (1984). *Managing public relations.* New York: Holt, Rinehart.

Harris, T. E. (1993). *Applied organizational communication: Perspectives, principles, and pragmatics.* Hillsdale, NJ: Lawrence Erlbaum Associates, Inc.

Hawes, L. C. (1975). *Pragmatics of analoguing: Theory and model construction in communication.* Reading, MA: Addison-Wesley.

Hazleton, V. (1992). "Toward a Systems Theory of Public Relations." In *Public Relations Als Wissenschaft: Grundlagen und Interdisziplinare Ansatze*, Horst Avenarius & Wolfgang Armbrecht (eds.). Westdeutscher Verlag: Berlin, 33–46.

Hazleton, V., and Botan, C. (1989). "The Role of Theory in Public Relations." In *Public Relations Theory*, Carl Botan & Vincent Hazleton (eds.). Lawrence Erlbaum Associates, Inc.: Hillsdale, N.J., 11–15.

Hazleton, V., and Cupach, W. (1986). "An Exploration of Ontological Knowledge: Communication Competence as a Function of the Ability to Describe, Predict, and Explain." *Western Journal of Speech Communication, 50,* 119–132.

Hazleton, V., and Cupach, W., and Canary, D. (1987). "Situation Perception: Interactions Between Competence and Messages," *Journal of Language and Social Psychology, 6,* 57–63.

Hazleton, V., and Strough, R. (1997) When Organizations Collide: Hostile Takeovers and Opposed Mergers as Interactive Crises. A paper presented at the annual meeting of the National Communication Association, Chicago, IL, November.

Hazleton, V. (1993). Symbolic resources: Processes in the development and use of symbolic resources. In H. Avenarius, W. Armbrecht, & U. Zabel (Eds.), *Image und PR* (pp. 87–100). Westdeutscher: Berlin.

Hazleton, V., & Cutbirth, C. (1993). Public relations in Europe: An alternative educational paradigm. *Public relations review, 19,* 187–196.

Hazleton, V. Jr., & Long, L. W. (1985, May). *The process of public relations: A model.* Paper presented to the International Communication Association, Honolulu, Hawaii.

Hazleton, V. Jr., & Long, L. W. (1988). Concepts for public relations education, research, and practice: A communication point of view. *Central states speech journal, 39,* 77–87.

Hazleton, V., & Kruckeberg, D. (1996). European public relations practice: an evolving paradigm. In H. M. Culbertson & N. Chen (Eds.), *International public relations: A comparative analysis* (pp. 367–377). Mahwah, NJ: Lawrence Erlbaum Associates.

Katz, D., & Kahn, R. (1966, 1978). *The social psychology of organizations* (1st and 2nd eds.). New York: Wiley.

Long, L., & Hazleton, V. (1987). Public relations: A theoretical and practical response. *Public Relations Review, 13*, 3–13.

Lustig, M. W., and King, S. W. (1980) The effect of communication apprehension and situation on communication strategy choice. *Human communication research, 7*, 74–82.

McCroskey, J. C. (1982) Communication competence and performance: A research and pedagogical perspective. *Communication Education, 31*, 19–32.

McCroskey, J. C. (1984). Communication: The elusive construct. In R. Bostrom (Ed.), *Competence in communication: A multidisciplinary approach.* Beverly, Hills, CA: Sage.

McLaughlin, M. L., Cody, M. J., and Robey, C. S. (1980). Situational influences on the selection of strategies to resist compliance-gaining attempts. *Human communication research, 7*, 14–36.

Miller, G., Boster, F., Roloff, M., and Seibold, D. (1977). Compliance-gaining message strategies: A typology and some findings concerning effects of situational differences. *Communication monographs, 44*, 37–51.

Page, K., and Hazleton, V. (1999). "An Empirical Analysis of Factors Influencing Public Relations Strategy Selection and Effectiveness." A paper presented at the annual meeting of the International Communication Association, San Francisco, May.

Putnam, L., and Roloff, M. E. (1992). *Communication and negotiation.* Newbury Park, CA: Sage.

Roloff, M. E., and Barnicott, E. F. (1978) The situational use of pro- and anti-social compliance gaining strategies by high and low Machiavellians. In B. D. Ruben (Ed.), *Communication yearbook 2* (pp. 193–205). Newbrunswick, NJ: Transaction Books.

Rubin, R. B., Martin, M. M., Bruning, S. S., & Powers, D. E. (1993). Test of a self-efficacy model of interpersonal communication competence. *Communication quarterly, 41*(2), 210–220.

Spitzberg, B. H., & Cupach, W. R. (1984). *Interpersonal communication competence.* Beverly Hills, CA: Sage.

Vasquez, G. (1996). Public relations as negotiation: An issue development perspective. *Journal of public relations research, 8*, 57–77.

Werder, K. P. (2005). An empirical analysis of the influence of perceived attributes of publics on public relations strategy use and effectiveness. *Journal of public relations research, 17*, 217–266.

Wieman, J. M. (1977). Explication and test of a model of communicative competence. *Human Communication Research, 3*(3), 195–213.

Grand Strategy, Strategy, and Tactics in Public Relations

Carl Botan
George Mason University

INTRODUCTION

This is chapter is not about theory in the same sense as some of the others in this book. It introduces a conceptual tool called grand strategy and provides a taxonomy of the various grand strategies (viz., organizational worldviews) that constrain and drive the publics→client→practitioner relationship. The chapter also identifies the three levels of planning and practice in public relations (grand strategy, strategy, and tactics) and how these levels are related.

Although not covered in this chapter, the model described here might also help in assessing which clients/employers are good to work for and which ones it would be wise to avoid. This model might also help in identifying and possibly resolving different assumptions made by those writing about

PR ethics, whose works are frequently incommensurate because they address various tactical, strategic, or grand strategic levels without specifying which. These authors also often fail to acknowledge their assumptions or how their work does, or does not, relate to the different levels.

The concepts discussed in this chapter are generally not new to academics or practitioners with experience in public relations, although one of the labels may be. This chapter employs the concept of grand strategy and applies it to public relations to help bring context and order to some of the widely disparate assumptions, findings, and advice in the public relations literature. To do this, the first section of the chapter explains the relationship between the idea of grand strategy and the more familiar ideas of strategy and tactics in public relations. The second section presents and discusses one possible taxonomy of grand strategies. The third section discusses the implication of these grand strategies for understanding major aspects of public relations, including publics and issues. The conclusion identifies, but does not exhaustively treat, a few of the ways this analysis might affect tactics, the conduct of campaigns, and the lives of PR practitioners.

GRAND STRATEGY—STRATEGY—TACTICS

As used in public relations the term *strategy* subsumes two distinct but overlapping concepts, grand strategy and strategy. The distinction is important because major differences underlie these two concepts. This chapter suggests that such failure to distinguish between concepts has contributed to a sometimes contradictory body of theoretic literature that has mixed disparate assumptions and levels of analysis. This first section of the chapter explains the importance of grand strategy, how it is distinct from strategy, and the relationship between grand strategy, strategy, and tactics.

Background

Strategy and tactics are deeply embedded concepts in public relations practice and scholarship. For example, the Public Relations Society of America (PRSA) has three regular publications, two of which are named *Strategist* (2005) and *Tactics* (2005).

Strategy and tactics are concepts originally developed in the military sciences, but acknowledging the military background of our terminology does not mean that public relations campaigns are in any meaningful way comparable to military campaigns. Indeed, only the most backward practitioner would suggest such a possibility.

Nevertheless, overlaying terms and their relationships from one theory or conceptual field onto another, so as to better understand a relationship under investigation, is an established theoretic practice known as analoguing. Hawes discussed analoguing at length in *Pragmatics of Analoguing* (1975, cf. pp. 7,

110–117), and Botan and Hazleton (1989) discussed its application to public relations in the first chapter of *Public Relations Theory.*

The authors of the books *Grand Strategy* (Sargeaunt & West, 1941) and *Strategy* (Hart, 1954) are among those who have distinguished between grand strategy and strategy based on the original work of Sun Tzu (500 BC/1963). For them strategy operates at the level of a campaign, whereas grand strategy operates far above the level of a campaign (or even of the whole military). *Grand strategy* involves questions of policy and planning at the highest levels, such as diplomacy and national alliances. *Strategy*, on the other hand, is a property of campaigns and is about planning and the maneuvering and allocation of resources. Sargeaunt and West explained the relationship as follows:

> We all try to keep informed on military strategy—the maneuvering of the general staff and the commanders in chief. But what of grand strategy...? This highest type of strategy emanates not from the military chiefs but from the war cabinets and their advisors, above all the Prime Minister or President. (p. vii)

In public relations the analog of the grand strategic level is organizational or even industry-level policy. The analogue of the strategic level is the campaign planning and evaluation function of public relations managers. The analogue of the tactical level is the work of public relations technicians.

Grand Strategy

Grand Strategy

Grand Strategy is the policy-level decisions an organization makes about goals, alignments, ethics, and relationship with publics and other forces in its environment.

Corporations, activist groups, and even publics have grand strategies for dealing with their environments that are analogous to, but fundamentally different from, the grand strategies of nations. For example, during the Cold War the United States had a grand strategy based on containment of Soviet influence and cooperation with several other developed countries through alliances such as NATO. This grand strategy operated far above the level of a single campaign strategy thought out by any military leader. Analogously, General Motors is a car maker with five advertising and marketing campaigns for five separate brands: Buick, Cadillac, Chevrolet, GMC, and Pontiac. The strategic marketing campaign for each of these is kept subordinate to a corporate grand strategy of different brands for different market segments, however, because corporate grand strategy operates far above the level of any one strategic marketing campaign.

Although grand strategies occur at a much higher level than do campaign strategies, what is most important is that they constrain or limit strategies. Strategic public relations decisions made to carry out the organization's grand strategies must accept certain goals and stay within certain bounds. For example, the grand strategy of General Motors limits and guides the strategies that can be used to sell each brand, and these, in turn, constrain the tactics, or specific activities, that can be used during a campaign. Public relations campaigns on behalf of one GM brand must be consistent with the organization's overall grand strategy, with, for example, Pontiac not directly competing with Cadillac for the luxury segment. Similarly, the public relations staff of the White House and the staff of Exxon-Mobil are constrained by the grand strategies of their organizations. Exxon-Mobil practitioners were no more free to admit wrongdoing after the *Exxon Valdez* oil spill than were Clinton White House practitioners during the Monica Lewinsky scandal.

Strategy

Strategy is the campaign-level decision making involving maneuvering and arranging resources and arguments to carry out organizational grand strategies.

So strategy is always constrained by grand strategy. That is, the strategic options that public relations practitioners have available for dealing with any issue are limited by the grand strategies of the organization. Adopting strategies inconsistent with the organization's grand strategic policies will not magically result in more ethical or effective public relations campaigns that change the organization. In fact, such strategies are more likely to result in a search for a new public relations practitioner. Finally, both tactics, the actual activities that comprise PR practice, and output objectives, the measurable units of work within a tactic, are similarly constrained by the strategy they are adopted to serve.

Tactics

Tactics are the specific activities and outputs through which strategies are implemented—the doing or technical aspect of public relations.

Grand strategies develop from, and with, the culture of an organization and define at least six dimensions of an organization's worldview that are critical to public relations. While other dimensions (e.g., top-level marketing strategy, mergers and acquisitions) may exist in particular organizations, the six dimensions discussed here appear to affect public relations practices in all organization. Thus, (1) organizational goals, and attitudes toward (2) change, (3) publics, (4) issues, (5) communication, and (6) public relations practitioners, define and constrain the practice of public relations in any one organization, as well as the quality of life and ethical limitations faced by practitioners. The next section of this chapter explains four generic grand strategies of organizations—intransigent, resistant, cooperative, and integrative—by providing an overview of the posture of each on these six dimensions.

GRAND STRATEGIC MODELS

Each organization develops its own unique grand strategy over time, so the number of actual grand strategies is almost infinite. However, attitudes involving the six areas important to public relations can be grouped into four archetypical grand strategies to help in understanding actual organizational grand strategies. Based on major differences in organizational goals and on attitudes toward change, publics, issues, communication, and public relations practitioners, the next section of this chapter sketches out what four generic grand strategies would look like. Identification of these generic grand strategies owes much to the earlier work of Jones and Chase (1979) and even more to that of Crable and Vibbert (1985), although both of those teams of researchers sought to address only strategic-level analysis.

Intransigent Grand Strategy

An intransigent view would be rare in organizations where leaders have any formal training. However, parts of it show up in a surprising number of individual organizational grand strategies. An *intransigent grand strategy* assumes that the group or organization can be autonomous and should seek to impose its decisions on the environment, even to conquer part of what is assumed to be a fundamentally hostile environment. The term *reactive* has been used to describe a similar attitude toward a single issue; for example, when an organization says, "let's stonewall this issue" (Jones & Chase, 1979, p. 16). The intransigent grand strategy is not just an option for handling single issues, however; it summarizes an organization's attitude toward all its relationships. Famous examples of intransigence include Enron after being caught in misleading financial statements and President Richard Nixon after the Watergate break-in was exposed.

Goal/Attitude Toward Environment

The goal of an intransigent grand strategy is to subordinate parts of the environment to the will of the organization. The aim is to "conquer," so negotiating with publics may be seen as a sign of weakness. Organizational autonomy is the highest good, and those calling for change are thought to represent outside interference in legitimate management/ownership prerogatives. Loyalty to the existing leadership and policies is the most important attribute, so partisan values (Sullivan, 1965; e.g., "my company right or wrong") are held in high esteem. Business is often seen as a contest between rival organizations to determine who is better at conquering problems, markets, and publics. When threatened, the first instinct is to, in effect, pull up the drawbridge, leaving stone walls to protect the organization, conserve its resources, and limit legal exposure. That is, the first instinct is to stop any give-and-take with elements of the environment, to shut publics out and real communication off.

In the nationally publicized case of sexual harassment at Diamond Star Motors (a joint auto manufacturing subsidiary of Mitsubishi and Chrysler), for example, the EEOC said Diamond Star "discouraged complaints and permitted retaliation against women who dared to complain [to government authorities]" (Annin & McCormick, 1997). These women were treated as if they posed a threat to the normal functioning of the company, or were disloyal. An intransigent grand strategy works from the implicit, and often even explicit, assumption that organizations make their best contribution to society by putting themselves first and beating all competitors. Whether this helps or hurts publics is irrelevant to them.

Attitude Toward Change

Intransigent organizations believe that change is bad and costs money. In addition, the need for change implies that someone in the leadership has failed in some way, so established leaders may try to block any change they do not initiate. At Diamond Star, for example, one EEOC official said, "We haven't seen evidence of real change" (*Diamond Star*, 9/29/97, p. 6). Even one Diamond Star worker, John Curtis, said, "Most people involved in the sexual harassment are still there. There's a good-old boys network" (Armour, 1998, p. A1). Those advocating change also run the risk of being seen as disloyal.

Attitude Toward Publics

Intransigent organizations treat publics as if they exist to meet the needs of the organization or are the foils of activist groups; they also view publics as dangerous. Most importantly, they believe publics have no legitimate stake in the organization except as defined by the organization and its leaders. For example, publics may be seen to have a legitimate role as customers but not as stakeholders in the environment. This view may be justified on the basis that publics do not know as many facts, or have as much experience, and are not as knowledgeable about a situation, as organizational leaders. Because these organizations believe publics lack both knowledge and any moral right to interfere, it is seen as right to limit the role of publics to the business relationship the organization wants. So, as was the case with the sexual harassment charges at Diamond Star Motors, internal and external publics, even government regulatory bodies, are viewed as troublemakers and agitators to be defeated, neutralized, or ignored.

Attitude Toward Issues

Issues are seen as impediments in an intransigent organization. They are typically seen as external assaults by a generally hostile environment. Those raising issues—particularly the media and activist publics—are defined as troublemakers and are sometimes even credited with creating issues. So it is assumed that the best way to protect the organization is to keep the media and special interest groups from getting information that could be used to interfere in the life of the organization. Publics may be seen as foils for activists and government regulators, but they are not seen as playing play a leading role in issues.

Attitude Toward Communication

Intransigent organizations believe they are already right, so the task of communication is to educate publics to that fact. This is an application of the "if you knew what I knew you'd make the same decision" assumption (Gaudino, Fritch, & Haynes, 1989). One-way campaigns often are thought to be sufficient for this purpose. In addition, since the organization is assumed to be in the right, it can justifiably withhold some critical information from publics, and even use deception occasionally.

Attitude Toward Practitioners

In an intransigent organization, public relations practitioners are technicians who are hired to use their skills to implement decisions already made by someone else. Their primary job is to explain management decisions and win people over to supporting them. These practitioners cede the authority to make decisions—including ethical judgments—to the organization's leadership. As technicians, practitioners are often restricted to lower- and middle-level positions because they carry out other people's judgments rather than having responsibility for make judgments.

How ethical a practitioner can be in an intransigent organization is entirely dependent on the ethical integrity of those making policy decisions. Practitioners often find that there is not enough opportunity for advancement, and many get tired of having to practice in ways that they believe are largely ineffective or wrong. Ironically, such ineffective practices can become a self-fulfilling prophecy, with the practitioner kept from engaging in the kinds of strategic practices that could help build valuable long-term relationships with publics, and the absence of such relationships taken as proof positive that public relations is only a technical skill.

Resistant Grand Strategy

A *resistant grand strategy* would also seek to keep the organization as free as possible from outside controls while making only the minimum changes necessary for survival. Again, the underlying goal is to defeat all competitors and challengers, but now with the fundamentally different understanding that the environment is the controlling force.

Goal/Attitude Toward Environment

A resistant grand strategy differs fundamentally from an intransigent one because intransigence is based on the assumption that the environment can or should be subordinated to the organization's needs, whereas a resistant grand strategy starts by acknowledging that the organization ultimately is subordinate to its environment. So, whereas the intransigent grand strategy seeks autonomy from the environment, except when advancing its own interests, the resistant grand strategy accepts that the organization is always interdependent with its environment. Issues are viewed as problems that are part of the cost of doing business in a particular environment.

For those familiar with systems theory, the difference between the intransigent and resistant grand strategies is easy to understand. Intransigent organizations would like to see themselves as a closed system—except for getting what they want out of the environment. Those with a resistant strategy accept the fact that they are part of an open system.

Attitude Toward Change

The need for change is not necessarily seen as reflecting failure in a resistant organization, but change is expensive and disruptive and should be avoided whenever possible. In other words, an organization with a resistant grand strategy knows it has to accept change, but it has to be dragged kicking and screaming into each change. It operates on a MiniMax principle in which the minimum amount of negotiation and change that publics will accept is the maximum amount that the organization will accept. These organizations often delay change as long as possible, keep it as small as possible, and try to declare it complete before it really is. For example, after the *Exxon Valdez* tanker hit a reef and spilled huge quantities of crude oil into Alaskan waters, the Exxon Corporation (which appeared to vacillate between intransigence and resistance during the matter) substantially damaged its own credibility by attempting to declare the cleanup finished before most publics thought it really was.

Publics looking in from outside cannot know what organizational leaders are thinking, so they have to watch leaders' actions and public statements. Although a resistant organization is fundamentally different from an intransigent one in its attitude toward change, it is so grudging about change that its publics often cannot see the difference. As a result, publics may end up treating a resistant organization as if it were an intransigent one. The irony comes when leaders of a resistant organization believe that they are being treated unfairly because publics, seeing any change as the result of outside pressure, give the organization little or no credit for its willingness to change or for the actual changes made. The *Exxon Valdez* spill may be an excellent example of this. Although it is true that we cannot know what was going on in the minds of corporate leaders, Exxon's behavior showed that they knew from the beginning they would have to answer to public opinion. However, Exxon appeared to be so resistant to being answerable to government bodies and publics that it may have wasted much of the cleanup money it spent. Many publics had a hard time seeing Exxon's foot-dragging as representing anything other than complete intransigence.

Attitude Toward Publics

Publics are powerful but dangerous in the eyes of a resistant organization, so publics are seen as a necessary evil, just as change is. Negotiating with publics is seen as disruptive to normal functioning and to be avoided or minimized whenever possible. The MiniMax principle holds here as well. Publics are more than just a foil, but they still are perceived to have more negative than positive potential.

Attitude Toward Issues

Issues are still impediments imposed on the organization by the environment, but they are also a normal part of the organization's environment. Even well-run organizations run into issues in the normal course of events. Issues are a problem to be gotten past. Crises can result when issues are not handled properly, but are most commonly seen as the result of meddling by activists, by the media, or by government regulators.

Attitude Toward Communication

Resistant organizations acknowledge that they need some two-way communication because feedback is important for the organization to adapt to its publics. These organizations also use communication to let publics know what the organization has done to meet their needs or to attempt to convince them to accept what the organization is willing to do. Therefore, the organization has to maintain effective channels of communication. Technical production skills are often highly valued, and Sullivan's (1965) craft values are often important.

Attitude Toward Practitioners

In the resistant grand strategy, as in the intransigent, practitioners are basically perceived as technicians who must possess the communication skills necessary to carry out decisions made by others. Practitioners are rarely involved at the organizational planning level. When part of marketing, or some other department, practitioners may have a chance for significant promotion, but the practice itself is typically a technical-level skill rather than a strategic one. It is appropriate to advise individual practitioners in resistant organizations to be more proactive, more strategic, and more ethical, and to work their way into the dominant coalition of the organization. But doing so, and affecting substantive ethical or grand strategic change by doing so, is often wishful thinking. Practitioners wishing to be more proactive and ethical might better invest their efforts in finding a different kind of organization to work for, although in some rare cases a single highly ethical and professional practitioner can succeed in altering the behavior of a whole organization.

Cooperative Grand Strategy

An organization using a *cooperative grand strategy* believes being a constructive part of its environment is both an opportunity and a duty, and that it has responsibilities that go beyond financial matters. Ongoing relationships with all publics are thought to be desirable, and change is accepted as natural.

Goal/Attitude Toward Environment

The goal of a cooperative grand strategy is shaping issues to meet the needs of the organization, particularly to make them less dangerous to the organization. Some authors (e.g., Crable & Vibbert, 1985; Jones & Chase, 1979) have labeled a similar attitude toward single issues in the public policy domain as *catalytic* or *dynamic*. Again, however, these authors discussed only a strategy for work in the domain of public policy, rather than a policy-level grand strategy. Cooperative organizations see themselves as interdependent with their environment.

Attitude Toward Change

Change is seen as a natural part of life that can sometimes even be good for the organization, but it is still essentially a negative experience that consumes already scarce organizational resources such as time and money. Because organizations are complex, a certain amount of change is to be expected, and it does not necessarily reflect failure on anyone's part. Skill at managing change is a valuable asset for upper managers and leaders, who are unlikely to get to those positions without it.

Attitude Toward Publics

In a cooperative grand strategy, publics are seen as a constructive force, so changing the organization to meet their needs is often good. In addition, publics are seen to have a legitimate stake in the behaviors of the organization, so they have a right to an opinion and to a wide array of information. They also have a right to attempt to implement both public and corporate policy in support of their views.

Attitude Toward Issues

Issues are seen as how publics inform organizations about necessary changes. Being attentive and doing issues research are key to making sure that small issues do not ripen into full-blown crises.

Attitude Toward Communication

Internal and external communication is the lifeblood of the cooperative organization, and two-way communication is thought to be the best. Management is often defined as a communication activity; skill as a communicator is seen as a prerequisite for leadership positions. Either party in the relationship can initiate communication. Dialogic skill is essential for any position involving public or media contact.

Attitude Toward Practitioners

In cooperative organizations, helping monitor and improve relationships between the organization and its publics is one of the primary jobs of leaders and members, including the CEO or president, so the practice of public relations is usually respected. The information public relations practitioners collect from publics plays an important strategic role in the organization, whether or not a public relations person takes it to the main table themselves. Public relations practitioners are seen as professionals in a cooperative organization rather than just technicians, so they are expected to have their own ethical standards and be able to make their own ethical decisions, or even to advise on ethical matters.

As communication specialists, practitioners are involved in one of the principal functions of the organization and thus may have a visible career path into the highest levels of the organization. In a cooperative organization, public relations may either be an independent department or be housed with other communication specialties in a department of corporate communication or some similar structure. A CCO (Chief Communication Officer) may be responsible for all internal and external communication and is part of high-level decision making.

Integrative Grand Strategy

An *integrative grand strategy* seeks to integrate the organization into an ever-evolving web of relationships in order to make the organization fully a part of its environment. Unlike the intransigent, resistant, or cooperative grand strategies, this view sees change as fundamentally positive and even something to be sought.

Goal/Attitude Toward Environment

The organization with an integrative grand strategy neither seeks to subordinate the environment to its will nor thinks of itself as just subordinate. Rather, it sees itself as an integral part of the environment, and its goal is to maintain that status. Other parts of the environment are understood to have legitimate interests and agendas of their own, and the organization seeks to integrate its goals with others so that stable relationships result. The primary means of achieving this goal is negotiating relationships that involve an exchange of persuasive or informational messages. An integrative organization accepts that it can best be integrated with its environment by opening itself to persuasive messages. Ethical and mutual persuasion is the key to an integrative grand strategy.

Attitude Toward Change

Whereas intransigent organizations try to put up a stonewall against all changes, resistant organizations have to be dragged kicking and screaming into each major change, and even cooperative organizations sea change as a painful and often unpleasant experience, integrative organizations believe change is "our element." The ability to change quickly and efficiently is seen as a major organizational strength. The organization expects to survive and flourish because it is better than others at identifying the need for change, and better at changing.

Organizations with an integrative grand strategy frequently are attracted to some of the tenets of management philosophies, such as Total Quality Management (TQM). TQM and various related management philosophies, including Continuous Quality Improvement, have their share of downsides so they should not be thought of as a panacea for public relations practitioners, but they do tend to have a healthy attitude toward change and in that sense are consistent with an integrative grand strategy.

Attitude Toward Publics

Publics play the central role in defining issues (Crable & Vibbert, 1985) and are themselves products of the process of communication (Botan &

Soto, 1998), so from an interpretive perspective, they cannot be external or a threat. Rather, the existence of publics is a normal part of the functioning of the public relations environment of which the organization is a part. In an integrative approach, publics and the organization mutually create and recreate one another. Thus, they are in every situation together, and negotiating with publics is seen as a little like working things out with close acquaintances. This position is a reversal of the intransigent grand strategy. From this perspective, publics are best understood not as static groups that react to organizational actions but as an ongoing process of agreement on how to interpret a phenomenon or situation (Botan & Soto, 1998).

Attitude Toward Issues

Integrative organizations see the development of issues as the result of the communication process. In other words, issues are the result of ongoing communication within and between publics. What an issue is and how it will affect the organization are determined by ongoing communication, which the organization can and should be a part of, but which it cannot and should not try to unilaterally control. As explained in the next section, an issue becomes an issue when significant publics say it is (Crable & Vibbert, 1985).

Attitude Toward Communication

From an integrative perspective, an organization is literally a product of the process of communication (as are publics). From a Structural-Functionalism perspective (Farace, Monge, & Russell, 1977), it is possible to have buildings, trucks, cash registers, shelves, bank accounts, incorporation papers, and so on, but still not have an organization. An organization comes into existence only when some communication takes place so that there can be shared goals, specialization of labor, and coordination of work. In an integrative organization, no one sees communication as a mere support or technical function. Communicators skilled in strategic communication and issues management are seen as core leaders of the organization.

Attitude Toward Practitioners

Practitioners are part of the central communication function of the integrative organization, so they can be a part of the strategic leadership function as well. The idea that the communication and executive functions are inseparable is a hallmark of modern management philosophies, but it is not at all new. For example, more than 60 years ago Chester Barnard, then President of AT&T, said, "The first executive function is to develop and maintain a system of communication. This involves both a scheme of organization and an executive personnel" (1938, pp. 271). In such organizations, public relations practitioners have an opportunity to play the role of strategic advisors because the organization is fully aware of the importance of negotiating relations with both internal and external audiences.

As summarized in Fig. 8.1, the four grand strategies discussed here are archetypes. Although real organizations do not precisely fit these archetypes, they do often reflect the main characteristics of a single grand strategy or two, so they can very loosely be described as, for example, resistant or cooperative/integrative. Because of how important publics and issues are to these grand strategies, the next section examines these two concepts in more depth.

PUBLICS AND ISSUES

All the dimensions of grand strategies just discussed are important to understanding public relations strategy and tactics in a particular organization but two, publics and issues, are most important because they are so central to public relations and to the strategies and tactics that can be employed in any given situation. To better see how attitudes toward publics and issues constrain strategies and tactics, this section further develops those two concepts and how they affect strategy and tactics.

Publics

Dewey (1927) said that a *public* is a group of people who see they have a common interest with respect to an organization and that "endeavor[s] to act through suitable structures and thus to organize itself for oversight and regulation" (p. 29). Dewey's definition of a public was pretty far ahead of its time for 1927, or for today. He thought publics "endeavor to act . . . to organize . . . for oversight and regulation," and he was on a track consistent with Cooperative or Integrative organizations.

By saying that publics "endeavor" to do something, Dewey adopted a humanistic perspective and acknowledged that publics have a kind of will of their own—that they are more than just reactive but rather seek to one degree or another to take charge of their destinies. Whether publics are merely reactive organisms, waiting for the organization to act toward them, or have some self-directing capacity of their own is the most important single issue for any organization to resolve about its view of publics. Those that view publics as passive and reactive—as convenient foils for activist groups and the media— have taken an important step toward adopting an intransigent or resistant grand strategy.

Botan and Soto (1998) suggested a view of publics that is more consistent with Dewey and more consistent with integrative and cooperative grand strategies when they said, "we can best understand a public as an ongoing process of agreement upon an interpretation, and that during this process a public

	Goal	Change	Publics	Issues	Communication	Practitioners
Intransigent	**Control** – Resist outside interference – Adapt environment to the organization – Stonewalling	**Negative** – Bad—to be avoided – Costs money – Any implies leadership failure	**Use** – Exist to meet org's needs – No legitimate "stake" beyond org's wishes	**Defensive** – Result of wrongful external attacks – Illegitimate tries at impeding right to manage	**One-Way** – Org is right – "Educate" publics – Withhold info for control	**Technicians** – Technicians only explain mgmt. decisions – Obey org's ethics – Loyalty primary
Resistant	**Control** – Avoid/resist outside influence – Adapt organization to environment	**Negative** – Bad/costly – May imply failure – Foot dragging – MiniMax Principle	**Use** – Powerful but dangerous – Appeasing is necessary evil	**Avoid/Solve** – Result of external interference – Natural occurrence – Get away as soon as possible	**Modified One-Way** – Mostly one-way – Some two-way for adaptation – Media work key	**Technicians** – Explain decisions – Obey org's ethics – Limited chance to influence org's values
Cooperative	**Share** – Interdependent w/ environment – Shape issues to org – "Enlightened" mgmt.	**Negative** – Natural but painful – Change managers valued for reducing pain	**Separate/Equal** – Constructive force – Legitimate stakeholders	**Solve** – Defined by publics – Part of org life – Avoid when can but learn from	**Lifeblood** – Comm is lifeblood of org – Dialog important	**Com Managers** – CEO is top one – Professionals with own skills – Strategic advisors
Integrative	**Share** – Integrate org into environment – Open to persuasive messages	**Positive** – "Our element" – Skill in change is how we beat competitors	**Together** – Legit interests & own agendas – Make org possible	**Build With** – Defined by publics – Issues = opportunity – Natural part of org life	**Produces Org** – Org is product of communication – Core function for all executives	**Strategic Team** – Internal and external advisors – Change managers – Ethics leaders

Keys: (1) *Intransigent* seeks to subordinate portions of the environment to the organization while resistant. cooperative and integrative accept that organization is subordinate to the environment so change is necessary. (2) *Resistant* seeks to avoid change so long it often appears to outsiders to be intransigent in spite of no. 1. (3) *Intransigent/resistant* believe issues are impositions from an essentially dangerous environment, *cooperative/integrative* accept that publics have legitimate agendas and define issues. (4) *Integrative* sees change as "our element" and therefore, publics and the issues they define as probable allies.

FIG. 8.1 **Summary of grand strategies.**

may well develop an interpretation that is more sophisticated, insightful, and socially linked than the understanding with which the practitioner/client started" (p. 21).

Publics, they thought, are best understood as an ongoing process rather than just an entity. It may sound strange to say a public, which we often speak of as a "thing," is really best understood as a process. But publics are engaged in a continuing process of agreeing on an interpretation. That is, whether one is a part of a public or not is determined by whether a shared interest is understood at a particular time. That interest can be objective or subjective. For example, the stockholders of a company are one of the important publics of that company because they have an objective relationship of partial ownership. Stockholders can interpret that as meaning they have something in common with other stockholders. People who sell their stock no longer belong to that public, because their objective status has changed. Stockholders are not all one public for management, however. Some interpret certain management actions one way and support the current management team, whereas others interpret change differently and are opposed to the current management team. This is a matter of interpreting management behavior and making choices.

Members of a pro-management public of an organization, for example, are in it because they interpret management actions or policies as in their best interest, whereas members of an antimanagement public (e.g., militant stockholders, environmental activists) are in it because they interpret the same actions as bad or ineffective. These two publics are not static but can shift and change from day to day. In fact, the process of interpreting management actions, and therefore deciding which public one belongs to, is continual. So a public is what I have called an *interpretive community* (Botan, 1992). In some cases publics even use their common understandings to organize themselves and initiate campaigns to which organizations and their practitioners respond.

One view of publics is foundational to the intransigent, and to a lesser extent the resistant, grand strategy, whereas a different view is equally foundational to the integrative or cooperative grand strategies. In any case, however, the assessment an organization has of publics is absolutely central to its grand strategy. A second assessment, what issues are, is dependent on an organization's view of publics and is equally central to its grand strategy.

Issues

This section discusses issues from an admittedly biased perspective that sees publics as both central and self-directing. So in some ways it assumes a view characteristic of cooperative and integrative organizations that might be flatly rejected in an intransigent or even resistant organization.

Although there can be numerous potential issues in any organization's environment, the organization only faces an issue when publics share the view that it needs to address something. If the public does not attach importance to a matter, it will not become an issue for the organization. This view of issues and the central role of publics in their creation is fundamentally humanistic and is the primary contribution of Crable and Vibbert (1985), who said, "an issue is created when one or more human agents attaches significance to a situation or perceived 'problem'" (p. 5).

Because publics define issues, publics play the central role in public relations. The stages through which publics move issues are important both because the idea of stages makes strategic planning possible and because some grand strategies are restricted as to which stages they can address issues in and what strategies they can use. The intransigent grand strategy, for example, is not equipped to address an issue as early in its development as the cooperative, and practitioners for an intransigent organization have far fewer strategic options available to them. This section, therefore, looks at the stages of issues.

Earlier research efforts treated issues management, and the strategic campaigns it uses, only as a management tool for protecting corporate interests and influencing the public policy process by, for example, getting a law passed or defeated. In fact, most authorities have discussed issues management only from the point of view of corporations and their influence on public policy. But such a limited view misses the fact that a consumer group can use strategic campaigns to influence IBM or Microsoft just as surely as corporations can use campaigns to influence federal legislation or the perceptions of quality in their products. No matter who takes the initiative, the key step in any campaign is identifying the issues on which publics share a view among themselves.

Such issues are not ready for resolution at all times. Indeed, the various stages in the life cycle of an issue, discussed later, emphasize that an issue is ready for decision at only a few points in its life cycle and that not all issues ever evolve to such a decision point. For example, the manufacturing of tobacco products went along for a century or more without becoming a public issue. In the 1990s, however, manufacturing and selling cigarettes became a big public issue, particularly when the targeted customers were teenagers. The reader would be right to point out that a number of consumer advocates, state attorneys general, and public health advocates worked long and hard through their own public relations campaigns to make selling tobacco into an issue embraced by significant publics. But it was not until major publics decided to attach significance to the question that it became a major issue. The same analysis could be applied to car safety, where antilock brakes and air bags were not major issues until large numbers of potential buyers decided they would be. Drivers have been driving drunk and causing accidents almost since there have been cars but it has been within the lifetime of the reader that drunk driving has stopped being handled with a wink and a nod and has been transformed by publics into a major issue.

Life Cycle of an Issue

Whether a matter will be a widely embraced issue is not an all-or-nothing proposition. Issues are not absent one moment and then spring into life full-blown the next. Rather, they go through a fairly predictable cycle of development. The existence of a life cycle for issues is crucial to the idea of strategic campaigns because if issues were random in their development, it would not be possible to approach them strategically. If, on the other hand, issues do have a life cycle made up of the various stages, it is possible to plan to employ different strategies to address them at different stages, either before or after they become widely embraced. Finally, that there is a normal set of developmental stages does not mean that every issue goes through all of them. Sometimes an issue is resolved or fades before becoming fully developed.

Up the Time Stream

When issues do move through several stages, they can be thought of as moving along a continuum that might be visualized as moving along, or down, a time stream. If so, the sine qua non of strategic issues management would be to move up that time stream as far as possible. This strategic option is all but foreclosed to the intransigent and resistant grand strategies because of their understanding of the role of publics in issues.

When an issue is identified early in its development, so that it has not yet gotten exposure in the media or been embraced by important publics, the sides may not have their feet set in concrete with hard-and-fast positions to which they are committed. Thus, many strategic options are likely to be available. The inverse is that the further down the time stream an issue gets, which the intransigent and resistant grand strategies play into, the fewer the strategic options available. Sometimes, however, an issue has to develop to a certain stage before it can be resolved.

Crable and Vibbert (1985) said that public policy issues go through five stages: potential, imminent, current, critical, and dormant. The stages of this life cycle are defined by which publics, and how many, decide to attach significance to an issue. As indicated earlier, this is a fundamentally humanistic approach because it acknowledges human will and decision making on the part of publics as the driving force in the development of issues.

As noted above, Crable and Vibbert's life cycle discussion was specific to public policy issue. Nevertheless, it is possible to summarize a more general five-phase life cycle for issues, while staying consistent with Crable and Vibbert's ground breaking contribution that publics play the central role in determining issues.

Preissues

Organizations exist within an environment on which they depend so most try to keep some kind of watch on their environment. This is known in public relations as *environmental scanning*. Environmental scanning is a kind of strategic research that involves watching for preissues, the trends that are "detectable changes which precede issues" (Jones & Chase, 1979, p. 11). If issues are what publics decide are important, then preissues are occurrences in the environment to which publics have not yet attached significance, but could. This is the farthest up the time stream that issues can be addressed, although they seldom are.

One reason issues typically are not addressed at the preissue stage is because there are so many. Most preissues will not develop into issues that are important to significant publics and so will not significantly affect the organization. It is, therefore, difficult to make the two critical risk assessments needed to allocate resources; the probability than a preissue will develop into a full issue, and how seriously that issue would affect the organization if it did. Organizations simply do not have the resources to assess every preissue in their environments. On the other hand, pre-issues are also often not addressed because the grand strategy of the organization dictates stonewalling until an issue has to be responded to, rather then working to influence its emergence. In the case of an extremely intransigent grand strategy, for example, the organization does not think publics have any right to an agenda of their own. Thus, the organization does not seek to engage publics about such views.

In addition, those organizations holding an intransigent grand strategy often do not have the communication links with their environment needed for early assessments (e.g., advisory councils, community involvement programs, social audits). Organizations holding intransigent or resistant views might also resist tracking preissues for other reasons, such as perceiving implicit criticism of those in authority and because openness to change is seen within the organization as indicating a lack of loyalty or not being a team player. Intransigent organizations, in particular, may assume that publics are not competent to understand the organization and its actions, and that if publics "only knew what I knew [they'd] make the same decision" (Gaudino et al., 1989). In other words, for these organizations, environmental scanning could only help to identify unqualified people making unqualified assessments about the organization.

Potential Issues

Preissues become potential issues when some group or important individuals attach significance to them. Although taking its name for Crable and Vibbert's (1985) potential stage, both the potential and imminent stages of issues for those authors fall into this stage. Here, the issue is not broadly known and most strategic options remain open. There are significantly fewer potential issues than preissues, although still too many for most organizations to attend to them all. Little damage has typically been done by this stage, although there are exceptions, and the parties often are not constrained by public positions they have taken. For example, a corporation facing a developing issue may be able to resolve the matter quietly by negotiating to change its behavior if its grand strategy permits such negotiations.

The potential stage can be fairly long for some issues and may contain several substages, depending on the field and the particular content of the issue. For example, issues of public health may have avoidance/rejection and outrage substages that call for very different strategies: education campaigns might be used for the former, and more persuasive or soothing strategies for the latter.

Organizations with an intransigent grand strategy may reject addressing an issue at the potential stages almost as much as at the preissue stage. Organizations with a merely resistant grand strategy may be willing to begin addressing issues at this stage, however, based on the realization that they are ultimately subordinate to their environments.

Public Issues

Once a developing issue is endorsed by major publics, such as consumer, environmental, or regulatory groups, the issue may acquire legitimacy in the eyes of others, often mass publics. For example, if a neighborhood association decided to oppose some new construction in a neighborhood and called a large meeting of concerned citizens, with local politicians and the press included, it could create a public issue for the organization in spite of the fact that only a few people are directly involved in the issue.

When an issue becomes public, it is recognized, regardless of which grand strategy is being followed. However, those with intransigent or resistant views may still deny their role or otherwise seek to avoid responsibility. Those with more cooperative or integrative views may seek to redress the issue before it can move any further and strategic options become even more limited.

Sometimes an intransigent or resistant grand strategy seems to "work" because the issue runs its course, or fails to gain the support of major publics, without the organization ever having to accept real responsibility. Legal strategies, for example, are often resistant or intransigent in nature and are defined as having worked if the organization is not sued or found legally guilty of anything. This, of course, ignores all the public relations damage that can be done when such strategies "work." On the other hand, a cooperative or integrative grand strategy enables the use of strategies and tactics that may actually help the organization enhance its relationships with publics under the same circumstances—depending, of course, on the nature and seriousness of the issue involved.

The usual route for an issue to attain public status, according to Crable and Vibbert (1985), is through media exposure, which means that the issue has met someone's definition of newsworthiness. A reporter or editor has made a professional judgment that the issue is important enough to warrant coverage in the media. In addition, once an issue makes the news, certain legitimacy is conferred on it in the minds of mass publics: It is on their agenda. Still, an issue must be embraced by large, or opinion-leading, publics before it becomes a public issue.

When issues become public, the positions of the parties are usually firm and the number of strategic options is diminishing quickly. Public exposure creates a situation in which all parties have a lot invested. Thus they often cannot risk being seen as the loser, even by compromising. Negotiated solutions are still possible, but frequently these involve careful, even scripted, language to ensure that no party is portrayed as the loser. A good example is the settlement of well-known court cases. Notice how, even in the most widely known cases, the paying party usually insists on a clause that guilt is not being admitted so that they can save face, maintain deniability, or avoid future legal exposure.

Media coverage is not the only way a developing issue can attain public status, however. Issues can become public by conversations in a community, door-to-door campaigns, petition drives, direct mail campaigns, demonstrations, pickets, protests, and a host of other methods. These methods of moving an issue to public status often draw media coverage of their own. Thus, although it may appear that the media coverage has made the issue public, the relationship between media coverage and the public status of an issue can be quite complex.

Whether media coverage is involved or not, movement from potential to public issue status can result from conscious efforts by activist or regulatory bodies as well as by other means such as investigative reporting or blogging. For example, an environmental group's press conference to publicize a threat to the environment can be interpreted as a conscious effort to move a potential issue up to a public stage by putting it onto the public agenda.

Critical Issues

Issues reach a critical stage when, as Crable and Vibbert (1985) said, they "are at a moment of decision" (p. 6). This means that the issue is ready for resolution in the minds of most publics. A failure to move toward some kind of resolution may be seen by publics as a suspect behavior, because they are ready for something to happen. This is quite different from the public stage, where many people are aware of the issue but are not pushing for a particular resolution. By the time the critical stage is reached, there is often little time or room for negotiation. Even at this very public stage, and with publics demanding some resolution, those with intransigent grand strategies may seek to deny wrongdoing and to duck responsibility, including President Nixon during Watergate and the Enron leadership after their financial dealings were exposed. Those with a resistant grand strategy part company with them, seeking to come to terms with important publics because they recognize that, ultimately, the organization is subordinate to its environment and must come to terms with it. The public relations strategies practitioners can use at this stage are severely constrained.

Crises are a particularly urgent form of critical issues. Crises are issues that have reached the critical stage and share two additional characteristics. First, a resolution is demanded in a time frame that is too short for the organization to engage in its normal decision-making process. The situation is underdetermined by the available data, as far as the decision makers are concerned. For example, with more time to make a decision, the sense of crisis might well not be present. This is why maintaining an ongoing environmental scanning and research function is like money in the bank for an organization. Having more relevant data reduces the time needed to make decisions and, thus, reduces the risk associated with a crisis. This also explains why a more experienced leadership team might be able to operate in noncrisis mode while handling a situation that would throw an inexperienced team into a full panic.

Second, a crisis represents a turning point for an organization such that it is unlikely to return fully to its precrisis state, whether for better or for worse. In effect, an organization has a lot of its chips on the table. If the amount the organization has at risk is reduced sufficiently, the sense of crisis will disappear, even if the time frame for decision making remains the same. Or, if the time frame for decision and action is extended sufficiently, the sense of crisis will disappear. In a crisis, the organization's reputation may be permanently damaged, as in the case of Exxon after the *Exxon Valdez* oil spill, or it may be permanently enhanced, as in the case of Johnson & Johnson after the Tylenol poisonings. Both were crises, neither organization returned to its precrisis state, and both had to make decisions and take action more quickly than they would have liked. The fact that Exxon had erred, whereas Johnson & Johnson had not, certainly influenced the eventual outcomes. However, Exxon was also limited because its strategies resulted from an intransigent or resistant grand strategy, whereas Johnson & Johnson had more strategic options partially because its strategies resulted from a cooperative grand strategy. The fact that Johnson & Johnson was "innocent" was certainly important, but had they adopted the organization-centered strategies characteristics of a resistant grand strategy, the outcome could well have been very different and very much more negative for Johnson & Johnson.

The loss of strategic versatility is often pronounced by the time matters have reached the critical/crisis stage. So strategic issues managers prefer to deal with issues while they are at an earlier stage, although this is not always possible.

Two practices, environmental scanning and the development of standing plans, can help avoid getting to the critical stage of issues more often than necessary.

Dormant Issues

Crable and Vibbert (1985) called issues that are resolved, or simply fade, *dormant*. This suggests that issues do not go away, but can come back to the preissue or developing stage where they should continue to be monitored and responses developed. This means that each resolution is temporary and each has the kernel of one or more new issues contained within it. The original issue can reappear if the client backslides or if conditions or publics change. If an issue reemerges after some resolution, it may not take as long to go through the stages as a new issue because much information is already known. In fact, having an issue re-emerge can be particularly dangerous for an organization because publics that were quite patient and forgiving the first time around can see its reemergence as reflecting intransigence or a broken promise

The fundamentally different views of publics held in different grand strategies lead to very different understandings of the issues faced by organizations and to very different strategic options and choices.

CONCLUSION

Grand strategies cover how the organization wants to relate to its publics and are part of the culture of the organization. Grand strategies are not under the control of the public relations department, of any one campaign staff, or of any one practitioner. Grand strategies do change but, as with the rest of the culture, such changes are typically quite gradual. A whole generation of organizational members may come and go in the time it takes to change a particularly well-entrenched grand strategy.

This analysis contributes to at least four lessons about the relationship of grand strategy, strategy, and tactics in public relations:

1. Grand strategy conditions strategy. Which strategies can be used in a given public relations campaign is primarily determined by the grand strategy of the organization. This is why, for example, the primary ethical decision a practitioner makes is often who they will work for. Once that decision has been made, much of the practitioner's future behavior, including the strategies he or she will be free to use, has been determined. Practitioners must therefore take ethical responsibility for their initial employment decision and the strategies and tactics that flow directly from it. Practitioners cannot duck ethical responsibility to publics with the claim that they were "just following orders."

2.   Strategy conditions tactics. Which tactics can be used in a given public relations situation is largely determined by the strategies used, which are in turn largely determined by the grand strategy of the organization. The voice of public relations technicians is, therefore, typically only a very small component in deciding how (and how ethically) they will practice.

3.   Evaluation of public relations strategies should begin with an assessment of the grand strategy constraining them, so that strategies are not evaluated against some unrealistically high—or low—unspoken standard. Then evaluation of public relations tactics should follow the same logic, beginning by assessing the strategy which constrains them. Finally, work on specifically measurable objectives, the actual units of work in public relations, should be evaluated using the same logic.

4.   Public relations practitioners need to be familiar with an organization's grand strategies so they can use strategies that are permissible within them.

REFERENCES

Annin, P., & McCormick, J. (1997, November 24). More than a tune-up: Tough going in a fight against sexual harassment. *Newsweek*, pp. 50–52.

Armour, S. (1998, June 12). Mitsubishi settles suit for '34 Millton. *USA Today*, 1A.

Barnard, C (1938). *The function of the executive*. Cambridge, MA: Harvard University Press.

Botan, C. (1992). International public relations: Critique and reformulation. *Public Relations Review, 18*, 149–159.

Botan, C., & Hazleton, V. (1989). *Public relations theory*. Hillsdale, NJ: Lawrence Erlbaum Associates.

Botan, C., & Soto, F. (1998). A semiotic approach to the internal functioning of publics: Implications for strategic communication and public relations. *Public Relations Review, 24*, 21–44.

Crable, R. E., & Vibbert, S. L. (1985). Managing issues and influencing public policy. *Public Relations Review, 11*, 3–16.

Diamond Star (1997, September 29). *Newsweek*, Vol. 130, Issue 13, p. 6.

Dewey, J. (1927). *The public and its problems*. Chicago: Swallow Press.

Farace, V., Monge, O., & Russell, H. (1977). *Communicating and organizing*. Menlo Park, CA: Addison-Wesley.

Gaudino, J. L., Fritch, J., & Haynes, B. (1989). "If you knew what I knew, you'd make the same decision": A common misperception underlying public relations campaigns. In C. Botan & V. Hazleton (Eds.), *Public relations theory* (pp. 281–298). Hillsdale, NJ: Lawrence Erlbaum Associates.

Hart, B. H. (1954). *Strategy*. Westport, CT: Praeger Press.

Hawes, L. C. (1975). *Pragmatics of analoguing: Theory and model construction in communication*. Reading, MA: Addison-Wesley.

Jones, B., & Chase, W. (1979). Managing public policy issues. *Public Relations Review, 2*, 3–23.

Sargeaunt, H. A., & West, G. (1941). *Grand Strategy*. New York: Thomas Y. Crowell.

Strategist (2005). Public Relations Society of America, New York.

Sullivan, A. J. (1965). Toward a philosophy of public relations images. In O. Lerbinger and A. Sullivan (Eds.). *Information, influence and communication: A reader in public relations* (pp. 240–249). New York: Basic Books.

Sun Tzu. (1963). *The art of war* (S. B. Griffith, Trans.). London: Oxford University Press. (Original work published 500 B.C.)

Tactics. (2005). Public Relations Society of America, New York.

9

Reformulating the Emerging Theory of Corporate Social Responsibility as Good Governance

Cornelius B. Pratt
U.S. Department of Agriculture

A clear sense of responsibility to and integration with the public welfare is a prerequisite to successful business management in today's complex world.
—Frank W. Abrams, chairman, the Standard Oil Company,
in Bowen (1953), p. 51

The purpose of this chapter is threefold. The first is to examine the conceptual foundation of the application of the emerging theory of corporate social responsibility (CSR) through a broader understanding of a range of activities that it symbolizes. That foundation reflects the evolution of dimensions of CSR from a strictly economic doctrine of profit-making for a firm's shareholders (Friedman, 1962, 1970) into corporate social responsiveness, into social issues management that includes issues identification and analysis and response management (Wartick & Cochran, 1985), and into the needs of community or society (Besser, 1998; Freeman, 1984).

The second is to analyze CSR within the circumstances of developing countries and to argue that the construct should be reformulated to better serve the needs of those countries; that is, CSR should reach beyond its traditional boundaries by contributing more directly to national constitutional discourse and to a society's well-being. For one thing, corporations increasingly understand that their goals and initiatives cannot be detached or insulated from those of the larger society. For another, corporate interests are consistent with those of their stakeholders for whom corporate responsibility, responsiveness, and accountability are key markers in their perceptions of, and continuing relationships with, business. Therefore, culture-specific models of communication practice based on economic, societal and political realities of a country (e.g., Holtzhausen, Petersen, & Tindall, 2003; Sriramesh, Kim, & Takasaki, 1999; Sriramesh & White, 1992) can provide the impetus for making CSR environmentally responsive.

The third purpose is to provide a basis for further research that examines the evolving theory of CSR within the framework of the unique sociopolitical and economic circumstances of developing nations in which the theory frames (or should frame) corporate actions.

Wood (1991) argues that although advances toward a theory of CSR can be identified, it is not yet a theory; however, the omnibus construct includes the affirmation of society's well-being by organizations in general—not by only corporations.

THE MEDIA INDUSTRY

The focus on Africa's media enterprises in this analysis is based on five considerations. First, perhaps no organization is more archetypal of attempts to reformulate the emerging theory of CSR than those in, or associated with, Africa's media industry. That industry, particularly its burgeoning independent companies, is a titan in national and community response to the need for societal well-being. Human rights, a function of good governance, are the crux of that need and are the fulcrum of the responsibilities of Africa's media, which are a tool for implementing sustainable development programs. Consequently, Oestreich (2002) urges the international business enterprise to respond politically to the growing phenomenon of antiglobalization protesters by recognizing human rights in developing countries as a basic concern.

Mbaku (1999) iterates the economic dimensions of those rights: "The [economic] freedom to engage in exchange and contract is a sine qua non for economic growth and development (i.e., economic progress). As a consequence, economic freedom is a very important determinant of sustainable development"

(p. 315). Mbaku further observes that such freedom is vital to Africa's develop-ment in three ways: (a) it protects citizens from "perverse economic policies" that interfere with their ability to create wealth; (b) it minimizes postconstitu-tional opportunism; and (c) it maximizes the participation of entrepreneurs to create wealth. It is the evolving responsibility of much of the media industry in Africa to ensure the protection of such a freedom—and its pervasive mani-festation as human rights and good governance. Thus that industry, alongside political parties that organize elections and interest groups that serve as inter-mediaries in the policy-making process, as a resource for those who govern and as a source of pressure on officials, influences government operations, the behavior of those who govern, and the outcomes of the governing process (Kumar & Jones, 2005). The continent's private media have assumed precisely those responsibilities, fostering economic, social, and political conditions con-ducive to attaining sustainable development—thereby extending the traditional practice of CSR well into the realm of good governance.

Second, absent a developed private sector in general, Africa's media or-ganizations have historically been the vanguard of the continuing struggle against neocolonialism and institutional decadence, a responsibility that has made them institutionalize management and operational structures that are much more developed than those commonly available in other industries. The fact is that the media sector—public and private—has developed alongside its country host; maturity of the latter translates into a concomitant maturity of the former.

Third, in various ways, the evolving operations of the media industry belie its advocacy and news-dissemination role by aligning its activities with one or more of the regnant dimensions of CSR theory that will be outlined presently. In essence, the industry is a business with as much financial as social stake in a nation.

Fourth, Africa's media industry continues to play key national roles enun-ciated by The Global Sullivan Principles for Corporate Social Responsibil-ity, launched in 1977. Embedded in those principles are human-rights issues, the fare of Africa's media industry's operations: (a) support universal human rights; (b) promote equal opportunity; (c) respect freedom of association; (d) provide economic and social opportunities; (e) protect human health and the environment; (f) promote fair competition, including intellectual and property rights; and (g) improve community life. More than 100 companies have so far endorsed those principles. Admittedly, the Sullivan principles focused on U.S. companies' operations in then-apartheid South Africa, but they have since been applied to companies of any size in any market.

Eribo (2001) argues that human rights, civil liberties, media freedom, and the propagation of a nation's democratic and economic ideals are conjoined. Similarly, Mwagiru (1997) argues that fundamental human rights and media rights coexist to the extent that no media practitioner can operate effectively without the guarantee of rights identified in the Universal Declaration of Human Rights and the International Covenant on Civil and Political Rights.

Finally, most communication practitioners on the continent still get their professional start in the media—either as print or broadcast journalists—whose strategies in fomenting public resistance to colonial administrations hold a legacy of communication excellence. The values of the media industry underpin the dominant press-agentry and public-information models of public relations on the continent—models that provide little of what Fobanjong (2004) describes as "an enabling forum for active policy debates, political participation, and democratic competition" (p. 208).

CHAPTER ORGANIZATION AND LIMITATIONS

This chapter is in six sections. The first outlines major dimensions of CSR theory. The second highlights the importance of CSR as a framework for preventing questionable management practices and as a means by which some U.S. businesses, particularly those in the securities industry, could be both accountable and responsible to their stakeholders. It also outlines examples of business' damage to Africa's natural resources. The third acknowledges the importance of CSR to Africa. The fourth presents the ethical framework of justice—a hallmark of the human-rights cause (à la good governance). The fifth makes a case for interpreting the struggle for human rights as synonymous with that for good governance. It argues for a more analytical framework for applying CSR to corporate activities on good governance. And the sixth places CSR theory within the specific, case-based context of good governance in African countries. It identifies touchstone issues (e.g., confrontations between human-rights, civil-society groups, and private media organizations on the one hand and governments on the other) that bear directly on human rights in three African nations: Ghana in western Africa, the Democratic Republic of Congo (DRC) in central Africa, and Zambia in southern Africa. It notes the extent to which confrontations are manifested in evolving media practices and democratic ideals. And it reformulates CSR theory by presenting a framework for corporate conduct for good governance as sustainable development.

The limitations of this chapter should be noted at the outset. First, it is largely a three-country-based analysis, not a descriptive presentation. Thus it does not identify corporate leaders' attitudes toward or stakeholder perceptions of CSR, or socially related practices of multinational corporations that operate in Africa, or those practices among indigenous businesses. Rather, based on community and political leaders' expectation of corporations, it suggests reformulating the evolving CSR theory as a beachhead toward furthering corporate efforts in Africa's development programs. The reason for this approach is based on the finding that corporations tend not to reveal information on their level of social responsibility (Besser, 1998; Griffin & Mahon, 1997).

Second, the prescriptive nature of this analysis justifies its reliance on the conceptualization of CSR from global perspectives and the interpretation of corporate or business actions within the theoretical framework offered by CSR.

Finally, it must be noted that in the media industry at some level one cannot speak about the media as a product- or service-producing enterprise in the same breath as we do about most businesses in Africa. The product of the media is essentially news (or its construction), which has a strong public-service component. Besides, the news industry, at least in much of Africa, does not have the financial holdings typical of the continent's natural resource-based enterprise, for example, the petroleum industry.

THE EMERGING THEORY OF CORPORATE SOCIAL RESPONSIBILITY

In the annals of recent world history, massive international attempts at nation-building occurred only once: in the aftermath of World War II, when U.S. President Harry S. Truman implemented the Marshall Plan. (Historians think that the absence of such a plan after World War I foreshadowed weak governance and contributed to the start of World War II.) Charges of three decades of misrule—the antithesis of good governance—resulted in the removal of Saddam Hussein's government and its key supporters: the Republican Guard, the Baath Party, and the Fedayeen Saddam. The resulting political vacuum and the dire need for reconstruction echo those that preceded the Marshall Plan. At this writing, the international community, led by the United States, is funding programs and projects to stabilize and rebuild Afghanistan and Iraq—perhaps on a scale comparable to that of the Marshall Plan.

Granted, such efforts are a sequela of military victories over the Taliban in Afghanistan and over the Baath Party in Iraq. Nevertheless, even if such victories were absent, the U.S. government's values would still have encouraged it to respond to the plight of ordinary citizens in those countries, whose economies and infrastructures have been damaged by decades of misrule and neglect by dictatorial regimes, whose political systems are in a shambles, and whose citizens are deprived of the essentials of normal living. The point here is that good governance as nation building is as much a governmental responsibility as it is that of the private sector. Thus, this analysis acknowledges, at both the national and community levels, the impact that corporate contributions—domestic and international—have on human-rights protections; on stable, growing economies; and on sustainable development.

Such international effort is not without precedence. It was perhaps in the mid-1940s that the business world began to pay particular attention to its "social consciousness"—that is, to the consequences of its actions in a sphere much wider than that covered by its profit-and-loss statements ("Fortune Management," 1946). Shortly thereafter, there was remarkable scholarly interest in the subject. One such early interest sought to define "the businessman's conception of his social responsibilities" (Bowen, 1953). Another argued that business should not become socially involved, and that society should even stop it from becoming so involved, because that involvement could turn a corporation to a 20th-century equivalent of the medieval church (Levitt, 1958). Another argued that advocating business' contributions to socially desirable outcomes is tantamount to socialism (Friedman, 1970). Yet another argued that dogmatic organizations dogged by rigidity and dominance are wont "to stifle, discredit, or eliminate any point of view which would make it appear as being socially non-responsible or irresponsible" (Loveland & Whatley, 1973, p. 17). And another early work presented reasons for a minimum business role in social responsibility and for a more significant role, and concluded that, "business institutions must move vigorously toward integrating social values into their decision-making machinery . . . or gradually sink into customer and public disfavor" (Davis, 1973, p. 321).

There were instances in which corporate support for socially responsible actions was just as poignantly expressed, as indicated in Abrams's quotation at the beginning of this chapter. Inarguably, the business world is much more complex today than it was in the 1950s; and stakeholders are even much more demanding today than they were then. Therefore, it is imperative that, as business environments become more complex, corporations embark on activities that respond to the ever-increasing conflict of interest among stakeholders, employees, and the public at large, and their collective and separate demands on business.

The preceding perspective and arguments have coalesced into a four-dimensional CSR construct: returns on investment, trustee management, self-interest, and corporate social performance.

Returns on Investment

This view took root in a business world characterized by the "public-be-damned" era of the last two decades of the 19th century. At that time, industrialists exploited both their consumers and their employees; their focus was profit-making. Friedman (1962), an ardent 20th-century exponent of this view, argued that the only social responsibility of business is

> to use its resources and engage in activities designed to increase its profits so long as it stays within the rules of the game, which is to say, engages in open and free competition, without deception or fraud. . . . Few trends could so thoroughly undermine the very foundations of our free society as the acceptance by corporate officials of a social responsibility other than to make as much money for their stockholders as possible. (p. 133)

Thus, the importance to the investor of maximizing profit becomes the impetus for corporate conduct—or misconduct. Although such outcomes are important in investment decisions of business, according to other views, they should not be an overriding interest.

Trustee Management

The hallmark of this view is the balancing role of business, which is vulnerable to push-pull, anthropogenic factors in complex environments. Because of the enormous power, resources, and influence of the corporation, that is, in comparison with small, owner-managed operations, it is important that it be balanced in its relationships with the disparate stakeholders who affect and are affected by it.

Self-Interest

This is indicative of the view that the public good is consistent with business interest, and that if business does not act in accordance with the expectations and interests of its stakeholders and community, it might be subject to public outcry for further oversight and regulation of the outcomes of its operations. Besides, socially responsible behavior can create a healthy, thriving community in which to do business, enabling a firm to reap benefits of its society-centered actions (e.g., Aram, 1989). It is in business interest, therefore, to identify ways in which it can serve at some level in the interest of its stakeholders.

Corporate Social Performance

CSR has also evolved into corporate social performance (CSP), which focuses on the social outcomes and ramifications of organizational behaviors. As a compendium view, CSP includes three activities: CSR itself, corporate social responsiveness, and the outcomes of corporate behavior (Wood, 1991). Business has an obligation to promote social betterment, to assist stakeholders in making their case for business' interest in the public, and to contribute to social discourse, programs and policies; in short, to adopt socially responsible practices. As Sethi and Steidlmeier (1995) affirm, "The large multinational corporation must become an active agent for social change if it is to make the world safe for democracy and indeed for capitalism" (p. 12).

It is this dimension of CSR that underpins the rest of the analysis in this chapter, in that responsibility to community development, as well as collaboration with communal partners, is an important topic in the economic and social contract between developing nations, whose governments devolve in community development and confront social problems, and (multinational) corporations, which often find it challenging to respond to ultra vires actions of social activists or to augment arguments for social experimentation (Boehm, 2002;

Cooper, 1998; Sethi & Steidlmeier, 1995). Altman (1998) argues that community relationships serve as a tool for achieving corporate citizenship.

All of this interest in corporate social responsibility coalesces in the effects of corporate activities on the environment and on society at large, not least in developing nations, particularly those in Africa. For one thing, Africa is in dire need of sustainable development. For another, corporate commercial activities have had palpable effects on Africa. For example, commercial logging, a corporate-intensive activity, threatens 79% of Africa's frontier forest cover, versus 72% for the rest of the world. (Frontier forests are virgin, undisturbed forests whose ecological properties produce clean water, improve air quality, and sustain fish and wildlife.) Invasive species, changes in fire regimes, and commercial hunting affect 41% of Africa's forests.

RESPONSIBILITY GAPS

Globally, consumer displeasure with global practices has been most palpably indicated in the continuing protests inflamed by the mere gathering of participants of the World Trade Organization (WTO). At issue is the demand for more transparency in WTO negotiations, which are viewed as undermining the economic interest of developing countries. And there is the companion issue of protection of human rights, which, as a factor in CSR, was brought to the fore recently in the Global Compact developed by Kofi Annan, U.N. secretary general, and launched in July 2000. The compact, inspired by the U.N. Universal Declaration of Human Rights, is a platform for disseminating good organizational practices based on universal principles.

In the United States particularly, 2001 was an annus horribilis for the corporate world. The reason: That was the year in which corporate scandals and greed of the magnitude of those of the mid- to late 1980s made a comeback. (During the 1980s, at least three corporate executives—Dennis Levine, Ivan F. Boesky, and Michael Milken—and a securities firm, Drexel Burnham Lambert, pleaded guilty to securities violations and paid hefty fines.) But perhaps the most disheartening thing is that, even on the cusp of a new millennium, the lessons of the 1980s seem lost on the corporate world, particularly in an era when the U.S. Securities and Exchange Commission is ever more vigilant about securities fraud.

The Enron Corporation, an energy-trading company and the seventh-largest Fortune 500 company, illustrates the debacle such organizations confront because of their demonstrably questionable accounting practices. In this case, such practice resulted, in 2001, in the largest corporate bankruptcy in the United States.

In October 2002, Sam Waksal, a former chief executive officer (CEO) of ImClone Systems, Inc., a biotech firm, was found guilty of securities fraud and perjury and given a prison sentence of more than 7 years.

In that same month, Steven B. Markovitz, a portfolio manager at Millennium Partners, a New York City-based hedge fund company, pleaded guilty to routinely violating, between 1999 and 2003, a 1968 law that required buyers who file their purchases of mutual fund shares after 4 p.m. to trade on next-day's price—a practice called late-day trading. Investigation of possible abuses in other financial companies, including Bank of America, Bank One Corporation, Prudential Securities, and Janus Capital Group, is expanding to include a much wider dragnet.

In June 2005, John J. Rigas, 80, the founder of Adelphia Communications Corp., received a 15-year sentence for fraud. In mid-July 2005, Bernard J. Ebbers, 64, former CEO of WorldCom Inc., was handed a 25-year prison sentence for his role in, perhaps, the nation's largest accounting fraud.

On September 19, 2005, L. Dennis Kozlowski, former chairman and CEO, and Mark H. Swartz, former chief financial officer, of Tyco International Ltd., were sentenced to $8\frac{1}{3}$ to 25 years in prison for looting the company, bilking investors of $600 million, and using part of the money for personal purposes. Both were also ordered to pay about $240 million in fines and restitution.

There has been at least one recent high-profile acquittal: the former CEO of HealthSouth, Richard M. Scrushy, was acquitted June 28 on charges of accounting fraud.

All of this occurred as business schools worldwide, but particularly in the United States, broadened their offerings to improve corporate financial success and social and environmental stewardship (Aspen Institute, n.d.); as those schools redesigned their curricula to include business ethics and values and corporate responsibility; as graduate management programs sought ways to best teach ethics as either integrated into the curriculum or as stand-alone ethics courses; as Fortune 500 companies and other leading organizations hire ethics officers or advisers and develop ethics programs to raise ethical awareness and train employees (Joseph, 2002; Steiner, 1976); as a corporation like Enron swore by its core values of respect, integrity, communication, and excellence even as it wantonly acted in ways that undermined those values; and as the U.S. government upped the ante on holding business executives accountable for corporate misdeeds that occurred on their watch, for those actions that (directly) compromised shareholder interest, or that undermined employee well-being.

Also in Africa, examples of responsibility gaps abound. Consider the following:

- Shell Petroleum Development Company, for almost a decade, defied public interest and used violence to quell community protests against its perceived failure to contribute to the socioeconomic development of Nigeria's Niger Delta, while reaping huge profits from its investment (Ogbondah & George, 2004).

- Talisman Energy of Canada has been publicly criticized for complicity in ethnic cleansing in communities adjoining its oil fields in southern Sudan, Africa's largest nation.

- Corporations account for 79% of forest loss in Africa; agriculture and energy exploration account for between 12% and 17% of loss in plant, mammal, and bird species (Economic Commission for Africa, 2001).

- Vegetation is removed from Africa is at about one-half the rate for the rest of the world, and land degradation accounts for 27.4% of that for the world, even though the continent has one-fifth of the world's total land area.

- Invasive species (an outcome of international trade), changes in fire regimes (an outcome of commercial logging), and commercial hunting affect 41% of Africa's forest cover, as against 13% in the rest of the world.

In light of corporations' gains from investing in Africa's natural resources, why should they take CSR seriously? Four factors justify its relevance. First, it enhances organizational attractiveness (Luce, Barber, & Hillman, 2001; Turban & Greening, 1997). Second, it improves corporate financial performance (Carpenter, 2003; McGuire, Sundgren, & Schneeweis, 1988; Orlitzky & Benjamin, 2001; Roman, Hayibor, & Agle, 1999; Stanwick & Stanwick, 1998). Third, it permits a firm to have low financial risk because it engenders stable relations with the government and financial community, shields the firm from fines and lawsuits, and expands its strategic options (McGuire et al., 1988). Finally, it can serve as a means by which a firm could signal its values, beliefs, and performance to potential customers, employees, investors, and suppliers, who could then use those positive signals in evaluating the firm (Jones & Murrell, 2001). Thus it should be expected that reformulating corporate role in community welfare would be a test of an organization's contributions to society and of how its various stakeholder groups respond to various actions by the firm.

CORPORATE SOCIAL RESPONSIBILITY IN AFRICA

In the absence of empirical studies that investigated community expectations of corporations in Africa, it is advisable that this analysis be informed by the inquiry undertaken, and by conclusions reached, by Reed (2002) regarding the implications of different environments for corporate responsibilities. By extension, we can also extrapolate from results evident in environments comparable to those in Africa (e.g., Boehm, 2002; Quanzi, 1997).

Reed (2002) argued that two factors impinge on corporations' activities in developing countries. The first is the different economic circumstance—weak financial markets and limited resources and the precolonial historic reasons that markets and an industrial economy did not emerge in these countries; political reality—how institutions are not necessarily structured to conform to defensible democratic principles; and sociocultural circumstances—where, for example, traditional values are dominant and a culture of consumerism less so, keeping large portions of the populations from being integrated into the market economy.

The second group of realities that ups the ante for corporations operating in developing countries is the normative bases for such increased corporate responsibilities: the obligation to act in accordance with the will of the people, to fulfill responsibilities not undertaken by other actors, to address problems of historic injustice (e.g., slavery or apartheid), and to rectify the ongoing results of structural injustice (e.g., unequal opportunities that emanate from racial, ethic or religious prejudice).

In essence, Reed prescribes unique sets of responsibilities particularly for the transnational corporation in developing countries: To the extent that governments fail in fulfilling their commitments to society whenever they do not undertake measures responsive to historic injustice, corporations similarly fail to contribute to societal good. Therein is the essence of corporate responsibility in developing countries:

> corporations . . . may have to assume responsibilities not taken up by other responsible agents. In this case, the primary responsible agent is the state, which should both effectively design and enforce company law in a way that protects shareholder rights and regulate markets so that they more closely approach perfects markets. In the absence of such government action, corporations take on greater responsibility . . . (p. 187)

CSR, Political Stewardship, and Development

Africa's major challenge is sustainable development—the capacity of a nation's resources for renewal, for recovery from a wide range of ecological disturbances, and for retention of their ecological properties, all in ways that enable the management of those resources to meet current and future needs of people who use them.

One area in which that is apparent is the environmental impact of corporations, particularly on natural resources. Therefore, this chapter examines corporate activities within the theoretical framework of CSR. It argues that organizations apply CSR as a pathway to responding more effectively to the challenges of the nation-states in which they operate. It argues that business organizations—as harbingers of much development in the developing world—apply normative core values of their social performance to evaluating and responding to community challenges and to collaborating with other organizations and community groups in charting their contributions to sustainable environmental development. A corporation that has a stake in natural resource management, for example, forest management, will be in default on its contract with society—and cannot legitimately claim public support—if it fails to deliver on its societal obligation to contribute to sustainable forest management. Thus one would argue that Isoroy, a French timber company with affiliates in Africa, falters on its social contract with the people of Gabon whenever its practices undermine, through excessive logging, that country's frontier forests.

Africa's natural resources (e.g., frontier forests, crude oil, and natural gas) are a major investment interest of multinational corporations such as ExxonMobil, Isoroy, Agip, and Shell Petroleum. They could also be institutions for nation-building, community-investing, and constitutional discourse. As the World Wide Fund for Nature, an organization that seeks to conserve the Earth's ecological diversity and to promote reduction of pollution and wasteful consumption of natural resources, notes, "While industry represents perhaps the single biggest threat to society and the natural world, it can also represent one of our greatest allies in our mission to safeguard it and provide for its sustainable development (Marsden 2000, p. 9).

The New Partnership for Africa's Development (NEPAD), an initiative approved July 11, 2001, by African leaders, describes the region's forests as one of humankind's most beneficial resources: they are its "ecological lung." Its rain forests, like forests elsewhere, absorb emissions and industrial effluents that are potentially hazardous to the environment. Yet an estimated 77% of its frontier forests is under moderate to high threat, much of it from unsustainable logging (Economic Commission for Africa, 2001), a largely commercial, corporate-intensive activity. Such threat, which results in a continuing high loss of forest cover, is broadly evident in one of Africa's most industrialized countries, South Africa, which accounts for 39% of the continent's emissions from fossil fuels and cement; it also has a higher annual per capita emission of carbon dioxide than the global average. CSR can provide the framework for implementing community-sensitive organizational actions and for fostering an ethic for the global corporation's contributions to sustainable forest management. And this is particularly important in many sub-Saharan African countries, where demands on agriculture and the policies and attitudes of governments and social-political institutions influence production and consumption patterns, and where the 0.8% annual average rate of net deforestation between 1990 and 2000 well exceeds the global rate of 0.2%.

Along with those challenges are Africa's deteriorating environment and ecosystems, its faltering agricultural productivity (most recently in Zimbabwe), its heavy-handed state intervention, its inadequate FDI, its improper political governance, its limited public health programs, its constrained business partnerships, and its social upheavals. A statement issued at the conclusion of the U.N. World Summit on Sustainable Development (WSSD), held in Johannesburg, South Africa, August 26 to September 4, 2002, underscored the enduring nature of those challenges: "Africa's efforts to achieve sustainable development have been hindered by conflicts, insufficient investment, limited market access opportunities and supply side constraints, unsustainable debt burdens, historically declining ODA [official development assistance] levels, and the impact of HIV/AIDS."

It is against that backdrop that this chapter focuses on the following question: How can organizational activities, particularly those of the media industry, be guided by the evolving theory of CSR to enable organizations to engage in environmental stewardship and in sustainable community and national development in Africa?

ETHICS: A CONCEPTUAL FRAMEWORK FOR GOOD GOVERNANCE

Business cannot operate long-term in a moral vacuum; it cannot insulate itself from ethical issues in its markets. Organizational values, by which CSR programs are grounded, have clear implications for good governance. It behooves an organization, then, to leverage its economic influence in taking a stand on moral issues, and to contribute to the institutionalization of values that could benefit society as a whole. As Oestreich (2002) notes, "Corporations should feel free to take steps that seem to increase justice where they can, and should not avoid having at times to make decisions on values" (p. 220).

For a nation to ensure that its citizens have human rights requires, at the minimum, a constitutional commitment to justice—and to equal justice for all. Ordinarily, such a commitment is provided in a nation's constitutional and legal systems. In more political terms, however, it is demonstrated in empowered citizens in ways that free them from unwarranted constraints. Both those perspectives are commonly described, respectively, as the egalitarian and the libertarian concepts of justice.

But, what is justice? Hazlitt (1972) defines justice as "the system of rules and arrangements that increase human peace, cooperation, production, and happiness, and Injustice whatever rules and arrangements stand in the way of these consequences" (p. 335). It is an indispensable element of human rights, not least because it enables citizens to have some degree of autonomy, independence or control over their own (business) decisions and, above all, over their own lives.

The Egalitarian Concept of Justice

Perhaps the best-known exponent of egalitarianism, from an ethics perspective, is Rawls (1971), a contemporary philosopher. Egalitarians argue that all members of society should be treated equally without regard to demographic and physiological circumstances. One perspective is drawn from Rawls's theory of distributive justice, which holds that rights, property, opportunities, and economic advantages should be distributed equally among members of society, but according to merit. Another is compensatory justice, which holds that compensation should be given for an injustice that produces harm. People, he argued, "have an equal right to the most extensive basic liberty compatible with a similar liberty for others" (p. 60).

To accomplish equal justice in society, he places everyone in a hypothetical "original position"; that is, behind a "veil of ignorance," which requires that, in evaluating situations, people step from their everyday, status-based roles into an egalitarian position behind a veil. In such a hypothetical position, self-serving criteria such as social and economic stratifications that are characteristic of the real world are eliminated. The goal is to develop a conception of justice or of the good from a disinterested, "equal" perspective. People are free to negotiate a new course of action or a new social contract that they might adopt when they emerge from their hypothetical position. The only social and economic inequalities that exist behind the veil are those that occur in accordance with equal access and justice and that are to everyone's advantage, particularly for the least advantaged in society.

The Libertarian Concept of Justice

This concept is consistent with the enduring search by corporations for liberalized markets and business environment. It requires that business be free of unnecessary governmental interference. Libertarians embrace market forces for determining the nature of their operations: The marketplace of ideas will be nurtured by a free flow of information and discourse and is only truly constrained by rational judgment regarding media or individual responsibility.

Worldwide, libertarianism has been as much the hallmark of media struggles for political and economic independence as it has been that for nonmedia enterprises seeking liberalized investment policies; it has also been a rationale for establishing privately owned media. The argument has been that organizations that depend almost exclusively on, say, government largesse are less likely to be editorially independent; they tend to be unwitting extensions of their benefactors.

HUMAN RIGHTS AS GOOD GOVERNANCE

Arguably, democratic traditions—and their protection of human rights—have unique roots in African societies. Democratic governance—for example, from "kinglessness" among the Tiv or the Ibo in Nigeria, to royalty-consciousness in Uganda or Ghana, to leadership by consensus in southern Sudan—preceded that of colonial governments (Conteh-Morgan, 1997; Deng & Lyons, 1998).

Therefore, non-Western definitions of democratic governance differed from those in, say, Africa. And the passing of time between the onslaught of colonialism and the emergence of independence had been fraught with political and cultural conflicts over power relationships, duties, and obligations.

Since the end of Africa's colonial governments, the continent's media organizations, particularly the press, have engaged in decades-long efforts to establish and maintain freedoms for their citizens and for their political and social institutions to contribute to economic growth, and to provide the framework for corporate—domestic and transnational—operations on the continent. Human rights have been pivotal to that struggle. And those rights are predicated on press freedom. Then as now, the salvoes in what has become an enduring battle for human rights in much of Africa were fired within the context of media freedom. The rationale for that struggle has been that no society can establish, let alone nurture, democratic ideals if its peoples and social institutions are not engaged strategically in a search for those ideals. Phiri (1999), for example, argues that Africa's transformation is linked to the response of civil-society entities such as the church, business, professional associations, and other nongovernmental organizations. In Zambia, the emergence of civil-society and human-rights groups, organizations, and associations enables political parties, newspapers, and magazines to flourish. But Africa's experience indicates that many of its governments still attempt to rein in the media, as those governments seek to deprive their citizens of a meaningful and an extensive input in civil and democratic governance and in social and economic enterprise.

African governments, even those that have evolved from multiparty democracies, have created environments conducive to having media practitioners attacked, killed, intimidated and harassed, as has been the case in Laurent Kabila's DRC, in Charles Taylor's Liberia, in Sani Abacha's Nigeria, in Robert Mugabe's Zimbabwe—and even in Levy Mwanawasa's Zambia. Nonetheless, media organizations in Zambia, Ghana, and Kenya and Nigeria have tenaciously played an advocacy role: criticizing government policies, urging democratic reforms, promoting grass-roots participation, exposing unwholesome corporate practices. As Ansah (1988) wrote, "In a democratic society, actions of the government, which is only a trustee of the collective will and power of the people, are expected to be regulated by the force of public opinion, and the press is the most appropriate medium gauging and reflecting public opinion" (p. 13).

Similarly, Kasoma (1995) affirms the importance of a free press in safeguarding democracy, noting that media that are not independent "cannot provide the people with all the information they require in order to make informed democratic decisions" (p. 539).

Historically, human-rights groups in Africa have largely been nonclandestine operations; they have, for the most part, operated above ground as "newspaper-supported, anti-colonial protests" (Hachten, 1971, p. 146). Newspapers were a medium for debates on political independence and human rights. Campaigns for political independence were a fillip for their establishment and nurturing. Even today, in an era of expanding multiparty democracy, such media sentiments are apparent, as the media have forced governments to be tolerant of diverse viewpoints and of criticisms.

REFORMULATING CORPORATE SOCIAL RESPONSIBILITY THEORY

Africa's economy is influenced by factors such as high rates of population growth, which exert a toll on natural resources; ineffective development policies and programs; inefficient production methods; unfavorable terms in international trade; debt burdens; and the environmental and economic effects of drought. African governments undertake nation-building roles as indicated in partnerships such as the U.S. African Growth and Opportunity Act, which is reforming economies while promoting democracy and good governance; the Corporate Council on Africa, a partnership that sponsors the biennial United States-Africa Business Summit, which tackles the challenges of doing business, and of identifying opportunities, in Africa; the Network for Environment and Sustainable Development in Africa; and NEPAD, which is encouraging inflows of foreign private direct investment to Africa.

During the past three decades, more than a dozen African governments established investment promotion agencies that transferred their holdings in state-owned enterprises to private interests in the understanding that the latter would be more efficient operationally and economically. For example, Zambia, among the first of a handful of African countries to adopt open-market policies, fueled in part by commentaries and exposés of media organizations, established the Industrial Development Corporation of Zambia Ltd., the Zambia Privatization Agency, and the Zambia Investment Promotion Center to create partnerships between the government and the private sector, to place greater control of the economy in the hands of the government, and to encourage indigenous entrepreneurship.

Additionally, a number of African governments launched policies to attract foreign direct investment (FDI) to the continent, which had the world's highest return on FDI in 2002 probably because the perceived higher risks in the region encouraged companies to invest only in high-yield projects. Since 1990, the rate of return of foreign affiliates of transnational corporations in Africa is 29% ("Foreign Direct Investment," 1999). Tanzania's return rate was 44%, Botswana's 30%, and Ghana's 29%. Front-runners in attracting that form of investment are Botswana, Egypt, Equatorial Guinea, Ghana, Morocco, Mozambique, Namibia, Nigeria, Tunisia, and Uganda. And there are additional examples of a continent on the mend: Countries such as Uganda and Mozambique average about 6% annually in GDP growth, and primary school enrollment in Mauritania is 90% whereas school access is 93% (African Development Bank, 2002). But continuing investment requires politically stable environments. Enter good governance.

To what extent do organizational actions have implications for good governance? This chapter argues that good governance, expressed within the context of human rights, is much more difficult to institutionalize in African countries whose media organizational role has been quiescent or reined in by the powers that be. Or, put differently, corporate intervention in national and community programs is more effective in politically pluralistic systems in which corporations benefit from liberal or liberalized investment policies and where their demonstrated responsibilities are consistent with those that appropriately define the fundamental rights and the civic obligations of citizens.

The North African country of Sudan offers meaningful opportunities for CSR in the context advanced in this chapter. Improvements, even if minuscule, in that nation's economic and political landscape, its intent to end its reputation as a sponsor of international terrorism, and its substantial oil deposits have enticed multinational corporations to forge new economic ties with it (Martin, 2002). A number of such corporations are prospecting for and producing oil; they are influencing the political and social outcomes and the development programs in the warring nation. Those companies include OMV (Austria), Talisman Energy (Canada), China National Petroleum Company, TotalFinaElf (Belgium and France), Agip (Italy), Petronas (Malaysia), Gulf Oil (Qatar), and Lundin Oil (Sweden). Some of those companies have been criticized for stoking Sudan's decades-long, low-intensity conflict; for destabilizing the region rather than encouraging peace; and for enabling slavery and religious persecution. They have been charged with allowing government troops to use their airstrips and roads to launch attacks on rebel forces or to clear civilians from oil-concession areas. But these companies could collectively leverage their investments to broker peace, to work with the international community to end more than three decades of a civil war now financed with the revenues that they generate for the country, and to build partnerships with community organizations to help translate a windfall into economic and political heft. At the very least, the companies have the opportunity to be at the center of efforts at national reconciliation.

Similar CSR challenges occur in Equatorial Guinea, a small West African country ruled by a strongman since 1979 and whose government, which, even though close to the West, has been charged with human-rights abuses, political repression and government corruption. The country's massive reserves of oil and natural gas attract private investors from the West (notably ExxonMobil, ChevronTexaco and Amerada Hess) and Asia (Petronas of Malaysia). The infusion of oil revenues into the economy is indicated only in limited economic development and in the affluence of family and friends of the president.

As noted earlier, although governments are necessarily the key players in any modern political system, a pluralistic economic system cannot function effectively without a series of "mediating" or enabling institutions. Mediating institutions—for example, a nation's economic and legal systems, investment institutions, political interest groups, and related nongovernmental organizations—are those whose policies and actions enable or constrain corporate actions and confer legitimacy on corporations. But mediating institutions cannot be effective unless their legitimacy is accepted by both the government and the citizenry; unless they develop in ways that arise from, and are consonant with, the national political culture; and unless they have basic freedoms. Finally, mediating institutions must be home-grown and indigenous, and, even if transplanted from other systems, be demonstrably sensitive to the internal dynamics of a nation.

Corporate organizations can serve as models for emerging democratic systems, offering a template for structures and processes—and their associated consequences—on which the rising leadership in emerging systems can make well-informed, grounded choices and decisions. ChevronTexaco, which, for decades, has supported health, education, labor rights, social and environmental initiatives in 52 African nations, can serve as one such model in Equatorial Guinea by engaging more forcefully its commitment "to conduct our business in a socially responsible and ethical manner, respect the law, support universal human rights, protect the environment and benefit the communities where we work" ("ChevronTexaco 2002").

In postcolonial Africa, a triangular interaction of factors also determines the fervor with which governments endorse human rights. The first is the deemphasis of dirigisme in preference for privatization, which has resulted in continent-wide business growth. The second is the development of multiparty parliamentary systems in more than two-thirds of the governments on the continent. The third is the structural adjustment policies that bolster weak social and political institutions and economies. Admittedly, those factors need to be examined for a fuller appreciation of the underpinnings of good governance on the continent, but, as this disquisition asserts, as an interplay among human rights, media independence, and good governance.

African countries have comparable human-rights experiences, a reflection of the political and economic challenges characteristic of the continent's emerging civil societies. For example, the mass media, as social institutions, develop pari passu with political institutions: broadly, privately owned media tend to play the role of political agitators; and government-owned media, that of unseemly propagandists for the government. The reason seems obvious. The mass media have always served as both the rallying point and the conduit for Africa's political interest groups. The latter's agendas are couched in terms used in the International Covenant on Civil and Political Rights: "Everyone shall have the right to freedom of expression; this right shall include the freedom to seek, receive and impart information and ideas of all kinds."

It is within the foregoing framework that a three-nation analysis is presented. The country-analysis approach is used because of its inherent strength: It focuses on an event or a series of related events of interest to the subject being discussed, identifying major issues that are as applicable to similar situations as they are instructive in understanding and analyzing contextually their larger meanings. To accomplish that analysis, and, because of the implications of ethics for human rights and press freedom, justice is used as its conceptual framework. The three nations indicate different levels of their commitment to human rights: a Freedom House (n.d.) survey of media freedom indicates that Ghana is "free," Zambia "partly free," and the DRC "not free." An assessment of their media industries indicates similar results, based on a composite score in three broad categories: (a) the legal environment that influences media content, (b) political influences over news content, and (c) economic pressures on the media (Karlekar, 2004). Therefore, organizational role vis-à-vis human rights in the three countries has implications for CSR in three areas: in constitutional discourse, in nation-building, and in community-investing.

Ghana: The Constitutional Basis for Good Governance

Among the three nations profiled here, Ghana is an outlier for two reasons. First, even though the government controls the two national daily newspapers—the *Ghana Times* and the *Daily Graphic*—and the major broadcasting organization—the Ghana Broadcasting Corporation—about a dozen nongovernment newspapers (that is, private enterprises) are published regularly. Further, privately run television stations and at least 15 private radio stations now broadcast throughout the nation. The implication of those developments for the country is that citizens who, hitherto, did not have direct access to a medium now have media in which to express their views. (A reformulated CSR, extended to other industries, will enable, say, community residents to avail themselves of a similar opportunity.)

Second, Ghana's independent and state-owned press is still among the most strident on the continent. As Ibelema, Land, Eko, and Steyn (2004) note, even though state-owned media have been marginalized by their independent counterparts in countries such as Nigeria, they remain major voices at newsstands in Ghana. Since the restoration of democracy in 1993, the media have played a central role in the country's development of procedures for home-grown democratic institution-building.

When developments in Ghana, particularly since 1993, are examined, it is clear that its media practitioners are cognizant of some of the lessons that can contribute to democratic development and civic education there. Since 1957, when the country attained independence, its media had not failed to provide a forum for debates and education and to promote democratic governance and a civil society, even during the military regimes of Gens. Akwasi A. Afrifa and Joseph Ankrah (1966–1969), Gen. Kutu Acheampong (1972–1978), and

Gen. Fred Akufo (1978–1979), and during the two periods (June–September 1979 and 1981–1993) of military rule by Ft. Lt. Jerry J. Rawlings. The assumption of the country's presidency by John Kufuor in 2000, following a presidential election, marked Ghana's first democratic transfer of power since attaining independence. So forceful were the media in promoting good governance and accountability—and in advocating freedoms in behalf of society—that, on January 7, 1993, former President Rawlings established a 15-member National Media Commission (NMC) to promote the freedom of Ghana's press for the greater good of society and to stifle undue governmental interference in state-owned media. In any event, the NMC was dissolved in 1996; attempts to reestablish it were futile.

Articles 12 through 30 of the Constitution of 1992 provide the impetus for human-rights causes: from the freedom and independence of the media themselves, to the right to life, to the prohibition of arbitrary arrest and forced labor. For one thing, those articles recognize the importance and protection of unfettered media and of free expression; for another, they offer guidelines for the unique contributions the media can make to the nation's well-being.

Chapter 18 of the Constitution mandates a body, the Commission on Human Rights and Administrative Justice, to investigate complaints of violations of fundamental human rights and freedoms and to educate the public on human-rights issues. The Rawlings administration was credited with formulating some of the country's most liberal media policies (e.g., the liberalization of the airwaves) and with approving constitutional provisions (e.g., media privatization that is occurring as a consequence of the country's structural adjustment and economic recovery program) (Gadzekpo, 1997).

Ghana's human-rights record is commendable; it is enabled by supportive free-market policies of the present administration of President John Kufuor. Inarguably, there have been shortcomings. The editors of two privately owned newspapers, *The Statesman* and *The Free Press*, reported receiving death threats for being critical of Rawlings's National Democratic Congress (Anokwa, 1997). And attempts by the Independent Media Corporation of Ghana (IMCG) to challenge the age-old monopoly of Ghana Broadcasting Corporation ended in protests against the latter and in a *melée*. Radio Eye, an independent, pirate FM station owned by IMCG had its equipment confiscated by the government on charges that it was broadcasting without a license.

Zambia: Good Governance and Open-Market Policies

In its 42-year postcolonial history, Zambia had perhaps only one crucial test of its human-rights policies: It occurred at dawn on October 28, 1997. On that day, Zambian army commandos seized the government radio station housed in the Mass Media Complex in Lusaka. Government troops regained control of the complex hours later. Thereafter, President J. T. Chiluba, with parliamentary approval, declared a state of emergency, which was in effect from October 29 through March 17, 1998. He ordered the detention of some of the hierarchs of the opposition parties, notably those of the former Zambia Democratic Congress and of the United National Independence Party.

At one time, more than 100 citizens were detained; it was also reported that some of the detainees had been tortured or abused in an attempt to get confessions. One such detainee, Robert Chiulo, died under suspicious circumstances in a military hospital.

Former President Chiluba's ruling party and the majority party in the current government, the Movement for Multiparty Democracy (MMD), had viewed the assault on the government media complex as attempted treason and had, accordingly, restricted rights of free expression, assembly, and association.

The government's response to allegations of torture was twofold. First, it set up a Permanent Human Rights Commission to investigate all charges. Second, it ratified the Convention Against Torture and Other Cruel, Inhumane or Degrading Treatment or Punishment. Even so, there were allegations of harassment, of intimidation, and of stonewalling on the part of government investigative agencies.

In May 1998, Joy Sata, a reporter at the government-owned *Zambia Daily Mail*, was threatened with disciplinary action for publicly criticizing her newspaper's practice of toning down editorials critical of the then-ruling Chiluba government. Sata made the comments April 27, 1998, on the government-owned Zambia National Broadcasting Corporation program, "National Watch." She said, "Most of the time, you may want to do a good story but you are told to start your story with a government position and not your own source."

In its front-page advertisement on April 30, 1998, the *Zambia Daily Mail* dissociated itself from the claims made by Sata, whom it described as a "mere reporter" and a "junior member of staff." It wrote, "She appeared on the program purely as a ZAMWA [Zambia Media Women's Association] representative and it is unfortunate that she chose to misrepresent the editorial board on which she does not even sit."

Investigative reporting by independent newspapers (e.g., *The Post*) has resulted in editorials on delusions and rifts within the MMD and in charges of corruption in government. In response to the latter, the government invoked legal procedures, filing scores of lawsuits against journalists. On March 9, 1999, the editorial offices of *The Post* were shut down for 48 hours on the orders of Chitalu Sampa, Zambia's former Minister of Defense, following the arrest and detention of its editor and five reporters for allegedly publishing an article on the previous day on Zambia's military strengths vis-à-vis Angola's. The government had argued that the article had demonstrated the newspaper's undisguised unpatriotic actions and of careless handling of security-related matters.

In November 2002, the government, headed by current President Levy Mwanawasa, thwarted the approval of three bills—the Freedom of Information Act, the Independent Broadcasting Act, and the Zambia National Broadcasting Corporation Act—that, in the view of the Zambia Independent Media Association and opposition members of parliament, would have ensured greater media freedom. But because the government expected the media to engage in a more dynamic social role, it introduced its own version of those bills, incorporating some of the key elements of the earlier version. That compromise version led to the establishment of the supposedly nonpartisan Independent Broadcasting Authority that regulates broadcast institutions. Even so, the Ministry of Information and Broadcasting Services in 2004 banned the broadcast of BBC programs on a community radio station, Breeze FM, in Chipata, on the basis that the government wanted to curb foreign influences on Zambia's airwaves.

Even against the backdrop of the preceding occurrences, there were no widespread threats to the media; freedom of speech and of the press, even if occasionally threatened by government pronouncements and actions, remained largely intact, enabling the media to contribute collectively to the urgent task of nation-building. From a strictly human-rights perspective, Zambia had generally been a beacon of hope for the continent. It has government-run radio and television stations, as well as several privately owned stations. And coverage of domestic issues by its media has usually been pointed.

Democratic Republic of Congo: A Failing Experiment in Social Responsibility

Zaire, as the DRC was known during the administration of Mobutu Sese Seko, was a classic case of personalization, centralization, and dictatorship. Shortly after Mobutu Sese Seko assumed power in 1965, he systematically annihilated the opposition either through co-opting or executing its adherents publicly or through weakening political participation. To consolidate and legitimize his power, in 1967 he created a political organization—the Mouvement Populaire de la Révolution—to replace all political parties. Five years later, he banned all religious radio and television broadcasts and youth movements. Mobutu's control over the legislative process was effected through his control over legislative and judicial appointments; even the Department of Citizens' Rights and Liberties, which he created, could not investigate incidents without the cooperation of other government departments (Leslie, 1993). Ibelema and Onwudiwe (1997) described Mobutu's political influence in these terms: "There has been a parliament, but its role has been more consultative than legislative, and its legislations have been subordinated to Mobutu's wishes— especially on sensitive and consequential issues" (p. 313).

Against the backdrop of abject poverty, widespread government-abetted corruption, and pervasive human-rights abuses, change in then-Zaire, Africa's third-largest country, could come only nonpolitically: on the battlefield.

In October 1996, Laurent Kabila created the Alliance of Democratic Forces for the Liberation of Congo. In just 7 months, it marched on Mobutu's strongholds, causing disaffection, toppling his 30-year regime, and raising hopes for the future of the country.

Upon assuming the presidency of what became known as the DRC in May 1997, Kabila promised to lead the country to presidential elections in 2 years. Meanwhile, a constitutional decree gave him legislative, executive, and judicial powers. Kabila has been cracking down on the media. Genocidal tendencies and terror reign in the country: Early in January 1999, for example, civilians were massacred and some 500 were slain in Makobola, in the eastern part of the country. Police, security agents, and vigilante groups disregard any semblance of justice and routinely humiliate government media staffers. In June 1998, the newly appointed director of the country's national television station was assaulted for failing to broadcast a government event.

The independent media were also publicly intimidated. For example, on April 18, 1998, Radio Amani, which transmitted BBC's African news and was run by the archdiocese of Kisangani, was shut down by the Interior Ministry because it had not respected "the schedule of conditions." And, in January 1999, a suspicious fire destroyed the studios of Radio Television Message de vie, Kinshasa, which was owned by an Angolan Pentecostal minister.

Also on April 18, Andre Ipakala, the editor of a private Kinshasa daily newspaper, *La Reference Plus*, was arrested on charges that he had reported unsubstantiated claims that some military officers had detained, in their private homes, civilians and had tortured them. At about the same period, the editors of two independent publications, *Le Potentiel* and *Le Palmares*, were detained for alleged editorial infractions. Similarly, Thierry Kyalumba, publications director of the independent twice-weekly newspaper, *Vision*, was arrested in May 1998 for "printing false information" on the trial of three political prisoners. Also in May 1998, Jose Kajangwa, director general of the National Radio and Television Agency, and four colleagues were arrested in Kinshasa for using video clips of civilian massacres on the air. More recently, on February 3, 1999, five *Le Potentiel* journalists were arrested for publishing articles critical of a new law regulating political parties.

Oscar Kangoa, a journalist at *Umoja*, a weekly newspaper, was sentenced May 31, 1998, to a 12-month jail term because an article he had written about Justice Minister Mwenze Kongolo's wedding to a U.S. citizen, a wedding to which several U.S. guests were invited at the minister's expense, was interpreted as a "slander against authorities." Kangoa was denied access to a defense lawyer.

Violence and conflicts between ethnic groups in neighboring countries spilled into Congo, creating allegiances and alliances and military incursions from rebel groups in Uganda. Angola, Chad, Namibia, and Zimbabwe intervened in Kabila's behalf, halting the fall of Kinshasa to rebel forces. Arguably, the Kabila government promised democratic reforms and the cessation of overt intimidation of the media.

But, historically, Congo has provided an environment that has not been conducive to human rights and media freedom. Justice, particularly its egalitarian and libertarian attributes, has been undermined continually. Its current president, Joseph Kabila, son of Laurent Kabila, presides over a new coalition government that places Congo on the path to reform and that represents a political transition from the vengeful, inept rule of his father (Duke, 2003).

CONCLUSIONS AND IMPLICATIONS FOR THEORY DEVELOPMENT

This chapter noted at the outset that responsibility gaps occur in corporate activities. Therefore, it is imperative that organizations take stock on how their programs affect both their reputation and profit margins. For Africa's media industry particularly, this chapter uses the ethical principle of justice to establish the notion of human rights as good governance in Africa—albeit in three countries south of the Sahara. It affirms the interplay among human rights, media independence, and good governance—within the overarching theory of CSR. It argues that the dynamic among them will, in the long run, make each to more directly embolden the other. The violation of human rights on the continent presents a continuing threat to justice, to civil liberties, and to good governance, and it compromises organizational efforts toward reformulating CSR as essentially good governance in the African context.

Civil society, democratic governance, and economic and social enterprise are a sine qua non for protecting human rights. Even so, they can promote private rights and can lead to sectional claims, polarization, ethnic rivalries, and reactionary responses (Diamond, 1997; Fatton, 1995).

To what extent, then, do the three nations profiled in this chapter uphold egalitarian and libertarian principles of justice—and, by implication, human rights and good governance? Even though it is difficult to answer that question forthrightly, three overarching conclusions can be drawn.

First, human rights, and by extension good governance, in the three case-study nations fall at different points on a continuum: Ghana at one extreme as a success story of a nation on the road to economic growth and stability; Zambia in the middle as an illustration of a donor-driven, donor-dependent economy; and Congo on the other extreme as an indicator of a failing experiment in CSR. The point on the continuum on which a nation falls—and the extent to which CSR can be repositioned as good governance for sustainable development—will be influenced by three considerations: (a) the extent to which its political system is pluralistic; (b) the extent to which its media organizations have frequent or occasional skirmishes with the government in their quest to contribute to sustainable development ; and (c) the extent to which its citizens are free to engage in practices conducive to personal development. The continuum can easily be misconstrued as a defense of government-dependent governance. The point here is that although governments have the responsibility to shape the push-pull factors that determine the landscape for reframing CSR as good governance, business has an equally critical (and proactive) role in that process.

Second, there is the issue of single-party dominance in countries that have held multiparty elections, as occurred in Kenya in 1992, 1997, and 2002, and in Zambia in 1991, 1996, and 2001. Even in the absence of ethnic conflicts, which are rife in Africa, that dominance raises questions about the relevance of multiparty democracy to media and individual freedoms, particularly in light of the increasing Western donor influence on both multipartyism and media operations.

Finally, as noted earlier, the pre-independence media in Africa were critical of foreign governments' colonial policies. Today, the targets of the media are as different as the issues of the day: they are in the main directed at domestic policies. Human rights, as a product of good governance, are fundamental to media role in contributing to societal well-being. But the extent to which they are embraced in the country examples indicates the fervor with which human-rights groups and media organizations—both independent and government-owned—synergistically protect, defend, and advocate them without the albatross of government policies, pronouncements, and coercive actions and contribute to the continent's development.

An implication of this analysis for theory development in the African context is that an evolving CSR theory assumes major importance well beyond that dictated by the evolving CSR theory in industrialized countries. Four propositions on such a theory are as follows:

- Societal, economic, and political factors in Africa will influence the emerging theory of CSR, as well as the continent's organizational communication models.

- Africa's business organizations will be (perceived as) truly socially responsible if they contribute more directly and forcefully to national and community political discourse, economic programs and social issues, and permit those responsibilities to define and guide their mission.

- The presence of national and community political discourse, economic programs, and social issues in organizational mission in Africa's business sector is essential to, or enhances, a firm reputation, firm risk management, and firm financial performance.

- Changes in economic growth at either national or community levels or both, in FDI flows, and in liberalization and investment policies will have significant effects on—and necessitate a shift in—CSR trends.

At the beginning of this chapter is Abrams's statement made one-half century ago, when he acknowledged how crucial an integration of corporate activities into public welfare is to assessing the real success of a corporation. And an earlier discussion provides examples of the gnawing responsibility gaps among some companies in the United States and among some that operate in Africa. Africa's media industry is not without blemish. Yet CSR is even more crucial in Africa, which, although at risk for a variety of economic, social, and political challenges, still enables business to earn high yields on investment. And the added organizational responsibility—informed by egalitarian and libertarian conceptions of justice—will further increase the benefits that accrue to CSR-driven organizations.

Inarguably, the media industry is at the forefront of the struggle for individual freedoms, human rights, and good governance. But the nonmedia enterprises can contribute as much to that struggle by reformulation their traditional CSR views—those on returns on investment, on trustee management, on self-interest, and on social performance—in response to the characteristics of the environments in which they do business. Business enterprises cannot risk accomplishing anything less.

Another implication is the need for multidisciplinary research to determine empirically the cross-cutting relevance of interpreting human rights as a major component of an extended, reformulated CSR theory. What variables (or factors) predict employees', communities', suppliers', customers', investors', and environmental groups' perceptions and expectations of companies regarding their CSR programs and activities? Inarguably, transnational corporations' practices indicate strong commitment to human rights as a desideratum of their social responsibilities. In 1996, Starbucks Coffee Company, for example, became the first U.S.-based agricultural commodity company to adopt a "Framework for a Code of Conduct" that iterates the company's commitment to human rights. Reebok International Ltd. was the first company anywhere to create a staff position—a vice president for human rights—to provide oversight for the company's human rights training and for its working conditions in company factories. And Rio Tinto, a global mining company, periodically assesses the effects of its activities on local communities and on the environment. It is, therefore, important that the traditional boundaries of the evolving theory of CSR be made ever more flexible to accommodate the expanding social and political role of organizations and of global corporations with operations in Africa, as well as those of Africa's indigenous fledgling industry (e.g., the media). That, perhaps more than anything else, will quicken the pace in which constraints on the good governance of the continent will lose significance.

REFERENCES

Author. (2002). *Achieving the millennium development goals in Africa: Progress, prospects, and policy implications (global poverty report)*. African Development Bank.

Altman, B. W. (1998). Transformed corporate community relations: A management tool for achieving corporate citizenship. *Business and Society Review, 102/103*, 43–45.

Anokwa, K. (1997). Press performance under civilian and military regimes in Ghana: A reassessment of past and present knowledge. In F. Eribo & W. Jong-Ebot (Eds.), *Press freedom and communication in Africa* (pp. 3–28). Trenton, NJ: Africa World Press.

Ansah, P. A. V. (1988). In search of a role for the African media in the democratic process. *Africa Media Review, 2*, 1–16.

Aram, J. D. (1989). The paradox of interdependent relations in the field of social issues in management. *Academy of Management Review, 14*, 266–283.

Aspen Institute and World Resources Institute (n.d.). Beyond grey pinstripes 2003: Preparing MBAs for social and environmental stewardship. www.BeyondGreyPinstripes.org (Retrieved July 25, 2005).

Besser, T. L. (1998). The significance of community to business social responsibility. *Rural Sociology, 63*, 412–431.

Boehm, A. (2002). Corporate social responsibility: A complementary perspective of community and corporate leaders. *Business and Society Review, 107*, 171–194.

Bowen, H. R. (1953). *Social responsibilities of the businessman*. New York City: Harper & Brothers.

Carpenter, D. (2003, November 3). Buy the right thing: Socially conscious investments do good; make good money. *The Washington Post Express*, p. 12.

ChevronTexaco 2002 CR report: Corporate responsibility strategy. *www.chevrontexaco.com/cr_report/overview_strategy/corporate_responsibility_strategy.asp* (Retrieved July 25, 2005).

Conteh-Morgan, E. (1997). *Democratization in Africa: The theory and dynamics of political transitions*. Westport, CT: Praeger.

Cooper, D. (1998). *Governing out of order: Space, law and the politics of belonging*. London: Rivers Oram Press.

Davis, K. (1973). The case for and against business assumption of social responsibilities. *Academy of Management Journal, 16*, 312–322.

Deng, F. M., & Lyons, T. (Eds.). (1998). *African reckoning: A quest for good governance*. Washington, DC: The Brookings Institution.

Diamond, L. (1997). *Prospects for democratic development in Africa* (Hoover Essays in Public Policy No. 74). Stanford University, Hoover Institution on War, Revolution and Peace.

Duke, L. (2003, November 5). The troubled inheritance of Joseph Kabila. *The Washington Post*, pp. C1, C9.

Economic Commission for Africa (2001). *State of the environment in Africa*. Addis Ababa, Ethiopia: Economic Commission for Africa.

Eribo, F. (2001). *In search of greatness: Russia's communication with Africa and the world*. Westport, CT: Ablex.

Fatton, R., Jr. (1995). Africa in the age of democratization: The civic limitations of civil society. *African Studies Review, 38*, 67–99.

Fobanjong, J. (2004). The quest for public relations in Africa: An introduction. In D. J. Tilson & E. C. Alozie (Eds.), *Toward the common good: Perspectives in international public relations* (pp. 203–214). Boston: Allyn & Bacon.

Foreign Direct Investment in Africa: Performance and Potential. (1999, June). Geneva: United Nations Conference on Trade and Development.

Fortune Management Poll. (1946, March). *Fortune, 33*, 197–198.

Freedom House (n.d.). Freedom in the world 2005: Table of independent countries, comparative measures of freedom. *www.freedomhouse.org/research/freeworld/2005/table2005.pdf* (Retrieved July 25, 2005).

Freeman, R. E. (1984). *Strategic management: A stakeholder approach*. Boston: Pitman.

Friedman, M. (1962). *Capitalism and freedom*. Chicago: University of Chicago Press.

Friedman, M. (1970, September 13). A Friedman doctrine—the social responsibility of business is to increase its profits. *The New York Times Magazine*, pp. 32–33, 122, 124, 126.

Gadzekpo, A. (1997). Communication policies in civilian and military regimes: The case of Ghana. *Africa Media Review, 11*, 31–50.

Griffin, J. J., & Mahon, J. F. (1997). The corporate social performance and corporate financial performance debate: Twenty-five years of incomparable research. *Business & Society, 36*, 5–31.

Hachten, W. A. (1971). *Muffled drums: The news media in Africa*. Ames: The Iowa State University Press.

Hazlitt, H. (1972). *The foundations of morality* (2nd ed.). Los Angeles: Nash.

Holtzhausen, D. R., Petersen, B. K., & Tindall, N. T. J. (2003). Exploding the myth of the symmetrical/asymmetrical dichotomy: Public relations models in the new South Africa. *Journal of Public Relations Research, 15*, 305–341.

Ibelema, M., Land, M., Eko, L., & Steyn, E. (2004). Sub-Saharan Africa (East, West and South). In A. S. de Beer & J. C. Merrill (Eds.), *Global journalism: Topical issues and media systems* (pp. 299–341). Boston: Allyn & Bacon.

Ibelema, M., & Onwudiwe, E. (1997). Congo (Zaire): Colonial legacy, autocracy and the press. In F. Eribo & W. Jong-Ebot (Eds.), *Press freedom and communication in Africa* (pp. 303–321). Trenton, NJ: Africa World Press.

Jones, R., & Murrell, A. J. (2001). Signaling positive corporate social performance: An event study of family-friendly firms. *Business & Society, 40*, 59–78.

Joseph, J. (2002). Integrating business ethics and compliance programs: A study of ethics officers in leading organizations. *Business and Society Review, 107*, 309–347.

Karlekar, K. D. (Ed.). (2004). *Freedom of the press 2004: A global survey of media independence*. Lanham, MD: Rowman & Littlefield.

Kasoma, F. P. (1995). The role of the independent media in Africa's change to democracy. *Media, Culture & Society, 17*, 537–555.

Kumar, M. J., & Jones, A. (2005). Government and the press: Issues and trends. In G. Overholser & K. H. Jamieson (Eds.), *The press* (pp. 226–247). New York: Oxford University Press.

Leslie, W. J. (1993). *Zaire: Continuity and political change in an oppressive state*. Boulder, CO: Westview.

Levitt, T. (1958, September–October). The dangers of social responsibility. *Harvard Business Review, 36*, 41–50.

Loveland, J. P., & Whatley, A. A. (1973). The threat of social responsibility. *Business and Society, 13*, 15–20.

Luce, R. A., Barber, A. E., & Hillman, A. J. (2001). Good deeds and misdeeds: A mediated model of the effect of corporate social performance on organizational attractiveness. *Business & Society, 40*, 397–415.

Marsden, C. (2000). The new corporate citizenship of big business: Part of the solution to sustainability? *Business and Society Review, 105*, 9–25.

Martin, R. (2002). Sudan's perfect war. *Foreign Affairs, 81*, 111–127.

Mbaku, J. M. (1999). The relevance of the state in African development: Preparing for the new century. *Journal of Asian and African Studies, 34*, 298–320.

McGuire, J. B., Sundgren, A., & Schneeweis, T. (1988). Corporate social responsibility and firm financial performance. *Academy of Management Journal, 31*, 854–872.

Mwagiru, M. (1997). A return to basics: Media rights as fundamental human rights. *Africa Media Review, 11*, 88–104.

Oestreich, J. E. (2002). What can businesses do to appease anti-globalization protestors? *Business and Society Review, 107*, 207–220.

Ogbondah, C. W., & George, A. (2004). Fire at Nigeria's treasure base: An analysis of Shell Petroleum's public relations strategies in the wake of the Niger Delta crisis. In D. J. Tilson & E. C. Alozie (Eds.), *Toward the common good: Perspectives in international public relations* (pp. 255–278). Boston: Allyn & Bacon.

Orlitzky, M., & Benjamin, J. D. (2001). Corporate social performance and firm risk: A meta-analytic review. *Business & Society, 40*, 369–396.

Phiri, I. (1999). Media in "democratic" Zambia: Problems and prospects. *Africa Today, 46*, 53–65.

Quanzi, A. M. (1997). Corporate social responsibility in diverse environments: A comparative study of managerial attitudes in Australia and Bangladesh. *Business & Professional Ethics Journal, 16*, 67–84.

Rawls, J. A. (1971). *A theory of justice*. Cambridge, MA: Harvard University Press.

Reed, D. (2002). Employing normative stakeholder theory in developing countries: A critical theory perspective. *Business & Society, 41*, 166–207.

Roman, R. M., Hayibor, S., & Agle, B. R. (1999). The relationship between social and financial performance. *Business & Society, 38*, 109–125.

Sethi, S. P., & Steidlmeier, P. (1995). The evolution of business' role in society. *Business and Society Review, 94*, 9–12.

Sriramesh, K., Kim, Y., & Takasaki, M. (1999). Public relations in three Asian cultures: An analysis. *Journal of Public Relations Research, 11*, 271–292.

Sriramesh, K, & White, J. (1992). Societal culture and public relations. In J. E. Grunig (Ed.), Excellence in public relations and communication management (pp. 597–614). Hillsdale, NJ: Lawrence Erlbaum Associates, Inc.

Stanwick, P. A., & Stanwick, S. D. (1998). The relationship between corporate social performance and organizational size, financial performance, and environmental performance: An empirical examination. *Journal of Business Ethics, 17*, 195–204.

Steiner, J. F. (1976). The prospect of ethical advisors for business corporations. *Business and Society, 16*, 5–10.

Turban, D. B., & Greening, D. W. (1997). Corporate social performance and organizational attractiveness to prospective employees. *Academy of Management Journal, 40*,658–672.

Wartick, S. L, & Cochran, P. L. (1985). The evolution of the corporate social performance model. *Academy of Management Review, 10*, 758–769.

Wood, D. J. (1991). Corporate social performance revisited. *Academy of Management Review, 16*, 691–718.

10

Building a Theoretical Model of Media Relations Using Framing, Information Subsidies, and Agenda-Building

Lynn M. Zoch
University of Miami

Juan-Carlos Molleda
University of Florida

This chapter focuses on an area of public relations that many nonpractitioners see as the *only* function of public relations—that of media or press relations. The vision of the practitioner as the press agent, the "mouthpiece" who tells the organization's good-news-only story or the TV-camera-blinded company spokesperson, has a long history.

Scott Cutlip (1994) traces the roots of today's public relations practitioners to the press agentry used by those promoting settlements on the East Coast of the United States in the 1600s. Modern public relations' use of media relations can be traced to the founding of The Publicity Bureau in mid-1900, and the firm's subsequent work for Harvard University, the railroads, and AT&T (Cutlip, 1994). The early careers of practitioners such as Ivy Lee, Edward Bernays, John Hill, and Carl Byoir were based on what was then called press agentry and today has evolved into media relations.

Although the public relations field has expanded well beyond the concept of one-way press agentry, no public relations textbook is complete without a chapter on media relations. Some textbooks use simple titles such as "Media Relations" (Baskin, Aronoff & Lattimore, 1997), "Publicity and Media" (Seitel, 1998), or "Media and Media Relations" (Cutlip, Center, & Broom, 2000), whereas others attempt to draw the focus away from the media by placing relationships with the media within a broader context such as two-chapter packages titled "Written Tactics" and "Spoken Tactics" (Wilcox, Ault, & Agee, 1998) or "Communication Channels and Media" and "Tactics and Techniques" (Newsom, Turk, & Kruckeberg, 2000). In whatever way it is presented, media relations is considered to be an important tool in the practitioner's skill set.

Knowing this, it was then surprising for us to discover in reviewing literature for this chapter that when the key words "media relations" were used to search the Communication Institute for Online Scholarship (CIOS) database, which covers the past 25 years of academic research in the field of communication, there were no matches. It was even more surprising that when we used "press relations" as the key words, only eight articles were cited, and six of those articles actually referred to the relationships between the "press" and various organizations or government bodies.

This, of course, does not mean that no research has been done in the area of public relations effect on the media coverage of organizations, issues, or events (see References). What it does mean is that the work being done may be hard to access through a simple search by a public relations student or practitioner interested in finding out which theories or models inform the practice of media relations.

To simplify the search for a theory with which to underpin media relations, in this chapter we attempt to create a theoretical framework, composed of three currently popular paradigms, through which the practice of media relations can be viewed. We describe it as an active process in which the public relations practitioner has, at the least, a modicum of control over the message she wishes to reach the public, its timing, the source of that information, and the effect on the media agenda of the issue presented.

The three areas we discuss, and from which we construct the theoretical framework, are framing theory, the concept of information subsidies, and the agenda-building paradigm. In this chapter we (1) discuss each of the three theoretical areas individually, (2) make interconnections between the areas,

(3) discuss implications of the three paradigms for practice, (4) develop a model of media relations using the three theoretical areas, and (5) end by discussing the model's implications for theory and research.

FRAMING

The concept of framing has been variously attributed to sociologist Erving Goffman (1974) and anthropologist Gregory Bateson (1955). Although Goffman credits Bateson with the first use of the word "frame" in the sense of a frame of interpretation or metamessage about what is going on in a particular situation, it is Goffman himself who carries the concept into the linguistic analysis of face-to-face interactions.

A number of elements are necessary to understand the concept of the "frame" or message "framing." Goffman (1974) defines a *frame* as a "schemata of interpretation" through which individuals organize and make sense of information or an occurrence (p. 21), whereas Reese (1997) notes that "[f]rames are organizing principles that are socially shared and persistent over time, that work symbolically to meaningfully structure the social world" (p. 5).

"Frames select and call attention to particular aspects of the reality described, which logically means that frames simultaneously direct attention away from other aspects" writes Entman (1993, p. 54). Here the metaphor of a window frame comes to mind. The message framer has the choice of what is to be emphasized in the message, as the view through a window is emphasized by where the carpenter frames, or places, the window. If the window had been placed, or framed, on a different wall, the view would be different.

Because framing involves selecting a particular viewpoint to bring to the fore as well as communicating some aspect of the whole to make it the salient point or points of the frame, it quickly becomes apparent that framing can take place in several locations along the path of any communication transaction. Entman (1993) identifies four locations where frames can occur in the communication transaction, and there serve their function of selecting and emphasizing, in the communication process: the communicator, the receiver, the text, and the cultural framework.

Frames or schemata of interpretation are present in both the communicator and the receiver from which they either build the message or the interpretation of the message. "The *text* [italics in original] contains frames, which are manifested by the presence or absence of certain keywords, stock phrases, stereotyped images, sources of information, and sentences that provide thematically reinforcing clusters of facts or judgments" (Entman, 1993, p. 52). Culture or a social grouping is the origin for many commonly accepted frames that are present in the thinking of a particular group of people. A good example of this is the issue of flying the Confederate battle flag over the state house in South

Carolina. The frame of one social grouping might be that the flag embodies the history and culture of the South and should be flown out of respect for the heritage of the state. Another social grouping works with the collective frame that the flag represents a repressive society and the enslavement of an entire race of people. Goffman (1974) separates frames into two broad classes—natural and social. Natural frames identify occurrences that are purely physical, such as the weather as given in a report. As public relations practitioners we are more concerned with social frames, which Goffman describes as "guided doings" where there is motive and intent to present a particular viewpoint, much like a public relations practitioner presenting information to the media about a particular issue or event. "Social frameworks ... provide background understanding for events that incorporate the will, aim, and controlling effort of an intelligence, a live agency, ... the human being" (Goffman, 1974, p. 22). Thus framing is critical to the construction of social reality—the way people view the world.

In his exhaustive literature review of framing and its relationship to public relations, Hallahan (1999) makes this connection to the practitioner:

> Implicitly, framing plays an integral role in public relations. If public relations is defined as the process of establishing and maintaining mutually beneficial relations between an organization and publics on whom it depends (Cutlip, Center, & Broom, 1995)(sic) the establishment of common *frames of reference* [italics in original] about topics or issues of mutual concern is a necessary condition for effective relations to be established (p. 207).

In terms of a public relations practitioner's use of framing to get out her organization's message, frames have four functions: (1) They define problems, or "determine what a causal agent is doing with what costs and benefits," in this case the organization; (2) they diagnose causes or identify what is causing the problem, either within or outside the organization; (3) they make moral judgments about the situation causing the problem; and (4) they suggest remedies or "offer and justify treatments for the problems" (Entman, 1993, p. 52).

A frame can also be viewed as an idea or central story line that organizes and provides meaning (Gamson & Modigliani, 1987) to the events related to a story or issue. Those looking for such frames can identify them through the use of five common devices: catchphrases, depictions, metaphors, exemplars, and visual images (Gamson & Modigliani, 1989).

From the media's perspective, frames allow journalists to work with large amounts of information quickly, assign that information to its place in the scheme of the story, and package it for the audience so that they too see where the information fits into the issue (Gitlin, 1980). Media framing thus takes into account not just the topic, but how the journalist or media in general cover and package an issue. By focusing attention on the language and defining the issue under consideration, "framing goes well beyond the traditional agenda-setting model, which tends to take issues as givens" (Kosicki, 1993, p. 113). Media can also affect the way issues are framed through the choices of journalists who cover a story, and those who may be chosen as sources (Kosicki & Pan, 1996). For public relations practitioners engaged in working with the media, this is an important point. As is discussed later in this chapter under information subsidies, positioning yourself as an accurate, dependable, and readily available source goes a long way toward getting your message into the media outlets.

A great deal of research has been done on how various topics are framed by both the media and what researchers often term *organizational policy actors*. Andsager and Smiley (1998) write, "Policy actors are entities—such as government agencies, large corporations, elite professional organizations and even citizen-activists—who are outside the media but, because of their size and influence, also possess the ability to intervene in the production of news. Policy actors employ public information officers to communicate their frames" (p. 185).

The largest body of framing research is based around how these policy actors attempt to frame their particular issue or event for the media. Health issues (Andsager & Smiley, 1998; Shriver, White & Kebede, 1998), race (Gandy, Kopp, Hands, Frazer & Phillips, 1997), the environment (Liebler & Bendix, 1996), political campaigns (Domke, Shah, & Wackman, 1998; Miller, Andsager & Riechert, 1998; Missika & Bregman, 1987; Rhee, 1997; Sullivan, 1989), nuclear issues (Entman & Rojecki, 1993; Meyer, 1995), war (German, 1995; Iyengar & Simon, 1993; Reese & Buckalew, 1995; Tankard & Israel, 1997), the government (Jasperson, Shah, Watts, Faber, & Fan, 1998), and political issues (Hanson, 1995; Iorio & Huxman, 1996; Norris, 1995; Woo, 1996) have each lent credence to the idea that the ability to frame the news is an exercise in power.

This chapter posits that along with the media's framing of events and issues, public relations practitioners who act as sources, whether or not they are public information officers for policy actors, also contribute to the framing of a story as presented in the media. They do this by highlighting or withholding specific information about a subject or issue from those covering the story.

The work done by Entman and by Gamson and Modigliani perhaps best inform the conscious framing by public relations practitioners. By using one or more of the five devices noted earlier, and creating a storyline to organize the message (Gamson & Modigliani, 1989), the practitioner can better emphasize her frame to the media. The work of Entman can help the practitioner best determine when use of a frame may be most effective—when defining problems, diagnosing causes or identifying what is causing the problem, making moral judgments about the situation causing the problem, or suggesting remedies for the problems (Entman, 1993, p. 52).

Those engaging in media relations must daily construct and process the information about their organization before releasing that information to the media. Pan and Kosicki (1993) state that framing may be considered a "strategy of constructing and processing news discourse or as a characteristic of the discourse itself" (p. 57). Another responsibility of those practicing media relations is to help the media outlet develop what Gamson (1984, 1989) calls media packages that arrange the assorted facts of a situation or event concerning an organization into a meaningful, organized whole.

INFORMATION SUBSIDIES

Public relations practitioners generate prepackaged information to promote their organizations' viewpoints on issues, and to communicate aspects of interest within those issues, to their internal and external publics. Publicity and public information strategies also assist organizations to meet legal demands of financial disclosure, to influence legislation, and, among other purposes, to publicize organizational actions and operations that could have an impact on their publics or could add to the formation of positive organizational images in the minds of their publics. Gandy (1982) describes the packaged information generated by public relations professionals as *information subsidies*, or the "efforts to reduce the prices faced by others for certain information in order to increase its consumption" (p. 8).[1]

The generation of information by media relations practitioners not only facilitates organizations to freely contribute to the marketplace of ideas, but also facilitates the newsgathering process of media organizations. Newsom et al. (2000) explain:

> Publicity is supposed to facilitate the newsgathering process. PR people expect news people to regard news releases critically, and to use or not use the news release at their own discretion. The release can be rewritten, incorporated with other materials, or not used at the time and used at a later date, sometimes in an unflattering way that is not helpful. That is part of the risk in being a source (p. 238).

The facilitation of the newsgathering process by public relations sources has economic implications for both the practitioners' organizations and media organizations. Organizations of all kinds invest human and monetary resources in producing information that expresses their viewpoints. Media organizations save these resources when they receive packaged information for free or significantly below the cost of production.

---

[1] Gandy derived this definition from Randall Bartlett's (1973) book *Economic Foundations of Political Power*.

The belief that "information is power" is applicable to the implicit value of information subsidies and their control. Turk (1986) writes, "Who has access to information and to what sources of information they have access, seems an important determinant of whose opinion and participation has the potential for influencing organizational life" (p. 1).

Information is seen as a commodity that has a value for those who provide and use it. Gandy (1982) states:

> Sources enter into an exchange of value with journalists in which (1) they reduce the costs of news work to increase their control over news content; (2) they reduce the costs of scientific research to increase their control over scientific and technical information; and (3) they even reduce the costs of writing and producing television fiction to increase their control over the cultural background against which social policy questions are generally framed. (p. 15)

Turk (1986) adds that "sources who make information quickly and inexpensively available to journalists through . . . 'information subsidies' increase the likelihood that the information will be consumed by the journalists and used in media content" (p. 3).

According to Gandy (1982), subsidized information could decrease or increase its value depending on how well disguised the quality of self-interest of the information is, how credible the sources are, and how diverse the available competing information is. Moreover, the value of an information subsidy increases in relation to its quality as perceived by reporters and editors. Editors who believe the authors of news releases share with them a similar education and training in news values are more likely to see the news release as more informational and less promotional (Kopenhaver, 1985, p. 41).

Scholars have studied information subsidies' effectiveness—mainly the generation and publication of news releases—in different types of organizations, such as state appellate courts (Hale, 1978), state agencies (Martin & Singletary, 1981; Turk, 1985, 1986, 1991; Walters & Walters, 1992), a comparison of U.S. and U.K. state agencies (Turk and Franklin, 1987), educational institutions (Bollinger 1999; Morton, 1988; Morton & Warren, 1992a, 1992b, 1992c; Rings, 1971), interest groups (Griffin & Dunwoody, 1995), and the scientific community (Walters & Walters, 1996). Other scholars have focused on wire service delivery of subsidized information (Morton and Ramsey, 1994) and the news media screening process of subsidized materials (Abbott & Brassfield, 1989; Berkowitz & Adams, 1990; Cameron & Blount, 1996).

Scholars have also focused on the information subsidy itself, exploring different characteristics of news releases that appear to contribute to their success in entering the media agenda. For instance, Hale (1978) explains that there seems to be a positive correlation between the length of new releases and the length of coverage. Nevertheless, most research has determined that although public relations practitioners do not have complete control over the outcome of their information subsidies, they can increase their value and chances for success if they focus on certain news values, such as thoroughness and accuracy. Martin and Singletary (1981) state, "Thoroughness and accuracy can be interpreted to mean that, when a reporter receives a news release, the facts should be checked with the news source. The reporter should be alert both to what it said and what it didn't say. It is further assumed that news releases are sometimes self-serving and hence should be rewritten" (p. 93).

News releases distributed through wire services appear to have a high rate of acceptance by newspapers (Gandy, 1992; Martin & Singletary, 1981; Walters & Walters, 1992). Not surprising to most public relations practitioners dealing with the media, releases of a negative or critical nature generate more published stories (Martin & Singletary, 1981). Newspapers, which because of competition increasingly focus mainly on local events, are more receptive to news releases generated by local sources than to releases issued by sources located in other cities or states (Martin & Singletary, 1981; Morton & Warren, 1992a). Similarly, both newspapers and television stations identified local focus, angle or relevance (Abbott & Brassfield, 1989; Berkowitz & Adams, 1990; Morton & Warren, 1992b; Turk, 1985), and timeliness (Abbott & Brassfield, 1989; Rings, 1971; Walters & Walters, 1992) as important factors for saving or rejecting a news release. In addition to standard news value, television stations place special emphasis on the visual possibilities for news releases.

Other aspects of a news release that are considered important by editors are accuracy (Kopenhaver, 1985), readers interests or benefit (Abbott & Brassfield, 1989; Kopenhaver, 1985; Turk, 1991), newsworthiness (Turk, 1991; Walters & Walters, 1992), avoidance of persuasive tactics or objectivity (Rings, 1971; Turk, 1991) and impact (Turk 1991; Griffin & Dunwoody, 1995). In contrast, Morton and Warren (1992a) note that there are three news elements that are difficult for the public relations practitioners to utilize despite the value those news elements have for journalists and editors: oddity, magnitude, and known principals.

The distinction between direct and indirect subsidies is explained by Gandy (1982): "The journalist receives a *direct* [italics in original] information subsidy, and the target in government receives an *indirect* subsidy when the information is read in the paper or heard on the news" (p. 62). When subsidized information is filtered through the media before it reaches its intended audience, usually the government, it becomes an indirect subsidy. Gandy (1992) further elaborates this concept of indirect subsidies:

> Policy actors provide indirect subsidies through a variety of means, most of which have to do with using a credible source to deliver a persuasive message. Journalists are blessed with a self-generated cloak of objectivity. Thus, material perceived as news, rather than as opinion, has a higher value to the decision maker. Indirect subsidies are therefore regularly provided through journalists and editors of print and electronic news media (p. 143).

Indirect subsidies are also delivered through the use of experts, grassroots lobbying, wire services, and satellite distribution (Gandy, 1992). Lobbyists combine subsidized information from their clients and data from their own research and expertise to influence legislation. Legislators use the indirect subsidy for decision making, and media report the development and outcome of this decision making process, which is a second use of that indirect subsidy provided by lobbyists.

By using the methods of direct and indirect subsidies, public relations practitioners wise in the ways of media, and aware of the needs of policy actors to obtain "objective" information about a particular issue, can make every effort to influence decision making for the benefit of their organizations. We also contend that when media outlets are provided a carefully framed message, perhaps even arranged into an organized media package to help facilitate their newsgathering, the benefits to a practitioner's organization increase geometrically. Following is the final piece necessary to build a complete model of active media relations.

AGENDA-BUILDING PROCESS

McCombs and Shaw (1972) introduced the concept of agenda setting to explain the impact of the news media in public opinion formation. The authors explained that the decisions made by editors, reporters, and broadcasters in choosing and reporting news plays an important part in shaping political reality. The findings of the first agenda-setting study, which was based on a political campaign, suggested a very strong relationship between the emphasis placed on different campaign issues by the media and the judgments of voters as to the salience and importance of various campaign topics.

In 1985, Weaver and Elliot asked the question, "Who sets the agenda for the media?" They argued that "it is not quite accurate to speak of the press *setting* [italics in the original] agendas if it is mainly passing on priorities set by other actors and institutions in the society" (p. 87). Earlier discussion in this chapter points out how a media relations practitioner can contribute to *building* the media agenda. For the purposes of our discussion the switch from a discussion of agenda setting to that of agenda building is perhaps most accurate.

This question of who builds media agendas was discussed by Cobb and Elder (1972) and Lang and Lang (1981) early in the development of the agenda-setting paradigm. On the one hand, Cobb and Elder explain that politicians act as opinion leaders and publicize particular issues creating a systematic and formal agenda through symbolic crusades. On the other hand, Lang and Lang (1981) suggest that the agenda-building is a collective and reciprocal process. More specifically, they state that the agenda-building process "is a continuous one, involving a number of feedback loops, most important among which are the way political figures see their own image mirrored in the media, the pooling of information within the press corps, and the various indicators of the public response" (p. 466).

Max McCombs has spent almost 30 years developing and tracking the agenda-setting paradigm (See for example: Brewer & McCombs, 1996; Lopez-Escobar, Llamas, McCombs & Lennon, 1998; McCombs, 1992; McCombs & Masel-Walters, 1976; McCombs & Shaw, 1972; McCombs & Shaw, 1993; Stone & McCombs, 1981; Wanta, Stephenson, Turk & McCombs, 1989). During that time he has presented and watched many changes in the way we view agenda setting. He has come to see agenda setting as a series of levels or phases and now writes of it in that way. Recently he has written that the currently evolving phase of agenda-setting research transformed the news agenda from independent variable to dependent variable, and that means the exploration of the sources that set the agenda to the media (McCombs, 1992; Roberts and McCombs, 1994). According to McCombs, "The outermost layer is the array of sources routinely used by journalists to obtain news. New agenda setting studies linked the interests of public relations researchers with work in the sociology of news. Other work expanded the scope of presidential studies to explore the agenda-setting influence of the nation's number one newsmaker" (1992, p. 816).

Johnson et al., (1996) explain that the collective and reciprocal agenda-building process means that the press, the public, and public officials influence one another and, at the same time, are influenced by one another. They conducted path analysis research and concluded with a model of agenda building that includes at least four stages: (1) real-world conditions set into motion the agenda-building process; (2) the news media increases coverage of the issue; (3) the public picks up salience cues from both real-world conditions and media coverage; and finally (4) the opinion leader (the president in this study) reacts to public concern.

In a similar attempt to explain a model of the agenda building process, Corbett and Mori (1999) point out how issues first arise in society (e.g., a disease epidemic); then interest groups become involved and take positions regarding those issues; third, those interest groups' positions influence the news media and the public; and finally, the news media's coverage influences interest groups that originally became involved in addressing the issue from their particular perspectives. Media coverage also influences the public and politicians.

Walters and Gray (1996) identify another starting point for the agenda-building process when studying how politicians match the agenda of issues important to voters. They argue that voters first set the agenda of issues for political candidates, then voters and candidates simultaneously or separately set the agenda for the news media, and finally the news media organize the agenda of issues of different candidates and groups or voters.

The different stages of the media agenda-building process summarized in Table 10.1 have implications for public relations practitioners in charge of

TABLE 10.1

Dynamic Agenda-Building Process

Researchers	Lang & Lang (1981)	Walters & Gray (1996)	Johnson et al. (1996)	Corbett & Mori (1999)
Process' label	Collective and Reciprocal	Matching Voters' Agenda	Reciprocal Agenda	Circular Relationship
Starting stage	▲ News media highlight events, activities, groups, and personalities	▲ Voters set the agenda of issues to candidates	▲ Real-world conditions set into motion the agenda-building process	▲ Issues arise in society (epidemic disease)
Second stage	▲ The object focus of attention is framed	▲ Both voters and candidates set the agenda to the news media	▲ The news media increase coverage of the issue	▲ Interest groups become involved and take positions regarding those issues
Third stage	▲ The buildup step links the object or event to secondary symbols and it becomes a continuing story	▲ News media organize the agenda of different candidates and sectors in society	▲ The public picks up salience cues from both real-world conditions and media coverage	▲ Interest groups influence the news media and the public
Final stage	▲ Spokespeople articulate demands and command media attention		▲ Opinion leaders react to public concerns	▲ The news media's coverage influences the public, interest groups, and politicians

media relations, as well as for the development of a theoretical framework and future research in the area. These implications will be discussed later in this chapter.

INTERCONNECTIONS BETWEEN THE CONCEPTS

Framing and information subsidies are just tools media relations practitioners can use to participate in the building process of the media agenda. After more than two decades of research regarding the effectiveness of news releases and other subsidized information, findings and implications clearly point to two additional factors that help determine the effectiveness of an information subsidy to influence the media agenda. Although information subsidies may set the stage for the presentation of particular viewpoints, they must be reinforced and complemented by interpersonal interaction and a variety of communication channels. Taking the news release as an example of a subsidy, Ohl, Pincus, Rimmer, and Harrison (1995) argue that it must "be considered more a 'stage setter' than a self-contained news package; that is, it provides basic facts and presents the sponsor's perspective, both of which hopefully whet reporters' appetites to seek further clarification and/or additional information from company sources" (p. 100).

In a previous section we discussed what seems to be a positive relationship between the quality of an information subsidy and the news media's rate of acceptance of it. The ideal outcome of information subsidies' efforts will be that the coverage reflects a similar viewpoint to the one presented in the subsidies. For instance, as early as 1978, Hale found that newspapers emphasized the same characteristics as the court-prepared and subsidized news releases on which the articles were based.

Researchers also have found that when sources of information (in this case public relations practitioners), reporters, and editors cultivate personal relationships with a high level of interpersonal contact based on similar approaches to news values, professional standards, and education level, the impact of those sources on the agenda-building process is greater (Berkowitz & Adams, 1990; Lipschultz, 1991).

Berkowitz (1987), too, argues that the literature regarding sources also facilitates the understanding of the agenda-building process. Some sources, because of their nature and placement within an organization, are seen as more believable than others. An understanding of media needs also helps a source to get information published or to get air play. A number of studies present high-ranking government officials and corporate executives as sources who dominate the agenda-building process by successfully providing their subsidized information to the news media (Berkowitz, 1987; Cameron & Blount 1996; Corbett, 1998; McCombs, Einsiedel & Weaver, 1991; Sachsman, 1976; Weaver & Elliot, 1985). Other sources that researchers find seem to grasp the attention of the media and, therefore, actively participate in building the media agenda are public relations practitioners and spokespersons (Duhé & Zoch, 1994–95; Kopenhaver, 1985; Ohl et al., 1995; Rings, 1971), the U.S. president (McCartney, 1994; Wanta, 1991; Wanta, Stephenson, Turk & McCombs, 1989), celebrities (Corbett & Mori, 1999; Denham, 1999), interest groups (Chang, 1999; Huckins, 1999), scientists (Dunwoody & Ryan, 1983), and court lawyers (Hale, 1978; Lipschultz, 1991).

A number of researchers have made a direct connection between information subsidies and agenda building, starting with Gandy (1982), although he does not use the words *agenda building*, choosing rather to use *agenda setting*. Turk (1986), in her study of public relations influence on the news, was the first to view the connection positively for media relations practitioners. While admitting that the agenda-building process is a complicated one, Berkowitz and Adams (1990) write, "The importance of studying the role of information subsidies in the agenda-building process is that it helps assess the magnitude of news source power" (p. 723). They conclude that the most powerful sources in local televisions news are those who both create news events and cultivate interpersonal relationships with reporters.

Framing also has a connection to agenda building. McCombs has designated it the "emerging second level of agenda setting" (McCombs, Llamas, Lopez-Escobar & Rey, 1997, p. 704) because rather than looking at issues, or what the authors call "objects," framing is involved with describing "*attributes,* [italics in original] those characteristics and properties that fill out the picture of each object" (p. 704). They contend that both the selection of objects and that of attributes are powerful agenda-setting roles. This is a role that the practitioner often plays while attempting to frame her organization's issue in such a way as to make it of interest to the media, because framing a message involves active decisions about the information to include or exclude, to emphasize or elaborate on, to evaluate or interpret. As McCombs et al. (1997) write, "In the language of the second level of agenda setting, framing is the selection of a small number of attributes for inclusion on the media agenda when a particular object is discussed" (p. 704).

As early as 1972 in their article about agenda building in politics, Cobb and Elder write about another aspect of framing. "The symbols, or language, in which an issue is phrased" will affect those who become aware of the issue (p. 162). The decisional aspect of choosing the right words or symbols to convey a particular meaning is part of a conscious effort to frame an issue in a certain way.

Few researchers discuss the use of message framing by sources in their attempt to provide information subsidies, perhaps because it seems too obvious to note. In one study that looked at presidential primaries and developed frames for the candidates based on press releases, the authors noted that these frames were transmitted by public relations practitioners. "This public relations function is referred to as providing information subsidies" (Miller et al., 1998, p. 313).

While no one researcher has previously interconnected the three concepts we have set out here—framing, information subsidies, and agenda building—it became obvious to us in our reading that each of the areas overlaps the other in informing the practice of media relations. We therefore decided to attempt to develop a theoretical model that would have practical implications for the media relations practitioner.

IMPLICATIONS OF THE THREE PARADIGMS

The quality and value of information subsidies to the originating source depend on numerous factors: the quality of the information provided in terms of traditional news values, how carefully the issue is framed to get across a particular issue, the relationship between the source and the reporter or editor, the media organization's news gathering and production process, the conditions present in the social environment, the individual judgment of the journalist, and organizational pressures within the newsroom. These factors affect each other and interact in multiple directions.

Because of these multiple interacting factors, there is also more than one direction or time sequence that can be used to describe the media agenda-building process. Characteristics of the news, where the information used was originally generated—a private organization, government, or a community group, for example—or who first detects an issue and generates the initial story determine which factors play the initial role in the agenda-building process.

Not every issue, or the consequences reported about it, evolves following the same pattern. An issue could arise from society, be produced by an organization, or be uncovered by a news medium. Following are descriptions of the different types of issue development that determine who initiates the media agenda building process.

1. The media agenda-building process could be initiated by the staff of an organization that knows an action or operation could affect one of its publics. This organization would take a proactive approach and design a communication plan to deal with the consequences of its actions or operations on that primary public. An example here would be a pharmaceutical company that developed and tested a new drug to reduce the potential for strokes in people over 65. The drug, as with any strong medication taken by a possibly fragile population, does have the potential to cause life-threatening side effects in a very few people.

The plan could include the production of subsidized information to facilitate the news-gathering process for the news media, and the organization would take the lead in releasing the organization's viewpoint on the issue. The message would be framed that the drug is safe if taken as directed, and the number of strokes it prevents far outweigh any risks of side effects from the medication.

Here the organization could initially control the situation, and media would depend on the organization for original information.

Once the information is released to the media, new actors will participate in the media agenda-building process, including journalists, editors, interest groups such as the American Association of Retired Persons (AARP), the Food and Drug Administration, and any others affected by the issue. The agenda-building process is a dynamic one, and if the media relations practitioner's responsibility is to gain control of the situation for the benefit of the organization she advocates, she needs to also understand how a public forms and evolves and how media follow interest or issue trends. Walters and Gray (1996) explain the dynamic agenda building process with a marketing approach in mind:

> [T]he public relations practitioners recognized, as do all good marketers, that bands of virtual publics linked not by proximity, but by interests and attitudes, define the marketplace.... The marketed public perspective not only recognizes that the agenda building process changes in harmony with the media business, it also changes in concert with society. Just as the concept of a homogeneous melting pot has given way to the view of a socially diverse salad bowl, and as the marketplace of ideas has become the menu of ideas, so too are there changes in the public and its power (p. 14).

2.   In contrast, the actions and operations of an organization could affect one of the organization's publics without the organizations having forecast it. Continuing with the example used above, a drug produced by the pharmaceutical company could have side effects on a group of people with certain unusual characteristics, and those side effects never showed up in drug trials because none of those in the test group had those characteristics (being more than 50% over healthy body weight for example). In this scenario the issue arises from society when a lobbying organization and/or interest group such as the AARP brings the issue to media and public awareness by staging events, taking the issue to the media, or publicly denouncing the company in some other way. Only at this point will the affected organization, the government, opinion leaders, and the news media have influence on the agenda-building they process, and thus they will not have initial control over how the issue is initially framed.

3.   Finally, the news media could become interested in an issue created by an organization or affecting a group in society, but one that has not yet reached the public agenda. To follow with our example, doctors may have contacted the pharmaceutical company about problems their severely overweight patients are having with the drug. The company is working with the FDA to include stronger warnings when the drug is dispensed. In this situation a news organization could initiate the agenda-building process by uncovering and reporting the issue before the organization releases information on the situation along with the steps it is taking to alleviate the problem.

Depending on the prominence and impact of the issue on society, and the activism of special interest groups such as the AARP, other news media will also follow suit in covering the issue. The organization and affected stakeholders will eventually be approached as sources of information or will attempt to provide information subsidies to reporters with whom they have previously worked, and only at that point will they become part of the media agenda-building process.

No matter who originates the coverage of an issue or in what stage of the agenda-building process that entity starts to participate, there are certain characteristics of issues as well as the corporate, media, or societal environments that could determine how information subsidies should be produced and handled. Griffin and Dunwoody (1995) explain that when information about health risks or related topics, such as the release of a new drug and its attendant side effects, is released, this type of information will be treated carefully by the organizations and news media involved in its dissemination. Subsidized information on these topics is valued by news organizations. The greater the impact on individuals or society, the more valuable is the subsidy; the greater the information scarcity, the better the chance that sources who control that information can influence the media agenda.

In both routine and crisis situations, journalists seek information from official sources. Nevertheless, the choices for the selection of sources in crisis situations could vary depending on the availability of the people knowledgeable about the situation. In these cases, organizations could be proactive and provide subsidized information to the news media so their positions are included in the coverage. In routine situations, reporters have more sources available, and so news organizations have more control over who and what is presented in the coverage. This implies that when only a few sources control the submission of information subsidies, these sources could produce subsidies according to the journalists' needs and still frame the information according to their organization's interest. The framing of the news should be done carefully to avoid the devaluation of the subsidy due to heavily self-serving content. Whatever the case, crisis or routine situations, a highly credible source has a greater chance to shape what enters the media agenda.

A MODEL OF MEDIA RELATIONS AND ITS IMPLICATIONS FOR PRACTICE

What we are about to discuss is an ideal vision of the process of media relations from an organizational viewpoint. The model was developed from the perspective of the public relations or media relations practitioner and takes into account all we have learned about positively affecting media coverage and the media agenda from our study of framing, information subsidies, and agenda

TABLE 10.2

A Model of Media Relations

Proactive *information management* and issues tracking entail ...

► Direct communication with organizational sources.

► Identify management positions regarding current or potential issues.

↓

Need to generate an *information subsidy* starts the process ...

1. Actions or operations will affect a public
2. A public reacts before the organization, which failed in tracking an issue/crisis
3. A real-world event produces consequences for the organization
4. The news media report an issue that involves the organization and publics

↓

Proceed with the Internal/external *news-gathering* process ...

• *Internal:* use information file/Intranet-Web site/organizational sources.

• *External:* use professional/industry associations, opinion leaders, experts, etc.

► Identify/seek authorization to express organizational viewpoint/position statement

► Produce information subsidy using traditional news values

► Carefully including organizational viewpoint through framing

↓

Provide news media, interest/grassroots groups with subsidized information ...

► Be ready/available with framed viewpoint for clarification/further inquiries from the news media.

► Monitor news media and audiences' responses/reactions.

► Follow up responses/possible generation of a sequence of information subsidies.

► Pay attention to competing sources—The more competing sources, the more difficult is to be heard.

↓

Evaluate the process and outcome to improve the media relations' efforts.

► Be sure to assess final interpretations/reactions of affected publics regarding organizational viewpoint.

---

building. In this section we are attempting to provide the practitioner with a theoretical and practical base from which to communicate with the media and other publics when an organizational issue arises.

The proposed model of media relations (Table 10.2) illustrates how the theoretical framework discussed in this chapter could be applied in the day-to-day production of framed information subsidies, the attempt by the media relations practitioner to participate in building the news media agenda, and ultimately inclusion on the public's agenda of issues. This model of media relations will also help in focusing future research on each of the stages of the process in an attempt to build a meta-theory that fully explains the complexity of media-public agenda building.

Information Management

Successfully conducting media relations starts long before the media ever become involved. The successful practitioner is constantly involved in a proactive internal information management process. The best position from which to do this, of course, is that of an upper-level manager, a person who participates in the management-level decision making of an organization. The IABC Excellence Study, which produced the book *Excellence in Public Relations and Communication Management* (1992), found in its study of 321 organizations that only those organizations in which public relations functions as an integral part of the management team could truly be considered excellent.

Although the media relations practitioner may not, herself, be part of an upper management team, she must have open access to those in upper management and keep direct communication open with important organizational sources such as the CEO, CFO, president, or vice presidents of important divisions or functions within the organization. Although every organization has its hierarchy and chain of command, employees such as media relations practitioners who are expected to interact quickly and accurately with important external publics must be accorded direct access to the sources they need to accurately explain the organization's stand on issues of concern.

In addition to direct access to important sources, public relations practitioners must engage in constant environmental scanning and issue identification. Environmental scanning is simply gathering information about an organization's publics and external environment in order to identify potential problems. Environmental scanning can be as simple and technical an activity as reading newspapers and journals relevant to an organization and clipping articles that relate to the organization or issues affecting it. It is also "ideally suited for a number of qualitative research techniques, including focus-group studies" (Dozier & Repper, 1992, p. 187). Other methods for such scanning include exploratory surveys and simple case studies.

If organizations deal with arising problems with publics when they are first identified through environmental scanning, public relations practitioners will never find themselves dealing with issues. Unfortunately, that is not usually the case, and a public will make an "issue" out of a situation that hasn't been resolved, thus attracting media coverage of the situation. Examples of common issues are consumer or neighborhood safety concerns, environmental problems involving clean air or water, community development or involvement concerns, and the financial health of the organization.

Need to Generate Information Subsidy

The need to generate an information subsidy starts the media relations portion of the process. We have identified four situations, based to some degree on research in agenda building, in which a practitioner would recognize the need to become involved with the media.

1. The first situation is a case where the organization recognizes that its actions or operations will affect one of its publics.

2. The second situation is when a public reacts before the organization, which has failed to track an emerging issue or situation, reacts. This situation, although in our case involving an organization, parallels the research done by Walters and Gray (1996) involving political candidates. In their study, voters set the agenda of issues for a candidate before the candidate publicly stated the issues he intended to focus on.

3. The third situation is a case where a real-world event produces consequences for an organization. For an organization this could mean the sudden death of a CEO, a natural disaster, or a coup in a country in which the organization operates. Research by Johnson et al. (1996) and Corbett and Mori (1999) (as described in Table 10.1) sets out the agenda-building process in cases where issues first arise in society or "the real world."

4. The final situation is one in which the news media report an issue that involves the organization and at least one of its publics, without the organization first initiating the information subsidy. Lang and Lang (1981), in an early agenda-building article, clearly describe the stages in the process when the media initiate a story or issue.

In the first three situations, the media relations practitioner can be proactive in contacting the news media, providing information subsidies, and carefully framing the organization's stand or viewpoint. In the fourth situation, the best a practitioner can do initially is to promptly attend to media requests for information, provide the organization's viewpoint as quickly and accurately as possible, provide properly prepared upper management spokespersons as required, and frame answers to the information requested as carefully and positively as possible.

Information-Gathering Process

Once it becomes obvious that there is a need to provide an information subsidy, the practitioner proceeds with internal and external information gathering.

This is a time to carefully review the organization's file of articles published about the organization, the issue in question, or related issues; conduct Internet searches for information about similar issues that may have affected competitors; call the relevant internal department, division, or individual to obtain the latest information available about the situation; interview upper management to cull good quotes; and begin to develop the frame with which the organization will discuss the issue. Developing a frame means deciding which information to include or exclude, particular words to use or avoid, visuals to provide, etc. Areas to consider when framing an issue will be discussed in more depth in the following section.

Producing the Information Subsidy

As we discussed earlier in this chapter, in the section on information subsidies, there are specific ways a media relations practitioner can improve her chances of getting the organization's viewpoint out to the ultimate target audience—the public—intact. Table 10.3 is a compilation of the important qualities of an information subsidy in order for it to be usable by the media, along with the

TABLE 10.3

Quality of Information Subsidy

Components of News	Author(s)
▶ **Impact** on the local community or business sector	Griffin & Dunwoody, 1995
▶ **Prominence** of the news source (This may emphasize to the media relations practitioner the importance of using a manager at the highest possible level from whom to extract quotes)	Weaver & Elliot, 1985
▶ **Credibility** of the news source (A source is more credible when he or she has no obvious interest in the outcome of an issue, so finding a credible, disinterested source may become a priority with some issues)	Gandy, 1982
▶ **Attractiveness** of the news source to the targeted public	Wanta, 1991
▶ Shape the information to fill the **journalists' needs**	Berkowitz & Adams, 1990
▶ **Access** to company executives may affect story length, point of view, and publication of lead paragraphs	Ohl et al., 1995
▶ Inclusion of **traditional news values**, such as thoroughness, accuracy, local focus, timeliness, visual possibilities (television-Internet), newsworthiness, readers' interests or benefit, avoidance of persuasive tactics, and impact	See pages 285 and 286 for a complete list of authors.
▶ **Quotability** of source	Culbertson & Stempel, 1984

TABLE 10.4

Elements of Framing

Media Relations Practitioner's Actions or Thought Process	Adapted From
▶ **Interpret** what is going on in a particular situation.	Bateson, 1954
▶ **Select and call attention** to particular aspects of the described issue or situation, which logically means directing attention away from other aspects.	Entman, 1993
▶ **Include or exclude** certain keywords, stock phrases, stereotyped images, and sources of information that thematically reinforce clusters of facts or judgments.	Entman, 1993
▶ **Establish** common *frames of reference* about topics or issues of mutual concern.	Hallahan, 1999
▶ **A frame has four functions**: (**1**) to define the problem, or state what the organization is doing with what cots and benefits; (**2**) they identify what is causing the problem, either within or outside the organization; (**3**) they make moral judgments about causing the problem; and (**4**) they suggest or justify solutions to the problem.	Entman, 1993
▶ **Use examples**, visual images or metaphors.	Gamson & Modigliani, 1989
▶ **Frames can be affected** by the journalist who covers a story, and sources used in providing the subsidy.	Kosicki & Pan, 1996

researchers who identified those qualities. It is also important to remember that a solid interpersonal relationship established over time between a practitioner and a reporter goes a long way toward getting an information subsidy a reading or hearing. Research also has shown that reporters repeatedly go to sources who are like themselves, and that they tend not to select sources who refute their own ideas (Powers & Fico, 1994). A media relations practitioner would do well to cultivate relationships with reporters who have shown themselves supportive, or at the least objective, about the sorts of issues that affect her organization.

Careful framing of the organization's position or stand on the issue is also an important step in preparing an information subsidy for the media. Table 10.4 reviews aspects of framing that should be considered by the media relations practitioners when constructing an information subsidy of any kind.

Organizational Authorization

Once the media relations practitioner has gathered all the information she considers relevant to the situation, and carefully framed the information to present the organization's viewpoint in an accurate yet positive way, she needs to verify the statement and collateral information she will present to the media. This is the time for the practitioner to recontact those individuals who were interviewed in the information-gathering process. This may also, depending on the issue, be the time to contact the legal or other regulatory departments within the organization.

In all situations, but especially in a situation where the organization is reacting to a media report, it is essential for the media relations practitioner to seek as high a level of authorization as possible to express the organizational viewpoint or position. This is a case where a public relations practitioner having unquestioned access to upper levels of management is essential to the organization.

Once the position statement has been authorized, and the information to be released to the media agreed upon, the media relations practitioner can move to the next step.

Contact the News Media

The message is framed, the subsidy prepared, and necessary authorizations received. If this is a situation in which the organization can be proactive, the media relations practitioner contacts the news media to provide the subsidy. In cases where the organization has not been the first to report an issue, and it has been reported first by the media, the public relations practitioner must be ready and available to talk with the media to clarify the organization's position on the issue and to answer any further inquiries. In such a case, the subsidy must be prepared and framed as carefully, if not more carefully, than if the organization had contacted the news media first.

Monitor Coverage and Responses

When the information subsidy is accepted by the news media and coverage starts appearing in various news outlets, the media relations practitioner begins to monitor this media coverage for accurate reporting of the organization's stand, completeness of information, how organizational sources are presented, and the media framing of the issue. It is important to remember that framing of an issue can be at the level of the source, the media, or the ultimate audience, and monitoring the media will only identify the first two levels.

The practitioner also monitors the reactions and responses not only of the general media audience (the newspaper reader or television viewer) but also of targeted publics and particular interest groups that themselves are affected by the issue at hand. Do the publics themselves respond in the media, or do they communicate directly with the organization? How close do the positions of the organization and the affected public or interest group appear to be, as reported in the media? From this monitoring, the media relations practitioner decides how any follow-up information should be framed and goes through the process of preparing further subsidies, as noted earlier.

Follow Up as Necessary

All responses from affected publics or interest groups must be noted and responded to. The practitioner should also prepare for possible generation of a sequence of information subsidies as the agenda on the issue is building in the media and the organization's environment. Continue to monitor media coverage of the issue, and pay particular attention to competing sources such as interest groups, community opinion leaders, politicians, or other organizations as they "weigh in" on the issue in the media. The more competing sources there are commenting on the issue, the more difficult it is to be heard, and the small amount of control the media practitioner has over the message the public is receiving through the media becomes even less.

It is at times like these, when the media are rife with competing viewpoints, that the practitioner must remember there are other ways to reach the organization's publics and stakeholders than through the mass media. Although the purposes of this chapter are to discuss media relations, how to frame messages targeted to the media, and how to produce information subsidies with the goal of building the media agenda, it would be remiss of us not to remind the reader that messages can be relayed and reinforced by means other than mass media.

Evaluate

The final step is to evaluate both the process of producing the subsidy and the outcome of media coverage in order to improve the media relations' efforts in the future. It is important to identify and assess the final interpretations and reactions of affected publics regarding the organizational viewpoint in this situation. It is also important to determine whether your theoretical framework—producing a carefully framed information subsidy in order to attempt to build the media agenda—for the media relations effort was effective.

Did the organization's position, as framed and provided through information subsidies, reach the publics? Did the publics understand the position? Were they swayed in their viewpoint? Does further communication activity, perhaps reaching beyond the media, need to take place with this public or interest group? Has the organization reached understanding with the affected groups?

The proposed model of media relations presents different stages on which researchers should focus.... Each stage has implications for the next. The output from one stage will be the input for the next, and a cycle develops. Even though we are presenting this model as linear, it is not linear in the world. According to the type of issue, crisis or noncrisis situations, the number of competing sources, and the quality of the relationships between media and source, the process will change.

IMPLICATIONS FOR RESEARCH AND THEORY

Becoming proficient in media relations is a complex process involving a deep understanding of media routines, interpersonal relations, and message construction; a savvy regard for timing, organizational factors, and news values; good research, both internal and external; awareness of current and potential environmental and public issues; and familiarity with organizational stakeholders, publics, and interest groups. Each of these areas holds potential for further research into the media relations process.

Much of the research we have quoted here has been undertaken from the viewpoint of the reporter or the media organization, a common problem also faced by other public relations researchers attempting to write about the relationship between public relations practitioners and the media. Cameron, Sallot, and Curtin, in their 1997 article on public relations and the production of news, write that although a "significant portion of the media sociology literature is devoted to source-reporter relations . . . most of this literature focuses on the routines and values of the reporter, not of the source" (p. 112).

Researchers would add significantly to the public relations body of knowledge simply by focusing their studies from the standpoint of the source rather than the receiver of information. Although some scholars complain that most public relations research is simply descriptive, we believe that with the dearth of research in this area, even descriptive studies will contribute if they are theoretically based. The areas discussed in this chapter—framing, information subsidies, and agenda building—offer the framework for three theories on which research studies can be built. Theories can also be pulled from management, interpersonal relations, sociology, and psychology to underpin further studies on organizational culture and its relationship to media relations, message construction, source-reporter and organization-public relationships, and the types of information subsidies that are most effective.

More work needs to focus on how framing theory is used by public relations practitioners, or sources in general, to influence not only media coverage, but the building of media agendas on particular issues. To date most mass communication research has focused on media use of framing in presenting issues to their audiences.[2]

Historically, in agenda-setting research, most studies have compared "Time One" to "Time Two" in order to assess the influence of the media agenda over the public agenda, and vice versa. Research undertaken to test the model introduced in the chapter, in which a media relations practitioner attempts to

---

[2] Framing theory's original focus was on interpersonal communication.

influence the agenda-building process through the use of carefully prepared and framed information subsidies, requires a multistage research process using both quantitative and qualitative methods.

For example, a story or issue could be the unit of analysis in a time sequence.

1. Measurement at Time 1 would be the production of the information subsidy. The researcher might study the influence of organizational, professional, and personal variables in the production of the subsidy. Specific framing techniques might also be quantified so they could be followed through the process to measure their inclusion in the other stages.

2. Time 2 would involve measuring the inclusion of the story or issue on the media agenda. The researcher would identify broadcast or print stories that identified, included, or followed the issue. Additional variables to study might be the influence of relationship quality between the source and reporter, competing sources, and media organization variables.

3. The final measurement at Time 3 in this example would be public understanding of the organization's framed position or viewpoint. Members of the ultimate target public who received the framed subsidy through the mass media could be studied. In this case, variables of interest might be the influence of competing sources and the quality of the indirect subsidy provided by the news media.

It would be appropriate to use a combination of research methods to conduct the proposed multistage research that is required to study the variables affecting the effectiveness of information subsidies in entering the media and public agendas of issues. Examples of possible methods are content analysis, interviews, survey research, focus groups, and path analysis.

Of course, other questions regarding information subsidies remain. A great deal of research has been done with regard to making the direct media subsidy as effective as possible, with researchers looking at timing, method of transmission, commonality of the source with the receiver, self-interest of the information, credibility of the source, and availability of competing information. Most research, however, has been conducted with a focus on media releases, or direct media subsidies. No work has been done to date to compare direct to indirect subsidies, or to even attempt to determine the efficacy of indirect subsidies, since Gandy's 1992 theoretical explication of the concept.

What we have done in this chapter is to review three existing theories or concepts in the communication literature in light of the potential impact of organizations and media for setting the agenda for the public. This allowed us to describe the media relations process based on theory, and thus to provide an example of the usefulness of combining theories or concepts to explain a phenomenon, in this case the media relations process.

The three concepts discussed here complement and inform each other and the practice of media relations. Not only do they provide a model of the practice of media relations, but we found this to be an excellent way to see the evolution of a theoretical approach such as agenda setting. After the first question—how do the media set the agenda of public issues?—we looked at who set the agenda for media. The third step was to identify how information is relayed (subsidies) and communicated (framing), and the final step was to pull together how practitioners can use all of this to better do their jobs.

In the case of two of the theories used in this chapter—framing and agenda building—we have taken concepts that have been used to explain the process from the media perspective and now here are being used to explain the process from the practitioner's perspective. Agenda building developed from agenda setting—the study of how the media act to identify issues the public needs to be concerned with. Agenda building takes the concept back one step to the source of the information used by the media. In the mass communication use of framing, framing theory was used to describe how media organizations presented information to the public. In this use, issues or stories were seen in certain ways by the reader or viewer because of the words and visuals used by reporters—how they "framed" the story. In this chapter we discuss how practitioners "frame" information to be presented to media representatives.

The same process of taking theories used in other contexts and applying them to pubic relations can be used to explain other aspects of practitioners' jobs. Perhaps to us the most exciting part about this type of exercise is the potential to generate new ways to conduct research and to combine theories from different fields into interdisciplinary explanations that can be used by public relations practitioners.

REFERENCES

Abbott, E. A., & Brassfield, L. T. (1989). Comparing decisions on releases by TV and newspapers gatekeepers. *Journalism Quarterly, 66*, 853–856.

Andsager, J., & Smiley, L. (1998). Evaluating the public information: Shaping news coverage of the silicone implant controversy. *Public Relations Review, 24*, 183–201.

Bartlett, R. (1973). *Economic foundations of political power*. New York: Free Press.

Baskin, O., Aronoff, C., & Lattimore, D. (1997). *Public relations: The profession—the practice (4th ed.)*. Brown, Benhmaks & Dubuque.

Bateson, G. (1954). A theory of play and phantasy. *Psychiatric Research Reports, 2*, 39–51.

Berkowitz, D. (1987). TV news sources and new channels: A study in agenda-building. *Journalism Quarterly, 64*, 508–513.

Berkowitz, D., & Adams, D. B. (1990). Information subsidy and agenda-building in local television news. *Journalism Quarterly, 67*, 723–731.

Bollinger, L. (1999). *Exploring the relationship between the media relations writer and the press: An analysis of the perceptions, goals and climate of communication.* Unpublished doctoral dissertation, University of South Carolina, Columbia.

Brewer, Marcus, & McCombs, Maxwell. (1996). Setting the community agenda. *Journalism and Mass Communication Quarterly. 73*, (1, Spring), 7–16.

Cameron, G. T., & Blount, D. (1996). VNRs and air checks: A content analysis of the use of video news releases in television newscasts. *Journalism and Mass Communication Quarterly, 73*, 890–904.

Cameron, G. T., Sallot, L. M., & Curtin, P. A. (1997). Public relations and the production of news: A critical review and theoretical framework. *Communication Yearbook, 20*, 111–155.

Chang, K. (1999). Auto trade policy and the press: Auto elite as a source of the media agenda. *Journalism and Mass Communication Quarterly, 76*, 312–324.

Cobb, R. W., & Elder, C. D. (1972). *Participation in American politics: The dynamics of agenda-building.* Baltimore: Johns Hopkins University Press.

Culbertson, Hugh M., & Stempel, Guido H., III. (1994). The prominence and dominance of news sources in newspaper medical coverage. *Journalism Quarterly. 61*, (3, Autumn), 671–676.

Corbett, J. B. (1998). The environment as theme and package on a local television newscast. *Science Communication, 19*, 222–237.

Corbett, J. B., & Mori, M. (1999). Medicine, media, and celebrities: News coverage of breast cancer, 1960–1995. *Journalism and Mass Communication Quarterly, 76*, 229–249.

Cutlip, S. M. (1994). *The unseen power: Public relations—a history.* Hillsdale, NJ: Lawrence Erlbaum Associates.

Cutlip, S. M., Center, A. H., & Broom, G. M. (1994). *Effective public relations (7th ed.)* (p. 6). Englewood Cliffs, NJ: Prentice Hall.

Cutlip, S. M., Center, A. H., & Broom, G. M. (2000). *Effective public relations (8th ed.).* Upper Saddle River, NJ: Prentice Hall.

Denham, B. E. (1999). Building the agenda and adjusting the frame: How the dramatic revelations of Lyle Alzado impacted mainstream press coverage of anabolic steroid use. *Sociolofy of Sport Journal, 16*, 1–15.

Domke, D., Shah, D. V., & Wackman, D. B. (1998). Media priming effects: Accessibility, association and activation. *International Journal of Public Opinion Research, 10*, 51–74.

Dozier, D. M., & Repper, F. C. (1992). Research firms and public relations practices. In J. E. Grunig (Ed.), *Excellence in public relations and communication management (pp. 185–215).* Hillsdale, NJ: Lawrence Erlbaum Associates.

Duhé, S. F., & Zoch, L. M. (1994–95). Framing the media's agenda during a crisis. *Public Relations Quarterly, 39*, 42–45.

Dunwoody, S., & Ryan, M. (1983). Public information persons as mediators between scientists and journalists. *Journalism Quarterly, 59*, 647–656.

Entman, R. M. (1993). Framing: Toward a clarification of a fractured paradigm. *Journal of Communication, 43*, 51–58.

Entman, R. M., & Rojecki, A. (1993). Freezing out the public: Elite and media framing of the U.S. anti-nuclear movement. *Political Communication, 10*, 155–173.

Gamson, W. A. (1984). *What's news: A game simulation of TV news.* New York: Free Press.

Gamson, W. A. (1989). News as framing. *American Behavioral Scientist, 33*, 157–161.

Gamson, W. A., & Modigliani, A. (1987). The changing culture of affirmative action. In R. G. Braungart & M. M. Braungart (Eds.), *Research in political sociology* (vol. 3, pp. 137–177). Greenwich, CT: JAI Press.

Gamson, W. A., & Modigliani, A. (1989). Media discourse and public opinion: A constructionist approach. *American Journal of Sociology, 95*, 1–37.

Gandy, O. H., Jr. (1982). *Beyond agenda setting: Information subsidies and public policy.* Norwood, NJ: Ablex.

Gandy, O. H., Jr. (1992). Public relations and public policy: The structuration of dominance in the information age. In E. L. Toth and R. L. Heath (Eds), *Rhetorical and critical approaches to public relations* (pp. 131–163). Hillsdale, NJ: Lawrence Erlbaum Associates.

Gandy, O. H. Jr., Kopp, K., Hands, T., Frazer, K., & Phillips, D. (1997). Rice and risk: Factors affecting the framing of stories about inequality, discrimination and just plain back luck. *Public Opinion Quarterly, 6*, 158–182.

German, K. M. (1995). Invoking the glorious war: Framing the Persian Gulf conflict through directive language. *Southern Communication Journal, 60*, 292–302.

Gitlin, T. (1980). *The whole world is watching: Mass media and the making and unmaking of the new left.* Berkeley: University of California Press.

Goffman, E. (1974). *Frame analysis: An essay on the organization of experience.* Cambridge, MA: Harvard University Press.

Griffin, R. J., & Dunwoody, S. (1995). Impacts of information subsidies and community structure on local press coverage of environmental contamination. *Journalism and Mass Communication Quarterly, 72*, 271–284.

Grunig, J. E. (Ed.). (1992). *Excellence in public relations and communication management.* Hillsdale, NJ: Lawrence Erlbaum Associates.

Hale, F. D. (1978). Press releases vs. newspaper coverage of California Supreme Court decisions. *Journalism Quarterly, 55*, 696–702/710.

Hallahan, K. (1999). Seven models of framing: Implications for public relations. *Journal of Public Relations Research, 11*, 205–242.

Hanson, E. C. (1995). Framing the world news: *The Times of India* in changing times. *Political Communication, 12*, 371–393.

Huckins, K. (1999). Interest-group influence on the media agenda: A case study. *Journalism and Mass Communication Quarterly, 76*, 76–86.

Iorio, S. H., & Huxman, S. S. (1996). Media coverage of political issues and the framing of personal concerns. *Journal of Communication, 46*, 97–115.

Iyengar, S., & Simon, A. (1993). News coverage of the gulf crisis and public opinion: A study of agenda-setting, priming, and framing. *Communication Research, 20*, 365–383.

Jasperson, A. E., Shah, D. V., Watts, M., Faber, R. J., & Fan, D. P. (1998). Framing and the public agenda: Media effects on the importance of the federal budget deficit. *Political Communication, 15*, 205–224.

Johnson, T. J., Wanta, W., Boudreau, T., Blank-Libra, J., Schaffer, K., & Turner, S. (1996). Influence dealers: A path analysis model of agenda building during Richard Nixon's war on drugs. *Journalism and Mass Communication Quarterly, 73*, 181–194.

Kopenhaver, L. L. (1985). Aligning values of practitioners and journalists. *Public Relations Review, 11*, 34–42.

Kosicki, G. M. (1993). Problems and opportunities in agenda-setting research. *Journal of Communication, 43*, 100–127.

Kosicki, G. M., & Pan, Z. (1996, May). *Framing analysis: An approach to media effects.* Remarks presented to the annual meeting of the International Communication Association, Chicago.

Lang, G. E., & Lang, K. (1981). Watergate: An exploration of the agenda-building process. *Mass Communication Review Yearbook, 2*, 447–469.

Liebler, C. M., & Bendix, J. (1996). Old-growth forest on network news: News sources and the framing of an environmental controversy. *Journalism & Mass Communication Quarterly, 73*, 53–65.

Lipschultz, J. H. (1991). A comparison of trial lawyer and news reporter attitudes about court-house communication. *Journalism Quarterly, 68*, 750–763.

Lopez-Escobar, E., Llamas, J. P., McCombs, M., & Lennon, F. R. (1998). Two levels of agenda setting among advertising and news in the 1995 Spanish elections. *Political Communication, 15*, 225–238.

Martin, W. P., & Singletary, M. W. (1981). Newspaper treatment of state government releases. *Journalism Quarterly, 58*, 93–96.

McCartney, J. (1994, September). Rallying around the flag. *American Journalism Review, 40*–46.

McCombs, M. (1992). Explorers and surveyors: Expanding strategies for agenda-setting research. *Journalism Quarterly, 69*, 813–824.

McCombs, M., Einsiedel, E., & Weaver, D. (1991). *Contemporary public opinion*. Hillsdale, NJ: Lawrence Erlbaum Associates.

McCombs, M., Llamas, J. P., Lopez-Escobar, E., & Rey, F. (1997). Candidate images in Spanish elections: Second level agenda-setting effects. *Journalism and Mass Communication Quarterly, 74*, 703–717.

McCombs, M., & Masel-Walters, L. (1976). Agenda-setting: A new perspective on mass communication. *Mass Communication Review, 3*, 3–7.

McCombs, M. E., & Shaw, D. L. (1972). The agenda setting function of mass media. *Public Opinion Quarterly, 36*, 176–187.

McCombs, M. E., & Shaw, D. L. (1993). The evolution of agenda- setting research: Twenty-five years in the marketplace of ideas. *Journal of Communication, 43*, 58–67.

Meyer, D. S. (1995). Framing national security: Elite public discourse on nuclear weapons during the cold war. *Political Communication, 12*, 173–192.

Miller, M. M., Andsager, J. L., & Riechert, B. P. (1998). Framing the candidates in presidential primaries: issues and images in press releases and news coverage. *Journalism and Mass Communication Quarterly, 75*, 312–324.

Missika, J. L., & Bregman, D. (1987). On framing the campaign: Mass media roles in negotiating the meaning of the vote. *European Journal of Communication, 2*, 289–309.

Morton, L. P. (1988). Effectiveness of camera-ready copy in press releases. *Public Relations Review, 14*, 45–49.

Morton, L. P., & Ramsey, S. (1994). A benchmark study of the PR News Wire. *Public Relations Review, 20*, 171–182.

Morton, L. P., & Warren, J. (1992a). News elements and editors' choices. *Public Relations Review, 18*, 47–52.

Morton, L. P., & Warren, J. (1992b). Proximity: Localization vs. distance in PR news releases. *Journalism Quarterly, 69*, 1023–1028.

Morton, L. P., & Warren, J. (1992c). Acceptance characteristics of hometown press releases. *Public Relations Review, 18*, 385–390.

Newsom, D., Turk, J. V., & Kruckeberg, D. (2000). *This is PR: The realities of public relations (7th ed.)*. Belmont, CA: Wadsworth.

Norris, P. (1995). The restless searchlight: Network news framing of the post-cold war world. *Political Communication, 12*, 357–370.

Ohl, C. M., Pincus, J. D., Rimmer, T., & Harrison, D. (1995). Agenda building role of news releases in corporate takeovers. *Public Relations Review, 21*, 89–101.

Pan, Z., & Kosicki, G. (1993). Framing analysis: An approach to news discourse. *Political Communication, 10*, 55–75.

Powers, A., & Fico, F. (1994). Influences on use of sources at large U.S. newspapers. *Newspaper Research Journal, 15*, 87–97.

Reese, S. D., & Buckalew, B. (1995). The militarism of local television: The routine framing of the Persian Gulf War. *Critical Studies in Mass Communication, 12*, 40–59.

Reese, S. D. (1997). *Framing public life: A bridging model for media study.* A synthesis keynote review presented at the inaugural conference of the Center for Mass Communications Research, College of Journalism and Mass Communications of the University of South Carolina, Columbia, SC.

Rhee, J. W. (1997). Strategy and issue frames in election campaign coverage: A social cognitive account of framing effects. *Journal of Communication, 47*, 26–48.

Rings, R. L. (1971). Public school news coverage with and without PR directors. *Journalism Quarterly, 48*, 62–72.

Roberts, M., & McCombs, M. (1994). Agenda setting and political advertising: Origins of the news agenda. *Political Communication, 11*, 249–262.

Sachsman, D. B. (1976). Public relations influence on coverage of environment in San Francisco area. *Journalism Quarterly, 53*, 54–60.

Seitel, F. P. (1998). *The practice of public relations (7th ed.).* Upper Saddle River, NJ: Prentice Hall.

Shah, D. V., Domke, D., & Wackman, D. B. (1996). "To thine own self be true": Values, framing, and voter decision-making strategies. *Communication Research, 23*, 509–560.

Shriver, T. E., White, D. A., & Kebede, A. (1998). Power, politics, and the framing of environmental illness. *Sociological Inquiry, 68*, 458–475.

Stone, G. C., & McCombs, M. E. (1981). Tracing the time lag in agenda-setting. *Journalism Quarterly, 58*, 51–55.

Sullivan, P. A. (1989). The 1984 vice-presidential debate: A case study of female and male framing in political campaigns. *Communication Quarterly, 37*, 329–343.

Tankard, J. W. Jr., & Israel, B. (1997). *PR goes to war: The effects of public relations campaigns on media framing of the Kuwaiti and Bosnian crises.* Paper presented at the annual convention of the Association for Education in Journalism and Mass Communication, Chicago, IL.

Turk, J. V. (1985). Information subsidies and influence. *Public Relations Review, 11*, 10–25.

Turk, J. V. (1986). Information subsidies and media content: A study of public relations influence on the news. *Journalism Monographs, 100*, 1–29.

Turk, J. V. (1991). Public relations' influence on the news. In D. L. Protess and M. McCombs (Eds.), *Agenda setting: Readings on media, public opinion, and policymaking* (pp. 211–222). Hillsdale, NJ: Lawrence Erlbaum Associates.

Turk, J. V., & Franklin, B. (1987). Information subsidies" Agenda-setting traditions. *Public Relations Review, 13*, 29–41.

Walters, L. M., & Gray, R. (1996). Agenda building in the 1992 presidential campaign. *Public Relations Review, 22*, 9–24.

Walters, L. M., & Walters, T. N. (1992). Environment of confidence: Daily newspaper use of press releases. *Public Relations Review, 18*, 31–46.

Walters, L. M., & Walters, T. N. (1996). It loses something in the translation: Syntax and survival of key words in science and nonscience press releases. *Science Communication, 18*, 165–180.

Wanta, W. (1991). Presidential ratings as a variable in the agenda-building process. *Journalism Quarterly, 68*, 672–679.

Wanta, W., Stephenson, M. A., Turk, J. V., & McCombs, M. E. (1989). How president's State of Union talk influenced news media agendas. *Journalism Quarterly, 66*, 537–541.

Weaver, D., & Elliot, S. M. (1985). Who sets the agenda for the media? A study of local agenda-building. *Journalism Quarterly, 62*, 87–94.

Wilcox, D. L., Ault, P. H., & Agee, W. K. (1998). *Public relations strategies and tactics (5th ed.)*. New York: Longman.

Woo, J. (1996). Television news discourse in political transition: Framing the 1987 and 1992 Korean presidential elections. *Political Communication, 13*, 63–80.

CHAPTER

11

Internal Public Relations, Social Capital, and the Role of Effective Organizational Communication

William R. Kennan
and Vincent Hazleton

Radford University

INTRODUCTION

The long history associated with organizational scholarship includes an extended and unresolved discussion of the ideal relationship that ought to exist between management and employees. That dialog has largely (although not exclusively) centered on the role of management, the lot of employees, and how those two very different groups might most effectively combine in ways that further organizational goals and objectives. More directly, it is fair to say that internal public relations is both grounded in and bounded by this relationship.

From the point of view of employees, and from the perspective of public relations, the most important public is management, whereas from management's perspective the most important public is employees. Ultimately, for both, being able to build and then explain a productive relationship to external publics is central to such goals as attracting investors, customers, and new employees.

This chapter is organized in the following manner. The first section provides a historical view of theories of organizational management and communication. It concludes with a discussion of the basic requirements for a theory of internal public relations. The second section discusses social capital as a theoretic perspective for a consideration of internal public relations. It includes a historical overview of this concept and a description of the theory and its components, and concludes by discussing its applications to internal public relations.

A HISTORICAL OVERVIEW

Every text written on organizational communication, management, and industrial psychology dwells in large measure on the inherent tension between those whose roles in organizations are identified as "management" and those whose roles define them as "workers." The relationship has never been an easy one, despite the fact that each is the other's most important public. The strain that traditionally marks this relationship has all too often resulted in frustration, hostility, and sometimes violence. And yet, the ability to achieve organizational success (however this term is ultimately defined) has always been connected directly to the ability to link the efforts of management and workers in useful ways. The means of doing so have ranged from what amounts to physical and mental coercion to more recent advances regarding the democratization of the workplace and the value of employee participation. Workers, for their part, have always sensed the power and political differentials that place them in secondary positions, whereas managers have often agonized over the gulf that separates them from fundamental human processes in the organization. This first section characterizes the historical nature of the internal public relationship.

What follows develops two key ideas that are of particular relevance for public relations scholars and practitioners. First, the discussion not only chronicles the emergent relationship between managers and employees, but it also makes clear the marginalized role of public relations in the internal public relations (IPR) process. The long history of this area largely ignores the role of the communication professional; in fact, in many of the works discussed, communication and public relations are mentioned not at all or only in passing. The perception that communication professionals are not relevant to basic organizational activities continues to persist at the start of the 21st century. Public relations managers, despite some progress (Watson-Wyatt, 1999), continue to perform technical rather than managerial roles in many organizations. Second, as discussed in more detail later, there is some evidence for a progression toward workplace democracy and, hence, an expanded role for the communication professional that may ultimately transform the technical IPR role into a managerial or strategic one. Fukuyama (1992, 1999, 2000) has written extensively about the historical nature of this progression, arguing that there is a historical trend in national governments toward liberal democracy. As he says, authoritarian states of all kinds have been "replaced with, if not well-functioning democracies, at least states that aspire to permit a greater degree of political participation" (p. 194). In his work Fukuyama cites several examples of countries once in the throes of totalitarian oppression that have progressed to become much more democratically oriented. In a similar vein, Fukuyama argues that organizations are also evolving into complex social systems where social capital and the connections between all sorts of people become essential to organizational success. In this new world employees of all sorts share responsibility and negotiate power in order to make organizations work. As Fukuyama notes, "Max Weber argued that rational, hierarchical authority in the form of bureaucracy was the essence of modernity. What we find in the second half of the twentieth century, instead, is that bureaucratic hierarchy has gone into decline in both politics and the economy, to be replaced by more informal, self-organized forms of coordination" (p. 194). This may be true for IPR as well. It may be that fundamental changes in the nature of contemporary organizations portend a fundamental shift in the role of the communication professional in the organization.

The Classical Tradition

Most textbooks and a great deal of writing on organizations begin with the classical management trinity of Frederick Taylor (1911), Henri Fayol (1949), and Max Weber (1947). Taylor is identified as the father of scientific management with its emphasis on efficiency, monetary reward, and control (Kanigel, 1999). Fayol describes the appropriate range of activities of a privileged managerial elite as the key to success. Weber subscribes to the notion that authority ought to reside exclusively in the organization's rule-defined relationships, as best reflected in a bureaucracy.

The employee relational environment that emerges in this view is one where employees are controlled because they ultimately cannot be trusted. Workers cannot become members of the managerial brotherhood, because they lack the capacity for the careful planning, commanding, and controlling that is the managerial birthright.

Communication in the classical view serves as a mechanism designed to engineer unquestioned compliance with managerial decisions that are scientifically and rationally based. The internal public relationship is primarily one-way, with communication flowing down the hierarchy to distribute information regarding policy, practice, and procedures. The internal public relationship, however, is not reciprocal. Management makes decisions on behalf of workers, presumably to ensure their welfare and that of the organization. Employees must accept this one-sided relationship as best for all concerned.

The Emergence of Doubt

Chester Barnard's book *The Functions of the Executive* (1938) is remarkable specifically because it expresses doubt about classical assumptions. Barnard was intimately familiar with American business as practiced, for example, by Carnegie and Morgan, and as expressed by Taylor, Weber, and Fayol. Barnard hesitated to blindly accept the dictum that managers must manage and workers must execute managerial directives. This doubt emerges because he sees organizational life from an interactive framework in which management and employees co-create the organizational fabric and the operative functions within it. He realized that management succeeds not because of superior knowledge, planning, or method, but because workers have chosen to cooperate in what they perceive to be a reasonable and justifiable managerial vision. Thus, the function of the executive is expanded to include the cultivation of support through networks of communication. Although Barnard ultimately does nothing to change the fundamental relationship between employees and management, he does expand and humanize the managerial imperative, providing an early recognition of the importance of communication in producing cooperation. In particular, this shift suggests recognition of employees as an audience for IPR and that this relationship must be cultivated through persuasive communication that leads to cooperation.

In this view, internal public relations are rooted in a communicative relationship where management seeks to convince employees that cooperation is in their best interest (acceptance theory). Management not only must envision the future, but must also persuade other audiences that their vision has merit. Ultimately, the gulf between the two cultures, although somewhat bridged through communicative interaction, remains largely intact because the vision remains management oriented and the range of employee options limited. That is, IPR remains primarily sender oriented and downward in its conception.

Beyond the Lamp Post

Elton Mayo (1933, 1945) and his work at the Western Electric Plant in Cicero, Illinois in the early 1920s earned him the title "Father of Human Relations Theory." The work of Mayo and his colleagues stands chronologically before that of Barnard. Conceptually, it advances the notion that task success is grounded irrevocably in the group relationship. According to Mayo, it is within the context of the group that human beings develop attitudes, beliefs, opinions, and values regarding their work life. It is this relational foundation that most directly influences an organization's ability to achieve goals and objectives.

Mayo's work has been repeatedly dissected since the date of its publication by critics of its method and conclusions. However, his work has been granted lawlike status by the many textbooks, articles, classroom lectures, and training sessions that take its key findings as axiomatic.

Human relations thinking argues that task success is rooted in the relationships that workers experience as a part of their work life. As work proceeds, employees enter relationships with each other and with management. The character of those relationships in various contexts constitutes a series of experiences that influence motivation and consequently work effectiveness. Low-quality relationships reduce motivation; more satisfying ones enhance the drive to succeed. Success at internal public relations, then, lies not in planning, control, or cooperation, but in the effective management of group relationships to produce an environment in which task accomplishment is enhanced. Again, the gulf between management and employees is not bridged, but the significance of individual relationships and needs is acknowledged and the managerial role expanded to reflect new message strategies and tactics.

The Person as Resource

The confluence of National Training Laboratories (NTL) work started by Kurt Lewin (Hirsch, 1988) and the quality improvement movement that emerges in the wake of World War II (Neave, 1990; Walton, 1986) coalesce to strike a new direction in which internal public relations is grounded in the recognition that human potential and the desire to leave one's mark are essential to organizational success. This direction is widely read by students in the work of McGregor (1960) and Likert (1961, 1967) and reinforced in the minds of managers through the work of such writers as Drucker (1994), Senge (1990), and Peters (1982).

This perspective is often tagged the *human resources model*. This position emphasizes the creative and intellectual potential of each individual while reconceptualizing the role of management. This new vision provides the asset base for any organization. In terms of motivation, for example, Maslow (1998) argues that what drives and transforms many organizational actors is the familiar self-actualization concept. Alderfer (1986) seeks to reinvent Maslow by creating the ERG model, recognizing that multiple needs may be at work and that employees may seek to emphasize other needs when some are frustrated. McClelland (1985) emphasizes need for achievement as a basic motive and as a counterpoint to Maslow's self-actualization concept. The point is that individuals come to the organization with the potential and desire for excellence. Consequently, the role of management is to cultivate and develop human resources to the fullest extent possible in order to maximize benefits for the organization. These benefits are frequently phrased in terms of a variety of outcomes including, but not limited to, quality, customer service, and on-time delivery.

The key words in this approach are *cultivation* and *facilitation*. Employees are seen as having skills and knowledge that provide direct benefits to the organization. Management is seen as the force in the organization with the ability to cultivate knowledge and skills as a part of the development of human resources. In addition, management is also seen as responsible for facilitating human accomplishment on behalf of the organization's goals and objectives. In this view, internal public relations consist of investments made to cultivate and facilitate human resources, rather than making investments to control and inhibit them.

Integrating People and Technologies

The movement identified as sociotechnical systems began in England with the work of Eric Trist (1981), which led, in turn, to the creation of the Tavistock Institute. The main argument made by scholars working in this tradition is that organizational success is ultimately rooted in the ability to balance two very different systems: human and technical. According to this perspective, these two basic systems exist side by side in every organization. The key is to find ways of integrating these two so that technology and humans blend together to the benefit of the larger enterprise.

The propensity of many organizations is to invest heavily in the technological side of the enterprise, such as computers, e-mail, pagers, robotics, and cell phones. The presumption is that humans will adjust themselves to new ways of working and doing to the betterment of the organization. This is often not the case. For example, e-mail, with all its potential for opening channels of communication, may not automatically produce the changes that organizational planners have imagined. One must also wonder how cell phones, with all of their capabilities and potential, will actually influence the work environment. Consequently, part of the work of effective internal public relations, from this perspective, is to find a balance between technological concerns and the humanity of employees.

It Depends

Contingency theorists argue that no one organizational approach will suffice in a world that has become increasingly turbulent and complex (Burns & Stalker, 1966; Woodward, 1965). Key organizational processes must remain dynamic to allow configuration and reconfiguration in response to new challenges and demands. Thus, a managerial approach to internal public relations that places an emphasis on open cooperation, cultivation, and facilitation is only operative as long as the environmental conditions that support it remain stable. As the environment changes, the approach to internal public relations must also change.

The work of management, in this view, becomes one of environmental scanning, a process embraced by public relations practitioners as a core value, and constant adjustment to new contingencies. Consequently, in this view effective IPR requires that flexibility with regard to change become internalized as a central organizational value. This is an idea embraced by public relations practitioners in general and crisis specialists in particular. It places special demands on management, and it pressures employees to accept change as a regular part of their work. The communicative relationship becomes crucial as the organization seeks to gather information critical for decision-making, and as it seeks to communicate that information and subsequent decisions to organizational members. Effective internal public relations then becomes the efforts directed at creating a flexible and adaptive workforce capable of surviving an environment in which reengineering, and restructuring, is a given.

Systems Theory

Systems theorists see organizations as organic wholes that interact dynamically with their various environments (Morgan, 1998). Communication is essential to the well-being of any organization because it is the central means by which organizations organize and structure themselves and simultaneously adapt themselves to often turbulent environments. Internal public relations emerge as a holistic concern for the manner in which various systemic components adjust to each other. An inability to maintain effective internal public relations manifests as an organization that loses flexibility and adaptability. Where internal public relations are effectively managed, the organization remains adaptive, open, and viable.

Complexity Theory

Management complexity theory (McMaster, 1996; Merry, 1995; Stacey, 1992, 1996; Wheatley, 1992) has been popularized by those who see in *chaos* a word capable of riveting the attention of readers on some of the key weaknesses that exist in contemporary managerial thought. The nexus of complexity theory is the canonization of change as a constant in organizational affairs. Basically, complexity theorists argue that organizations are self-organizing entities that constantly experience the pressure to change from their various overlapping and interdependent environments. The environments that produce the motivation for change are themselves extremely complex and, hence, are difficult to explain or predict. These environments organize quickly and often demand an immediate response from the organization to ensure survival. The volatility of these environments places tremendous stress and strain on organizations. Further, complexity theorists argue that small changes in various organizational features can produce unexpected and significant outcomes for organizations.

The essence of organizational success is to create a supple and adaptable structure that can react quickly and confidently to increasingly turbulent, difficult-to-anticipate, and often violent changes in organizational environment. Needless to say, the essence of organizational success is a relational environment where the capacity for rapid adaptation and change is institutionalized as a foundational cultural element.

The Critical Perspective

Critical theorists argue that organizations subjugate various constituencies through a desire to exert hegemony. Hegemony provides the organization with the unquestioned and unthinking allegiance of employees. The internal public relationship is really no relationship at all; rather, it is a one-sided effort on the part of organizations to groom organizational actors as unconscious and unwitting proponents of core organizational values, beliefs, and behaviors.

Critical theorists justifiably and forcefully demand a careful reconsideration of basic assumptions and ways of thinking that create and recreate contexts and that are rarely, if ever questioned. For example, this chapter has repeatedly used the words *manager, employee, success,* and *worker.* These symbols carry an inherent and unchallenged set of meanings and assumptions that define the basic work relationship. In doing so, these symbols limit actions and vision. These limitations are absorbed by organizational members, who then create and re-create relationships that are embedded at the deepest level in the symbols that are used unconsciously to describe basic organizational relationships. Inherent in the meanings associated with these symbols is a basic relationship, one in which managers are responsible for basic organizational decisions while employees and workers are responsible for seeing that those decisions are put into practice. What a different it might make were these symbols understood for the reality they create, and new ways of conceptualizing this most basic relationship were conceived? What a difference it might make for the life that managers, employees, and workers lead in their organizations. What a difference it might make in the way organizations approach their work.

This, then, is the contribution of critical theory to the historical progression of thinking regarding the relationships that exist among people who live and work in organizations. In this view, the essence of internal public relations must be seen as fundamentally and essentially manipulative. Communication is central to the discussion because it is the mechanism whereby meanings are created, conveyed, and maintained, and it becomes the mechanism whereby individuals and groups become aware of the situation they are in and discover means to exert control over their lives.

Synthesis

The theoretical perspectives just discussed chronicle the uncertain and frequently turbulent relationship that has always existed between management and employees. This conversation has continued over the years, in large measure, because there exists the feeling that effective internal public relations can have a desirable impact on those processes and outcomes that optimize the organization. With the possible exception of the critical perspective, theorists have rarely been interested in internal public relations solely because of the potential impact on the lives of employees. Rather, much of the dialogue has focused on internal public relations as a potentially important independent variable in a managerial equation focused on specific outcomes. Hence, internal public relations, as critical theorists remind us, frequently becomes a kind of exploitative activity where employees are asked to provide "more" toward organizational goals and objectives without a true and continuing commitment of the organization to them.

The essence of this historical progression of thinking about internal public relations for the purposes of this chapter is twofold, as indicated earlier. First, there appears to be a historical progression toward increasing workplace democracy. There is a difference between theory and practice, and it is probably fair to say that theory has advanced at a far greater pace than has practice. However, it is fair to claim that the conventional wisdom regarding internal public relations has significantly changed over the years toward increasing democratization and participation. Second, this progression demonstrates the need for an increased sensitivity to and skill regarding internal public relations. The added emphasis on communication and relationships correspondingly brings with it the need for a vision that must include communication at the strategic rather than the purely technical level. In other words, as organizations have evolved, so too have their communication needs, to the point that the expertise residing in the public relations function becomes of central rather than peripheral strategic value.

The Significance of Relationships

One of the striking things that stands out in this discussion is the historical progression of ideas regarding internal public relations, from highly autocratic and control-oriented visions of organizations and organizational communication to a contemporary vision that values transparency, democracy, openness, flexibility, social concerns, ethics, change, and environmental responsibility, among other important characteristics. Regardless of perspective, the underlying relational issue emerges as a consistent theme, whether the emphasis is on efficiency or facilitation. Ultimately, the fundamental and enduring question centers on the nature of the relationship that can and should be established between two very different organizational constituencies. Although the progression of ideas regarding internal public relations has been evolutionary (placing increasing value on the internal public relationship over time), the discussion is not complete, and widespread uncertainty exists among scholars, managers, and employees as to the potential for their productive association.

Relationships and Outcomes

The dialogue continues unabated, in part, because considerable uncertainty exists as to the appropriate character of the internal public relationship. That is, do relationships where employees are seen as valuable assets actually contribute significantly to organizational outcomes? In many respects, this is the central issue that has driven much of the historical dialogue. Given the tendency to see internal public relations as one concern among a constellation of concerns that may be connected to outcomes, the tendency has been to see internal public relations as something to be acknowledged, but whose impact is difficult to evaluate.

The Role of Communication

This historical dialogue regarding internal public relations has dealt either implicitly or explicitly with communication. The classicists rarely mentioned communication, and then only as a downward mechanism designed to control the unpredictable nature of employees. The emphasis on efficiency and structure, for example, foreshadowed a de facto communication approach that emphasized control, authority, and downward information flow and placed importance on task-related concerns. In more contemporary formulations, the role of communication is expanded to include person-oriented issues, conflict, and diversity, especially where employees are seen as organizational assets.

The Relatedness of Contexts

The theoretical perspectives just discussed consider the internal public relationship in various contexts (e.g., interpersonal, group, public, organizational, and technological). However, it is rare for the various contexts for relational development to be connected in ways that affect broader organizational concerns. For example, a great deal of research focuses on the interpersonal context; however, little discussion is provided as to how those relationships form, coalesce, and merge to affect on how the organization, seen as a whole, succeeds or fails. Much the same is true at the group level. Group theorists focus on groups and group formation, but fail to connect group processes with broader organizational concerns. At some point these various contexts and context-dependent theories must be seen in broader perspective with regard to holistic organizational concerns.

Theoretical Requirements

The preceding analysis leads to five requirements for a theory of internal public relations:

1. It must ground itself in relationships and relational activity.
2. It must provide a framework in which a clear empirical connection exists between internal public relations and desired organizational outcomes.
3. It must clarify the role of communication behavior as central to effective internal public relations.
4. It must provide a connection between micro-level actions and macro level outcomes.
5. It must place its focus at the strategic level.

The following section builds on these five requirements and advances a theoretical perspective based in social capital theory to address the concerns just identified.

SOCIAL CAPITAL

Despite its relative youth as a concept, social capital has been variously defined (Astone, Nathanson, Schoen, & Kim, 1999). As with so many concepts, conceptual clarity is at a premium, leaving significant gaps in treatment, method, and theoretical development. Some researchers, for example, have defined social capital at the macro level by focusing on national and cultural trends in social capital and subsequent desirable or undesirable outcomes (Fukuyama, 1995; Putnam, 1995, 2000), whereas others have focused primarily on the individual level (Coleman, 1988; Granovetter, 1973). Social capital research has included organizations by focusing on the relationship as a human asset (Leanna & Van Buren, 1999). Researchers have also focused on schools and school systems (Helliwell & Putnam, 1999; Morgan & Sorenson, 1999), poverty (Dordick, 1997; Narayan, 1999), community development, gender related concerns (Burt, 1998; Ibarra, 1992, 1995; Parks-Yancy, 2004), downsizing (Brockner, 1990, 1992; Shah, 2000), and economic development (Easterly, 2000; Knack & Keefer, 1997; Rodrik, 1999a, 1999b).

Since Coleman's (1988a, 1988b) and Putnam's (1995, 2000) popularization of this concept, the rush to apply social capital in almost "snake oil" fashion has led to serious problems with conceptual clarity. Each paper published contains a slightly different vision of the concept, including corresponding variations in treatment of operationalization, method, analysis, and conclusions. This situation leaves large gaps in the literature, and consequently little emerges in the way of comparable perspectives, questions, approaches, or results.

Social capital is defined here as the ability that organizations have of creating, maintaining, and using relationships to achieve desirable organizational goals (Portes, 1998). In particular, social capital is seen as something that can be acquired, stored, and expended and that can be used to facilitate action that can result in a competitive advantage for individuals, groups, and organizations. The account balance of available social capital emerges from the communication among individuals, groups, and organizations that allows them to successfully form, maintain, and utilize relationships.

This definition contains several ideas that will guide the following discussion and that connect directly with the theoretical requirements discussed earlier. First, it identifies relationships and relational concerns as central to all organizational activity. Second, it asserts that the social capital relationship affects organizational outcomes. Third, it implies that communication behavior serves as a mechanism for the production, maintenance, and expenditure of social capital. Fourth, it suggests the possibility of linking social capital activity occurring in many different locations to form a broader vision of organizational outcomes.

Theoretical Origins

Contemporary notions of social capital developed independently in the work of two theorists: Bourdieu (1979, 1980, 1986) and Coleman (1988a, 1988b, 1990, 1993, 1994a, 1994b). Althogh Bourdieu's work precedes Coleman's work, Coleman's work was the first to receive widespread recognition, which served to popularize the concept and led to a rapidly developing body of research (Woolcock, 2001).

Coleman defines social capital functionally as "a variety of entities with two elements in common: They all consist of some aspect of social structures, and they facilitate certain actions of actors—whether persons or corporate actors—within the structure" (Coleman, 1988a, p. s98). It is the emergence of the forms of social structure in various contexts that produces social capital (Baker, 1990; Coleman, 1988a). Social capital emerges through the rich, varied, and textured communicative exchanges that occur among various organizational actors who are embedded in various contexts. These communicative exchanges involve individuals, groups, organizations, cultures, and nations, producing a shifting sea of relational creation, maintenance, and dissolution that forms that framework for successful organizational activity.

Bourdieu takes a slightly different approach, defining the concept as "the aggregate of the actual or potential resources which are linked to possession of a durable network of more or less institutionalized relationships of mutual acquaintance or recognition" (Bourdieu, 1986, p. 248). Bourdieu's definition is important because it distinguishes between two critical elements: (1) the social relationship itself that allows a variety of actors to access resources held by their associates, and (2) the amount and quality of those resources.

To refine our understanding of resources, it is important to distinguish resources from the ability to obtain, maintain, and utilize those resources. It is the communicative exchange that produces and defines the available resources, and it is also communication that allows actors to access and make use of them. Information (intellectual capital) and economic and other forms of physical, human, and cultural capital may all be cultivated through the utilization of social capital. However, the possession of social capital does not necessarily mean that it will be maintained or spent effectively. Social capital is best understood as potential and its utilization recognized as influence. Further, like economic capital, social capital is not always used wisely and can produce negative consequences for actors (Portes & Landolt, 1996).

The following sections explain the distinctive features of social capital as they relate to internal public relations.

Obligations and Expectations

Coleman (1988a) describes the essential components of the relationship and its basic components by making two distinctions: obligations and expectations. Both are created through the communicative exchange and the both contain actor beliefs about past and future exchanges. As Coleman (1988a) notes:

> If A does something for B and assumes that B will reciprocate in the future, an expectation is established in A and an obligation incurred on the part of B. This obligation can be conceived as a credit slip held by A for the fulfillment of an obligation by B. These credit slips constitute a relational deposit that has a value that A can spend to accomplish various goals and objectives—unless, of course, the actor who has the obligation defaults on the debt. (p. S102)

Some clarification is necessary at this point. One must understand that a financial obligation is fungible, whereas a social capital obligation is not. For example, a debt can be sold or passed on to another individual or organization. Unlike financial or economic obligations, social capital is rooted in and constrained by the particular relationship in which it emerges. One could not tell

Fred that he ought to buy John lunch because John had bought Sam lunch last Tuesday. The relationship and the social capital exist only between John and Sam and within a particular context.

Dimensions of Social Capital

Social capital, grounded in social relationships, is complex and multidimensional. Identifying the nature of social behaviors and relational constructs that parsimoniously account for economic and other consequences is a critical feature of the development of a theory of internal public relations grounded in social capital theory. Putnam (1995, 2000) recognized the tendency to proliferate concepts and argued that a high priority should be placed on clarifying the dimensions of social capital. Consequently, Hazleton and Kennan (2000) modify the work of Nahapiet and Ghoshal (1998) and consequently proposed a three-dimensional model of social capital: structural, communicative, and relational. These elements are described in the following sections.

The Structural Dimension

Structural characteristics, imposed by history and culture, define a range of opportunities and limitations for relational activities. An organization where technology has a heavy impact on communication exchange experiences inherent limitations on the kind, quantity, quality, and number of relationships that can emerge. This, in turn, influences the organization's basic ability to configure and reconfigure itself with regard to the manner in which publics are accessed.

Structure is a necessary condition for the development and utilization of social capital. The system of network connections is, consequently, a fundamental structural concept. When more than two actors are connected, the configuration of the network itself influences relational outcomes. Communication scholars have a long history of interest in communication networks (Farace, Monge, & Russell, 1987; Monge, 1987). Elements of configuration such as network density, hierarchy, and connectivity are all structural components that affect the ability to create social capital.

Burt (1992), for example, identifies three features of networks: access, timing, and referral. *Access* describes the opportunity to send or receive messages, as well as knowledge of the appropriate network channels to use in social capital formation, maintenance, and expenditure. Knowledge of formal and informal networks facilitates both strategic choices and the efficiency of communication. Knowing whom to talk with about what is important, and it reflects what people know and intuitively understand about the nature and character of their networks (Garfinkel, 1967).

Timing is a consequence of both knowledge and network structures. However, all other factors being equal, organizations that can communicate more quickly and in an appropriate chronological frame are likely to possess an organizational advantage. For example, an organization that encounters a new market competitor can only succeed if the response is immediate and if information about this challenge is available in a chronological frame that enables effective decision making. Beyond this, however, the issue has to do with when the response should occur. When, for example, should the market response occur?

Referrals indicate the network processes that provide information to actors about availability and accessibility of additional network ties. That is, some networks are more open and accessible than others. Also, inclusion in one network can make membership in other networks possible. Networks with high referral potential are more likely to produce more social capital from more different relationships than networks with low referral potential.

The final feature of network structure has to do with Coleman's idea of the appropriable social organization (1988a). This concept describes the ability of networks or organizations formed for one purpose to be utilized for other purposes. Fukuyama (1995), for example, describes the transfer of trust from family and religious affiliations into work situations. Coleman (1990) shows how social capital formed in personal relationships are appropriated for business purposes. Burt (1992) describes how social capital that emerged in personal relationships was then expended to create organizations.

Applications of these concepts to our understanding of internal public relations are clear and direct. Public relations practitioners are those with the capacity to cultivate, maintain, and expend social capital on behalf of their organizations in an effort to cultivate functional internal public relationships. For example, the relationships established with media and other publics constitutes a deposit of social capital, which the organizations may expend to secure fair media coverage, gather information, and build alliances with other groups or organizations. Thus, access, referral, timing, and the appropriable social organization as basic characteristics of networks may be used to better understand how internal public relations works, and it also affords the opportunity to create a series of metrics that can help assess the effectiveness of the internal public relations practitioner.

Similarly, the connectedness of practitioners to internal networks is likely to be an indicator of the influence of public relations on the organization. Ties to the dominant hierarchy alone are not likely to produce excellent public relations. Rather, excellent public relations are best conceptualized by understanding the nature of the social capital accessible by the organization, including the practitioner, and the manner in which available social capital is expended to achieve important goals and objectives. This perspective offers something unique: a conceptualization of excellent public relations as a distinctively communication-grounded phenomenon that produces a commodity that can be observed and measured and that can be connected directly to the organization's efforts to succeed.

The Relational Dimension

Expectations and obligations have previously been defined as central features of the social capital relationship. The amount and nature of both are central features in understanding an organization's relations with its internal publics. Further, as noted previously, this most basic of all human activities clarifies the role of communication in building excellent public relations.

Whether or not B repays A depends on a number of factors. One of these factors is the motivation to meet obligations through resource allocation (Portes, 1998). Two different relational consequences of communication are important in our model: trust and identification. Both help us to understand motivation with regard to retiring relational debt.

Trust is the primary relational feature of social capital in Coleman's (1988a) formulation and the most frequently studied concept linked to other social outcomes from a social capital perspective (Portes, 1998). Trust on the part of an actor supplying resources assumes the "anticipated cooperation" (Burt & Knez, 1996) of the actor seeking resources. Organizational trust becomes an "orientation toward risk" and an "orientation toward other people and toward society as a whole" (Kramer, 1999).

Trust as a basic component of social capital may be further clarified. Trust may be fragile or resilient (Leanna & Van Buren, 1999; Ring, 1996; Ring, & Van de Ven, 1992). Fragile trust is dependent on the immediate likelihood of rewards, and it is not likely to survive where benefits and costs are not perceived as equal. A contractor agrees to frame a house based on the expectation of prompt payment. This is contracting, or what Rosseau (1995) calls *transacting*, as opposed to relationship building. Relationships based on fragile trust emphasize formal communication exchanges that constitute a public obligation (Leanna & Van Buren, 1999). This does not lead to a deeper level of association and does not lead to an exchange if the reward structure is not clarified through some contractual arrangement.

Resilient trust is based on stronger and more numerous links and is not likely to be disrupted by occasional unequal exchanges (Leanna & Van Buren, 1999). Further, resilient trust reflects a transaction based on a handshake rather than a complex set of requirements embodied in a written contract. Resilient trust requires little maintenance because it inheres in a history characterized by stable, principled, and ethical interactions. However, resilient trust is easily destroyed through thoughtless acts that can immediately and irrevocably destroy the relationship.

Identification refers to the extent to which actors view themselves as connected to other actors. Portes (1998) identifies two forms of identification. The first is bounded solidarity. Grounded in Marx's concept of emergent class consciousness (Marx, [1894] 1967; Marx & Engels, [1848] 1947), the production of social capital is a product of the emergent awareness of a common fate. Originally, the concept referred to situations bounded by community. That is, individuals who are residents of a community sense their connectedness in terms of goals, values, and beliefs and identify with each other on that basis. Out-group members are identified based on their lack of solidarity with a particular community. This concept must be expanded, however. It is possible for the motivation to seek solidarity to cross social boundaries where contextual factors drive together groups, forming alliances previously impossible.

The second form of identification arises when A and B hold membership in a common social structure. Unlike the bounded solidarity situation, the expectation of repayment is not dependent on a perceived common fate, but on norms operational with the community. In some instances, the actual repayment to A may come not from B but from the community. For example, the benefit to an employer who creates a day-care center for employee children does not accrue from the children themselves or even necessarily from their parents. Rather, the reward emanates from the approval of the broader community of employees in that organization.

Both trust and identification are made operational where there is an adequate degree of social system closure. Coleman (1988) argues that trust and trustworthiness, for example, are essential, but they do not, by themselves, constitute an adequate normative force ensuring repayment. System closure provides effective sanctions that add normative force to trust and identification processes. Social capital emerges more readily where some system (formal or informal) of constraints operates to discourage violations of trust and identification.

The Communication Dimension

Communication, as a visible and manifest activity, provides the process through which internal public relationships are accomplished. As such, human communication provides the symbolic mechanism through which social capital is acquired and the mechanism through which it is expended in ways designed to produce desired internal public relations outcomes. Communication is not a dichotomous variable. Its mere presence or absence cannot account for social capital formation. Although its presence may be necessary for social capital formation and use, a careful explanation will require theories that explain and describe variations in communication content and strategy.

One particular means of viewing the communication is provided by Hazleton (1998), who advances a set of messaging strategies that could be connected to social capital creation, maintenance, and expenditure. He suggests that organizations exhibit two types of goals: instrumental and relational. He argues that public relations are central to the achievement of relational goals and that the achievement of relational goals is necessary for the achievement of instrumental goals. This is consistent with our view and understanding of the concept of social capital and its role in cultivating internal public relations.

Hazleton (1992, 1993) has also proposed a taxonomy of seven public relations strategies phrased in terms of individual functions that are useful in understanding the communicative dimension of social capital: facilitative, informative, persuasive, promise and reward, threat and punishment, bargaining, and cooperative problem solving. Page (1998; 2000a, 2000b, 2000c, 2003; Page & Hazleton, 1999; Werder, 2003, 2004, 2005) in a series of studies has explored the use of the public relations strategies identified by Hazleton. Her research demonstrates both the utility and validity of the strategy taxonomy for studying public relations communication, demonstrating empirical linkages between perceived attributes of publics, and perceived public relations effectiveness.

One would expect that communicative strategy will systematically vary with social capital processes. Some of these strategies are associated with the formation of social capital, whereas others either drain the available stock of social capital or inhibit its development. Different communication strategies are likely to characterize differing levels and types of social capital. Facilitative strategies that enable others to overcome constraints and achieve their goals clearly have implications for social capital formation. Both bargaining and promise and reward, for example, are more likely to be used in situations where trust is "fragile" rather than "resilient," that is, when resilient trust is in demand. On the other hand, effective and fair use of some of these strategies over time may create more social capital and facilitate the use of additional communication strategies.

Communication, in addition to laying the foundation for the emergence of social capital, is also the mechanism whereby the available stock of social capital can be accessed and expended to further individual, group, and organizational goals and objectives. Informative strategies, cooperative problem-solving strategies, and informative strategies may all be useful in the transformation of social capital into other forms of capital (Coleman, 1988) as communicators indicate their needs and goals to employees or other publics with a sense of obligation to the organization.

Communication is a primary concept in the theory of social capital. Unfortunately, we do not have the time or space here to develop this area of our theory more fully. The particular ways in which these communication strategies for acquisition and expenditure of social capital operate provide a clear avenue for future investigation.

Consequences of Social Capital

As communication is employed to expend the available deposit of social capital, various organizational outcomes emerge. These outcomes may be either positive or negative depending on the manner in which social capital is expended. This serves as a reminder that social capital is potential and that desirable outcomes depend on its effective expenditure. That is, the mere presence of social capital does not necessarily lead to positive outcomes. An individual who has a sum on deposit at the local bank possesses the potential for desirable outcomes based on the prudent expenditure of his money. If, however, the individual spends that money in frivolous ways, the outcome may in fact be negative. In the same sense, social capital provides the potential for success depending on its judicious expenditure. Here again is a direct connection to the practice of internal public relations and communication. The professional communicator, in whatever capacity, is the one individual in the organization positioned to make strategic decisions about both the cultivation and expenditure of social capital.

In this regard there are three classes of potentially positive outcomes: increased and/or more complex forms of social capital, reduced transaction costs, and organizational advantage. As noted earlier, these outcomes can be either positive or negative and can be characterized along a continuum that ranges from the highly concrete to the highly abstract. Outcomes are often less easily observed and more uncertain than other types of exchanges (Bourdieu, 1979, 1980).

The effective use of communication to allocate deposits of social capital may produce additional social capital and/or expressions or byproducts of social capital, e. g., intellectual capital (Nahapiet and Ghoshal, 1998) or human capital (Coleman, 1988), new relationships, and new or enhanced networks. This is an important feature of internal public relations. In this case, effective relational management through campaigns and message management done well can produce additional social capital, thus retaining a strong account balance available for disbursement. More specifically, the judicious expenditure of social capital creates an environment in which important organizational initiatives, such as restructuring and change management, can occur in a more timely and successful way. This recognition places the internal public relations function in the center of important organizational activities rather than as a valuable but somewhat peripheral activity. There are also a variety of activities that can benefit from effectively managed social capital, including increased commitment to management and the broader organizational framework, improved community relations based on positive employee responses to change, and the fact that media could come to identify the organization as excellent.

Fukuyama (1995) identifies transaction costs as those costs that accrue to organizations or cultures in the absence of social capital. Fukuyama argues that simpler and less expensive systems, based on trust, come to be replaced by "a system of formal rules and regulations, which have to be negotiated, agreed to, litigated, and enforced, sometimes by coercive means" (p. 27). Transaction costs (Coase, 1937, 1961; Williamson, 1975) are costs incurred by individuals, groups, and organizations that are associated with human interaction. The concept of transaction costs has been variously defined (Klaes, 2000), and hence, as with many concepts, conceptual confusion is the norm rather than the exception. The approach taken in this chapter acknowledges the work of theorists such as Coase (1937, 1961), Marschak (1959), Malmgren (1961), Alchian (1965), and Williamson (1975). It builds on the notion of contracts, policing, exchanges, negotiation, etc., contained in those visions to see transaction costs as being associated with human interaction, that is, communication.

Those costs might include, but are not limited to, brokering solutions to problems, negotiating and managing conflict, creating contracts to regulate the behavior of others, and creating an information environment in which people are connected to each other and to information. In the absence of the ability to successfully acquire and expend social capital, transaction costs tend to proliferate. These costs can assume a variety of guises within the context provided earlier: the costs of sexual harassment suits, age discrimination suits, and disability claims are often manifestations of the absence of social capital. In addition, increased information costs, increased conflict, legal costs, employee theft, and labor-union-based grievances are also transaction costs. Rather than reflecting purely economic costs associated with market activities, transaction costs reflect a lack of social capital. Transaction costs demand additional expenditures of social and financial capital beyond what is necessary to achieve organizational objectives, imposing a limit on what the organization can ultimately achieve. Employee theft, for example, reflects either the absence of social capital or a poorly managed set of relationships that has emerged as dysfunctional employee, group, or organizational behavior. Employee monitoring devices, as another example, are transaction costs because they require added financial inputs to attempt behavioral control, where a more effective expenditure of social capital could have produced less costly and more desirable outcomes.

Expenditures of social capital via communication can result in increases in organizational advantage: productivity, efficiency, quality, customer satisfaction, net asset value, stock value, employee satisfaction, employee commitment, organizational adaptation, etc. But these aren't the only important outcomes that are possible and desirable. Social capital also connects to ethical behavior, transparency, and a more livable organization that is sustainable in terms of both individual and organizational needs. Organizational advantage refers to outcomes that improve the ability of the organization to achieve self-defined goals and objectives by adapting to changing environments.

Here again internal public relations becomes a central strategic and tactical concern rather than a peripheral one. Effective internal public relations provides a constraint on transaction costs. Hence, the value of managed relational activity lies both in enhanced goal attainment and in the management of transaction costs. For example, an organization that experiences grievances and perhaps legal action regarding gender-based relations has incurred a transaction cost. In this case, it is the cost of dysfunctional human interaction. Where effectively managed internal public relations occurs and where it is targeted toward gender-based interaction problems, transaction costs can be mitigated. This does not mean that transaction costs will disappear, because an infrastructure must exist to cultivate and maintain human interaction. However, it does suggest that the role of internal public relations is a central organizational activity targeted toward social capital formation and expenditure designed to manage transaction costs. This in turn facilitates and enables organizational goal attainment.

The pursuit of associations between social capital expenditures and the three categories of outcomes must be understood. First, outcomes are complex, turbulent, and uncertain because of the nature of the relationships that give rise to them. This can be more easily understood by recognizing that outcomes are characterized by unspecified obligations, uncertain time horizons, and potential violations of reciprocity expectations (Bourdieu, 1979, 1980). One does not know exactly how actors might construe their obligations based on social capital, because the types of outcomes that can emerge are contextually embedded. A manufacturing organization, for example, might have built a sizeable account of social capital with employees based on the long-standing cultivation of positive internal public relations. How, then, do employees see their obligation, and how are they likely to respond based on their perceptions of those obligations? Will they invest greater effort in their work, will they improve quality, or will they simply express more positive attitudes toward their organization among themselves?

Further, it is difficult to understand when obligations will be repaid (uncertain time horizons). When can one expect an obligation to be repaid? Will actors perceive reasons for reciprocating at all? Actors may also violate reciprocity expectations. For example, an actor lends an acquaintance $20. The actor expects that the loan will be repaid promptly. The acquaintance seeks to meet the obligation by offering to buy lunch in some unspecified time frame. Although the intent is to repay the obligation, the manner in which the obligation is to be met fails to meet conventional expectations and may become the source of conflict rather than a resource that can be applied to future needs.

Within this context, researchers have sought associations among communication and organizational advantage, for example, in an effort to satisfy bottom-line demands. The overall strategy has been to seek correlations between traditionally valued organizational outcomes and some measure of communication, often embodied as participation (Cotton, et al., 1988; Doucouliagos, 1995; Leana and Van Buren, 1999; Locke and Schweiger, 1979; Miller and Monge, 1986; Schweiger and Leana, 1986; Seibold and Shea, 2001; Wagner and Gooding, 1987). If net asset value, for example, is not significantly associated with some measure of communication-related activity, then the search is often interpreted to have been in vain. Unexpected interpretations and violations of obligation and expectations introduce a level of complexity and uncertainty that makes the link between communication and outcomes more challenging to identify, but potentially richer in its implications for organizational practice. How to proceed?

An approach to this relationship requires a twofold focus. First, although correlations with organizational advantage variables may be modest, the associations with social capital and with transaction costs may provide a better picture, especially when seen as additive with organizational advantage concerns. Second, over time associations among organizational advantage, transaction costs, and the emergence of additional forms of social capital may interact synergistically to produce additional unanticipated effects. Consequently, the more productive approach is to focus on explicating which outcomes (and what types) actually emerge, their net effect, and their potential interactions.

CONCLUSION

This chapter has argued that effectively managed internal public relations offers an important and useful means of understanding the difficult relationship between those who fill management roles and those defined as employees or workers. Social capital theory and transaction cost economics blended with a focus on communication behavior offers a unique and profitable way of envisioning this process and its impact on organizational competitiveness. This view places public relations practice in a central position with regard to the strategy associated with internal public relations. Our argument suggests that those who are able to understand and manage internal public relations from this perspective are more likely to adapt effectively to their relevant environments and fulfill their most deeply held aspirations.

REFERENCES

Alchian, A. A. (1965). Some economics of property rights. In A. A. Alchian (Ed.), *Economic forces at work* (pp. 127–149). Indianapolis, IN: Liberty Press.

Alderfer, C. (1986). An intergroup perspective on group dynamics. In Lorsch, J. (Ed.), *Handbook of organisational behaviour*. Englewood Cliffs, NJ: Prentice Hall.

Astone, N. M., Nathanson, C. A., Schoen, R., & Kim, Y. J. (1999). Family demography, social theory and investment in social capital. *Population and Development Reviw, 25*, 1–32.

Aupperle, K. E., Carroll, A. B., & Hatfield, J. D. (1985). An empirical examination of the relationship between corporate social responsibility and profitability. *Academy of Management Journal, 28*, 446–463.

Baker, W. E. (1990). Market networks and corporate behavior. *American Journal of Sociology, 96*, 589–625.

Barnard, C. (1938). *The functions of the executive*. Cambridge, MA: Harvard University Press.

Bourdieu, P. (1979). Les trois etats du capital culturel. *Acres Rech. Sci. Soc., 30*, 3–6.

Bourdieu, P. (1980). Le capital social: notes provisoires. *Acres Rech. Sci. Soc., 31*, 2–3.

Bourdieu, P. (1986). The forms of capital. In J. G. Richardson (Ed.), *Handbook of theory and research for the sociology of education* (pp. 241–258). New York: Greenwood.

Brockner, J. (1990). Scope of justice in the workplace: How survivors react to coworker layoffs. *Journal of Social Issues, 46*, 95–106.

Brockner, J. (1992, Winter). Managing the effects of layoffs on survivors. *California Management Review*, 9–27.

Burns, T., & Stalker, G. M. (1966). *The management of innovation*. London: Tavistock.

Burt, R. S. (1992). *Structural holes: The social structure of competition*. Cambridge, MA: Harvard University Press.

Burt, R. (1998). The gender of social capital. *Relationships and society, 10*, 5–36.

Burt, R. S., & Knez M. (1996). Trust and third-party gossip. In R. M. Kramer & T. R. Tyler (Eds.). *Trust in organizations: Frontiers of theory and research* (pp. 68–89). Thousand Oaks, CA: Sage Publications.

Cline, C. G., McBride, M. H., & Miller, R. E. (1989). The theory of psychological type congruence in public relations and persuasion. In V. Hazleton Jr. & C. Botan (Eds.), *Public relations theory* (pp. 221–239). Hillsdale, NJ: Lawrence Erlbaum Associates.

Coase, R. (1937). The nature of the firm. *Economica, 4*, 386–405.

Coase, R. (1961). The problem of social cost. *Journal of Law and Economics, 3*, 1–44.

Coleman, J. S. (1988a). Social capital in the creation of human capital. *American Journal of Sociology, 94*, S95–S120.

Coleman, J. S. (1988b). The creation and destruction of social capital: Implications for the law. *Notre Dame Journal of Law, Ethics, & Public Policy, 3*, 375–404.

Coleman, J. S. (1990). *Foundations of social theory*. Cambridge, MA: Belknap Press of Harvard University Press.

Coleman, J. S. (1993). The rational reconstruction of society. *American Sociological Review, 58*, 1–15.

Coleman, J. S. (1994a). A rational choice perspective on economic sociology. In N. J. Smelser & R. Swedberg (Eds.), *Handbook of economic sociology* (pp. 166–180). Princeton, NJ: Princeton University Press.

Coleman, J. S. (1994b). The realization of effective norms. In R. Collins (Ed.), *Four sociological traditions: Selected readings* (pp. 171–189). New York: Oxford University Press.

Conine, T. F., & Madden, G. P. (1986). Corporate social responsibility and investment value. In W. D. Guth (Ed.), *Handbook of business strategy 1986/1987 yearbook*. Boston: Warren, Gorham, & Lamont.

Cotton, J. L., Vollrath, D. A., Froggatt, K. L., Lengnick-Hall, M. L., and Jennings, K. R. (1988). Employee participation: Diverse forms and different outcomes. *Academy of Management Review, 13*, 8–22.

Dordick, G. (1997). *Something left to lose: Personal relations and survival among New York's homeless*. Philadelphia, PA: Temple University Press.

Doucouliagos, C. (1995). Worker participation and productivity in labour-managed and participatory capitalist firms: A meta-analysis. *Industrial and Labour Relations Review, 49*, 58–77.

Drucker, P. (1994). *The post capitalist society*. New York: Harper Business.

Easterly, W. (2000). The middle class consensus and economic development. *Policy Research Working Paper* 2346. Washington, DC: The World Bank.

Farace, R. V., Monge, P. R., & Russell, H. M. (1977). *Communicating and organizing.* Reading, MA: Addison-Wesley.

Fayol, H. (1949). *General and industrial management.* London: Pitman.

Fombrun, C., & Shanley, M. (1990). What's in a name? Reputation building and corporate strategy. *Academy of Management Journal, 33*, 233–258.

Fukuyama, F. (1992). *The end of History and the last man.* New York: Free Press.

Fukuyama, F. (1995). *Trust: The social virtues and the creation of prosperity.* New York: Free Press.

Fukuyama, F. (1999). *The great disruption: Human nature and the reconstitution of human nature.* New York: Free Press.

Fukuyama, F. (2000). *Social capital and civil society.* Washington: International Monetary Fund, IMF Institue.

Garfinkel, H. (1967). *Studies in ethnomethodology.* Englewood Cliffs, NJ: Prentice Hall.

Granovetter, M. (1973). The strength of weak ties. *American Journal of Sociology, 78*, 1360–1380.

Grunig, J. E. (1989). Symmetrical presuppositions as a framework for public relations theory. In V. Hazleton Jr. & C. H. Botan (Eds.), *Public relations theory* (pp. 3–15). Hillsdale, NJ: Lawrence Erlbaum Associates.

Harris, T. (1993). *Applied organizational communication.* Hillsdale, NJ: Lawrence Erlbaum Associates.

Hazleton, V. (1992). Toward a systems theory of public relations. In H. Avenarius & W. Ambrecht (Eds.), *Ist Public Relations eine Wissenschaft?* (pp. 33–46). Berlin: Westdeutscher Verlag.

Hazleton, V. (1993). Symbolic resources: Processes in the development and use of symbolic resources. in H. Avenarius, W. Armbrecht, & U. Zabel (eds.), *Image und PR* (pp. 87–100). Berlin: Westdeutscher-Verlag.

Hazleton, V. (1998). *Implications of a theory of public relations competence for crisis communication: Balancing concerns for effectiveness and eppropriateness.* Paper presented at the annual meeting of the National Communication Association, New York.

Hazleton, V., & Botan, C. H. (1989). The role of theory in public relations. In C. H. Botan & V. Hazleton (Eds.), *Public relations theory* (pp. 3–15). Hillsdale, NJ: Lawrence Erlbaum Associates.

Hazleton, V., & Kennan, W. (2000). Relationships as social capital: Reconceptualizing the bottom line. *Corporate Communication: An International Journal, 5*, 81–86.

Helliwell, J. F. and Putnam, R. D. (1999). *Education and social capital.* NBER Working Paper No. 7121. Cambridge, MA: National Bureau of Economic Research.

Hirsch, J. I. (1988). *The history of the national training laboratories, 1947–1986: Social equality through education and training.* New York: Peter Lang.

Ibarra, H. (1992). Homophily and differential returns: Sex differences in network structure and access in an advertising firm. *Administrative Sciences Quarterly, 37*, 422–438.

Ibarra, H. (1995). Race, opportunity, and diversity of social circles in managerial networks. *Academy of Management Journal, 18*, 673–703.

Kanigel, R. *The one best way: Frederick Winslow Taylor and the enigma of efficiency.* New York: Viking.

Klaes, M. (2000). The birth of the concept of transaction costs: Issues and controversies. *Industrial and Corporate Change, 9*(4), 567–593.

Knack, S., & Keefer, P. (1997). Does social capital have an economic payoff? A cross-country investigation. *Quarterly Journal of Economics, 112*(4), 1251–1288.

Kramer, R. M. (1999). Trust and distrust in organizations: Emerging perspectives, enduring questions. *Annual Review of Psychology, 50,* 569–598.

Leanna, C. R., & Van Buren III, H. J. (1999) Organizational social capital and employment practices. *Academy of Management Review, 24*(3), 538–555.

Ledingham, J. A., & Bruning, S. D. (1999). *Public relations as relationship management: A relational approach to the study and practice of public relations.* Mahwah, NJ: Lawrence Erlbaum Associates.

Likert, R. (1961). *New patterns of management.* New York: McGraw-Hill.

Likert, R. (1967). *The human organization: Its management and value,* New York: McGraw-Hill.

Locke, E. A. and Schweiger, D. M. (1979). Participation in decision making: One more look. In B. M. Staw (Ed.), *Research in organizational behavior* (pp. 285–339). Greenwich, CT: JAI Press.

Lustig, M. W., & King, S. W. (1980). The effect of communication apprehension and situation on communication strategy choices. *Human Communication Research, 7,* 74–82.

Malmgren, H. B. (1961). Information, expectations, and the theory of the firm. *Quarterly Journal of Economics, 75,* 399–421.

Marschak, J. (1959). Remarks on the economics of information. In J. Maarschak (ed.), *Economics of information, precision and prediction: Selected essays* (*Vol. 2* pp. 91–117). Dordrecht: Reidel.

Marx, K. (1967 [1894]). *Capital, (Vol. 3).* New York: International.

Marx, K., & Engels, F. (1947 [1848]). *The German ideology.* New York: International.

Maslow, A. (1998). *Maslow on management.* New York: Wiley.

Mayo, E. (1933). *The human problems of an industrial civilization.* New York: Macmillan.

Mayo, E. (1945). *The social problems of an industrial civilization.* Andover, MA: Andover Press.

McClelland, D. (1985). *Human motivation.* Glencoe, IL: Scott, Foresman.

McCloskey, D., & Klamer, A. (1995). One quarter of GDP is persuasion.*American Economic Review, 85,* 191–195.

McGregor, D. (1960). *The human side of enterprise.* New York: McGraw-Hill.

McLaughlin, M. L., Cody, M. J., & Robey, C. S. (1980). Situational influences on the selection of strategies to resist compliance-gaining attempts. *Human Communication Research, 7,* 14–36.

McMaster, M. D. (1996). *The intelligence advantage: Organising for complexity.* Newton, MA: Butterworth-Heinemann.

Merry, U. (1995). *Coping with uncertainty: Insights from the new sciences of chaos, self organization and complexity.* Westport, CT: Praeger.

Miller, G. R., Boster, F., Roloff, M., & Seibold, D. (1977). Compliance-gaining message strategies: A typology and some findings concerning effects of situational differences. *Communication Monographs, 44,* 37–57.

Miller, K. I., & Monge, P. R. (1986). Participation, satisfaction, and productivity: A meta-analytic review. *Academy of Management Journal, 29,* 727–753.

Monge, P. R. (1987). The network level of analysis. In C. R. Berger & S. H. Chaffee (Eds.), *The handbook of communication science* (pp. 239–270). Newbury Park, CA: Sage.

Monge, P. R., & Contractor, N. S. (1995). Communication networks. In A. Kuper & J. Kuper (Eds.), *Social science encyclopedia* (2nd ed.). London: Routledge.

Morgan, G. (1998). *Images of organization*. Thousand Oaks, CA: Sage.

Morgan, S., & Sorensen, A. (1999). Parental networks, social closure, and mathematical learning: A test of Coleman's social capital explanation of school effects. *American Sociological Review, 64*(5), 661–681.

Nahapiet, J., & Ghoshal, S. (1998). Social capital, intellectual capital, and the organizational advantage. *Academy of Management Review, 23*: 242–267.

Narayan, D. (1999). *Bonds and bridges: Social capital and poverty*. Policy Research Working Paper No. 2167. Washington, DC: The World Bank.

Neave, H. (1990). *The Deming dimension*. Knoxville, TN: SPC Press.

Page, K. G. (1998). *An empirical analysis of factors influencing public relations strategy use and effectiveness*. Unpublished master's thesis, Radford University, Radford, VA.

Page, K. G. (2000a, March). *An exploratory analysis of goal compatibility between organizations and publics*. Paper presented at the meeting of the Public Relations Division of the Southern States Communication Association, New Orleans, LA.

Page, K. G. (2000b, June). *Prioritizing relations: Exploring goal compatibility between organizations and publics*. Paper presented at the meeting of the Public Relations Division of the International Communication Association, Acapulco, Mexico.

Page, K. G. (2000c, August). *Determining message objectives: An analysis of public relations strategy use in press releases*. Paper presented at the meeting of the Public Relations Division of the Association for Education in Journalism and Mass Communication. Phoenix, AZ.

Page, K. G. (2003, May). *Responding to activism: An experimental analysis of public relations strategy influence on beliefs, attitudes, and behavioral intentions*. Paper presented at the meeting of the Public Relations Division of the International Communication Association. San Diego, CA.

Page, K., & Hazleton, V. (1999, May). *An empirical analysis of factors influencing public relations strategy selection and effectiveness*. Paper presented to the annual meeting of the International Communication Association, San Francisco.

Parks-Yancy, R. (2004). The impact of social capital on African-American and women survivors of organizational downsizing. In N. Ditomaso and C. Post (Eds.), *Diversity in the workforce*. New York: Elsevier.

Peters, T. (1982). *In search of excellence*. New York: Harper & Row.

Portes, A. (1998). Social capital: Its origins and applications in modern sociology. *Annual Review of Sociology, 22*, 1–25.

Portes, A., & Landolt, P. (1996). Unsolved mysteries: The Tocqueville files II. *The American Prospect, 7*(26). The American Prospect Web site: http://www.prospect.org/print/V7/26/26-cnt2.html

Putnam, R. D. (1995). Bowling alone: America's declining social capital.*Journal of Democracy, 6*, 65–78.

Putnam, R. D. (2000). *Bowling alone: The collapse and revival of American community*. New York: Simon & Schuster.

Ring, P. S. (1996). Fragile and resilient trust and their roles in economic exchange. *Business and socity, 35*, 148–175.

Ring, P. S., & Van de Ven, A. H. (1992). Structuring cooperative relationships between organizations. *Strategic Management Journal, 13*, 48–498.

Rodrik, D. (1999a). *The new global economy and developing countries: Making openness work*. Baltimore, MD: Johns Hopkins University Press.

Rodrik, D. (1999b). Where did all the growth go? External shocks, social conflicts, and growth collapses. *Journal of Economic Growth, 4*(4), 385–412.

Roloff, M. E., & Barnicott, E. F. (1978). The situational use of pro- and anti-social compliance-gaining strategies by high and low Machiavellians. In B. D. Ruben (Ed.), *Communication yearbook, 2* (pp.193–205). New Brunswick, NJ: Transaction.

Rosseau, D. M. (1995). *Psychological contracts in organizations: Understanding written, and unwritten agreement.* Thousand Oaks, CA: Sage.

Rothman, M. A. (1972). *The cybernetic revolution.* New York: Franklin Watts.

Scott, J. C. III, & O'Hair, D. (1989). Expanding psychographic concepts in public relations: The composite audience profile. In V. Hazleton Jr. and C. Botan (Eds.), *Public relations theory* (pp. 193–202). Hillsdale, NJ: Lawrence Erlbaum Associates.

Schweiger, D. M., and Leana, C. R. (1986). Participation in decision making. In E. A. Locke (Ed.), *Generalizing from laboratory to field settings* (pp. 147–166). Lexington, MA: Lexington Books.

Seibold, D. R., & Shea, B. C. (2001). Participation and decision making. In Jablin F. M. and Putnam L. L. (Eds.), *The new handbook of organizational communication: Advances in theory, research, and methods.* Thousand Oaks, CA: Sage.

Senge, P. (1990). *The fifth discipline: The art and practice of the learning organization.* New York: Doubleday.

Shah, P. P. (2000). Network destruction: The structural implications of downsizing. *Academy of Management Journal, 43*, 101–112.

Shiller, R. J. (1989). *Market volatility.* Cambridge: MIT Press.

Shleifer, A., & Summers, L. H. (1988). Breach of trust in hostile takeovers. In A. J. Auerbach (Ed.), *Corporate takeovers: Causes and consequences* (pp. 33–56). Chicago: The University of Chicago Press.

Spitzburg, B. H., & Cupach, W. R. (1984). *Interpersonal communication competence.* Beverly Hills, CA: Sage.

Stacey, R. D. (1992). *Managing the unknowable: Strategic boundaries between order and chaos in organizations.* San Francisco: Jossey-Bass.

Stacey, R. D. (1996). *Complexity and creativity in organizations.* San Fransisco: Berrett-Koehler.

Taylor, F. W. (1911). *The principles of scientific management.* New York: Harper Brothers.

Trist, E. (1981). *The evolution of sociotechnical systems: A conceptual framework and an action research program* (Occasional Paper No. 2). Toronto: Ontario Quality of Working Life Center.

Wagner, J. A., & Gooding, R. (1987). Shared influence and organizational behavior: A meta-analysis of situational variables expected to moderate participation. *Academy of Management Journal, 44*, 621–639.

Walton, M. (1986). *The Deming management method.* New York: Dodd, Mead.

Watson-Wyatt (1999). *Linking communications with strategy to achieve business goals.*

Watson-Wyatt Web site: http://www.watsonwyatt.com/research/resrender.asp?id=W-252&page=1.

Weber, M. (1947). *The theory of social and economic organization.* London: Free Press of Glencoe.

Werder, K. P. (2003, August). *An empirical analysis of the influence of perceived attributes of publics on public relations strategy use and effectiveness.* Paper presented at the meeting of the Public Relations Division of the Association for Education in Journalism and Mass Communication, Kansas City, MO.

Werder, K. P. (2004, August). *Responding to activism: An experimental analysis of public relations strategy influence on attributes of publics*. Paper presented at the meeting of the Public Relations Division of the Association for Education in Journalism and Mass Communication, Toronto, Canada.

Werder, K. P. (2005). An empirical analysis of the influence of perceived attributes of publics on public relations strategy use and effectiveness. *Journal of Public Relations Research, 17*, 217–266.

Wheatley, J. J. (1992). *Leadership and the new science: Learning about organization from an orderly universe*. San Francisco: Berett-Koehler.

Williamson, O. E. (1975). *Markets and hierarchies: Analysis and anti-trust implications: A study in the economics of internal organisation*. New York: Free Press.

Woodward, J. (1965). *Industrial organization: Theory and practice*. London: Oxford University Press.

Woolcock, M. (2001). The place of social capital in understanding social and economic outcomes. *ISUMA: Canadian Journal of Policy Research, 2*(1), 65–88.

PART

II

Tools for Tomorrow

CHAPTER

12

Public Relations Theory and Practice in Nation Building

Maureen Taylor and Michael L. Kent
Western Michigan University

INTRODUCTION

What is a nation? How are nations created? When does a nation cease to exist? For example, at what point did the region of the United States of America cease being an English colony and instead become a nation? Was it when the War of Independence ended (a war that the British call the American Revolution)? Was it when the United States first signed its Constitution? Or was it much later, perhaps after the Civil War, when Americans could clearly articulate a common vision of the nation that they belonged to? Questions about nations are not easily answered because building a nation requires more than just a declaration of independence. Nation building is a process that necessitates interactions between citizens and between the state and other nations. Indeed, as Burke points out in *Language as Symbolic Action,* identification is based on the idea of similarity (1973, pp. 263–275) and differences, or negatives (1966, pp. 3–24). That is, individuals and nations understand themselves in relation to others, and in relation to what they are not. An approach to nation building that looks at how communication can contribute to national identity and unity is a timely endeavor. Communication, especially mass communication, has been discussed as a central part of most nation-building programs. However, nation building is a dynamic human process. A public relations approach to nation building utilizes a more elaborate model of communication that focuses on how meanings such as national identity, national unity, and the nation state are socially constructed.

Much attention has been given to defining a nation and exploring how nations are created and maintained (James, 1996). At the most basic level, a nation exists by the consent of its people and by recognition of a common heritage that is communicated by various social practices (Hobsbawm, 1994; Yack, 1999). Nations in all stages of economic, social, and political development rely on nation building to accomplish specific national goals. Nation building is a strategic process that involves various resources and policies, and communication is one of the most important of those resources.

Over the past 15 years there has been a growing interest in the application of public relations in the nation-building process. This chapter explores the role that public relations can play in the nation-building process. The first sections of the chapter explain the phenomenon of nation building and ground nation building in theories of political science and public relations. Relationship building is a dynamic activity. Relationships that foster nation building occur between governments and publics as well as between nation-states and publics in other countries. The next sections of the chapter explore various public relations theories and practices in internal and external nation building strategies. The chapter concludes with a discussion of public relations as a strategic and ethical approach to building national and international relationships.

POLITICAL FOUNDATIONS OF NATION BUILDING

The term *nation building* is associated with building political institutions in newly formed (or transformed) states (Huntington, 1968). The goal of the political institutions is to mediate the infrastructure demands by citizens for roads, schools, fire protection, and personal safety, with the political capabilities of the government. Nation building in this approach most accurately describes institution building. The creation of institutions such as political parties, nonpartisan professional organizations, and nongovernmental organizations (NGOs) supportive of the government is an important part of the nation-building process. Other less tangible conditions are also necessary. For instance, creation of national identity and national unity are integral parts of the nation-building process.

National Identity

The creation of a national identity is a foundation of the nation building process (Scott, 1966). A *national identity* can be defined as the conscious identification of a group of people with shared national goals. People often have many different identities—religious, ethnic, professional—that define who they are and what values they hold. Efforts to build national identity seek to create a loyalty to the nation that supersedes local or ethnic loyalties and will help a nation to maximize its development potential (Scott, 1966). Communication campaigns can be used to create national identities that allow a nation's people to think together and act together (Deutsch, 1963). Communication is a central part of nation building because communication channels act as relationship-building tools that bring citizens together and, in times of crisis or threats, can help to unify them. A national identity is a prerequisite to national unity and, therefore, must be part of the initial stages of nation building.

National Unity

National unity refers to cultural orientations about events and institutions that bring people together and enable them to cooperate to achieve national goals (Emerson, 1966). National unity most often emerges when there is some kind of threat to a people who share common identifications. Nation unity creates a common ground that facilitates cooperative efforts for the benefit of the state. Creating and maintaining national unity is difficult in culturally diverse states where citizens do not already share national visions or have common enemies and goals (Foltz, 1966).

Examples of events in the United States that work to create shared identities and national unity include Thanksgiving celebrations, remembrance ceremonies and holidays for war veterans, and public events of mourning, such as what occurred as a result of the attacks on the World Trade Center and the Pentagon on September 11, 2001. Every nation enacts ceremonies to celebrate religious, cultural, and social institutions as a means of building national unity.

National unity, national identity, and nation building are all created, maintained, and nurtured through strategic communication efforts. Interpersonal communication, mass media campaigns, and government policies all contribute to important national communication initiatives. Benier (1999), however, noted that state-controlled broadcast media (radio and television) are primary tools in many nation-building programs. Connor (1994) agreed, suggesting that one-way communication, from a national government to the people, is the preferred means of nation building. Although the link between communication and nation building is clear, the majority of the research that has addressed the linkage is not found in the communication literature, but rather, in the political science literature. An examination of the two schools of thought that have most thoroughly explored the role of communication in nation building shows why a communication approach, grounded in public relations theory and practice, may help better explain nation building as a public-centered process.

THEORETICAL FOUNDATIONS OF NATION BUILDING

Taylor (2000b) reviewed the literature on nation building and found that the field of political science has most clearly described the relationship between nation building and communication. The political science literature is split between two schools of thought: the primordialists and the integrationists. The primordialist approach is most often associated with anthropologist Clifford Geertz and political theorist Walker Connor. Geertz (1973) first described primordial sentiments as competing loyalties between groups. Geertz observed that ethnic or religious groups prefer to stay within their own community and will minimize contact with others. This practice is known as in-group and out-group identification. When taken to extremes, primordial sentiments can undermine the political and social balance within a culturally plural nation. Primordial sentiments often inhibit national unity efforts because heterogeneous ethnic affiliations create the "basis for the demarcation of autonomous political units" (Geertz, 1973, p. 110), rather than harmonious relations. In other words, primordial groups often oppose efforts aimed at national harmony and instead support interests of value to their own members. Nations where political parties encompass only one ethnic group, such as the United Malay National Organization (UMNO) in Malaysia, and the Serb Nationalist party (SNS) in Bosnia-Herzegovina, are examples of how primordial sentiments can have negative repercussions for the nation-building process.

Primordialist scholars have argued that in developing, multiethnic nations increased communication through radio, newspapers, and television can end the historical isolation of ethnic groups. However, when previously unrelated groups receive mediated messages about national and local issues, members of primordial groups become even more aware of the differences between themselves and other groups. In response to the new awareness of difference, groups often try to minimize contact with others. Primordialist scholars believe that communication can have negative repercussions for the nation state, because the increased communication between groups in culturally plural states can lead to secessionist movements and even civil wars.

Walker Connor (1972, 1992, 1994), a primordialist, has posited that one-way communication from governments to national publics increases ethnic identification and brings ethnic and religious issues to national attention. Connor argued that if the government officials who create the nation-building messages differ in language, dialect, or colloquialisms from their intended publics, their messages might strengthen the cultural heterogeneity of the social group and draw attention to divisive rather than common traits. Thus, the primordialists argue, increased communication among different ethnic groups will foster conflict and separatism, rather than achieving the intended goal of nation building.

Although the primordialist approach acknowledges the role of communication, it does not explain why and how in some situations ethnic conflicts in the developing world has been minimized by communication. The ethnic conflicts in Rwanda, Bosnia, and Kosovo, although horrific, are the exceptions and not the rule for culturally plural states. In most nations, government communication serves an integrative function rather than a demarcative function.

A second approach to the role of communication in nation building can be found in the integrationist approach. Karl W. Deutsch argued that individuals and small groups became nations when various communication mediums allow people to share common social habits (1963, 1966a, 1966b). For Deutsch, social integration of individuals, groups, associations, and institutions is directly related to communication channels. Communication channels transfer information from one group or network to another and build the relations necessary for attaining national goals. More specifically, a nation is enacted by the communicative competency of both the government and its citizens (Deutsch, 1963). Communication competency allows nations, especially ethnically diverse nations, to foster cooperative relationships that achieve national goals.

Integration, through various communication channels, is the means through which nations are built. Integration, through communication, creates a collective national consciousness. Mediated messages through the print and broadcast channels, and now the Internet, create a collective consciousness that leads to national integration. However, there is much more to nation building than one-way communication. Mediated channels alone cannot, and never will, be the sole communicative element of national unity and nation building. Interpersonal communication and inter-organizational relationships are also needed.

If we were to shift nation-building research to focus on relationships, where would it fall in the communication research spectrum? The answer is obvious, public relations. Public relations theory and practice has the unique potential to create, maintain, and change relationships between citizens and governments. Public relations campaigns can be used to improve citizens' lives and to promote democracy in the developing world. For instance, literacy campaigns using public relations strategies and tactics can empower the uneducated and offer them opportunities to participate in the political process. Information campaigns about family planning can help women take control over their own futures. And campaigns for voter registration, voter education, and getting out the vote can provide marginalized individuals and groups with the knowledge and relational skills to articulate their needs in a political system. Given public relations' focus on relationship building, mediated communication, and organizational adaptation, nation building might fall within a relationship-building framework as a subspecialty in public relations.

RELATIONSHIP BUILDING

An approach to nation building that looks at how communication can contribute to national identity and unity is a timely endeavor. The political science literature on nation building reflects a political communication bias. Communication is viewed only as a channel or network in this literature. However, nation building is a dynamic human process. A public relations approach to nation building utilizes a more elaborate model of communication that focuses on how meanings are socially constructed. A public relations approach to nation building picks up where the integrationists leave off, because it offers a focus on communication and relationships. Although integrationism provides a starting point for a public relations approach to nation building, a communicative approach to nation building differs because it treats the process of communication rather than the content of messages, as that which shapes the collective consciousness of individuals, groups, communities, and the nation.

Although the uses for communication in the nation-building process are numerous, most considerations of communication in the nation building process have been limited to discussions of media ownership and control, national development programs, and mass communication technology and hardware (Bates, 1988; Hornik, 1988; Stevenson, 1988). Few dispute that communication acts as an important tool in the nation-building practices of developing nations. Recent research about development communication and nation building is starting to take a more participatory approach (Gudykunst & Moody, 2002). The next section of this chapter builds on the recent shift to participatory approaches to nation building. We argue that the importance of communication in nation building is found not so much in technological advances or the amount of information disseminated but in the relationships that communication creates, maintains, and alters.

Relationship Building With National Publics

A new understanding of the relationship-building role that communication plays in the nation-building process is needed. Public relations offers a valuable lens through which to view the nation-building process. Early public relations assumptions held that public relations was a business and management function. However, today there are different perspectives that show how public relations contributes to relationship building and nation building. For instance, Kruckeberg and Starck (1988) identified public relations as a way to rebuild community. Extending the Chicago School's concept of community, Kruckeberg and Starck argued:

> public relations is better defined and practiced as the active attempt to restore and maintain a sense of community. Only with this goal as a primary objective can public relations become a full partner in the information and communication milieu that forms the lifeblood of United States society and, to a growing extent, the world. (1988, p. xi; cf. also, Starck & Kruckeberg, 2001)

If public relations can be used to rebuild communities in the United States, then it can also be used to create and recreate communities around the world. Moreover, Botan (1992) argued that public relations should be viewed as a tool to build relationships between previously unrelated social systems or as a tool to modify existing relationships between organizations and publics. When communication and public relations are viewed as tools for creating and maintaining relationships nationally, then the nation state emerges as a truly communicatively constructed system.

All nation-building campaigns include large communication components that are essentially public relations campaigns. Deutsch's integrationist theory provides the framework for a focus on the relationships that are created and maintained through communication. Public relations, as a tool for building relationships between previously unrelated social systems, offers a new approach to nation building. Because public relations focuses on how communication efforts are used to establish, maintain, or change relationships between organizations and publics, primarily mass publics, public relations is an appropriate, yet underutilized, approach to the study of nation building. For the past 15 years there has been a growing interest in the link between public relations and nation building, and the following applied examples show how public relations has been enacted in nation building efforts in Africa, Asia, and Eastern Europe.

Africa is one of many regions in the world that would benefit from nation-building efforts. The nations of Africa, created by colonialism with little regard for ethnic or cultural boundaries, have experienced political, economic, and social upheaval. Pratt (1985, 1986) discussed nation building in articles about public relations practitioners who represent multinational corporations (MNCs) in Africa. Pratt (1985) noted that developing nations in Africa attempt to establish practices that are "consistent with their political ideologies, level of development, established patterns of symbolic communication, and sociopolitical controls" (p. 12). Pratt's treatments of public relations in the developing world emerged as early and valuable contributions to our understanding of international public relations. Pratt's articles offered a different perspective on public relations practice, and much of the current work on international public relations and nation building is based on Pratt's analyses.

Africa is not alone in its need for nation building. The emerging democracies in Asia also recognize the value of public relations as a nation-building function. Mohd Hamdam Adnan, Honorary Secretary of the Institute for Public Relations in Malaysia, has outlined how public relations programs served the nation-building process in his country. Adnan (1986) highlighted public relations practices and government-sponsored communication programs utilizing two-way communication to "create permanent mutual understanding and harmony among individuals and organizations" (p. 42). Malaysian public relations activities attempted to "build a good image" and create unity for all members of the Malaysian society (p. 42).

Hamadah Karim also included nation building as a function of public relations. Karim (1989) described the Filipino and Singaporean governments' use of public relations offices to serve as nerve centers linking governmental agencies with various media sources. Practitioners facilitate relationship building between the government and the people and help create processes that allow for communication and feedback. Karim viewed nation building as an essential governmental function that helps to build the national character of developing nations. Moreover, nation building is linked to the creation and maintenance of national values. Public relations practitioners who assist with nation-building efforts need to understand the priorities and values of the host culture(s) and government structure. Karim (1989) acknowledged that the practice of public relations in developing nations "will become in time a part of the government's tool for nation building" (p. 21).

Van Leuven (1996) has also addressed the topic of nation building and public relations. After a 4-month study in Singapore and Malaysia, Van Leuven reported that public relations in Southeast Asia has progressed through a nation-building phase in which "virtually all public relations work emanated from government information ministries" (p. 210) to a regional interdependence phase whereby public relations departments and agencies create the majority of strategic communication messages. In the nation-building phase Van Leuven reported that the relationship between government and the media and government and the public is a one-way relationship. The government dominated the tone and content of communication. However, as the economy developed and new relationships were formed, Van Leuven acknowledged the government–media relationship as well as the government–public relationship has matured. Van Leuven's observations are correct. In many nations public relations has progressed from a complete monopoly of government control over national communication to a shared-power situation. However, nation building does not end once a nation begins to develop economically. More specifically, public relations for nation building must continuously ensure that all public voices are tolerated and valued, and government–public relationships are allowed to mature.

Taylor and Botan (1997), and Taylor (2000b), examined a nation building campaign in Malaysia. The Neighborliness Campaign was a public education campaign that attempted to build relationships between people of different ethnic groups in Malaysia. Worth noting is that the outcomes of nation-building campaigns like the Neighborliness Campaign are not always congruent with the stated goals of the planners. Nation building campaigns often have unanticipated and detrimental results for national identity and unity (Taylor, 2000b). In the case of the Neighborliness Campaign, interethnic tensions may have actually been exacerbated by the government's nation-building efforts. Taylor (2000b) found that Malaysians in the Neighborliness communities had lower levels of national unity and lower levels of national identity. One reason for this outcome may be the disconnect between the message of the Neighborliness Campaign which stated that all Malaysians were equal, and the government programs which favored one ethnic group over the others. The Malaysian government's failure to create consistent messages and enact consistent policies congruent to the goals of Neighborliness Campaign no doubt contributed to the unanticipated consequences of the effort.

Also worth noting is that governments are not the only organizations that can participate in creating nation-building messages. In a study of Bosnia, Taylor examined how NGOs contribute to nation building and civil society efforts (2000a; cf. also, Taylor & Kent, 2000). Many different types of social and political organizations seek to influence the direction of Bosnian civil society. Through news releases, news conferences, and invitations to the media to cover newsworthy events, NGOs seek to reach publics with pro-democracy and civil society messages. Increased dialogue with media representatives adds up to a new level of relationship building between the organizations that seek to improve the situation in a nation and the various publics who benefit from NGO actions. There is, however, another way that public relations theory and practice contribute to nation building—relationships at the international level.

Relationship Building With International Publics

According to Boulding (1956), all societies have a stock of images, created by discourse, that represent organizations and nation-states. "The basic bond of any society, culture, subculture, or organization is a 'public image'" (Boulding, 1956, p. 64). Citizens have particular images (or conceptions) of their own nation in relations to other nations, and those images reflect specific values and emotions. People in one nation make attributions about those living in other nations even when they have not visited a particular country. And when individuals discuss their personal images with others, they contribute to the creation of public images. The public images of nation-states emanate from a "universe of discourse" (Boulding, 1956, p. 15). For instance, consider the number of people who have never visited Iraq or Afghanistan, yet have an image of the nation and the people who live there?

Nations, like individuals and organizations, attempt to manage their image and create favorable impressions for particular audiences. Although national images can be changed through new information or experience, they are relatively enduring (Boulding, 1956). Efforts to shape national images are not a recent phenomenon. Nations throughout history have consciously attempted to alter national images for both domestic and international audiences. Indeed, the building, maintaining, and dismantling of national images has been traced back through biblical times and even to the ancient Egyptians (Kunczik, 1990).

An image that portrays a unified, stable, and quickly developing nation is a prerequisite for attracting and maintaining business ventures as well as gaining international development aid (Pratt, 1985). Nations that do not present a unified national image are often unable to attract foreign investment even when there is development potential. For example, South Africa and some of the former East Bloc nations regularly invite foreign investment, but, because they do not project an image of political stability to corporate audiences, they fail to gain international trust. Many nations are also focusing nation-building efforts on external publics. There are several reasons for this, but economic development may be one of the most important reasons why nations cultivate their image for external audiences. Although a unified national image is an important factor for any nation, for "small nations in particular, it is often crucially important for economic reasons to cultivate their national image abroad" (Kunczik, p. 22).

In a text directed toward readers in developing nations, Kunczik presented an historical overview of image cultivation by a variety of governments and offered practical applications on international image cultivation for practitioners and government leaders. International image cultivation is based on research about public relations, advertising, prejudice, attitudes, and political decision making (p. 7). Moreover, Kunczik's text explained dozens of successful and unsuccessful attempts by nations to cultivate their image in the international arena. In Kunczik's text, case studies are accompanied by prescriptions for public relations practitioners and governments on how to create bonds with journalists, prepare material for press kits, manage a press conference, and correct negative media portrayals. Kunczik's approach offered an overview of what variables are involved in the creation or changing of a national image in the international arena. Kunczik offered practical applications of international image cultivation and attempted to link the case studies in his book with traditional scientific research. Kunczik's final statement argued that "the conclusion to be drawn from the research findings and the experiences of the practitioners is that clearly the best form of image cultivation for states is for them to be democratic, to observe human rights, and to pursue policies of openness" (p. 282).

Other public relations scholars have discussed government public relations with international audiences. Signitzer and Coombs (1992) discussed how public diplomacy and public relations share similar assumptions and also share similar methodological practices. L'Etang (1998) also argued that the fields of diplomacy and public relations are historically linked. Manheim (1994) explored strategic public diplomacy, a communication process that "is practiced less as an art than as an applied social science of human behavior. It is . . . the practice of propaganda in the earliest sense of the term, but enlightened by half a century of empirical research into human motivation and behavior" (p. 7). Nations have employed strategic public diplomacy either to cultivate a positive international image or to minimize negative publicity. For instance, a 1983 study that focused on the impact of public relations campaigns in Rhodesia (now Zimbabwe) showed that "when Rhodesia hired a public relations firm to advise it, negative comment declined sharply in the *New York Times*, although incidents of violence remained virtually unaffected" (Albritton & Manheim, 1983, p. 622).

Albritton and Manheim (1983, 1985) examined how the public relations campaigns by developing nations are portrayed in the United States media. Their studies revealed that when developing nations such as Argentina, Indonesia, Korea, the Philippines, and Turkey retained American public relations agencies, the national image of each country, as portrayed in *New York Times* stories, improved (1985). Manheim (1994) later examined the strategic public diplomacy efforts of developing nations such as the Philippines, Korea, Kuwait, Turkey, Pakistan, Iran and Argentina on United States policy makers and the American public. He found that public diplomacy campaigns were created and implemented "for purposes of improving the setting for which foreign policy decisions of interest . . . are made, and of stimulating or deterring . . . decision making" (1994, p. 158).

Clearly public relations plays an important role on the international level of relationship building at home and abroad. At home, nations seek to create their own national identities that will encourage citizens to differentiate themselves from their regional neighbors. Simultaneously, nations also attept to create positive national images and to influence international media coverage for their own benefit. One question needs to be asked about public relations and nation building: What theories can be used to guide the practice and extend scholarly development? The next section discusses several theoretical models that have implications for public relations as a framework for nation building.

IMPLICATIONS FOR PUBLIC RELATIONS THEORY

The practice of nation building continues today, and it will always continue as long as the nation-state exists as a viable economic, political, and social entity.

Nations are using strategic communication to build relationships between national governments and indigenous publics, as well as to build relationships with publics in other nations. Most of the nation-building communication follows a top-down model and serves the needs of the governments in power rather than the public in general. From a public relations standpoint, the focus on communicating the state's needs to the public, rather than developing stable relationships that cut across racial and ethnic boundaries, is problematic. Diamond (1990) suggests that in multiethnic nations, crosscutting cleavages or broad patterns of social alignment are central to creating a tolerant and enlightened citizenry. Indeed, the assumption of the top-down approach presupposes that a small group of decision makers, often from the elite class, knows what is best for all citizens.

A public relations approach to nation building assumes that what is ultimately more important is to create stable interpersonal and intergroup relationships, and to foster trust in the nation state as a viable and responsive social entity. Trust and cooperative relationships serve as foundations for stable nations (Taylor & Doerfel, 2003). Trust and cooperation are important because nations do not draw their strength from placating, silencing, suppressing, or privileging one group over another. Nations are strong when there exist many long-term relationships among various ethnic, social, and political groups. With relationships at the core of the nation-state, a public relations approach to nation building can be both practical and ethical.

Theories to Guide Nation Building

Relational theory may offer a useful framework for a public relations perspective. If, as most definitions of public relations suggest, one of public relations' central strengths is its emphasis on relationship building as a means of creating trust and support among publics, then an approach to nation building that focuses on relational stability is warranted. Three public relations theoretical approaches that provide practical and ethical frameworks to nation building include coorientation, dialogue, and civil society.

Coorientation theory may help governments and organizations to identify and measure issues where organizations and publics differ. Stable interpersonal relationships (and by extension, inter-group relationships) are premised on the notion of intersubjectivity, or interpersonal behavioral models that help explain the actions of others. Coorientation theory examines how groups see each other and what they believe the other groups think about them. That is, in any interaction, individuals and groups have at least three perspectives to consider: (1) how they think about themselves (as honest, strategic, powerful, etc.), (2) how they view other individuals or groups (as self-serving, manipulative, elitist, etc.), and (3) how they think other individuals and groups view them.

Coorientation encompasses efforts to come to honest or objective understanding of other groups or organizations' position and to understand how other groups think about one's own group or organization. When (or if) both parties in an exchange share the same view(s) of the other, intersubjectivity has been achieved. Intersubjectivity is difficult and often unobtainable depending upon the degree of ideological, economic, or social distance between parties. A lack of intersubjectivity on the part of individuals is why it is so difficult for people in many nations of the world to understand why other nations fear, hate, or mistrust them.

Coorientation involves a commitment among individuals and groups to try to understand others' perceptions of reality and events, in spite of whether that definition is shared. For intersubjectivity to be achieved, both parties in an interaction must be willing to see the world differently and accept that the other's view of the world is not necessarily "wrong," only different (Broom, 1977; Springston & Keyton, 2001).

One approach to measuring or identifying coorientation is the idea of public relations field dynamics (PRFD). Springston and Keyton (2001) suggest that PRFD is a tool for coorientation "to identify which publics are potentially open for collaboration and which publics are not. In addition, PRFD can be used to determine the views of other publics on the issue central to the situation" (p. 123). The PRFD approach would be especially important for NGOs and social activist organizations to identify strategic partners when they seek to leverage activities. And, PRFD would also help governments to identify organizations, whether indigenous or external, that share similar national development objectives.

One of the starting points of a coorientational approach to nation building is understanding and tolerance. From a nation-building standpoint, efforts to promote cultural understanding and tolerance are practiced all the time. The Neighborliness Campaign in Malaysia is an example, although an unsuccessful one, where the government encouraged citizens from different ethnic groups (Malay, Chinese, and Indian) to come together in an attempt to promote understanding and tolerance among citizens. In the United States an assortment of secular events (speeches, parades, picnics, etc.) are used to bring together citizens from all walks of life in an effort to promote tolerance and intergroup understanding.

But coorientation is more than just tolerance. From a public relations standpoint, coorientation means that two or more individuals or parties have an awareness of how they are actually perceived by others not just a guess about what they think the other group or public thinks about them. They know. Coorientation requires individuals or groups to engage the other to learn about how they see the world and what they actually believe. To give a local example, for the United States to practice a coorientational perspective with other nations would require that the United States interact with citizens and leaders of other nations and not just dismiss them as fanatics. Through interaction, United States leaders would eventually learn what the citizens of other nations actually think and believe about the United States—not from third-hand briefing reports by intelligence agencies but through actual interaction. Such a bold step would be an eye opener for any government. Although, as suggested above, nations can engage in formal coorientational assessment (through PRFD and other techniques), on the most basic level coorientation requires a commitment to understanding, a willingness to listen, and the capacity to change.

Dialogic theory is a second public relations approach to nation building that may be helpful for both scholars and practitioners. Like coorientational theory, dialogic theory suggests that understanding and tolerance of other individuals and groups is central to effective government–public relationships. Unlike coorientational theory, however, dialogue is about fostering honest and mutually beneficial relationships with individuals rather than groups. Dialogue is ideal for creating government–public relationships. That is, while coorientation may be useful for nations to understand how other nations or groups think about each other, dialogue necessitates a commitment to effective organization–individual relations. As Kent and Taylor (2002) explain, "dialogue is not about the 'process' used, it is about the products that emerge— trust, satisfaction, sympathy" (p. 32). According to Kent and Taylor:

> Dialogue as an orientation includes five features: *mutuality*, or the recognition of organization–public relationships; *propinquity*, or the temporality and spontaneity of interactions with publics; *empathy*, or the supportiveness and confirmation of public goals and interests; *risk*, or the willingness to interact with individuals and publics on their own terms; and finally, *commitment*, or the extent to which an organization gives itself over to dialogue, interpretation, and understanding in its interactions with publics. (Kent & Taylor, 2002, pp. 24–25, authors' emphasis)

A dialogic approach to nation building necessitates public forums and open decision making practices as a means to provide the framework for public participation. Indeed, although the dialogic approach to nation building does not require democratic political structures per se, it does privilege liberal democratic notions in which public participation and public voice are emphasized.

Dialogic theory in the nation-building process can be studied by examining the communication structures within a nation—the mass media, Internet and government Web sites, and government–citizen outreach efforts. Ultimately, successful nation building is premised on the development of civil society structures that try to meet the needs of an assortment of publics rather than simply serving the needs of those in power.

Civil society theory may provide a third framework for theorizing a public relations approach to nation building. When there is coorientation and dialogue between publics and government officials, then there is the potential for civil society. Civil society describes a system whereby groups and organizations mediate the relationship between citizens and government. Taylor (2000a) described civil society development in Bosnia, noting that "public relations, through its focus on media relations and relationship-building, is an integral part of the civil society function. Civil society organizations need to reach various publics with information and create links between like-minded groups" (p. 3). Thus, examining relationships between groups and between governments and publics is one way to bring public relations and relational theory into nation building.

Civil society can be studied by examining the interpersonal and inter-organizational linkages created and changed as citizens participate in groups that cross racial, ethnic, religious, class, and geographic regions and allegiances. In a civil society, people belong to many groups that focus on different interests. Network methodology can be used to measure relationship building in civil society efforts. Taylor and Doerfel (2003) measured the strength of a civil society movement in Croatia. Using measures such as network density, structural holes, and multiplex links, Taylor and Doerfel were able to identify the organizations that were most central to the civil society movement. Moreover, the researchers identified which types of organizations serve necessary network roles. Coorientation, dialogue, and civil society theories provide both practical and ethical frameworks for enacting and studying nation building.

Importance of Public Relations to Nation Building

The previous sections have shown that there are a variety of ways to look at the relationship between communication and nation building. The practice of nation building includes efforts by developing national governments to promote a national identity and unity. Many developing nations are still recovering from the vestiges of colonialism and communism. These countries create national communication campaigns to assist in their political, social, and economic development. Because many developing nations encompass various ethnic and religious groups, governments often sense a need for unifying national ideologies to maintain popular support (or the status quo). Developed nations such as those from the former Eastern Bloc have similar nation-building needs for identity building. Communication campaigns can help people during difficult times of social, economic, and identity transformation.

Although the importance of a unifying national vision is obvious—it leads to collective action on the part of citizens, it allows a government to conserve resources and focus national energies—a stable nation cannot be built at the expense of segments of its citizenry. Top-down public relations efforts by officials, whether elected or appointed, that attempt to create national identities superseding local and ethnic loyalties to solidify support for a non-democratic government are self-serving. These one-way campaigns are doomed to fail to achieve their goals because they fail to address the real needs of a transitional nation—strong interpersonal and inter-organizational relationships that will strengthen the nation state. The coorientation, dialogue, and civil society theories of nation building, however, offer better models because of their ability to create solidarity, tolerance, and mutual understanding among citizens, governments, groups, organizations, and international publics.

CONCLUSION

This chapter has discussed how public relations has been involved in many facets of nation building in Asia, Africa, and Europe. Inherent in nation building is the idea of connectiveness and linkages that build relationships between governments and publics as well as between publics that have been previously unrelated. Relationships between governments and publics created through public relations are an important part of the national development process. Moreover, relationships are not limited to relationships between governments and internal publics. Communication for national development also includes public diplomacy practices and communication to multinational corporations.

Public relations has enormous democratic potential both as a strategic communication function and as a relationship-building function. Through both strategic campaign activities and relational communication activities, public relations can improve citizens' lives and promote democracy throughout the world. Public relations professionals need to look at how communication in general and public relations in particular can be used in all parts of the world to help identify and solve local and national problems. Many nations already employ communication campaigns as a tool to maintain or alter relationships. Communication campaigns can educate and empower, level the playing field, and bring the nation to a state of equilibrium in which all people have the opportunity to develop to their fullest potential.

Relationship building includes those efforts that attempt to create the conditions under which people of various ethnic groups can be mobilized to cooperate with each other. Moreover, relationship building helps to achieve national goals such as mobilization during times of external threat or for national development objectives.

A public relations approach to nation building, with an explicit focus on relationships at both the interpersonal and organization–public levels, can extend both the primordialist and integrationist models. Relationship building is not easily accomplished; and creating relationships among individuals of various ethnic groups and between individuals and the government still requires additional study. However, several assumptions about communication, relationships, and public relations campaigns that guide nation building already exist.

Interpersonal and inter-organizational relationships can be encouraged through dialogic, coorientational, and civil society efforts. Communication campaigns are one vehicle for relationship building. Relationships must also be negotiated between individuals and governments. Negotiation involves compromise, trust, risk, mutuality, and respect for other parties—features of dialogue. Communication campaigns need to be flexible, and organizations must be able to address the diverse needs of publics.

The principles of dialogue and mutuality serve as the foundation for a public relations approach to nation building and call for both interpersonal and organization–public relationships. Mutual understanding and the recognition that some change on the part of the interactants must be the goal of communication efforts. The assumptions of the coorientational, dialogic, and civil-society approaches also provide a rationale for the locus of control of nation building to be placed not with the government, but with the people who participate in civil society organizations. Jacobson and Jang (2002) noted that NGOs and civil-society organizations have "influenced forums that are traditionally dominated by state actors. They facilitate informed participation in policy processes at both the national and international levels" (p. 350). Indeed, in many societies the civil society organizations play the most influential role in citizens' lives. Coorientational, dialogic, and civil-society approaches may be best to explain and describe this new type of grass-roots development.

The nation-building principles discussed here are only a starting point. Perhaps our most important contribution to the study of nation building is the attempt to reframe the way that researchers examine communication in the nation-building process. Communication as a tool for nation building must be understood as that which creates and maintains relationships, and not simply as a channel or medium for government communication efforts.

REFERENCES

Adnan, M. H. (1986). Public relations for neighborliness: Malaysian experiences. *International Public Relations Review, 10*, 41–45.

Albritton, R. B., & Manheim, J. B. (1983). News of Rhodesia: The impact of a public relations campaign. *Journalism Quarterly, 60*, 622–628.

Albritton, R. B., & Manheim, J. B. (1985). Public relations efforts for the Third World: Images in the news. *Journal of Communication, 35*, 43–59.

Bates, B. J. (1988). Information as an economic good: Sources of individual and social value. In V. Mosco, & J. Wasko, (Eds.), *The political economy of information*. Madison: University of Wisconsin Press.

Benier, R. (1999). *Theorizing nationalism*. Albany, NY: SUNY Press.

Botan, C. H. (1992). International public relations: Critique and reformulation. *Public Relations Review, 18*, 149–159.

Boulding, K. E. (1956). *The image: Knowledge in life and society*. Ann Arbor: University of Michigan Press.

Broom, G. M. (1977). Coorientational measurement of public issues. *Public Relations Review, 3*, 110–119.

Burke, K. (1973). The rhetorical situation. In L. Thayer (Ed.), *Communication: Ethical and moral issues* (pp. 263–275). London: Gordon & Breach Science Publishers.

Burke, K. (1966). *Language as symbolic action: Essays in life, literature, and method.* Berkeley: University of California Press.

Connor, W. (1972). Nation-building or nation destroying? *World Politics, 24*, 319–355.

Connor, W. (1992). When a nation? *Ethnic and Racial Studies, 13*, 92–103.

Connor, W. (1994). *Ethnonationalism: The quest for understanding.* Princeton, NJ: Princeton University Press.

Deutsch, K. W. (1963). *Nationalism and social communication.* Cambridge, MA: MIT Press.

Deutsch, K. W. (1966a). *The nerves of government: Models of political communication and control.* New York: The Free Press.

Deutsch, K. W. (1966b). *Nation-building.* New York: Atherton Press.

Diamond, L. (1990). Nigeria: Pluralism, statism and the struggle for democracy. In L. Diamond, J. Linz & S. Lipset (Eds.), *Politics in developing countries: Comparing experiences with democracy* (pp. 351–409). Boulder, CO: Rinner Publishers:

Emerson, R. (1966). Nation building in Africa. In K. W. Deutsch, & W. J. Foltz (Eds.), *Nation building* (pp. 95–116). Chicago: Atherton.

Foltz, W. J. (1966). Building the newest nations: Short run strategies and long run problems. In K. W. Deutsch & W. J. Foltz (Eds.), *Nation building* (pp. 117–131). Chicago: Atherton.

Geertz, C. (1973). *The interpretation of culture.* New York: Basic Books.

Gudykunst, W., & Moody, B. (2002). *The handbook of intercultural and international communication.* Thousand Oaks, CA: Sage.

Hobsbawm, E. (1994/1983). The nation as invented tradition. In J. Hutchinson & A. D. Smith (Eds.), *Nationalism* (pp. 76–83). New York: Oxford University Press.

Hornik, R. C. (1988). *Development communication: Information, agriculture, and nutrition in the third world.* New York: Longman.

Huntington, S. P. (1968). *Political order in changing societies.* New Haven, CT: Yale University Press.

Jacobson, T. L., & Jang, W. Y. (2002). Media, war, peace, and global civil society. In W. Gudykunst & B. Moody (Eds.), *The handbook of intercultural and international communication* (pp. 343–358). Thousand Oaks, CA: Sage.

James, P. (1996). *Nation formation: Toward a theory of abstract community.* London: Sage

Karim, H. (1989). Development of public relations in Asia/Pacific: A Malaysian view. *International Public Relations Review, 12*, 17–24.

Kent, M. L., & Taylor, M. (2002). Toward a dialogic theory of public relations. *Public Relations Review, 28*, 1, 21–37.

Kruckeberg, D., & Starck, K. (1988). *Public relations and community: A reconstructed theory.* New York: Praeger.

Kunczik, M. (1990). *Images of nations and international public relations.* Bonn, Germany: Friedrich-Ebert Stiftung.

L' Etang, J. (1998). State propaganda and bureaucratic intelligence: The creation of public relations in 20th century Britain. *Public Relations Review, 24*, 413–441.

Manheim, J. (1994). *Strategic public diplomacy and American foreign policy: The evolution of influence.* New York: Oxford University Press.

Pratt, C. (1985). The African context. *Public Relations Journal, 41*, 11–16.

Pratt, C. (1986). Professionalism in Nigerian public relations. *Public Relations Review, 10*, 27–40.

Scott, R. E. (1966). Nation building in Latin America. In K. W. Deutsch, & W. J. Foltz (Eds.), *Nation building* (pp. 73–83). Chicago: Atherton.

Signitzer, B., & Coombs, T. (1992). Public relations and public diplomacy: Conceptual convergences. *Public Relations Review, 18*, 137–147.

Springston J. K,. & Keyton, J. (2001). Public relations filed dynamics. In R. L. Heath, & G. Vasquez, *Handbook of public relations* (pp. 115–126). Thousand Oaks CA: Sage.

Starck, K., & Kruckeberg, D. (2001). Public relations and community: A reconstructed theory revisited. In R. L. Heath & G. Vasquez, *Handbook of public relations* (pp. 51–60). Thousand Oaks CA: Sage,

Stevenson, R. (1988). *Communication, development, and the third world: The politics of information.* New York: Longman.

Taylor, M. (2000a). Media relations in Bosnia: A role for public relations in building civil society. *Public Relations Review, 26*, 1–14.

Taylor, M. (2000b). Toward a public relations approach to nation building. *Journal of Public Relations Research, 12*, 2, 179–210.

Taylor, M., & Botan, C. H. (1997). Public relations campaigns for national development in the Pacific Rim: The case of public education in Malaysia. *Australian Journal of Communication, 24*, 115–130.

Taylor, M., & Doerfel, M. L. (2003). Building inter-organizational relationships that build nations. Human *Communication Research, 29*(2), 153–181.

Taylor, M., & Kent, M. L. (2000). Media transition in Bosnia: From propagandistic past to uncertain future. *Gazette 62*, 5, 355–378.

Van Leuven, J. K. (1996). Public relations in South East Asia: From nation building campaigns to regional interdependence. In H. M. Culbertson & N. Chen (Eds.), *International public relations: A comparative analysis* (pp. 207–222). Mahwah, NJ: Lawrence Erlbaum Associates.

Yack, B. (1999). The myth of the civic nation. In R. Benier (Ed.), *Theorizing nationalism* (pp. 103–118). Albany, NY: SUNY Press.

Overcoming System and Culture Boundaries: Public Relations from a Structuration Perspective

Diane F. Witmer

California State University, Fullerton

INTRODUCTION

Since the early 1980s, public relations theory has been guided largely by systems theory. Some scholarly work focuses on public relations as a rhetorical endeavor (e.g., Bostdorff, 1994; Coombs, 1992; Heath, 1988; Vasquez, 1993). However, with the exception of Kuhn's (1997) structurationist perspective of issues management and Banks' (1996) social-interpretive approach to multicultural public relations, the predominance of mainstream public relations research is undergirded by a systems perspective. Scholarship in this tradition includes such foundational areas as identification of practitioner roles and functions (e.g., Broom, 1982; Dozier & Broom, 1995; Lauzen, 1994), issues management (e.g., Arrington & Sawaya, 1984; Crable & Vibbert, 1985; Ewing, 1990; Wartick & Rude, 1986), negotiation (e.g., J. Grunig & L. Grunig, 1992; Vasquez, 1996), and identification of publics (e.g., J. Grunig, 1978, 1982, 1983, 1984, 1989a, 1992; J. E. Grunig & L. Grunig, 1992; Grunig & Hunt, 1984). However, limitations in common theoretic approaches to public relations scholarship such as systems theory are creating a need to adopt newer, more robust, and broader theoretic perspectives.

This chapter recommends structuration theory as a logical extension to systems theory that enables public relations scholars to overcome some in the limitations inherent in the traditional systems perspective. It first provides an overview of systems theory, and then describes the theory's limitations for the field of public relations. These limitations concern the organizational/environmental interface and environmental scanning, the ongoing communicative practices of social organizations, and the recursive nature of institutional structures through human interactions. The chapter also offers a brief background on organizational culture studies and their relationship to public relations. Finally, it provides a very brief overview of structuration and its potential contribution to public relations scholarship.

The next section offers a very brief recap of systems theory for those not fully comfortable with the terminology of that theory. A reader well-versed in systems theory might wish to jump to the section immediately following, on implications of systems theory for public relations.

SYSTEMS THEORY

First proposed by biologist Ludwig von Bertalanffy (1968), general systems theory has evolved into an academic field of its own. One of the major advantages of systems theory is that it accounts for complex behaviors of and relationships between system components. Systems are generally defined as interrelated sets of parts or components that create a unique, bounded entity (e.g., Athey, 1982). Systems function within the contexts of their immediate surroundings or environments, although not all systems are particularly sensitive to environmental influences. As a result, systems are categorized according to their relative openness to environment.

Closed systems are, as the name implies, functionally unresponsive and have internal controls for adaptation to environmental influences. An example of a closed system is a key-wound clock, which neither recognizes nor adjusts to external conditions. *Open systems*, on the other hand, constantly strive to survive by responding to environmental forces that act on them and to maintain a healthy balance or homeostasis between input and output. Open systems utilize resources from the environment as input, transform those resources during throughput, and produce an output of some sort. Biological systems, for example, use nutrients to produce energy, system functionality, and waste.

Cybernetic systems are the most open of open systems, in terms of their relative sensitivity to environmental influences. A cybernetic system is sensitive to its environment, and it contains internal mechanisms that allow it to adapt to environmental changes. An example of a cybernetic system is a plant, which is sensitive to changes in the environmental light and temperature and makes internal adjustments to enable growth and reproduction.

Systems are generally considered hierarchical, in that their components may also be viewed as interdependent systems. This means that the definition of what constitutes a system is relatively arbitrary, depending upon the locus of research. Looking again at the biological example, the plant or animal within which a system, such as the circulatory system, resides is the immediate environment or the suprasystem. Components of a circulatory system are bounded by the vessels through which blood flows (or in the case of plants, xylem or phloem), and the cells that make up the blood and vessels are components of the circulatory system. However, although the circulatory system is a subsystem or component of a larger biological system (a plant or an animal), similarly, the components of that circulatory system are bona fide systems in their own rights. Cellular systems, for example, comprise such organelles as mitochondria, ribosomes, and nuclei that interact to utilize resources for system functions such as reproduction. Similarly, social systems, such as organizations, use resources of goods and services to produce output of new goods and services.

IMPLICATIONS OF SYSTEMS THEORY FOR PUBLIC RELATIONS

Organizational systems are considered cybernetic systems and often are characterized by permeable boundaries (e.g., Stohl, 1995), in that environmental elements freely enter and leave them. People live, work, and play in a variety of social systems, including churches, schools, businesses, and clubs. We join them, we abandon them, we are hired into them, and we graduate from them. In each case, we influence the characteristics and cultures of our social systems even as they influence us.

From a systems perspective, public relations functions as both system component and boundary spanner (e.g., Vasquez, 1996), whether the practitioner's role is that of technician or manager (Broom & Dozier, 1986; Dozier, 1984, 1992) or a combination of both (e.g., Newsom, Turk, & Kruckeberg, 1996; Toth, Serini, Wright, & Emig, 1998). Environmental scanning brings information into the organization, and external communications send information into the organizational environment (see Dozier, 1990, for a comprehensive overview of research in this area). Therefore, public relations activities serve a feedback function that helps the client systems interpret their environments in order to maintain homeostasis.

Beyond providing a functional understanding of the public relations role, systems theory has undergirded descriptive public relations models. Grunig and Hunt (1984), for example, developed a four-model overview of public relations that emphasizes the boundary-spanning and feedback roles of public relations in organizations. The Grunig and Hunt models address evolutionary changes in public relations practices and focus largely on one-way versus two-way communication between a public relations client and its target publics.

Systems theory also provides a foundation for the situational theorists' typology of publics (e.g., Grunig, 1989a, 1989b; Grunig & Repper, 1992). The situational theory of publics proposes the communication behaviors and public participation of audiences or publics as a locus of public relations research. This approach entails an analysis of the levels of a public's organized cognitions about an issue (Dyer, 1996; Grunig, 1989a, 1989b), or a public's public opinion and issues orientation (Berkowitz & Tunmire, 1994). Strategic publics are typically defined in terms of actions regarding their agreement or disagreement with an organization's policies or positions (Grunig, 1992; Grunig & Hunt, 1984).

LIMITATIONS OF SYSTEMS THEORY FOR PUBLIC RELATIONS

Although systems theory has been a major influence on both public relations research methodology and theoretical advances, it may limit the degree to which we can extend our understanding of the processes and the functions of public relations in light of developing trends, particularly the increasing importance of communication technologies and globalization. Four key areas characterize those limitations: poor differentiation of time and space from structure, artificial delineation between systems and their environments, inability to address the human interaction that creates and recreates publics, and inadequate conceptualization of culture as lived experience.

First, although systems theory accounts for complex behaviors of system components and of system interactions with environmental factors, it tends to be time bound. Time and space are concepts that are separated by the modern differentiation of lived time from social structures. The systems perspective deemphasizes the development of internal and external opinions and trends over time that enable forecasting and long-term planning. Instead, it focuses on complex interactions of system components and system environment as stable influences, and does not differentiate time from structure.

Second, the underlying assumption of systems theory, that a system and its environment are discrete entities, discounts the recursive nature of system interactions with environmental interfaces (Cozier & Witmer, 2000). Systems theory oversimplifies the interconnections between the micro- and macro-level institution, the ways in which organizations both create and are created by their structures, and the disembedding and re-embedding of global systems within local systems. Global corporate structures, for example, may be embedded into local divisions by organizational members. Furthermore, those members may have multiple roles as organizational consumers, employees, and stockholders.

Third, systems theory does not adequately account for the creation and re-creation of publics through shared experiences (Branham, 1980; Branham & Pearce, 1985) or their changeability over time (e.g., Lauzen & Dozier, 1992; Thomsen, 1995). Communicative interactions between people form discursive communities that transcend time and space through communication technologies (Cozier & Witmer, 2000) and discursively organize latent, closed publics or nonpublic into active publics. In other words, the traditional, systems-based approach to publics underemphasizes the communicative interactions by which publics are formed. Because an organization's publics may be constituted in part or in whole by organizational members, the discursive communities and cultures they form also create organizational cultures. This brings us to a fourth limitation of the systems perspective.

Much of the practice of public relations is organizationally situated, and organizational culture is a critical aspect of organizational public relations (Kendall, 1996). However, systems theory does not adequately facilitate the explication of culture in organizations. Everyday living, including organizational life, tends to fall into patterns, routines, habits, rites, and rituals, which enact and reproduce organizational culture. Systems theory cannot adequately address organizational culture because it is a product of human experience and social interactions. The following sections provide a brief overview of scholarship in organizational culture, and then offer ways in which the structurationist perspective not only can overcome the incommensurabilities of those studies, but also can overcome the limitations of systems theory.

RESEARCH IN ORGANIZATIONAL CULTURE

The concept of organizational culture, first appropriated from cultural anthropologists, is studied widely for academic research (e.g., Amsa, 1986; Barley & Kunda, 1992; Barney, 1986; Brown, 1992; Cooke & Rousseau, 1988; Frost, Moore, Louis, Lundberg, & Martin, 1991; Golden, 1992; Gordon, 1991; Gorman, 1989; Harrison & McIntosh, 1992; Hofstede, Neuijen, Ohayv, & Sanders, 1990; Laabs & McDougall, 1992; Martin & Meyerson, 1988; Martin & Siehl, 1983; McDonald, 1988; Moran & Volkwein, 1992; Pratt & Beaulieu, 1992; Rousseau, 1990; Sackmann, 1991; Saffold, 1988; Schein, 1983, 1985; Shamir, 1991) and for practical application (e.g., Deal & Kennedy, 1982; Kendall, 1996; Ouchi, 1981; Peters & Waterman, 1982). However, organizational culture scholarship tends to be paradigmatically disparate and contradictory (Frost et al., 1991; Martin, 1992).

Martin (1992) identified three dominant perspectives for the study of organizational culture (described earlier by Frost et al., 1991; Martin & Meyerson, 1988; Meyerson & Martin, 1987). Each perspective both acknowledges and disavows some aspects of what culture is and how it might be conceptualized. In general, the perspective used most widely is that of *integration*, which focuses on consensus (Martin, 1992). The *differentiation* perspective recognizes inconsistencies within organizations that may be undervalued by the integration perspective. It therefore focuses on subcultural forces (Martin, 1992). Finally, the *fragmentation* perspective of organizational culture addresses ambiguities, complexities, inconsistencies, and multiplicitous understandings in organizations (Martin, 1992). Martin notes that the three perspectives are inherently incommensurable at a number of conceptual levels, and that it is both possible and desirable to use a multiperspective approach to cultural research that blends the three concepts.

The concept of structuration offers one approach that resolves the complexities noted by Martin (1992) because it is sensitive to the interconnectedness of agents and institutions, it facilitates contextualization, and it explores organizational phenomena from the superficial to the deeply embedded (Witmer, 1997). To draw again on the biological analogy, organizational systems can be studied simultaneously at all levels, much like viewing an organism through a microscope. The viewer is able to focus on the organizational whole (e.g., an amoeba) and its interactions with other organisms, or use a higher magnification to view the substance of and interactions between internal particulars (e.g., mitochondrion, ribosome, or nucleus). Whereas higher lens powers provide differentiated (or even fragmented) views of system components lower powers provide views of entire organisms and their interactions with each other. It is the aggregation of these multiple perspectives that provides a viewer with holistic conceptualizations of the organism and its functions and processes. Similarly, structuration permits the communication scholar to study the complexity of organizational culture, at the same time overcoming the paradigmatic incommensurabilities of a multiperspective approach (Witmer, 1997).

Beyond the study of culture, structuration also is widely used as a metatheoretical approach for a wide range of communication scholarship. The next section describes some communication studies from a structurationist perspective, and then outlines very briefly some key concepts of structuration.

STRUCTURATION THEORY AND COMMUNICATION

Communication scholars have adopted structuration as a way to explore a broad range of phenomena, including communication in groups (e.g., Corman & Scott, 1994; Gouran, 1990; Meyers & Seibold, 1990; Sunwolf & Seibold,

1998), written genre (e.g., Berkenkotter & Huckin, 1993), identity in the workplace (e.g., Scott, Corman, & Cheney, 1998), organizational climate (e.g., Bastien, McPhee, & Bolton, 1995; Helmer, Martin, & Poole, 1985; Poole, 1985; Poole & McPhee, 1983), power and democracy in organizations (e.g., Harrison, 1994; Riley, 1983, 1992), organizational structure (e.g., Browning, 1992), organizational culture (e.g., Witmer, 1997), organizational members in organizational change (e.g., Howard & Geist, 1995), standards formation in organizations (e.g., Browning & Beyer, 1998), and technology (e.g., Barley, 1986; Contractor & Seibold, 1993; Contractor, Seibold, & Heller, 1996; Parsons, 1989; Poole & DeSanctis, 1989, 1992; Scott, Quinn, Timmerman, & Garrett, 1998). Developed primarily through the work of Anthony Giddens (1976, 1979, 1981, 1984), structuration frames social structures as being formed by and through human interactions.

Banks and Riley (1993) offered one of the most cogent explications of structuration to date and outlined four central concepts of structuration: "agency and reflexivity, the duality of structure, praxis and time/space distanciation, and social/system integration and institutional reproduction" (p. 171). The first concept of *agency and reflexivity* refers to the idea that human agency is extant through stocks of knowledge. People know how to proceed in social interactions on the basis of mutually understood norms and learning experiences. Because human beings are self-reflexive, they are able to articulate goals and motivations, although not all human action is consciously motivated (Giddens, 1984).

Duality of structure refers to the notion that "the structural properties of social systems are both the medium and outcome of the practices they recursively organize" (Giddens, 1984, p. 25). Structures are the rules and resources people use in social interaction, and there are three basic types: legitimation (normative action), domination (allocation or authorization of resources), and signification (symbolic action and language).

The concept of *distanciation of time and space from praxis,* the third key concept of structuration, indicates that structures exist only as actors' remembrances across spans of time and geographic distances. Structures have no reality beyond the social interactions that create them. Thus, whereas actions may occur in a particular place and at a particular time, the relationship between them and the reproduction of their institutional practices extend across time and space, as stocks of knowledge upon which human agents draw to engage in everyday life.

Finally, *social integration* refers to the interactive nature of systems; that is, there must be reciprocity over time in social interactions. From a structurationist perspective, systems are conventionalized patterns that produce social structures. The structures that become most deeply embedded within systems are typically the oldest and most durable (Giddens, 1979) and become institutionalized. However, as Banks and Riley (1993) noted, "Social life is not emergent per se but is reproduced by knowledgeable, self-reflexive agents" (p. 176), and practices are reproduced "across time and space, articulating relationships that transcend spatiotemporal moments of social action" (p. 176). Banks and Riley (1993) proposed that communication scholars use structuration as "a set of ontological principles and entailments from which they can derive questions, base research explanation, and ground the development of communication theory across the field's many subspecialties" (p. 168). As an ontological approach, structuration can undergird a wide range of scholarship in public relations.

IMPLICATIONS OF STRUCTURATION FOR PUBLIC RELATIONS

Structuration offers public relations three expanded avenues for research. First, it offers new ways to conceptualize the organizational/environmental interface and environmental scanning. Second, structuration is sensitive to the ongoing communicative practices of a social organization. Third, structuration accounts for the recursive nature of institutional structures through human interactions to facilitate an understanding of organizational culture. This section addresses each of these points in turn.

The Organizational/Environmental Interface

Structuration permits a focus on the ways in which organizational members recursively reproduce social structures. At the same time, it is sensitive to the organizational/environmental interconnections that both create and are created by an organization and its members. The concepts of social integration and duality of agent/institution/agency relationships recognize the coconstruction of an organization, its constituents, and its publics through social interaction, rather than characterizing them as discrete entities. Thus, a structurationist perspective of public relations overcomes the limitations of general systems theory for exploring the recursive nature of system interactions and environmental interfaces (Cozier & Witmer, 2000). In addition, structuration overcomes the time boundedness of general systems theory because it accounts for the development of internal and external opinions and trends over time to facilitate and encourage forecasting and long-term planning.

Publics as Discursive Communities

Structuration encourages a view of publics as created and re-created through shared experiences (Botan & Soto, 1998), which enables an understanding of their changeability over time. In an age of global communication through technology, this is essential, because: "New Publics arise as discursive organizations through members' shared experiences. In on-line communicative interactions, members of New Publics utilize their experiences to constitute and enact dominant 'ideological meaning systems' (Deetz & Mumby, 1990; Mumby, 1989), which both mobilize them toward and constrain them from action" (Cozier & Witmer, 2000, p. 1).

Organizational Culture as Lived Experience

Finally, structuration overcomes the classic macro/micro dichotomy of organizational research (Banks & Riley, 1993; Bastien et al., 1995), which obfuscates the relationships between organizational actors and institutions. There is an interconnection, according to Giddens, between "globalizing influences" and "personal dispositions" (p. 1) in organizations. Giddens (1991) proposes that "modernity must be understood on an institutional level; yet the transmutations introduced by modern institutions interlace in a direct way with the individual" (p. 1). This interconnectedness occurs between agent and institution, between local and global structures, and between external global or local forces and agent/institution. As a result, a structurationist view of organizational culture addresses the ways in which culture is created through the interactions of human actors, both as organizational members and as constituents of organizational publics, which overcomes a limitation of systems theory.

In sum, a structurationist perspective of public relations offers potential solutions to the limitations of traditional systems-based research, because it (1) offers new ways to conceptualize the organizational/environmental interface and environmental scanning, (2) accounts for the recursive nature of institutional structures through human interactions to facilitate an understanding of organizational culture, and (3) is sensitive to the ongoing communicative practices of a social organization that may typically be associated with a latent, closed public or a nonpublic as it discursively organizes toward becoming an active or target public. Clearly, as communication technologies continue to proliferate, both environmental interfaces and the development of new publics are critical areas for research.

REFERENCES

Amsa, P. (1986). Organizational culture and work group behaviour: An empirical study. *Journal of Management Studies, 23*, 347–363.

Athey, T. H. (1982). *Systematic systems approach: An integrated method for solving systems problems*. Upper Soddle River, NJ: Prentice-Hall.

Arrington, C. B., Jr., & Sawaya, R. N. (1984). Managing public affairs: Issues management in an uncertain environment. *California Management Review, 26*, 148–160.

Banks, S. P., & Riley, P. (1993). Structuration theory as an ontology for communication research. In S. A. Deetz (Ed.), *Communication yearbook, 17* (pp. 167–196). Newbury Park, CA: Sage.

Barley, S. R. (1986). Technology as an occasion for structuring: Evidence from observation of CT scanners and the social order of radiology departments. *Administrative Science Quarterly, 31*, 78–108.

Barley, S. R., & Kunda, G. (1992). Design and devotion: Surges of rational and normative ideologies of control in managerial discourse. *Administrative Science Quarterly, 37*, 363–400.

Barney, J. B. (1986). Organizational culture: Can it be a source of sustained advantage? *Academy of Management Review, 11*, 656–666.

Bastien, D. T., McPhee, R. D., & Bolton, K. A. (1995). A study and extended theory of the structuration of climate. *Communication Monographs, 62*, 87–109.

Berkenkotter, C., and Huckin, T. N. (1993). Rethinking genre from a sociocognitive perspective. *Written Communication, 10*, 475–509.

Berkowitz, D., & Tunmire, K. (1994). Community relations and issues management: An issue orientation approach to segmenting publics. *Journal of Public Relations Research, 6*, 105–123.

(von) Bertalanffy, L. (1968). *General systems theory*. New York: Braziller.

Bostdorff, D. (1994). The rhetoric of deflection: John F. Kennedy and the Cuban missile crisis of 1962. *The Presidency and the rhetoric of foreign crisis* (pp. 25–55). Columbia, SC: University of South Carolina.

Botan, C. H., & Soto, F. (1998). A semiotic approach to the internal functioning of publics: Implications for strategic communication and public relations. *Public Relations Review, 24*, 21–44.

Branham, R. J. (1980). Ineffability, creativity, and communication competence. *Communication Quarterly* 11–20.

Branham, R. J., & Pearce, B. (1985). Between text and context: Toward a rhetoric of contextual reconstruction. *Quarterly Journal of Speech, 71*, 19–36.

Broom, G. M., (1982). A comparison of sex roles in public relatoins. *Public Relations Review, 8*, 17–22.

Broom, G. M. & Dozier, D. M. (1986). Advancement for public relations role models. *Public Relations Review, 12*(1), 37–56.

Brown, A. (1992). Organizational culture: The key to effective leadership and organizational development. *Leadership & Organization Development Journal, 13*(2), 3–7.

Browning, L. D. (1992). Lists and stories as organizational communication. *Communication Theory, 2*, 281–302.

Browning, L. D., & Beyer, J. M. (1998). The structuring of shared voluntary standards in the U.S. semiconductor industry: Communicating the reach agreement. *Communication Monographs, 65*, 220–243.

Contractor, N. S., & Seibold, D. R. (1993). Theoretical frameworks for the study of structuring processes in group decision support systems: Adaptive structuration theory and self-organizing systems theory. *Human Communication Research, 19*, 528–563.

Contractor, N. S., Seibold, D. R., and Heller, M. A. (1996). Interactional influence in the structuring of media use in groups: Influence in members' perceptions of group decision support system use. *Human Communication Research, 22*, 451–481.

Cooke, R. A., & Rousseau, D. M. (1988). Behavioral norms and expectations: A quantitative approach to the assessment of organizational culture. *Group & Organization Studies, 13*, 245–274.

Coombs, W. T. (1992). The failure of the Task Force on Food Assistance: A case study of the role of legitimacy in issue management. *Journal of Pubic Relations Research, 4*, 101–122.

Corman, S. R., and Scott, C. R. (1994). Perceived networks, activity foci, and observable communication in social collectives. *Communication Theory, 4*, 171–190.

Cozier, Z. R. & Witmer, D. F. (2000) The development of a structuration analysis of New Publics in an electronic environment. In R. Heath & G. Vasquez, (Eds.). *Handbook of Public Relations* (pp. 615–623). Thousand Oaks, CA: Sage.

Crable, R. E., & Vibbert, S. L. (1985). Managing issues and influencing public policy. *Public Relations Review, 11*, 3–16.

Cutlip, S. M., & Center, A. H. (1952). *Effective public relations: Pathways to public favor.* New York: Prentice Hall.

Cutlip, S. M., Center, A. H., & Broom, G. M. (1994). *Effective public relations* (7th ed.). Englewood Cliffs, NJ: Prentice Hall.

Deal, T., & Kennedy, A. (1982). *Corporate cultures.* Reading, MA: Addison-Wesley.

Deetz, S., & Mumby, D. K. (1990). Power, discourse, and the workplace: Reclaiming the critical tradition. In J. Anderson (Ed.), *Communication Yearbook, 13* (pp. 18–47). Newbury Park, CA: Sage.

Dozier, D. M. (1984). Program evaluation and roles of practitioners. *Public Relations Review, 10*(2), 13–21.

Dozier, D. M. (1990). The innovation of research in public relations practice. Review of a program of studies. In L. A. Grunig & J. E. Grunig (Eds.), *Public Relations Research Annual, 2* (pp. 3–28). Hillsdale, NJ: Lawrence Erlbaum Associates.

Dozier, D. M. (1992). The organizational roles of communication and public relations practitioners. In J. E. Grunig (Ed.). *Excellence in public relations and communication management* (pp. 327–356). Hillsdale, NJ: Lawrence Erlbaum Associates.

Dozier, D. M., & Broom, G. M. (1995). Evolution of the managers role in public relations practice. *Journal of Public Relations Research, 7*, 3–26.

Dyer, S. C. (1996). Descriptive modeling for public relations environmental scanning: A practitioner's perspective. *Journal of Public Relations Research, 8*, 137–150.

Ewing, R. P. (1990). Moving from micro to macro issues management. *Public Relations Review, 16*, 19–24.

Frost, P., Moore, L., Louis, M., Lundberg, C., & Martin, J. (1991). *Reframing organizational culture.* Newbury Park, CA: Sage.

Giddens, A. (1976). *New rules of sociological method: A positive critique of interpretative sociologies.* New York: Basic Books.

Giddens, A. (1979). *Central problems in social theory: Action, structure and contradiction in social analysis.* Berkeley: University of California Press.

Giddens, A. (1981). *A contemporary critique of historical materialism.* Berkeley: University of California Press.

Giddens, A. (1984). *The constitution of society: Outline of the theory of structuration.* Berkeley: University of California Press.

Giddens, A. (1991). *Modernity and self-identity: Self and society in the late modern age.* Stanford, CA: Stanford University Press.

Golden, K. A. (1992). The individual and organizational culture: Strategies for action in highly-ordered contexts. *Journal of Management Studies, 29*, 1–22.

Gordon, G. G. (1991). Industry determinants of organizational culture. *Academy of Management Review, 16*, 396–416.

Gorman, L. (1989). Corporate culture. *Management Decision, 27*, 14–20.

Gouran, D. S. (1990). Exploiting the predictive potential of structuration theory. *Communication Yearbook, 13*, 313–322.

Grunig, J. E. (1978). Defining publics in public relations: The case of a suburban hospital. *Journalism Quarterly, 55*, 109–118.

Grunig, J. E. (1982). The message-attitude-behavior relationship: Communication behaviors of organizations. *Communication Research, 9*, 163–200.

Grunig, J. E. (1983). Washington reporter publics of corporate public affairs programs. *Journalism Quarterly, 60*, 603–615.

Grunig, J. E. (1984). Organizations, environments, and models of public relations. *Public Relations Research & Education, 1*(1), 6–29.

Grunig, J. E. (1989a). Publics, audiences and market segments: Segmentation principles for campaigns. In C. T. Salmon (Ed.), *Information campaigns: Balancing social values and social change* (pp. 199–228). Newbury Park, CA: Sage.

Grunig, J. E. (1989b). Sierra club study shows become activists. *Public Relations Review, 15*, 3–24.

Grunig, J. E. (1992). *Excellence in public relations and communication management.* Hillsdale, NJ: Lawrence Erlbaum Associates.

Grunig, J. E., & Grunig, L. A. (1992). Models of public relations and communication. In J. E. Grunig (Ed.). *Excellence in public relations and communication management* (pp. 285–325). Hillsdale, NJ: Lawrence Erlbaum Associates.

Grunig, J. E. & Hunt, T. T. (1984). *Managing public relations.* New York: Holt, Rinehart and Winston.

Grunig, J. E., & Repper, F. C. (1992). Strategic Management, Publics, and Issues. In J. E. Grunig (Ed.), *Excellence in public relations and communication management* (pp. 117–159) Hillsdale, NJ: Lawrence Erlbaum Associates.

Harrison, J. R., & McIntosh, P. (1992). Using social learning theory to manage organizational performance. *Journal of Managerial Issues, 4*, 84–106.

Harrison, T. M. (1994). Communication and interdependence in democratic organizations. *Communication Yearbook, 17*, 247–274.

Heath, R. L. (1988). *Strategic issues management: How organizations influence and respond to public interests and policies.* San Francisco: Jossey-Bass.

Helmer, J., Martin, K., & Poole, M. S. (1985, October). *A new view of organizational climate and communication: A qualitative study of organizational climates.* Paper presented at the annual meeting of the Speech Communication Association, Chicago.

Hofstede, G., Neuijen, B., Ohayv, D. D., & Sanders, G. (1990). Measuring organizational cultures: A qualitative and quantitative study across twenty cases. *Administrative Science Quarterly, 35*, 286–307.

Howard, L. A., & Geist, P. (1995). Ideological positioning in organizational change: The dialectic of control in a merging organization. *Communication Monographs, 62*, 110–131.

Kendall, R. (1996). *Public relations campaign strategies.* New York: HarperCollins.

Kuhn, T. (1997). The discourse of issues management: Agenre of organization communication. *Communication Monographs, 62*, 110–131.

Laabs, J. J., & McDougall, L. M. (1992). Corporate anthropologists. *Personnel Journal, 71*, 81–88.

Lauzen, M. M. (1994). Public relations practitioner role enactment in issue management. *Journalism Quarterly*, 356–369.

Lauzen, M. M. & Dozier, D. M. (1992). The missing link: The public relations manager role as mediator of organizational environments and power consequences for the function. *Journal of Public Relations Research, 4*, 205–220.

Martin, J. (1992). *Cultures in organizations: Three perspectives.* New York: Oxford University Press.

Martin, J., & Meyerson, D. (1988). Organizational culture and the denial, channeling and acknowledgment of ambiguity. In L. Pondy, R. Boland, R., Jr., & H. Thomas (Eds.), *Managing ambiguity and change* (pp. 93–125). New York: Wiley.

Martin, J., & Siehl, C. (1983). Organizational culture and counterculture: An uneasy symbiosis. *Organizational Dynamics, 12*, 52–64.

McDonald, P. (1988). The Los Angeles Olympic Organizing Committee: Developing organizational culture in the short run. In P. J. Frost, L. F. Moore, M. Louis, C. Lundberg, & J. Martin (Eds.), *Organizational culture* (pp. 26–38), Newbury Park, CA: Sage.

Meyers, R. A., & Seibold, D. R. (1990). Perspectives on group argument: A critical review of persuasive arguments theory and an alternative structurational view. *Communication Yearbook, 13*, 268–302.

Meyerson, D., & Martin, J. (1987). Cultural change: An integration of three different views. *Journal of Management Studies, 24*, 623–647.

Moran, E. T., & Volkwein, J. F. (1992). The cultural approach to the formation of organizational climate. *Human Relations, 45* (1), 19–48.

Mumby, D. K. (1989). Ideology & the social construction of meaning: A communication perspective. *Communication Quarterly, 37*, 291–304.

Newsom, D., Turk, J., & Kruckeberg, D. (1993). *This is PR.* New York: Wadsworth.

Ouchi, W. G. (1981). *Theory Z.* Reading, MA: Addison-Wesley.

Parsons, Patrick R. (1989). Defining cable television: Structuration and public policy. *Journal of Communication, 39*(2), 10–26.

Peters, T. J., & Waterman, R. H. (1982). *In search of excellence: Lessons from America's best-run companies.* New York: Harper & Row.

Poole, M. S. (1985). Communication and organizational climates: Review, critique, and a new perspective. In R. McPhee, & P. Tompkins (Eds.), *Organizational communication: Traditional themes and new directions* (pp. 9–108). Beverly Hills, CA: Sage.

Poole, M. S., & McPhee, R. (1983). A structurational theory of organizational climate. In L. Putnam, & M. Pacanowsky (Eds.), *Communication and organizations: An interpretive approach* (pp. 195–219). Beverly Hills, CA: Sage.

Poole, M. S., & DeSanctis, G. (1989). Understanding the use of group decision support systems: The theory of adaptive structuration. In J. Fulk & C. Steinfeld (Eds.), *Organization and communication technologies* (pp. 173–193). Newbury Park, CA: Sage.

Poole, M. S., & DeSanctis, G. (1992). Microlevel structuration in computer-supported group decision making. *Human Communication Research, 19*, 5–49.

Pratt, J., & Beaulieu, P. (1992). Organizational culture in public accounting: Size, technology, rank, and functional area. *Accounting, Organizations and Society, 17*, 667–685.

Riley, P. (1983). A structurationist account of political culture. *Administrative Science Quarterly, 28*, 414–437

Riley, P. (1992). Arguing for "ritualistic" pluralism: The tension between privilege and the mundane. In S. A. Deetz (Ed.), *Communication yearbook 16* (pp. 112–121). Newbury Park, CA: Sage.

Rousseau, D. M. (1990). Normative beliefs in fund-raising organizations: Linking culture to organizational performance and individual responses. *Group & Organization Studies, 15*, 448–461.

Sackmann, S. A. (1991). Uncovering culture in organizations. *Journal of Applied Behavioral Science, 27*, 295–318.

Saffold, G. S. III, (1988). Culture traits, strength, and organizational performance: Moving beyond "strong" culture. *Academy of Management Review, 13*, 546–559.

Schein, E. H. (1983). The role of the founder in creating organizational culture. *Organizational Dynamics, 12*, 13–28.

Schein, E. H. (1985). *Organizational culture and leadership.* San Francisco: Jossey-Bass.

Scott, C. R., Corman, S. R., and Cheney, G. (1998). Development of a structurational model of identification in the organization. *Communication Theory, 8*, 298–336.

Scott, C. R., Quinn, L., Timmerman, C. E., & Garrett, D. M. (1998). Ironic uses of group communication technology: Evidence from meeting transcripts and interviews with group decision support system users. *Communication Quarterly, 46*, 353–374.

Shamir, B. (1991). Meaning, self and motivation in organizations. *Organization Studies, 12*, 405–425.

Stohl, C. (1995) *Organizational communication: Connectedness in action.* Thousand Oaks, CA: Sage.

Sunwolf, & Seibold, D. R. (1998). Jurors' intuitive rules for deliberation: A structurational approach to communication in jury decision making. *Communication Monographs, 65*, 282–307.

Thomsen, S. R. (1995). Using online databases in corporate issues management. *Public Relations Review, 21*, 103–122.

Toth, E. L., Serini, S. A., Wright, D. K., & Emig, A. (1998). Trends in public relations roles: 1990–1995. *Public Relations Review, 24*(2), 145–163.

Vasquez, G. M. (1993). A Homo Narrans paradigm for public relations: Combining Bormann's symbolic convergence theory and Grunig's situational theory of publics. *Journal of Public Relations Research, 5*, 201–216.

Vasquez, G. M. (1996). Public relations as negotiation: An issue development perspective. *Journal of Public Relations Reearch, 8*, 57–77.

Wartick, S. L., & Rude, R. E. (1985). Issues management: Corporate fad or corporate function? *California Management Review, 24*, 124–140.

Witmer, D. F. (1997) Communication and recovery: Structuration as an ontological approach to organizational culture. *Communication Monographs, 64*, 324–349.

CHAPTER

14

Reframing Crisis Management Through Complexity

Dawn Gilpin and Priscilla Murphy
Temple University

The field of crisis management has generated a rich body of theoretical and practical research in the relatively short period of time since its formal recognition as an organizational theme in the 1980s. Various disciplines have explored the causes, consequences, and behaviors involved when an organization is faced with a crisis situation and suggested ways of averting crises and attenuating the damage suffered by the organization when crises do occur.

Organizational crises are by nature not entirely predictable. Some are avoidable, such as those resulting from deliberate deception by or of the organization in question, while others may be the result of an interplay between events that no one can realistically predict or avoid. One or more apparently minor problems can spiral into a major crisis situation in surprising ways, as Weick (2001) noted: "What is striking is that crises can have small, volitional beginnings in human action. Small events are carried forward, cumulate with other events, and over time systematically construct an environment that is a rare combination of unexpected simultaneous failures" (p. 228).

Although authors have suggested a variety of methods organizations should use to prepare for crisis events, a certain consensus has emerged from the literature. In particular, organizations are urged to prepare as much as possible during non-crisis times so that they will be able to act swiftly and effectively to prevent and/or manage any untoward situations that arise. This preparation is generally assumed to take the form of planning.

A significant part of the planning process involves gathering and analyzing information. Indeed, many authors (Coombs, 1999; Mitroff & Anagnos, 2001; Regester & Larkin, 2002) consider environmental monitoring and establishing clear internal and external communication channels to be among the most important aspects of crisis preparedness. These authors argue that early awareness of potential crisis situations is one of the best forms of defense for organizations, and therefore they urge managers to invest considerable material and human resources in these areas.

However, this type of planning can actually narrow the vision rather than expand it. Existing literature on crisis management focuses primarily on the need for organizations to develop crisis awareness, in an attempt to break through what social psychologists term *optimistic bias,* or the belief that one is less susceptible to risk than one's peers (Joffe, 1999). To overcome this barrier the mechanistic approach of detailed planning deliberately oversimplifies the complex. By reducing the uncertainty of the situation to a set of rules and steps, the perceived risk is reduced and the world is made to appear more controllable (Dörner, 1996). Yet this approach ignores the multiplicity of factors that, as described earlier and in the next section, can contribute to or aggravate organizational crises, or can cause a crisis to shift and change while in process, making much crisis planning obsolete even as it is applied.

For this reason, some scholars have suggested that planning to control, or even predict, a complex event such as a crisis is an impossible goal: "precise, accurate and unequivocal communication about the behavior of complex systems is inherently inaccurate" (Seeger, 2002, p. 332; see also Murphy, 1996, 2001). Instead, they have advocated a different overarching theoretical framework, one that seeks to avoid any potential reductionism, because crises are often complex in nature and have a tendency to become rapidly more complex as they play out. Such a framework may be found in the realm of complexity: the study of interaction processes within complex systems, including social systems such as organizations.

Theories of complexity are attracting growing attention in the management community (Ashmos, Duchon, McDaniel, & Reuben, 2000; Dent, 1999; Haeckel, 1999; Lissack, 1997; Lissack & Roos, 1999; McElroy, 2000; McKelvey, 1999; Stacey, 2001; van Uden, Richardson, & Cilliers, 2001). However, these theories pose a serious challenge to embedded organizational practices. As Mirvis (1996) observed, "Long range requirements to acknowledge and live with uncertainty, to accept role ambiguity and conflict, and to expect and embrace errors run counter to organizational preferences for predictability, order and control" (p. 20). At the same time, by acknowledging the inherent disorderliness of everyday occurrences rather than attempting to simplify for clarity, complexity offers a potentially powerful tool for managers, who must face a multifaceted and rapidly changing world. The choice of complexity theory seems especially appropriate to the topic of organizational crises, given its focus on uncertainty and unpredictability and the central role it affords relationships and the communicative process. It therefore offers a new way of examining and making sense of organizational crises and how they occur, which in turn can lead scholars to formulate new suggestions for how organizations might approach crises from a practical standpoint.

This chapter delineates certain concepts from complexity theory that have particular relevance to organizational crisis management. It identifies underlying assumptions that inform the mainstream model of crisis management in public relations, as viewed through the lens of complexity. It then probes for inconsistencies and brings to light any conflicts, and it uses the tools provided by complexity theories to suggest a new approach to crisis management. Finally, working from the complexity-based framework outlined here, it suggests how future studies and projects may examine the effects of organizational behavior before, during and after crises.

Snowden (2000) suggested that one way of developing a new perspective on organizational problems is to "take an existing . . . issue and associated organic practice, reviewing it in the context of complexity theory, and applying the revisions in a visible way that on articulation enables a shift in thinking and understanding" (p. 55). Using Snowden's approach, this chapter does not seek to devalue the entire traditional crisis management paradigm. Rather, it is an attempt to use the poststructuralist tool of deconstruction to seek out the unspoken and unacknowledged assumptions underlying its prescriptions, questioning their validity, and proposing alternative viewpoints where appropriate.

ASSUMPTIONS UNDERLYING TRADITIONAL CRISIS MANAGEMENT

The first step in applying Snowden's approach is to define the assumptions that inform the current dominant approach to crisis management. As Table 14.1 indicates, these assumptions are divided into three general categories, arranged along a loose continuum from a broad perspective to those assumptions that relate more narrowly to crisis management. *Philosophical assumptions* imply a certain general outlook on "how things work," whereas *assumptions about organizations* suggest a given way of thinking about organizations and their

TABLE 14.1

Assumptions Underlying the Dominant Crisis Management Paradigm

More general	Philosophical Assumptions	It is possible to control events and/or perceptions of events by directly influencing the system at large.
		Ambiguity and uncertainty are undesirable states that should be overcome through various communication and action strategies.
		Stability is a desirable and attainable state, and the preferred outcome of a crisis situation.
	Assumptions about organizations	The organization may be likened to a mechanical system.
		There are clear boundaries between the organization and its external environment, including stakeholders. The organization should learn as much as possible about this environment in order to adapt appropriately.
More specific		Organizational culture is an identifiable, measurable variable that may be manipulated as needed, also as a means of overcoming (silencing) conflict and dissent.
	Assumptions about crisis management	The primary aim of crisis management is to avoid or limit the loss of organizational assets and maintain or restore organizational legitimacy in the eyes of key stakeholders as quickly as possible.
		The best response by an organization in crisis is to centralize information and decision-making procedures around a designated crisis management team.
		The best way to handle time-sensitive, critically important situations is to follow a detailed procedure previously prepared using analytical decision-making techniques.
		An organization will learn the necessary lessons from a crisis if the crisis team examines the data gathered during the crisis containment stage to identify any mistakes that may have been made, and updates the crisis plan accordingly.

characteristics. Finally, *assumptions about crisis management* deal specifically with organizational crises and how best to prevent and manage them.

However, these assumptions also suggest a reductionist approach that hampers the dominant crisis management paradigm. It focuses on the parts of the organization, its environment (viewed as an objective entity external to the organization), and breaks down the crisis management process into discrete components. This approach attempts to eliminate or control ambiguity, paradox and uncertainty rather than accept these as unavoidable and uncontrollable characteristics inherent in our world. As we see in the following section, such a view is diametrically opposed to complexity-based thinking, which posits a recognizable but unknowable future and the absence of stability in any but inert systems. Such a fundamental philosophical divergence cannot help but be reflected in every aspect of the model.

COMPLEX SYSTEMS AND EMERGENCE

A complex system may be defined as one that is more than the sum of its parts, as a result of interaction among those parts (van Uden et al., 2001). No matter how complete our familiarity with the parts, we cannot predict with certainty how or in what direction the system as a whole will develop (Boje, 2000). Complex systems have a number of distinguishing characteristics, examined later. It is worth noting, though, that according to Fioretti (1998), complexity is not an inherent property of a given system, but instead describes the relationship between the observer and the system: "a system is seen as 'complex' by its observer when, due to the presence of a self-referential loop, the observer can never compile a finite list of the behaviors the system will exhibit" (p. 6). This subjective definition takes into account the role of the observer not as a separate entity but as an active element within the system itself. This characteristic has special relevance to social systems such as organizations, in which observers are embedded in the experience of an organizational crisis.

A key consequence of the densely interconnected relationships within complex systems is that cause-and-effect relationships become difficult—even impossible—to isolate; "we are now confronted with incredibly intricate interacting networks of cause and effect rather than the relatively easily identifiable chains of cause and effect apparent in complicated, or linear, systems" (van Uden et al., 2001, p. 56). Attempts to predict outcomes can be wildly inaccurate, and even the most thorough efforts to retrace events—for example, in seeking out the causes of a crisis—often become inextricably mired in a tangle of interrelated details that provide no clear answers.

In addition, a given complex order may give way to new forms of complex order, since a complex system is never in a state of perfect, ongoing stability. One of the major themes of complexity science is that of *emergence*, which refers to unpredictable yet recognizable patterns of order that appear through a process of self-organization. This notion of complex order is one feature that distinguishes complexity from chaos theory,[1] and may be conceptualized as the "realm between simple order and chaos" (Byrne, 1998, p. 5) that may emerge from either extremity. The nonlinearity of this emergence process also means that the effects of change may be highly unpredictable:

> In nonlinear systems small changes in causal elements over time do not necessarily produce small changes in other particular aspects of the system, or in the characteristics of the system as a whole. Either or both may change very much indeed, and, moreover, they may change in ways which do not involve just one possible outcome. (Byrne, 1998, p. 14)

Nobel Prize-winning chemist Ilya Prigogine developed a notion of "dissipative structures" that explained why, instead of dissolving into entropy, in open systems the dissipated energy self-organizes into complex systems of its own (Abel, 1998). *Dissipative structures* are systems that go beyond mere adaptation to external or internal conditions: They are capable of complete self-organization. These systems are neither chaotic nor tending toward stability, existing instead in a "far from equilibrium" state (Mathews, White, & Long, 1999). In addition, dissipative structures do not have an environment per se, as the two are not conceptualized as distinct entities existing at separate hierarchical levels but as inextricably intertwined. The system dissipates energy until it reaches a transition state (also often defined as the "edge of chaos"), at which it may either self-destruct or self-organize into a new, emergent form: "This is the period of morphogenetic change in which existing functional relationships among components, patterns of interaction, rules, values, and belief systems that provided the source of equilibrium and stability for the system now breaks down" (Mathews et al., 1999, p. 26).

---

[1] The term *complexity* is often used interchangeably with the term *chaos*, but strictly speaking, complexity theory and chaos theory are somewhat different fields. Goldberg and Markóczy (1998) defined the differences thus: "The study of chaos generally involves the study of extremely simple non-linear systems which lead to extremely complicated behavior, and complexity is generally about the (simple) interactions of many things (often repeated) leading to higher level patterns" (p. 4). *Chaos theory*—often the favored term in sciences such as biology, physics and mathematics—aids in studying, and making predictions from, nonlinear dynamical systems. By contrast, complexity theory

> is really about how a system which is complicated (usually by having many interactions) can lead to surprising patterns when the system is looked at as a whole. For example, each of the billions of water molecules does its own thing when it joins up with others as it freezes to others, given some constraints on what each of them can do, something recognizably snow flake shaped can emerge. Complexity theory is about how the interaction of billions of individual entities can lead to something that appears designed or displaying an overall system level pattern. (Goldberg & Markóczy, 2000, pp. 75–76)

Although these emergent structures may be more or less complex than those that preceded the transition, some authors allege that they are necessarily better able to contend with complex conditions (Cilliers, 1998; Mathews et al., 1999; Seeger, 2002). Other authors argue that no such guarantee of optimization may be offered, because of the underlying teleology that is not presumed to evolve toward an idealized form (Stacey, 2001; Stacey, Griffin & Shaw, 2000).

Whether emergent structures are optimizing or merely new, they differ radically from merely complicated systems with multiple interconnected elements passively reacting to external stimuli according to established rules (Haeckel, 1999). Instead, emergent structures are "dynamic complex networks that are capable of initiating systemic changes as well as responses to exogenous changes" (Black, Fabian, & Hinrichs, 2000, p. 4). Some complexity theorists (Stacey, 2001; Stacey et al., 2000) have brought together both the self-organizing, autonomous nature of emergent social systems and the unpredictability of the future, under the rubric of "complex responsive processes," or CRP. Stacey (2001) described CRP as "a view of causality in which the future is under perpetual construction in the detail of interaction between entities" (p. 59).

With respect to crises, CRP specifically acknowledges the duality between control and unpredictability. It brings together social systems and human agency within a framework that concedes both autonomous action by individuals and the limits of individual order. As such, it is an apt descriptor for the new approach to crisis management advocated here: an approach that emphasizes flexibility and alertness over rigidity and an "autopilot" response to threats, and takes into account the truly unpredictable nature of how crises unfold.

REFRAMING THE DOMINANT CRISIS MANAGEMENT MODEL

The very nature of the crisis management field poses serious challenges to traditional research methods. As Pearson and Clair (1998) acknowledged, some challenges arise from the infrequency of organizational crises, so that researchers are not in the right place at the right time. In other cases, organizations may be "reluctant to open current or past 'wounds' to external examination and speculation," or may simply lose the evidence over time. Successful crisis management may be invisible to external and even internal publics. Finally, "organizations that survive crises tend to be reluctant to share perspectives, perceptions, and lessons learned with the uninitiated" (p. 73).

These difficulties suggest that the very nature of organizational crisis may make classic empirical data collection impossible. From a complexity perspective, no two crisis situations are alike or even similar enough to permit direct comparison, since even seemingly minor contextual factors may have important consequences within the framework of the crisis event, and emergent behavior makes prediction impossible. A more suitable approach for public

TABLE 14.2

Reframing the Assumptions of the Dominant Crisis Management Paradigm

	Dominant Paradigm	Reframed for Complexity
Philosophical assumptions	The future is, at least to some extent, predictable.	The future is unknowable yet recognizable, the product of everyday microinteraction among people, entities, and the environment.
	It is possible to control events and/or perceptions of events by directly influencing the system at large.	It is not possible to control the perceptions of events in a crisis, nor many events themselves, as they depend on too many exogenous and complex interactions factors. The organization can only control its own behavior and develop new patterns of interaction.
	Ambiguity and uncertainty are undesirable states that should be overcome through various communication and action strategies.	Ambiguity and uncertainty are unavoidable states that should be accepted and embraced through various communication and action patterns, which may allow the organization to both enact and adapt to changing circumstances.
	Stability is a desirable and attainable state and is the preferred outcome of a crisis situation.	Stability is possible only in an inert (dead) system, and hence is an undesirable state. Even apparent stability in a social system is actually dynamically changing through patterns of microinteraction.
Assumptions about organizations	The organization may be likened to a mechanical system.	The organization is a complex entity that demonstrates emergent behavior, quite unlike a mechanical system.
	There are clear boundaries between the organization and its external environment, including stakeholders. The organization should learn as much as possible about this environment in order to adapt appropriately.	The organization is defined by fluid, changing, socially constructed boundaries that form a tenuous separation between the organization (and its stakeholders) and the environment. Members of the organization should actively engage with this environment so as to enact and be part of changes.

	Organizational culture is an identifiable, measurable variable that may be manipulated as needed, and also as a means of overcoming (silencing) conflict and dissent.	Organizational culture is a paradoxically identifiable yet dynamic trait that is constantly in flux, a blend of multiple conflicting voices that is constantly produced and reproduced through microinteraction and everyday behavior, inside and outside the organization as well as across organizational boundaries.
Assumptions about crisis management	The primary aim of crisis management is to avoid or limit the loss of organizational assets and maintain or restore organizational legitimacy in the eyes of key stakeholders as quickly as possible.	The primary aim of crisis management is to avoid or limit the loss of organizational assets and maintain long-term organizational legitimacy in the eyes of key stakeholders, by engaging in double-loop learning that may require internal change.
	The best response by an organization in crisis is to centralize information and decision-making procedures around a designated crisis management team whose members convene and work together solely and specifically on crisis-related matters.	The best response by an organization in crisis is by an experienced team whose members possess the necessary expertise and authority to take immediate action, recognize their limitations, and know where to find other information they realize they need.
	The best way to handle time-sensitive, critically important situations is to follow a detailed procedure previously prepared using analytical decision-making techniques.	The best way to handle time-sensitive, critically important situations is to develop the expertise necessary for skillful improvisation.
	An organization will learn the necessary lessons from a crisis if it the crisis team examines the data gathered during the crisis containment stage to identify any mistakes that may have been made, and updates the crisis plan accordingly.	An organization will learn the necessary lessons from a crisis if it takes the time to reflexively examine the multiple, complex causes behind the situation, to engage in double-loop learning, and to make the necessary changes to ensure long-term legitimacy.

relations scholars and practitioners to further their understanding of crises might thus be to examine the underlying assumptions of the dominant crisis management paradigm through the lens of complexity-based thinking, and determine whether these assumptions remain valid from this alternative standpoint. Where there is a discrepancy, it may be possible to elaborate a new assumption more in line with complexity, and thus reframe the model of crisis management in new terms.

To facilitate these comparisons, Table 14.2 places assumptions made by the institutionalized approach to crisis management within the public relations field alongside alternative assumptions that reflect a complexity perspective, using the dominant assumptions about crisis management in the three categories of philosophical assumptions, assumptions about organizations, and assumptions about crisis management. All three areas show stark discrepancies between traditional and complexity-based views of crisis management. In each instance, complexity-based crisis management reframes the traditional perspective's quest for stability and certainty, so that the future is accepted as unknowable, stability is deemed impossible, and uncertainty and ambiguity are accepted as qualities that will help the organization adapt to circumstances it cannot control. For example, where a traditional perspective may see an organization as a mechanical system, to be handled through well-specified procedures and centralized decision making, a complexity-based perspective sees an organization as a dynamic entity, whose boundaries shift and whose culture emerges from contextual interactions that lie beyond strict controls. These contrasts are further elaborated in the section that follows.

COMPLEXITY REDUCTION/ABSORPTION

The concepts of complexity reduction and complexity absorption in organizations help to explain the reasoning behind some of the reframed assumptions in Table 14.2. Ashmos et al. (2000) examined organizations that reacted in two diametrically opposed ways to a turbulent, complex environment. They distinguished between behavioral strategies aimed at "complexity reduction," that attempt to increase control and predictability in a struggle to contain the perceived complexity, and those that instead embrace the nature of complexity in an attempt to adapt through "complexity absorption."

Organizations that adopt complexity absorption strategies enact four types of behaviors. First, they gather ongoing information about their own nature, the environment, stakeholders, and evolving conditions. Second, they recognize and encourage multiple, even conflicting, organizational goals. Third, they emphasize numerous, tight relationships, internally and externally, both as an aid to sensemaking in light of the disorder deriving from the pursuit of conflicting goals, and as conduits for gathering information and producing knowledge. Fourth, they flexibly self-organize as a result of the new information gathered and knowledge created, and the resulting new goals formulated, through the ever-denser network of relationships.

In contrast, organizations that pursue a strategy of complexity reduction attempt to impose order on a chaotic world by simplifying their internal structure, minimizing and narrowing goals, formalizing and centralizing decision-making processes, and seeking to achieve a state of predictably stable equilibrium. Ashmos et al. (2000) observed that complexity reduction is the traditional approach taken by managers and advocated by management books and MBA programs alike, noting that "good managers are often judged as those who achieve stability and balance in a system, and are able to minimize sudden and unpredictable change" (p. 580). Those who fail to do so are deemed incompetent by a society that values order and predictability.

From this standpoint, complexity reduction is not unlike the concept of threat-rigidity, Studies of threat-rigidity responses suggest that meticulous planning may be counterproductive. For example, Barnett and Pratt (2000) described the effects of a threat as causing an organization to adopt a defensive pose, leading it to self-limit its information gathering and processing capacity and narrow decision options as a means of reducing uncertainty. Other researchers have also found evidence to support this position (D'Aveni & Macmillan, 1990; Penrose, 2000). However, if an organization has limited its options a priori by specifying a fixed set of procedures, it may fail to absorb information or consider decisions that fall outside this predetermined range of options (Pfeffer & Sutton, 1999). Managers who prefer to allow the company to "go into auto-pilot" (Thayer, 1998) willingly adopt this mindset as a means of reducing confusing stimuli.

In contrast to this managerial rigidity, Ashmos et al. (2001) operationalized several measures of internal and environmental complexity, and developed a survey to determine the behavioral strategy adopted by organizations. They then examined a sample of Texas hospitals to determine which strategy proved most effective. Their findings suggest that, although complexity absorption is more difficult to implement (not least because it deviates from what is considered "standard" organizational behavior), this approach is more effective in adapting to a turbulent environment. The authors recognized the deep impact such a conclusion has on the identity of an organization, as well as the definition of management:

> There is no doubt that when managers see the inherent nature of their systems as complex and adaptive, the job of managing is much different than traditional management theory would suggest. The problems—the conflict, ambiguity, disorder—will be the same, but the manager will work with these problems rather than impose a simplified order on them. For example, rather than try to eliminate conflict, managers will see it as an inevitable part of the sensemaking process which is normal and necessary. (p. 591)

This radical change of perspective poses a serious challenge to entrenched ways of thinking. Hence Weick (1995) warned against falling prey to "Cartesian anxiety," or the belief that knowledge must be clearly delineated and stable, the sole alternative being chaos. In fact, as McKie (2001) pointed out, public relations has been particularly prone to this view ever since it was espoused by Edward Bernays, who associated chaos with "the mess of democracy" and "unacceptable disorder," in contrast to the "engineering" of public consent (p. 89). Cartesian—or Bernaysian—anxiety is essentially the old trap of the false dichotomy. Complexity is the antithesis of this black-and-white approach, seeking instead to understand the infinite shades of gray. In fact, as the following section points out, it is possible to temper the rigid structure of positivist thinking without advocating total anarchy. Such a balance becomes possible within an "enacting organization."

THE ENACTING ORGANIZATION

The concept of the enacting organization was put forward by Daft and Weick (2001), who characterized organizations according to their attitudes and behaviors in environmental scanning. They identified two dimensions in each respect: attitude toward the environment, seen as either rational and definable or complex and impossible to analyze, and whether the organization takes an active or passive stance toward environmental events. This classification process resulted in four organizational categories, of which the most effective in handling unforeseen events was the group they called "enacting" organizations.

Enacting organizations assume the world to be indeterminate, yet actively engage with it rather than passively reacting to occurrences. They are therefore less likely to rely on so-called hard data or analytical decision models, and are more involved in testing actions, experimenting with new processes and programs, and attempting to shape the environment through their behavior. Enacting organizations are heavily invested in learning by doing. Managers in these organizations play an active part in the entire interpretation cycle, from awareness to sensemaking to learning and back again. This model characterizes organizations as "more than transformation processes or control systems" (Daft and Weick, 2001, p. 255). Daft and Weick furthermore warned that "to survive, organizations must have mechanisms to interpret ambiguous events and to provide meaning and direction for participants" (p. 255). These reframed assumptions depict an organization that focuses on developing skills and knowledge, along with effective information-sharing and learning processes, as a means of handling rapid, unforeseen change. These processes are flexible rather than rigid, situated rather than sweeping, gently indicative rather than strictly prescriptive. The following sections describe practical implications of the complexity-based paradigm for public relations, as well as possible areas of future research for scholars of crisis management interested in a complexity-based perspective.

IMPROVISED TEAMWORK

One way to incorporate a complexity approach is by developing expertise in improvisation. Yet many people balk at the thought of improvisation as a strategy, because they mistake improvisation for unskilled decision-making. Instead, successful improvisation requires a synthesis of skills and abilities that must be honed to where the individual or group can call upon them as needed, in what Weick (2001) referred to as "just-in-time strategy." He also explained why improvisation is more suited to a complex, changing environment than traditional planning methodologies: "When it is assumed that survival depends on variation, then a strategic plan becomes a threat because it restricts experimentation and the chance to learn that old assumptions no longer work" (p. 151).

Thus improvisation deals with the unforeseen, it works without a prior stipulation, and it works with the unexpected. For example, Klein (1998) explained that expert rock climbers must learn to identify the leverage points they use to progress in their climb. These points have no single common characteristic; they may be a crevice or a protrusion in the rock, something to be grasped by a hand, a notch just large enough to insert the toes, a ledge too narrow to stand on but wide enough to take some of the weight off the upper body, or to serve as a launching pad to jump to a larger shelf. What is more, there are no "absolute" leverage points: the environment (visibility, wet or dry, hot or cold) and condition of the climber (fresh or tired, relative strength, size and weight) all play a part in determining what may be used. "For these reasons," Klein explained, "no one can examine a photograph and identify the holds" (1998, p. 114). The same holds won't work for everyone, even on the same climb. Rock climbers must learn to make rapid and effective real-life decisions: They must learn to improvise.

Similarly, then, crisis teams need to learn to improvise. However, the only way to gain expertise is through practice, which in the area of crises presents something of a problem. A crisis may be a learning experience, but an organization cannot simply wait for a crisis to appear on the horizon. Therefore, crisis managers have advocated a range of training methods, of which simulated crises are among the most frequent.

Mainstream crisis management authors commonly urge managers to perform simulations as a test of the crisis plan and to keep it current (Caponigro, 2000; Coombs, 1999; Dyer, 1995; Fearn-Banks, 1996). The commonly recommended frequency for these simulations is once or twice a year. However, such infrequent simulations do not appear very efficacious. For example, Klein (1998) observed a number of organizational crisis management teams as they carried out their simulations and called them "the worst ones we have observed" (p. 238). Teams were led by the CEO, and the other team members were lower-level managers such as the director of security. The companies observed held training exercises and crisis management seminars "a few times a year." Despite this training—which reflected at least the basic level recommended by the mainstream literature—the crisis teams suffered from a variety of problems, ranging from communication breakdowns to a tendency to micromanage situations. Team members hesitated to make decisions, as they tried to gather all possible information before committing to a course of action. They failed to recognize cues and opportunities. There were power struggles within the team itself as certain members attempted to take control and micromanage the work of others. Team members gave orders to subordinates but lacked awareness of how long it would take to execute those orders, throwing off the pace of the entire exercise. In the end, Klein pronounced himself "surprised by their incompetence" (p. 238).

Clearly, then, infrequent simulations are not sufficient in order for a team to develop group intuition and a shared sense of identity. Simulations are often expensive and disruptive exercises. Someone in the organization must spend the time and money to develop a plausible scenario, make all the necessary arrangements, perhaps even hire actors to play a part in the simulation. The crisis team members are taken away from their other responsibilities for extended periods. Such a full-scale effort obviously cannot be made very often. Still, between simulations, the team can practice its skills through other forms of training and education.

Training people to become—or at least think like—experts is often too time-consuming and costly a project for organizations to undertake. However, Klein (1998) suggested that it is possible to teach people to "learn like experts" (p. 104). The process he described consists of four essential steps: (a) engaging in deliberate practice; (b) accumulating a rich array of experiences; (c) obtaining ready and accurate diagnostic feedback; and (d) reviewing past experiences, including those of others, to learn from mistakes and gain new understanding.

Synthesizing these approaches, Gavetti and Levinthal (2000) proposed combining "offline" cognitive methods such as scenario development and planning exercises with the "online" results of experience—as well as "grey area" practices such as simulations—to maximize decision-making results. Although they found that experience accounts for the largest degree of enhanced performance, adding offline processes shortens the learning cycle, reduces risk, and provides a broader array of options.

Scenario planning, in particular, is an exercise that encourages managers to "think different" and imagine a situation in great detail, turning it into a sort of future narrative (Brown & Starkey, 2000; De Geus, 1999; Schwartz, 1998; Smallman & Weir, 1999). The exercise of planning offers the advantage of practice in reasoning processes without producing, as its final output, a set of procedures to which the organization is expected to adhere. Scenario planning is essentially a way of encouraging executives to leave behind assumptions that normally go unquestioned, as a means of learning through mental exploration. Brown and Starkey explained that "the premise [behind scenario planning] is that our present ways of knowing, and what we already know, form an inadequate basis for learning about an uncertain future" (2000, p.112).

Researchers have also discerned several of the learnable competencies that are to be practiced, as recommended by the first stage of Klein's process, to expedite the development of proficiency. Canon-Bowers and Bell (1997) identified these competencies as: (a) *metacognitive skills*, or the ability to recognize the limits of one's own understanding, knowledge of where to acquire the missing information or knowledge, and skill in determining which decision strategies are most appropriate to a given situation; (b) *reasoning skills*, both analytical and creative; (c) *domain-specific problem solving skills*; (d) *mental simulation skills*, which require both reasoning and imagination and avoid the need for extensive, time-consuming, and costly trial-and-error methods; (e) *risk-assessment skills*, as decision makers working in extreme conditions must be able to estimate and balance the risks and potential payoff of various decision options; and (f) *situation awareness skills*, or the faculty of noticing details within an overall complex scenario that weigh on the decision to be made, and understanding the significance of those details. Additionally, Canon-Bowers and Bell highlighted the need to foster an infrastructure of knowledge organization to support intense decision-making efforts.

CONCLUSION: IMPLICATIONS FOR PRACTICE

A complexity-based approach to crisis management poses a challenge to researchers and practitioners accustomed to thinking along traditionally positivist lines. At the same time, complexity science offers an exciting new way to approach events, such as crises, that do not fit comfortably into the neat categories of traditional organizational science. Rather than attempting to identify every potential threat and response, crisis managers and researchers are free to actively explore new areas of interrelating. This approach therefore embraces the emergent properties of complex systems, instead of striving to contain, control, and predict them. By acquiring knowledge and gaining expertise through action and reflexive sensemaking, those who make crisis-related decisions can hone their individual and group decision-making skills.

Numerous other areas remain fertile ground for study and application. For example, the role of storytelling as a means of sharing complex knowledge within an organization, and the development of communities of practice that effectively become basins of specific expertise within the organization and across its boundaries, are two fields that hold a great deal of promise for organizations in general, and that may be applied within a complexity-based crisis management framework. Scenario planning deserves further attention as a less costly, yet potentially effective, process for simulating crisis situations and experimenting with different reactions; it also incorporates some of the benefits of storytelling, thanks to its narrative format.

Continued research in the area of naturalistic decision-making will also be useful in providing specific tools and techniques for training teams and individuals in a wide range of real-world decision-making situations. Finally, the lens of complexity may offer a novel means of examining the very nature of organizational knowledge and learning, and the role these play in causing, averting, managing, and learning from crises.

REFERENCES

Abel, T. (1998). Complex adaptive systems, evolutionism, and ecology within anthropology: Interdisciplinary research for understanding cultural and ecological dynamics. *Georgia Journal of Ecological Anthropology, 2*, 6–29.

Argyris, C. (1977). Double loop learning in organizations. *Harvard Business Review,* 115–124.

Ashmos, D. P., Duchon, D., & McDaniel, R. R., Jr. (2000). Organizational responses to complexity: The effect on organizational performance. *Journal of Organizational Change Management, 13*(6), 577–594.

Barnett, C., & Pratt, M. G. (2000). From threat-rigidity to flexibility: Toward a learning model of autogenic crisis in organizations. *Journal of Organizational Change Management, 13*(1), 74–88.

Black, J. A., Fobian, F., & Hinrichs, K. (2000). *Fractals, stories and the development of coherence in strategic logic.* Paper presented at Competence 2000: Fifth International Conference on Competence-Based Management, Helsinki University of Technology, Espoo (Helsinki), Finland.

Boje, D. M. (2000). Phenomenal complexity theory and change at Disney: Response to Letiche. *Journal of Organizational Change Management, 13*(6), 558–566.

Brown, A. D., & Starkey, K. (2000). Organizational identity and learning: A psychodynamic perspective. *Academy of Management Review, 25*(1), 102–120.

Byrne, D. S. (1998). *Complexity theory and the social sciences: An introduction.* London: Routledge.

Canon-Bowers, J. A., & Bell, H. H. (1997). Training decision makers for complex environments: Implications of the naturalistic decision making perspectives. In C. E. Zsambok & G. Klein (Eds.), *Naturalistic decision making* (pp. 89–110). Mahwah, NJ: Lawrence Erlbaum Associates.

Caponigro, J. R. (2000). *The crisis counselor: A step-by-step guide to managing a business crisis.* Lincolnwood, IL: Contemporary Books.

Cilliers, P. (1998). *Complexity and postmodernism.* London: Routledge.

Coombs, W.T. (1999). *Ongoing crisis communication: Planning, managing and responding.* Thousand Oaks, CA: Sage.

D'Aveni, R. A., & Macmillan, I. C. (1990). Crisis and the content of managerial communications: A study of the focus of attention of top managers in surviving and failing firms. *Administrative Science Quarterly, 35*, 634–657.

Daft, R. L., & Weick, K. E. (2001). Toward a model of organizations as interpretation systems. In K. E. Weick (Ed.), *Making sense of the organization* (pp. 241–257). Oxford: Blackwell.

De Geus, A. (1999). *The living company*. Nicholas Brealey.

Dent, E. B. (1999). Complexity science: A worldview shift. *Emergence, 1*(4), 5–19.

Dörner, D. (1996). *The logic of failure: Recognizing and avoiding error in complex situations*. Reading, MA: Perseus Books.

Dyer, S. C. (1995). Getting people into the crisis communication plan. *Public Relations Quarterly, 40*(3), 38–40.

Fearn-Banks, K. (1996). *Crisis communications: A casebook approach*. Mahwah, NJ: Lawrence Erlbaum Associates.

Fioretti, G. (1998). A concept of complexity for the social sciences. *Revue Internationale de Systemique, 12*(3), 285–312.

Gavetti, G., & Levinthal, D. (2000). Looking forward and looking backward: Cognitive and experiential search. *Administrative Science Quarterly, 45*(March), 113–137.

Goldberg, J., & Markóczy, L. (2000). Complex rhetoric and simple games. *Emergence, 2*(1), 72–100.

Haeckel, S.H. (1999). Adaptive enterprise: Creating and leading sense-and-respond organizations. Boston: Harvard Business School Press.

Joffe, H. (1999). *Risk and "the other."* Cambridge, UK: Cambridge University Press.

Klein, G. (1998). *Sources of power: How people make decisions*. Cambridge, MA: The MIT Press.

Lissack, M. R. (1997). Of chaos and complexity: managerial insights from a new science. *Management Decision, 35*(3–4), 205–219.

Lissack, M., & Roos, J. (1999). *The next common sense: The e-manager's guide to mastering complexity*. London: Nicholas Brealey.

Mathews, K. M., White, M. C., & Long, R. G. (1999). The problem of prediction and control in theoretical diversity and the promise of the complexity sciences. *Journal of Management Inquiry, 8*(1), 17–31.

McElroy, M. W. (2000). Integrating complexity theory, knowledge management and organizational learning. *Journal of Knowledge Management, 4*(3), 195–203.

McKelvey, B. (1999). Complexity theory in organization science: Seizing the promise or becoming a fad? *Emergence, 1*(1), 5–32.

McKie, D. (2001). Updating public relations: "New science," research paradigms, and uneven developments. In Robert L. Heath (Ed.), *Handbook of public relations* (pp. 75–91). Thousand Oaks, CA: Sage.

Mirvis, P. H. (1996). Historical foundations of organizational learning. *Journal of Organizational Change Management, 9*(1), 13–31.

Mitroff, I. I., & Anagnos, G. (2001). *Managing crises before they happen*. New York: AMACOM.

Murphy, P. (1996). Chaos theory as a model for managing issues and crises. *Public Relations Review, 22*(2), 95–113.

Murphy, P. (2001). Symmetry, contingency, complexity: Accommodating uncertainty in public relations theory. *Public Relations Review, 26*(4), 447–462.

Pearson, C. M., & Clair, J. A. (1998). Reframing crisis management. *Academy of Management Review, 23*(1), 59–76.

Penrose, J. M. (2000). The role of perception in crisis planning. *Public Relations Review, 26*(2), 155.

Pfeffer, J., & Sutton, R. (1999). *The knowing-doing gap.* Boston: Harvard Business School Press.

Regester, M., & Larkin, J. (2002). *Risk issues and crisis management: A casebook of best practice.* London: Kogan Page.

Schwartz, P. (1998). *The art of the long view.* West Sussex, UK: Wiley.

Seeger, M. W. (2002). Chaos and crisis: Propositions for a general theory of crisis communication. *Public Relations Review, 28*(4), 329–337.

Smallman, C., & Weir, D. (1999). Communication and cultural distortion during crises. *Disaster Prevention and Management, 8*(1).

Snowden, D. J. (2000). New wine in old wineskins: From organic to complex knowledge management through the use of story. *Emergence, 2*(4), 50–64.

Stacey, R. D. (2001). *Complex responsive processes in organizations: Learning and knowledge creation.* London: Routledge.

Stacey, R. D., Griffin, D., & Shaw, P. (2000). *Complexity and management.* London: Routledge.

Thayer, W. (1998, April 1). An inside look at the scary world of food safety scares. *Frozen Food Age,* pp. 1, 12, 38.

van Uden, J., Richardson, K. A., & Cilliers, P. (2001). Postmodernism revisited? Complexity science and the study of organisations. *Tamara—Journal of Critical Postmodern Organization Science, 1*(3), 53–67.

Weick, K. E. (1995). *Sensemaking in organizations.* Thousand Oaks, CA: Sage.

Weick, K. E. (2001). *Making sense of the organization.* Oxford, UK: Blackwell.

Sense-Making Methodology: A Theory of Method for Public Relations

Gael Walker

University of Technology, Sydney

INTRODUCTION

Sense-Making assumes that there is a fundamental discontinuity in how people, such as the publics we need to communicate with, move from one point in time to another. It challenges the belief that a person's actions are easily predictable, as if people were not making choices all the time. The underlying metaphor for Sense-Making relates to the gap between where a person is and where they wish to be. Such an approach fits with a process worldview rather than the static assumptions that often exist with audience segmentation.

The origins of Sense-Making methodology and the theoretical premises on which it is based are outlined. This wider communication theory is then linked to the field of public relations to show how it can help our practice and research. A useful technique developed by Sense-Making scholars is a particular type of interview, a simplified example of which is presented and analyzed. The chapter then draws on some recent uses of the methodology to make this theoretical approach more real to public relations students and practitioners by referring to studies in which it has been used in public communication campaigns.

THE ROLE OF METATHEORY

Students of public relations theory need to know the connections among metatheory, methodology, and methods and the substantive theories they generate, because the everyday work of communicators draws subconsciously on this knowledge. This understanding is vital not just for scholars building basic theory about communicative practice and public relations, but also for practitioners who are drawing on theory whenever they design campaigns or evaluate their effectiveness. This is because our own metatheoretical assumptions affect the way we approach research and communication practice, whether these assumptions are explicit or implicit. The metatheoretical assumptions underlying Sense-Making can affect how research questions are framed, how interviews are designed, and how the results of research are analyzed and applied.

Sense-Making methodology is "a theoretic net, a set of assumptions and propositions, and a set of methods which have been developed to study the making of sense that people do in their everyday experiences" (Dervin, 1992, p. 61). Originated by Professor Brenda Dervin at Ohio State University and used in a series of studies since 1972, this methodology provides a means to understand how publics act so that we can develop more effective approaches to studying and practicing communication. It provides "a theory of method for theorizing. ... Methodology is theory for research step-taking, including theory of the methods of theorizing as well as theory of the methods of observing and analyzing" (Dervin, 1996a, pp. 21–23).

Like all methodologies, Sense-Making is based on metatheoretical presuppositions about the nature of reality and human beings (ontology) and the nature of knowing (epistemology). Space, time, and movement through space and time are basic concepts in the metatheory of Sense-Making. Its scholars attempt to be explicit about the bridge it makes between metatheoretic assumptions and methods. They see reality as something that human beings have the capacity to know, and they insist that reality will vary for an individual across time and across space, differing for each new situation they encounter. Sense-Making avoids both subjectivist and realist views of reality and enters theorizing in what it calls the "in-between," in that it is the actor who must interpret their inner and outer worlds, yesterday and today, themselves and others and all aspects of their situation. Reality is seen to exist in constant

Sense-Makings and sense-unmakings as actors move through time and space, testing and retesting, responding and adapting and inventing.

Sense-Making as a methodology guides us toward techniques or methods that are consistent with its underlying assumptions. It regards the common division of research methodologies into qualitative or quantitative as a false dichotomy (Dervin, 1993). It favors neither approach and claims that any method or combination of methods may be needed in a particular situation.

LINK TO PUBLIC RELATIONS

As a communication-based methodology for researching communicating behaviors, attitudes, and beliefs, Sense-Making might interest scholars and students of public relations because its metatheoretical presuppositions are similar in many ways to the worldview on which two-way symmetrical communication is based. J. Grunig (1989a) claimed that organizations with a symmetrical worldview typically use the following presuppositions: interdependence, open system, moving equilibrium, equity, autonomy, innovation, decentralized management, responsibility, conflict resolution, and interest-group liberalism. Each of these presuppositions applies equally to the Sense-Making methodology, with its principle that dialogue is essential for communities to be created.

Some of the insights Sense-Making offers could be useful to public relations scholars and practitioners who may encounter an implicit assumption of order and certainty in public relations practice, a tendency to believe that human beings are cognitive and rational, that reality is fixable, and that information and knowledge describe that reality (Dervin, 1998). In an article in *Public Relations Research and Education*, Volume 1 (1984), Dervin suggested that this emerging theoretic perspective would be relevant to public relations practice. Two decades later, there are still opportunities for students and for researchers to use the insights Sense-Making provides our growing field of practice as well as our domain of communication scholarship.

Methodology provides the link between metatheory and public relations practice, as expressed in the methods we use when we approach a particular formal or informal research task. It provides a comprehensive and integrated account of how we should make theories, observe behavior, analyze its significance, and interpret what it all means. It is not just a list of the methods we could use, but an explanation of how these methods fit alongside the assumptions underlying our metatheory. Because it consists of a "coherent set of theoretically derived methods for studying human Sense-Making" (Dervin, 1992, p. 62), Sense-Making guides us toward appropriate ways to research a situation. It makes us concentrate on movement and fluidity, rather than on fixed and unchanging circumstances. It mandates a dialogic approach in which we as researchers attempt to understand the interpretations of people who themselves are capable of interpreting their own situations. It demands that the researcher work with publics as partners in research.

Connections Between Sense-Making and Research

The public relations industry around the world is demanding more research and measurement, part of its professionalizing move to evaluate its contribution and relative value to society and the economy. This can lead to a temptation to act as if we can transfer information gathered in a particular context to another time and space, as if this information remains accurate. However, whenever we assume that research from one time and space will apply to other times and different circumstances, we are using a conception of information as something static and objective. A researcher can develop concepts and propositions that will create a substantive theory for a particular situation, but must keep in mind that the resulting theory will not apply to all times and all places.

Sense-Making approaches the research situation as "an applied communication situation involving attempts to understand how others have designed their senses of their worlds" (Dervin, 1999b, p. 47). Rather than prescribe set procedures that a researcher must follow, Sense-Making provides philosophical guidance for approaching research. It cautions against a mechanical use of tools or procedures, reminding us to think of what we are doing and to be aware of the assumptions underlying our actions. Sense-Making as a methodology has been used to study a variety of phenomena, most frequently information seeking and use, but also technology use, media reception, and attitudes toward issues that are the focus of public communication campaigns. Some examples of studies related to public relations are provided at the end of this chapter.

Segmentation of Publics

Dervin's concern about an overuse of segmentation has some similarities to concerns expressed by public relations scholars. For example, J. Grunig wrote in 1989 that the "literature in marketing, public relations, and mass communication seems to offer a seemingly inexhaustible and disorganized list of concepts for segmenting populations" (1989b, p. 205). In 1992 Grunig and Repper found that most research firms had "greater knowledge of market research techniques than of techniques applicable to public relations. Thus, public relations managers more often buy research to identify markets than to identify publics" (p. 140). The problem is that publics are not markets.

As a public relations theorist, J. Grunig pointed out the tendency to use the more easily obtainable objective variables such as demographics and geographic location, rather than more reliable inferred variables that required direct questioning of publics. He responded to this problem by developing a new model for public relations: nested segmentation concepts showing the value of moving from the outer nests of less powerful indicators such as demographics, geodemographics, and psychographics, toward the inner nests of communities and publics, and finally to individual communication behaviors and effects. This last category refers to an individual confronting a problem that arises in a particular situation and recognizing the constraints that affect him or her.

This model reflects the value of what Grunig described as "the variables that predict individual communication behaviors and effects—the perfect concepts for segmentation if it were feasible to organize campaigns for individuals" (1989b, p. 206). The emphasis that Sense-Making places on the individual in a situation and facing a gap offers an additional level of analysis for understanding how this individual is likely to respond to the situation and bridge the gap.

Sense-Making scholars express reservations about treating communication and information as commodities with an objective reality and applying a technique that works well in another domain to the intrinsically different application of communicating with publics. Dervin (1984) criticized attempts to predict audience use of messages that seek stable portraits across time and space using demographic or lifestyle characteristics. Such an approach can lead us to assume that segmentation approaches provide an appropriate model for human communication. According to Dervin and Schaefer (1999), "communication between representatives and stakeholders has now degenerated to the point where stakeholders have become the targets of segmentation and strategic marketing communication" (p. 20).

Despite the fact that factors such as geodemographics can be useful in public relations in understanding people's general positions on issues, Grunig and Repper (1992) claim that most uses of audience segmentation in public relations "have been asymmetrical—that is, communication managers target clusters most likely to agree with their position and then direct messages to mobilize support" (p. 145). They relate such categorization of publics to an asymmetrical approach to communication that "provides a map of how to describe or position a product or organisation so that people will accept it, rather than a map of the people affected by an organisation and the problems they face" (p. 134). Sense-Making warns that such an ability to manipulate publics will lead to knowledges created by those in power while others are subjugated (Dervin, 1989a, p. 70).

Sense-Making's concern is consistent with the reminder by Grunig and Repper (1992) that a "public, a market, or any other segment of a population exists only because a researcher or practitioner uses a particular theoretical concept to identify it" (p. 129). It sees other problems in treating "traditional categories of users" as if they are real when this may result in reifying systems, intensifying inequities, and hampering new technologies. Dervin suggests that segmentation categories are "all rooted in essentially the same mechanistic, transmission-oriented, objectivity-oriented model of communication" (1989b, p. 217).

Some segmentation of publics is essential, to allow a communicator to identify which publics need to be addressed, and to avoid the waste of resources of attempting to communicate with a whole population, whether salient to an issue or not. Grunig's situational theory of identifying publics (Grunig and Hunt, 1984, pp. 147–149) takes the emphasis away from outside characteristics of a public toward attempting to understand how a person acts in a particular situation. This is consistent with a Sense-Making approach that sees differences between how publics are described by others and how the publics actually behave (Dervin, 1998).

Market research needs to treat situated behavior as a legitimate and meaningful subject of study, rather than an aberration or mistake. Rather than completely abandon market segmentation or demographic, lifestyle, and personality approaches, Sense-Making reconceptualizes them in terms of how such characteristics are relevant to a person in a particular situation, with his or her own typical approaches to decision-making. For Sense-Making, the important thing is to identify those conditions under which behavior responds uniquely to situations, those conditions where it is habitual, and those conditions where these interplay with each other, and then to use a methodology that allows all of this to be studied.

THEORETIC ASSUMPTIONS OF SENSE-MAKING

Regardless of the phenomenon studied, Sense-Making conceptualizes the phenomenon as communication, more specifically as communicatings. In its early years, Sense-Making was defined by Dervin as a constructivist approach (Dervin, 1983), but in her later writings she describes it as a "verbing" approach, as beyond constructivism and even beyond postmodernism. Sense-Making walks a line between such polarizations in the field of communication and the social sciences generally and attempts to capture the contributions of constructivism and postmodern approaches.

Sense-Making requires communication to be studied self-consciously or reflexively, which means that the researcher should not be separate or apart from the topic or the object of study, but should seek an immersion and connectedness (Dervin, 1998). It is an approach that involves researchers deeply, because they cannot simply seek answers, but must be fully present in the situation, each time. Such an approach to research cannot be mechanical and fixed because of the flexibility demanded by the study of diverse, uncontrolled, and complex human activity (Dervin, 1998).

A Sense-Making approach to research is not so much about using different research methods, but more about a new way of thinking about research practices and making choices about them. It attempts to steer between a set, standard, unvarying, simplistic approach and the utter confusion of allowing all influences to affect us without any way of creating order (Dervin, 1998).

Using Sense-Making affects how we research and work with publics. It requires us to consider humans in all their aspects, not just intellectual but also emotional, physical, and spiritual. Because Sense-Making does not define the individual as solely a cognitive being, it aims to discover what really activates people, even when they may not be aware of their full range of motivations. The interactions with a subject that develop from interviews based on this methodology are often revealing even to the person involved. They are constructed in such a way that hidden choices and directions-not-taken are made explicit and explored in depth, revealing motivations originally beyond the consciousness of the actor.

Sense-Making conceptualizes each person as a social theorist with the capacity to develop ideas and theories about his or her own experience. If people are theorists and knowledge-makers in their own worlds (Dervin, 1998), a researcher must involve the person being researched as a thinking and contributing participant in research. Such an approach to research cannot pretend to think for individuals or presume to develop their perceptions for them. It requires a partnership between the researcher and the individual whose world is made available for study, rather than the all-too-conventional expectation of access to data. This methodology demands a constant personal involvement and cannot be performed to a formula or in a predetermined way.

A significant underlying assumption of this theoretical approach is *discontinuity*, a concept developed by Richard Carter as described by Dervin (1992, p. 82). The concept of discontinuity has also influenced the work of J. Grunig (2003), who credited Carter's work as changing the way he "looked at communication and eventually, at public relations" (p. 85). *Discontinuity* refers to the assumption that there is no automatic movement from each moment or action to the next. If we assume that there is always some kind of gap between our reality and our publics, our perceptions and theirs, the time in which we are situated and all other times, the space where we are and all other spaces, the particular message we are interested in and all other messages, then we will place more importance on human characteristics than on institutional factors. Such an approach to behavior suggests that what we do is ultimately controlled by ourselves rather than being completely determined by rules, standards or organizations.

Adopting the perspective of the actor enables us to study how people use information, and hence how we should design programs to communicate with them. As public relations communicators we often need to understand why a public is not using a service or a product, and what is really going on when a public seems to be alienated and resists what others may define as a benefit. However, as observers we do not share the same world as any actor and are likely to ask the wrong questions or misconstrue their response. With Sense-Making it is possible to remove some of the barriers between the external understanding of a situation and what participants see themselves as experiencing and the helps or uses that are relevant to them.

Move from Static to Process Worldview

The common approach to explaining and predicting human behavior focuses on what are called *state conditions*. We use different levels of analysis to study public behavior by describing it as, for example, interpersonal or organizational. We study the topical contexts in which people communicate, such as health or political communication. In public relations, a whole range of objective characteristics are used to attempt to understand publics. Demography, personality type, and education level are examples of static categories developed to be stable and useful in all situations, but they do not explain and predict how a person will behave in a particular time, place, and context.

According to Sense-Making, knowing about such state conditions is not enough to successfully explain and predict human behavior. Its alternative focus on process conditions is concerned with how individuals respond to and use information: the communicatings that Sense-Making calls "step-takings." These can be internal responses such as comparing, categorizing, liking, disliking, polarizing, or stereotyping. Some common external responses are shouting, ignoring, agreeing, disagreeing, attending, or listening.

Sense-Making has a complex construction of the individual as the living element of agency that works within or against structures, the creator and at the same time the critic of order, as well as the reason that domination gets exercised over people or that it gets resisted. According to Savolainen (1993), Sense-Making draws "at least implicitly, on the structuration theory of Anthony Giddens (1984)" (p. 20). Dervin describes structure as "energized by, maintained, reified, changed and created by individual acts of communicating" (1992, p. 67) and describes communication scholarship as "where structure and agency meet, both implemented in communicatings" (1993, p. 52). What public relations scholars and professionals need to understand is "what happens in the elusive moments of human communicatings" (Dervin, 1993, p. 53).

Dervin challenges us to reconceptualize theory and to move from conceiving of entity to process and from state to dynamic. She suggests we should focus on verbs rather than nouns, and study the making of meaning rather than the meanings that people have made. The problem with any continuing inadvertent use of the transmission model is that it makes us confuse "communication as process" with "communication as product," which leads to inappropriate research and campaign design.

The term *target public* clearly illustrates the transmission metaphor in the field of public relations practice, and it discloses a theoretical assumption that will undermine attempts at dialogue. According to Dervin (1991), what happens in communication is that "human beings draw on their understandings of the world and make observations that they construct into ideas and then encode into messages that they then 'send' out where other human beings use their understandings of the world, and so on" (p. 63). When done to transmit information to a public, even for a service that will ultimately benefit them, this practice fails to engage in two-way symmetrical communication.

Accounting for Power

Issues relating to the use of power and the rights of the consumer are integral to Sense-Making methodology, not as an afterthought but as part of its deepest underlying assumptions. Rights are not restricted to researchers, whether academic or policy driven, and hence, as every good public relations person should expect, there needs to be a symmetrical relationship between researcher and researched. It would be inconsistent to devise a dialogic communication situation that is based on any notion of exploitation in collecting data.

Dealing with power is difficult when it promotes or enforces acceptable answers or approaches. Sometimes this is hidden. Sense-Making is critical of a stakeholder model of democratic participation that assumes that all participants can participate fully and have dialogue with other stakeholders. With new technologies being controlled by powerful interests, a general expectation of access to participation can no longer be relied on. This attempt to control often uses the tool of marketing segmentation. In contrast to such an approach, Sense-Making pays attention to individuals and "explicitly, and necessarily, privileges the ordinary person as a theorist involved in developing ideas to guide an understanding of not only her personal worlds but also collective, historical, and social worlds" (Dervin, 1999b, p. 46).

Sense-Making research takes particular care to allow disagreement by using interviewing techniques that do not push people toward approved responses. When studying a group of people, Sense-Making looks for communality and contest by seeking agreement and disagreement. Dervin (1998) calls this "the circling of perspectives or frameworks, the surrounding of the phenomena in order to reach for that which can never be touched or held still" (p. 41). It achieves this by questions focusing on a person's "struggles, constraints, barriers, hurts and hindrances as well as the user's assessments of the relationships between a given moment of Sense-Making and the power structures of an organisation or society" (Dervin, 1998, p. 41). "Audience research, conceptualized within the framework of a communication-as-dialogue perspective, is a new way of listening to the public" (Dervin, 1989a, p. 76).

> A Sense-Making methodology can inform the design of public relations campaigns when researchers are encouraged to be responsive to and to listen to their publics but to be able to do this they need an approach that allows it. Sense-Making researchers report the success of such an approach and that "users have been willing to tell us things that ordinary surveys miss entirely." (Dervin, 1998, p. 41)

Sense-Making develops a detailed picture of the ways people build cognitive strategies in gap-bridging situations, and this results in a direct benefit to research participants, who often gain more understanding of their individual approaches and their limitations in solving problems in their everyday life settings. In working with the actors involved to identify their actions in a particular situation, Sense-Making can perform an indirect emancipatory role (Savolainen, 1993).

The underlying equity assumptions of Sense-Making are reflected in its suspicion of traditional user categories, which can lead to constructing communication systems that make haves and have-nots inevitable. Such systems are criticized for reinforcing inequities and guiding exploitation. "Based as they are on population segmentation and marketing principles, the traditional categories thus can lead only to conclusions that reify systems based on the same categories. Such systems may be inherently antidemocratic" (Dervin, 1989b, p. 221).

Dervin (1998) claims that if researchers seek dialogue rather than control and that if their "contributions to the knowledge base are anchored in verbs and in the material conditions in which they arose, an important result is a higher capacity of all parties to understand each other" (pp. 41–42). Public relations scholars and practitioners working toward achieving symmetrical communication will already have a commitment to the dialogical design of communication. The additional element Sense-Making adds is the focus on process and the situation as inseparable and integral influences of an action.

THE SENSE-MAKING METAPHOR

This metaphorical framework proposes that we can understand more about people by using the metaphor of travel through time and space in which each instant, each location is in some ways different from all others (Dervin, 1998). It forms the basis of Sense-Making interviewing which analyses each step or choice that a person has made to bridge the gaps they faced.

Figure 15.1 draws on the core Sense-Making discontinuity notion that as human beings move in time and space, they constantly face gaps that they will need to find a way across. It illustrates a person who comes to a particular situation from that person's unique history, constraints, and forces. The person is facing a gap, such as a block or a barrier, and can choose from various helps or uses to bridge this gap. The person will choose particular strategies based on her own information values to answer her questions, form ideas, and obtain resources with which to bridge the gap and gain the outcome she wants to achieve.

There are likely to be patterns in how people respond to particular situations because of their organizational context as well as the effects of culture and history. People behave systematically when conceptualized as an entity behaving

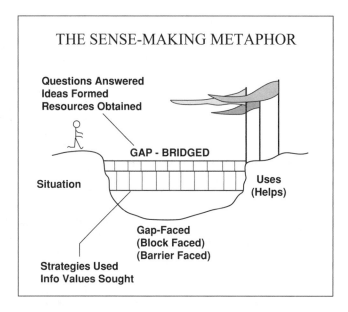

FIG. 15.1   The Sense-Making metaphor (Dervin, 1996b). Based on Dervin's
Sense-Making Workshop, Sydney.

at a moment in time and in space. This is because individuals construct ideas
of these moments and develop particular strategies to deal with them, sometimes depending on what they have done in the past and sometimes creating
new approaches. An individual's use of information and systems will vary
depending on a particular situation as he perceives it. This is very much up to
the individual and his own choices. However, Sense-Making shows us that the
way in which a person defines gaps and attempts to bridge discontinuities can
be explained and predicted from understanding that person's decision-making
strategies.

   To illustrate the theoretic possibilities of this focus on how people bridge
gaps, Dervin and Clark (1993) lay out a two-dimensional grid with six situation-
defining strategies on one axis and nine generalized communicative tactics
on the other. The model proposes that at each intersection there are a set of
potential communicatings (i.e., verbings) by which people make and unmake
sense. Some of these situation-defining strategies have been identified as the
individual relating to self, the individual relating to other individuals, and
collectively to the relating individual. Some of the communicative tactics are
creating ideas, finding connection, opposing, and mediating. According to
Savolainen (1993), the gap metaphor can help us understand people by studying
the "context of how they meet the challenges of the discontinuities of everyday
life" (p. 23).

TABLE 15.1
Process-Oriented Categories of Interpersonal Communication

Categories	Examples
1. The actor's situation	The complexity of the situation, its clarity, the diversity of elements involved, the number of people involved, the power and constraints operating, and the barriers in the way
2. The gaps in the actor's Sense-Making	How the actor responds to the gap she perceives
3. The purpose as defined by the actor	Some purposes might be to get ideas, find direction, acquire skills, connect with others, get support, achieve goals
4. The actor's information-using strategy	Strategies could include browsing, grouping, interpreting or connecting
5. The actor's values for evaluating communication	These might include timeliness, accuracy, specificity and newsworthiness
6. The actor's communication preferences	How the actor is expected to respond

(Based on Dervin, 1989b, p. 225.)

Dervin provides a set of process-oriented categories to describe a person at a particular moment in time and space, as shown in Table 15.1. To understand how a person will communicate in an interpersonal, group, or organizational context, the researcher needs to explore these six categories.

The Importance of the Situation

The knowledge or information that we as public relations practitioners may want to share with a public is not what we should concentrate on. We may have our own view of how knowledge about better nutrition or stopping smoking may benefit a public, but these are our understandings, and it is not wise to construct campaigns based on such a limited approach. We must find out what such knowledge means to our publics. The research of Dervin (1998) and her Sense-Making colleagues has shown that "information and knowledge are rarely ends in themselves; they are rather means to ends . . . [we need to learn how to] leave users free to define what is informing on their own terms" (p. 40). She also claims that "it is rarely person attributes (traits and predisposition) or task or organizational attributes but rather how users conceptualize their movement through time-space and their gap bridging that predicts Sense-Making and sense-unmaking best" (p. 40).

Sense-Making can contribute to our understanding of publics and capacity to predict how they are likely to behave by its "set of universal categories of situation-facing based on the concepts of time, space, movement, gap, constraint" (Dervin, 1998, p. 40). When a person feels that he is stopped at a moment in time-space, he can feel that two or more roads lie ahead; that something blocks the road; that the road has disappeared; that someone or something is pulling him down the road; that the road is spiraled and has no direction; or he may feel "blanked out." All of these categories relate to situation movement. Sense-Making research has compared these situation movement categories with demographic indicators in studies, and "in each case, situation movement has accounted for far more variance in user internal and external behavior" (Dervin, 1998, p. 40), whether for individual or collaborative work.

Grunig and Repper (1992) focused on the concept of a situation and claimed that it "allows the aggregation of individuals into publics in a way that is more useful for symmetrical communication programs than do the concepts of attitudes and cognitions" (p. 134). They also pointed out that variables affecting a situation include "physical and social surroundings, time, the specific task for which a product is used, personal state of mind at purchase, social or financial pressure, uncertainty, or a situation served inadequately by existing products" (p. 134). A communicator should also consider whether the person is relating simply to herself, to another person, to another group of people, or within a group to which she belongs.

J. Grunig's situational theory of publics demonstrates that three variables help explain why people engage in a behavior and communicate in the process of planning that behavior. These are problem recognition, level of involvement, and constraint recognition. "The concept of problem recognition is tied to the concept of a situation. . . . J. Grunig has defined involvement as an individual's cognitive perception of a situation: It is a person's perception that he or she has a connection with a situation" (Grunig and Repper, 1992, 136). There is a strong relationship between these aspects and the way a person approaches information. Problem recognition and constraint recognition increase information seeking and information processing. A high level of involvement also increases information seeking (Grunig and Hunt, 1984, p. 149).

Grunig used situational concepts to explain the behavior of publics, especially as they relate with each other. "Publics, therefore, begin as disconnected systems of individuals experiencing common problems, but they can evolve into organized and powerful activist groups engaging in collective behavior" (Grunig and Repper, 1992, p. 138). Publics have "similar levels of problem recognition, constraint recognition, and involvement for the same issues or problems" (Grunig and Repper, 1992, p. 139).

These definitions of publics suggest that publics consist of individuals who detect the same problems and plan similar behaviors to deal with those problems. Grunig and Hunt (1984) explain that "we can define a public as a loosely structured system whose members detect the same problem or issue, interact either face to face or through mediated channels, and behave as though they were one body" (p. 144). They claim that "to say that attitudes and behaviors are situational means that people do not think and act in relation to broad values that they apply to all situations, but they change their attitudes and behaviors to fit the situation" (Grunig and Hunt, 1984, p. 130).

Application of the Gap Metaphor

The Sense-Making metaphor is an abstract methodological approach that provides a way to research and understand the communicatings and actions of a person. Dervin uses this metaphor to create a deeper understanding of publics and their needs and to set a foundation for the relationship between the researcher and the researched (1998). "Humans, Sense-Making assumes, live in a world of gaps: a reality that changes across time and space and is at least in part gappy at a given time-space" (Dervin, 1998, p. 36).

The Sense-Making assumption that humans are mandated to make and remake sense is captured in its central metaphor of a gap. Theoretically, each micro-moment of experience is a micro-moment of gap-bridging mandated by the human condition. Whereas most research and practice focuses on results, Sense-Making focuses on the processes by which people bridge the gaps they encounter. It sees an integral connection between how we conceptualize a situation and how we choose to deal with it.

The Sense-Making metaphor is the opposite of the transmission metaphor, in that it makes no attempt to transmit information or to influence people with magic bullets. It simply asks actors how they bridged their own gaps. The reason Sense-Making makes this assumption is that when it comes to communication, what people make of messages is as important, if not more important, than the actual message.

There is always a gap between reality and perceptions, different times, different spaces, a message meant and a message actually sent. The gap relates to the human factor and the fact that behavior is controlled internally rather than by outside forces. The idea of the gap applies to all aspects of communication, including research and communication design, management, and practice.

Four tasks central to public relations activity can be guided by the Sense-Making metaphor: "thinking about people, talking to them, asking questions of them, and designing systems to serve them" (Dervin, 1998, p. 39). Each of these tasks is regularly done by communication managers who need to develop an in-depth understanding of publics and their needs before producing any campaign or designing any system for them. The gap concept can guide them when framing questions, interviewing people, and analyzing their responses. Sense-Making focuses on how a person deals with a particular gap rather than trying to develop a picture of this from our own understandings (Dervin, 1998).

Conventional practice pays attention to the needs of publics, but from a different perspective, that of the researcher or program designer. It is extremely difficult to bypass our own understandings of a situation no matter how much we try to "put ourselves in the other person's shoes." Public information campaigns often reflect the worldview of campaign designers, who have done research into the attitudes and beliefs of a salient public, but still use their own framework to interpret what they find. This trap is particularly common in public information campaigns that target the public good and can be noted in countless efforts to stop people from smoking or from driving too fast.

Actor's Information Using Strategy

It is only by investigating what particular knowledge means to our publics that we can provide the information they really need. It may not even be more information that they need. Carl Weick (1995) also uses the term "sensemaking," but quite differently from Dervin, to describe an approach that is a mandate to attend to the phenomena of sensemaking. His work is relevant to this discussion because it demonstrates the completely different communication strategies required when people are uncertain, in which case they may be assisted by more information, compared with when they are equivocal, in which case providing further information only aggravates their confusion.

Dervin (1992) presents the gap concept as "the essence of the communicating moment" (p. 66) that describes and explains the situation as the actor experiences it and that can allow the involved observer to predict the behavior of the actor in that moment. She claims that the most useful way to understand communicating is to use the perspective of the gap, and to imagine that each time a person defines himself or herself as facing a gap, that person will use different tactics depending on the moment and the gap. Public relations practitioners' ability to communicate about an issue depends on them knowing how the public has defined the issue for themselves and attempted to deal with it, to bridge the metaphorical gap it presents to them.

USING A SENSE-MAKING METHOD

Dervin (1989a) describes Sense-Making as taking a communication-as-dialogue approach to audience research. It does not propose methods as recipes but invites us to "enter the research situation in the 'in between,' between order and chaos, structure and individual, culture and person, self 1 and self 2, and so on. It focuses on how humans make and unmake, develop, maintain, resist, destroy, and change order, structure, culture, organisation, relationships, self" (Dervin, 1999b, p. 45).

It emphasizes the importance of creating an environment in which a person being interviewed will be assisted to present his own individual approach without being influenced by the interviewer or her questions "to provide the interviewee with the freedom and power of self-description and explanation" (Shields and Dervin, 1993, p. 74). The interviewing approach most commonly used in Sense-Making is called the *micro-moment time-line interview*. The respondent is asked to recollect a critical situation and to explain what happened over the period of time in the following manner:

> For each time-line event, in terms of the situations (e.g., barriers, constraints, history, memory, experience), gaps (e.g., confusions, worries, questions, muddles), bridges (e.g., ideas, conclusions, feelings, opinions, hypotheses, hunches, stories, values, strategies, sources), and outcomes (e.g., helps, facilitations, hurts, hindrances, outcomes, effects, impacts). (Dervin, 1999b, p. 47)

The time-line interview requires the interviewer to ask the interviewee to describe in detail what happened in a situation step by step; analyze these events one at a time by asking him to indicate any questions, puzzles, or confusions associated with the events; and analyze the nature of each of these questions by asking a series of specifying questions that reflect the dimensions of the situation, the gap, and the uses/helps (Savolainen, 1993, p. 24).

The following example provides some ideas of how Sense-Making directs the approach to an interview, although it is not strictly a time-line interview, which would be too complex for my purpose here. A real time-line interview would have triangulations of elements at each step in the time-line, and then for each step it would ask the person about his thoughts, ideas, conclusions, questions, feelings, etc. For each of these, the person would be asked how the thought or idea connected to his life and the impact it had on him.

In my simplified adaptation of the time-line interview, I was interested in a campaign designed to reduce smoking, and I wanted to conduct some research into the attitudes, behavior, and beliefs of salient publics. This extract from an interview with one individual demonstrates some features of this method in action at just one of its steps.

This woman had agreed to tell me about a time she had decided to stop smoking. She was then asked:

Q. What made you decide to stop smoking then?

A. A close relative had heart by-pass surgery. This gave me a shock.

Q. How did you go about it?

A. I just stopped buying cigarettes.

Q. What other options did you consider?

A. I considered the possibility of patches and hypnotherapy.

Q. Why didn't you go ahead with the patches?

A. They seemed to be targeted toward heavy smokers and I wasn't. I think they have more nicotine in them than I took in a week by smoking. Also they are quite expensive as I think they are sold as a whole course.

Q. Why didn't you use hypnotherapy?

A. I've known people who used hypnotherapy and it didn't work.

Q. Why do you think it didn't work for them?

A. Because if you don't want to stop it can't make you.

Q. What happened when you stopped buying cigarettes?

A. Initially nothing because I wasn't a heavy smoker but it became more difficult later.

Q. What made it difficult?

A. Having a drink with friends when they smoke and they offer you one of theirs. And if you have a stressful situation you immediately reach for a cigarette . . . or want one.

Q. What would have helped you?

A. If they weren't as readily available . . . if other people who smoked wouldn't give you one of theirs. Perhaps nicotine chewing gum . . . but I'm not certain how it works.

Q. Would you have tried the gum if you knew more about it?

A. Yes.

Q. When you think back about trying to stop smoking, what made it harder?

A. It's the addiction and the social thing . . . a way of relaxing, something you do with your hands and your mouth.

Q. What would have made it easier to stop smoking?

A. Knowing how that gum works would have been a real help.

A first analysis of this simplified example shows that there are several related situations here, each with its own gap to bridge, questions to get answered, and helps to find. In the first situation the individual wants to make a change to her life by stopping smoking. She faces a gap between her wish to make the change and actually achieving it. In her attempt to bridge the gap she uses one of many possible strategies, after considering several others and rejecting them for different reasons. In moving to bridge the gap, she had questions about several different strategies she could use, and she has formed ideas about the different strategies she knew about.

A communicator attempting to devise a campaign to help a public such as this individual stop smoking may gain some advantage from knowing her demographic and psychographic profiles, but the real insights come from considering the person in a particular situation taking steps to move through an experience that was important to her. As a response to her relative's heart disease, she has defined this gap as vital for her own future, introducing an element of desperation. However, she seems insistent on taking control of her own decision and distrusts other approaches she could have used. The social situation of interacting with friends sets up another Sense-Making situation of its own, in which she would have made some decisions about how to get the outcome she wanted while not harming her standing in the group. Looking back on the situation some time afterwards, we can now see a third situation in which she has introduced the idea of a new element, the gum, that in retrospect she thinks would have been the help she needed to have been successful at the time.

Researching the attitudes, beliefs, knowledge, and behavior of publics is richer when we work cooperatively with the people involved to try to understand the situation as they see it. No amount of empathy from an uninvolved researcher could disclose the very private responses of a person actually involved in this situation and the meanings she makes of it.

SENSE-MAKING STUDIES RELEVANT TO CAMPAIGN DESIGN

It would be useful to present a brief review of the work of Sense-Making scholars working in areas relevant to public communication campaign design. The first exemplar of Sense-Making as an alternative approach to understanding a public is provided by Dervin, Harpring, and Foreman-Wernet (1999). Their dialogic interviews focused on specific situations that had been faced by drug-addicted pregnant women when they had a need for information, what they called their "moments of concern." From this they learned how these women inform themselves and how public communication campaigns could address their needs. Compared with remedial correction public communication campaigns based on fear and guilt, this Sense-Making research provided insights into the real needs of the people involved and showed how fear and guilt appeals were counterproductive.

In another study, Brendlinger, Dervin, and Foreman-Wernet (1999) criticized the top-down transmission model underlying the HIV/AIDS prevention strategy and its reliance on close-ended traditional surveys that impose institutional worldviews. They compared a traditional survey with a Sense-Making survey using similar respondents and the same topic. Using a Sense-Making audience survey to listen to people talk about HIV/AIDS from within their own phenomenological worlds, they discovered that seven out of 10 said they knew the official facts about AIDS. Comparing the Sense-Making survey with a matched traditional survey, they found a different way of framing knowledge and a much less limited map. This showed that the audience was not obstinate, but that they operated from a different worldview from the institution.

Madden (1999) used Sense-Making to explore the meaning of environmental campaigns for a particular public. She showed the uselessness of delivering information to people unless it helps them manage their own situations and find their own solutions. Campaign information was shown to be irrelevant to people who were attempting to come to terms with their own beliefs and feelings about environmental responsibility. This approach moves the responsibility to act from the public and enables the researcher to understand how people feel about being more environmentally friendly, giving them the prerogative to define what they want to discuss and to set their own priorities. Madden noted an unintended effect of using Sense-Making: A wider and more inclusive group were willing to be part of the study when they realized that they didn't have to answer set survey questions and that they could describe their own experiences. This is a useful reminder of how surveys by their very nature may be excluding that part of the population we need most to understand.

Frenette's research (1999) into meaningful use of health communication messages in Canada explored how adolescents make sense of anti-smoking messages. As a Sense-Making scholar, she assumed that the audience was inherently active and that they were searching for their own understandings. For her research she gathered teenagers' analyses of advertisements and categorized messages according to whether they were perceived as helps, as neutral, or as hindrances. This enabled her to identify the characteristics of effective communication to teenagers about smoking and to conclude that successful communication must be based in young smokers' lived context and relate to what they are struggling with and to what they are attempting to achieve. This very interesting study shows how a particular public makes sense of the media (such as public service announcements) and how this intersects with their Sense-Making about an issue.

Dervin (1997) evaluated the consumer education plan developed for restructuring electricity in California. She highlighted the pitfalls that can face public relations practitioners who do not understand how people meet their everyday information needs. Marketing plans were used instead of public communication or education. Community education was confused with creating brand awareness. The experiences and concerns that informed the campaign were those of the institution, whereas the life experience of the users of electricity was ignored. Through this study Dervin illustrates a convincing commercial imperative to avoid the stereotyping of publics and to use methods such as

Sense-Making that can provide the rich and authentic knowledge that comes with interactivity.

Dervin and Shields (1999) investigated the ways people understand telephone privacy issues. Their research revealed a variety of ways in which people construct telephone privacy and how people are likely to respond to what they see as invasions of their privacy. They compared the predictive capacity of demography, context, and situation and concluded that "restricting policy analyses to demographic predictions alone yields ironically both a too shallow and a too chaotic portrait of users" (p. 434).

Andsager (2001) investigated how women's magazines report on breast cancer and silicone implants and revealed a woman-centered approach to dealing with these issues. Based on a Sense-Making methodology, this research helped to demonstrate the impact of media coverage on women's health consciousness.

Murphy (1999) provides a final example of Sense-Making research relevant to the design of public communication campaigns. Murphy sought to understand the human experience of wilderness, an essential starting point for any campaign to save this aspect of the environment. He described his use of a highly structured open-ended questioning format in which there was virtually no content, but in which informants were directed toward their own wilderness experiences and asked to describe these experiences. From this research Murphy was able to show the role of the media in creating the meaning of wilderness, particularly for those of us with no direct experience of it, and to provide insights for constructing communication campaigns to preserve it.

Each of these Sense-Making scholars has demonstrated, in a different way, the ability of this approach to take them to a deeper and more meaningful understanding of the publics with whom they need to communicate. They have approached their publics in a very situated manner and constructed a dialogic communication that resulted in reliable knowledge on which campaigns can be built. As public relations scholars, students, and practitioners we could enrich our capacity to communicate by learning more about Sense-Making as a methodology. Sense-Making offers insights that can be valuable in helping us concentrate on the individual as a whole person dealing with a particular and unique set of circumstances, and it provides ways to listen more closely to what our publics can tell us.

In conclusion, it is a challenge to try to bring together some of the relevant ideas from a living and growing theoretical area and attempt to make these ideas available to scholars and students from a different but related field. Although more than 100 researchers around the world are using Sense-Making in their research and practice, it still centers around its originator, Brenda Dervin, whom I thank for allowing me to attempt to share its insights and theoretical approach with my academic and professional domain of communication, and for providing me with valuable feedback and help as I prepared this chapter.

Students of public relations who would like to know more about the Sense-Making approach to communication will find a complete bibliography, articles, and exemplars at http://communication.sbs.ohio-state.edu/sense-making.

REFERENCES

Andsager, J. (2001). Framing womens' health with a Sense-Making approach: Magazine coverage of breast cancer and implants. *Health Communication, 13*(2), 163-186.

Brendlinger, N., Dervin, B., & Foreman-Wernet, L. (1999). When respondents are theorists: An exemplar study in the HIV/AIDS context of the use of Sense-Making as an approach to public communication campaign audience. *The Electronic Journal of Communication, 9* (2, 3, & 4). Accessed 25 August 2005 http://www.cios.org. ezproxy.lib.uts.edu.au/getfile/ Brendlin_V9N23499.

Dervin, B. (1983, May). *An overview of Sense-Making research: Concepts, methods, and results to date.* Paper presented at the annual meeting of the International Communication Association, Dallas, TX.

Dervin, B. (1984). A theoretic perspective and research approach for generating research helpful to communication practice. *Public Relations Research and Education, 1*(1), 30–45.

Dervin, B. (1989a). Audience as listener and learner, teacher and confidante: The Sense-Making approach. In R. Rice & D. Atkin (Eds), *Public communication campaigns* (2nd Ed., pp. 67–86). Newbury Park, CA: Sage.

Dervin, B. (1989b). Users as research inventions: How research categories perpetuate inequities. *Journal of Communication, 39*(3), 216–232.

Dervin, B. (1991). Comparative theory reconceptualised: From entities and states to processes and dynamics. *Communication Theory, 1*(1) 59–69.

Dervin, B. (1992). From the minds eye of the user: The Sense-Making qualitative-quantitative methodology. In J. Glazier and R. Powell (Eds), *Qualitative research in information management* (pp. 61–84). Englewood, CO: Libraries Unlimited.

Dervin, B. (1993). Verbing communication: A mandate for disciplinary invention. *Journal of Communication, 43*(3), 45–54.

Dervin, B. (1996a, August). *Given a context by any other name: Methodological tools for taming the unruly beast.* Keynote paper at ISIC 96: Information seeking in context. Tampere Finland. August 14–16.

Dervin, B. (1996b, August 24). *A day with Brenda Dervin: Sense and Sense-Making methodology workshop.* University of Technology, Sydney.

Dervin, B. (1997, June 20). *Evaluation of the May 30, 1997 Electric Restructuring Education Group (EREG) Consumer Education Progress (CEP) proposed Marketing plan.* Report to California Public Utilities Commission, Consumer Services Division, San Francisco, CA.

Dervin, B. (1998). Sense-Making theory and practice: An overview of user interests in knowledge seeking and use. *Journal of Knowledge Management, 2*(2), 36–46.

Dervin, B. (1999a). On studying information seeking methodologically: The implications of connecting metatheory to method. *Information Processing and Management, 35*, 727–750.

Dervin, B. (1999b). Chaos, order, and Sense-Making: A proposed theory for information design. In R. Jacobson (Ed.), *Information design* (pp. 35–57). Cambridge, MA: MIT Press.

Dervin, B., & Clark, K. D. (1989) Communication as cultural identity: The invention mandate. *Media Development, 36*(2), 5–8.

Dervin, B., & Clark, K. D. (1993). Communication and democracy: A mandate for procedural invention. In S. Splichal & J. Wasko (Eds.), *Communication and democracy* (pp. 103–140). Norwood, NJ: Ablex.

Dervin, B., Harpring, J., & Foreman-Wernet, L. (1999). In moments of concern: A Sense-Making study of pregnant drug-addicted women and their information needs. *Electronic Journal of Communication, 9*(2, 3, & 4). Accessed 25 August 2005 http://www.cios.org.ezproxy. lib.uts.edu.au/getfile/Devin2_V9N23499.

Dervin, B., & Schaefer, D. (1999). Peopling the public sphere. *Peace Review, 11*(1), 17–23.

Dervin, B., & Shields, P. (1999). Adding the missing user to policy discourse: Understanding U.S. user telephone privacy concerns. *Telecommunications Policy, 23,* 403–435.

Frenette, M. (1999). Explorations in adolescents' sense-making of anti-smoking messages. *Electronic Journal of Communication, 9*(2, 3, & 4). Accessed 25 August 2005 http://www.cios. org.ezproxy.lib.uts.edu.au/getfile/Frenette_V9N23499.

Giddens, A. (1984). *The constitution of society: Outline of the theory of structuration.* Cambridge, UK: Polity Press.

Grunig, J. E. (1989a). Symmetrical presuppositions as a framework for public relations theory. In C. H. Botan & V. Hazleton, Jr. (Eds.), *Public relations theory* (pp. 17–44). Hillsdale, NJ: Lawrence Erlbaum Associates.

Grunig, J. E. (1989b). Publics, audiences and market segments: Segmentation principles for campaigns. In Salmon, C. T. (Ed.), *Information campaigns: Balancing social values and social change* (pp. 199–228). Newbury Park, CA: Sage.

Grunig, J. E. (2003). Constructing public relations theory and practice. In B. Dervin & S. Chaffee (with L. Foreman-Wernet) (Eds.), *Communication, a different kind of horserace: Essays honouring Richard F. Carter* (pp. 85–116). Cresskill, NJ: Hampton Press.

Grunig, J. E., & Hunt, T. (1984). *Managing public relations.* New York: Holt, Rinehart & Winston.

Grunig, J. E., & Repper, F. C. (1992). Strategic management, publics, and issues. In Grunig, J. E. (Ed.), *Excellence in public relations and communication management,* (pp. 117–157). Hillsdale, NJ: Lawrence Erlbaum Associates.

Madden, K. M. (1999). Making sense of environmental messages: An exploration of households' information needs and uses. *Electronic Journal of Communication, 9*(2, 3, & 4). Accessed 27 August 2005 http://www.cios.org.ezproxy.lib. uts.edu.au/getfile/Madden_V9N23499.

Murphy, T. P. (1999). The human experience of wilderness. *Electronic Journal of Communication, 9*(2, 3, & 4). Accessed 27 August 27 August 2005 http://www. cios.org.ezproxy.lib.uts.edu.au/ getfile/Murphy_V9N23499.

Savolainen, R. (1993). The Sense-Making theory: Reviewing the interests of a user-centered approach to information seeking and use. *Information Processing and Management, 29*(1), 13–28.

Shields, V. R., & Dervin, B. (1993). Sense-Making in feminist social science research: A call to enlarge the methodological options of feminist studies. *Women's Studies International Forum, 16*(1), 65–81.

Weick, C. (1995). *Sensemaking in organisations.* Thousand Oaks, CA: Sage.

CHAPTER

16

The Technology–Image Expectancy Gap: A New Theory of Public Relations

Dean Kazoleas
and Lars Georg Teigen

Illinois State University

In the wake of the attacks on the United States in September of 2001, many victims, families of victims, citizens, and leaders of our country asked the same question: Given all of our technological advancements and abilities, how could these attacks occur? The realization of our true vulnerability and the false sense of security given to us by that technology were exemplified by an editorial that appeared in the *Chicago Tribune* on September 12, 2001: "And then, come a Tuesday in September, we realize that for all our progress, all our technology, our cities are infinitely more vulnerable to attack than were the coarse, walled cities of medieval Europe" (University of Wisconsin historian Stan K. Schultz, *The Vulnerabilities*, p. 22, 2001).

While unrealistic beliefs about the absolute abilities of technology to protect our nation from attack are reflected in the dialogues following 9/11, these

415

misperceptions about the ability of technology can create issues in everyday life for many organizations. For example, an article in the November 2000 edition of the *Journal of the American Medical Association* (Kravitz, 2000) focuses on a new everyday crisis faced by physicians across the United States. Patients see ads for new drugs on television, or are exposed to media coverage of the announcement of new drugs (often focusing on the very positive results of clinical trials and ignoring qualifiers). The patients then rush off to their doctors and demand access to these new, often very expensive drugs, which appear to offer risk-free miracle cures. In the face of unrealistic patient expectations, doctors are facing a crisis: They and their sponsoring medical organizations look bad if they refuse to prescribe the drugs, but they also run the risk of reputational damage if they do prescribe the medication, and it then does not deliver the unrealistic expected results.

This chapter presents a new theory of technology and public relations. As opposed to dealing with the way that technology aids the practitioner or increases communication ability, this theory identifies a series of processes that create scenarios where the image and very survival of many organizations become threatened. Simply stated, this theory suggests that the marketing of technology, coupled with media coverage of technological advances, creates unrealistic expectations as to the ability of organizations to meet the needs of their stakeholders. Moreover, this theory gives a set of propositions predicting that the advancement of technology in our society and the marketing of technologically based products, coupled with heavy media coverage of such advances, affects public perceptions of the ability of the technology to deliver all that is promised. Furthermore, this theory argues that the heavy emphasis on technology in the media creates unrealistic expectations among stakeholders regarding the quality of goods and services that most organizations deliver, the speed and effectiveness of organizational response to inquiries, and the extent to which organizations can monitor their internal and external environments. Additionally, this theory suggests that organizations, upon seeing the heavy focus of society on technology, often chose to emphasize (and perhaps overemphasize) their technological abilities to enhance their image, thereby increasing organization-specific expectations of performance. Last, this theory suggests that these expectations are often unrealistic and can lead to crisis and reputational damage when the organization's performance cannot meet the unrealistic expectations of its stakeholders.

In sum, the Technology–Image Expectancy Gap says that when consumers see ads portraying a young man trading stocks and bonds while sitting on a park bench, using a very small computer that is displaying the data flawlessly at blazing speed on the inside of his glasses; or when consumers watch the media cover the new "talking" computers at COMDEX (a large computer trade show), unrealistic expectations are created. The unrealistic expectations are not limited to expectations about the true ability of computers; they are also about the abilities, safety, and reliability of other products, the abilities of health care providers and pharmaceuticals, the abilities of the government, and the abilities of organizations to communicate and respond to their stakeholders. Simply stated, consumers begin to believe that "with all this technology" doctors can't make mistakes, that food and products will be 100% safe, that the government can track all persons inside and outside our borders, and that endeavors such as space travel are fairly safe, as opposed to risky.

The Technology–Image Expectancy Gap model is built on the assumptions and research offered by a number of well-established media, consumer behavior, persuasion, and public relations models. Therefore, a discussion of Expectancy theories, agenda-setting models, cultivation theories, and impression management theories is also presented.

EXPECTANCY THEORY

The foundations of the technology–image gap are grounded in expectancy theory. *Expectancy theory* suggests that individuals' perceptions of events, persons, or messages are not static in nature, but to some extent are based on the actual discrepancy between expectations and observed behavior. The notion that attitudes towards product, people, and organizations are based on the discrepancy between their actual performance and our expectations is not a new one. For example, models of consumer behavior often posit that our satisfaction with a product or the services of an organization is a function of the discrepancy between the expectations of the consumer and the actual performance of the product or organization. Figure 16.1 highlights this model.

In this consumer-relations-based model, satisfaction with people, products, or the organization occurs only when the consumers' expectations regarding performance are met. There has been a great deal of research on the predictors of consumer satisfaction, and a body of literature that both tests and supports the disconfirmation of expectations model (for examples see: Oliver, 1980; 1993, 1994; Oliver and Bearden, 1983; Oliver and DeSarbo, 1984; Wirtz and Matilla, 2001). Wirtz and Matilla (2001) have recently taken this line of research further by using path models, which examined the roles of need/desire congruence and expectations on satisfaction These models clearly indicate that high levels of performance do not always equal success or satisfaction. If the expectations are very high, success or satisfaction can be almost impossible to obtain. Although the experimental causal model oriented research such as the studies performed by Spreng, MacKenzie, & Olshavsky (1996) and Wirtz and Matilla (2001) suggests that to some extent the disconfirmation of expectations may not be the only direct predictor of satisfaction, they nonetheless find statistically significant and substantial effects on satisfaction for the violation of expectations. Moreover, the causal models that they test imply that the violation of expectations for involved consumers may even be more of a predictor of

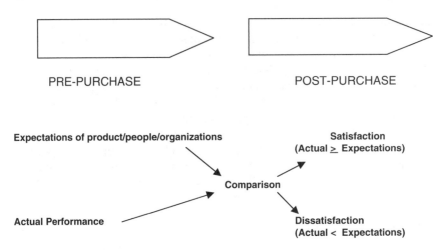

PRE-PURCHASE   POST-PURCHASE

FIG. 16.1   Expectancy model of consumer satisfaction (taken from Wilkie, W., 1990, *Consumer Behavior,* **p. 629).**

satisfaction, and that need/desire congruence or the extent to which needs are unmet will increase dissatisfaction. The findings for need/desire congruence are important because they indicate that merely limiting expectations (e.g., expecting poor performance) will not increase satisfaction if needs or desires are not met. Finally, the implications of the results reported by Spreng et al. (1996) and Wirtz and Matilla (2001) also indicate that need/desire congruence (i.e., the extent to which needs or desires are met) is also a statistically significant predictor of satisfaction. This means that as more products and services are delivered via technologically mediated mechanisms such as the Internet, and in place of human interaction, the probability of expectations being violated because of poor technological management or unrealistic expectations will increase as well.

This theory also predicts that media discussions of technological advancements, and the marketing and hyping of technology (how many consumers are still waiting for the promised reliable and easy-to-use speech-to-text computer programs?), coupled with organizations' use of their technological achievements and/or abilities to enhance their image or market their products, all create unrealistic expectations. These might include expectations that products will be 100% reliable, that communication will be instantaneous ("If I can email you at 2 a.m., you should respond by 8 a.m."), that an employer will always know exactly what every employee is doing on the job, or that a government is able to track every foreign visitor or worker who enters a country. A *Newsweek* article entitled "The Hijackers We Let Escape," for example, highlights the discussion and accusations of intelligence failure surrounding 9/11, and the tracking of known terrorists in the United States prior to their suicide attacks on September 11th 2001 (Isikoff et al., 2002).

Finally, as more organizations use technology such as the Internet or enhanced voice-mail systems to deliver services and value, more violations of expectations may occur as rapid response expectations are unmet, or as need and congruence decreases because needed and important services are not reliably delivered.

A perhaps more familiar use of expectancy theory within the communication discipline is found in Fishbein's Expectancy Value (1967a, 1967b) model of influence and persuasion. In this model Fishbein sets forth the notion that our beliefs and attitudes toward a person, object, or entity will be based on our beliefs and expectations regarding the object's or person's ability to actually perform to promised levels, coupled with the salience of the attributes, actions, or consequences. Thus, in Fishbein's model, the promise of a positive outcome, result, or reward is not enough to predict positive attitudes; rather, the ability to meet expectations moderates the impact of those factors on attitudes and judgments. In short, the Technology–Image Expectancy Gap suggests that stakeholders have unrealistic beliefs regarding the ability of the related organization to perform, to produce, or to meet their needs.

TECHNOLOGY AND EXPECTATIONS

Interestingly, the general issue of technology and unrealistic expectations has been briefly discussed in several different contexts. For example, West (1996) discusses the concept of *technological utopianism*, which refers to the promises that the developers of technology often make in regard to the impacts of their products on society and nations. He gives several examples, including AT&T's marketing of the videophone at the 1933 and 1964 World's Fairs, and its offer of service as early as the 1960s. AT&T promised that the videophone would reduce distance between families and revolutionize communications. They even invested millions into setting up systems and service. However, the technology never really delivered results. West also uses examples of the promises that technology often makes to improve society as a whole, improvements in the communications and infrastructure of nations, and the claims of the ability of technology to enhance our everyday lives (predictions of personal robots have been made for the past 40 years). As always, the technology rarely lives up to its predicted and stated potential.

Similarly, in his book entitled *Media Morphosis: Understanding New Media,* Fidler (1990) discusses the difficulty of separating hype from reality, in terms of technological advances, and discusses failed technologies. In this context he discusses and redefines a concept that he calls *technomyopia* (the original concept was called "Macro-Myopia" by P. Saffo, 1992). Technomyopia is a strange phenomenon that causes us to overestimate the potential short-term impacts of new technology. Then, when the world fails to conform to our inflated expectations, we turn around and underestimate the long-term implications. First we overshoot, then we undershoot.

TECHNOLOGY AND IMAGE

The Role of the Internet

Today, it is hard to find opposing views on the notion that the Internet is here to stay, and that it will affect many aspects of society and business, as we know it. More specifically, the characteristics of communication have changed significantly. There are four important changes in the characteristics of communication (Holtz, 1999; Kaye & Medoff, 1998) that must be taken into account when we discuss the technology–expectancy gap, and how to deal with it.

According to Kaye and Medoff (1998), the first important change is the move from few-to-many communication to many-to-many communication. Businesses, nonprofit organizations, and news organizations, to name a few, are establishing their presence on-line, in part because the technology exists to do so, but also in part because relevant publics use the technology as a communication medium and have the expectation that information will be available through the on-line medium (Kaye & Medoff, 1998). Additionally, Kaye and Medoff note, the Internet provides a wider variety of information, because the availability and low cost of the technology empowers almost any individual with the minimal ability that is needed to disseminate information. As a result, organizations and individuals compete for attention in the same arena, which puts greater pressure on larger organizations to differentiate themselves from smaller and less capable competitors. From the perspective of the Technology–Expectancy Image Gap, this often means that smaller organizations can create communication systems and campaigns that make them look like larger competitors, creating larger expectations than they can perhaps meet, while larger organizations promise more and more technological advancements as a method of increasing brand placement relative to smaller brands. A good example of this phenomenon are the many membership organizations that exist in the United States. Through the use of the Internet and advanced telecommunication technologies, they can create an image of a large service provider, and deliver a large amount of value, while at the same time maintaining low overhead costs by limiting staffing and facility costs.

A second major change in the characteristics of communication is the shift from producer-driven communication to receiver-driven communication (Kaye & Medoff, 1998). New Internet technologies have been developed that allow individuals to search for and select information based on personal preferences or to meet very specific needs. As a result of this receiver-oriented perspective, the consumer has become more demanding and often takes a "I-want-what-I-want-when-I-want-it" attitude toward communication, even when such demands are unreasonable or impossible to satisfy. Moreover, in order to compete for attention, organizations now have to promise better and faster technology to differentiate themselves from others and establish themselves as a premier provider of services. The danger, according to the Technology–Image Expectancy Gap Theory, is that in order to get attention and appear competitive, the organization has to promise better products, as well as better and faster service (see Pellet, 2002, for examples). This process of escalation increases expectations and the probability of disappointment.

A third major change is that communication is becoming more access-driven According to Kaye and Medoff (1998), it is driven by the audiences accessing the Web to get information. The Web is becoming the tool of choice for individuals seeking to retrieve specific information quickly. Organizations had better be sure they are providing it through their official channels of communication, or publics might get the information from unofficial sources that may be biased against the organization. The dilemma here is that the organization may be forced to offer access to services that may not be reliable, or to incorporate technology into their communications that requires expertise that is not available, resulting in a higher risk of failure and stakeholder dissatisfaction.

The fourth and final change predicted by Kaye and Medoff (1998) in the characteristics of communication change is that the emergence of on-line communication makes organizations able to break down their segments into microsegments. Targeted messages are often the ultimate goal of communication, based on the assumption that they are the most powerful form of communication. Through advanced database management systems that can track on-line information on customers and visitors, and through the use of real-time dynamic Web pages, organizations are able to personalize the communication. The inherent danger here is that whereas some organizations have the ability and resources to supply targeted access to services, many organizations do not. Thus, although the organizations that do offer such services gain credibility, smaller or less capable organizations may lose credibility because generalized expectations are created in the minds of stakeholders and consumers.

Net Relations

With the growth of technology and the Internet, organizations are now faced with a growing demand to provide services, information, and products online. In many ways the on-line arena has become the face of the organization in the 21st century. Because of this shift, the term *net relations* has begun to be used as a theoretical and practical framework for the management of relationships through the Internet. Mike Spataro first introduced the term in 1998. He defines *net relations* as "the intersection of traditional direct marketing, public relations and the Internet" (p. 16) and as media relations on the Internet. Moreover, net relations "combines direct marketing and public relations to deliver messages directly to the audience as well as using online writers to reach audiences. It includes communicating directly with target audiences by delivering information directly to them or by attracting them to web sites where that information resides" (pp. 16–17).

The definition of *net relations* is based on an approach to public relations that is oriented toward the simultaneous management of symbolic and behavioral relationships (Grunig, 1993). Likewise, Botan (1992) suggested that public relations is the use of communication to negotiate relationships among different groups. A general definition of net relations can be derived from these perspectives: *Net relations is the management of relationships between an organization and all its relevant publics through the use of the Internet and Web technology.*

The Internet as a Symbolic Reality

Rapid advancements in technology have created a new high-velocity phenomenon in the financial world, which some call webonomics (Schwartz, 1997). Because of the intense pressure to compete in this new "tech economy," businesses are expanding their marketing and sales strategies to the Internet— not to mention all the remaining dot-coms that are competing for a chunk of a projected market size of $300–600 billion worldwide in 2005. Subsequently, corporations worldwide are moving from a physical presence/location to a virtual presence/location. All together, this means that the interaction between an organization and its audience will increasingly be carried out through the use of Web sites. Images and symbols are exchanged through a Web site, and publics interact with organization via the Web. Because the Internet is virtual, so also is the experience of the people using the Internet: The use of the technology and its interface is the experience on which memories and judgments are based. Through the interaction between users and an organization's Web site, a virtual reality is created—*virtual* in the sense that it only exists through the interaction and exchange of messages and manifested in the experience of the reader. For some people, the experience might even share some of the characteristics of hyper-reality, as described by Baudrillard (1983). Thus, the reality, as the reader experiences it, is a symbolic reality created trough the exchange of symbols. The receiver brings into this reality her own set of expectations regarding the ability of the organization to meet her needs, respect her values, and provide high quality service.

This has implications for the public relations practitioner. Public relations, according to Grunig (1993), is concerned with both symbolic and behavioral relationships. He considers long-term behavioral relationships to be the essence of public relations, but he does not dismiss symbolic relationships. According to Grunig, "symbolic and behavioral relationships are intertwined like strands of a rope" (p. 123). This is certainly true for Net relations as well. Nevertheless, we believe that because the Internet can be described as a virtual environment, the symbolic component of relationship management on-line may be emphasized compared to the behavioral. The symbolic component of relationship building is for the most part concerned with the image of the organization. This basically suggests a stronger emphasis on the messages and images that the organization communicates through the Internet. At the very least, it suggests that PR practitioners should be aware that an organization's Web site (and the degree to which it meets expectations) will be the primary communication vehicle that carries and promotes the image of the organization.

THE IMAGE OF TECHNOLOGY

Corporations, organizations, and individuals are dependent on their images, and they deal with this in different ways. The image is essential for every open system dealing with its surroundings. A number of approaches to the concept of image have been suggested. Treadwell and Harrison (1994) explain that "image is often used to refer to representations of and organization that exist for an external public, but not exclusively so since the organizational images of members themselves are thought to be the basis for the development of public images" (p. 63). Researchers have conceived organizational image in various ways. Recently, it seems like the field is moving away from the notion that image is a single impression shared by an audience (Benoit, 1997). For example, Moffitt (1994), from a cultural studies approach, suggested the articulation model of meaning as a model for theorizing the process where audience members take on *multiple images* of a single organization. However, drawing on the different perspectives, and in accordance with Treadwell and Harrison (1994), we adopt a multifaceted approach, viewing image as "a set of cognitions, including beliefs, attitudes, as well as impressions about organizationally relevant behaviors, that a person holds with respect to an organization" (pp. 65–66). In contrast to some public relations approaches that view image as a result of the communicative efforts of an organization, we conceptualize image as "an individual's self-reported subjective responses to an organization emerging from any interaction, planned or unplanned, persuasive or non-persuasive, mediated or interpersonal" (p. 66). The current technology–expectancy theory suggests that those responses are a function of the discrepancy between expected and actual outcomes that occur through the use of technology or that are dependent on processes that rely on technology.

Impression Management Theory

We have noted that our society and the media have become "tech savvy" and very demanding of technology and information. To meet these expectations, and to succeed in the new arena of competing agendas and messages on-line

TABLE 16.1

Impression Motivation	Impression Construction
Goal-relevance of impression	Self-concept
Value of desired goals	Desired and undesired identity images
Discrepancy between desired and current image	Role constraint
image	Target's values
	Current or potential social image

in a technology-saturated environment, companies are forced to market their technological abilities to establish brand placement and brand differentiation. Given this drive for a positive technological image, impression management theories may be able to explain some of the important issues that should be taken into account in the framework of net relations. Although impression management theory is a symbiotic (interdisciplinary) communication theory derived from the social psychological school of research, we still believe that some of its basic components can be applied to the context of net relations, and in turn may have explanatory power.

According to Leary and Kowalski (1990), impression management "refers to the process by which individuals attempt to control the impressions others form of them" (p. 34) and involves two distinctly different processes. The first process they call impression motivation, and the second impression construction. *Impression motivation* is associated with "the desire to create particular impressions in other's minds" (p. 35), whereas *impression construction* deals with "how people may alter their behaviors to affect other's impressions of them" (p. 35). Both impression motivation and construction are affected by different factors. They are illustrated in the Table 16.1 (Leary & Kowalski, 1990, p. 36).

In general, impression management is a way to manipulate information available to others in order to control their impressions. Kacmar, Delery, and Ferris (1992) write that this manipulation can take "various general forms such as embellishing or withholding information available to others during an interaction, or more explicit forms, such as the specific verbal impression management tactics" (p. 1251). These tactics include *exemplification* (e.g., acting as a role model), *entitlements* (e.g., taking major responsibility for positive events in one's background), *enhancements* (e.g., attempting to increase the value of an event in order to make the outcome appear even more positive), *self-promotion* (e.g, describing positive attributes of oneself, in this case a high level of technological ability), *other enhancement* (e.g., flattering another person), *opinion conformity* (e.g., agreeing with other's opinions), *favor doing* (e.g., making other people owe you something), and *feigned helplessness* (e.g., trying to look helpless to make other people offer their help) (Kacmar et al., 1992).

In sum, the use of communication campaigns to bolster image, and thus affect the public's perception as suggested by impression management theory, can on the one hand generate unrealistic perceptions, while on the other hand it can help moderate these expectations. However, overpromotion of an organization's technological abilities to manage image can defeat attempts to create realistic perceptions of the organization's capabilities to produce and deliver high-quality goods and services.

THE TECHNOLOGY–IMAGE EXPECTANCY GAP

This theory posits that because so much of the media and the public eye is focused on technology, many organizations believe that technological advances must be an integral part of their existence. It is no longer good enough to be an organization that provides excellent products or services. To be successful today, an organization is almost required to have a technological presence. (There is general perception that to be "tech savvy" in the 21st century, an organization has to simply add an "E" to their name or brand.)

The problem with this approach to image marketing, this theory suggests, is that by touting the use of technology, organizations are more likely to create unrealistic expectations as to their ability to produce high-quality and reliable products, deliver fast, reliable service, or solve customer problems. Similarly, at the macro level, the intense media focus on technology also creates generalized expectations about every organization's ability to handle issues, monitor employee behavior, and to some extent compensate employees. Examples of where unrealistic expectations may have been created include the following:

- Successes in NASA's programs and the highlighting of its technology, even in the wake of the failures of the Mars probe program, created an unrealistic perception of the risks involved in space exploration, which has always been considered a high-risk endeavor. The investigation into the *Columbia* disaster (CAIB, 2003) acknowledges these misperceptions when the report notes, on p. 208:

> Because of the dangers of ascent and re-entry, because of the hostility of the space environment, and because we are still relative newcomers to this realm, operation of the Shuttle and indeed all human spaceflight must be viewed as a developmental activity. It is still far from a routine, operational undertaking. Throughout the *Columbia* accident investigation, the Board has commented on the widespread but erroneous perception of the Space Shuttle as somehow comparable to civil or military air transport.... The Board urges NASA leadership, the architects of U.S. space policy, and the American people to adopt a realistic understanding of the risks and rewards of venturing into space.

- The FDA has currently shut down experimental trials for genetically engineered treatments for disease. Although these trials were known to be of high risk, the recent highly publicized death of a teen undergoing treatments has motivated the FDA to stop the tests. The teen's parents complained that the risks were not communicated and that they were downplayed to get compliance. (Philipkoski, 2000)
- In 2000, Toys"R"us decided to compete in the *e*-commerce arena, launching ToysRus.com, and promising their customers to deliver toys for their children by Christmas. Although Toys"R"us was able to take thousands of orders, it did not have the similar capacity to deliver them on time, resulting in dissatisfied customers, bad press, and a costly consumer satisfaction program that awarded customers with delayed orders with a $100 gift certificate. (Bacheldor & Konicki, 2000)
- The call for investigations into intelligence failures and the extent to which the Bush administration could have predicted or prevented the attacks of September 11, 2001, are an example of unrealistic expectations regarding the performance of technology and the organizations that deploy it (Elliot et al., 2002; Isikoff, et al., 2002; Mann, 2002; Nather, Barstay, & McCutcheon, 2002).

Adding to the underlying threat to the stability of organizations is the notion many companies and organizations have that problems can't happen to them because they use so much technology. In other words, they put their trust in the technology (e.g., the disbelief surrounding the events of September 11th and the lack of forewarning). This ancillary prediction for the technology–expectancy gap suggests that perhaps employees of organizations begin to believe in their own marketing efforts, when they should instead be aware of their own technological limitations. Any doubts are limited, however, by a false sense of confidence in the availability of technology and its capability to reliably solve problems.

Technologically Based Expectancy Cycles

At a conceptual level, what this theory argues is that a cycle begins that creates larger and larger expectations from individuals and publics regarding the capabilities of organizations and their products or services. Society, the media, and individuals come to expect that companies can create products that are 100% reliable, are never defective, and are always safe, and that if individuals need to communicate, organizations will provide the means to do so effectively 24/7.

The advancement of technology has spawned a cycle where much of our lives revolve around the technologies we use, and we have become dependent on those technologies. Given the central focus and role of technology in our

FIG. 16.2   A model of the parallel expectancies created by the marketing of technology.

society, the media in turn focuses much of their attention on the technology, and perhaps often presents us with a unrealistic picture of how the technology is predicted to work, without providing an accurate picture of what it takes to get the technology to work, or its limitations.

Technology Can Create False Expectations

Moreover, this model suggests that two sets of false expectations are created. First, as technologies are presented and discussed in society and the media, a generalized sense of expectations is developed. This means that overall we expect better products, better and faster service, and more on the whole from technology. More importantly, when organizations emphasize their technological prowess or their technological abilities as part of their marketing efforts, they create organization-specific expectations, which may resonate with the generalized expectations that have already been cultivated. The model in Fig. 16.2 highlights this process.

Although this the technology–image expectancy gap model explains the motivation for organizations to overpromote their abilities, the role of the media in either creating or fueling this cycle is best explained by a number of theories from the literature on mass media effects.

AGENDA SETTING

Agenda-setting theory suggests that the media tells us not what to think, but what to think about. (For seminal research and reviews see McCombs, 1992; McCombs & Shaw, 1982, 1993). That is to say, the media often provides us with the topics that fill our daily conversations. Much of the public relations function is often oriented toward placing an issue on the "public agenda" or relating an issue into the current topics on the agenda.

In the 1990s a large part of the agenda was technology. As noted earlier, the rapid advancement in technology has created a new technology-based economy, where stock is bought and sold on the promises of technological advancement, products are becoming increasingly technically complex, and even the most basic of organizations is required to have a Web presence. These advances have put pressure on the media to report these advancements, to highlight changes in technology, and perhaps also to highlight the latest and greatest technologies that are available, without the accompanying qualifiers or limitations. A cycle has been created where society is enamored of and driven by technology, technologies are marketed using advertising and publicity-based strategies, the media reports on it, and in turn this drives society into a higher level of technological salience. The end result of all of these processes is to create the perception that to succeed, organizations must promote their technological abilities and their supremacy in the area of technological advancements relative to their competitors. Given a perceptual need to appear to be technologically advanced and part of the new economy, organizations secure or, better, develop technology that they can highlight. This of course creates competition among the developers of technology to supply their customers with faster and more powerful technology. This, when marketed, catches the media's attention, and they in turn report on the latest advances. In sum, an escalating cycle is created that drives both the expectations of technology and the actual advancement of technology to better meet the needs of a technologically hungry society.

CULTIVATION EFFECTS

Cultivation Theory suggests that the media (frequently the entertainment media) depict an unrealistic view of the world (for a review, see Gerbner, Gross, Morgan, & Signorelli, 1986, 1994). Additionally, other research suggests that the media play a large role in the construction of social reality (Searle, 1995) and may have effects on both lower-order and higher-order beliefs (Elliot, Kelly, & Byrd, 1992). Cultivation Theory suggests that heavy users of the media develop more unrealistic views of the world. Furthermore, this theory set also argues that the media often present unrealistic presentations across genres (and may even be spreading across news), so that consumption across genre and media type reinforces a false view of the world. Moreover, because some parts of the view depicted by the media are reflected in actual society and in the viewer's realm of direct experience, the perceptions will resonate and may become very convincing. Thus, the cultivation model predicts that these effects are more likely to occur among heavy users.

However, in contrast to cultivation theory, the technology–image expectancy gap model suggests that a curvilinear relationship exists between use of the media and the expectations from technology and organizations. In classic cultivation theory, a linear relationship is predicted to exist between the use of media and unrealistic perceptions. Examples include heavy news viewing and unrealistic expectations of the world, and heavy use of pornography and unrealistic expectations of relational partners. However, the technology expectancy

Moderate Media Use

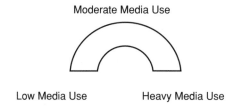

Low Media Use   Heavy Media Use

FIG. 16.3   A representation of media use and unrealistic expectations.

gap predicts a curvilinear relationship between use of the media and unrealistic expectations (see Fig. 16.3). In this model the low media consumer is not familiar with technological advances. Because this consumer pays little attention to consuming media and has little exposure to information about technology, he or she is less likely to develop unrealistic expectations.

In contrast, the heavy consumer of media, especially technology-specific media, will be exposed to a great deal of information about the capabilities of new technology, including its limitations. In this case, although an initial expectation may be created, over time the consumer will obtain more information on the actual performance of the technology, qualifying its abilities. The end result is a more accurate view of the ability of new technology, and hence of the ability of organizations to use that technology to deliver goods and services.

The distinction between the light consumer of media and the heavy viewer is thus twofold. The light consumer of media is less likely to have unrealistic expectations created. In contrast, the heavy consumer is initially likely to have the expectation created, but in time those expectations are put in perspective because information regarding the actual abilities and limitations of the technology is eventually obtained.

The largest effects in this model are predicted to be on the moderate consumer of media. These individuals will be exposed to enough information about technology that expectations are created, but are less likely to get more in-depth information on the specific abilities and limitations of the technology and the way that organizations can use that technology to deliver goods and services.

BREAKING THE TECHNOLOGY–EXPECTANCY CYCLE

It might be easy to suggest a fast way to break this expectancy cycle: to not use technology to promote the image of the organization. This logic fails on several accounts. First, this theory argues that societal focus on technology coupled with intensive media coverage fosters at least a moderate generalized level of expectation regarding the production and delivery of goods and services. So although an individual organization may refrain from using a technology-based image appeal with a goal of managing organization-specific expectations, that organization's stakeholders may still have an increased generalized level of expectations due to media and societal exposure to advances in technology. The question, therefore, is how to deal with both the general and specific expectations created about the organizations' abilities to deliver goods and services.

The answer lies in a public relations theory that often receives much attention: Grunig's two-way model (Grunig & Hunt, 1984), better known as two-way communication. The two-way model suggests that organizations gather information from relevant publics and use that information to balance the good of the publics with the activities of the organization. To avoid creating this expectancy–reality gap, organizations need to monitor publics' expectations regarding their products, services, or behavior. Communication strategies have to be developed to reflect the organization's best abilities without creating false expectations. This application of the two-way model requires frequent monitoring to gauge the level of generalized as well as specific expectations generated by the increased focus on technology. Carefully tracking expectations and creating targeted messages to help maintain a realistic sense of expectations is the best defense against disappointment and dissatisfaction. Some business-related examples of such behavior are reported by Pellet (2002): anecdotal evidence provided by a number of CEOs who claim that they only way to stay ahead of consumers' often unrealistic expectations is to carefully monitor their needs and learn what they expect before producing and marketing products and services.

TESTING TECHNOLOGY–IMAGE EXPECTANCY GAP THEORY

Testability implies that the ability to be falsified is a requirement for any theory. The theory presented in this chapter makes a number of very specific predictions regarding the impact of media coverage of technology, stakeholder exposure to information about technology, and stakeholder expectations regarding technology and an organization's ability to deliver goods and services. The theory sets out a set of testable propositions, which are outlined here:

> *Proposition 1.* As technological advancements become more of a focus in a society, so will the generalized expectations that individuals will have regarding the uses of that technology.

> *Proposition 2.* As technological advancements become more of a focus in a society, the media through the agenda-setting process will devote more coverage and discussion to technology and technology-based issues.

> *Proposition 3.* As the media increase their coverage of technological innovations, the number of unrealistic expectations will also increase. This may be manifested by unrealistic expectations about the quality of

products and services in general, and perhaps in the underassessment of risks in traditionally risk-laden activities.

Proposition 4. As the media focus on technology increases, organizations (particularly those that are publicly traded) will increase the emphasis of technology in their image-building, image-enhancing, and reputation-management strategies.

Proposition 5. As organizations increase their emphasis on technology as part of their image, the specific expectations regarding the quality of goods, products, services, and behavior will also increase.

Proposition 6. Organizations can moderate the expectancy gap by monitoring relevant publics' perceptions and expectancies, and by creating message strategies that are targeted at creating more realistic expectations of organizational abilities.

Research to test these propositions is currently in progress. No matter what the outcome, identifying public relations processes and strategies that affect organizational performance is of the utmost importance to a field that may still be in its infancy. If public relations scholars want to be taken seriously by scientists and humanistic researchers, they must begin to identify processes that may be unique to the public relations process and can contribute to the practice of that discipline.

REFERENCES

Bacheldor, B., & Konicki, S. (2000, August 7). Long arm of the law. *Information Week.* http://www.informationweek.com/798/ftc.htm.

Baudrillard, J. (1983). The ecstasy of communication. In Foster (Ed.), *The anti-aesthetic: Essays on postmodern culture.* Townsend, WA: Bay Press.

Benoit, W. L. (1997). Image repair discourse and crisis communication. *Public Relations Review, 23*(2), 177–186.

Botan, C. (1992). International public relations critique and reformulation. *Public Relations Review, 18*(2), 149–159.

Carter, R. F., Stamm, K. R., & Heintz-Knowles (1992). Agenda setting and consequentiality. *Journalism Quarterly, 69,* 868–877.

Columbia Accident Investigation Board (CAIB) (2003). *Columbia Accident Investigation Board Report* (Vol. 1, p. 208).

Elliott, M., Calabresi, M., Carney, J., Duffy, Michael, Shannon, E., Waller, D., Weisskopf, M., Schwartz, D., Crumley, B., & McAllister, J. (2002). How the U.S. missed the clues. *Time, 159*(21), 24–31.

Elliot, W. R., Kelly, J. D., & Byrd, J. T. (1992). *Synthetic history and subjective reality: The impact of Oliver Stone's JFK.* Paper presented at the communication and research methodology division of AEJMC, MontreaL, Canada. [Note: Description and citation taken from Severin, W., & Tankard, J. W. (1997). *Communication theories: Origins, methods, and uses in the mass media* (p. 318). New York: Longman.]

Fidler, R. (1997). *Media morphosis: understanding media*. Thousand Oaks, CA: Pine Forge Press.

Fiur, Merton. (1988). Public relations faces the 21st century. In R. Hiebert (Ed.), *Precision Public Relations* (pp. 337–355).

Fishbein, M. (1967a). A behavior theory approach to the relations between beliefs about an object and the attitude toward the object. In M. Fishbein (Ed.), *Readings in attitude theory and measurement* (pp. 389–400). New York: Wiley.

Fishbein, M. (1967b). A consideration of beliefs, and their role in attitude measurement. In M. Fishbein (Ed.), *Readings in attitude theory and measurement* (pp. 257–266). New York: Wiley.

Gerbner, G., Gross, L., Morgan, M., & Signorelli, N. (1986). Living with television: The dynamics of the cultivation process. In J. Bryant and D. Zillman (Eds.), *Perspectives on media effects*, pp. 17–40. Hillsdale, NJ: Lawrence Erlbaum Associates.

Gerbner, G., Gross, L., morgan, M., and Signorelli, N. (1994). Growing up with television: The cultivation perspective. In J. Bryant and D. Zillman (Eds.), *Media effects: Advances in theory and research* (pp. 17–41). Hillsdale, NJ: Lawrence Erlbaum Associates.

Grunig, J. E. (1993). Image and substance: From symbolic to behavioral relationships. *Public Relations Review, 19*(2), 121–139.

Hansen, G. (1998). Smaller may be better for web marketing. *Marketing News, 32*(2), 10–13.

Holtz, S. (1999). *Public relations on the Net*. New York: Amacom.

Isikoff, M., Klaidman, D., Hosenball, M., Lipper, T., Clift, E., Murr, A., & Reno, J. (2002, June 10). The hijackers we let escape. *Newsweek, 139*(23), 20–28.

Iyengar, S., Peters, M. D., and Kinder, D. R. (1982). Experimental demonstrations of the "not-so-minimal" consequences of television news programs. *American Political Science Review, 76*, 848–858.

Kacmar, K. M., Delery, J. E., & Ferris, G. R. (1992). Differential effectiveness of applicant impression management tactics on employment interview decisions. *Journal of Applied Social Psychology, 22* 1250–1272.

Kaye, B. K., & Medoff, N. J. (1998). *The World Wide Web: A mass communication perspective*. Mountain View, CA: Mayfield.

Kravitz, R. L. (2000). Direct-to-consumer advertising of prescription drugs: Implications for the patient–physician relationship. *Journal of the American Medical Association, 284*, 2244.

Leary, M. R., & Kowalski, R. M. (1990). Impression management: A literature review and two-component model. *Psychological Bulletin, 107*, 34–47.

Mann, P. (2002). White house firmly denies hijacking intelligence failure. *Aviation Week & Space Technology, 156*(20), 19.

McCombs, M. E. (1992). Explorers and surveyors: Expanding strategies for agenda setting research. *Journalism Quarterly, 69*, 813–824.

McCombs, M. E., & Shaw, D. L. (1982). The agenda setting function of mass media. *Public Opinion Quarterly, 36*, 176–187.

McCombs, M. E., & Shaw, D. L. (1993). The evolution of agenda setting research: Twenty five years in the marketplace of ideas. *Journal of Communication, 43*, 58–67.

Moffitt, M. A. (1994). Collapsing and integrating concepts of "public" and "image" into a new theory. *Public Relations Review, 20*, 159–170.

Nather, D., Barstay, J., & McCutcheon, C. (2002, May 25). Politics muddies the waters around the September 11th investigation. *CQ Weekly*, 1366–1369.

Oliver, R. L. (1980). A cognitive model of the antecedents and consequences of satisfaction decisions. *Journal of Marketing Research, 17*, 460–469.

Oliver, R. L. (1993). Cognitive, affective and attribute bases of the satisfaction response. *Journal of Consumer Research, 20*, 418–430.

Oliver, R. L. (1994). Conceptual issues in the structural analysis of consumption emotion, satisfaction and quality. *Advances in Consumer Research, 21*, 16–22.

Oliver, R. L., & Bearden, W. (1983). The role of involvement in satisfaction processes. *Advances in Consumer Research, 10*, 250–255.

Oliver, R. L., & DeSarbo, W. (1988). Response determinants in satisfaction judgments. *Journal of Consumer Research, 14*, 495–507. *Management, 6*, 17–33.

Palvik, J. (1996). *New media technologies.* Boston: Allyn and Bacon.

Pellet, J. (2002). Unleashing the power of the consumer-driven profit machine. *Chief Executive, 181*, 78–84.

Philipkosi, K. (1999). Another chance for gene therapy? http://www.wired.com/news/technology/0,1282,34148,00.html.

Philipkosi, K. (2000). Science + Business: A Bad Mix? http://www.wired.com/news/technology/0,1282,34148,00.html.

Saffo, P. (1992). Paul Saffo and the 30 year rule. *Design World, 24*, 18.

Schwartz, E. L. (1997). *Webonomics.* New York: Broadway.

Searle, J. (1995). *The social construction of reality.* New York: Free Press.

Spataro, M. (1998). Net relations: a fusion of direct marketing and public relations. *Direct Marketing, 61*(4), 16–20.

Spreng, R. A., & Olshavsky, R. W. (1993). A desires congruency model of consumer satisfaction. *Journal of the Academy of Marketing Science, 21*(3), 169–177.

Spreng, R. A., MacKenzie, S. B., & Olshavsky, R. W. (1996). A re-examination of the determinants of consumer satisfaction. *Journal of Marketing. 60*(3), 15–32.

The vulnerabilities we cherish. (2001, September 12). [Editorial]. *The Chicago Tribune*, sec. 1, p. 22.

Treadwell, D. F., & Harrison, T. M. (1994). Conceptualizing and assessing organizational image: Model images, commitment, and communication. *Communication Monographs, 61*, 63–85.

Ware, T. (2001, Sept. 24). Bush: We're at war. *Newsweek, 138*(13), 26–35.

Westbrook, R. A., & Oliver, R. L. (1981). Developing better measures of consumer satisfaction: Some preliminary results. *Advances in Consumer Research, 8*, 94–99.

West, J. (1996). Utopianism and national competitiveness in technology rhetoric: The case of Japan's technology infrastructure. *The Information Society, 12*, 257–272.

Zillmann, D. (1999). Exemplification Theory: Judging the whole by some of it's parts. *Media Psychology, 1*, 69–94.

Public Diplomacy: A Specific Governmental Public Relations Function

Benno Signitzer and Carola Wamser

University of Salzburg, Austria

Our world is diverse, complex, and intertwined. Challenges are no longer confined within the borders of a single nation, but they are truly global in scope. The combined forces of the telecommunications revolution, the world-wide spread of democracy and market economies are placing foreign publics at center stage (USAC, 1999, p. 1)—for multinational corporations as well as for nation-states. Both have to pursue "communication across international boundaries for the procurement of certain objectives" (Sonnesyn & Williams, 1999, p. 1), and the respective communication functions of (international) public relations and public diplomacy should thus show a certain degree of conceptual convergence. Nonetheless, to date these two fields have little in common; they act mostly separately from one another; they do not have a common culture; and they do not form a community—either academically or professionally. While the business side treats the planned establishment of relations with publics of other nations under international public relations (and hence in the domain of public relations), the management of communicative relationships of nation-states, countries, or societies remains largely in the academic home of international relations (as a part of political science).

This divide leads to the conclusion that, at the moment, public relations theory may be well suited to explain and to predict the communication behavior of ordinary organizations in both the profit and nonprofit fields, whereas theories of international relations are better suited to the understanding of diplomacy, "the management of international relations" (Webster cit., after Sonnesyn & Williams 1999, p. 1).

But does this divide make sense? The assumption that overcoming this divide can be more than fruitful for both areas is strengthened by developments in the field of international relations. Formal political relations are becoming more and more closely connected with actors other than national governments. There is a shift away from the traditional, state-level diplomacy[1] and toward public, citizen-level diplomacy.[2] There is a shift from the level of government-to-government/diplomat-to-diplomat to the level of government-to-people (of foreign countries), respectively, people-to-people (Manheim, 1990). And this shift brings about even more similarities between public relations and international relations, explicitly between public relations and the branch of international relations known as public (and cultural) diplomacy.

In the following, we explore areas and possibilities for the integration of public diplomacy with public relations. To do so we address three crucial areas. First, we define public diplomacy and its related concepts to clarify the theoretic background and establish a common understanding of where we are starting. Second, we look into similarities and differences of both public diplomacy and public relations in practice and theory. In practice we do so by looking at their role in an organized whole, their functional equivalence, and economic and political conditions. In theory we do so by examining their academic history and compatibility regarding levels of analysis and various strategic concepts and theories. This allows us insight into what a common future of public diplomacy and public relations could look like. Third, we discuss what could be done to enhance public relations' and public diplomacy's convergence and consider future research concerns.

---

[1] Traditional diplomacy has been practiced by nations since their inception and was formalized at the 1648 Treaty of Westphalia (Sonnesyn & Williams, 1999, p. 1).

[2] Public diplomacy, which opens the doors of international relations to proactive global citizens, has existed for generations, but has only been recognized as a valid model for conducting international affairs in the last decades. Though relatively new, it is now undoubtedly the emerging trend in the diplomatic field (Sonnesyn & Williams, 1999, p. 1).

PUBLIC DIPLOMACY DEFINED: A CONCEPTUAL OUTLINE
AND OUTLOOK

"Strictly defined, the field of International Relations (IR) concerns the relation-ships among the world's national governments" (Goldstein 1994, p. 1). And, strictly defined, (traditional) diplomacy concerns the "art of conducting nego-tiations between governments" (Deutsch, 1966, p. 81). But what if we are less strict? That international relations have changed: international relations are now—as the world economy becomes globally integrated—closely connected with (1) additional actors such as inter-[3] and nongovernmental organizations,[4] substate actors[5] that are increasingly also becoming transnational actors[6] and individuals, and (2) other social relationships such as economics and culture. Because of the exponential growth in instantaneous global communications, combined with the rapid spread of democratic institutions and market-oriented economies, the close connection between foreign and domestic politics, grow-ing mass participation in foreign politics, and the mediatization of politics, international relations have now begun to extend beyond the interactions of national governments (PDF, 1999a, Signitzer 1993, p. 201). Hence, modern diplomacy has changed, too, and is now defined as being "concerned with the management of relations between states and between states and other ac-tors" (Barston, 1997, p. 1). The inclusion of other actors acknowledges the novel types of interactions, described with terms such as *public diplomacy, cultural diplomacy*, and *media diplomacy*. According to some practitioners in the field, these interactions may make up 90% of diplomacy (PDF, 1999a, p. 1).

The core idea of public diplomacy can be seen as "one of direct commu-nication with foreign peoples, with the aim of affecting their thinking and,

---

[3] Intergovernmental organizations (IGOs) are "organizations whose members are national gov-ernments": e.g. UN, World Bank, OPEC, NATO (Goldstein, 1994, p. 11).

[4] Nongovernmental organizations (NGOs) are private organizations that interact with states, multinational corporations, and other NGOs and are increasingly "being recognized, in the UN and other forums, as legitimate actors along with states, though not equal to them" (Goldstein, 1994, p. 11). Some of them have a humanitarian purpose, and some a political, technical, or economic one. Examples for NGOs are Greenpeace, the Catholic Church, and the International Studies Association.

[5] Substate actors are groups within states that operate below the state level and influence the state's foreign policy through political action committees, lobbying, and other means. Such substate actors are, for instance, certain branches of industry, which have interests in foreign economic policy (to reduce imports of competing products made abroad, etc.), and farmers who wish to influence their governments' positions in negotiations concerning agricultural trade (Goldstein, 1994, p. 9f).

[6] When actors operating below the state level also operate across state borders, they are becoming transnational actors. Very influential transnational actors are the thousands of multinational corporations (MNCs) (Goldstein, 1994, p. 10f.).

ultimately, that of their governments" (Malone, 1985, p. 199). It is based on the assumption that in a more democratic world, people do have an increasing influence on the positions, policies, and attitudes of their elected governments. It makes a lot of political sense to deal with those people, consider their views, and help them understand the ideals and policy of a foreign country along with the full spectrum of its citizens' diverse opinions (PDF, 1999a, p. 1). In terms of content, the range of public diplomacy extends from (1) a press interview of the American President with Russian journalists in the run-up to a state visit in Russia, in which the position of the United States on a point at issue might be stated and explained (level: government-to-peoples), to (2) a staff exchange program between U.S. and Austrian universities (level: people-to-people). These examples mark the end points of a continuum of possible strategies and functions of public diplomacy as ideal types. The press interview serves the purpose of persuasion of foreign publics, whereas the staff exchange program aims at mutual understanding between domestic and foreign publics. This dualism of purpose and outlook is also reflected in definitions by public diplomacy practitioners. Whereas Malone (1988, p. 3) sees the aim of public diplomacy as influencing "the behavior of a foreign government by influencing the attitudes of its citizens," Tuch (1990, p. 3) is of the opinion that "public diplomacy is a government's process of communicating with foreign publics in an attempt to bring about understanding for its nation's ideas and ideals, its institutions and cultures, as well as its national goals and current policies."

These differing views go back to an interesting distinction developed by Deibel and Roberts (1976), using concepts advanced by James (1955). They distinguished between the tough-minded and the tender-minded schools in public diplomacy, between *political information* (persuasion) and *cultural communication* (understanding). The tough-minded want to exert influence on attitudes of foreign audiences using persuasion and propaganda, conveying hard political information through *fast media* such as radio, television, newspapers, and news magazines to attain fairly short-term policy ends. The tender-minded school sees public diplomacy as a predominantly cultural function that—in the long-range—should create a climate of mutual understanding through *slow media* such as academic and artistic exchanges, films, exhibitions, and language instruction. Political information is usually administered by a political section of the foreign ministry or by a political secretary of an embassy and, hence, rather close to political decision makers; cultural communication, on the other hand, is mostly entrusted to a cultural section of the foreign ministry, a cultural institute abroad, or some type of semiautonomous body (e.g., the Fulbright Commission, the British Council, or the German Goethe Institute). These distinctions and others that follow in this section are articulated in Fig. 17.1.

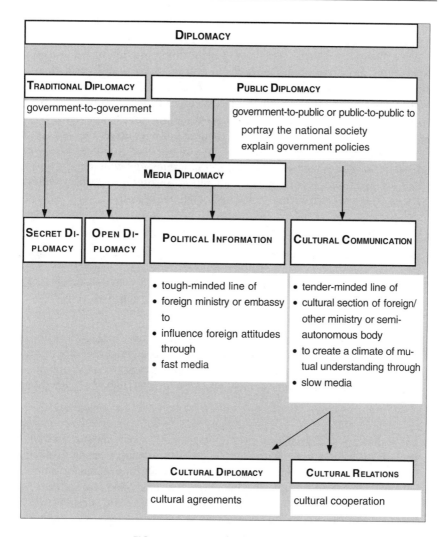

FIG. 17.1   System of public diplomacy.

This distinction was later confirmed by Malone (1988, pp. 3–4) with some slight modification. He calls the political information side of public diplomacy *political advocacy* and sees in cultural communication not only the purpose to "help foreign citizens gain a better understanding of the United States, its culture and institutions" but also to foster "mutual understanding between our people and those of other countries." This alludes to the convergence model of communication by Rogers and Kincaid (1981), who define communication as a "process in which the participants create and share information with one another in order to reach a mutual understanding" (p. 63).

A level below this distinction is the further differentiation of cultural communication into cultural diplomacy and cultural relations. British theorist Mitchell (1986)[7] describes *cultural diplomacy* as the creation of cultural agreements in the formal sense, and its goal as the conveyance of a favorable image of one's culture abroad with a view toward facilitation of diplomatic activities as a whole. *Cultural relations*, in contrast, is viewed as the "execution of these agreements and the conduct of cultural relations flowing from them" and, hence, as the content side of cultural communication, which might be delegated by governments to agencies and cultural institutions. Ideally, cultural relations does not look for unilateral advantage, but tries to

> achieve understanding and cooperation between national societies for their mutual benefit. Cultural relations proceed ideally by the accretion of open professional exchanges rather than by selective self-projection. They convey an honest picture of each country rather than a beautified one. They do not conceal but neither need to make a show of national problems. (Mitchell, 1986, p. 5)

These conceptual distinctions between the mutual understanding and the persuasion dimensions of public diplomacy notwithstanding, constant oscillations between the two (Burke, 1966; Miller, 1989) appear to be the rule rather than the exception and become evident when we look at Tuch's[8] (1990) choice of words:

> Public diplomacy, in its attempt to affect the attitudes and opinions of foreign publics, involves the entire communications spectrum, modern communication technology as well as such other methods of intercultural communication as cultural and educational exchange, libraries, publications, and people (among them professionally qualified Foreign Service officers). And it includes our own learning experience, because we must understand the hopes, fears and hang-ups of other peoples if we are going to be successful in persuading them to understand us. (p. 10)

The centrality of this perpetual change led Malone (1988) at one point to question the usefulness of the generic term *public diplomacy*, as it suggests

---

[7] The focus is here on cultural communication because political information currently lacks further differentiation (except the study of press attaches; e.g., de Jong, 1977); Fankhauser, 1985; Fischer, 1985.

[8] Tuch's definition earlier in this section could be seen as an example of the tender-minded approach to public diplomacy.

more conceptual and empirical unity than there actually is[9] or even should be. Critics of this concept have further pointed out that it may lead to the misunderstanding that public diplomacy was the mere exposure of traditional diplomacy (e.g., state visits) to the media, public opinion and the glare of publicity (for which the term *open diplomacy* is usually employed).

So, should the public diplomacy concept be pursued, or should alternatives be sought? Arguments for its use are its broad acceptance both in practice and in academic discourse and its relative consistency in regard to the foreign policy concept—namely through the component *diplomacy*, which denotes the level of implementation of foreign policy (Pitterle, 1995). But the very connection with the foreign policy system is also a certain drawback, as this orientation may tend to neglect the international relations system in which an ever larger part of the (strategic) communicative relations of nation-states take place.

A somewhat broadened concept of public diplomacy may be tentatively termed *international nation public relations* or, alternatively, *international governmental public relations*. It would address the international dimension of communication and allow the integration of views, which postulate the growing interconnectedness of national and international levels.[10] The element *nation* connects the concept with the political system and helps to clarify relationships with the many actors who differ in regard to closeness or distance to the nation state; the *public relations* component emphasizes the communicative dimension and makes its store of theories and experienced instruments accessible to public diplomacy—a store whose potential is explored through delineations of conceptual convergence and combined models of international nation/governmental public relations and public relations as such in the following sections. Still, for the sake of clarity, the *public diplomacy* concept will be used throughout this chapter, albeit vested with the enlarged meaning as discussed earlier.[11]

PUBLIC DIPLOMACY AND PUBLIC RELATIONS: SIMILARITIES AND DIFFERENCES

Both public relations and public diplomacy are strategic communicative functions of either organizations or nation-states, and typically deal with the reciprocal consequences a sponsor and its publics have upon each other.

---

[9] A theoretical analysis of the whole complex of public diplomacy is lacking.

[10] Pitterle (1995), for example, distinguishes between *internal* and *external* foreign-policy public relations.

[11] This also testifies to the view that it is not newly coined wrapping that entails the convergence of concepts, but the substance of the phenomenon itself.

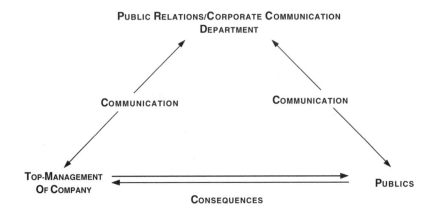

FIG. 17.2 Model of the public relations function in an organization (adopted from Grunig & Hunt, 1984, p. 10).

These consequences upon one another create a public relations problem, which is illustrated by Grunig and Hunt's (1984) "Model of the Public Relations Function in an Organization" (Fig. 17.2).

The arrows at the base of the triangle indicate that organizations and publics have reciprocal consequences for each other, which explains why organizations need public relations. An organization's management decisions may have consequences for publics. And when publics learn about these consequences, they often take actions that have consequences for the organization, whether good or bad.

The arrows that form the sides of the triangle show how a public relations department functions to solve public relations problems. Generally, the role of a public relations department is two-way communication with both management and publics. In communicating with publics, the public relations department seeks to explain the organization to publics through the mass media or interpersonally and to learn how the publics view the organization through more or less formal research. In communicating with management, it provides counsel on the publics' points of view so that management has the benefit of that knowledge when making decisions. And the public relations department has to listen to management, to understand its decisions and behaviors, so that it can explain them to publics.

Adapted to public diplomacy, the model in Fig. 17.2 looks like that shown in Fig. 17.3.

Again, the arrows at the base of the triangle indicate that a government and publics have reciprocal consequences for each other. The arrows that form the sides of the triangle show how public diplomacy departments function to solve public diplomacy problems, fulfilling the same functions as PR departments do for organizations.

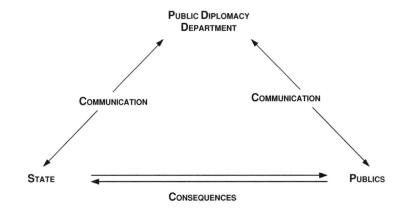

FIG. 17.3   Model of the public diplomacy function (adopted from Figure 17.2, by Grunig & Hunt, 1984, p. 10).

Both public relations and public diplomacy personnel are performing a boundary-spanning role[12]: "They function at the edge of the organization [organized whole/state], serving as a liaison between the organization [state] and the external groups and individuals. They have one foot in the organization and one outside" (Grunig & Hunt, 1984, p. 9). Both diplomats and public relations practitioners are "crossing cultures (whether organizational or national) and bridging cultural gaps" (L'Etang, 1996, p. 16).

Functional Equivalence

Both diplomats and public relations practitioners—following organizational and communication literature and particularly L'Etang's metaphorical approach (1996)—fulfill the functions of intelligence gathering (research, environmental scanning), being representational (rhetoric, oratory, advocacy), dialogic (negotiation, peacemaking), and advisory (counseling).

Whereas intelligence gathering underscores the issues management function and conjures up connotations of "a military function carried out at least partly secretly" (L'Etang, 1996, p. 15), representational functions need to be passed on to the public. This implies strategies of promotion and persuasion. In contrast to this, neutrality and mutuality are stressed by dialogic metaphors. Counseling activities are (or at least should be) the result of the other functions taken together of an evaluation of the situation in regard to goals and an election of alternative strategies of communication (including the respective instruments) to reach those goals.

---

[12] In public diplomacy, the term *boundary role* even has a literal meaning.

Obviously, these various functional approaches to public relations as well as public diplomacy practice must not be seen in isolation from one another. They are interwoven, and more than one is used in the course of a relationship[13] and the management of public opinion. This constitutes a mastery whose power public relations scholars have long recognized: "The power of public opinion must be faced, understood, and dealt with. It provides the psychological environment in which organizations prosper or perish" (Cutlip & Center, 1958, p. 58). Nicolson (1954, p. 51), for example, a diplomat himself, says that the thinking that "no policy could succeed unless it had national opinion behind it" goes back to Richelieu, who was also the first to introduce a system of domestic propaganda[14] (Nicolson, 1954, pp. 51–52).

Economic and Political Conditions

But it is not only the similar functions public relations and public diplomacy practitioners have to fulfill. It is also that both spheres are becoming more and more intertwined in our times: "Numerous large organizations today explicitly act in a political manner and see themselves as doing so" (Cheney & Vibbert, 1987, p. 188). As many multinational organizations are economically as big as or bigger than small or developing countries, governments are highly dependent on industries, which then consciously develop their own political goals and have "direct political influence without being identified as political groups" (Cheney & Vibbert, 1987, p. 188). This "may lead to the formation of a wider diplomatic culture within which an extended chain of agency relationships exists; these agency relationships may not be formalized or even recognized" (L'Etang, 1996, p.18).

Whether intended or not, public relations and public diplomacy are growing together in practice:

> Public diplomacy combines the skills of the traditional diplomat with those of the specialist in mass communication and the social researcher. The diplomat formulates the ideas that he [sic] would like to have communicated to a foreign public, the social researcher studies the intended audience, and the communications specialist chooses the most appropriate media and composes the messages. (Davison,[15] 1976, p. 399)

Following practical developments, the time to attempt a coordination of theoretical concepts, theories, and models appears to have come.

---

[13] This takes us back to the comments on advocacy and mutual understanding.
[14] Richelieu used pamphlets to educate and "create a body of informed opinion favorable to his policies" (Nicolson, 1954, p. 51).
[15] W. Phillips Davison was one of public diplomacy's earliest academic professionals.

THEORY: ON ITS WAY TO CONVERGENCE?

Academic History

Looking at the development of public diplomacy and public relations within academia, one is surprised that both pursued separate tracks and that there has been little or no discussion about convergence. In fact, they do share much common ground:

1. Public diplomacy and public relations are dealing with similar phenomena, showing strong relations to specifically defined areas of practical application. At times, this basis in practice produces tensions between academics and practitioners because of their differing perspectives. Besides, it can be "difficult for academics to obtain access to certain types of information or activity regarded as politically or commercially sensitive" (L'Etang, 1996, p. 25).

2. Both fields have, in practice, quite long traditions and even antecedents in classical literature: What Aristotle's *The Art of Rhetoric* and Plato's *Gorgias* are for public relations, Thucydide's *History of the Peloponnesian War* and Machiavelli's *The Prince* are for diplomacy.

3. Both are relatively new fields of academic study and facing similar problems: German scholars Ronneberger and Rühl (1992, p. 10) find faults with deficits in academic public relations research and a lack of an institutionalized scientific community. Similarly, L'Etang (1996) complains about the dearth of theoretical work on diplomacy within the field of international relations. And whatever work is available on diplomacy is often of the "how-to" variety[16] (as is the majority of the work in public relations). Diplomacy is "not, therefore, seen as a field of study in itself, but as a technique used to achieve certain ends" (L'Etang, 1996, p. 24). Lack of knowledge and dependence on other disciplines lead to disputes followed by harsh methodological debates between the Traditionalists[17] and the Behavioralists.[18] Hence, public diplomacy as well as public relations must be prepared to face ongoing epistemological and methodological debates, questions of boundaries, legitimacy, credibility and ethic.

---

[16] Examples describing diplomatic customs precedent, but including no theoretical debate, are *Satow's Guide to Diplomatic Practice* (Gore-Boothe, 1978), first published in 1917 and still used by the British Foreign and Commonwealth Office, and Nicolson's *The Evolution of the Diplomatic Method*, asserting that the essence of diplomacy is common sense (a view held by many practitioners as well, which is another similarity to public relations).

[17] The Traditionalists thought accurate prediction to be impossible in the field of international relations.

[18] The Behavioralists argued that "all assumptions should be clearly spelt out and only empirically verifiable hypotheses should be produced" (L'Etang, 1996, 27).

4. Both are responding to similar intellectual currents such as systems theory (which was quite influential in international theory in the 1970s and is still one of the pillars of public relations theory today), structuralism, critical theory, and postmodernism. A common area of interest is also the theory of communicative action, which is in the focus of some public relations academics as well as international theorists, as it emphasizes "the emancipatory potential within IR [PR]—both as a discipline and a social practice" (Burkart, 1993; Hoffman, 1994, p. 38; Pearson, 1989).

5. And both show different levels of analysis. Whereas the lowest levels focus on small, disaggregated units like individuals, the highest ones trace macro processes such as global trends.

Hence, the different levels of analysis that can be labeled as micro, meso, and macro theories (which has proven useful in social sciences) could serve as a starting point to draw up a comparison between the two functions of public relations and public diplomacy.

Levels of Analysis

The systems of public relations of Ronneberger and Rühl (1992)—in which the macro level designates the society as a whole, the meso level characterizes societal systems such as the political, economic, or legal systems, and the micro level is equated with organizations—can be transformed to the *global*, *interstate* (international, systemic), and *domestic* (state, societal) levels (Goldstein, 1994, p. 13) of international relations. This juxtaposition also shows that international relations has—considering that the global level is only a recent addition[19]—to offer one further level, namely the individual one. This level finds its counterpart on the public relations side in the (again) triplefold, but differently organized differentiation of Kunczik (1990), who places micro theories on the level of individuals and small groups. Meso theories relate—according to him—to organizations, and macro theories try to clarify the importance of public relations for societies. We may conclude from this that it might be helpful not to quarrel about which social reality should be labeled how, or which one should be left out in the scheme, but to somehow fine-tune the otherwise practicable threefold differentiation and simply add another level—as is done in international relations. This comparison is represented in Fig. 17.4.

---

[19] But one that was absolutely necessary considering the growing importance of global-level processes such as the "evolution of human technology, of certain worldwide beliefs, and of humans' relationship to the natural environment" which "are all processes at the global level that permeate down to influence international relations" (Goldstein, 1994, p. 14)—not to speak of the worldwide scientific, technical, and business communities.

PUBLIC RELATIONS	INTERNATIONAL RELATIONS
GLOBAL SOCIETAL LEVEL seeks to explain the contributions of public relations to make societies/the global society work	**GLOBAL LEVEL** seeks to explain the international outcomes in terms of global trends and forces that transcend the interactions of states themselves
MARKET LEVEL concerns the coordination of pluralistic interests of public relations in the (free) market	**INTERSTATE LEVEL** concerns the influence of the international system (e.g. states' geographic locations, their relative power positions in the international system) upon outcomes
ORGANIZATIONAL LEVEL concerns the contributions of public relations to help the organization reach its goals	**DOMESTIC LEVEL** concerns the aggregations of individuals (e.g. interest groups, political organizations, and government agencies) within states that influence state actions in the international arena
INDIVIDUAL LEVEL concerns the perception, choices, and actions of individual human beings (e.g. theories of persuasion)	**INDIVIDUAL LEVEL** concerns the perceptions, choices, and actions of individual human beings

FIG. 17.4 Levels of public relations and international relations.

In both public relations and international relations, scholars often focus their study on one level of analysis only, neglecting the fact that other levels may bear on a problem simultaneously. But thinking in terms of multiple levels would remind scholars and students alike to "look beyond the immediate and superficial aspects of an event to explore the possible influences of more distant causes. IR [PR] is such a complex process that there is rarely any single cause that completely explains outcomes" (Goldstein, 1994, p. 14). And there is so much complexity, a feature social sciences have in common. Not only are there complex layers and levels of analysis, but theories and approaches need to be complex as well. That is what organizational researchers were starting to recognize in the 1950s, when they began to discover that traditional all-or-none theories of management worked only some of the time. In this contingency view of management, no one approach is appropriate all of the time and for all conditions. There is no one best way to organize. What is the best approach depends on the nature of the organization and the nature of the environment in which it must survive. The same is true for public relations. There is no one best way to communicate. The situational theory of publics, an approach quite well developed in public relations, takes account of that and could have a stimulating effect on public diplomacy.

Situational Approach: A Strategic Dimension

The development of the situational theory of publics began with the assumption that John Dewey and Herbert Blumer, two classic theorists of public opinion,[20] first made about publics: namely, that publics arise around issues or problems that affect them (Grunig & Hunt, 1984, pp. 143–145). Beginning as disconnected systems of individuals they can, when they are experiencing common problems, evolve into organized and powerful activist groups. At its current level of development, the situational theory consists of three independent[21] and five dependent variables; the independent ones are problem recognition,[22] constraint recognition,[23] and level of involvement.[24] They describe how people perceive specific situations (which create publics that change over time); the dependent ones are active and passive communication behavior (also known as information seeking and information processing[25]), and cognitive, attitudinal, and behavioral effects (Grunig, 1997, pp. 10–11). The logical interconnection between these concepts could briefly be described as follows:

> People are more likely to be motivated to think, evaluate, and act in situations that involve them, which they view as problematic, and in which they feel unconstrained.... Consistently, research has shown that the more active a public, the more active its communication behavior, and the more likely it is that members of the public will construct cognitions and attitudes and participate in behaviors. (Grunig, 1997, p. 20)

---

[20] That public opinion is a central concept for public relations as well as for international relations became evident when we viewed the functional similarities of both areas. Its centrality becomes even more evident in the following statement: "Public opinion is one of the most vital and enduring concepts in the social sciences. It is widely applied in psychology, sociology, history, *political science* and *communication research*, both in academic and applied settings. Few concepts have engendered as much broad social concern, scientific interest, or intellectual debate. Certainly very few have roots that run as deeply into Western thought" (Price, 1992, p. 1; italics ours).

[21] The designation *independent* remained from the original formulation of Grunig's situational theory, in which he maintained that problem recognition, level of involvement, and constraint recognition were independent of each other. In the meantime most of his research has shown that the three variables are correlated with each other—especially level of involvement and problem recognition (Grunig, 1997, p. 30).

[22] "People detect that something should be done about a situation and stop to think about what to do" (Grunig, 1997, p. 10).

[23] "People perceive that there are obstacles in a situation that limit their ability to do anything about the situation" (Grunig, 1997, p. 10).

[24] "The extent to which people connect themselves with a situation" (Grunig, 1997, p. 10).

[25] Clarke and Kline described information seeking (which they called *premeditated information seeking*) as the "planned scanning of the environment for messages about a specified topic," and information processing (which they named *message discovery*) as the "unplanned discovery of a message followed by continued processing of it" (cit. after Grunig, 1997, p. 9).

Identification of Publics

The situational theory is teleological in that it attempts to predict—from the situational variables—when people will think and communicate purposively about situations, when they will develop cognitions and attitudes about situations, and when they will act. It should, therefore, be able to predict communicative situations of competition and complementarity, risks and chances, and show ways to handle competitors and partners (on different levels) in the field of public opinion. It should be able to identify which publics are most likely to have some cognition or attitude, which publics will communicate most about organizational consequences, and which publics will be most likely to develop ideas and evaluate those ideas. The theory allows for the definition of four types of publics: (a) non-publics,[26] (b) latent publics,[27] (c) aware publics,[28] and (d) active publics.[29]

If this theory was utilized for international relations in general and public diplomacy in particular, a state could conceptually identify such groups as Amnesty International and Greenpeace as additional publics to be rated and treated situationally. From a public relations perspective of public diplomacy, these activistic (and sometimes antagonistic) groups, which are using worldwide operating media and information systems, would not be anything fundamentally new or extraordinary. In addition to the potential of endangering a state's communicative interests, they also hold the potential of offering new and efficient channels of communication to not-yet-reached publics (Signitzer, 1998, p. 503).

Detecting publics and interpreting them is only one, albeit a key, element in the planning process. Other such elements will be addressed as we now immerse ourselves in the strategic dimension of public relations, trying to explore to what extent developments in public relations strategy can be applied to public diplomacy.

Strategy: What Else Needs to Be Considered?

Emphasizing the strategic dimension of communication, public relations can help ask the right questions to get the right answers. It is worth considering whether such a procedure may apply to public diplomacy as well.

1. Which are the basic goals of my organization? Which are the basic goals of my state?

---

[26] Persons who are not linked to the *organization*.

[27] Persons who are linked to the *organization*, but have not realized it yet.

[28] Persons who are linked to the *organization* and have already realized it.

[29] Persons who are linked to the *organization*, have realized it, and have organized themselves to handle this linkage.

2. Which of these goals of my organization/state can be reached exclusively by means of communication, and to the attainment of which of these goals can communication only contribute?

3. Which are the publics of my organization/state?

4. Which communicative goals do I pursue, for which respective public of my organization/state?

5. Which public relations/public diplomacy programs do I have to set up to reach my communicative goals with a given public of my organization/state?

6. Which public relations/public diplomacy instruments do I employ to reach these communicative goals?

7. Did the employment of the specific public relations/public diplomacy instruments contribute to the attainment of my communicative goals with the respective publics? Did the attainment of those communicative goals contribute to the attainment of the overall goals of my organization/state?

Next we start with exploring possible communicative goals of public diplomacy[30] and confront them with public relations goals to find out about their similarities/differences. Furthermore, we want to explore how the hierarchy and the matrix models, both showing communicative goals that can be reached by different communicative behaviors, could benefit from one another.

Hierarchy of Goals in Communication Studies

Communication researchers have constructed models of a hierarchy of effects,[31] which usually range from being simple to being very difficult to reach. An example of such a hierarchy of effects is the following:

(a) *Contact*, which simply means to succeed in establishing contact respectively communication between the organization/state and (one of) its publics

(b) *Retention*, which wants the publics to understand and remember correctly—at least for a certain period—what the organization/state tells them

---

[30] That they go hand in hand with the goals of the state (as they are derived from them) should be obvious from the foregoing.

[31] Grunig and Hunt (1984). The hierarchy of effects concept is still a valuable starting point. Remember, however, that the linear progression of effects does not always occur (Ray, 1973). Also, newer public relations research has questioned some aspects of this hierarchy (e.g., Dozier & Ehling, 1992, p. 163ff.).

(c) *Acceptance*, which means that the publics accept what the organization (state) tells them as the opinion or view of the organization (state); this goal does not yet imply consent, but it may lead to it

(d) *Attitude*, which designates the goal of forming a positive reaction to the opinion or view of the organization (state) and the adoption of this opinion by the publics; it can mean that publics have to change their (for the organization/state unfavorable) attitudes or that they maintain their (for the organization/state favorable) attitudes

(e) *Behavior*, which means that publics change or maintain their behavior according to the goals of the organization (state); this goal is usually the most difficult to reach and only topped by the goal that those publics who have already changed their behaviors are willing to influence other publics in the interest of the organization (state)[32]

Matrix of Goals in Public Diplomacy

In contrast to the foregoing hierarchy of communicative goals/effects, which was developed in the field of communications, public diplomacy, or, more precisely, the cultural communication dimension of it,[33] has drawn up a *matrix* of goals: a matrix developed by German author Peisert (1978), whose work was informed by extensive investigations into the cultural communication practices of four different countries, namely the United States, Italy, United Kingdom, and France. He tried to grasp and summarize the wide range of political, economical, humanitarian, religious, and ecological goals, etc. (which themselves show a great variety[34]—even within the modern pluralistic and democratic societies just listed—not to speak of different political systems or regimes and states on different levels of development). The result is Fig. 17.5, depicting possible goal structures of cultural communication (adopted and slightly modified from Signitzer & Coombs, 1992, pp. 143–146).

The goal *one-way transmission of own culture abroad* does not ascribe equal rights to both partners and is, thus, unbalanced in its structure. All communicative activities are subordinated to an overall strategy prescribed and supervised by a central institution, close to foreign policy. Everything centers around persuasion, and systematic language policy—as language is primarily

---

[32] This shows parallels to the two-step strategy of persuasion employed in public diplomacy, which seeks to influence foreign publics with regard to influencing through them foreign governments.

[33] We have to deal with this aspect of public diplomacy as there is, as far as we know, no theoretic analysis of the overall complex of public diplomacy.

[34] They reach from preserving national security to the expansion or creation of new frontiers, from economic expansion at any costs to a preservation of nature above all, from the support of religious freedom to absolutistic subordination to a state religion, and so on.

The acting country	is interested in the culture and cultural issues of the other country	is disinterested in the culture and cultural issues of the other country
aims at cultural changes in the other country	EXCHANGE AND COOPERATION	ONE-WAY TRANSMISSION OF OWN CULTURE ABROAD
accepts the cultural status quo in the other country	IMAGE ADVERTISING[a]	SELF-PORTRAYAL

FIG. 17.5   Goal structures of cultural communication.

seen as an instrument of persuasion (rather than information exchange)—is a major vehicle in this approach. The realization of systematic language policy is secured by a network of language schools abroad, which is a typical institutional pattern.

In the *self-portrayal* approach, which aims at the conscious drawing of a specific picture abroad of one's own country, an organization (again close to foreign policy) also centrally plans and coordinates all activities according to the picture envisioned. Typical examples for such organizations are cultural institutes with a strong national profile and a staff who are experts about their own country.[35]

The *image advertising* model seeks to create abroad understanding and sympathy for one's own country. In this model contacts with foreign policy are diminished in favor of close contacts with the cultural and scientific community, and institutions in the other country monitor relevant social and cultural developments. Language courses and other measures are only offered when there is a clear demand for it that cannot be met by domestic efforts.

Peisert's most demanding model, *exchange and cooperation*, ascribes both partners equal rights they use to join together in combined efforts to solve

---

[a] In the original model (and also in Signitzer & Coombs, 1992) this was labeled *information*, but now it appears that the concept of advertising better covers the persuasive intent.

[35] Tuch describes the qualifications that U.S. practitioners of public diplomacy should meet as follows:

First, they must have a solid foundation in the history, institutions, and culture of America and the American people. Second, public diplomats must know the purpose and substance of the policy that is to be represented and promulgated. Third, FSOs [= Foreign Service Officers] specializing in public diplomacy must have an understanding of the people in the country to which they are assigned—their traditions, their culture, and their psychology. And finally, they must be competent communicators, knowledgeable in the methods of conveying the message. (Tuch, 1990, p. 39) scientific, social, and cultural problems. The ultimate goal, thus, is to replace national with international loyalties. Typically, there are no national institutions abroad, but some sort of central institution—which is autonomous and shielded from day-to-day foreign policy—may collect information at home as well as abroad and pass it on to professional and academic bodies. These bodies then actually carry out the exchange and cooperation activities such as international scholarship and visiting programs and joint research projects.

Converging Goal Models

Both hierarchy and matrix show goals that can be reached by different communicative behaviors. The advantage of the hierarchy model is that it draws our attention to the different levels of difficulty in reaching the respective goals by making them explicit—and with it the fact that the more difficult the goals, the more complex the communication models that have to be used.

But Peisert's models[36] can be brought into certain accordance with different public relations models, too. This was shown by the Austrian researchers (i.e., Weiss, 1988; Signitzer, 1993) who related the Peisert models of cultural communication with the Grunig and Hunt (1984) models of public relations, namely by connecting:

1. One-way transmission of one's own culture abroad with press agentry/publicity:
   * Both are one-way
   * Both are unbalanced and, in a way, propagandistic
2. Self-portrayal with public information
   * Both are one-way
   * Both want to convey comprehensible contents in which persuasion plays a secondary role
3. Image-advertising with two-way asymmetric communication
   * Both are unbalanced two-way[37]
   * Both use feedback and scientific planning to persuade others into sympathy and acceptance

---

[36] They can serve a useful organizing purpose in a study of (the cultural) communication styles of different countries.

[37] This means that they do not have the intention of changing their own behavior; however, whereas in public relations the asymmetric model implies an intention on the part of the organization to change the *other's* (=the public's) behavior, the respective public diplomacy model by Peisert (1978) does not imply such intention, but rather the acceptance of the (cultural) status quo in the other country.

4. Exchange and cooperation with two-way symmetric communication
    - Both are balanced two-way[38]
    - Both assume that combined efforts can produce best results and
      lead into a win-win zone

Although the convergence of public diplomacy and public relations is most
apparent in the exchange and cooperation and two-way symmetric communication models,[39] it is these very models that are rarely found in practice—
especially in public diplomacy. Weiss (1988), for example, found that in
cultural communication, two-way communication is more of two one-way
exchanges (e.g., a French art exhibition in Austria for an Austrian one in
France)[40] rather than the sender–receiver model being substituted by a participant A–participant B construct (Rogers & Kincaid, 1981). It would appear,
then, that public relations can help public diplomacy in developing its scope
and in advancing—not only in theory, but also in practice—from one-way
information models to more two-way communication models.

Digression: Symmetry—Ethical Communication or Totalitarian Ideology?

Considering the foregoing, it becomes evident that the symmetrical position
is a prominent one. It stands out not only because of the degree of convergence or because it seems most difficult to achieve, but also because it holds
a very prominent position within (international) public relations. Specifically,
it is often equated with being both ethical and most effective: "Symmetrical
public relations would eliminate most ethical problems of international public relations. More importantly, it would make public relations more effective
in producing international understanding and collaboration" (Grunig, 1993,
p. 162).

That it would be more effective in producing international understanding
and cooperation than other models and that this could, ideally, result in peaceful
coexistence, might be true. But what is already implied in Grunig's statement,
as well as in reality, in which symmetrical communication is found least often,
is that it is not most effective. And it is certainly not most efficient—in producing persuasion; a strategy applied widely[41] and mostly to satisfy the "strong
desire for gain of those involved in international relations [and also in public
relations]" (L'Etang, 1996, p. 33).

---

[38] This means that both sides are equally willing to change their behavior.

[39] When one has the goal *exchange and cooperation*, it is evident that two-way-symmetric
communication is a very important alternative that is able to guarantee coordination and
cooperation.

[40] It should be noted, however, that more research is needed to confirm this finding.

[41] Whether as crude propaganda or, more refined, as asymmetric two-way-communication, which
seeks to influence more effectively through feedback.

Although symmetrical communication is not well developed in public diplomacy or international relations theory, critical implications of symmetrical thoughts are namely that the symmetrical position implies

> fundamental change in political architecture but the potential for transformation is not explored in public relations theory. This raises a problem for the public relations theory where there seems to be a tension between achieving the goal of symmetry and retaining existing structural and organizational frameworks. The concept of *symmetry* has implications for the potential disintegration of organizations as we know them and their possible transformation as they reintegrate in some different form. (L'Etang, 1996, p. 33)

Moreover, it is hegemonic in that—through the application of one overall framework—the potential for disagreement may be restricted and hence it cannot only offer free expression but is at the same time a potentially totalitarian ideology (L'Etang, 1996, p. 34). The theory this can be deduced from can be found in Wight's framework of diplomacy dating from the 1950s,[42] which conceptualized diplomacy as consisting of three positions: the Machiavellian (realist), the Grotian[43] (rationalist), and the Kantian (revolutionist) (Wight, 1994).

Grunig's Models of Public Relations and Wight's Framework of Diplomacy

For the *Machiavellian* (realist) approach, the world is a competitive, hostile, difficult, and changeable arena, and international relations equal international anarchy. Motivations of peoples and states are seen in fear and greed in the Heraklithian *panta rhei* condition of world control, and a self-interested position of strength is the only thing that counts; pressure and inducements are the only chance to pursue one's own interests, and the only valuable relationships are those based on contract. Proceeding on this worldview, the goal is the coercion/persuasion of publics by force, a persuasion that mirrors the basic model of traditional public diplomacy—which was mostly employed in antagonistic relationships[44]—as well as the press agentry/publicity model and the two-way asymmetrical model of Grunig and Hunt (1984) on the public relations side.

The *Grotian* (rationalist) position banks on building relationships through truthfulness and promise keeping, which results in reliability

---

[42] Unfortunately his promising work has undergone only few attempts to be developed further.

[43] Hugo Grotius was a Dutch diplomat who preferred moderate negotiation; his "De Jure Belli et Pacis" was published in 1625 (L'Etang, 1996, p. 28).

[44] During the Cold War, for example, both the United States and the Soviet Union developed and extensively used public diplomacy in order to shape favorable public attitudes all over the world toward their respective rival ideologies (Manheim, 1994).

and trustworthiness. It holds a position of enlightened self-interest[45] and reciprocity—but a reciprocity that is mostly reduced to the sum of customary (often commercial) exchanges to achieve mutually beneficial acts for both (organization/state and publics). Or, to speak in terms of public relations, of (mutual) public information (Grunig & Hunt, 1984)—although the boundaries of this position are not very rigid in the direction of the third tradition, namely the Kantian one.

The *Kantian* (revolutionist) position goes further, as it magnifies reciprocity so that it sees existing national governments as obstacles to the fulfillment of the human potential because they try to manipulate public opinion to their own ends. So it favors an international society comprising a world-state, nation-states having diminished influence. The ultimate goal is transcendental mutual satisfaction and understanding between peoples through absolute symmetry, leaving "little space for those who wish to deviate form the accepted norm" (L'Etang, 1996, p. 30). This peacemaking approach of international theory finds its public relations equivalent in the two-way symmetric model, which becomes quite explicit in quotes such as "In the two-way symmetric model, finally, practitioners serve as mediators between organizations and their publics. Their goal is mutual understanding between practitioners and their publics" (Grunig & Hunt, 1984, p. 22). A societally beneficial role of public relations— actually quite crucial in processes of professionalization—may also be deduced from such an approach. Somewhat bombastically, Black and Sharpe (1983, vii, emphasis added) state: "Public relations serves society by mediating conflict... PR plays a major role in resolving cases of competing interests in society.... *Blessed are the peacemakers*" (Black & Sharpe, 1983, vii); and Hiebert (1988, p. 1) maintains: "I believe the more we understand one another, the more we will reduce the chances of war, or terrorism, and of man's violence against man. Fortunately, public relations can aid us in that understanding."

The equivalence is not perfect, however. While the "revolutionist doctrine in international relations posits an international state or community which can override nation-state," the "symmetrical doctrine in public relations does not currently propose an equivalent body which can override organization-states. The implications of the convergence of public relations theory and international theory may be that we have to rethink our concept of organizations, organizational goals, and organizational boundaries"[46] (L'Etang, 1996, p. 33). What if an organization's or state's interests are irreconcilable with the public's or people's interests? What if the idealistic, utilitarian goal to maximize happiness for everyone cannot be reached? Is absolute agreement always the desirable state of affairs? These are questions posed by international theory

---

[45] *Enlightened self-interest* presupposes that one can estimate the interests of other parties, which might pose problems.

[46] It may even lead us to rethink metatheoretical positions such as systems theory.

transferred to the realm of public relations: questions that could help scrutinize some of the more orthodox public relations concepts.

Discussions between public relations and public diplomacy/international theory would, therefore, prove more than fruitful for both areas. Also concerning programs and instruments/media, which takes us—now turning to the implementation of public diplomacy—explicitly[47] back to practice, at the same time maintaining the theoretic concepts explored earlier such as the "environment in which they are practiced, the objectives they are to achieve, and the targets they are to address or involve" (Tuch, 1990, p. 58).

Programs and Instruments/Media

In regard to programs and instruments/media,[48] the previous differentiation within public diplomacy, namely that between political information and cultural communication, serves again as a borderline. It is a not very rigid, but it is a useful borderline, which could also help public relations—often using the same tools—classify its instruments according to their effectiveness in reaching respective (short- or long-time) goals pragmatically. Public relations in turn could help to offer the following:

(a) Explanations why the practicable classification works, as it can explore the different media in regard to one- or two-way communication possibilities. These are possibilities that determine the attainability of specific goals to a large extent.

(b) Its experience in dealing with the mass media. The media on the one hand act quite autonomously and according to their own operating principles, removing themselves to a great extent from an organization's influence (concerning production as well as control) and on the other hand are dependent on organizations as sources of information conveyed via press releases and media relations. Therefore, public relations could help interpret in a public diplomacy context the specific meaning of the time-honored practitioner's dictum: "More important than the question, of how the media can manipulate me, is the question, of how *I* can manipulate the media."

Whereas, according to public diplomacy, fast media such as radio, television, newspapers, and news magazines are suitable for conveying hard political information (including political advocacy), slow media such as academic and

---

[47] "Explicitly," therefore, as all theoretic concepts have practical relevance insofar, as they are able to improve practice through analytical reflection.

[48] Programs and instruments/media are dealt with together—not because the value of analytical differentiation is not considered important and not only because the practice of public diplomacy does so (PDF, 1999b), but also because of the fact that conducting public diplomacy programs implies the use of media.

artistic exchanges, films, exhibitions, and language instruction are better for cultural communication (with a view to creating a climate of mutual understanding). A deeper insight into differing goal structures is given by the Public Diplomacy Foundation (1999b), which distinguishes the U.S. activities[49] of public diplomacy into (a) information activities with the subsection of (b) international broadcasting and (c) educational and cultural exchanges.

Information Activities

1. *"Wireless File"*: It is the oldest media tool, nowadays using high-speed computer-to-computer transmissions via telephone lines and satellite links. It provides a full menu of information and foreign policy-related material on a timely and authoritative basis to U.S. embassies and USIA's[50] overseas offices.

On the public relations side this medium could be compared to intranets[51] of (multinational) corporations, which are expanding tremendously. Concerning programs, the "Wireless File" and intranet, respectively, could be a medium backing up especially employee and member relations.

2. *Publications and Electronic Media*: They include a broad range of booklets, pamphlets, brochures, and other special publications, often in multiple language editions.

These media are used exactly the same way in public relations and could be very useful in promotion, community relations, educational relations, etc.

3. *Book Programs and Information Resource Centers*: Book programs include the translation and production of selected titles by foreign publishers to enter foreign commercial markets and serve Information Resource Centers.

In public relations books usually play only a minor role, but could also be imagined to make sense (e.g., in educational relations). The Information Resource Centers, however, could be equated with after-sales service or call centers on the business side as they get the client the information he needs or wants.

4. *Foreign Press Centers*: They provide a variety of services to more than 1,600 resident foreign journalists along with those thousands coming to the United States each year.

---

[49] The reason why the U.S. activities are cited here instead of public diplomacy activities of another country is, that—according to most international relations scholars—the United States is now the world's only superpower and, hence, the most important of the state actors, greatly affecting the outcomes in international relations (Goldstein, 1994, p. 9).

[50] USIA, United States Information Agency.

[51] Although—concerning the advances in communication technology in recent years—they (will) also hold the potential for two-way communication (chat and discussion programs, whiteboard software, e-mail, workflow software, teleconference programs, etc.) they are still used mostly as information media.

Foreign Press Centers could be equated with press agencies (of MNCs[52]), which handle media relations for them.

5. *Speakers, Specialists and Professionals-in-Residence*: Americans representing government, business, academia, media, and community organizations conduct short-term speaking programs under USIA's auspices,[53] and professional specialists in such fields as law, business, public administration, and the media spend some time in a country serving as advisors to non-academic institutions.

In the sphere of business, specialists could be involved in relations with active publics (e.g. consumers, environmentalists) or in lobbying efforts. Further they could be used for instrumental activities in community relations.

International Broadcasting

International broadcasting was traditionally included under the rubric of "Information Activities," but now is thought to merit a separate section. It includes the following:

1. Voice of America (VOA), USIA's international radio service, which provides news and information in dozens of languages

2. VOA's "Affiliate" Broadcasters, which are "affiliate" radio stations throughout the world to expand its listening audience

3. Worldwide Television and Film Service, which presents U.S. perspectives on important domestic and international events, explains U.S. government policies to a global audience, and transmits a visual image of American culture, history, and scientific and technological achievements

4. Radio and TV Marti, directed toward Cuban audiences

5. Radio Free Europe/Radio Liberty, directed to Central Europe and the former Soviet Union

6. Radio Free Asia, which seeks to promote the rights of freedom of opinion and expression (including freedom to seek, receive, and impart information and ideas through any medium regardless of frontiers) and broadcasts to listeners who do not have access to full and free news media in China, Tibet, Burma, Vietnam, etc.

MNCs—except media enterprises—mostly do not own broadcasting media of their own. Therefore, they have to rely exclusively on their media relations to convey their message to mass audiences.

---

[52] MNC, multinational corporation.

[53] Speakers unable to travel are linked with audiences overseas through teleconference programs.

Educational and Cultural Exchanges

1. Academic exchanges such as the Fulbright Program
2. Study of the United States, which promotes better understanding of the United States by helping establish and maintain quality U.S. studies programs at foreign universities and secondary schools
3. International Visitors Program, which brings people to the United States for about a month to meet and confer with professional counterparts
4. Citizen Exchange Program, which develops international exchange grant projects with American nonprofit institutions (including voluntary community organizations, professional associations, and universities)
5. Program for Building Democratic Institutions, which helps emerging democracies worldwide build institutions that support democratic reform
6. Performing and Visual Arts Program, under which American arts are presented to audiences overseas
7. English Teaching (PDF, 1999b, pp. 1–3).

The programs of cultural communication could probably best be compared to educational relations as well as *community relations*, which—in this case—should be named more adequately global (community) relations, as the environments in which MNCs and states are operating concern almost the whole world. These measures mostly use people and their creations (e.g., art) as media to stabilize the conditions of constant flux by analyzing them and, therefore, making them more predictable.

Research Paves the Way

What remains is the question to what extent public relations/public diplomacy programs and instruments/media such as the foregoing are actually making a contribution to reaching the communicative goals with the respective publics, and to what extent such activities are furthering the goals of the organization/state as a whole. The way to systematically answer both of these questions is through summative and formative evaluation research, which seems to be widely acknowledged not only in academic circles but by some public diplomacy practitioners as well. Witness G. Garin, president of a commercial research firm, who recently said, "There are times the U.S. wants to deliver a specific message abroad. What is persuasive to us might seem illogical to foreigners. Polling can help craft a message that is logical and persuasive to foreign audiences" (1999, p. 2). It may be useful for public diplomacy practitioners to think of our behaviors as embedded in processes that individuals and systems (organizations as well as states) go through to plan and select their respective behaviors (in our case public relations or public diplomacy activities). They may be more successful in adapting to and controlling their environments, if they follow a behavioral molecule that can be seen as an example of a management information system. The behavioral molecule confirms the value of research and theory in public relations/public diplomacy, as the molecule would consist of little more than the behave segment without it (Grunig & Hunt, 1984, p. 108).

Future Research Concerns

As demonstrated previously in this chapter, both public diplomacy (international relations) and public relations share a lot of common ground, as they are

linked to fundamental positions about the way individuals organize themselves into collectivities (whether publics or nations), form identities and relate to other collectivities. Assumptions about what is considered appropriate in organizational and international intercourse and about the rights of organizations and nations to define and fulfill their destinies are as important as the communicative acts that are undertaken in the name of those represented." (L'Etang, 1996, p. 34)

Therefore, both could profit from one another and answer the questions posed by their (similar) functions with common efforts. To do so, they would have to rely on some shared paradigms. Metatheoretical positions such as equivalence-functionalism[54] or systems theory[55]—which is established within public relations and applicable across disciplines— could offer some potential for integration. To clarify, systems theory could help do the following:

1. Make theories of different levels of both areas comparable (e.g., image concepts)
2. Interpret states as organizations that are situated in an arena of international competition
3. Detect input-output circles, specify the respective positions of subsystems and supersystems, and, hence, be useful for a theoretical analysis of the whole complex—an analysis that is not fully developed, not in public relations and definitely not in public diplomacy[56]

---

[54] It could emphasize the boundary-spanning role of both areas.
[55] Even if international theory turned its back on it after the 1970s.
[56] There are separate analyses of the concepts of cultural communication (e.g., Peisert 1978) and political information (e.g., Pitterle 1995), but no comprehensive ones.

4. Clarify the interdependence between internal and external public relations and public diplomacy strategies

5. Understand the teleological and situational dimensions of (communicative) behaviors

6. Transfer ethnocentric models (exemplified in business writings by Illman[57] (1980) and polycentric views[58] of international public relations to the public diplomacy models of political information and cultural communication

7. Pursue the mediatization of politics and the politization of media

8. Evaluate the employment of professional communicators (public relations agencies) for public diplomacy and international relations

9. And, it could help to develop systems theory as such.[59]

A reciprocal stimulation could, therefore, answer (meta)theoretical and analytical as well as concrete and practical questions and meet the requirements posed by an ever more dynamic reality.

REFERENCES

Barston, R. (1997). *Modern diplomacy* (2nd ed.). London: Longman.

Black, S., & Sharpe, M. (1983). *Practical public relations.* Englewood Cliffs, NJ: Prentice Hall.

Botan, C. (1992). International public relations: Critique and reformulation. *Public Relations Review, 18*(2), 149–159.

Burkart, R. (1993). *Public Relations als Konfliktmanagement. Ein Konzept für verständigungsorientierte Öffentlichkeitsarbeit.* Vienna: Braumueller.

Burke, K. (1966). *Language as symbolic action.* Berkeley: University of California Press.

Cheney, G., & Vibbert, S. (1987). Corporate discourse: Public relations and issue management. In F. Jablin, L. Putnam, K. Roberts, & L. Porter (Eds.), *Handbook of organizational communication: An interdisciplinary perspective.* London: Sage.

Cohen, Y. (1986). *Media diplomacy.* London: Frank Cass.

Cutlip, S. M., & Center, A. H. (1958). *Effective public relations.* Englewood Cliffs, NJ: Prentice Hall.

Davison, W. P. (1976). Mass communication and diplomacy. In J. N. Rosenau, K. W. Thompson, & G. Boyd (Eds.), *World politics: An introduction.* New York: Free Press.

---

[57] Illman (1980) assumed that there is no major difference between persuading people at home and in other countries as they are functionally the same everywhere. "Activities at the overseas operations are directed by the international headquarters staff in the corporation's home country" (Kinzar & Bohn, cit. after Botan, 1992, p. 150).

[58] In polycentric models, host country public relations practitioners, who know and understand the host country, exercise a high degree of autonomy. Local public relations may, thus, be effective, but global coordination might pose a problem (Botan, 1992, p. 151).

[59] For example, by critical discussions of symmetry, which are better developed in international relations than in public relations.

de Jong, J. G. (1977). The press attache: Background, status, task. *Gazette, 23*, 171–184.

Deibel, T. L., & Roberts, W. R. (1976). *Culture and information. Two foreign policy functions.* Beverly Hills, CA: Sage.

Deutsch, K. W. (1966). *Nationalism and social communication: An inquiry into the foundations of nationality.* Cambridge, MA: MIT Press.

Dozier, D. M., & Ehling, W. P. (1992). Evaluation of public relations programs: What the literature tells us about their effects. In J. E. Grunig (Ed.), *Excellence in public relations and communication management* (pp. 159–184). Hillsdale, NJ: Lawrence Erlbaum Associates.

Fankhauser, M. M. (1985). *Diplomatie und Öffentlichkeit—Am Beispiel der Entwicklung der Öffentlichkeitsarbeit der österreichischen Diplomatie. Eine Fallstudie zu den Berufsfunktionen der österreichischen Presseattaches im auswärtigen Dienst.* Unpublished doctoral dissertation, University of Salzburg, Salzburg.

Fischer, H. D. (Ed.). (1985). *Kommunikations-Diplomaten im internationalen Dialogsystem. Presseattaches an Auslandsmissionen zwischen Informationspolitik und publizistischen Rahmenfaktoren.* Bochum: Brockmeyer.

Friberg, R. (1989, June). *Problems in profiling small countries.* Paper presented at the annual meeting of the International Public Relations Association, Helsinki, Finland.

Garin, G. (1999, August 29). *Global Public Opinion Research.* Retrieved August 29, 1999, from http://www.usia.gov/usiahome/pdforum/rostrum/acpage.htm.

Goldstein, J. S. (1994). *International relations.* New York: HarperCollins College.

Gore-Boothe, L. (1979). *Satow's guide to diplomatic practice.* New York: Longman.

Grunig, J. (1993). Public relations and international affairs: effects, ethics and responsibility. *Journal of International Affairs, 47*, 137–162.

Grunig, J. E. (1997). A situational theory of publics: Conceptual history, recent challenges, and new research (pp. 3–48). In D. Moss et al. (Eds.), *Public relations research.* London: International Thomson Business Press.

Grunig, J. E., & Hunt, T. (1984). *Managing public relations.* New York: Holt, Rinehart & Winston.

Hiebert, R. (Ed.). (1988). *Precision public relations.* London: Pearson Education.

Hoffman, M. (1994). Normative international theory: approaches and issues. In A. J. R. Groom & M. Light (Eds.), *Contemporary international relations: A guide to theory.* London: Pinter.

Illman, P. E. (1980). *Developing overseas managers and managers overseas.* New York: Amacom.

James, W. (1955). *Pragmatism.* Cleveland: World.

Kunczik, M. (1990). *Die manipulierte Meinung. Nationale Image-Politik und internationale Public Relations.* Köln: Böhlau.

L'Etang, J. (1996). Public relations as diplomacy. In J. L'Etang & M. Pieczka (Eds.), *Critical perspectives in public relations* (pp. 14–34). London: International Thomson Business Press.

Malone, G. D. (1985). Managing public diplomacy. *The Washington Quarterly, 8*, 199–213.

Malone, G. D. (1988). *Political advocacy and cultural communication. Organizing the nation's public diplomacy.* Lanham, MD: University Press of America.

Manheim, J. B. (1990, August). *"Democracy" as international public relations.* Paper presented at the annual conference of the American Political Science Association, San Francisco.

Manheim, J. B. (1994). *Strategic public diplomacy and American foreign policy: The evolution of influence.* New York: Oxford University Press.

Miller, G. R. (1989). Persuasion and public relations. Two "ps" in a pod. In C. H. Botan & V. Hazleton, Jr. (Eds.), *Public relations theory* (pp. 45–66). Hillsdale, NJ: Lawrence Erlbaum Associates.

Mitchell, J. M. (1986). *International cultural relations*. London: Allen & Unwin.

Nicolson, H. (1954). *The evolution of the diplomatic method*. London: Weidenfeld.

PDF (Public Diplomacy Foundation) (1999a, August 29). *Public diplomacy in a restructured foreign affairs community*. http://www.publicdiplomacy.org/3.htm.

PDF (Public Diplomacy Foundation) (1999b, August 29). *Typical public diplomacy activities and programs*. http://www.publicdiplomacy.org/9.htm. Retrieved August 29, 1999.

Pearson, R. (1989). Business ethics as communication ethics: Public relations practice and the idea of dialogue. In C. H. Botan & V. Hazleton, Jr. (Eds.), *Public relations theory* (pp. 111–131). Hillsdale, NJ: Lawrence Erlbaum Associates.

Peisert, H. (1978). *Die auswärtige Kulturpolitik der Bundesrepublik Deutschland: Sozialwissenschaftliche Analysen und Planungsmodelle*. Stuttgart: Klett-Cotta.

Pitterle, E. (1995). *Aussenpolitische Öffentlichkeitsarbeit: Struktur-, Begründungs- und Funktionszusammenhang*. Unpublished doctoral dissertation, University of Salzburg, Austria.

Price, V. (1992). *Public opinion*. Newbury Park, CA: Sage.

Ray, M. (1973). Marketing communication and the hierarchy of effects. In P. Clarke, (Ed.), *New models for communication research*. Newbury Park, CA: Sage.

Rogers, E. M., & Kincaid, D. L. (1981). *Communication networks: Towards a paradigm for research*. New York: Free Press.

Ronneberger, F., & Rühl, M. (1992). *Theorie der Public Relations. Ein Entwurf*. Opladen: Westdeutscher Verlag.

Signitzer, B. (1988). Public Relations-Forschung im Überblick. *Publizistik, 33*, 92–116.

Signitzer, B. (1993). Anmerkungen zur Begriffs- und Funktionswelt von Public Diplomacy. In W. Armbrecht et al. (Eds.), *Image und Public Relations* (pp. 199–211). Opladen: Westdeutscher Verlag.

Signitzer, B. (1995). Public Relations und Public Diplomacy. In W. A. Mahle (Ed.), *Deutschland in der internationalen Kommunikation* (pp. 73–81). Konstanz: Universitätsverlag Konstanz.

Signitzer, B. (1998). Staaten im internationalen System. In O. Jarren, U. Sarcinelli, & U. Saxer (Eds.), *Politische Kommunikation in der demokratischen Gesellschaft. Ein Handbuch mit Lexikonteil* (pp. 496–505). Opladen: Westdeutscher Verlag.

Signitzer, B., & Coombs, T. (1992). Public relations and public diplomacy: Conceptual convergences. *Public Relations Review, 18*, 137–147.

Sonnesyn, M., & Williams, M. (1999, August 29). *Diplomacy*. Retrieved August 29, 1999, from http://www.prin.edu/pac/diplom.htm.

Tuch, H. N. (1990). *Communicating with the world. U.S. public diplomacy overseas*. New York: St. Martin's.

USAC (United States Advisory Commission on Public Diplomacy) (1999, August 29). *Bipartisan Presidential Comission says public diplomacy crucial in global communications age*. Retrieved August 29, 1999, from http://www.advcomm.fed.fov/98presre.htm.

Weiss, M. (1988). *Kulturelle Kommunikation und Öffentlichkeitsarbeit: Eine Untersuchung von Kongruenzen und Divergenzen am Beispiel der Auslandskulturpolitik von Frankreich*. Unpublished master's thesis, University of Salzburg, Austria.

Wight, M. (1994). *International theory: The three traditions*. London: Leicester University Press.

Relationship Management: A General Theory of Public Relations

John A. Ledingham
Capital University

INTRODUCTION

Publics—people who are somehow mutually involved or interdependent with . . .
organizations.

— Cutlip, Center, and Broom (2000)

The relationship perspective of public relations suggests that balancing the interests of organizations and publics is achieved through management of organization-public relationships. From that perspective, public relations is seen as "the management function that establishes and maintains mutually beneficial relationships between an organization and the publics on whom its success or failure depends" (Cutlip, Center, & Broom, 1994, p. 2). The notion of public relations as a *management* function provides a framework for conducting programs and campaigns within the four-step process of analysis, planning, implementation and evaluation, and offers a systematic means for determining return on investment from public relations initiatives, outcome documentation that has been lacking in the practice since its inception.

The relational perspective has been applied to various public relations functions, including issues management (Bridges & Nelson, 2000), crisis management (Coombs, 2000), community relations (Ledingham & Bruning, 2001), media relations (Ledingham & Bruning, in press), and public affairs (Ledingham, 2003b), among others. In addition, the notion of relationship management is consistent with major concepts such as systems theory and the two-way symmetrical model of Grunig and Hunt (1984), and also accommodates middle-range theories such as Ledingham and Bruning's (1997) theory of public loyalty.

The essence of public relations as the management of organization-public relationships is captured in Center and Jackson's (1995) observation: "The proper term for the desired outcomes of public relations practice is public *relationships*. An organization with effective public relations will attain positive public *relationships*" (p. 2). Moreover, the relational perspective is said to clarify the function of public relations within an organizational structure and to provide a framework for determining the contribution of public relations to attainment of organizational goals (Ledingham & Bruning, 1998). Further, the application of managerial concepts, as part of the relationship management process, increases opportunities for public relations experts to join the ranks of upper-level management (Ledingham & Bruning, 2000a). And, a cornerstone of relationship management theory is its focus on managing organization-public relationships to generate benefit for organizations, and publics alike (Ledingham & Bruning, 2000b).

The notion of relationship management represents a fundamental change in the function and direction of public relations, a movement away from traditional impact measurements, such as the quantity of communication messages produced or number of stories placed in the mass media, and toward evaluation of public relations initiatives based on their impact on the quality of the relationship between an organization and the publics with which it interacts. Moreover, the notion of public relations as a management function also elevates public relations from a crafts-driven tactical endeavor to one in which strategic planning is central.

In addition, relationship management theory shifts the central focus of public relations from communication to relationships, with communication acting as a tool in the initiation, nurturing, and maintenance of organization-public relationships. Within that framework, the value of the communication rests on its contribution to the quality of the organization-public relationship (Dozier, 1995; Ledingham & Bruning, 1998).

Further, relationship management theory provides a paradigm for scholarly inquiry, serves as a perspective for public relations education, equips practitioners with an outcome-based means of accounting for the cost of program initiatives, and mandates that public relations managers be conversant with management concepts and practices such as goal setting, strategic planning, and evaluation.

This chapter traces the emergence of the relational perspective and the shift in focus from communication practices to the management of organization-public relationships. Moreover, the importance of expectations in the development and nurturing of relationships is explored. The author also reviews emerging models of the organization-public relationship and summarizes what is known concerning that relationship. The author then summarizes criteria for constructing theory and demonstrates how relationship management meets those criteria. The author also argues for relationship management as a general theory of public relations and constructs a relational paradigm for future research. Implications of the theory for the study, teaching, and practice of public relations also are offered.

EMERGENCE OF THE RELATIONAL PERSPECTIVE

Four pivotal developments spurred the emergence of the relational perspective as a paradigm for public relations study and practice (adapted from Ledingham, 2003b).

1. *Recognition of the central role of relationships in the study and practice of public relations.* Ferguson's (1984) notion that relationships—"not . . . the organization, nor the public, nor the communication process"—should be the unit of study of public relations set the scene for a major shift in the way in which public relations is conceptualized. The idea of *relationships* between organizations and their publics provided an organizing concept for the relational perspective.

2. *Reconceptualizing public relations as a management function.* The notion of *managing* organization-public relationships brought into play management concepts understood and appreciated by senior management. Particularly, reconceptualization pointed up the need for public relations managers to be proficient in analysis, planning, implementation, and evaluation in addition to traditional communication skills.

3. *The emergence of measurement strategies, relationship components and types of organization-public relationships, and linkage of organization-public relationships to public attitudes, perceptions, knowledge and behavior.* The distillation of relationship attributes from interorganizational and interpersonal literature contributed to a better understanding of the composition of organization-public relationships. That, in turn, set the stage for exploring the value of organization-public relationships as predictors of public

behavior and for development of measurements of organization-public relationship quality.

4. *The construction of models that accommodate relationship antecedents, process, and consequences.* A pioneering model of relationship management included antecedents, properties, and consequences of organization-public relationships. The model was later augmented to include direct observation and a definition of organization-public relationships. A further expansion offered maintenance and monitoring strategies. A model based on the development of interpersonal relationships also was constructed, followed by a multistep process model to guide the management of organization-public relationships. Numerous other models have been advanced in an effort to explain part or all of the process of managing organization-public relationships.[1]

IMPORTANCE OF THE RELATIONAL CONCEPT

It would be difficult to overstate the importance of emergence of the notion of relationship management to the study, teaching and practice of public relations. Ledingham and Bruning (2000a) contend that "the emergence of relationship management . . . calls into question the essence of public relations—what it is and what it does or should do, its function and value within the organizational structure and the greater society, and the benefits generated not only for sponsoring organizations but also for the publics those organizations serve and the societies in which they exist" (p. xiii). Ehling (1992) suggests that the notion of public relations as relational represents a shift from manipulation toward the building, nurturing, and maintenance of relationships and is "an important change in the primary mission of public relations" (p. 662). Similarly, Dozier (1995) has observed that "the purpose and direction of an organization (its mission) is affected by *relationships* with key constituents (publics) in the organization's environment" (p. 85).

Additionally, Dozier has suggested that within the perspective of relationship management, communication becomes "a strategic management function (that helps) manage relationships with key publics that affect organizational mission, goals and objectives" (p. 85). Similarly, Ledingham and Bruning (1998) have noted that while "goals are developed around relationships . . . communication is used as a strategic tool in helping to achieve those goals (and that) while measurement of communication efficiencies should certainly be part of the evaluation process, their importance eventually may rest upon their ability to impact the achievement of relationship objectives" (p. 63).

---

[1] Adapted from: Ledingham, J. A. (2001). Government-Community Relationaships: Extending the Relational Theory of Public Relations. *Public Relations Review, 27,* 285–295.

Moreover, Broom and Dozier (1990) argue that an inappropriate focus on communication has resulted in validation of public relations initiatives in terms of communication *output*, rather than relational or behavioral *outcomes*.

THE NEED FOR NEW THEORY

The shift in the central focus of public relations from a communication-centered function to one in which the management of organization-public relationships is central requires a reconceptualization of public relations theory. According to Littlejohn (1995), the purpose of research is to build theories to solve the problems researchers face in working in a domain. Thus, theory building begins with an examination of the presuppositions of a domain, and collectively those presuppositions constitute a "worldview" that drives scholarship and practice. Further, theories also may be thought of as organizing mechanisms shaped by the presuppositions of that domain (Grunig, 1989). Moreover, the source of the suppositions presumed within a discipline serve as a framing mechanism for the development of theory. Thus, a shift in domain from communication to relationships requires a corresponding shift in the theoretical constructs of the field. With relationships—not communication—as the domain of public relations, the overarching principles of public relations must be derived not from communication theory, but from that of relationships.

Effective relationship management also encompasses the need for management skills among those public relations practitioners aspiring to leadership positions. For example, Broom and Dozier (1986) documented that public relations practitioners often are categorized in terms of technicians concerned with the production and dissemination of communication messages, and managers charged with developing policy and strategies consistent with the overall goals of the organization. They further found that those solely with public relations training more often were assigned the technician role, whereas managers tended more often to be selected from disciplines such as business, marketing or related fields, because those fields generally require management training.

LITERATURE REVIEW

Scholarship concerning the management of organization-public relationships has increased dramatically in recent years. A review of the scholarly literature of public relations found research reports concerning how organization-public relationships develop (Broom, Casey, & Ritchey, 1997), dimensions and types of organization-public relationships (Ledingham & Bruning, 1998), strategies for maintenance of organization-public relationships (Ledingham & Bruning, 2000a), the importance of expectations in organization-public relationship quality (Coombs, 2000; Thomlison, 2000); the impact of time on organization-public relationships (Ledingham, Bruning, & Wilson, 1999), and developmental and process models of organization-public relationships grounded in the relationship management perspective (Broom, Casey, & Ritchey, 1997, 2000; Grunig & Huang, 2000; Ledingham, 2000). In addition, two definitions of an organization-public relationship are found in the literature.

Ledingham and Bruning's (1998) definition links relationships and impact:

> [An organization-public relationship is] the state which exists between an organization and its key publics, in which the actions of either can impact the economic, social, cultural or political well being of the other (p. 62).

The definition offered by Broom, Casey, and Ritchey (2000) focuses more on the transactional aspect of the relationship:

> Relationships consist of the transactions that involve the exchange of resources between organizations ... and lead to mutual benefit, as well as mutual achievement (p. 91).

Measuring the Quality of an Organization-Public Relationship

As noted earlier, the notion of managing organization-public relationships provides a means for determining the impact of public relations initiatives. Several researchers have suggested ways of doing so. For example, Broom and Dozier (1990) offered an approach centered on the degree of agreement or accuracy between organizations and publics. They recommended that researchers (1) determine levels of agreement between organizations and publics on key issues, and (2) identify the degree to which an organization and its key publics can accurately predict each other's position on a given issue. In fact, Ledingham's (2001) study of government-citizenry relationships confirmed that the perception of agreement between organizations and publics is linked to relationship quality and, ultimately, to public behavior.

Moreover, Ledingham, Bruning, Thomlison, and Lesko (1997) identified 17 dimensions that various relationship scholars have held to be central to interpersonal relationships, marketing relationships, and other relationships. The initial list of 17 dimensions then was reduced to five dimensions and operationalized through research with public members (Ledingham & Bruning,

1998). In that way, *trust* was operationalized as an organization "doing what it says it will do" and *openness* was operationalized as "sharing the organization's plans for the future with public members." *Involvement* was seen as "the organization being involved in the welfare of the community," *investment* as "the organization investing in the welfare of the community," and *commitment* as "the organization being committed to the welfare of the community" (p. 62). Ledingham and Bruning (1998) then examined the linkage between the five operationalized dimensions and attitudes toward an organization, finding that higher scoring of the relationship dimensions correlated with a favorable predisposition toward the organization. In further research, Bruning and Ledingham (1998) found that the dimensions of trust, openness, involvement, commitment, and investment affected consumer satisfaction.

Based on that study, Bruning and Ledingham (1998) advised that "the relationship between an organization and its key publics should be considered when developing customer satisfaction initiatives and should be included in future models of satisfaction research" (p. 199). Additional research (Bruning & Ledingham, 2000) found that those relationship dimensions operate in an organization-organization relationship as well as in the context an organization-public relationship. In addition, L. A. Grunig, Grunig, and Ehling (1992) have suggested that the quality of organization-public relationships can be measured through the dimensions of reciprocity, trust, mutual legitimacy, openness, mutual satisfaction, and mutual understanding (p. 136).

Relationship Quality and Loyalty

Ledingham and Bruning (1997) also found relationships linked to social and political issues, as well as revenue stream. Their research further showed that consumers who ranked an organization high with regard to that organization's support of community interests more often said they would continue to subscribe to that organization's services rather than sign up with a new marketplace competitor. They concluded that, "to be effective and sustaining, relationships need to be seen as mutually beneficial, based on mutual interest between an organization and its significant publics [and] the key to managing successful relationships is to understand what must be done in order to initiate, develop and maintain that relationship" (p. 27).

Ledingham and Bruning (1998) then expounded on the linkage between organizational support for a community and public support for that organization:

> Organizational involvement in and support of the community in which it operates can engender loyalty toward an organization among key publics when that involvement/support is known by key publics [and] what emerges is a process in

which organizations must (1) focus on the relationships with their key publics, and, (2) communicate involvement of those activities/programs that build the relationship to members of their key publics. (p. 63)

As the result of a test of "the loyalty theory," Wilson (2000) concluded, "There is support (for) the application of (the) theory to . . . community and employee publics as well (and the theory) provides an exciting new direction of inquiry in the field of public relations . . . a giant step forward in providing practitioners concrete principles that lead toward success" (p. 12).

Typologies of Organization-Public Relationships

Bruning and Ledingham (1999) also found that indicators of relationship quality cluster together into three relationships types—interpersonal, professional, and community. Those dimensions formed the basis for of a multi-item, multidimensional scale to measure relationship quality. An additional study by Ledingham, Bruning, and Wilson (1999) found that organization-public relationships can and do change over time, and that it may require decades, in some cases, to solidify an organization-public relationship. As a result, the researchers stressed the need to maintain attention to an organization-public relationship throughout its life cycle, not simply when the relationship is initiated or when it is declining.

At this point, linkage between perceptions and loyalty toward an organization has been documented within the context of the utilities industry, local government, the insurance industry, banking, and higher education (see Ledingham & Bruning, 2000a).

Another attempt to categorize organization-public relationships is found in Grunig's (1993) notion of "symbolic and behavioral" relationships. He has suggested that:

> When symbolic (communication-based) relationships are divorced from behavioral relationships (grounded in actions and events), public relations practitioners reduce public relations to the simplistic notion of image building [which] offer[s] little of value to the organizations they advise because they suggest that problems in relationships with publics can be solved by using the proper message— disseminated through publicity, or media relations—to change an image of an organization. (p. 136)

The Importance of Expectations in Organization-Public Relationships

Littlejohn (1992) suggests that "a relationship is defined not so much by what is said as by the partner's expectations for behavior" (p. 262). The literature supports that viewpoint. The notion of *social exchange*, which holds that entities in a relationship have a level of expectations regarding others in the relationship and that failure to meet or exceed expectations will decide whether a relationship continues, has been explored within the domain of public relations. Thomlison (2000) has suggested that when the expectations one holds for another are met, the relationship endures. However, when those expectations are not met, one may seek other means for fulfilling expectations. In that same way, Coombs (2000) has argued that damage to a relationship "tends to be a result of either (1) incongruence between the public and private definitions of a relationship, or (2) the people involved in the relationship have different expectations of each other" (p. 2). In addition, Coombs (2000) introduced the notion of relationship history as a variable in organization-public relationship quality.

Models of the Organization-Public Relationship

Models are an illustration of theories in action, and models of organization-public relationships are found in the recent literature of public relations. Broom, Casey, and Ritchey (1997) advanced a model of organization-public relationships that included *antecedents* to a relationship, *subsequent* states of the relationship, and relationship *consequences*. They suggest that "antecedents... include perceptions, motives, needs, behaviors... posited as contingencies or causes in the formation of relationships... (and) antecedents are the sources of change pressure or tension... derived from the environment." Consequences of organization-public relationships were seen as "the outputs that have the effect of changing the environment and of achieving, maintaining or changing goal states both inside and outside of the organization" (p. 94). In a later iteration of the model, Broom et al. (2000) suggested that transactions are part of the process of fulfilling needs and can be used to describe, categorize, and evaluate the quality of relationships. In that model, the communication-centered patterns of accessing, storing, and using information (a need) as well as communication engagement (social exchange) are seen as indicators of relationship state, and also may provide a method for constructing typologies of organization-public relationships.

The Broom et al. model also includes three dimensions of relationships— degree of formalization, standardization, and complexity—as well as the intensity and reciprocity of two additional relationship processes, information flow and resource flow. Grunig and Huang (2000) reconceptualized Broom et al.'s early model of antecedents, states and consequences as characteristics that describe the publics with which organizations need relationships (*antecedents*), maintenance strategies (*relationship states*), and outcomes of those strategies (*consequences*). They then suggested methods for monitoring each of the three components of the model; environmental scanning for the antecedents phase, ongoing observations by management and publics for relationship states, and, coorientational measurement for *consequences* (Fig. 1, p. 94).

In addition, Dimmick, Bell, Burgiss, and Ragsdale (2000) constructed a model that illustrates the steps in the development of a physician-patient relationship, moving from current state to desired state in a process of ongoing monitoring and adjustment. As measures of the quality of behavioral relationships, Dimmick et al. suggested reciprocity, trust, credibility, openness, mutual legitimacy, mutual satisfaction, and mutual understanding. They further offered symmetry, intensity, frequency, duration, valance and content as measures of communication linkage attributes (Fig. 6.1, p. 132). Moreover, Toth (2000) advanced a view of public relations as interpersonal, encompassing personal influence and interpersonal influence. She described two types of public relations practice: (1) a personal influence approach in which "interpersonal communication is used to dominate individuals, to accept either the organization's or public's position, closed and static in attributes," and (2) an interpersonal influence approach in which "interpersonal communication (is) used to find mutual definitions, mutuality of understanding, agreement, consensus, open and dynamic in attributes" (p. 214). Toth also suggested, "The end goal of interpersonal communication is to establish and maintain successful relationships" (p. 217), adding that "some conceptual elements to examine along an individual continuum are mutuality of understanding, trust, credibility, emotion, intimacy and similarity, immediacy, and dominance-submission" (p. 218). Toth further called for research "to make this (interpersonal) model of use in managing public relationships" and suggested, "One starting point would be to study qualitatively how much individuals in negotiation situations attribute their success to their own choices and motivations and how much their agency is influenced and distinctly built in the negotiation relationship" (p. 217).

A process model of relationship management—"SMART PR"—was constructed (Bruning & Ledingham, 1999) and expanded in a later iteration to SMARTS PR (Ledingham, 2000). SMARTS is shorthand for Scan (analysis), Map (plan), Act (produce), Rollout (implement), Track (evaluate), and Steward (adjust). The model specifies the steps that must be taken in managing organization-public relationships. It also lists monitoring strategies, methods for pretesting public relations initiatives, recommendations for implementing programs, and evaluation and nurturing strategies. Bruning and Ledingham (2002) subsequently constructed an organization-public relationship developmental model based on Knapp's (1984) model of the five stages of the coming together and five stages of the coming apart of an interpersonal relationship. In developing the model, members of a public relations firm were asked to operationalize Knapp's stages in terms of an agency-client relationship. The results indicated that changes in symbolic and behavioral patterns are associated with rises and declines in relationship quality, and that the relationship stages model can serve as a basis for developing strategies to initiate, nurture and maintain agency-client relationships.

Summary Points

This short review of the literature has not been exhaustive of the large body of literature on organization-public relationships but, when combined with the background pieces for articles reviewed here, leads to several summary points about organization-public relationships. Specifically;

1. Relationship presuppositions act as a foundation for theory building, teaching, and practice. Also, within that perspective, the use of communication *output* as the measure of programmatic accountability is replaced with relational and behavioral *outcomes*.

2. The central unit of measures of public relations success is the organization-public relationship.

3. Interpersonal relationship principles, complete with guidelines for initiating, maintaining, and improving relationships, can serve as a framework for the exploration of organization-public relationships.

4. Organization-public relationships involve an ongoing exchange of needs, expectations, and fulfillment.

5. Organization-public relationship dimensions define the state, or quality, of an organization-public relationship, which, in turn, acts as a predictor of public behavior.

6. Organization-public relationship types include symbolic and behavioral relationships, as well as personal, professional, and community-related relationships.

7. Organization-public relationships can and do change over time.

8. The desired outcome of effective organization-public relationship management is mutual understanding and benefit.

9. Successful organization-public relationships develop around common interests and shared goals.

10. Relationship state is reflective of perceptions of needs and expectations fulfillment.

11. Mutual benefit strategies not only respond to ethical considerations, but also can generate economic, societal, and political gain both for organizations and publics.

RELATIONSHIP MANAGEMENT THEORY

In order to explicate the notion of relationship management as a theory of public relations, it is helpful to offer a brief review of the concept of theory itself. In that regard, Hazelton and Botan (1989) suggest that "a theory consists of at least two concepts and a statement explaining or predicting the relationship between those concepts" (p. 7). And, according to Littlejohn (1995), "all theories are abstractions" that "focus on certain aspects of process" (p. 12) and "represent various ways in which observers see their environments" (p. 13). Littlejohn further suggests that theory is the result of a *process* of asking questions, observing phenomena, and constructing answers in which "the scholar attempts to define, to describe and explain, to make judgments" (p. 9).

Littlejohn also specifies eight functions of theory: (1) organizing and summarizing, (2) focus, (3) clarifying, (4) observation, (5) predictability, (6) heuristic, (7) communicative, and (8) control (p. 13). And, he shares Hawes' view that theory serves as an explanation, whereas a model illustrates the "interrelationships among the parts of the modeled process" (p. 12). Littlejohn also stresses the usefulness of a theory, noting that "questioning a theory's usefulness is wiser than questioning its truthfulness" (p. 13).

In discussing their initial model, Broom et al. (1997) called for an articulation of the relational theory. With that in mind, this author suggested, "Effectively managing organizational relationships around common interests and shared goals, over time, results in mutual understanding and benefit for interacting organizations and publics" (Ledingham, 2003, p. 190).

Examination of that theoretical statement of relationship management found that it meets Littlejohn's (1983, pp. 13–14) eight conditions because it (1) serves as an organizing concept for the study of public relationships and the knowledge generated from that study; (2) focuses on the core of the domain, relationships, and answers the question: "What will I look at?", (3) helps to clarify what is observed and what the field of study is about, (4) specifies the concepts of the domain and the interaction of those concepts, (5) lends itself to observation by pointing out how to observe the process through operational definitions and models of the phenomenon, (6) sets the direction for future research by identifying concepts and examining the relationships between them, (7) lends itself to communicative efforts through the presentation and/or publication of scholarly work, and (8) not only is descriptive, but also is normative in that it sets requirements for performance in terms of expectation fulfillment, and mutuality of understanding and benefit.

Relationship management theory also responds to the concerns of Leichty and Springston (1993) in that it identifies the elements of an organization-public relationship (organizations, publics), as well as the phenomenon (mutual benefit), and the elements of the condition that produce an instance of the phenomenon (effective management, common interests, shared goals). The theory also explains that mutual benefit occurs when organization-public relationships are effectively managed, and specifies how a symmetrical organization-public relationship emerges (by management focused, over time, on common interests and shared goals). The theory further specifies measurable outcomes (mutual benefit for interacting organizations and publics). Moreover, the scholarly literature indicates that research concerning relationship management in differing contexts has produced similar findings. That research also demonstrates the usefulness of the relational perspective by identifying measurable outcomes that transcend communication frequency, and also by providing practitioners with a means of demonstrating the contribution of public relations initiatives to the economic, cultural, and social well-being of an organization and the communities in which it operates.

The notion of mutuality, central to the relationship management perspective, has practical implications; longitudinal research (Ledingham & Bruning, 2000b) has shown that mutuality is the concept upon which long-term organization-public relationships are constructed. Those findings are supported by research concerning the organization-public relationship in differing contexts and industries (Ledingham & Bruning, 2000a). Similarly, research has demonstrated the importance of common interests and shared goals to organization-public relationship quality (Ledingham & Bruning, 1998), and previously cited research has noted how changes in organization-public relationships occur over time (Ledingham et al., 1999). Further, the relationship management theory meets the requirements of explication set forth by Broom et al. (2000) in that it specifies the act (effective management) that produces a result (mutual understanding and benefit) under specified conditions (focus on shared goals, common interests over time).

RELATIONSHIP MANAGEMENT AS A GENERAL THEORY OF PUBLIC RELATIONS

> One can think of many theories that apply . . . but it is more difficult to think of *a* public relations theory . . . that has not been borrowed from another . . . (Grunig, 1989, p. 18)

A *general theory* is a concept that unifies a discipline, providing an overarching framework for exploring issues within that discipline. Leichty and Springston suggest:

> If the relationship management metaphor is to be taken seriously, a theory of how relationships between organizations and publics develop, change and are maintained [is needed]. The varying ways in which organization-public relationships change across time should be a focus of analysis. In particular, a normative theory of public relations would instruct practitioners on how to try to develop or change an from one relational phase to a more desirable one. (p. 334)

They added, "What we need is a theory that tells us when and how to build toward a two-way symmetrical exchange between organizations and publics" (p. 335).

Moreover, a general theory must be specific to the degree that it can predict outcomes and the conditions under which those outcomes occur. Such a theory also needs to be sufficiently broad to have application in various environments, over time, but also to accommodate subtheories—those that Prior-Miller (1989) terms "middle-range" (p. 68). Middle-range theories explain parts of a process or specify standards of outcome. However, they are not sufficiently comprehensive to serve as a framework for examining a process in its entirety. Many middle-range theories can be subsumed under the broader framework of relationship management. These include, among others, Ledingham and Bruning's (1998) notion of public loyalty toward an organization.

For example, the notion of public loyalty advanced by Ledingham and Bruning and ameliorated by Wilson (2000) explains and prescribes ways in which an organization can engender public loyalty (by meeting the needs of a public). In that way, the loyalty theory does illuminate a part of the process of relationship management. However, in failing to address how publics can gain the support of organizations, it lacks the comprehensive view needed to encompass all the elements and interactions involved in the organization-public relationship-building process.

However, the overarching notion of relationships as an organizing concept for public relations offers an appropriate umbrella for subtheories such as loyalty. And, the relationship management theory provides both scholars and practitioners with a framework that is easily understood and that responds to the functional imperatives of organizations, publics, and the greater society. Most importantly, the relational theory is predicated on the notion that the appropriate domain of public relations is that of relationships. Thus, the guiding principles of relationship building should be paramont in the study, teaching, and practice of public relations.

The collective findings from the literature review also support the notion that organizational relationships are transactional and dynamic: They change over time. Moreover, organizational relationships also are goal oriented, have antecedents and consequences, and can be analyzed in terms of relationship quality, maintenance strategies, relationship type, and those involved in the relationship. In addition, organizational relationships are driven by the perceived needs and wants of interacting organizations and publics, and the continuation of an organization-public relationship depends on whether those needs and expectations are met. Indeed, those needs are expressed in interactions between organizations and publics. And, while organizational relationships involve communication, it is not the sole instrument of relationship building. Relationships are affected by relational history, the nature of the transaction, the frequency of exchange, and reciprocity. In addition, the literature indicates that organizational relationships can be described by type (personal, professional, community) independent of the perceptions of those relationships, and that organization-public relationships may be viewed as symbolic or behavioral. The literature further supports the notion that the appropriate domain of public relations is relationships—not communication—and that communication alone cannot sustain long-term relationships in the absence of supportive organizational behavior. Finally, the literature indicates that effective management of organizational relationships results in mutual benefit, and that the relationship perspective is applicable throughout the public relations process and with regard to all public relations techniques.

IMPLICATIONS

Concepts such as *relationship management* focus attention on the need for new ways of thinking about the field. For example, the field needs to come to agreement once and for all that public relations is not a collection of practice activities, but a way of viewing the interaction of organizations and publics (and, for that matter, of organizations with organizations, and publics with publics). It would seem that the immediate challenge to scholars is to validate the value of effectively managing relationships around common interests and shared goals, over time, to generate mutual understanding and benefit for interacting organizations and publics.

With regard to public relations education, public relations graduates increasingly are expected to be proficient not only in messaging, but in strategic planning and evaluation as well. In fact, an understanding of management principles is essential for those who aspire to higher-level management positions. It is essential, then, that students be prepared to develop and manage organization-public relationships in addition to proficiency in traditional communication skills.

Moreover, the relational theory—as illustrated in the process models—provides a beginning for answering long-standing questions concerning the value of public relations to an organization. For example, the literature suggests that programs designed to generate mutual benefit as part of the relational process can engender public support, which in turn affects the ability of an organization to meet public expectations and to achieve organizational goals. And, an organization's ability to measure the impact of meeting the common needs, wants, and expectations of interacting publics is both appropriate and, in both the short and long term, productive.

A RELATIONAL PARADIGM FOR FUTURE RESEARCH

The theory of relationship management sets the stage for exploration of numerous streams of research. For example, there is a need for a greater understanding of the different types of organization-public relationships that are operating and their importance in organization-public interaction. Similarly, treating the quality of organization public relations as a continuum, and determining how quality evolves—as well as the myriad elements that affect it—represents another promising areas of investigation. Moreover, the matter of management philosophy and style, as applied to public relations, is an area that is largely unexplored.

A matrix that specifies organization type, management approach, and problem context for those charged with responsibility for applying management relationship principles in various situations would be highly useful. In addition, much of the research concerning relationship management has focused exclusively on one side or the other of the relationship equation: either the organization or a key public. A coorientational approach such as that utilized by Ledingham and Bruning (2006) could yield perceptions of the relationship from organizations and publics alike, and in that way provide insights for strategic planning.

Finally, to provide a framework for future relational research, the author offers the following Laswellian type of paradigm:

> What management practices are most effective in focusing, over what increments of time, on what types of interests and shared goals, to generate what degree of mutual understanding and benefit?

It is hoped this chapter provides a foundation for those seeking to explore the notion of relationship management, as well as for those in need of a conceptual framework to assess the value of public relations initiatives to publics, organizations, and the environment they share.

REFERENCES

Bridges, J. A., & Nelson, R. A. (2000). Issues management: A relational approach. In J. A. Ledingham & S. D. Bruning (Eds.), *Public relations as relationship management: A relational approach to public relations*. Mahwah, NJ: Lawrence Erlbaum Associates.

Broom, G., Casey, S., & Ritchey, J. (1997). Toward a concept and theory of organization-public relationships. *Journal of Public Relations Research, 9*(2), 83–98.

Broom, G., Casey, S., & Ritchey, J. (2000). Toward a concept and theory of organization-public relationships: An update. In J. A. Ledingham & S. D. Bruning (Eds.), *Public relations as relationship management: A relational approach to public relations*. Mahwah, NJ: Lawrence Erlbaum Associates.

Broom, G., & Dozier, D. (Spring, 1986). Advancement for public relations role models. *Public Relations Review, 12*(1), 37–56.

Broom, G. M., & Dozier, D. M. (1990). *Using research in public relations: Applications to program management.* Englewood Cliffs, NJ: Prentice Hall.

Bruning, S. D., & Ledingham, J. A. (1998). Organization-public relationships and consumer satisfaction: Role of relationships in the satisfaction mix. *Communication Research Reports, 15*(2), 199–209.

Bruning, S. D., & Ledingham, J. A. (1999). Relationships between organizations and publics: Development of a multi-dimensional scale. *Public Relations Review, 25*(2), 157–170.

Bruning, S. D., & Ledingham, J. A. (2000). Organization and key public relationships: Testing the influence of the relationship dimensions in a business-to-business context. In J. A. Ledingham & S. D. Bruning (Eds.), *Public relations as relationship management: A relational approach to public relations.* Mahwah, NJ: Lawrence Erlbaum Associates.

Bruning, S. D., & Ledingham, J. A. (2002). Identifying the communication behaviors and interaction patterns of agency-client relationships in development and decline. *Journal of Promotional Management, 18*(2), 21–34.

Center, A. H., & Jackson, P. (1995). *Public relations practices: Management case studies and problems* (5th ed.). Englewood Cliffs, NJ: Prentice Hall.

Coombs, T. (2000). Crisis management: Advantages of a relational perspective. In J. A. Ledingham & S. D. Bruning (Eds.), *Public relations as relationship management: A relational approach to public relations.* Mahwah, NJ: Lawrence Erlbaum Associates.

Cutlip, S. M., Center, A. H., & Broom, G. M. (1994). *Effective public relations.* Englewood Cliffs, NJ: Prentice Hall.

Cutlip, S. M., Center, A. H., & Broom, G. M. (2000). *Effective public relations.* Englewood Cliffs, NJ: Prentice Hall.

Dimmick, S. (with Bell, T. E., Burgiss, S. G., & Ragsdale, C.) (2000). Relationship management: A new professional model. In J. A. Ledingham & S. D. Bruning (Eds.), *Public relations as relationship management: A relational approach to public relations.* Mahwah, NJ: Lawrence Erlbaum Associates.

Dozier, D. M. (with Grunig, L. A., & Grunig, J. E.) (1995). *Manager's guide to excellence in public relations and communication management.* Mahwah, NJ: Lawrence Erlbaum Associates.

Ehling, W. P. (1992). Estimating the value of public relations and communication to an organization. In J. E. Grunig, D. M. Dozier, W. P. Ehling, L. A. Grunig, F. C. Repper, & J. White (Eds.), *Excellence in public relations and communication management* (pp. 617–638). Hillsdale, NJ: Lawrence Erlbaum Associates.

Ferguson, M. A. (1984, August). *Building theory in public relations: Interorganizational relationships.* Paper presented to the Association for Education in Journalism and Mass Communication, Gainesville, FL.

Grunig, J. E. (1989). Symmetrical presuppositions as a framework for public relations theory. In C. H. Botan & V. Hazelton, Jr. (Eds.), *Public relations theory.* Hillsdale, NJ: Lawrence Erlbaum Associates.

Grunig, J. E. (1993, Summer). Image and substance: From symbolic to behavioral relationships. *Public Relations Review, 19*, 121–139.

Grunig, L. A., Grunig, J. E., & Ehling, W. P. (1992). What is an effective organization? In J. E. Grunig, D. M. Dozier, W. P. Ehling, L. A. Grunig, F. C. Repper, & J. White (Eds.), *Excellence in public relations and communication management.* Hillsdale, NJ: Lawrence Erlbaum Associates.

Grunig, J. E., & Huang, Y.-H. (2000). From organizational effectiveness to relationship indicators: Antecedents of relationships, public relations strategies, and relationship outcomes. In J. A.

Ledingham & S. D. Bruning (Eds.), *Public relations as relationship management: A relational approach to public relations*. Mahwah, NJ: Lawrence Erlbaum Associates.

Grunig, J. E., & Hunt, T. (1984). *Managing public relations*. New York: Holt, Rinehart & Winston.

Hazleton, V., Jr., & Botan, C. (1989). The role of theory in public relations. In C. Botan & V. Hazleton, Jr. (Eds.), *Public relations theory*. Hillsdale, NJ: Lawrence Erlbaum Associates.

Knapp, M. (1984). *Interpersonal communication and interpersonal relationships*. Boston: Allyn and Bacon.

Ledingham, J. A. (2000, May). Relationship management: Where do we go from here? Paper presented at the Annual Convention of the International Communication Association, Acapulco, Mexico.

Ledingham, J. A. (2001). Government-community relationships: Extending the relational theory of public relations. *Public Relations Review, 27*, 285–295.

Ledingham, J. A. (2003a). Explicating relationship management as a general theory of public relations. *Journal of Public Relations Research, 15*(2); 181–198.

Ledingham, J. A., & Bruning, S. D. (1997). Building loyalty through community relations. *The Public Relations Strategist, 3*(2); 27–29.

Ledingham, J. A., & Bruning, S. D. (1998). Relationship management and public relations: Dimensions of an organization-public relationship. *Public Relations Review, 24*, 55–65.

Ledingham, J. A., & Bruning, S. D. (2000a). Background and current trends in the study of relationship management. In J. A. Ledingham & S. D. Bruning (Eds.), *Public relations as relationship management: A relational approach to public relations*. Mahwah, NJ: Lawrence Erlbaum Associates.

Ledingham, J. A., & Bruning, S. D. (2000b). A longitudinal study of organization-public relationship dimensions: Defining the role of communication in the practice of relationship management. In J. A. Ledingham & S. D. Bruning (Eds.), *Public relations as relationship management: A relational approach to public relations*, Mahwah, NJ: Lawrence Erlbaum Associates.

Ledingham, J. A., & Bruning, S. D. (2001). Community relations. In R. L. Heath (Ed.), *Handbook of public relations*. Thousand Oaks, CA: Sage.

Ledingham, J. A., & Bruning, S. D. (2006, Autumn). Media relationships. *Journal of Promotional Management* (in press).

Ledingham, J. A., Bruning, S. D., Thomlison, T. D., & Lesko, C. (1997). The transferability of interpersonal relationship dimensions into an organizational setting: A qualitative approach. *Academy of Managerial Communications Journal, 1*, 23–43.

Ledingham, J. A., Bruning S. D., & Wilson, L. J. (1999). Time as an indicator of the perceptions and behavior of members of a key public: Monitoring and predicting. *Journal of Public Relations Research, 11*(2); 167–183.

Leichty, G. & Springston, J. (1993, Winter). Reconsidering public relations models. *Public Relations Review, 19*(4), 327–339.

Littlejohn, S. W. (1992). *Theories of human communication* (4th ed.). Belmont, CA: Wadsworth.

Littlejohn, S. W. (1995). *Theories of human communication* (5th ed.). Belmont, CA: Wadsworth.

Prior-Miller, M. (1989). Four major social science theories and their value to the public relations researcher. In C. Botan & V. Hazelton, Jr. (Eds.), *Public relations theory*. Hillsdale, NJ: Lawrence Erlbaum Associates.

Thomlison, T. D. (2000). An interpersonal primer with implications for public relations. In J. A. Ledingham & S. D. Bruning (Eds.), *Public relations as relationship management: A relational approach to public relations*. Mahwah, NJ: Lawrence Erlbaum Associates.

Toth, E. (2000). From personal influence to interpersonal influence: A model for relationship management. In J. A. Ledingham & S. D. Bruning (Eds.), *Relationship management: A relational approach to public relations*. Mahwah, NJ: Lawrence Erlbaum Associates.

Wilson, L. J. (2000). Building employee and community relationships through volunteerism: A case study. In J. A. Ledingham & S. D. Bruning (Eds.), *Public relations as relationship management: A relational approach to public relations*. Mahwah, NJ: Lawrence Erlbaum Associates.

The Role and Ethics of Community-Building for Consumer Products and Services

With Some Recommendations for New-Marketplace Economies in Emerging Democracies

Dean Kruckeberg
University of Northern Iowa

Kenneth Starck
Zayed University

Marina Vujnovic
University of Iowa

INTRODUCTION

Many manufacturers and service providers nurture "communities" of consumers, raising the question, "What are the social ethics of such consumer
communities for these organizations and their public relations practitioners?"
Further, do these "consumer communities" provide an authentic "sense of community" as advocated by Kruckeberg and Starck (1988), who argue that public
relations is the active attempt to restore and maintain the sense of community
that has been lost in contemporary society? This definition of public relations
suggests significant differences between public relations' role and function
in contrast to those of marketing and advertising—both in the traditional literature of the three communication specializations as well as in the context
of Duncan and Moriarty's (1997) consideration of "brand relationships" and
"mission marketing" of integrated marketing communication.

Distinctions between *publics* and *markets* are widely recognized—if not
fully understood or discretely conceptualized—by scholars and practitioners
in public relations, marketing, and advertising. Nevertheless, marketers and advertisers too often see public relations as a tactical tool for their sales missions,
whereas public relations practitioners commonly see an encompassing role for
public relations, in which public relations practitioners have a societal—as
well as an organizational—function that may in fact coopt and include the
marketing and advertising roles as subfunctions. For example, scholars such
as Kruckeberg and Starck (2000) have examined consumer "communities," arguing that public relations practitioners should be primarily responsible within
their corporations for the development and nurturing of the consumer communities that are formed around corporations' products and services. Although not
restricting public relations responsibilities only to consumers, the two scholars nevertheless maintain that the societal implications of today's consumer
communities extend far beyond the traditional objectives of organizations'
marketing and advertising departments, as well as beyond the perceived tunnel vision of marketers and advertising executives. Rather, Kruckeberg and
Starck (2000) emphasize that consumer communities—when appropriately
formed and nurtured—have an impact on individuals and society at large, an
impact that is best considered from a public relations, rather than a marketing
or advertising, worldview. Indeed, public relations scholars frequently criticize
marketing concepts such as "relationship marketing" as being grossly inadequate in their heuristic value in any theoretical consideration of the scope of
organizations' publics, that is, as no more than "markets" to be cultivated for
sales rather than as an all-encompassing array of publics for which organizations have expanded responsibilities. Finally, Starck and Kruckeberg (2003)
argue that the most important public of any organization is society itself.

Thus, corporations' attempts to develop relationships with the pervasive
"consumer communities" of 21st century global society are significant both

theoretically and ethically—strongly suggesting the need for (a) a deeper consideration of both the role and the ethics of public relations as its practice relates to consumer communities; (b) a fuller exploration and examination of contemporary consumer culture in global society; and (c) specific recommendations for emerging democracies that are developing new-marketplace economies in societies that have not shared the culture and traditions of Western Europe and North America. Some of these considerations are presented in this chapter.

RELEVANCE OF COMMUNITY

Kruckeberg and Starck (2000) remind us that public relations advocacy has always had its limitations, both in its effectiveness in achieving its goals and ethically. Although relationship-building models of public relations might be noble and ethical and beneficial to organizations and their stakeholders, the authors have argued that it is through community-building that public relations best serves society as well as its organizations. Indeed, although contemporary models of public relations, such as Grunig and Hunt's (1984) two-way symmetrical model and Ledingham and Bruning's (2000) relationship management model, are undoubtedly superior to earlier models, one could nevertheless argue that they are not the best normative models of public relations—having inherent weaknesses that must be addressed by scholars. For example, a preoccupation with earning membership in an inherently asymmetrical "dominant coalition" and modeling an organization's relationships to be centered at the hub of a perceived social system, that is, a worldview from which spokes of communication and relationships extend from the organization outward to satellites of stakeholders along a boundary rim, is arguably inferior to a community-building model, in which the organization is not centered so self-importantly. Such a model recognizes that the organization is only an organic part of the whole social system of society, and therefore its responsibility to society is greater—with the public relations practitioners' responsibilities likewise dramatically increased.

Kruckeberg and Starck (1988, p. xi) argue that a fundamental reason why public relations practice exists today is the loss of community resulting from new means of communication and transportation. They maintain that both the history and the definitions of public relations as they have been presented are inadequate, with histories not accounting for the larger social forces operating within the social environment—especially communication technology and transportation. Rather, public relations scholars have tended to settle on simple, one-dimensional explanations of the evolution and contemporary practice of public relations.

In 1988 (p. xi), the authors argued that public relations was commonly practiced as a vocation utilizing persuasion communication to obtain a vested goal on behalf of a represented client, with the goal vaguely defined as goodwill, albeit often linked to marketing objectives. Kruckeberg and Starck (1988) said that only with a goal of restoration and maintenance of a sense of community as a primary objective can public relations become a full partner in the information and communication milieu that has formed the lifeblood of U.S. and global society.

More than a decade later, Starck and Kruckeberg (2001) re-affirmed their belief in their original thesis. They argued that, in light of massive societal changes that had evolved since 1988, and especially the escalating development of communication/transportation technology, multiculturalism, and globalism, community in contemporary society has remained urgently important. Warning of the power of corporations, they observed:

> We believe that . . . corporations ultimately operate by consent of society, which remains in fact the ultimate stakeholder of such corporations to which these organizations are answerable. Society has the right—indeed the obligation—to examine these corporations in light of their power and influence as well as their effect on society. And threats to democracy must be substantively removed.
>
> All of this is best accomplished, however, not by societal restrictions but rather by proactive efforts on the part of corporations to be accountable to society and answerable to all governments and peoples where they operate as well as to the inherent democratic principles of such nations. (p. 59)

The authors suggested that community-building can be proactively encouraged and nurtured by corporations with the guidance and primarily leadership of these organizations' public relations practitioners. In their community-building efforts, these practitioners must consider, their environmental constituencies, that is, everyone potentially affected by these corporations. The authors argued that this new approach to accountability is predicated on the idea that the very existence of corporations depends on public authorization: "Corporations must recognize that the greatest stakeholder—the ultimate environmental constituency—is society itself, to which such corporations are ultimately and irrefutably answerable" (p. 59).

The most important concept in this community-building theory is *community* itself. In examining the writings of the Chicago School of Social Thought, Kruckeberg and Starck (1988, p. 56) identified six elements prevalent in the Chicago School's usage of this term:

1. An individual ordinarily belongs primarily to one community.
2. The individual participates in the common life of the community, is aware of and interested in common ends, and regulates activity in view of those ends. For this, communication is required.
3. Functional differentiation occurs to some extent because people have diverse occupations and activities.

4. People in a community occupy a definable geographic area.

5. Institutions spring up and become prerequisites to community formation.

6. A community develops particular cultural characteristics.

The first criterion identified by the Chicago School of Thought would only apply to the most parochial and provincial individual today, although tendencies might still exist to think of oneself within the context of one primary community. However, those in contemporary society have the sense of belonging to many different communities because of the ease of doing so through contemporary communication technology. The early work of the Chicago School of Thought and the related work of Kruckeberg and Starck (1988) support the idea that a sense of community was lost because of communication/transportation technology. Although this was true with early communication/transportation technologies, new communication technologies have shown promise for an ever-increasing capacity for communicative interactivity, and therefore for the individual's greater participation within the community. Whereas new communication technologies a century ago may have disrupted and dissolved communities, the potential exists today for a sense of community to re-evolve through the ease of community participation that is now available.

The second criterion continues to define the individual both by himself and by others. Membership in the community is defined in part by the community and in part by the individual, himself or herself. Ultimately, an individual's level of participation determines his or her true community membership. To a great extent, the individual controls his or her membership in a community by that individual's participation in this community. The participation requires communication, however. Nevertheless, other community members must recognize and accept the individual's membership in the community.

The third criterion is more pronounced today than ever before, because of the increasing diversification and specialization of individuals' roles and functions in society. People might feel they are members of many communities, but by-and-large they will be identified primarily with only one of these communities. Some might feel more connected and will identify more with their occupational communities, whereas others might identify more with other communities to which they belong, such as consumer communities. Without question, society and communities within society are more complex today than in the past.

The fourth criterion may no longer be true today, as communication technology allows new forms of community to exist. The Chicago School viewed geographic proximity as essential to a community. This view was derived from the Chicago School's traditional belief regarding the necessity of geographic proximity to form a community, a requisite at an earlier time for a high level of participation in a community. Other types of communities were possible, of course, but individuals' level of participation was limited. Today's communication technologies allow for a high level of participation: Web interest groups, teleconferences, newsletters, e-mail, etc. Therefore, geographic proximity no longer plays this important role in defining a community.

The fifth criterion recognizes the need for a communication infrastructure to maintain cultural values and norms. The Chicago School argued that a society's institutions were the foundation upon which communities could be built. An *institution* is an inherent sociological concept that Berger (1963) defined as a "distinctive complex of social actions" (p. 87). He also borrows the explanation of the concept from Arnold Gehlen, who "conceives of an institution as a regulatory agency, channeling human actions in much the same way as instincts channel animal behavior" (p. 87). So institutions are essential for channeling the actions of the people to build the communities that, themselves, become institutions through which people achieve their individual and common goals.

The sixth criterion refers to cultural characteristics that distinguish community members from those outside the community. This is an important criterion to acknowledge, as the massive literature of diffusion and adoption of innovation illustrates. In addition, these cultural values can be and often are spread beyond the members of a community and might be adopted by the larger society as well as become a central value of other communities.

The beginning of the 21st century begs the question what it means to be human within contemporary Western society. New-marketplace economies, especially within emerging democracies, have even redefined the concept of wealth from that of net financial worth to that of the amount and quality of consumer products an individual possesses. In an era of unprecedented personal debt and aggressive marketing of an ever-expanding range of consumer products and services, wealth can no longer be measured according to individual financial worth, and even the concept of debt has become by-and-large meaningless.

A modern household will subscribe to Internet and Web services, to television cable services that offer huge numbers of channels, and to cellular telephones—all unheard of even a few decades ago. The concept of leasing automobiles that individuals could not otherwise afford to drive, of astronomical housing costs, and the plethora of "need for" products and services that were unknown by past generations all point to a society that defines itself by its consumption more than any other criterion. To be human means to possess and to consume. Even higher education has become more of a commodity to be purchased than a degree of achievement to be sought and attained. Where is the community in all of this? This is a particularly poignant question for those who had enjoyed the security of collectivistic societies in the newly emerging democracies that have rapidly adopted marketplace economies. Are there lessons that can be learned from the excesses of a consumer society that would be helpful to those countries that are adopting marketplace economies?

DEFINITIONS OF CONCEPTS

As noted earlier, many concepts important to our discussion—including that of community itself—are subject to diverse interpretations. Although we do not want to give the impression that we possess the pure meaning or the only definitions of these terms, we do want to indicate how we view the concepts that are pertinent to this inquiry. Some of these concepts may, in fact, be peripheral or seem irrelevant to our discussion, but nevertheless may help in understanding our approach and analysis.

Bell (1988, pp. 21–22) says that *mass society* brings people into closer contact with one another and binds them together in new ways because of advances in transportation and communication technology. Division of labor makes individuals more interdependent on one another, while, ironically, becoming more estranged from one another. The standards of an educated *elite* no longer shape opinions and taste, resulting in society's uncertainty about mores and morals, while individuals in society become tangential or compartmentalized. Meanwhile, greater mobility—spatial and social—intensifies individuals' concern over status, and people assume multiple roles—requiring them to constantly prove themselves in a succession of new situations. The individual loses a coherent sense of self, and his or her anxieties increase, together with an ensuing search for "new faiths." This concept of mass society is important because it relates to the loss of the sense of community decried by Kruckeberg and Starck (1988). Bell (1988, p. 51) agrees with Mills, who defines *elite* primarily on the basis of "institutional position," although the term can have broader dimensions in a consumer community.

Goodstein, Nolan, and Pfeiffer (1993, p. 60) regard *culture* as a pattern of deeply held common beliefs and expectations. These beliefs give rise to values that are cherished by a social unit and its members. These values, then, give rise to situational norms that are evidenced in observable behavior. Normative behavior becomes the basis for the validation of beliefs and values from which the norms originated.

Dicken Garcia (1989, p. 15) notes that the term *values* refers to the broad dominant social attributes, behaviors, and larger goals that are advocated, promoted and defended by a society. Dicken Garcia accepts John Finnegan Jr.'s definition of *culture* as "shared ideation behind social behavior among groups"; *society* as a "group of people in social and behavioral interdependence"; *social structure* as the manifestation of "the nature of social and behavioral independence"; and *values* as "ideals"—"desirable, preferable ends that . . . correspond to a pattern of choices or actions." *Wealth* may be defined as the value of the assets of the owner of this wealth (Gwartney and Stroup, 1990, p. 204), although, as mentioned before, consumer communities broaden this definition from that of net financial worth to that of the amount and quality of consumer products and services.

Finally, we define *consumer community*. Our definition is a group of enthusiasts who believe in the superiority of a product or service whose members individually and as a group publicly identify with this product or service. Of course, individual members of these consumer communities remain a part of mass society; however, membership in consumer communities will—in most instances—be elitist and exclusionary because members distinguish themselves from mass society through their use of the product or service.

We argue that consumer community should possess these elements:

1. Continuing presence within the community of the service or product, with enthusiasm for the product or service nurtured by both the corporation and the members of the community.

2. Belief among those in the community concerning the merits of the service or product (the belief is almost religious in the fervor of its adherents, e.g., those abandoning the service or product for a competitor are viewed as heretics).

3. Shared culture as it revolves around the service or product (members of the community create their own meanings and create and share symbols, e.g., participants in a cyberspace community create and share symbols that are used exclusively within and among members of the community; in addition to shared culture, an important factor is shared values as they relate to the service or product).

4. Normative behavior in relation to product or service (members of the community adopt similar behaviors toward the product or service, e.g., the Corvette "wave." Although members of the community might be diverse in other areas of their lives, as their behavior relates to the service or product, it is highly shared. Rules of behavior might be extremely strict as they relate to the service or product, and several rituals might exist that will be centered around this service or product. A substantial knowledge regarding the service or product brings prestige to individual members of the community).

5. Assumed identities related to the product or service (identity created in a consumer community might as strong or stronger than the individual's professional/occupational identity).

6. Members of the community have inordinate power to promote or abandon the product or service, far beyond that of normal customers.

7. Generally, tremendous competition exists for the service or product, with loyalists taking great pride in it while deriding competing brands.

8. Dynamism of the community exists, particularly in the exchange of information about the service or product. Brands create bonds among those who would otherwise not come into contact with one another. In fact, consumer communities are oftentimes global.

ISSUES RELATED TO CONSUMER COMMUNITIES

Germane to public relations scholars and practitioners is the question of the role and function of public relations in a consumer society, that is, what is public relations' societal role that distinguishes its practice from the related—yet distinctly different—practices of marketing and advertising. Indeed, the question is not how public relations must distinguish itself from marketing and advertising, an essentially reactive question, but rather how it defines itself professionally to best serve the needs of organizations and their stakeholders—a proactive approach in which this professional specialization takes the initiative in defining itself. Public relations theorists must challenge—indeed must free themselves from—the past literature of public relations. In this quest, distinctions between public relations and related practices will quickly become apparent as a collateral outcome of this theoretical examination.

What are the dialectics of today's consumer communities? What new forms of democracy can be developed, forms that are perhaps more compatible with collectivist cultures of former communist countries that do not share the histories and traditions of Western Europe and North America? What can be learned from alternative societies and philosophies, ranging from the Amish to those practicing yoga?

Addressing and answering such questions will help public relations practitioners further define and redefine their role and function, not only in their own organizations, but within society itself. Examining these questions will make public relations practitioners a proactive element of organizational management and leadership. Thus, the question becomes, not how does public relations reconcile territoriality, but rather what will public relations become and what must it become in a 21st century global society having consumer communities? These questions must not be addressed reactively, to distinguish public relations from marketing and advertising, but must be addressed philosophically and theoretically and with a truly global worldview.

Kruckeberg and Starck (1988, pp. 112–117) identified eight ways in which public relations practitioners can restore and maintain a sense of community in their organizations and among stakeholders/publics:

1. Practitioners can help community members and the organizations they represent become conscious of common interests that are the basis for both their contentions and their solutions.

2. Practitioners can help individuals in the community to overcome alienation in its several forms.

3. Practitioners can help their organizations assume the role that Dewey reserved for the public schools, that is, in helping to create a sense of community.

4. Public relations practitioners should encourage leisuretime activities of citizens to enhance their sense of community.

5. Practitioners who are concerned with persuasion and advocacy should encourage consummate communication, that is, self-fulfilling communication.

6. Practitioners can help individuals find security and protection through association with others.

7. Practitioners can address interest in community welfare, social order, and progress.

8. Practitioners can help foster personal friendships.

The role of public relations practitioners in the new consumer communities is expanded beyond these eight elements of the concept in what are exciting and highly complex ways, such as in providing understanding of the dynamics of a 21st century society in which consumerism, good or bad, right or wrong, is inextricably linked to people's lives in ways that are not readily obvious or understandable.

Several public relations concepts need to be revisited and further scrutinized, such as the concept of the *nonpublic*, which in a community-building model arguably cannot exist because of everyone's importance within the community and therefore everyone's membership in at least one of an organization's publics. In this context, the long-discredited "general public" is given new meaning—indeed ultimate importance, if society is an organization's most important stakeholder.

The concept of *organic public relations* has heuristic value in the context of Durkheim's (1933) organic solidarity. Also of considerable heuristic value is the concept of *social capital*. Putnam (2000) says social capital can be understood in relation to other forms of capital that interact in a mutually productive way. Physical capital, such as tools, technology, and resources, and human capital, such as skills and education, both have value. Interacting with one another, these two forms of capital have the potential to enhance productivity, both individually and collectively. However, social capital—or networks of people—has the same capability, according to Putnam. He defines *social capital* as referring "to connections among individuals—social networks and the norms of reciprocity and trustworthiness that arise from them" (p. 19).

Social capital may be equated with "civic virtue," and the power of civic virtue, as Putnam points out, rests in "a dense network of reciprocal social relations" (p. 19). If there is social capital, what is the potential for the public relations theoretical development of a "social capitalism"?

The implications of community-building theory for "consumer communities" are many in number, and they are immense in their impact: For example is a consumer community reconcilable to the ideals of the Chicago School of

Social Thought, who envisioned community as having a higher purpose than to use and take pride in a specific product or service? The Eastern European countries, new to democracy and a free-marketplace economy, have embraced all of the negativities and excesses of consumerism in a way that distorts their traditional societal values. Community-building theory applied to consumer communities can provide a philosophical and ideological theoretical framework to help reconcile the new emphasis on consumerism and the affront to traditional values. This is not to say that consumerism and "consumer communities" should be embraced in such new-marketplace economies, nor that public relations practitioners' charge is to "educate" people to be consumers; rather, public relations practitioners have a perhaps unique responsibility to help stakeholders/publics to understand consumer communities and to become more responsible consumers. This role is within the realm of organizations' corporate social responsibility, which is getting greater attention globally as the excesses of powerful corporations become increasingly criticized and as those in traditional societies learn to cope with the cultural implications of the power of consumer communities.

IMPLICATIONS FOR PUBLIC RELATIONS AND FUTURE DIRECTIONS FOR RESEARCH

In a type of "any-community-is-better-than-no-community" mindset, Kruckeberg and Starck (1988) noted that corporations could contribute to community-building in a way that is functional and beneficial for society at large as well as for individual members of society. Maximum benefits will only result, however, if the development and maintenance and nurturance of consumer communities are not viewed narrowly from a marketing perspective.

What are the social ethics of consumer communities? An important issue is elitism, i.e., does membership in a consumer community detract from membership in other communities that might be considered more beneficial to the individual as well as to society, and does a we/they exclusivity result in divisiveness among members of society? Because consumer communities' membership is predicated on the consumption of a specific product or service, the person whose identity is primarily or exclusively based on a consumer product or service might ponder the comparative value of other communities to which he or she might belong, that is, those communities having greater benefit to society.

Do consumer communities provide an authentic "sense of community"? Yes, they have this potential, but consumer communities can be functional or dysfunctional. In societies having a long-time tradition of marketplace economies, consumer communities have the potential to be highly functional, whereas in societies having newly emerging marketplace economies, the potential for dysfunction remains great.

Another important ethical issue is the influence and control of the organization over the consumer community. Consumer communities are voluntary in their membership, as are many other communities, but—unlike many other communities—the organizations providing the products and services have considerable influence over members of these communities, arguably a predominant influence. Thus, an organization must view itself, and members of the consumer community must view it, as only one member of the consumer community rather than the "ruler" or even the "leader" of this community.

We conclude that the public relations practitioner should be primarily responsible in the corporation for fostering and nurturing these consumer communities, making every attempt to encourage the positive benefits of such communities while minimizing and hopefully eliminating the potential negative outcomes, that is, to the individuals within these communities, to society at large, and to other elements of our social environment. Public relations scholars must pay increasing attention to consumer communities and not leave their theoretical foundation to the tunnel vision and singular motives of those only concerned with marketing these products and services. Scholarly inquiry should include why consumer communities exist and their impact on society and on individuals. Also to be explored are the differences between virtual and real communities.

Existing theories in public relations may not be adequate for the challenges provided by consumer communities. Theory-building must consider community-building in the broadest sense that extends beyond the heuristic value of two-way symmetry and relationship-building. Consumer-based marketplace economies challenge the concept of community as envisioned by the Chicago School of Social Thought as well as the theoretical perspective of community-building as proposed by Kruckeberg and Stark (1988) and Stark and Kruckeberg (2001). This chapter did not make an attempt to resolve these theoretical challenges. Rather, this chapter argues that consumer communities must not go unchallenged. They are too much a part of 21st century global society to be ignored by public relations theorists and practitioners.

REFERENCES

Bell, D. (1988). *The end of ideology*. Cambridge, MA: Harvard University Press.
Berger, P. L. (1963). *Invitation to sociology: A humanistic perspective*. Garden City, NY: Anchor Books.
Dicken Garcia, H. (1989). *Journalistic standards in nineteenth-century America*. Madison: University of Wisconsin Press.
Duncan, T., & Moriarty, S. (1997). *Driving brand value: Using integrated marketing to manage profitable stakeholder relationships*. New York: McGraw-Hill.
Durkheim, E. (1933). *The division of labor in society*. New York: Free Press.

Goodstein, L., Nolan, T., & Pfeiffer, J. W. (1993). *Applied strategic planning: A comprehensive guide*. New York: McGraw-Hill.

Grunig, J. E. & Hunt, T. (1984). *Managing public relations*. New York: Holt, Rinehart & Winston.

Gwartney, J. D., & Stroup, R. L. (1990). *Economics: Private and public choice*. San Diego: Harcourt Brace Jovanovich.

Kruckeberg, D., & Starck, K. (1988). *Public relations and community: A reconstructed theory*. New York: Praeger.

Kruckeberg, D., & Starck, K. (2000, November 10) *The role and ethics of community building for consumer products and services*. Paper presented at the convention of the National Communication Association, Seattle, Washington.

Ledingham, J. A., & Bruning, S. D. (Eds.). (2000). *Public relations as relationship management: A relational approach to the study and practice of public relations*. Mahwah, NJ: Lawrence Erlbaum Associates.

Putnam, R. D. (2000). *Bowling alone: The collapse and revival of American community*. New York: Simon & Schuster.

Starck, K., & Kruckeberg, D. (2001). Public relations and community: A reconstructed theory revisited. In R. L. Heath (Ed.), *Handbook of public relations* (pp. 51–59). Thousand Oaks, CA: Sage.

Starck, K., and Kruckeberg, D. (2003). Ethical obligations of public relations in an era of globalisation. *Journal of Communication Management: An International Journal, 8*(1), pp. 29–40.

Building Public Affairs Theory

Elizabeth L. Toth

University of Maryland

This chapter builds theory of the public affairs specialization of public relations by defining public affairs, describing the concepts of public affairs, and proposing theories and research that could help build public affairs theory. Researchers are challenged to test societal corporatism as a useful worldview of public affairs, the findings of the Excellence study and other theories such as activism, social capital, and situational theory.

Public affairs is the specialization of public relations that concerns building public policy relationships between organizations. To be successful, all organizations must understand and build public policy relationships through active collaboration with local, state, and federal public officials. Organizations must strategically differentiate their public affairs relationships from those of their commercial activities, or fail to acknowledge how public policy activities dramatically reduce their autonomy, let alone their efforts to thrive. For example, real communication failures by U.S. pharmaceuticals created public scorn and government threats to ignore drug patents, in order to help millions of South Africans who carry HIV ("Pharmaceuticals Face Uphill Communications Challenge," 2001). J. P. Garnier, CEO of GlaxoSmithKein, retorted to mounting criticism: "We're a very major corporation. We're not insensitive to public opinion. That is a factor in our decision-making" (p. 1).

Definitions of public affairs focus this specialization on the building of relationships in the public policy arena. Paluszek (1995) defined *public affairs* as addressing public policy: "Public affairs helps an organization develop and maintain quality relationships with the various groups of people ('publics') who can influence the future. Public affairs is the public relations practice that addresses public policy and the publics who influence such policy" (xvii). J. E. Grunig (1992) emphasized the public policy concept in his definition of public affairs: "Public affairs applies to fewer communication activities than does public relations/communication management. Public affairs applies to communication with government officials and other actors in the public policy area" (pp. 5–6). Dennis (1995), editor of *Practical Public Affairs*, stated: "The public affairs issues the practitioner has to deal with often have public policy impact. This, in reality, is oftentimes in the public interest however defined, and is thus the public affairs professional's overriding obligation and concern" (p. ix).

Public affairs as a specialization of public relations is found in many types of organizations. As a reflection on this breath of organizations, the 1982 *Public Affairs Handbook* spoke of public affairs from corporate, agency, association, and academic perspectives (Nagelschmidt, 1982). The most recent public affairs handbook, *Practical Public Affairs in an Era of Change*, included experts writing on business, government, agencies, and colleges (Dennis, 1995).

The U.S. federal government is "one of the world's largest governmental employers of public information or public affairs personnel with over 10,000 practitioners (Baker, 1997, p. 454). Government public affairs officers develop political and administrative responses to various government actions, such as public policy-making, public programs, and lobbying for legislation. They are central to developing relationships between bureaucratic governments and their constituencies (Cutlip, Center, & Broom, 2000). Government public affairs officers provide political communication, and information services, develop and protect positive institutional images, and generate public feedback (Baker,1997, pp. 456–458). A first public affairs handbook, *Informing the People: A Public Affairs Handbook* (Helm, Hiebert, Naver, & Rabin, 1981), gave an exclusively governmental perspective.

The U.S. federal government originated the title "public affairs," selecting it over "public relations" because of a 1913 Act of Congress, the Gillett Amendment (Section 107, Title V, U.S. Code), prohibiting "appropriated funds to pay a publicity expert unless specifically appropriated for that purpose." (L. A. Grunig, 1998, p. 103). This language continues, according to a government public affairs officer, "to intimidate those who work in government public relations" (Cutlip, Center Broom, 2000, p. 501.)

Public affairs is a specialization of for-profit and other nonprofit organizations as well. Corporate public affairs dates to the early 1960s (Dennis & Holcomb 1995), combining many communication specializations, such as "government relations, public relations, marketing communication, corporate philanthropy and community relations" (Reynolds, 1995, p. 27).

The most prominent professional association of corporate public affairs officers, The Public Affairs Council, defines *public affairs* as "an organization's efforts to monitor and manage its business environment. It combines government relations, communications, issues management and corporate citizenship strategies to influence public policy, build a strong reputation and find common ground with stakeholders." (What is public affairs 2005).

The Public Affairs Council reported, based on a 1996 Foundation for Public Affairs/Boston University School of Management survey, a list of functions that public affairs officers reported carrying out. These results suggested that a very broad set of functions are connected to public affairs. However, the functions most frequently noted, such as "federal governmental relations (75%), state government relations (75%), community relations (71%) local governmental relations (69%), contributions (69%), and grassroots programs (68%), focus on building public policy relationships" (Public Affairs Council, 2001).[1]

Public affairs as a specialization of public relations seems similar to *issues management,* another specialization of public relations focused on public policy issues. However, issues management refers specifically to a strategic planning process. The Public Relations Society of America defined issues management as the "systematic identification and action regarding public policy matters of concern to an organization" (1987, p. 9). Gaunt and Ollenburger (1995) distinguish public affairs and issues management in this way: "Issues management can be a valuable tool for professionals engaged in public affairs" (p. 199). Heath (1997) defined issues management as "the identification, monitoring, and analysis of trends in key publics' opinions that can mature into public policy and regulatory or legislative constraint on the private sector" (p. 7). Ramsey (1993) reported that members of the Issues Management Association were "more positively involved with two procedures—'environmental scanning for emerging issues' and 'developing communication plans about the issues'—than were other public affairs practitioners" (p. 261). Doug Pinkham

---

[1] The complete listing is as follows: Advertising 39%, Community Relations 71%, Consumer Affairs 17%, Contributions 69%, Educational Affairs/Outreach 44%, Employee Communications 58%, Environmental Affairs 29%, Federal Governmental Relations 75%, Grassroots Programs 68%, Institutional Investor/Financial Relations 23%, International Public Affairs 35%, Issues Management 67%, Local Government Relations 69%, Media Relations 66%, Action Committee 66%, Public Interest Group Relations 51%, Public Relations 64%, Regulatory Affairs 43%, State Government Relations 75%, Stockholder Relations 24%, Volunteer Program 41% (Public Affairs Council, 2001).

(2003), president of the Public Affairs Council, defined issues management as "the process of prioritizing and proactively addressing public policy and reputation issues that can affect an organization's success."

Few corporate public affairs practitioners or people in governmental public affairs define themselves as issues managers. Corporate public affairs officers describe their work in much broader terms, such as relations with a number of constituencies: state, local, and federal government officials, the community, and political action groups, to name a few. Therefore, this chapter takes a broad perspective of public affairs: a perspective that encompasses the many communication specializations of the "noncommercial environment" and that includes relationship building in the public policy arena by both for-profit and governmental organizations.

Public affairs is not only a U.S. subspecialization of public relations. It is a global term, actually preferred over *public relations* in European countries (Vercic, White, & Moss, 1998). Unfortunately, most literature on global public affairs is descriptive rather than theoretical (see Miller & Schlesinger, 2000; Vercic et al.,1998). One example of theory development was the addition of a public relations model, based on the work of K. Sriramesh (1991), Lyra (1991), and Huang (1990) and called the *personal influence model* used in international relations (J. E. Grunig, L. A. Grunig, Siramesh, Lyra, & Huang, 1995). Huang (1990) gave an example of unsavory personal influence in Taiwan where practitioners flatter public officials or provide them with drinks, food, and gifts.

This chapter synthesizes the academic and trade public relations literature on public affairs. The first section describes concepts that distinguish the public affairs practice from other specializations of public relations: the noncommercial environment; public policy, the public policy process; and publics' opinions, community, and communal relationships. The second section synthesizes from the academic and trade literature some of the theoretical work of public relations that is related to further our understanding of public affairs. These theories include the situational theory of publics; worldviews of political systems; communitarianism; social capital theory; theories from the Excellence study; and activism theory. Concluding comments make suggestions for developing research in public affairs.

CONCEPTS OF PUBLIC AFFAIRS

Although the public affairs specialization of public relations has a long history of practice, there is no agreement on what the central concepts of the public affairs domain are. Three characteristics may help shape its study (Toth, 1986). First, public affairs should focus on the political and social issues emerging from an organization's private interests. Deetz (1995) argued that public decisions are made at private sites. For example, corporations can no longer exist separated from the political effects of their activities. "Corporations have come to have powerful effects on social decision making" (p. 36). Second, the success of public affairs is interdependent on many interests outside the control of specific organizations. For example, Bovet (1994) concluded that to do successful environmental affairs, counselors would need to "build coalitions, bring about consensus, influence legislation, and help resolve difficult questions about such issues as siting and waste management" (p. 4). Third, public affairs crosses organizational boundaries, providing a window out, to learn about external change, and a window in, though which society can affect corporate policy (Post, 1980). "Public affairs is, then a boundary-spanning function with one foot firmly planted in the organization and the other one in the social and political environment" (p. 23). From these summary characteristics and definitions, there seem to be at least five concepts of the public affairs domain: the noncommercial environment; public policy, public policy process, public opinion, community, and communal relationships.

The Noncommercial Environment

Organizational theorists such as Robbins (1990) identified the environment as one of five determinants of how organizations structured themselves. Organizations recognized that beyond their boundaries were potential economic markets and social and political activities that may be opportunities or constraints on organizational goals.

One of the first public relations researchers to write about the noncommercial environment was J. E. Grunig (1984). J. E. Grunig called the public relations behaviors of organizations generated by a political/regulatory environment "public affairs." He proposed a typology of public relations models based on the political/regulatory environment. His independent variables were the extent of environmental constraints and environmental uncertainty. He hypothesized that "the symmetry of public relations activities has a curvilinear relationship to the extent of environmental constraints" (p. 23). When organizations completely dominated their political/regulatory environments, as Enron reportedly did, or are highly constrained, such as the U.S. Congress, whose delegates must stand for election every 2 years, they would practice asymmetrical public relations. When environmental uncertainty was low, such as in public school districts, organizations would have little reason to provide information and would limit this to one-way communication models such as press agentry or public information. "It was at a middle level of environmental constraint that the organization is more likely to practice symmetrical public relations" (J. E. Grunig, 1984, p. 23).

Toth (1986) recommended research, based on J. E. Grunig's 1984 work, to examine the kinds of political/social issues that made up the public affairs organizational environment. "The more varied the political/social issues an organization faces, the more likely the organization faces an uncertain environment. Whether these issues remain stable or changed over time would predict the amount of environmental constraint" (p. 34).

Although "the environment" poses challenges to organizations, such as building the appropriate structures to accomplish organizational goals, Vercic and J. E. Grunig (1995) also contended that organizations gained competitive advantages through successful relationships with the actors of their environments—competitors, governments, and other stakeholder publics.

> For example, a corporation that successfully solves its environmental problems, usually when pressured by environmental activism, will gain an advantage from relationships with stockholders, consumers, employees, government, and communities that can support or constrain the corporation. Likewise, a government agency that responds well to pressures from its constituents will be more likely to gain support from those publics as it competes for limited funding. (J. E. Grunig & L. A. Grunig, 1997, pp. 2–3)

More recent public relations research suggests that the environment is less of an influence than the people who choose which aspects of the environment are important to their organizations. Those in power, the *dominant coalition,* ultimately perceive and control the definitions of the environment (Dozier, L. A. Grunig & J. E. Grunig, 1995, p. 15). Robbins (1990) refers to this as "strategic choice" and states that "perceptions and evaluations of events are an important intervening link between environments and the actions of organizations" (p. 242).

Public Policy

Little has been written in the public relations literature defining or describing what *public policy* is. Heath (1997) used Buchholtz's (1988) definition of *public policy* as "a specific course of action taken collectively by society or by a legitimate representative of society, addressing a specific problem of public concern that reflects the interests of society or particular segments of society" (p. 53). Public policy is the result of several groups or constituencies coming together to decide what to do about specific problems of public concern.

Public policy does not refer to decisions made through public opinion, as the word "public" might suggest. Rather, makers of public policy guide the actions of others. Public policy makers impose their will on institutions and individuals. Gandy (1992, p. 135) noted that traditionally we believe that the public policy role is confined to government organizations. Legislatures, executive agencies, courts, and local governments make public policy. However, he argued that the corporate and foundation boardrooms are also important policy centers. As a by-product of their existence and pursuit of profit, corporations can potentially create policies that affect various publics, including individuals who have limited recourse (Gandy, 1992, pp. 135–136). Consider how corporations push for favorable trade policies even at the cost of U.S. jobs.

The Public Policy Process

Public policy formation is a form of collective decision making. Gandy (1992) defined the process of formation as "the negotiation of agreements among policy actors with standing and resources about the nature of the problem to be addressed" (p. 136).

There has been very little written in the public relations literature about the concept of a public policy arena or process. Reynolds (1995) hints at a process in these tips in moving from public relations to public affairs: "Get a book on the agency with which you are dealing and how it works; get a guide to how Congress works; and learn how the law and regulations affect your problem" (p. 4). Gandy (1992) discussed one policy process model and the critical role of public relations in providing information. The phases of the public policy process included the identification phase; efforts to formulate alternative solutions presented for adoption by actors with formal authority; implementation of the policy; and specification of the procedures to be followed to make sure that the intent of the policy makers is evident to its administration (p. 136).

According to Gandy (1992), public relations provides "the objective facts," (p.138) but also provides information that helps to structure the problem, identify options and marginalizes the opposition" (pp. 138–140). Public relations does this through information subsidies (see also the work of Turk, 1986, and Turk & Franklin, 1987), relevant information provided conveniently and "for free" to policy-makers. Subsidized information comes through direct methods such as reports, testimony, and hearings. It comes indirectly as well through use of the media and grass-roots lobbying. Gandy noted that technology would enhance information subsidies, a prediction that has clearly come true 10 years after he wrote this opinion.

Public's Opinions, Not Public Opinion

Public affairs practitioners have to work with external information about social and political issues through assessments of public opinion. As boundary spanners, they must identify what that opinion is and communicate it to their organizations. However in the public relations literature, there exists oversimplified views of what public opinion means. Public relations people have defined pubic opinion as "perceptions, cognitions, or attitudes" that cause behavior. They seek to determine opinion through surveys and polls, snap-shots in time of samples of mass audiences or populations.

Data based on survey research come with three faulty assumptions (J. E. Grunig, 1994). Assumption 1: There is such a thing as the public opinion, an average of individual views. Realistically, there are people in groups, samples, and society that have opinions on issues. But, not all people pay attention to all issues equally. They rarely spend time developing opinions about all issues. Instead, whether individuals have opinions depends on several things, such as access to information, time, and interest. Assumption 2: For one person, there is one vote. Many people do not exercise their right to vote, a form of expressing one's opinions. Indeed, public policy makers have to be very specific about what kinds of votes will count when attempting to influence legislation and election campaigns. Assumption 3: Gaining public opinion support means "getting out the word," typically through the mass media. This assumption shows complete ignorance about mass media effects and how indeed people select and choose to be influenced. Yet, still public relations people try to "get out the word" to gain public opinion support (J. E. Grunig, 1994), even when there's no opinion there.

We need to think conceptually about not one public opinion, but many publics and their opinions. J. E. Grunig (1994) defined opinion, as "outcomes" of the communication behavior. He argued that conceptualizing many distinct publics and their communication behaviors made for much more precision in public relations planning and evaluation:

> It is important, therefore, to sort out what outcomes are possible before choosing objectives for public relations programs and developing measures of those objectives for evaluation purposes—just as it is to conceptualize the publics with which organizations need to build relationships before developing communication programs. (p. 4)

John Dewey defined a *public* as "an active social unit consisting of all those affected who recognize a common problem for which they can seek common solutions" (Cutlip, Center & Broom, 2000, p. 268). This definition of public becomes problem or opportunity specific, recognizing that groups of people organize and disperse around problems, issues, or actions that they recognize as being important enough so that they will become actively engaged in them. Publics form around issues and organizations because of what these organizations attempt to achieve. Publics are dynamic rather than static; public relations people rarely have the luxury of choosing their publics. Instead, publics choose organizations and issues to address.

J. E. Grunig (Grunig and Hunt, 1984) built on Dewey's definition of publics by proposing that this definition would imply four groups: a *nonpublic* that has no consequences for an organization and vice versa; a *latent public* that fails to recognize problems; *aware publics* that do recognize a problem; and *active publics* that organize and do something about their problems (p. 145). L. A. Grunig (1992) added to this categorization the *activist public*: "a group of two or more individuals who organize in order to influence another public or publics through action that may include education, compromise, persuasion, pressure tactics, or force" (p. 504).

Community, Communal Relationships

The concepts of *community* and *communal relationships* describe actions taken for the collective rather than the individual good. Kruckeberg and Starck (1988) took the position that public relations should produce a sense of community. They defined community in this way: "Community encompasses what we also refer to as environmental constraints, that is, all those groups that affect or are affected by an organization" (Stark & Kruckeberg, 2001, p. 56). Under the heading of "Democracy," they challenged corporations "to consider larger questions that deal with society and ultimately, with life itself and the values that give life meaning for each of us" (p. 54).

Hon and Grunig (1999) have proposed as one measure of effective relationships the exchange-communal measure, which will vary along a line that defines the kinds of relationships produced in marketing versus the kind of relationships produced in public relations. In marketing, the focus of the relationship between an organization and its customers is one of exchange. "In an exchange relationship, one party gives benefits to the other only because the other has provided benefits in the past or is expected to do so in the future" (Hon & Grunig, p. 20). Cutlip, Center, & Broom (2000) described the exchange relationship as "quid-pro-quo" (p. 8), something for something.

Hon and Grunig (1999) continue that often an exchange relationship is not enough. "Publics expect organizations to do things for the community for which organizations get little or nothing in return (p 21). Organizations engage in communal relationships because it is the right thing to do; it is socially responsible behavior. Communal relationships may or may not benefit the organization, but they may reduce the likelihood of negative consequences, such as public policy decisions that restrict organizational activities. Hon and Grunig give a public affairs example that illustrates the exchange-communal continuum:

A Nuclear Reactor in a Residential Community. The story is very familiar for organizations that must deal with toxic waste. Radioactive waste from the nuclear reactor at a national laboratory leaks into the ground water. Laboratory officials say nothing. Soon, however, someone tests the water for a well. Pollution is spotted in a stream. Local media report the leakage. Community activists are enraged. They feel they have no control over their own health. The laboratory has said little about the problem, so residents do not trust what they say in the future. The exchange of jobs for health is insufficient for the activists. Obviously, residents feel dissatisfied with the relationship and believe that the laboratory has no commitment to the welfare of its neighbors.

Active involvement of the community and complete openness to the media, however have begun to repair the relationship. The laboratory needs to do its research; the community wants to preserve its health and safety. Working with a citizen advisory panel and local leaders, trusting, communal, and mutually satisfactory relationship are developing between the lab and its neighbors. (p. 23)

All of the concepts described in this section sharpen the focus of public affairs. The actors, processes, and communication strategies are more clearly defined as issue or situation specific, with power distributed to coalitions of publics, individuals, and organizations, accommodating as well as competing for support for the resolution of issues that have communal implications.

THEORIES FOR PUBLIC AFFAIRS

Although there is little public affairs theory, there are several theories of public relations that suggest starting points for a theoretical discussion of public affairs. These theories seem germane to public affairs because they touch on public affairs concepts and functions: the situational theory of publics; worldviews of political systems; relationship building to support the community; social capital as a measure of effective relationships; the results of the Excellence Study; and theories of activism.

Situational Theory of Publics

The situational theory of publics, first presented in 1984 by J. E. Grunig and Hunt in *Managing Public Relations*, advanced significantly the theory on public opinion by defining publics and their opinions as communication behavior. This approach helped explain how public relations people could categorize publics more strategically. Whereas others have defined publics based on demographics, geographics, psychographics, community, power, membership, reputation, and role in the decision-making process, (Broom & Dozier, 1990, pp. 32–36; Grunig and Repper, 1992), J. E. Grunig defined publics based on communication behavior that was "purposive and active: a tool for solving problems" (J. E. Grunig, 1994, p. 7).

The situational theory is based on three independent variables and their influence on information-seeking behavior: The independent variables were problem recognition, constraint recognition, and level of involvement:

- *Problem recognition.* People detect that something should be done about a situation and stop to think about what to do.
- *Constraint recognition.* People perceive that there are obstacles in a situation that limit their ability to do anything about the situation.
- *Level of involvement.* The extent to which people connect themselves with a situation.

These independent variables influence two communication outcomes or dependent variables: active information seeking or passive information seeking. Situational theory stated that "high problem recognition and low constraint recognition increased both active information seeking and passive information processing. Level of involvement increases information seeking but has less effect on information processing" (J. E. Grunig, 1994, p. 7). People who recognize problems and believe they can do something about them seek information. They are more likely to form groups and try to do something about the situation.

The basic situational theory of publics led to finding a set of segmented profiles of active and passive information-seeking publics. Initially, J. E.Grunig believed that these profiles would be different for each issue. However, his analysis defined the same profiles even over different issues:

- *All-issue publics.* Publics active on all of the problems.
- *Apathetic publics.* Publics inattentive to all of the problems.
- *Single-issue publics.* Publics active on one or a small subset of the problems that concerns only a small part of the population.
- *Hot-issue publics.* Publics active only on a single problem that involves nearly everyone in the population and that has received extensive media coverage. (J. E. Grunig, 1994, p. 9)

Recent research in situational theory has added cognitive, attitudinal, and behavioral effects to the list of dependent variables. J. E. Grunig concluded that cognitions, attitudes, and behaviors are communication outcomes and not causes. "In that way, research can help us understand our publics, but we are not drawn into the asymmetrical presupposition that the research will allow us to control the behavior of publics" (J. E. Grunig, 1994, p. 27).

Advantages to examining public affairs from the situational perspective include the premise that communication behaviors are situation specific, an important premise in public affairs because each issue is a focal point around which organizations choose to enter or retreat from the public policy process. Second, situational theory focuses on groups of people in relationships with organizations rather than aggregates of individuals. Given that we can learn whether publics are active or passive information seekers, we can design public affairs strategies accordingly.

Political System Worldviews

Public affairs officers make assumptions on a daily basis about the political system values in which they operate. However, they may not theoretically consider how these shape the public policy objectives that they pursue. For example, Berger (2001) used as his theoretical perspective on public policy influence the "elitist" worldview. "Elitist theorists argue that corporate interest groups influence policy through significant financial expenditures and established connections with policy makers; economic power equates political power" (p. 94).

However, according to J. E. Grunig and Jaatinen (1998), political scientists have paid the most attention to pluralist and corporatist theories (p. 70). Pluralism represented the relationship between organizations and publics as one of competition. "All organizations, including corporations and nonprofits, believing in a pluralistic worldview, would see the relationship between government agencies and publics as one of competition—a competition among interest groups for access to government funds and services."(Grunig & Jaatiinen, 1998, p. 70)

Pluralism is the political system worldview that assumes "that ideas freely complete with one another in a marketplace of ideas" (Coombs, 1993, 112). "In essence, pluralism is the *ideal* type of government where all parties have equal access to and equal power in the policy making process" (Coombs, 1993, p. 112, quoting Smith). Governments sometimes involved themselves in this competition when it is in the interests of the citizenry to do so. But, governments also opened the door to everyone equally without giving preference to any individual interest. According to Cawson (1986): "In a pluralist system, there are multiple voluntary organizations competing with each other for power and influence on political decision-making. The general means of influence is to exert pressure on the elected leaders" (pp. 27–30).

Generally, there is criticism that a pluralistic worldview has become outdated (Coombs, 1993; Grunig & Jaatinen, 1998). Among the criticisms of this worldview are that pluralism assumed that access is equally available to all parties. Researchers recognized that access is not equal and that groups must have money, status, and media support, to identify a few influencing variables (Coombs, 1993, p. 113). Critics attack pluralism because it does not consider power differences in groups, which would translate into access to government

Pluralism_____SocietalCorporatism_____Corporatism
Pure Advocacy	Collaborative Advocacy	Pure Collaboration
Private Interests	Balancing of self-interests with interests of others	Collaborative Interests

FIG. 20.1   Three political views of society: pluralism, social corporatism, and corporatism.

officials. Two other criticisms deal with counter balances in the policy-making process and the self-interests of policy makers. Counter balances are built into the political system, but critics argue that power differences do not disappear because of this. Finally, public policy makers use power to promote their own self-interests, a variable not even considered in pluralism (Coombs, 1993, p. 113).

Corporatism was pluralism's opposing worldview. This worldview considered that society valued the rights of the collectivity over the individual. Coombs (1993) described corporatism as a policy-making process denying access to groups that do not have clientelistic relationships with government departments or agencies (p. 112). Cawson (1986) described corporatism in this way:

> There is a concentration of power to the economically powerful who are granted a representational monopoly in their own sphere of competence by the state and who act as self-regulating agents implementing the decisions. The interest groups are a part of government administration negotiating policies with state agencies. (pp. 32–38)

Corporatist theorists saw the relationship between organizations and publics as one of pure collaboration between organizations and publics (Grunig, 2000). Examples of corporatism given are bureaucratically structured and controlled systems that predominated in Eastern Europe (Grunig, 2000). Coombs (1993) and Grunig (2000) do not develop corporatism as a worldview much further because it is an extreme for which we can find little practice in our modern global societies.

Grunig and Jaatinen (1998) posited that many political systems fall between the ends of a pluralism/corporatism continuum, and pluralism and corporatism exist at the same time. They stated that such political systems represent a *societal corporatism* worldview (see Figure 20.1). In them, society is made up of relationships between governments and publics (private and public interest groups). Publics compete for government support through legislation and regulation of issues, and governments attempt to gain support and persuade interest groups.

> Societal corporatism represents a relationship between governments and publics (interest groups in the language of comparative politics) that incorporate aspects of pluralism (in which publics compete for government attention) and corporatism (in which governments attempt to co-opt and dominate publics and interest groups attempt to capture government for their own purposes. (Grunig, 2000, p. 40)

Grunig and Jaatinen (1998) further describe societal corporatism as making possible both pressure politics and negotiation. Groups could not merely dominate or be granted monopolies to implement public policy, but would have to practice strategic, symmetrical public relations. The relationships of a societal corporatist political system would encourage more of a situational view and would encourage collaboration rather than the individualistic competition of the pluralist view.

Societal corporatism implies that one takes a situational perspective to public policy issues. "In societal corporatism, interest groups exert influence either through pressure politics or negotiation, depending on the sphere a group is operating in" (J. E. Grunig & Jaatinen, 1998). Societal corporatism suggests the making of different choices of public affairs strategies, based on specific issues. Societal corporatism as a worldview also pushes groups to win-win solutions, rather than win-lose. Societal corporatism seems also to respect the kinds of social networks and relationships that develop over time between organizations and publics. J. E. Grunig (2000) values this kind of democracy because "government agencies collaborate and bargain with publics they are supposed to serve or regulate to balance the interest of those publics and society at large" (p. 41). The communication strategy in this perspective is collaborative advocacy.

Spicer (1997) provided an example of collaborative advocacy in his book on organizational public relations. A City School District (CSD) faced considerable public pressure over a program for highly capable children known as the Horizon program. The program identified gifted children and placed them in advanced classes at area elementary schools. The result was the formation of a task force composed of parents, teachers, and two district administrators. Their charge was to recommend an effective model to deliver this program to the school district. Over the course of the next 2 years, the task force met weekly to struggle with the issue of highly capable education. A solution to this challenge came only after the task force expanded the original issue and established more of a collaborative relationship with the several groups involved. Spicer (1997) concluded:

Over time, as the task force rumbled and grumbled its way toward an emotionally and politically accepted proposal, a somewhat more collaborative frame was established. This came about primarily because the task force, seeking to gain support for highly capable education in a hostile environment, expanded the scope of the original charge. The task force adopted a larger arena, one that allowed for the incorporation of numerous other programs, thereby alleviating fears of administrators and teachers. (p. 261)

Although J. E. Grunig argues that societal corporatism provides a clearer picture of democracy, few public relations scholars have tested this position. What little has emerged seems to continue to reflect the pluralist position. For instance, Dozier and Lauzen (1998) called for a study of a different kind of public relations that would help less powerful groups such as activist organizations, because they could not compete with established organizations in the public policy arena. To J. E. Grunig (2000), assumptions of pluralism—competition, confrontation, and individualism—are too limiting a view of public relations. "In contrast, I believe that we can—and should—look at a democratic society as a society based on collaboration as well as advocacy" (p. 39). Societal corporatism has as its outcome collaboration, achieving a win-win outcome for community and individual goals. Communitarian theory continues to argue for the balancing of individual rights and community goals.

Communitarianism

Sense of community as an important public affairs concept also comes from theoretical work of public relations researchers on *communitarianism* (Culbertson & Chen, 1997; K. A. Leeper, 1996; R. Leeper, 2000). Communitarianism is an approach to balancing individual rights with community responsibilities, established in 1990 by a group of ethicists, social philosophers, and social scientists (K. Leeper, 1996, p. 165). K. Leeper described communitarianism's critical look at the political system, citing founder Amitai Etzioni: "The public's current loss of control over our political institutions calls for a new progressive movement, a major social effort to energize a package of reforms that will reduce the role of special interests in the government of our local and national communities" (Etzioni, 1993, p. 234). Culbertson and Chen promoted communitarianism's stress on balancing rights and responsibilities, citizen empowerment, and the reduction of social fragmentation. R. Leeper (2000) argued that communitarianism served as a metatheory for public relations. He summarized themes from this worldview as "a rebalancing between individualism and community; a conception of human beings as integrally related to the communities of culture and language that they create; the opposite of liberalism and its emphasis on the individual" (p. 96). R. Leeper focuses communitarianism on the situated self. "The situating of the self entails participatory interaction with a public arena that produces common ends and agreed-on basic values" (p. 98). This theoretical view emphasizes respect and trust throughout an active participative problem-solving process because of the highest value of all parties on the community.

Social Capital Theory

Another theory that shows promise for explaining how public affairs works is *social capital theory*. Social capital theory considers the relationships that people create through their involvement in groups. It has promise for a theory of public affairs because it gives specificity to how individuals in organizations build relationships that lead to overall decision-making. Social capital theory moves away from a "rational" model of decision-making that focuses on the logical or factual outcomes.

Hazleton and Kennan (2000, June 26 and July 24) argued that social capital emerges through social structures that facilitate communication exchanges. "These exchanges involve individuals, groups, organizations, cultures & nations, producing a shifting sea of relational creation, maintenance & dissolution that forms the framework for successful organizational activity" (Hazleton & Kennan, 2000, June 26.) Out of the communication exchanges come social relationships, which can be banked, analogously to financial capital. Social network participants build and bank obligations and expectations that can be spent on accomplishing various goals and objectives.

Organizational structures that permit emerging relationships have five dimensions. The first dimension is a system of network connections, which influences relationship outcomes. Elements of this configuration make up the next four dimensions. The second dimension is access or opportunity to send and receive messages as well as knowledge of appropriate network channels for communication. The third dimension is timing, a consequence of knowledge and network structures. Speed is often critical to compete in the marketplace. But, timing refers to appropriateness of contact as well. The fourth dimension is referral. Some networks required that others refer one for membership. The fifth dimension is appropriable social organization. "Social capital from personal relationships may be aggregated to create organizations." (Hazleton and Kennan, 2000, July 26, p. 2).

Hazleton and Kennan propose that social capital is a means of evaluating public relations success for two reasons. First, public relations effectiveness can be predicted based on access, referral, timing, and appropriate social characteristics of networks (2000, June 26, p. 2). Second, they hypothesized that "the connectedness of practitioners to internal networks is likely to be an indicator of the influence of public relations on the organization" (p. 2). If a public relations person has social capital throughout an organization, through connectedness, access, timing, and appropriate social organization, he/she is achieving excellent public relations (Hazleton & Kennan, June 26).

There are three consequences of social capital. As organizations use social capital, there can be increased and/or more complex forms of social capital to emerge; there is reduction in transaction costs because relationships are already established; and, there may be organizational advantage. Some public relations outcomes include "increased commitment to management and the organizational framework, better community relations based on employee responses and positive media attention (Hazleton & Kennan, 2000, July 24, p. 2) Hazleton and Kennan connect social capital theory to communication excellence because it gives a clearer measure of how public relations relates to organizational goals. Social capital theory would seem to have applicability to the networking and interpersonal relations that are part of lobbying and government relations.

Theories from the Excellence Study

Theories from the Excellence Study that relate to theory building in public affairs included the practical application of the symmetrical model with constituent groups, activism, and how excellent practices of public relations played out in governmental organizations. The Excellence Study of 1992 (J. E. Grunig, 1992; Dozier, Grunig, L.A., & Grunig, J. E., 1995) was the most comprehensive original research project ever done to examine how public relations contributed to organizational effectiveness. A team of researchers developed an extensive set of hypotheses on the roles, models, and organizational influences that would determine the most excellent practices of public relations. There were 321 organizations in the study from three countries. Of these organizations, there were 148 corporations, 58 nonprofits, 44 associations, and 71 government agencies.

The results of this study included a 20-item Excellence factor. This factor, based on an examination of surveys of chief communicators, senior management, and employees, suggested that communication excellence had three parts: a knowledge base of the communication department to play the communication manager role and to use both two-way symmetrical and asymmetrical models of public relations; shared expectations about communication with senior management, and an organizational culture that was supportive of female employees and participative rather than authoritarian.

The Excellence study included qualitative case study research of 24 organizations ranking high on the Excellence scale. From this analysis, the team proposed a series of propositions on how public relations should be carried out: listen to all strategic constituencies; telling the story of the organization; communicating continuously; acknowledging the legitimacy of all constituent groups; having expertise to use two-way symmetrical public relations; and determining effectiveness over the long run, rather than in short-term wins and losses. Finally, the team posted that pubic relations must be in or close to the dominant coalition.

Activism

Theories of activism and public affairs practices are linked in important ways. First, activist groups present the most challenge to organizations because they are organized and seek purposefully to make organizations change their behaviors. Second, activist groups seek partnerships with governments, "trying to enlist the support of a governmental body in a crusade against an offending organization (L. A. Grunig, 1992, p. 511). Third, L. A. Grunig noted that Mintzberg (1983) listed activist or special interest groups as one of three categories of powerful external publics (along with the mass media and government).

A theory of how public relations and activist organizations could build successful relationships first appeared in the 1992 Excellence Study literature review (L.A. Grunig). The Excellence study considered when and why the efforts of public relations practitioners were effective or excellent, as related to issues of activist groups. Based on a series of case studies, L. A. Grunig presented these propositions about activism. First, activism is a major problem for organizations because activist groups apply public opinion pressure against organizations, threatening resulting government regulation. There are a wide variety of activist organizations that use a variety of techniques to court public opinion. Activist groups and organizations rely on public relations communication. More than a few organizations have tried to ignore pressure from outside publics. All of J. E. Grunig's (1984) models of public relations were found in the organizations that communicated with activist groups. L. A. Grunig's results were inconclusive about the use of two-way symmetrical public relations as the most effective model, although the press agentry, public information, and two-way asymmetrical models did not seem successful in coping with activism.

On activism, the Excellence team hypothesized that activism would push organizations toward excellence in public relations and communication management:

> Organizations that face activist pressure would be more likely to assign public relations a managerial role, include public relations in strategic management, communicate more symmetrically with a powerful adversary or partner, and develop more participative cultures and organic structures that would open the organization to its environment. (J. E. Grunig & L. A. Grunig, 1997, p. 10)

The team found moderate support for this hypothesis. Activism stimulated excellent public relations, defined as strategic, managerial, symmetrical, and diverse (p. 12). "They succeed more often in their dealings with activists; and this success does not appear to come at the expense of activists failing to achieve their goals" (p. 12).

The Excellence team posited that activist groups would practice public relations in the same ways as any other kind of organization or group. J. E. Grunig and L. A. Grunig (1997) proposed five steps in the development of a theory of public relations in activist organizations: Use the logic of the situational theory; use strategic public relations planning and coalition building to enlarge the power of the original group; make an attempt to communicate symmetrically; but if the organization does not respond, use asymmetrical techniques; once media pressure, government intervention, or the courts have forced the organization to consider the problem, return to symmetrical public relations and conflict resolution (p. 38).

Excellence in Government Organizations

The Excellence Study team posited that a theory of strategic public relations management would not be based on type of organization. Although there were differences among corporation, nonprofit and government organizations, "the range of differences was slight and of no practical significance" (Dozier, et al., 1995, p. 181). Excellence in public relations across organizations will look the same. This finding supports a theory of public affairs that is not specific to type of organization.

However, based on the Excellence Study findings, J. E. Grunig and Jaatinen (1998) concluded that "although organizations are more likely to be effective when their public relations function helps to build strategic symmetrical relationships, specific applications of this theory will differ in a government agency" (p. 67).

> There will be more stakeholders and there will be conflicting stakeholders for a government agency to take into account. In addition, the leaders who provide strategic direction for a government agency are not only the 'managers' of that agency but also legislators and the chief executive of the nation, state or locality. (Grunig & Jaatinen, 1998, p. 67)

J. E. Grunig and Jaatinen posited that there needs to be a government communication theory that adapts the Excellence principles to the government setting. They provided this theoretical basis by reviewing the theories of pluralism, corporatism, and societal corporatism.

The Excellence Study team recently attempted to globalize the theory of excellence. They identified 10 major principles from the Excellence Study that they believed would be general principles that could be used throughout the world. Important to public affairs research, two variables considered to influence the application of the 10 generic principles were the political system and the extent of activism.

THEORY BUILDING FOR PUBLIC AFFAIRS

In the context of public relations, there is little theory about public affairs. Although the subspecialization is well established within the public relations domain, there still needs to be developed explanations of why public affairs is practiced as it is, the processes of public affairs, and public affairs' contribution to organizational effectiveness. The concepts that belong in this discussion are the noncommercial environment, public policy, the public policy process, and publics' opinions', community and communal relationships. The theories from public relations that show promise are the situational theory of publics; political system worldviews; social capital theory, activism; and benchmark criteria from the Excellence study. This section proposes the direction and types of research that might develop theory about public affairs.

Initially, more audits should be done of public affairs practitioner roles and contributions to their organizations. Although some descriptive research is available, continuing to count the numbers of people, budgets and activities of public affairs units would be helpful over time as an inductive approach to theory building.

Research and theory building about public affairs should focus on how public policy relationships are built. Researchers should consider the external relationships of organizations with their potential and many different and ever-changing groups, publics, and stakeholders. As situations, issues, or problems of public affairs change, how will these alliances change? What will be the worldviews, values, and communication models to use in public affairs, or will these change based on such variables as power, environment, and community?

Public affairs, like public relations, should be measured for excellence, using the 20-item excellence factor. There should be no difference in excellence by specialization or by type of organization. However, there will be different applications of the theories of excellence because of influencers such as the political system and amount of activism.

Researchers should test the usefulness of the societal corporatism worldview of democracy, contrasting this to the older political science views of pluralism and corporatism.

Researchers should take the next steps in testing these starting points by looking for cases of public affairs' contributions to public policy-making and whether best public affairs practices were evident. These best practices should include a push for collaborative advocacy and relationship building that stresses the community over organizational or individual gain. What ideal public affairs practices would achieve in the public policy process is a win-win zone for all the policy-makers. The excellent processes of policy-making should provide evidence of situational analysis rather that taking stances based on history or organizational preferences. There should be an analysis of specific publics' communication behavior. Public affairs practitioners may use social capital, information subsidies, public hearings, and position papers as several of the tactics to advance collaborative advocacy.

Public relations scholars should claim the public affairs subspecialization as a rich opportunity to learn more about a critical communication management practice. They should work from previous public relations theory, but they should also look further at the political science and public administration theories on public policy processes and makers. The political science body of knowledge puts public policy making on a larger stage than the processes of communication involved. Political scientists rarely look at public relations theory as a means of informing their theory making. Public relations, political science; and public administration collaboration is possible and worth pursuing because public affairs should add the vital and missing strategic communication piece.

REFERENCES

Baker, B. (1997). Public relations in government. In C. L. Caywood (Ed.)., *The handbook of strategic public relations and integrated communications* (pp. 453–480). New York: McGraw-Hill.

Berger, B. K. (2001). Private issues and public policy: Locating the corporate agenda in agenda-setting theory. *Journal of Public Relations Research, 13*(1), 91–126.

Bovet, S. F. (1994, April). Environmental affairs practice today requires sophisticated counselors. *Public Relations Journal, 50*, 4.

Broom, G. M., & Dozier, D. M. (1990). *Using research in public relations: Applications to program management.* Englewood Cliffs, NJ: Prentice Hall.

Buchholz, R. (1988). Adjusting corporations to the realities of public interests and policies. In R. L. Heath (Ed.), *Strategic issues management*, (pp. 50–72). San Francisco: Jossey-Bass.

Cawson, A. (1986). *Corporatism and political theory.* New York: Basil Blackwell.

Coombs, W. T. (1993). Philosophical underpinnings: Ramifications of a pluralistic paradigm. *Public Relations Review, 19*(2), 111–119.

Culbertson, H. M., & Chen, N. (1997, Summer). Communitarianism: A foundation for communication symmetry. *Public Opinion Quarterly, 42*(2), 36–41.

Cutlip, S., Center, A. H., & Broom, G. (2000). *Effective public relations* (8th ed). Upper Saddle, NJ: Prentice Hall.

Deetz, S. (1995). *Transforming communication, transforming business.* Cresskill, NJ: Hampton Press.

Dennis, L. B. (Ed.) (1995). *Practical public affairs in an era of change: A communications guide for business, government and college.* Lanham, MD: University Press of America.

Dennis, L. B., & Holcomb, J. M. (1995). Historical antecedents: Public affairs in full flower—1975–1985. In. L. B. Dennis (Ed.), *Practical public affairs in an era of change: A communications guide for business, government and college.* (pp. 17–31). Lanham, MD: University Press of America.

Dozier, D. M., Grunig, L. A, & Grunig, J. E. (1995). *Manager's guide to excellence in public relations and communication management.* Mahwah, NJ: Lawrence Erlbuam Associates.

Dozier, D. M., & Lauzen, M. M. (1998, August 8). *The liberation of public relations: Activism and the limits of symmetry in the global market.* Paper presented to the Public Relations Division, Association for Education in Journalism and Mass Communication Annual Conference: Baltimore, MD.

Etzioni, A. (1993) . *The spirit of community: The reinvention of American society.* New York: Simon and Schuster.

Gandy, O. W. (1992). Public relations and public policy: the structuration of dominance in the information age. In Toth, E. L., & Heath, R. L. (Eds.), *Rhetorical and critical approaches to public relations* (pp. 131–163). Hillsdale, NJ: Lawrence Erlbaum Associates.

Gaunt, P. & Ollenburger, J. (1995, Fall). Issues management revisited: A tool that deserves another look. *Public Relations Review, 21*(2), 199–210.

Grunig, J. E. (1984, Winter). Organizations, environments and models of public relations. *Public Relations Research and Education, 1*(1), 6–29.

Grunig, J. E. (1992). Communication, public relations, and effective organizations: An overview of the book. In J. E. Grunig (Ed.). *Excellence in public relations and communication management,* (pp. 1–28). Hillsdale, NJ: Lawrence Erlbaum Associates.

Grunig, J. E. (1994, July). *A situational theory of publics: Conceptual history, recent challenges and new research.* Paper presented to the International Public Relations Symposium, Bled, Slovenia.

Grunig, J. E. (2000). Collectivism, collaboration, and societal corporatism as core professional values in public relations. *Journal of Public Relations Research, 12*(1), 23–48.

Grunig, J. E., & Grunig, L. A. (1992). Models of public relations and communication. In J. E. Grunig (Ed), *Excellence in public relations and communication management* (pp. 285–326). Hillsdale, NJ: Lawrence Erlbaum Associates.

Grunig, J. E, & Grunig, L. A. (1997, July). *Review of a program of research on activism: Incidence in four countries, activist publics, strategies of activist groups, and organizational responses to activism.* Paper presented to the Fourth Public Relations Research Symposium. Bled, Slovenia.

Grunig, J. E., Grunig, L.A., Sriramesh, K., Lyra, A., & Huang, Y. H. (1995). Models of public relations in an international setting. *Journal of Public Relations Research, 7*(30), 163–186.

Grunig, J. E., & Hunt, T. (1984). *Managing public relations.* New York: Holt, Rinehart & Winston.

Grunig, J. E., & Jaatinen, M. (1998). Strategic, symmetrical public relations in government: From pluralism to societal corporatism. In D. Vercic, J. White, & D. Moss (Eds.), *Government relations and public affairs.* Bled, Slovenia: Pristop Communications.

Grunig, J. E., & Repper, F. C. (1992). Strategic management, publics, and issues. In E. J. Grunig (Ed.), *Excellence in public relations and communication management* (pp. 117–157). Hillsdale, NJ: Lawrence Erlbaum Associates.

Grunig, L. A. (1992). Activism: How it limits the effectiveness of organizations and how excellent public relations departments respond. In J. E. Grunig (Ed.), *Excellence in public relations and communication management* (pp. 503–530). Hillsdale, NJ: Lawrence Erlbaum Associates.

Gtunig, L. A. (1998). Implications of gender and culture for government public affairs. In D. Vercic, J. Whites & D. Moss (Eds.) *Government and public affairs* (pp. 101–112). Bled, Slovenia: Pristop Communications.

Hazleton, V., & Kennan, W. (2000, June 26). Toward a social capital theory of public relations: Part I. *Tips and Tactics, 28*(8), 1–2.

Hazelton, V., & Kennan, W. (2000, July 24). Toward a social capital theory of public relations: Part II. *Tips and Tactics, 38*(9), 1–2.

Heath, R. L. (1997). *Strategic issues management: Organizations and public policy changes.* Thousand Oaks, CA: Sage.

Helm, L. M., Hiebert, R. E., Naver, M. R., & Rabin, K. (Eds.). (1981). *Informing the people: A public affairs handbook.* New York: Longman.

Hon, L. C., & Grunig, J. E. (1999). *Guidelines for measuring relationships in public relations.* Gainesville, FL: The Institute for Public Relations.

Huang, Y. H. (1990). *Risk communication, models of public relations and antinuclear activism: A case study of a nuclear power plant in Taiwan.* Unpublished master's thesis, University of Maryland, College Park.

Kruckeberg, D., & Starck, K. (1988). *Public relations and community: A reconstituted theory.* New York: Praeger.

Leeper, K. A. (1996, Summer). Public relations ethics and communitarianism: A preliminary investigation. *Public Relations Review, 22*(2); 163–179.

Leeper, R. (2000). In search of a metatheory for public relations: An argument for communitarianism. In R. L. Heath (Ed.), *Handbook of public relations* (pp. 93–104). Thousand Oaks, CA: Sage.

Lyra, A. (1991). *Public relations in Greece: Models, roles and gender.* Unpublished master's thesis, University of Maryland, College Park.

Miller, D., & Schlesinger, P. (2000). The changing shape of public relations in the European union. In R. L. Heath (Ed.), *Handbook of public relations* (pp. 675–683). Thousand Oaks, CA: Sage.

Mintzberg, H. (1983). *Power in and around organizations.* Englewood Cliffs, NJ: Prentice Hall.

Nagelschmidt, J. (Ed.) (1982). *The public affairs handbook.* Washington, DC: Amacom.

Paluszek, J. L. (1995). Editorial note: Defining terms. In L. B. Dennis (Ed.), *Practical public affairs in an era of change: A communications guide for business, government, and college* (p. xvii). Lanham, MD: University Press of America.

Pharmaceuticals face uphill communications challenge (2001). *pr Reporter, 44*(24), 1–2.

Pinkham, D. (2003). *Issues management.* Retrieved July 20, 2005. www.pac.org/public/issues_management.shtml

Post, J. (1980). Public affairs and management policy in the 1980s. *Public Affairs Review,* p. 23.

What is public affairs (2005). Public Affairs Council. http://www.pac.org/page/FAQ.shtml. Retreived July, 20, 2005.

Public Relations Society of America. (1987). Report of special committee on terminology. *International Public Relations Review, 11*(2), 6–11.

Ramsey, S. A. (1993). Issues management and the use of technologies in public relations. *Public Relations Review, 19*(3), 261–275.

Reynolds, M. (1995, January–February). From PR to PA: A natural fit. *Communication World, 12*(1), 27.

Robbins, S. P. (1990). *Organizational theory: Structure, design, and applications.* (3rd ed). Englewood Cliffs, NJ: Prentice Hall.

Spicer, C. (1997). *Organizational public relations: A political perspective.* Mahwah, NJ: Lawrence Erlbaum Associates.

Sriramesh, K. (1991). *The impact of societal culture on public relations: An ethnographic study of south Indian organizations.* Unpublished doctoral dissertation, University of Maryland, College Park.

Starck, K., & Kruckeberg, D. (2001). Public relations and community: A reconstructed theory revisited. In R. L. Heath (Ed.), *Handbook of public relations* (pp. 51–59). Thousand Oaks, CA: Sage.

Toth, E.L. (1986). Broadening research in public affairs. *Public Relations Review, 12*(2), 27–36.

Turk, J. V. (1986, December). Information subsidies and media content: A study of public relations influence on the news. *Journalism Monographs*, No. 100.

Turk, J. V., & Franklin, R. (1987). Information subsidies: Agenda-setting traditions. *Public Affairs Review, 13*(4), 29–41.

Vercic, D., & Grunig, J. E. (1995, July). *The origin of public relations theory in economics and strategic management.* Paper presented to the Second International Public Relations Research Symposium, Bled, Slovenia.

Vercic, D., White, J., & Moss, D. (Eds.) (1998). *Government relations & public affairs.* Bled, Slovenia: Prestop Communications.

Index